A History
of
the
Modern
World

Contemporary Europe

0 100 200 300 miles

ICELAND

ARCTIC OCEAN

LAPLAND

NORWAY

Trondheim

SWEDEN

GULF OF BOTHNIA

FINLAND

FAEROE I.
(Denmark)

SHETLAND I.

Bergen

Oslo

Helsinki

Viborg

Leningrad

Göteborg

Stockholm

Tallinn
ESTONIAN
S.S.R.

ORKNEY I.

SCOTLAND

Skagerrak

NORTH SEA

Riga
LATVIAN S.S.R.

ATLANTIC OCEAN

NORTHERN
IRELAND

Edinburgh

DENMARK

Copenhagen

Klaipeda

LITHUANIAN
S.S.R.

UNITED
KINGDOM

Kaliningrad

Minsk

IRELAND
(EIRE)

Dublin

Liverpool

Hull

Gdansk
(Danzig)

BYELO-RUSSIAN

WALES

ENGLAND

NETHERLANDS

Amsterdam

Hamburg

GERMAN
DEMOCRATIC
REPUBLIC

Szczecin

Berlin

Oder R.

POLAND

Warsaw

Vistula R.

PRIPET
MARSHES

London

Rhine R.

HANOVER

Elbe R.

ENGLISH CHANNEL

Brussels

BELGIUM

LUX.

Cologne
Bonn

Dresden

Wroclaw

(Silesia)

Lvov

Dniester

BRITTANY

NORMANDY

Seine R.

Rouen

Paris

LORRAINE

Strasbourg

GERMANY

GERMAN
FEDERAL
REPUBLIC

Prague

BOHEMIA

MORAVIA

CZECHOSLOVAKIA

SLOVAKIA

CARPATHIAN MTS.

RUTHENIA

ALSACE

BADEN

BAVARIA

Munich

Vienna

AUSTRIA

Budapest

TRANSYLVANIA

MOLDAVIA

Loire R.

Tours

FRANCE

Berne

SWITZERLAND

HUNGARY

RUMANIA

BAY OF BISCAY

Geneva

Lyons

Rhone R.

SLOVENIA

Trieste

CROATIA-
SLAVONIA

BANAT

WALLACHIA

Bucharest

La Coruña

Bordeaux

Milan

VENEZIA

Venice

BOSNIA

YUGOSLAVIA

Belgrade

Danube R.

GALICIA

Bilbao

GASCONY

PIEDMONT

LOMBARDY

Po R.

Sarajevo

SERBIA

BULGARIA

Oporto

LEÓN

NAVARRE

Ebro R.

Genoa

Florence

MONTE-
NEGRO

Sofia

Duero R.

OLD CASTILE

ARAGON

LANGUEDOC

PROVENCE

Marseilles

Toulon

TUSCANY

ADRIATIC SEA

PORTUGAL

Tagus R.

Madrid

SPAIN

CATALONIA

Barcelona

ANDORRA

CORSICA
(France)

Rome

ITALY

CAMPANIA

APULIA

Tirana

ALBANIA

Salonica

Lisbon

NEW CASTILE

Valencia

Palma

Naples

AEGEAN

Cordoba

LA MANCHA

BALEARIC I.
(Spain)

SARDINIA
(Italy)

GREECE

Seville

ANDALUSIA

Malaga

Gibraltar (Britain)

Palermo

SICILY

Athens

Tangier

Ceuta (Spain)

Melilla
(Spain)

Oran

Algiers

Tunis

MALTA

Rabat

Casablanca

Fez

MEDITERRANEAN SEA

MOROCCO

ALGERIA

TUNISIA

Tripoli

Bengazi

TRIPOLITANIA

LIBYA

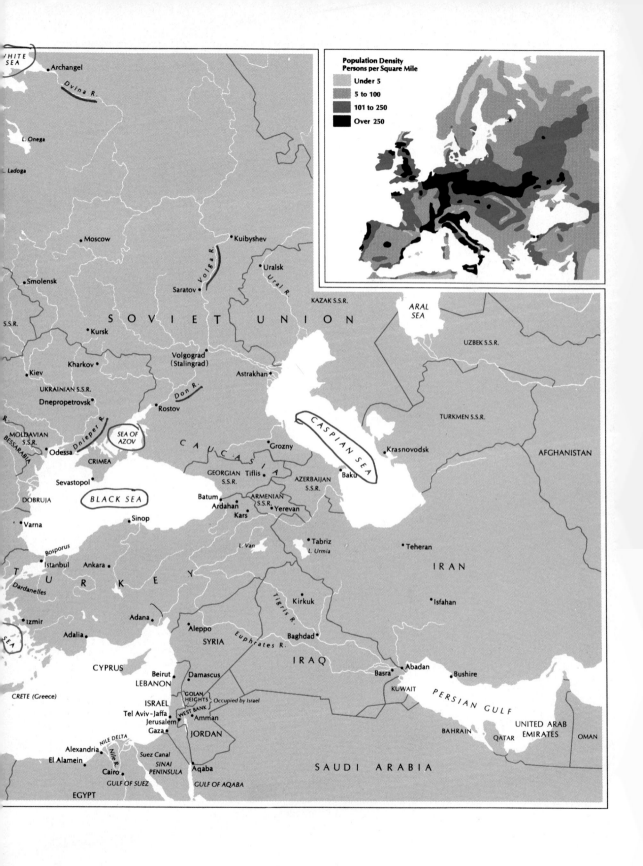

Population Density
Persons per Square Mile

- Under 5
- 5 to 100
- 101 to 250
- Over 250

WHITE SEA
• Archangel
Dvina R.
L. Onega
L. Ladoga
• Moscow
• Kuibyshev
• Uralsk
Volga R.
Saratov •
Ural R.
• Smolensk
KAZAK S.S.R.
ARAL SEA
S O V I E T   U N I O N
UZBEK S.S.R.
S.S.R.
• Kursk
Volgograd
(Stalingrad)
• Astrakhan
TURKMEN S.S.R.
• Kiev
• Kharkov
UKRAINIAN S.S.R.
Don R.
• Dnepropetrovsk
• Rostov
Dnieper R.
R.
MOLDAVIAN S.S.R.
BESSARABIA
• Odessa
SEA OF AZOV
C A U C A S I A
CASPIAN SEA
• Grozny
Krasnovodsk •
AFGHANISTAN
CRIMEA
GEORGIAN Tiflis
S.S.R.
AZERBAIJAN S.S.R.
Baku •
• Sevastopol
BLACK SEA
Batum •
ARMENIAN S.S.R.
Ardahan •
• Yerevan
DOBRUJA
Kars •
• Sinop
• Varna
Bosporus
L. Van
• Tabriz
L. Urmia
• Teheran
Dardanelles
• Istanbul
Ankara •
T U R K E Y
I R A N
SEA
• Izmir
Adalia •
• Adana
Tigris R.
• Kirkuk
• Isfahan
• Aleppo
Euphrates R.
Baghdad •
CYPRUS
SYRIA
I R A Q
Basra •
• Abadan
• Bushire
CRETE (Greece)
• Beirut
LEBANON
• Damascus
KUWAIT
P E R S I A N   G U L F
GOLAN HEIGHTS *Occupied by Israel*
ISRAEL
WEST BANK
UNITED ARAB EMIRATES
Tel Aviv-Jaffa •
Jerusalem •
• Amman
BAHRAIN
• Gaza
JORDAN
QATAR
OMAN
• Alexandria
NILE DELTA
Nile R.
El Alamein •
Suez Canal
SINAI PENINSULA
• Aqaba
S A U D I   A R A B I A
Cairo •
GULF OF SUEZ
GULF OF AQABA
EGYPT

sixth edition

A History
of
the
Modern
World

To 1815

R. R. PALMER
JOEL COLTON

Alfred A. Knopf
New York

THIS IS A BORZOI BOOK PUBLISHED BY ALFRED A. KNOPF, INC.

Library of Congress Cataloging in Publication Data

Palmer, Robert Roswell, 1909–
   A history of the modern world.

   Bibliography: p.
   Includes index.
   1.   History, Modern.   I.   Colton, Joel G., 1918–
joint author.   II.   Title.
D209.P26   1984b   909.08   83–13580
ISBN 0–394–33599–6 (pbk. : v. 1)
ISBN 0–394–33600–3 (pbk. : v. 2)

Published July 24, 1950. Reprinted seven times.

Second edition, revised, reset, and printed from new plates, with new maps, 1956. Reprinted fourteen times.

Third edition, revised, with new maps, 1965. Reprinted five times.

Fourth edition, revised, reset, and printed from new plates, with new maps and illustrations, 1971. Reprinted five times.

Fifth edition, revised, reset, and printed from new plates, with new maps and illustrations, 1978. Reprinted seven times.

Sixth edition, revised, reset, and printed from new plates, with new maps and illustrations, 1983.

Sixth Edition
987654321

ACKNOWLEDGMENT IS HEREBY MADE FOR PERMISSION TO QUOTE FROM THE FOLLOWING WORK:

The World's Food: A Study of the Interrelations of World Populations, National Diets and Food Potentials, by M. K. Bennett, 1954. Reprinted by permission of Harper & Row.

Manufactured in the United States of America

Preface

[Publisher's Note: In order to provide an alternative to the hardcover edition, *A History of the Modern World* is being made available in a two-volume paperbound edition. Volume 1, *To 1815*, includes chapters I–X; volume 2, *Since 1815*, chapters XI–XXII. The page numbering in these chapters remains the same as in the hardcover text, and footnotes refer to pages in both volumes.]

Once again we take pleasure in offering a new edition, now the sixth, of a work that continues to be well received. In structure, content, and coverage *A History of the Modern World* remains very much what it was in the fifth edition. Both of us, however, have carefully worked together over the whole volume in another effort to make it more useful and attractive.

The new features include a short geographical introduction, a new section on popular culture, more references to the role of women, a few revisions in treatment of the Enlightenment, more attention to Latin American independence, a new picture essay, and numerous smaller alterations in many places. Some of these changes are in response to comments made by readers, who may perhaps agree that the scale of the book, large as it is, allows too little to be said on many topics. The two concluding chapters on the years since the Second World War are as usual the most thoroughly revised, and have been brought abreast of contemporary developments. The bibliography, which has always been a special feature of the book, has been reviewed and pruned but remains extensive; it has also been brought up to date and now may contain as many as four thousand titles, classified by subject according to the plan of the book as a whole. In general, we have done what we could to make so long and complex a volume more manageable and digestible. The whole structure of chapters, sections and subsections, the frequent cross-references, the chronological tables, and the detailed index are intended for this purpose. A student's Study Guide is also available for those who may wish to use it.

Since its first edition the book has been designed to set forth the modern history of Europe and European civilization as a unit, and in its later chapters it attempts to tell the story of an integrated, or at least interconnected, world. Emphasis falls on situations and movements of international scope, or on what Europeans and their descendants have done and faced in common. National histories are therefore somewhat subordinated, and in each national history the points of contact with a larger civilization are treated most fully. Historic regional differences within Europe, as between eastern and western Europe, are brought out, and the history of the Americas is woven into the story at various points, as are developments of the last century in Asia and Africa. A good deal of institutional history is included. Considerable space is given to the history of ideas, not only in special sections devoted to ideas, but throughout the book in close connection with the account of institutions and events. Social and economic development bulks rather large, as does the impact of wars and revolutions. Since our own age is one in which much depends on political decision, we think of this volume as political history in the broadest sense, in that matters of many kinds, such as religion, economics, social welfare, and international relations, have presented themselves as public questions requiring public action by responsible citizens or official persons. It seems to us that many subjects of current research interest, such as women's history, family history, the history of the laboring classes, the history of minorities, or demographic and quantitative studies, are best understood when seen within a wider framework such as this book attempts to provide.

We are again glad to thank all those who have helped with the book over the years, and in particular the half-dozen persons who have acted as consultants for this sixth edition. We are indebted to David Follmer, June Smith, and David Rothberg of Alfred A. Knopf, Inc., the former for his initiative in bringing this new edition into being, the latter two for their careful work on the manuscript. Since they have left the important decisions to us, and all the actual writing is ours, we assume all responsibility for errors, imperfections, questionable judgments, and other possible shortcomings. Esther Palmer and Shirley Colton have contributed in innumerable ways to the newest edition of this history, which can stand as some kind of continuing monument to marriage, friendship, and intellectual collaboration.

R. R. PALMER
JOEL COLTON

Contents

ILLUSTRATIONS

MAPS AND CHARTS

A History
of
the
Modern
World

A Few
Words on
Geography

istory is the experience of human beings in time, but it takes place also in space, on the planet Earth, so that geography always underlies it. It is the business of geography not merely to describe and map the earth and its various areas, but to study the changing relationships between human activities and the surrounding environment.

The earth is over four billion years old. The entire history of mankind since the Middle Stone Age has occupied less than a hundred-thousandth of the time in which the earthly habitat has been developed. Some minerals now put to human use were formed in the earliest ages of the planet, others such as coal and petroleum were not laid down until a few hundred million years ago, but none that are now being consumed in a flicker of geologic time can ever be replaced. Oceans and continents have moved about, changing in size, shape, and location with respect to one another and to the North and South Poles. There was a time when dinosaurs could walk from North America to Europe (as we now call them) on solid land in a warm climate. The continents as we now know them became fully distinct less than a hundred million years ago. It is only a few thousand years since the end of the most recent glacial age, which may not be the last. The melting back into the ocean of water frozen over a mile thick in Antarctica and in large parts of North America and Europe produced the coastlines, offshore islands, inland seas, straits, bays, and harbors that we see on a map today, as well as some of the largest river systems and lakes. It is only about three hundred years since the first French explorers saw Niagara Falls, which then looked quite different, because by eating away the underlying rock the falls have receded several hundred feet since that time.

At present, the oceans cover more than two-thirds of the surface of the globe. By no means is all the remaining third suited for occupation by human beings, or indeed by most other animal or vegetable organisms, for much of the land still lies under perpetual ice in Antarctica and Greenland, much is tundra, much is desert, and some is along the windswept ridges of high mountains. Like the oceans, these desolate regions have been important in human history, first in earlier times by acting as barriers. Man, as the anthropologists call him (and her), is now thought to have originated in Africa. He (and she) eventually spread to every continent except Antarctica. In doing so, human groups became isolated from each other for thousands of years, separated by oceans, deserts, or mountains, and so became differentiated into the modern races, though all are derived from the same source and belong to the same species. The same is true of cultures or civilizations over a time period measured in centuries rather than millennia. It is such separation that accounts for the historic cultural differences between Africa, pre-Columbian America, China, India, the Middle East, and Europe. On a smaller scale it explains the differences in languages and dialects.

Separation has also produced differences in flora and fauna, and hence in the plants and animals by which humans live. Wheat became the most usual cereal in the Middle East and Europe, millet and rice in East Asia, sorghum in tropical Africa, maize in pre-Columbian America. The horse, first domesticated in central Asia, was for centuries a mainstay of Europe for muscle power, transportation, and combat, while the less versatile camel was adopted later and more slowly in the Middle East, and America had no beasts of burden except the llama. Not until Europeans began to cross the oceans, taking plants and animals with them, and bringing others back, did these great differences begin to diminish.

The present book is concerned primarily with Europe, and with the last few hundred years. And as a traveler setting out on a journey may provide himself with a map, and carry its contents as much as possible in his head, so the reader is invited to examine the map of Europe on pages 6 and 7, and keep it in mind while reading the following history. The map shows the topographical features that have remained unchanged in historic times.

Europe is physically separated from Africa by the Mediterranean Sea, which however has been as much a passageway as a barrier. A more effective barrier was created when the Sahara Desert dried up only a few thousand years ago. The physical separation of Europe from Asia has always been less clear; the conventional boundary has long been the Ural Mountains in the Soviet Union, but the Soviet Union recognizes no such distinction. The Urals are in any case low and wide, and it can be argued that Europe is not a continent at all, but a cultural conception arising from felt differences from Asia and Africa. Europe, even with European Russia, contains hardly more than 6 percent of the land surface of the earth. It has about the same area as the United States including Alaska. It is a little larger than Australia, and a little smaller than Antarctica.

If we consider only its physical features Europe is indeed one of several peninsulas jutting off from Asia. It is altogether different, however, from the Arabian and Indian peninsulas, which also extend from the mass of Asia, as shown on the back endpaper of the present book. For one thing, the Mediterranean Sea is unique among the world's bodies of water. Closed in by the Strait of Gibraltar, which is only eight miles wide, it is more shielded than the Caribbean or East Asian seas from the open ocean. Hence it has very little tide, and is protected from the most violent ocean storms. Though over two thousand miles long, it is subdivided by islands and peninsulas into lesser seas with an identity of their own, such as the Aegean and the Adriatic, and it gives access also to the Black Sea. It is possible to travel for great distances without being far from land, so that navigation developed from early times, and one of the first civilizations appeared on the island of Crete. It is possible also to cross between Europe and Asia at the Bosporus and between Europe and Africa at Gibraltar, so that populations became mixed by early migrations, and various historic empires—Carthaginian, Roman, Byzantine, Arabic, Spanish, Venetian, and Turkish—have used the Mediterranean as an avenue between their component parts. After the Suez Canal was built the Mediterranean became a segment in the "lifeline of empire" for the British Empire in its heyday.

In southern Europe, north of the Mediterranean and running for its whole length, is a series of mountains, produced geologically by the pushing of the gigantic mass of Africa against this smaller Eurasian peninsula. The Pyrenees shut off Spain from the north, as the Alps do Italy; the Balkan Mountains have always been difficult to penetrate; and the only place where one can go at water level from the Mediterranean to the north is by the valley of the Rhone River, so that France, since it came together in the Middle Ages, is the only country that clearly belongs both to the Mediterranean and to northern Europe. North of the mountains is a great plain, with branches in England and Sweden, extending from western France through Germany and Poland into Russia and on into Asia, passing south of the Urals through what is called the Caspian Gate, north of the landlocked Caspian Sea. One might draw a straight line from Amsterdam eastward through the Caspian Gate as far as the borders of western China, and although this line would reach the distance from New York to a point five hundred miles west of San Francisco, one would never in traveling along it be higher above sea level than central Kansas. The continuity of this level plain has at various times opened Europe to Mongol and other invasions, enabled the Russians to move east and create a huge empire, and made Poland a troubled intermediary between Western Europe and what is now the Soviet Union.

The rivers as shown on the map are worth particular attention. Until quite recent times rivers offered an easier means of transportation than any form of carriage by land. The principal rivers also give access to the sea. Most are navigable, especially in the north European plains. With their valleys, whether in level country or confined between mountains, they provided areas where intensive local development could take place. Thus we see that some of the most important older cities of Europe are on rivers—London on the Thames, Paris on the Seine, Vienna and Budapest on the Danube, Warsaw on the Vistula. In northern Europe it was often possible to move goods from one river to another, and then in the eighteenth century to connect them by canals; and the networks of rivers and canals still carry much heavy traffic by barges. The importance of water is shown again by the location of Copenhagen, Stockholm, and Leningrad (formerly St. Petersburg) on the Baltic, which is a kind of inland lake, and of Amsterdam and Lisbon, which grew up after the ocean could be traversed by Europeans.

There are many important geographical conditions that a topographic map cannot show. One is climate, which depends on latitude, ocean currents, and winds that bring or withhold rainfall. In latitude Europe lies as far north as the northern United States and southern Canada, with Madrid and Rome in the lati-

ICELAND

NORWEGIAN SEA

SCANDINAVIAN PENINSULA

FAEROE I.

SHETLAND I.

HEBRIDES

ORKNEY I.

ATLANTIC OCEAN

BRITISH ISLES

GRAMPIANS

SCOTTISH LOWLANDS

Edinburgh

PENNINE CHAIN

NORTH SEA

FINNISH LAKE REGION

KÖLEN MOUNTAINS

GULF OF BOTHNIA

Dal R.

Oslo

L. Vanern

L. Vättern

Stockholm

ALAND I.

Helsinki

GULF OF FINLAND

L. Peipus

GOTLAND

ÖLAND

Riga

Dvina R.

BALTIC SEA

IRISH Dublin CENTRAL PLAIN

IRISH SEA

St. George's Channel

THE WASH

MIDLAND PLAIN

Bristol Channel

Thames R.

London

JUTLAND PENINSULA

HELIGOLAND

FRISIAN I.

Amsterdam

Ijsselmeer

Copenhagen

Danzig

Niemen R.

Masurian Lakes

Weser R.

Elbe R.

NORTH GERMAN PLAIN

Berlin

Warta R.

Vistula R.

Bug R.

Warsaw

SCILLY I.

LAND'S END

ENGLISH CHANNEL

Strait of Dover

USHANT I.

BRITTANY PENINSULA

PLAIN OF FRANCE

Scheldt R.

Maas R.

Rhine R.

ARDENNE

Meuse R.

Moselle R.

Marne R.

Seine R.

Paris

Loire R.

VOSGES MTS.

JURA MTS.

BLACK FOREST

Main R.

HARZ MTS.

ERZ MTS.

SUDETEN MTS.

Prague

BOHEMIAN PLAIN

BOHEMIAN FOREST

Danube R.

Inn R.

L. Constance

Vienna

CARPA

Tisza R.

BAY OF BISCAY

CAPE FINISTERRE

CANTABRIAN MTS.

Douro R.

PYRENEES

Garonne R.

MASSIF CENTRAL

CEVENNES

Rhône R.

Saône R.

L. Geneva

ALPS

PLAIN OF LOMBARDY

Po R.

Trieste

ISTRIA

Drave R.

Save R.

L. Balaton

PLAIN OF HUNGARY

Budapest

IRON GATE

Belgrade

TRANSYL

Morava R.

BAL

IBERIAN PENINSULA

SPANISH

Ebro R.

GUADARRAMA

Madrid

PLATEAU

Tagus R.

Lisbon

Guadiana R.

SIERRA MORENA

Guadalquivir R.

SIERRA NEVADA

CAPE TRAFALGAR

Strait of Gibraltar

Gibraltar

BALEARIC I.

IVIZA

MINORCA

MAJORCA

SARDINIA

CORSICA

ELBA

Arno R.

Rome

ITALIAN PENINSULA

Mt. Vesuvius

TYRRHENIAN SEA

APENNINES

ADRIATIC SEA

DALMATIA

DINARIC ALPS

BALKAN PENINSULA

PINDUS MTS.

Sofia

Vardar R.

IONIAN I.

IONIAN SEA

MOREAN PENINSULA

Algiers

LITTLE ATLAS MOUNTAINS

Tunis

PANTELLERIA

Mt. Etna

SICILY

Strait of Messina

MALTA

Fez

MIDDLE ATLAS MOUNTAINS

SAHARAN ATLAS MOUNTAINS

MEDITERRANEAN SEA

GREAT ATLAS MOUNTAINS

ALGERIAN SAHARA

Tripoli

GULF OF SIDRA

Skagerrak

Kattegat

Neisse R.

Oder R.

WHITE SEA

N. Dvina R.

L. Onega

L. Ladoga

Leningrad

NORTH RUSSIAN PLAIN

CENTRAL RUSSIAN HIGHLANDS

Moscow

Oka R.

Volga R.

Kama R.

URAL MOUNTAINS

Tobol R.

Ishim R.

KIRGHIZ STEPPE

Ural R.

VOLGA REGION

VOLGA HEIGHTS

ARAL SEA

Syr Darya

Areas Below Sea Level

0   100   200   300 miles

Pripet R.

PRIPET MARSHES

Kiev

Dnieper R.

Donets R.

Don R.

BLACK EARTH

CASPIAN DEPRESSION

Volga R.

TURANIAN PLAIN

Amu Darya

Bug R.

DONETS HEIGHTS

Dniester R.

Prut R.

SEA OF AZOV

Odessa

CRIMEA

CAUCASUS MOUNTAINS

CASPIAN SEA

Danube R.

Bucharest

PLAIN of WALLACHIA

BLACK SEA

ARMENIAN HIGHLANDS

Araxes R.

ELBURZ MTS.

 AN ALPS

AN MTS.

Maritsa R.

HODOPE MTS

Bosporus

Istanbul

SEA OF MARMARA

Kizilirmak

Ankara

L. Van

L. Urmia

Teheran

Dardanelles

ASIA MINOR (ANATOLIAN PENINSULA)

ZAGROS MTS.

AEGEAN SEA

Athens

Meander R.

TAURUS MOUNTAINS

MESOPOTAMIAN PLAINS

Tigris R.

DODECANESE I.

RHODES

CYPRUS

Euphrates R.

Baghdad

CRETE

SYRIAN DESERT

PERSIAN GULF

SEA OF GALILEE

Jordan R.

Jerusalem

DEAD SEA

Alexandria

NILE DELTA

Suez Canal

Cairo

SINAI PENINSULA

GULF OF SUEZ

Nile R.

GULF OF AQABA

NEFUD DESERT

tude of New York, and with Stockholm and Leningrad as far north as the middle of Hudson Bay. All Europe thus is within what is called the temperate zone, somewhat misleadingly, since the temperate zone is by definition the region of pronounced difference between winter and summer. But the parts of Europe that are near the sea have less extreme temperatures than the corresponding northerly regions of America, and the Mediterranean countries have more sunshine and less severe winters than either northern Europe or the northern United States. Everywhere, however, the winters are cold enough to keep out certain diseases by which warmer countries are afflicted. They have also obliged the inhabitants to expend more effort on clothing, housing, and heating. Warm summers with their growing seasons have produced an annual cycle of agriculture, for which rainfall has been adequate but not excessive. Although the Spanish plateau is arid, and the Mediterranean shores are subject to seasonal variations of rainfall, Europe is the only continent that has no actual desert. Thanks to a combination of causes, including rainfall, ground water, deposits left by retreating glaciers, the character of the underlying rock, and the alternate freezing and thawing, Europe is also for the most part a region of fertile soils. In short, since the end of the Ice Age, or since humans learned how to survive the winters, Europe has been one of the most favored places on the globe for human habitation. In recent times it has been, as shown by the insets of the two endpaper maps in this book, one of the few large regions, along with China and India, of very high density of population.

Climate itself can change. The Roman ruins in the interior of Morocco and Tunisia remind us that the climate there was once more favorable. Studies of tree rings, fossil plants, and alpine glaciers show that average temperatures were warmer from the end of the Ice Age throughout ancient and medieval times, and then fell during what is called the "little Ice Age" from about 1400 to 1850, when the winters lengthened and the growing season shortened, without drastic consequences for the people, who by that time could simply wear more wool, so that sheep raising and the woolen trade became a main staple of European commerce.

There is no geographical determinism. Climate and the environment not only set limits but provide opportunities for what human beings can do. What happens depends on the application of knowledge and abilities in any particular time and place. A broad river is an obstruction and hence a good boundary under simple conditions; it is less so after bridges connect the two sides. The oceans that long divided mankind became a highway for the Portuguese, Spanish, Dutch, French, and English, and later for others. Distance, which any good map will show by its scale, also varies in its effects according to the means of transportation; it must be remembered that for most of human history neither persons, information, nor commands could travel much more than thirty miles a day, so that localism prevailed, and large organizations, in trade or government, were hard to create and to maintain. For most of its history Europe was in fact made up of a diversity of small local units, pockets of territory each having its own customs, way of life, and manner of speech, each largely unknown to the others and looking inward upon itself, rather than of the blocks called "Germany" or "France" that we take for granted on a map today. A "foreigner" might come from a thousand miles away, or from only ten.

What constitutes a natural resource varies with the state of technology and the possibilities of exchange. The tin of Cornwall at the western tip of Britain became an important resource as long ago as the early Bronze Age, when despite its remoteness it gave rise to some of the first long-distance European trade. Deposits of coal lay little noticed and scarcely exploited until the nineteenth century, and petroleum was of no significance nor even known, until about a century ago. It is a big fact of human history, rather than of geologic history, that some of the world's greatest coal beds happened to be in northwestern Europe and the United States, which could the more readily industrialize because they had easy access to abundant fuel, over which they had control, an advantage that was lost as they became more dependent on natural gas and oil. If the future is like the past, it will see a similar conversion of natural materials into natural resources.

The Mediterranean coasts were more wooded three thousand years ago than they are today. It was not only the change of climate that changed their appearance. Many human generations spent in cutting timber, pasturing goats, and planting vines and olives brought about erosion and depletion of the soil. Europe north of the mountains was heavily forested before human intervention. Trees were cut down and burned there as in America centuries later, so that the landscape slowly became an orderly expanse of carefully tended fields, still interrupted by woodlands. The state of agriculture obviously depends on natural conditions. But it depends historically also on the invention and improvement of the plow, the finding of appropriate crops, the rotation of fields to prevent soil exhaustion, and the introduction of livestock from which manure can be obtained as a fertilizer. Socially, agriculture benefits from the existence of stable village communities, and is affected by demographic changes; if a population falls as a result of war or epidemics, some fields will be abandoned and return to "nature"; if population grows, new and less fertile or more distant areas will be brought under cultivation. Nor can agriculture be improved without the building of roads, a division of labor between town and country, and some degree of regional specialization, so that some areas may grow cereals, others raise livestock, and still others be devoted to orchards and vineyards. Basic to agriculture, as to other enterprises, is elementary security. Farming cannot proceed, nor food be stored over the winter, unless the men and women who work the fields can be protected from attack by marauders, brigands, barbarian invaders, warring chiefs, or hostile armies. Such protection, or what might be called the normalcy of peace, was for several centuries imposed by the Roman Empire, in more recent times (barring wars) by the national state, and in between by barons who at least protected the peasants who worked for them, and by kings attempting to pacify their kingdoms.

For maps with exact detail, or extensive coverage, it is best to consult a good historical atlas, of which several are listed in the bibliography at the end of this book. Over fifty maps are included in the present volume, but some are only diagrams rather than true maps; all are intended to supplement the written text, by showing the location and geographical spread of matters under discussion. Many of the maps are mainly designed to show political boundaries at particular dates. Readers in looking at them can use their imagination to fill in the mountains and rivers that these maps cannot show but which can be important for an understanding of the extent of political power. Readers can also, by using their imagination and consulting the scale, convert space into time, remembering that until the invention of the railroad both people and news traveled far more slowly than today, or that at a rate of thirty miles a day it would take three weeks to travel from London to Venice, and at least six weeks for an exchange of letters. In human terms Europe has not been such a small place after all.

I.
The Rise
of Europe

I t may seem strange for a history of the modern world to begin with the European Middle Ages, for Europe is not the world and the Middle Ages were not modern. But most of what is now meant by "modern" made its first appearance in Europe, and to understand modern Europe it is necessary to reach fairly far back in time. To understand the modern world it is likewise necessary to begin by looking at Europe.

Over the centuries Europe created the most powerful combination of political, military, economic, technological, and scientific apparatus that the world had ever seen. In doing so, Europe radically transformed itself, and also developed an overwhelming impact on other continents and other cultures in America, Africa, and Asia, sometimes destroying them, sometimes stimulating or enlivening them, and always presenting them with problems of resistance or adaptation. This European ascendancy became apparent about 300 years ago. It reached its zenith with the European colonial empires at the beginning of the twentieth century. Since then, the position of Europe has relatively declined, partly because of conflicts within Europe itself, but mainly because the apparatus which had made Europe so dominant can now be found in other countries. Some, like the United States, are essentially offshoots of Europe. Others have very different and ancient backgrounds. But whatever their backgrounds, and willingly or not, all peoples in the twentieth century are caught up in the process of modernization or "development," which usually turns out to mean acquiring some of the skills and powers first exhibited by Europeans.

Chapter Emblem: The symbolic Chi-Rho, or crossed X and P, standing for the first two letters of the Greek Khristos. From a Roman sarcophagus. "P" is the Greek letter rho, for small "r," so that the symbol stands for Christ.

There is thus in our time a kind of uniform modern civilization which overlies or penetrates the traditional cultures of the world. This civilization is an interlocking unity, in that conditions on one side of the globe have repercussions on the other. Communications are almost instantaneous and news travels everywhere. If the air is polluted in one country, neighboring countries are affected; if oil ceases to flow from the Middle East the life of Europe and North America may become very difficult. The modern world depends on elaborate means of transportation, on science, industry, and machines, on new sources of energy to meet insatiable demands, on scientific medicine, public hygiene, and methods of raising food. States and nations fight wars by advanced methods, and negotiate or maintain peace by diplomacy. There is an earth-encompassing network of finance and trade, loans and debts, investments and bank accounts, with resulting fluctuations in monetary exchanges and balances of payments. About 160 very unequal and disunited members compose the United Nations. The very concept of the nation, as represented in that body, is derived from Europe.

In most modern countries there have been pressures for increased democracy, and all modern governments, democratic or not, must seek to arouse the energies and support of their populations. In a modern society old customs loosen, and ancestral religions are questioned. There is a demand for individual liberation, and an expectation of a higher standard of living. Everywhere there is a drive for more equality in a bewildering variety of meanings—for more equality between sexes and races, between high and low incomes, between adherents of different religions, or between different parts of the same country. Movements for social change may be slow and gradual, or revolutionary and catastrophic, but movement of some kind is universal.

Such are a few of the indexes of modernity. Since they appeared first in the history of Europe, or of the European world in the extended sense in which the United States is included, the present book deals mainly with the growth of European society and civilization, with increasing attention, in the later chapters, to the earth as a whole. There have also been antimodern movements and protests; when they occur in Asia or Africa, as in the recent Islamic revival, they are called anti-Western, as if to show that Europe and the "West" have been at the heart of the problem.

If "modern" refers especially to a certain complicated way of living, it has also another sense, meaning merely what is recent or current. As a time span the word "modern" is purely relative. It depends on what we are talking about. A modern kitchen may be as much as 5 years old, modern physics is less than 100 years old, modern science over 300, the modern European languages about 1,000. Modern civilization, the current civilization in which we are living, and which may be passing, is in one sense a product of our own twentieth century, but in other senses it is much older. In general, it is agreed that modern times began in Europe about the year 1500. Modern times were preceded by a period of 1,000 years called the Middle Ages, which set in about A.D. 500, and which were in turn preceded by another 1,000 years of classical Greco-Roman civilization. Before that reached the long histories of Egypt and Mesopotamia, and, further east, of the Indus Valley and of China. All times prior to the European Middle Ages are commonly called "ancient." But the whole framework—ancient, medieval, and modern—is largely a matter of words and convention, without meaning except for Europe. We shall begin our history with a running start, and slow down the pace, surveying the scene more fully in proportion as the times grow more "modern."

1. ANCIENT TIMES: GREECE, ROME, AND CHRISTIANITY

Europeans were by no means the pioneers of human civilization. Half of recorded history had passed before anyone in Europe could read or write. The priests of Egypt began to keep written records between 4000 and 3000 B.C., but two thousand years later the poems of Homer were still being circulated in the Greek city-states by word of mouth. Shortly after 3000 B.C., while the pharaohs were building the pyramids, Europeans were laboriously setting up the huge, unwrought stones called megaliths, of which Stonehenge is the best-known example. In a word, until after 2000 B.C., Europe was in the Neolithic or New Stone Age. This was in truth a great age in human history, the age in which human beings learned to make and use sharp tools, weave cloth, build living quarters, domesticate animals, plant seeds, harvest crops, and sense the returning cycles of the months and years. But the Near East—Egypt, the Euphrates and Tigris valley, the island of Crete, and the shores of the Aegean Sea (which belonged more to Asia than to Europe)—had reached its Neolithic Age two thousand years before Europe. By about 4000 B.C. the Near East was already moving into the Bronze Age.

After about 2000 B.C., in the dim, dark continent that Europe then was, there began to be great changes that are now difficult to trace. Europeans, too, learned how to smelt and forge metals, with the Bronze Age setting in about 2000 B.C. and the Iron Age about 1000 B.C. There was also a steady infusion of new peoples into Europe. They spoke languages related to languages now spoken in India and Iran, to which similar peoples migrated at about the same time. All these languages (whose interconnection was not known until the nineteenth century) are now referred to as Indo-European, and the people who spoke them, merging with and imposing their speech upon older European stocks, became the ancestors both of the classical Greeks and Romans and of the Europeans of modern times. All European languages today are Indo-European with the exceptions of Basque, which is thought to be a survival from before the Indo-European invasion, and of Finnish and Hungarian, which were brought into Europe from Asia some centuries later. It was these invading Indo-Europeans who diffused over Europe the kind of speech from which the Latin, Greek, Germanic, Slavic, Celtic, and Baltic languages were later derived.[1]

The Greek World

The first Indo-Europeans to emerge into the clear light of history, in what is now Europe, were the Greeks. They filtered down through the Balkan peninsula to the shores of the Aegean Sea about 1900 B.C., undermining the older Cretan civilization, and occupying most of what has since been called Greece by 1300 B.C. Beginning about 1150 B.C., other Greek-speaking tribes invaded from the north in successive waves. The newcomers consisted of separate barbaric tribes and their coming ushered in several centuries of chaos and unrest before a gradual stabilization and revival began in the ninth century. The *Iliad* and the *Odyssey*, written

[1] Formerly the term "Aryan" was sometimes used to denote Indo-European. In Germany, under Adolf Hitler, much nonsense was written about an Aryan race, and the term Aryan was made in practice to mean simply non-Jewish. The grain of truth in all this was simply that Hebrew is not an Indo-European but a Semitic language, closely related to Arabic (which is also Semitic) and less closely to the language of the ancient Egyptians. There is no Indo-European (Aryan) or Semitic "race"; persons speaking these languages no more had to be of one physical descent than are persons who speak English today.

down about 800 B.C., but composed and recited much earlier, probably refer to wars between the Greeks and other centers of civilization, of which one was at Troy in Asia Minor. The siege of Troy is thought to have occurred about 1200 B.C.

The Greeks proved to be as gifted a people as mankind has ever produced, achieving supreme heights in thought and letters. They absorbed the knowledge of the, to them, mysterious East, the mathematical lore of the ancient Chaldeans, the arts and crafts that they found in Asia Minor and on voyages to Egypt. They added immediately to everything that they learned. It was the Greeks of the fifth and fourth centuries B.C. who first became fully conscious of the powers of the human mind, who formulated what the Western world long meant by the beautiful, and who first speculated on political freedom.

As they settled down, the Greeks formed tiny city-states, all independent and often at war with one another, each only a few miles across, and typically including a coastal city and its adjoining farmlands. Athens, Corinth, Sparta were such city-states. Many were democratic; all citizens (i.e., all grown men except slaves and "metics," or outsiders) congregated in the marketplace to elect officials and discuss their public business. Politics was turbulent in the small Greek states. Democracy alternated with aristocracy, oligarchy, despotism, and tyranny. From this rich fund of experience was born systematic political science as set forth in the unwritten speculations of Socrates and in the *Republic* of Plato and the *Politics* of Aristotle in the fourth century before Christ. The Greeks also were the first to write history as a subject distinct from myth and legend. Herodotus, "the Father of History," traveled throughout the Greek world and far beyond, ferreting out all he could learn of the past; and Thucydides, in his account of the wars between Athens and Sparta, presented history as a guide to enlightened citizenship and constructive statecraft.

Perhaps because they were a restless and vehement people, the Greeks came to prize the "classical" virtues, which they were the first to define. For them, the ideal lay in moderation, or a golden mean. They valued order, balance, symmetry, clarity, and control. Their statues revealed their conception of what man ought to be—a noble creature, dignified, poised, unterrified by life or death, master of himself and of his feelings. Their architecture, as in the Parthenon, made use of exactly measured angles and rows of columns. The classical "order," or set of carefully wrought pillars placed in a straight line at specified intervals, represented the firm impress of human reason on the brute materials of nature. The same sense of form was thrown over the torrent of human words. Written language became contrived, carefully planned, organized for effect. The epic poem, the lyric, the drama, the oration, along with history and the philosophic dialogue, each with its own rules and principles of composition, became the "forms" within which, in Western civilization, men long continued to express their thoughts.

Reflecting on the world about them, the Greeks concluded that something more fundamental existed beyond the world of appearances, that true reality was not what met the eye. With other peoples, and with the Greeks themselves in earlier times, this same realization had led to the formation of myths, dealing with invisible but mighty beings known as gods and with faraway places on the tops of mountains, beneath the earth, or in a world that followed death. Greek thinkers set to criticizing the web of myth. They looked for rational or natural explanations of what was at work behind the variety and confusion that they saw. Some, observing human sickness, said that disease was not a demonic possession, but a natural sequence of conditions in the body, which could be identified, understood, foreseen, and even treated in a natural way. Others, turning to physical nature, said that all matter was in reality composed of a very few things—of atoms or elements—which they usually designated as fire, water, earth, and air. Some said that change was a kind of illusion, all basic reality being uniform; some, that only change was real, and that the world was a flux. Some, like Pythagoras, found the enduring reality in "number," or mathematics. The Greeks, in short, laid the foundations for science. Studying also the way in which the mind worked, or ought to work if it was to reach truthful conclusions, they developed the science of logic. The great codifier of Greek thought on almost all subjects in the classical period was Aristotle, who lived in Athens from 384 to 322 B.C.

Greek influence spread widely and rapidly. Hardly were some of the city-states founded when their people, crowded within their narrow bounds, sent off some of their number with equipment and provisions to establish colonies. In this way Greek cities were very early established in south Italy, in Sicily, and even in the western Mediterranean, where Marseilles was founded about 600 B.C. Later the Greek city-states, unable to unite, succumbed to conquest by Philip of Macedon, who came from the relatively crude northern part of the Greek world, and whose son, Alexander the Great (356–323 B.C.), led a phenomenal and conquering march into Asia, across Persia, and on as far as India itself. Alexander's empire did not hold together, but Greek civilization, after having penetrated the raw world of the western Mediterranean, now began to revivify the ancient peoples of Egypt and the Near East. Greek thought, Greek art, and the Greek language spread far and wide. The most famous "Greeks" after the fourth century B.C. and on into the early centuries of the Christian era usually did not come from Greece but from the Hellenized Near East, and especially from Alexandria in Egypt. Among these later Greeks were the great summarizers or writers of encyclopedias in which ancient science was passed on to later generations—Strabo in geography, Galen in medicine, Ptolemy in astronomy. All three lived in the first and second centuries after Christ.

The Roman World

In 146 B.C. the Greeks of Greece were conquered by a new people, the Romans. The Romans, while keeping their own Latin language, rapidly absorbed what they could of the intellectual and artistic culture of the Greeks. Over a period of two or three centuries they assembled an empire in which the whole world of ancient civilization (west of Persia) was included. Egypt, Greece, Asia Minor, Syria all became Roman provinces, but in them the Romans had hardly any deep influence except in a political sense. In the West—in what are now Tunisia, Algeria, Morocco, Spain, Portugal, France, Switzerland, Belgium, and England—the Romans, though ruthless in their methods of conquest, in the long run acted as civilizing agents, transmitting to these hitherto backward countries the age-old achievements of the East and the more recent culture of Greece and of Rome itself. So thorough was the Romanization that in the West Latin even became the currently spoken language. It was later wiped out in Africa by Arabic but survives to this day, transformed by time, in the languages of France, Italy, Spain, Portugal, and Rumania.

In the Roman Empire, which lasted with many vicissitudes from about 31 B.C.

to the latter part of the fifth century A.D., virtually the entire civilized world of the ancient West was politically united and enjoyed generations of internal peace. Rome was the center, around which in all directions lay the "circle of lands," the *orbis terrarum*, the known world—that is, as known in the West, for the Han Empire at the same time in China was also a highly organized cultural and political entity. The Roman Empire consisted essentially of the coasts of the Mediterranean Sea, which provided the great artery of transport and communication, and from which no part of the empire, except northern Gaul (France), Britain, and the Rhineland, was more than a couple of hundred miles away. Civilization was uniform; there were no distinct nationalities; the only significant cultural difference was that east of Italy the predominant language was Greek, in Italy and west of it, Latin. Cities grew up everywhere, engaged in a busy commercial life and exchange of ideas with one another. They remained most numerous in the east, where most of the manufacturing crafts and the densest population were still concentrated, but they sprang up also in the west—indeed, most of the older cities of France, Spain, England, and western and southern Germany boast of some kind of origin under the Romans.

The distinctive aptitude of the Romans lay in organization, administration, government, and law. Never before had armies been so systematically formed, maintained over such long periods, dispatched at a word of command over such distances, or maneuvered so effectively on the field of battle. Never had so many peoples been governed from a single center. The Romans had at first possessed self-governing and republican institutions, but they lost them in the process of conquest, and the governing talents which they displayed in the days of the empire were of an authoritarian character—talents, not for self-government, but for managing, coordinating, and ruling the manifold and scattered parts of one enormous system. Locally, cities and city-states enjoyed a good deal of autonomy. But above them all rose a pyramid of imperial officials and provincial governors, culminating in the emperor at the top. The empire kept peace, the *pax Romana*, and even provided a certain justice as between its many peoples. Lawyers worked on the body of principles known ever afterward as Roman law.

Roman judges had somehow to settle disputes between persons of different regions, with conflicting local customs, for example, two merchants of Spain and Egypt. The Roman law came therefore to hold that no custom is necessarily right, that there is a higher or universal law by which fair decisions may be made, and that this higher, universal, or "natural" law, or "law of nature," will be understandable or acceptable to all men, since it arises from human nature and reason. Here the lawyers drew on Greek philosophy for support. They held also that law derives its force from being enacted by a proper authority (not merely from custom, usage, or former legal cases); this authority to make law they called *majestas*, or sovereign power, and they attributed it to the emperor. Thus the Romans emancipated the idea of law from mere custom on the one hand and mere caprice on the other; they regarded it as something to be formed by enlightened intelligence, consistently with reason and the nature of things; and they associated it with the solemn action of official power. It must be added that Roman law favored the state, or the public interest as seen by the government, rather than the interests or liberties of individual persons. These principles, together with more specific ideas on property, debt, marriage, wills, etc., were in later centuries to have a great effect in Europe.

The Coming of Christianity

The thousand years during which Greco-Roman civilization arose and flourished were notable in another way even more momentous for all the later history of mankind. It was in this period that the great world religions came into being. Within the time bracket 700 B.C.–A.D. 700 the lives of Confucius and Buddha, of the major Jewish prophets, and of Muhammad are all included. At the very midpoint (probably about 4 B.C.), in Palestine in the Roman Empire, was born a man named Jesus, believed by his followers to be the Son of God. The first Christians were Jews; but both under the impulse of its own doctrine, which held that all men were alike in spirit, and under the strong leadership of Paul, a man of Jewish birth, Roman citizenship, and Greek culture, Christianity began to make converts without regard to former belief. There were certainly a few Christians in Rome by the middle of the first century. Both Paul and the elder apostle, Peter, according to church tradition, died as martyrs at Rome in the time of the Emperor Nero about A.D. 67.

The Christian teaching spread at first among the poor, the people at the bottom of society, those whom Greek glories and Roman splendors had passed over or enslaved, and who had the least to delight in or to hope for in the existing world. Gradually it reached other classes; a few classically educated and well-to-do people became Christians; in the second century Christian bishops and writers were at work publicly in various parts of the empire. In the third century the Roman government, with the empire falling into turmoil, and blaming the social troubles on the Christians, subjected them to wholesale persecution. In the fourth century (possibly in A.D. 312) the Emperor Constantine was converted to Christianity. By the fifth century the entire Roman world was formally Christian; no other religion was officially tolerated; and the deepest thinkers were also Christians, men who combined Christian beliefs with the now thousand-year-old tradition of Greco-Roman thought and philosophy.

It is impossible to exaggerate the importance of the coming of Christianity. It brought with it, for one thing, an altogether new sense of human life. Where the Greeks had demonstrated the powers of the mind, the Christians explored the soul, and they taught that in the sight of God all souls were equal, that every human life was sacrosanct and inviolate, and that all worldly distinctions of greatness, beauty, and brilliancy were in the last analysis superficial. Where the Greeks had identified the beautiful and the good, had thought ugliness to be bad, and had shrunk from disease as an imperfection and from everything misshapen as horrible and repulsive, the Christians resolutely saw a spiritual beauty even in the plainest or most unpleasant exterior and sought out the diseased, the crippled, and the mutilated to give them help. Love, for the ancients, was never quite distinguished from Venus; for the Christians, who held that God was love, it took on deep overtones of sacrifice and compassion. Suffering itself was proclaimed by Christians to be in a way divine, since God himself had suffered on the Cross in human form. A new dignity was thus found for suffering that the world could not cure. At the same time the Christians worked to relieve suffering as none had worked before. They protested against the massacre of prisoners of war, against the mistreatment and degradation of slaves, against the sending of gladiators to kill each other in the arena for another's pleasure. In place of the Greek and pagan self-satisfaction with human accomplishments they taught humility in the face of an almighty Providence, and in place of proud distinctions between high and low, slave and free, civilized and barbarian, they held that all men were brothers because all were children of the same God.

On an intellectual level Christianity also marked a revolution. It was Christianity, not rational philosophy, that dispelled the swarm of greater and lesser gods and goddesses, the blood sacrifices and self-immolation, or the frantic resort to magic, fortune-telling, and divination. The Christians taught that since there was only one God, the pagan gods must be at best lesser demons, and even this idea was gradually given up. The pagan conception of local, tribal, or national gods disappeared. It was now held that for all the world there was only one God, one plan of Salvation, and one Providence, and that all mankind took its origin from one source. The idea of the world as one thing, a "universe," was thus affirmed with a new depth of meaning. The very intolerance of Christianity (which was new to the ancient world) came from this overwhelming sense of human unity, in which it was thought that all men should have, and deserved to have, the one true and saving religion.

It was for their political ideas that the Christians were most often denounced and persecuted. The Roman Empire was a world state; there was no other state but it; no living human being except the emperor was sovereign; no one anywhere on earth was his equal. Between gods and human beings, in the pagan view, there was moreover no clear distinction. Some gods behaved very humanly, and some human creatures were more like gods than others. The emperor was held to be veritably a god, *divus Caesar, semper Augustus*. A cult of Caesar was established, regarded as necessary to maintain the state, which was the world itself. All this the Christians firmly refused to accept. It was because they would not worship Caesar that the Roman officials regarded them as monstrous social incendiaries who must be persecuted and stamped out.

The Christian doctrine on this point went back to the saying gathered from Jesus, that one should render to Caesar the things that were Caesar's, and to God those that were God's. The same dualism was presented more systematically by St. Augustine about A.D. 420 in his *City of God*. Few books have been more influential in shaping the later development of Western civilization.

The "world," the world of Caesar, in the time of St. Augustine, was going to ruin. Rome itself was plundered in 410 by heathen barbarians. Augustine wrote the *City of God* with this event obsessing his imagination. He wrote to show that though the world itself perished there was yet another world that was more enduring and more important.

There were, he said, really two "cities," the earthly and the heavenly, the temporal and the eternal, the city of man and the City of God. The earthly city was the domain of state and empire, of political authority and political obedience. It was a good thing, as part of God's providential scheme for human life, but it had no inherently divine character of its own. The emperor was a man. The state was not absolute; it could be judged, amended, or corrected from sources outside itself. It was, for all its majesty and splendor, really subordinate in some way to a higher and spiritual power. This power lay in the City of God. By the City of God Augustine meant many things, and all sorts of meanings were found by readers in later ages. The heavenly city might mean heaven itself, the abode of God and of blessed spirits enjoying life after death. It might mean certain elect spirits of this world, the good people as opposed to the bad. It might, more theoretically, be a system of ideal values or ideal justice, as opposed to the crude approximations of the actual world. Or it was later thought, by some, to mean the organized church and its clergy.

In any case, with this Christian dualism the Western world escaped from what is called Caesaropapism, the holding by one man of the powers of ruler and of pontiff. Instead, the spiritual and the political power were held to be separate and independent. In later times popes and kings often quarreled with each other; the clergy often struggled for worldly power, and governments at various times (including the twentieth century with its totalitarian systems) have attempted to dictate what men should believe, or love, or hope for. But speaking in general of European history neither side has ever won out, and in the sharp distinction between the spiritual and the temporal has lain the germ of many liberties in the West. At the same time the idea that no ruler, no government, and no institution is too mighty to rise above moral criticism opened the way to a dynamic and progressive way of living in the West.

As for Augustine himself, he lived to see the world grow worse. He died in A.D. 430. In 429 the Roman province of Africa, where he had been a bishop, was pillaged by a wild Germanic tribe called the Vandals.

2. THE EARLY MIDDLE AGES: THE FORMATION OF EUROPE

There was really no Europe in ancient times. In the Roman Empire we may see a Mediterranean world, or even a West and an East in the Latin- and Greek-speaking portions. But the West included parts of Africa as well as of Europe, and Europe as we know it was divided by the Rhine-Danube frontier, south and west of which lay the civilized provinces of the empire, and north and east the "barbarians" of whom the civilized world knew almost nothing. To the Romans "Africa" meant Tunisia-Algeria, "Asia" meant the Asia Minor peninsula; and the word "Europe," since it meant little, was scarcely used by them at all. It was in the half-millennium from the fifth to the tenth centuries that Europe as such for the first time emerged with its peoples brought together in a life of their own, clearly set off from that of Asia or Africa.

The Disintegration of the Roman Empire

First of all the Roman Empire went to pieces, especially in the West. The Christianizing of the empire did nothing to impede its decline. The Emperor Constantine, who in embracing Christianity undoubtedly hoped to strengthen the imperial system, also took one other significant step. In A.D. 330 he founded a new capital at the old Greek city of Byzantium, which he renamed Constantinople. (It is now Istanbul.) Thereafter the Roman Empire had two capitals, Rome and Constantinople, and was administered in two halves. Increasingly the center of gravity moved eastward, as if returning to the more ancient centers in the Near East, as if the "modern" experiment of civilizing the West were to be given up as a failure.

Throughout its long life the empire had been surrounded on almost all sides by barbarians—wild Celts in Wales and Scotland, Germans in the heart of Europe, Persians or Parthians in the East ("barbarian" only in the ancient sense of speaking neither Greek nor Latin), and, in the southeast, the Arabs. (In the south the empire simply faded off into the Sahara.) These barbarians, always with the exception of Persia, had never been brought within the pale of ancient civilization. Somewhat like the Chinese, who about 200 B.C. built the Great Wall to solve the same problem, the Romans simply drew a line beyond which they themselves rarely ventured and would not allow the barbarians to pass. Nevertheless the barbarians filtered in. As early as the third century A.D. emperors and generals recruited bands of them to serve in the Roman armies. Their service over, they would receive farmlands, settle down, marry and mingle with the population. By the fourth and fifth centuries a good many individuals of barbarian birth were even reaching high positions of state. At the same time, in the West, for reasons that are not fully understood, the activity of the Roman cities began to falter, commerce began to decay, local governments became paralyzed, taxes became more ruinous, and free farmers were bound to the soil. The army seated and unseated emperors. Rival generals fought with each other. Gradually the West fell into decrepitude and an internal barbarization so that the old line between the Roman provinces and the barbarian world made less and less difference.

After some centuries of relative stability, the barbarians themselves, pressed by more distant peoples from Asia, rather suddenly began to move. Sometimes they first sought peaceable access to the empire, attracted by the warmer Mediterranean climate, or desiring to share in the advantages of Roman civilization. More often, tribes consisting of a few tens of thousands, men, women, and children, moved swiftly and by force, plundering, fighting, and killing as they went. At first most of the barbarians threatening the empire were Germanic, going under many names. The Angles and Saxons overran Britain about 450, the Franks invaded Gaul at the same time, the Vandals reached as far as Roman Africa in 429, the East Goths appeared in Asia Minor in 382 and in Italy in 493, the West Goths lunged toward Constantinople about 380, tore through Greece in 396, sacked Rome itself in 410, and reached Spain about the year 420. In 476 the last Roman emperor in the West was deposed by a barbarian chieftain. Sometimes in the general upheaval wild Turkman peoples fresh from Asia were intermixed. Of these the most famous were the Huns, who cut through central Europe and France about 450 under their leader Attila, the "scourge of God"—and then disappeared. Nor were these invasions all. Two centuries later new irruptions burst upon the Greco-Roman world on its opposite side, where hitherto outlying peoples poured in from the Arabian deserts. The Arabs, aroused by the new faith of Islam (Muhammad died in 632), fell as conquerors upon Syria, Mesopotamia, Persia, occupied Egypt about 640, the old Roman Africa about 700, and in 711 reached Spain, where they destroyed the Germanic kingdom set up there by the West Goths.

Beneath these blows the old unity of the Greco-Roman or Mediterranean world was broken. The "circle of lands" divided into three segments. Three types of civilization now confronted each other across the inland sea.

The Byzantine World, the Arabic World, and the West about A.D. 700

One was the Eastern Roman, Later Roman, Greek, or Byzantine Empire (all names for the same thing) with its capital at Constantinople, and now including only the Asia Minor peninsula, the Balkan peninsula, and parts of Italy. It represented the most direct continuation of the immemorial civilization of the Near

East. It was Christian in religion and Greek in culture and language. Its people felt themselves to be the truest heirs both of early Christianity and of the Greeks of the golden age. Art and architecture, trades and crafts, commerce and navigation, thought and writing, government and law, while not so creative or flexible as in the classical age, were still carried on actively in the eastern Empire, on much the same level as in the closing centuries of ancient times. For all Christians, and for heathen barbarians in Europe, the emperor of the East stood out as the world's supreme ruler, and Constantinople as the world's preeminent and almost fabulous city.

The second segment, and the most extensive, was the Arabic and Islamic. It reached from the neighborhood of the Pyrenees through Spain and all North Africa into Arabia, Syria, and the East. Arabic was its language; it became, and still remains, the common speech from Morocco to the Persian Gulf. Islam was its religion. It was organized in the caliphate in which all Muslims were included, and the caliph was regarded as the true religious and military successor to Muhammad himself. The Arabic world, like the Byzantine, built directly upon the heritage of the Greco-Romans. In religion, the early Muslims regarded themselves as successors to the Jewish and Christian traditions. They considered the line of Jewish prophets to be spokesmen of the true God, and they put Jesus in this line. But they added that Muhammad was the last and greatest of the prophets, that the Koran set forth a revelation replacing that of the Jewish Bible, that the New Testament of the Christians was mistaken because Christ was not divine, and that the Christian belief in a Trinity was erroneous because there was in the strictest and most rigid sense only One True God. To the Muslim Arabs, therefore, all Christians were contemptible infidels.

In mundane matters, the Arabs speedily took over the civilization of the lands they conquered. In the caliphate, as in the Byzantine Empire, the civilization of the ancient world went its way without serious interruption. Huge buildings and magnificent palaces were constructed; ships plied the Mediterranean; merchants ventured over the deserts and traversed the Indian Ocean; holy or learned men corresponded over thousands of miles; taxes were collected, laws were enforced, and provinces were kept in order. In the sciences the Arabs not only learned from but went beyond the Greeks. The Greek scientific literature was translated: some of it is known today only through these medieval Arabic versions. Arab geographers had a wider knowledge of the world than anyone had possessed up to their time. Arab mathematicians developed algebra so far beyond the Greeks as almost to be its creator ("algebra" is an Arabic word), and in introducing the "Arabic" numerals (through their contacts with India) they made arithmetic, which in Roman numerals had been a formidably difficult science, into something that every schoolchild can be taught.

The third segment was Latin Christendom, which about A.D. 700 did not look very promising. It was what was left over from the other two—what the Byzantines were unable to hold, and the Arabs unable to conquer. It included only Italy (shared in part with the Byzantines), France, Belgium, the Rhineland, and Britain. Barbarian kings were doing their best to rule small kingdoms, but in truth all government had fallen to pieces. Strange and uncouth peoples milled about. Usually the invading barbarians remained a minority, eventually to be absorbed. Only in England, and in the region immediately west of the Rhine, did the Germanic element supersede the older Celtic and Latin. But the presence of the

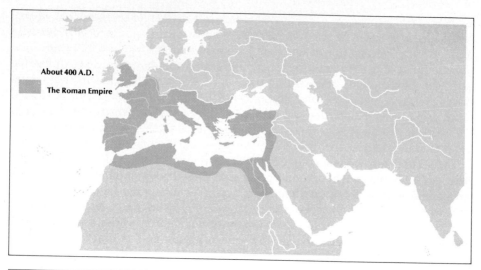

About 400 A.D.

The Roman Empire

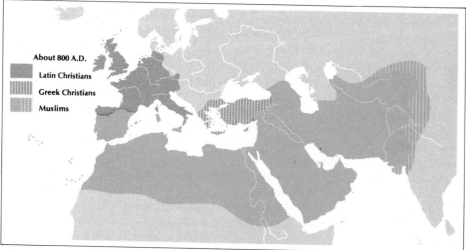

About 800 A.D.

Latin Christians

Greek Christians

Muslims

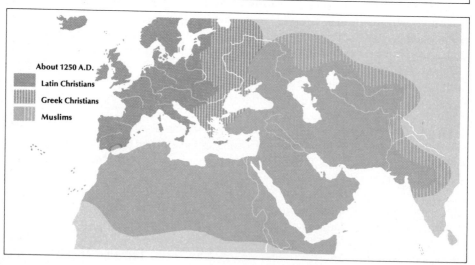

About 1250 A.D.

Latin Christians

Greek Christians

Muslims

invaders, armed and fierce amid peasants and city dwellers reduced to passivity by Roman rule, together with the disintegration of Roman institutions that had gone on even before the invasions, left this region in chaos.

The Western barbarians, as noted, were Germanic; and the Germanic influence was to be a distinctive contribution to the making of Europe. Some Germans were Christian by the fourth century, but most were still heathen when they burst into the Roman Empire. Their languages had not been written down, but they possessed an intricate folklore and religion, in which fighting and heroic valor were much esteemed. Though now in a migratory phase, they were an agricultural people who knew how to work iron, and they had a rudimentary knowledge of the crafts of the Romans. They were organized in small tribes, and had a strong sense of tribal kinship, which (as with many primitive peoples) dominated their ideas of leadership and law. They enjoyed more freedom in their affairs than did the citizens of the Roman Empire. Many of the tribes were roughly self-governing in that all free men, those entitled to bear arms, met in open fields to hold council; and often the tribe itself elected its leader or king. They had a strong sense of loyalty to persons, of fealty to the acknowledged king or chief; but they had no sense of loyalty to large or general institutions. They had no sense of the state—of any distant, impersonal, and continuing source of law and rule. Law they regarded as the inflexible custom of each tribe. In the absence of abstract jurisprudence or trained judges, they settled disputes by rough and ready methods. In the ordeal, for example, a person who obstinately floated when thrown into water was adjudged guilty. In trial by battle, the winner of a kind of ritualistic duel was regarded as innocent. The gods, it was thought, would not allow wrong to prevail.

The Germans who overran the old Roman provinces found it difficult to maintain any political organization at more than a local level. Security and civil order all but disappeared. Peasant communities were at the mercy of wandering bands of habitual fighters. Fighters often captured peasant villages, took them under their protection, guarded them from further marauders, and lived off their produce. Sometimes the same great fighting man came to possess many such villages, moving with his retinue of horsemen from one village to another to support himself throughout the year. Thus originated a new distinction between lord and servant, noble and commoner, martial and menial class. Life became local and self-sufficient. People ate, wore, used, and dwelled in only what they themselves and their neighbors could produce. Trade died down, the cities became depopulated, money went out of circulation, almost nothing was bought or sold. The

THE MEDITERRANEAN WORLD ABOUT A.D. 400, 800, AND 1250

Greco-Roman civilization, centered about the Mediterranean, was officially Christian and politically unified under the Roman Empire in A.D. 400, but broke apart into three segments in the early Middle Ages. Each segment developed its own type of life. Each segment also expanded beyond the limits of the ancient Mediterranean culture. By 1250 Latin Christendom reached to the Baltic and beyond, to include Iceland and even an outpost in Greenland. Greek Christendom penetrated north of the Black Sea, to include the Russians. The Muslim world spread into inner Asia and black Africa. In 1250, and until 1492, the Muslims, or Moors, still held the southern tip of Spain. There continued to be Greek, Armenian, and other Christians under Muslim rule in the eastern Mediterranean, and Jews in varying numbers in each of the three segments.

Roman roads fell into neglect; people often used them as quarries for ready-cut building blocks for their own crude purposes. The West not only broke up into localized villages, but also ceased to have habitual contacts across the Mediterranean. It became isolated from the eastern centers from which its former civilization had always been drawn. The West was reverting. From roughly A.D. 500 on, Europe was in the so-called Dark Ages.

The Church and the Rise of the Papacy

Only one organized institution maintained a tie with the civilized past. Only one institution, reaching over the whole West, could receive news or dispatch its agents over the whole area. This institution was the Christian church. Its framework still stood; its network of bishoprics, as built up in late Roman times, remained intact except in places like England where the barbarian conquest was complete.

In addition, a new type of religious institution was rapidly spreading with the growth of monasteries. The serious and the sensitive, both men and women (though not together, to be sure), rejected the savagery about them and retired into communities of their own. Usually they were left unmolested by rough neighbors who held them in religious awe. In a world of violence they formed islands of quiet and of peace. In a society of burly barbarians they lived the life of contemplation. Their prayers, it was believed, were of use to all the world, and their example might at the least arouse in obstreperous worldlings the pangs of shame. The monastic houses generally adopted the rule of St. Benedict (c. 480–543), and were generally governed by an abbot. Dedicated to the same ideals, they formed unifying filaments throughout the chaos of the Latin West.

Bishops, abbots, and monks looked with veneration to Rome as the spot where St. Peter, the first apostle, had been martyred. The bishop of Rome corresponded with other bishops, sent out missionaries (to England, for example), gave advice on doctrine when he could, and attempted to keep in mind the situation throughout the Latin world as a whole. Moreover, with no emperor any longer in Rome, the bishop took over the government and public affairs of the city. Thus the bishop of Rome, while claiming a primacy over all Christians, was not dominated by any secular power. In the East the great church functionaries, the patriarchs, fell under the influence of the emperor who continued to rule at Constantinople, so that a tradition of Caesaropapism grew up in the East; but in the West the independence of the bishop of Rome now confirmed in practice a principle always maintained by the great churchmen of the West—the independence of the spiritual power from the political or temporal.

In this way was built up the authority of the popes. It was fortified by various arguments. St. Peter, it was held, had imparted the spiritual authority given to him by Christ himself to the Roman bishops who were his successors. This doctrine of the "Petrine supremacy" was based on two verses in the Bible, according to which Christ designated Peter as the head of the church, giving him the "power of the keys," to open and close the doors of eternal salvation.[2] As for the

---

[2] "Thou art Peter, and upon this rock I will build my church; and the gates of hell shall not prevail against it. And I will give unto thee the keys of the kingdom of heaven, and whatsoever thou shalt bind on earth shall be bound in heaven; and whatsoever thou shalt loose on earth shall be loosed in heaven." Matthew xvi, 18–19. In Greek the name Peter meant a "rock"; a play upon words was involved. The pun is still evident in some modern languages, as in French, where *pierre*, a rock, is the same as *Pierre*, Peter.

pope's temporal rule in Rome, it was affirmed that the Emperor Constantine had endowed the bishop with the government of the city. This "Donation of Constantine" was accepted as historical fact from the eighth century to the fifteenth, when it was proved to be a forgery.

It was the church which incorporated the barbarians into a higher way of life, and when a barbarian embraced a more civilized way of living it was the church that he entered. As early as about A.D. 340, the church sent out Ulfilas to convert the Goths; his translation of the Bible represents the first writing down of any Germanic language. About 496 the king of the Franks, Clovis, was converted to Christianity. A hundred years later, in 597, the king of Kent in southeast England yielded to the persuasions of Augustine of Canterbury, a missionary dispatched from Rome, and the Christianization of the Anglo-Saxons gradually followed. Missionaries from Ireland also, to which Christians of the Roman Empire had fled before the heathen barbarians, now returned to both Britain and the Continent to spread the gospel. By some such year as A.D. 700, after three centuries of turmoil, the borders of Christianity in the West were again roughly what they had been in late Roman times. Then in 711, as we have seen, the Arabs conquered Spain. They crossed the Pyrenees and raced toward central Europe, but were stopped by a Christian and Frankish army in 732 at Tours on the river Loire. Islam was not destined to reach beyond Spain.

The Empire of Charlemagne, A.D. 800

Among the Franks, in what is now northern France and the German Rhineland, there had meanwhile arisen a line of capable rulers of whom the greatest was Charlemagne. The Frankish kings made it their policy to cooperate with the pope. The pope needed a protector against depredations by his barbarian neighbors and against the political claims of the Byzantine Empire upon the city of Rome. The Frankish kings, in return for protection thus offered, won papal support to their side. This made it easier for them to control their own bishops, who were more often seen on horseback than in the episcopal chair, and was of use in pacifying their own domains and in wars of conquest against the heathen. In the year 800, in Rome, the pope crowned Charlemagne as emperor of the West. Frankish king and Roman bishop both believed that if only the Roman Empire could be restored peace and order might once more reign. Church and empire, the spirit and the state, were to be as two mighty swords employed in the same holy cause.

Charlemagne crossed the Pyrenees and won back the northeastern corner of Spain to Christian rule. He overthrew and subordinated the barbarian kings who had set themselves up in Italy. He sent forces down the Danube, penetrated into Bohemia, and proceeded against some of the still heathen Germans (the Saxons) who lived along the river Elbe, and whom he either massacred or converted to Christianity. All these regions he brought within his new empire. Except for England and Ireland, which remained outside, the borders of his empire were coextensive with those of the Latin Christian world.

Once more, to a degree, the West was united. But a momentous change had occurred. Its capital was now not Rome and did not lie in the ancient world of the Mediterranean. Its capital was at Aix-la-Chapelle, or Aachen, near the mouth of the Rhine. Its ruler, Charlemagne, was a German of an ethnic group which ancient civilization had left outside. Its people were Germans, French, and Italians, or the ancestors from whom these nationalities were to be developed. In the Greco-Roman world the north had always been at best provincial. Now the north became a center in its own right. Charlemagne dispatched embassies to the emperor at Constantinople, and to Harun al-Rashid, the great caliph at Baghdad. In intellectual matters, too, the north now became a capital. Centuries of violence and confusion had left ignorance very widespread. Charlemagne himself, though he understood Latin, could barely read and never learned to write. He used his authority to revive the all but forgotten ancient learning and to spread education at least among the clergy. To his palace school came scholars from England, Germany, France, Italy, Spain. They wrote and spoke in Latin, the only Western language in which any complicated ideas could at the time be expressed. Disintegrating ancient manuscripts were copied and recopied to assure a more abundant supply for study—always by hand, but in a more rapid script than had before been used, the so-called Carolingian minuscule, from which come the small letters of the modern Western alphabet, only the capitals being Roman. Commerce also, which had virtually disappeared, Charlemagne undertook to foster. He created a new and more reliable coinage, which was based on silver, the gold coins of the Roman Empire having long since vanished. A pound of silver was divided into 20 *solidi* or 240 pennies. This scheme of values, though long used in many parts of Europe, survived longest in the country that remained outside Charlemagne's empire, namely, in England, the last country to replace it with a decimal currency, and then not until the twentieth century.

Ninth-Century Invasions; Europe by A.D. 1000

It is in Charlemagne's empire that we can first see the shape of Europe, as a unit of society and culture distinct from the Mediterranean world of antiquity. The empire did not last. The troubled era was not yet over. New hordes of barbarians assailed Western Christendom in the ninth century. The Magyars (called in Latin "Hungarians") terrified various parts of Europe until they settled down on the middle Danube about the year 900. New Germanic tribes uprooted themselves, coming this time from Scandinavia, and variously known as Norsemen, Vikings, or Danes. Bursting out in all directions, they reached Kiev in Russia in 864, discovered Iceland in 874, and even touched America in 1000. In the Christian world they assaulted the coasts and pushed up the rivers but settled in considerable numbers only in the Danelaw in England and in Normandy in France. Meanwhile the Arabs raided the shores of France and Italy and occupied Sicily. Nowhere was the power of government strong enough to ward off such attacks. Everywhere the harassed local population found its own means of defense or, that failing, was slaughtered, robbed, or carried off into slavery.

Gradually the second wave of barbarians was incorporated as the first had been, by the same process of conversion to Christianity. By the year 1000 the process was nearly complete. In 1001 the pope sent a golden crown to the Magyars to crown St. Stephen as their first king, thus bringing Hungary within the orbit of the Latin West. Poland, Bohemia, and the Scandinavian homelands of the Norsemen were being rapidly Christianized. In older Christian countries, such as France, the last remote and isolated rustics—the "heathen" who lived in the "heath"—were finally ferreted out by missionaries and brought within the Christian fold. In Christian countries Christianity now permeated to every corner, and the historic peoples of western Europe had come together within the spreading system of the Latin church.

Meanwhile West and East continued to drift apart. The refusal of Greek patriarchs at Constantinople to recognize the claims to primacy of the bishop of Rome, whom they regarded as a kind of Western barbarian, and the refusal of the Roman pontiff to acknowledge the political pretensions of the Byzantine Empire, led to the Great Schism of East and West. This schism, after developing for three centuries, became definite in 1054. It divided the Christian world into the Latin or Roman Catholic and the Greek Orthodox churches. It was from Constantinople that Christianity reached the peoples of Russia. The Russians, like the Balkan peoples, remained out of contact with the West during the centuries when spiritual and intellectual contacts were carried through the clergy. They believed, indeed, that the Latin West was evil, heretical, contumacious, and unholy. The Latin West, at the same time, by the schism, cut one more of its ties with antiquity and emerged the more clearly as an independent center of its own civilization.

By the year 1000, or soon thereafter, the entity that we call Europe had been brought into existence. From the turbulence that followed the collapse of the Greco-Roman civilization had issued the peoples and the countries of modern Europe. A kingdom of France was in being, adjoining the great ill-defined bulk of Germany to the east. There were small Christian kingdoms in northern Spain and a number of city-states in the Italian peninsula. In the north there were now a kingdom of England and a kingdom of Scotland; Denmark, Norway, and Sweden had also taken form. In the east rose the three great kingdoms of Poland, Bohemia, and Hungary, the first two predominantly Slavic, Hungary predominantly Magyar, but all Latin and Catholic in culture and religion, and Western in orientation. The east Slavs, or Russians, and the Slavs and other peoples of the Balkan peninsula also formed kingdoms of their own. Their way was diverging from the West. Christianized by Byzantine missionaries, they were Greek and Orthodox in culture and religion and oriented toward Constantinople.

The civilization of the West, in the year 1000, was still not much to boast of in the more polished circles of Byzantium or Baghdad. It might still seem that the West would suffer more than the East from their separation. But the West began at this time to experience a remarkable activity, ushering in the European civilization of the High Middle Ages.

3. THE HIGH MIDDLE AGES: SECULAR CIVILIZATION

Changes after A.D. 1000

Some historical periods are so dynamic that a person who lives to be fifty years old can remember sweeping changes that have come in his own lifetime. Such a time has been the last century of the modern age. Such a time, also, began in Europe in the eleventh century. People could see new towns rise and grow before their eyes. They could observe new undertakings in commerce or government. It is hardly too much to say that all the cities that Europe was to know before the modern industrial era sprang up between about 1050 and 1200. The population of western Europe, which had been sparse even in Roman days, and which was even more sparse after 500, suddenly began to grow more dense about the year

1000, and expanded steadily for two or three hundred years. The people of the High Middle Ages did not develop the conception of progress, because their minds were set upon timeless values and personal salvation in another world, but the period was nevertheless one of rapid progress in nonreligious or "secular" things. It was a period in which much was created that remained fundamental far into modern times.

The new era was made possible by the process of growth in population which went along with agricultural changes. After the Norse and Magyar inroads had stopped, Europe was spared the assaults of barbarians. There came to be more security of life and limb. A farmer could plant with more confidence that he would reap. A man could build a house and expect to live his life in it and pass it on to his children. Hence there was more planting and building. Sometime before the year 1000 a heavier plow had been invented, which cut a deeper furrow. Better methods of harnessing horses had been found than the ancients had ever known. The Romans had continued simply to throw a yoke over a horse's neck, so that the animal in pulling a weight easily choked. Europeans, before the year 1000, began to use a horse collar that rested on the animal's shoulders. The single horse could pull a greater load, or several horses could now for the first time be hitched in tandem. The amount of available animal power was thus multiplied, at a time when animals were the main source of power other than human muscle. Windmills also, unknown to the ancients, were developed in the Low Countries about this time. They too offered a new source of power. Thus at the very beginning of a specifically "European" history, one may detect a characteristic of European civilization—a faculty for invention, a quest for new sources of energy.

With such labor-saving devices people continued to work very hard, but they obtained more results by their efforts. Probably the use of such inventions, together with the influence of the Christian clergy, accounts for the gradual disappearance of slavery from Europe and its replacement by the less abject and less degrading status of serfdom. It is true that medieval Christians, when they could, continued to enslave whites as they were later to do with blacks. Usually such slaves were captives in war, taken from tribes not yet converted to Christianity, and sometimes exported as a form of merchandise to the Byzantine and Muslim worlds. As the successive European peoples became Christianized, the supply of slaves dried up. Medieval Christians did not enslave each other, nor was slavery essential to any important form of production.

Not only did population increase, and work become more productive, but groups of people became less isolated from one another. Communications improved. The roads remained poor or nonexistent, but bridges were built across the many European rivers, and settlers filled in the wildernesses that had formerly separated the inhabited areas. Trees were felled and land cleared, as they would be long afterward in the United States during the westward movement. But where the forest gave way in America to an agricultural world of detached individual farmsteads, in medieval Europe the rural population clustered in village communities. The "nucleated" village gave more security, more contact between families, and readier access to the blacksmith or the priest. It also made possible a communally organized agriculture.

Better ways of using land were introduced in the "three-field" system, which spread almost everywhere where cereal crops were the staple. In this "system" the peasant village divided its arable fields into three parts. In a given year one part was sown with one crop, such as wheat, a second part with another, such as barley, and the third was left to lie fallow. The three parts were rotated from year to year. Thus soil exhaustion was avoided at a time when fertilizers were unknown. Formerly half or less of the available fields had been cultivated at any one time. With the three-field system two-thirds of the land came into annual use. This fact, reinforced by better plowing and more effective employment of animals, led to a huge increase in the supply of food.

The peace and personal security necessary to agriculture were also advanced, in the absence of effective public authority, by the growth of institutions that we know as "feudalism." Feudalism was intricate and diverse, but in essence it was a means of carrying on some kind of government on a local basis where no organized state existed. After the collapse of Charlemagne's empire the real authority fell into the hands of persons who were most often called "counts." The count was the most important man of a region covering a few hundred square miles. To build up his own position, and strengthen himself for war against other counts, he tried to keep the peace and maintain control over the lesser lords in his county, those whose possessions extended over a few hundred or a few thousand acres. These lesser lords accepted or were forced to accept his protection. They became his vassals, and he became their "lord." The lord and vassal relation was one of reciprocal duties. The lord protected the vassal and assured him justice and firm tenure of his land. If two vassals of the same lord disputed the possession of the same village, the lord decided the case, sitting in council (or "court") with all his vassals assembled, and judging according to the common memory or customary law of the district. If a vassal died young, leaving only small children, the lord took the family under his "wardship" or guardianship, guaranteeing that the rightful heirs would inherit in due time. Correspondingly the vassal agreed to serve the lord as a fighting man for a certain number of days in the year. From other "unauthorized" fighting and squabbling the vassal was supposed to refrain. The vassal also owed it to the lord to attend and advise him, to sit in his court in the judging of disputes. Usually he owed no money or material payment; but if the lord had to be ransomed from captivity, or when his children married, the vassal paid a fee. The vassal also paid a fee on inheriting an estate, and the income of estates under wardship went to the lord. Thus the lord collected sporadic revenues with which to finance his somewhat primitive government.

This feudal scheme, which probably originated locally, gradually spread. Lords at the level of counts became in turn the vassals of dukes. In the year 987 the great lords of France chose Hugh Capet as their king, and became his vassals. The kings of France enjoyed little real power for another two hundred years, but the descendants of Hugh occupied their throne for eight centuries, until the French Revolution. Similarly the magnates of Germany elected a king in 911; in 962 the German king was crowned emperor, as Charlemagne had been before him; thus originated the Holy Roman Empire of which much will be heard in the following chapters.

To England, in these formative centuries, it was not given to choose a king by election. England was conquered in 1066 by the Duke of Normandy, William. The Normans (the old Norsemen reshaped by a century of Christian and French influence) imposed upon England a centralized and efficient type of feudalism which they had developed in Normandy. In England, from an early date, the king and his central officials therefore had considerable power. In England there was more civil peace and personal security than on the Continent. Within the framework of a strong monarchy self-governing institutions could eventually develop with a minimum of disorder.

The notable feature of feudalism was its mutual or reciprocal character. In this it differed from the old Roman imperial principle, by which the emperor had been a majestic and all-powerful sovereign. Under feudalism no one was sovereign. King and people, lord and vassal, were joined in a kind of contract. Each owed something to the other. If one defaulted, the obligation ceased. If a vassal refused his due services, the king had the right to enforce compliance. If the king violated the rights of the vassal, the vassals could join together against him. The king was supposed to act with the advice of the vassals, who formed his council or court. If the vassals believed the king to be exceeding his lawful powers, they could impose terms upon him. It was out of this mutual or contractual character of feudalism that ideas of constitutional government later developed.

Feudalism applied in the strict sense only to the military or noble class. Below the feudal world lay the vast mass of the peasantry. Here, in the village, the lowliest vassal of a higher noble was lord over his own subjects. The village, with its people and surrounding farmlands, constituted a "manor," the estate of a lord. In the eleventh century most people of the manor were serfs. They were "bound to the soil" in that they could not leave the manor without the lord's permission. Few wanted to leave anyway, at a time when the world beyond the village was unknown and dangerous, and filled at best only with other similar manors in which opportunities were no different. The lord, for his part, could not expropriate the villagers or drive them away. He owed them protection and the administration of justice. They in turn worked his fields and gave him part of the produce of their own. No money changed hands, because there was virtually no money in circulation. The manorial system was the agricultural base on which a ruling class was supported. It supported also the clergy, for the church held much land in the form of manors. It gave the protection from physical violence and the framework of communal living without which the peasants could not grow crops or tend livestock.

Many consequences flowed from the rise of agricultural productivity. Lords and even a few peasants could produce a surplus, which they might sell if only they could find a market. The country was able to produce enough food for a town population to live on. And since population grew with the increase of the food supply, and since not all the new people were needed in agriculture, a surplus of population also began to exist. Restless spirits among the peasants now wanted to get away from the manor. And many went off to the new towns.

The Rise of Towns and Commerce

We have seen how the ancient cities had decayed. In the ninth and tenth centuries, with few exceptions, there were none left in western Europe. Here and there one would find a cluster of population around the headquarters of a bishop, a great count, or a king. But there were no commercial centers. There was no merchant class. The simple crafts—weaving, metalworking, harness making—were carried on locally on the manors. Rarely, an itinerant trader might appear with such semiprecious goods as he could carry for long distances on donkeys—Eastern silks, or a few spices for the wealthy. Among these early traders Jews were often important, because Judaism, penetrating the Byzantine and Arabic worlds as well as the Western, offered one of the few channels of distant communication that were open.

Long-distance trading was the first to develop. The city of Venice was founded about A.D. 570 when refugees from the barbarians settled in its islands. The Venetians, as time went on, brought Eastern goods up the Adriatic and sold them to traders coming down from central Europe. In Flanders in the north, in what is now Belgium, there developed manufacturers of woolen cloth. Flemish woolens were of a unique quality, owing to peculiarities of the atmosphere and the skill of the weavers. They could not be duplicated elsewhere. Nor could Eastern goods be procured except through the Venetians—or the Genoese or Pisans. Such goods could not possibly be produced locally, yet they were in demand wherever they became known. Merchants traveled in increasing numbers to disseminate them. Money came back into more general circulation; where it came from is not quite clear, since there was little mining of gold or silver until the end of the Middle Ages. Merchants began to establish permanent headquarters, settling within the deserted walls of ghostly Roman towns or near the seat of a lord or ecclesiastic, whose throngs of retainers might become customers. Craftsmen moved from the overpopulated manors to these same growing centers, where they might produce wares that the lords or merchants would wish to buy. The process once started tended to snowball: the more people settled in such an agglomeration the more they needed food brought to them from the country, and the more craftsmen left the villages the more the country people, lords and serfs, had to obtain clothing and simple tools and utensils from the towns. Hence a busy local trade developed also.

By 1100, or not long thereafter, such centers existed all over Europe, from the Baltic to Italy, from England as far east as Bohemia. Usually there was one about every twenty or thirty miles. The smallest towns had only a few hundred inhabitants, the larger ones two or three thousand, or sometimes more. Each carried on a local exchange with its immediate countryside and purveyed goods of more distant origin to local consumers. But their importance was by no means merely economic. What made them "towns" in the full sense of the word was their acquisition of political rights.

The merchants and craftsmen who lived in the towns did not wish to remain, like the country people, subject to neighboring feudal lords. At worst, the feudal lords regarded merchants as fat possessors of ready money; they might hold them up on the road, plunder their mule trains, collect tolls at river crossings, or extort cash by offering "protection." At best, the most well-meaning feudal lord could not supervise the affairs of merchants, for the feudal and customary law knew nothing of commercial problems. The traders in the course of their business developed a "law merchant" of their own, having to do with money and money-changing, debt and bankruptcy, contracts, invoices, and bills of lading. They wished to have their own means of apprehending thieves, runaway debtors, or sellers of fraudulent goods. They strove, therefore, to get recognition for their own law, their own courts, their own judges and magistrates. They wished, too, to govern their towns themselves and to avoid payment of fees or taxes to nearby nobles.

Everywhere in Latin Christendom, along about 1100, the new towns struggled to free themselves from the encircling feudalism and to set themselves up as self-governing little republics. Where the towns were largest and closest together—along the highly urbanized arteries of the trade routes, in north Italy, on the upper Danube and Rhine rivers, in Flanders, or on the Baltic coast—they emancipated themselves the most fully. Venice, Genoa, Pisa, Florence, Milan became virtually independent city-states, each governing a substantial tract of its surrounding country. In Flanders also, towns like Bruges and Ghent dominated their localities. Along the upper Danube, the Rhine, the North Sea, the Baltic, many towns became imperial free cities within the Holy Roman Empire, each a kind of small republic owing allegiance to no one except the distant and usually ineffectual emperor. Nuremberg, Frankfurt, Augsburg, Strasbourg, Hamburg, and Lübeck were free cities of this kind. In France and England, where the towns in the twelfth century were somewhat less powerful, they obtained less independence but received charters of liberties from the king. By these charters they were assured the right to have their own town governments and officials, their own courts and law, and to pay their own kind of taxes to the king in lieu of ordinary feudal obligations.

Often towns formed leagues or urban federations, joining forces to repress banditry or piracy or to deal with ambitious monarchs or predatory nobles. The most famous such league was the Hanse; it was formed mainly of German towns, fought wars under its own banner, and dominated the commerce of the North Sea and the Baltic until after 1300. Similar tendencies of the towns to form political leagues, or to act independently in war and diplomacy, were suppressed by the kings in England, France, and Spain.

The fact that Italy, Germany, and the Netherlands were commercially more advanced than the Atlantic countries in the Middle Ages, and so had a more intensive town life, was to be one cause (out of many) preventing political unification. Not until 1860 or 1870 were nationwide states created in this region. In the west, where towns also grew up, but where more of a balance was kept between town and country, the towns were absorbed into nationwide monarchies that were arising under the kings. This difference between central and western Europe was to shape all the subsequent history of modern times.

The liberties won by the towns were corporate liberties. Each town was a collective thing. The townsman did not possess individual rights, but only the rights which followed from being a resident of a particular town. Among these were personal liberty; no townsman could be a serf, and fugitive serfs who lived over a year in a town were generally deemed to be free. But no townsman wanted individual liberty in the modern sense. The world was still too unsettled for the individual to act alone. The citizens wanted to join together in a compact body, and to protect themselves by all sorts of regulations and controls. The most obvious evidence of this communal solidarity was the wall within which most towns were enclosed. The citizens in time of trouble looked to their own defense. As the towns grew they built new walls farther out. Today, in Paris or Cologne, one may still see remains of different walls in use from the tenth to the thirteenth centuries.

Economic solidarity was of more day-to-day importance. The towns required neighboring peasants to sell foodstuffs only in the town marketplace. They thus protected their food supply against competition from other towns. Or they forbade the carrying on of certain trades in the country; this was to oblige peasants to make purchases in town, and protect the jobs and livelihood of the town craftsmen. They put up tariffs and tolls on the goods of other towns brought within their own walls. Or they levied special fees on merchants from outside who did business in the town. In Italy and Germany they often coined their own money; and the typical town fixed the rates at which various moneys should be exchanged. The medieval towns, in short, at the time of their greatest liberty, followed in a local way the same policies of protectionism and exclusiveness which national governments were often to follow in modern times.

Within each town merchants and craftsmen formed associations, or "guilds," for collective supervision of their affairs. Merchants formed a merchant guild. Stonemasons, carpenters, barbers, dyers, goldsmiths, coppersmiths, weavers, hatters, tailors, shoemakers, grocers, apothecaries, etc., formed craft guilds of their own. The guilds served a public purpose, for they provided that work should be done by reliable and experienced persons, and so protected people from the pitfalls of shoddy garments, clumsy barbers, poisonous drugs, or crooked and flimsy houses. They also provided a means of vocational education and marked out a career for young men. Typically a boy became an apprentice to some master, learned the trade, and lived with and was supported by the master's family for a term of years, such as seven. Then he became a journeyman, a qualified and recognized worker, who might work for any master at a stated wage. If lucky, he might become a master himself, open his own shop, hire journeymen, and take apprentices. So long as the towns were growing, a boy had some chance to become a master himself; but as early as 1300 many guilds were becoming frozen, and the masters were increasingly chary of admitting new persons to their own status. From the beginning, in any case, it was an important function of the guilds to protect their own members. The masters, assembled together, preserved their reputation by regulating the quality of their product. They divided work among themselves, fixed the terms of apprenticeship, the wages to be paid to journeymen, and the prices at which their goods must be sold. Or they took collective steps to meet or keep out the competition of the same trade in nearby towns.

Whether among individuals within the town itself, or as between town and country, or between town and town, the spirit of the medieval economy was to prevent competition. Risk, adventure, and speculation were not wanted. Almost no one thought it proper to work for monetary profit. The few who did, big merchants trading over large areas, met with suspicion and disapproval wherever they went.

The towns, although in many ways they tried to subject the peasants' interests to their own, nevertheless had an emancipating influence on the country. A rustic by settling in town might escape from serfdom. But the town influence was more widespread, and far out of proportion to the relatively small number of people who could become town dwellers. The growth of towns increased the demand for foods. Lords began to clear new lands. All western Europe set about developing a kind of internal frontier. Formerly villages had been separated by dark tracts of roadless woods, in which wolves roamed freely shadowed by the gnomes, elves, and fairies of popular folklore. Now pioneers with axes cleared farmlands and built villages in these immemorial forests. The lords who usually supervised such operations (since their serfs were not slaves, and could not be moved at will) offered freer terms to entice peasants to go and settle on the new lands. It was less easy for the lord of an old village to hold his people in serfdom when in an adjacent village, within a few hours' walk, the people were free. The peasants, moreover, were now able to obtain a little money by selling produce in town. The lords now wanted money because the towns were producing more articles which money could buy. It became very common for peasants to obtain personal freedom, holding their own lands, in return for an annual money payment to the lord for an indefinite period into the future. As early as the twelfth century serfdom began to disappear in northern France and southern England, and by the fifteenth century it had disappeared from most of western Europe. The peasant could now, in law, move freely about. But the manorial organization remained; the peasant owed dues and fees to the lord, and was still under his legal jurisdiction.

The Growth of National Monarchies

Meanwhile the kings were busy, each trying to build his kingdom into an organized monarchy that would outlast his life.[3] Monarchy became hereditary; the king inherited his position like any other feudal lord or possessor of an estate. Inheritance of the crown made for peace and order, for elections under conditions of the time were usually turbulent and disputed, and where the older Germanic principle of elective monarchy remained alive, as in the Holy Roman Empire, there was periodic commotion. The kings sent out executive officers to supervise their interests throughout their kingdoms. The kings of England, adopting an old Anglo-Saxon practice, had a sheriff in each of the forty shires; the kings of France created similar officers who were called bailiffs. The kings likewise instituted royal courts, under royal justices, to decide property disputes and repress crime. This assertion of legal jurisdiction, together with the military might necessary to enforce judgments upon obstinate nobles, became a main pillar of the royal power. In England especially, and in lesser degree elsewhere, the kings required local inhabitants to assist royal judges in the discovery of relevant facts in particular cases. They put men on oath to declare what they knew of events in their own neighborhood. It is from this enforced association of private persons with royal officers that the jury developed.

The kings needed money to pay for their governmental machinery or to carry on war with other kings. Taxation, as known in the Roman Empire, was quite unknown to the Germanic and feudal tradition. In the feudal scheme each person was responsible only for the customary fees which arose on stated occasions. The king, like other lords, was supposed to live on his own income—on the revenue of manors that he owned himself, the proceeds of estates temporarily under his wardship, or the occasional fees paid to him by his vassals. No king, even for the best of reasons, could simply decree a new tax and collect it. At the same time, as the use of money became more common, the kings had to assure themselves of a money income. In England, in the twelfth century, the customary obligation of the vassal to render military service to the king was being converted into a money payment, called "scutage" or shield money. As the towns grew up, with a new kind of wealth and a new source of money income, they agreed to make certain payments in return for their royal charters.

The royal demands for money, the royal claims to exercise jurisdiction, were regarded as innovations. They were constantly growing and sometimes were a source of abuse. They met with frequent resistance in all countries. A famous case historically (though somewhat commonplace in its own day) was that of Magna Carta in England in 1215, when a group of English lords and high churchmen,

[3] See pp. 29–30.

joined by representatives of the city of London, required King John to confirm and guarantee their historic liberties.

The king, as has been said, like any lord, was supposed to act in council or "court" with his vassals. The royal council became the egg out of which departments of government were hatched—such as the royal judiciary, exchequer, and military command. From it also was hatched the institution of parliaments. The kings had always, in a rough sort of way, held great parleys or "talks" (the Latin *parliamentum* meant simply a "talking") with their chief retainers. In the twelfth and thirteenth centuries the growth of towns added a new element to European life. To the lords and bishops was now added a burgher class, which, if of far inferior dignity, was too stubborn, free-spirited, and well furnished with money to be overlooked. When representatives of the towns began to be normally summoned to the king's great "talks," along with lords and clergy, parliaments may be said to have come into being.

Parliaments, in this sense, sprouted all over Europe in the thirteenth century. Nothing shows better the similarity of institutions in Latin Christendom, or the inadequacy of tracing the history of any one country by itself. The new assemblies were called *cortes* in Spain, diets in Germany, Estates General or provincial estates in France, parliaments in the British Isles. Usually they are referred to generically as "estates," the word "parliament" being reserved for Britain, but in origin they were all essentially the same.

The kings called these assemblies as a means of publicizing and strengthening the royal rule. They found it more convenient to explain their policies, or to ask for money, to a large gathering brought together for that purpose than to have a hundred officials make local explanations and strike local bargains in a hundred different places. The kings did not recognize, nor did the assemblies claim, any right of the parliament to dictate to the king and his government. But usually the king invited the parliament to state grievances; his action upon them was the beginning of parliamentary legislation.

The parliaments were considered to represent not the "nation" nor "people" nor yet the individual citizen, but the "estates of the realm," the great collective interests of the country. The first and highest estate was the clergy, the second the landed or noble class; to these older ruling groups were added, as a "third estate," the burghers of the chartered towns. Quite commonly these three types of people sat separately as three distinct chambers. But the pattern varied from country to country. In England, Poland, and Hungary the clergy as a whole ceased to be represented; only the bishops came, sitting with lay magnates in an upper house. Eventually the burghers dropped out in Poland, Bohemia, and Hungary, leaving the landed aristocracy in triumph in eastern Europe. In Castile and Württemberg, on the other hand, the noble estate eventually refused to attend parliament, leaving the townspeople and clergy in the assemblies. In some countries—in Scandinavia, Switzerland, and in the French Estates General—even peasants were allowed to have delegates.

In England the Parliament developed eventually in a distinctive way. After a long period of uncertainty there came to be two houses, known as the Lords and the Commons. The Lords, as in Hungary or Poland, included both great prelates and lay magnates. The House of Commons developed features not found on the Continent. Lesser landholders, the people who elsewhere counted as small nobles, sat in the same House of Commons with representatives of the towns. The

Commons was made up of "knights and burgesses," or gentry and townsmen together, a fact which greatly added to its strength, for the middle class of the towns long remained too weak to act alone. The mingling of classes in England, the willingness of townsmen to follow the leadership of the gentry, and of the gentry to respect the interests of townsmen, helped to root representative institutions in England more deeply than in other countries, in many of which the parliaments tended to die out in later times, in part because of class conflict. Moreover, England was a small country in the Middle Ages, even smaller than it looked on the map because the north was almost wild. There were no provincial or local parliamentary bodies (as in France, the Holy Roman Empire, or Poland) which might jealously cut into the powers of the central body or with which the king could make local arrangements without violating the principle of representative government. And finally, as a reason for the strength of Parliament in England, the elected members of the House of Commons very early obtained the power to *commit* their constituents. If they voted a tax, those who elected them had to pay it. The king, in order to get matters decided, insisted that the votes be binding. Constituents were not allowed to repudiate the vote of their deputy, nor to punish or harass him when he came home, as often happened in other countries. Parliament thus exercised power as well as rights.

In summary, the three centuries of the High Middle Ages laid foundations both for order and for freedom. Slavery was defunct and serfdom expiring. Politically, the multitude of free chartered towns, the growth of juries in some places, the rise of parliaments everywhere, provided means by which peoples could take some part in their governments. The ancient civilizations had never created a free political unit larger than the city-state. The Greeks had never carried democracy beyond the confines within which people could meet in person, nor had the Romans devised means by which, in a large state, the governed could share any responsibilities with an official bureaucracy. The ancients had never developed the idea of representative government, or of government by duly elected and authorized representatives acting at a distance from home. The idea is by no means as obvious or simple as it looks. It first appeared in the medieval monarchies of the West.

4. THE HIGH MIDDLE AGES: THE CHURCH

So far in our account of the High Middle Ages we have told the story of Hamlet without speaking of the Prince of Denmark, for we have left aside the church, except, indeed, when some mention of it could not be avoided. In the real life of the time the church was omnipresent. Religion permeated every pore. In feudalism the mutual duties of lord and vassal were confirmed by religious oaths, and bishops and abbots, as holders of lands, became feudal personages themselves. In the monarchies, the king was crowned by the chief churchman of his kingdom, adjured to rule with justice and piety, and anointed with holy oils. In the towns, guilds served as lay religious brotherhoods; each guild chose a patron saint and marched in the streets on holy days. For amusement the townspeople watched religious dramas, the morality and miracle plays in which religious themes were enacted. The rising town, if it harbored a bishop, took especial care to erect a new cathedral. Years of effort and of religious fervor produced the Gothic cathedrals which still stand as the best known memorials of medieval civilization.

The Development of the Medieval Church and Papacy

If, however, we turn back to the tenth century, the troubled years before 1000, we find the church in as dubious a condition as everything else. The church reflected the life about it. It was fragmented and localized. Every bishop went his own way. Though the clergy was the only literate class, many of the clergy themselves could not read and write. Christian belief was mixed with the old pagan magic and superstition. The monasteries were in decay. Priests often lived in a concubinage that was generally condoned. It was customary for them to marry, so that they had recognized children, to whom they intrigued to pass on their churchly position. Often rough laymen dominated their ecclesiastical neighbors, with the big lords appointing the bishops, and the little ones the parish priests. When people thought about Rome at all, they sensed a vague respect for something legendary and far away; but the bishop of Rome, or pope, had no influence and was treated in unseemly fashion in his own city. The popes of the tenth century were the creatures of the unruly Roman nobles. Marozia, daughter of a Roman "senator," became the mistress of one pope, by whom she had a son who became pope in turn, until she imprisoned him so that another son, by another father, could claim the papacy also.

The Roman Catholic church is in fact unrecognizable in the jumble of the tenth century. So far at least as human effort was concerned, it was virtually created in the eleventh century along with the other institutions of the High Middle Ages.

The impulse to reform came from many quarters. Sometimes a secular ruler undertook to correct conditions in his own domains. For this purpose he asserted a strict control over his clergy. In 962 the Holy Roman Empire was proclaimed. This Empire, like the Carolingian and Roman empires which it was supposed to continue, was in theory coterminous with Latin Christendom itself, and endowed with a special mission of preserving and extending the Christian faith. Neither in France nor in England (nor, when they became Christian states, in Spain, Hungary, Poland, or Scandinavia) was this claim of the Holy Roman Empire ever acknowledged. But the Empire did for a time embrace Italy as well as Germany. The first emperors, in the tenth and eleventh centuries, denouncing the outrageous conditions in Rome, strove to make the pope into their appointee.

At the same time a reform movement arose from spiritual sources. Serious Christians took matters into their own hands. They founded a new monastery at Cluny in France, which soon had many daughter houses. It was their purpose to purify monastic life and to set a higher Christian ideal to which all clergy and laity might look up. To rid themselves of immediate local pressures, the greed, narrowness, ignorance, family ambition, and self-satisfied inertia that were the main causes of corruption, the Cluniacs refused to recognize any authority except that of Rome itself. Thus, at the very time when conditions in Rome were at their worst, Christians throughout Europe built up the prestige of Rome, of the idea of Rome, as a means to raise all Latin Christendom from its depths.

As for the popes in Rome, those who preserved any independence of judgment or respect for their own office, it was their general plan to free themselves from the Roman mobs and aristocrats without falling into dependence upon the Holy Roman Emperor. In 1059 Pope Nicholas II issued a decree providing that future popes should be elected by the cardinals. The cardinals, at that time, were the priests of churches in the city of Rome or bishops of neighboring dioceses. By entrusting the choice of future popes to them, Pope Nicholas hoped to exclude all influence from outside the clergy itself. Popes have been elected by cardinals ever since, though not always without influence from outside.

One of the first popes so elected was Gregory VII, known also as Hildebrand, a dynamic and strong-willed man who was pope from 1073 to 1085. He had been in touch with the Cluniac reformers, and dreamed of a reformed and reinvigorated Europe under the universal guidance of the Roman pontiff.

To understand what followed, the reader must exert his imagination. In his mind's eye he must see a world in which all political barriers have dropped away. In this world people have no nationality. They do not live in the state, as in modern times; they live in the church. Society itself is a great religious community. Its leaders are the clergy, to which all educated persons belong. The public personage with whom people come into most frequent contact is the priest, and the most important public official is the bishop. The chief public buildings are churches, abbeys, and cathedrals. Secular interests, those of kings and dukes, of merchants and artisans, are earthbound and shortsighted. All persons, even kings, in addition to secular interests, have a higher concern. All are living in the religious community and preparing their souls for eternal life. The religious community, or church, reaches in principle as far as the borders of the known world. It is universal, for all men must be saved. At its head stands the bishop of Rome, the Vicar of Christ, the successor to Peter, the keeper of the keys, the *servus servorum Dei*, the servant of the servants of God.

Some such vision filled the mind of Gregory VII, and with it he founded the papal supremacy of the High Middle Ages. He believed that the church should stand apart from worldly society, that it should judge and guide all human actions, and that a pope could judge and punish kings and emperors if he deemed them sinful. His ideal was not a "world state," but its spiritual counterpart, a world church officered by a single-minded and disciplined clergy, centralized under a single authority. He began by insisting that the clergy free itself of worldly involvements. He required married priests to put aside their wives and families. Celibacy of the clergy, never generally established in the Greek Orthodox church, and later rejected by Protestants in the West, became and remained the rule for the Roman Catholic priesthood. Gregory insisted also that no ecclesiastic might receive office through appointment by a layman. In his view only clergy might institute or influence clergy, for the clergy must be independent and self-contained.

Gregory soon faced a battle with that other aspirant to universal supremacy and a sacred mission, the Holy Roman Emperor, who at this time was Henry IV. In Germany the bishops and abbots possessed a great deal of the land, which they held and governed under the emperor as feudal magnates in their own right. To the emperor it was vitally important to have his own men, as reliable vassals, in these great positions. Hence in Germany "lay investiture" had become very common. "Lay investiture" meant the practice by which a layman, the emperor, conferred upon the new bishop the signs of his spiritual authority, the ring and the staff. Gregory prohibited lay investiture. He supported the German bishops and nobles when they rebelled against Henry. Henry proving obstinate, Gregory excommunicated him, i.e., outlawed him from Christian society by forbidding any priest to give him the sacraments. Henry, baffled, sought out the pope at Canossa in Italy to do penance. "To go to Canossa" in later times became a byword for submission to the will of Rome.

In 1122, after both original contenders had died, a compromise on the matter of lay investiture was effected by which bishops recognized the emperor as their feudal head but looked to Rome for spiritual authority. But the struggle between popes and emperors went on unabated. The magnates of Germany, lay lords as well as bishops, often allied with the pope to preserve their own feudal liberties from the emperor. The emperor in Germany was never able to consolidate his domains as did the kings in England and France. In Italy, too, the popes and emperors quarreled, the foes of each commonly siding with the other. The unwillingness of lords and churchmen (and of towns also, as we have seen) to let the emperors build up an effectual government left its mark permanently upon Europe in two ways. It contributed to the centralization of Latin Christendom under Rome, while it blocked national unity in central Europe.

The height of the medieval papacy came with Innocent III, whose pontificate lasted from 1198 to 1216. Innocent virtually realized Gregory's dream of a unified Christian world. He intervened in politics everywhere. He was recognized as a supreme arbiter. At his word, a king of France took a wife, a king of England accepted an unwanted archbishop, a king of León put aside the cousin whom he had married, and a claimant to the crown of Hungary deferred to his rival. Innocent advised the kings of Bohemia, Poland, and Denmark on weighty matters, and the kings of England, Aragon, and Portugal acknowledged him as feudal overlord within their realms. Huge revenues now flowed to Rome from all over Latin Christendom, and an enormous bureaucracy worked there to dispatch the voluminous business of the papal court. As kings struggled to repress civil rebellion, so Innocent and his successors struggled to repress heresy, which, defined as doctrine at variance with that of the church at large, was becoming alarmingly common among the Albigensians of southern France.

4th lateran Council

In 1215 Innocent called a great church council, the greatest since antiquity, attended by 500 bishops and even by the patriarchs of Constantinople and Jerusalem. The council labored at the perplexing task of keeping the clergy from worldly temptations. By forbidding priests to officiate at ordeals or trials by battle, it virtually ended these survivals of barbarism. It attempted to regularize belief in the supernatural by controlling the superstitious traffic in relics. It declared the sacraments to be the channel of God's saving grace and defined them authoritatively.[4] In the chief sacrament, the Eucharist or Mass, it promulgated the dogma of transubstantiation, which held that, in the Mass, the priest converts the substance of bread and wine into the substance of Christ's body and blood. Except for heretics, who were suppressed, the acts of the Fourth Lateran Council were accepted with satisfaction throughout Latin Europe.

Intellectual Life: The Universities, Scholasticism

Under the auspices of the church, as rising governments gave more civil security, and as the economy of town and country became able to support men devoted to a life of thought, the intellectual horizon of Europeans began to open. The

---

[4] A sacrament is understood to be the outward sign of an inward grace. In Catholic doctrine the sacraments were and are seven in number: baptism, confirmation, penance, the Eucharist, extreme unction, marriage, and holy orders. Except for baptism, a sacrament may be administered only by a priest. A dogma is the common belief of the church, in which all the faithful share and must share so long as they are members of the church. Dogmas are regarded as implicitly the same in all ages; they cannot be invented or developed, but may from time to time be clarified, defined, promulgated, or proclaimed.

twelfth and thirteenth centuries saw the founding of the first universities. These originated in the natural and spontaneous coming together of teachers and pupils which had never wholly disappeared even in the Dark Ages. By 1200 there was a center of medical studies at Salerno in south Italy, of legal studies at Bologna in north Italy, of theological studies at Paris. Oxford was founded about 1200 by a secession of disgruntled students and professors from Paris, Cambridge shortly thereafter. By 1300 there were a dozen such universities in Latin Europe, by 1500 almost a hundred.

As the early agglomerations of traders developed into organized towns, so the informal concourses of students and teachers developed into organized institutions of learning, receiving the sharp corporate stamp that was characteristic of the High Middle Ages. It was in having this corporate identity that medieval universities resemble our own and differed from the schools of Athens or Alexandria in ancient times. A university, the early University of Paris, for example, was a body of men, young and old, interested in learning and endowed by law with a communal name and being. It possessed definite liberties under some kind of charter, regulated its own affairs through its own officials, and kept its own order among its often boisterous population. It gave, and even advertised, courses and lectures, and it decided collectively which professors were the best qualified to teach. It might consist of distinct schools or "faculties"—the combination of theology, law, and medicine, as at Paris, was the most usual. It held examinations and awarded degrees, whose meaning and value were recognized throughout the Latin West. The degree, which originated as a license to teach, admitted its holder to certain honors or privileges such as those of a craft guild. With it, a professor might readily move from one university to another. Students moved easily also, the language being everywhere Latin and the curriculum much the same. The university, moreover, though typically it began in poverty, was as a corporate body capable of holding property; and the benefactions of pious donors, as the years went on, often built up substantial endowments in lands and manors. So organized, free from outside control, and enjoying an income from property, the university lived on as an institution beyond the lifetime of all living men, through good times and bad.

The queen of the sciences was theology, the intellectual study of religion. Many in Europe, by the eleventh century, were beginning to reflect upon their beliefs. They continued to believe but could no longer believe with naïve or unthinking acceptance. It was accepted as a fact, for example, that the Son of God had been incarnated as a man in Jesus Christ. But in the eleventh century an Italian named Anselm, who became archbishop of Canterbury, wrote a treatise called *Cur Deus Homo?*—"Why Did God Become Man?"—giving reasoned explanations to show why God had taken this means to save mankind.[5] Soon afterward Abélard, who taught at Paris, wrote his *Sic et non*—"Yes and No" or "Pro and Con"—a collection of inconsistent statements made by St. Augustine and other Fathers of the Church. Abélard's purpose was to apply logic to the inherited mass of patristic writings, show wherein the truth of Christian doctrine really lay, and so make the faith consistent with reason and reflection.

---

[5] It may be useful to note that the Latin *homo* refers to all members of the human race, male and female, children and adults, the word for an adult male being *vir*. In English there is only the one word "man" to serve in both senses. Thus in modern biology and anthropology all members of the genus *homo*, of which *homo sapiens* is the only living species, are "man." In the present book the use of "man" in this generic sense will occur from time to time. In such contexts the pronouns "he," "his," and "him" are of indeterminate gender.

Meanwhile, in the twelfth century a great stream of new knowledge poured into Europe, bringing about a veritable intellectual revolution. It was derived from the Arabs, with whom Christians were in contact in Sicily and Spain. The Arabs, as has been seen, had taken over the ancient Greek science, translated Greek writings into Arabic, and in many ways added further refinements of their own. Bilingual Christians (assisted by numerous learned Jews who passed readily between the Christian and Muslim worlds) translated these works into Latin. Above all, they translated Aristotle, the great codifier of Greek knowledge who had lived and written in the fourth century B.C. The Europeans, barely emerging from barbarism, were overwhelmed by this sudden disclosure of an undreamed of universe of knowledge. Aristotle became The Philosopher, the unparalleled authority on all branches of knowledge other than religious.

The great problem for Europeans was how to digest the gigantic bulk of Aristotle, or, in more general terms, how to assimilate or reconcile the body of Greek and Arabic learning to the Christian faith. The universities, with their "scholastic" philosophers or "schoolmen," performed this useful social function. Most eminent of scholastics was Thomas Aquinas (1225–1274), the Angelic Doctor, known also to his own contemporaries as the Dumb Ox from the slow deliberation of his speech. His chief work, appropriately called the *Summa Theologica*, was a survey of all knowledge. The thought of Aquinas, as recently as 1879, was pronounced by Pope Leo XIII to be the foundation of official Catholic philosophy.

The chief accomplishment of Thomas Aquinas was his demonstration that faith and reason could not be in conflict. By reason he meant a severely logical method, with exact definition of words and concepts, deducing step by step what follows and must follow if certain premises are accepted. His philosophy is classified as a form of "realism." It holds, that is, that the general idea is more "real" than the particular—that "man" is more real than this or that man or woman, that "law" as such is more real and binding than this or that particular law. He derived his philosophy from what he took to be the nature of God, of man, of law, of reason, of beings in general. He taught a hierarchic view of the universe and of society, of which God was the apex, and in which all things and all men were subordinated to God in a descending order, each bound to fulfill the role set by its own place and nature. It was the emphasis on the superior reality of abstractions that enabled men in the Middle Ages to believe steadfastly in the church while freely attacking individual churchmen, to have faith in the papacy while denouncing the popes as scoundrels—or to accept without difficulty the mystery of transubstantiation, which declared that what admittedly looked and tasted like bread and wine was, in real inner substance, the body of Christ.

The scholastic philosophy, as perfected by Thomas Aquinas, was not very favorable to the growth of natural science, because, in its emphasis on an inner reality, it drew attention away from the actual details and behavior of concrete things. On the other hand, the scholastic philosophy laid foundations on which later European thought was to be reared. It habituated Europeans to great exactness, to careful distinctions, even to the splitting of hairs. It called for disciplined thinking. And it made the world safe for reason. If any historical generalization may be made safely, it may be safely said that any society that believes reason to threaten its foundations will suppress reason. In Thomas' time, there were some who said that Aristotle and the Arabs were infidels, dangerous influences that must be silenced. Any reasoning about the faith, they warned, was a form of weakness.

Thomas' doctrine that faith could not be endangered by reason gave a freedom to thinkers to go on thinking. Here Latin Christendom may be contrasted with the Muslim world. It was ruled, in about the time of Thomas Aquinas, that valid interpretation of the Koran had ended with the Four Great Doctors of early Islam. As Muslims said, the Gate was closed. Arabic thought, so brilliant for several centuries, went into decline.

The Crusades; New Invasions; Europe by 1300

Meanwhile, the West was expanding. Europe in the eleventh century took the offensive against Islam. All Latin Christendom went on the Crusades. War itself was subordinated to the purposes of religion.

The most ambitious, best remembered, and least successful of such expeditions were the Crusades to win back the Holy Land. The First Crusade was preached in 1095 by Pope Urban II, who hoped thereby to advance the Peace of God by draining off bellicose nobles to fight the infidels, and to build up the leadership of Rome, just asserted by Gregory VII, through raising a universal cause of which the pope might be the head. Crusades to the Holy Land, with varying success, and sometimes departing woefully from their religious aims, went on intermittently for two hundred years. It was the growth of Italian shipping in the Mediterranean, the rise of more orderly feudal monarchies, the increasing sense of a Europe-wide common purpose, that made possible the assembly and transport of considerable forces over a great distance. It is sometimes said that the Crusades, by bringing contacts with the East, stimulated the development of civilization in the West, but it seems more likely that, as Europe's counterthrust against Islam, the Crusades were the consequence of Europe's own growing strength. For a century the Latin Christians occupied parts of Palestine and Syria. But in the thirteenth century they had to withdraw, and the Muslims remained in possession.

THE MEETING OF ST. ANTHONY AND ST. PAUL
by Sassetta (Italian, 1392–1450)

Here we can see something of the medieval way of thinking. The picture tells a religious story. St. Anthony appears in three places, walking alone, converting a centaur, and meeting and embracing St. Paul. There is no attempt to present him as a unique individual person; his head and features disappear behind those of St. Paul in the principal scene. The picture gives the "idea" of the story. The two figures are typical saints, with the halos which conventionally designated sacred persons. The artist has painted the "idea" or "essence" of a forest, i.e., many trees; he has not shown the actual appearance of a particular forest, with underbrush, shadows, trees of different sizes, and foliage of different kinds. His hills are hills in general, i.e., mounds of earth; his cave is a cave in general, i.e., a dark hole. When the two saints embrace, their arms and legs are placed where the mind knows that they ought to be, not where the eye would see them concretely in any particular situation. The picture thus illustrates, on a simple level, what is meant by the abstractness or "realism" (the realism of ideas) of medieval thought. A child today, or an artistically untrained adult, draws in the same way, portraying the idea rather than the physical actuality. The idea of a forest is, after all, "many trees"; all else is special or incidental, not of the essence. Courtesy of the National Gallery of Art, Washington, D.C., Samuel H. Kress Collection.

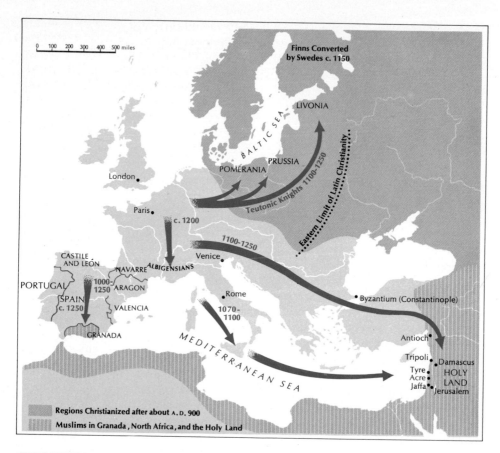

CRUSADING ACTIVITY, 1100–1250

Medieval Christendom expanded geographically until about A.D. 1250. Darker regions are those Christianized shortly before and after A.D. 1000. Arrows indicate organized military-religious expeditions, which by 1250 had recovered most of Spain from Muslim control, but had failed to do so in the Holy Land. Dates are rounded and very rough.

Other crusades (for such they were) had more lasting results. A party of Normans won Sicily from the Arabs about 1100. Iberian Christians, descending from the mountains of northern Spain, carried on a *reconquista* of two centuries against the Moors. By 1250 they had staked out the Christian kingdoms of Portugal, León, Castile, Aragon, and Valencia, leaving the Muslims only Granada in the extreme south, which was conquered much later, in 1492. In southern France, an Albigensian crusade in the thirteenth century put down the heretics, those born in the faith but erring from it. Against remaining European heathen, those born in ignorance of the faith, of whom a few were still found along the Baltic coast, crusading expeditions were also launched. The Teutonic Order, a military-religious society of knights founded originally to fight in the Holy Land, transferred its operations to the north. Christianity, and with it the civilization of the Latin West, was brought by the sword to primitive Prussia and the east Baltic regions.

About the year 1250 there developed a new threat of invasion from Asia. As the

Huns had burst out of Asia in the fifth century, and the Magyars in the ninth, so now the Tartars appeared in the thirteenth century, to be followed in the fourteenth by the Ottoman Turks. We shall see how the Turks long continued to press upon central Europe. But, on the whole, by the thirteenth century, Europe was capable of resistance. Always until then it had lain open, an outlying, backward, thinly populated protuberance from the Eurasian land mass. It had lain open in the remote past to wandering Indo-Europeans, then to Roman imperial conquerors, to Germanic barbarians, to Huns, Magyars, and, in part, the Arabs. All these were assimilated. The blood of all flowed in European veins. In spirit all were assimilated by the Roman church, the Latin language, the common institutions of feudalism, monarchy, a free town life, parliamentary assemblies, and scholastic learning, which ran as an almost seamless web from England to Sicily and from Portugal to Poland.

By 1300 the "rise of Europe" was an accomplished fact. The third of the three segments into which the Greco-Roman world had divided, the one which in A.D. 700 had been the most barbarous, now some six hundred years later had a civilization of its own. It was still only one among the several great cultures of the world, such as the Islamic, Byzantine, Indian, and Chinese. It enjoyed no preeminence. The Chinese empire, for example, in the thirteenth century, had cities whose population reached into millions. It had an affluent merchant class, great textile manufactures, and an iron industry that produced over 100,000 tons a year. The arts and sciences were assiduously pursued. Government was centralized and complex; it issued paper money, and employed a civil service recruited by competitive examinations. Books on religious, technical, and agricultural subjects, including whole multivolume encyclopedias, were printed in enormous numbers, even though the lack of an alphabet and use of thousands of characters made it difficult for literacy to become widely spread. The Venetian Marco Polo was dazzled by the China that he lived in from 1275 to 1292.

Many have asked why China did not generate, as Europe did in these centuries, the forces that ultimately led to the modern scientific and industrial world. One answer is suggested by the fact that it was Europeans like Marco Polo who went to China, not Chinese who went to Europe. It was the Chinese who invented printing, but it was Europe that was revolutionized by printed books. The Chinese knew of gunpowder, but the Europeans invented guns. Chinese merchant vessels traded with India in the twelfth century, but did not pursue the advantage; Europeans did so three centuries later, and they also discovered America. Somehow Europe was more enterprising and restless. It was already on the alert for something new. In Europe there was no all-embracing empire as in China, but kings, lords, and towns that competed with each other. Conformity was not one of the primary virtues. With religion and the church kept distinct from the state, the questions of what one should do with one's life were less dependent on the political powers than in China. Europe was disorderly and full of conflict—rivalries and wars between kings, quarrels between kings and their barons, disputes between church and state, clashes between lords and their peasant workers. In such disorder there was also a kind of freedom, and a dynamism which promoted change.

II.
The Upheaval in Christendom, 1300-1560

I n the transition from a traditional to a more modern form of society all the old civilizations have had to reexamine their religious base. Today we can observe this process at work everywhere: the Chinese reconsider the age-old teachings of Confucius, the Muslims enter into wider activities than those known to the Koran, and the peoples of India attempt to found a society in which historic Hindu practices no longer form the dominant pattern. It is not necessarily that peoples reject their ancestral religion. They may even reaffirm it, but they try also to modernize it, to adapt it, to make room for new and nonreligious interests. The process of developing a variety of activities outside the sphere of religion is called "secularization."

Latin Christendom was the first of the world's major civilizations to become "secularized." In the very long run it was those aspects of European civilization that were least associated with Christianity, such as natural science and industrial technology, or military and economic power, that the "non-European" world from Islam to East Asia proved to be most willing to adopt. If in our own time there has come to be such a thing as a world civilization, it is because all the world's great traditional cultures have been increasingly secularized.

The Europe which by the thirteenth century was so triumphantly Christian soon entered upon a series of disasters. The Mongols after about 1240 held Russia in subjugation for two hundred years. The Ottoman Turks, who had originated in central Asia, penetrated the Byzantine Empire, crushed the medieval Serbian state in 1389, spread over the Balkans, and took Constantinople itself in 1453. Eastern Christianity continued to exist, but under alien political domination. Latin

Chapter Emblem: A medal struck in honor of Pico della Mirandola, Florentine humanist of the fifteenth century.

Christianity, reaching from Poland and Hungary to the Atlantic, remained independent but was beset with troubles. The authority of the papacy and of the Roman Catholic church was called into question. Eventually the Protestant churches emerged. The whole of medieval civilization was undermined. Yet new forces also asserted themselves, alongside or outside the religious tradition. Government, law, philosophy, science, the arts, material and economic activities were pursued with less regard for Christian values. Power, order, beauty, wealth, knowledge, and control of nature were regarded as desirable in themselves.

In this mixture of decline and revival, of religious revolution and secularization, medieval Christendom began to take on the outlines of modern Europe.

5. DISASTERS OF THE FOURTEENTH CENTURY

The Black Death and Its Consequences

During the fourteenth century, and quite abruptly, almost half the population of Europe was wiped out. Some died in sporadic local famines that began to appear after 1300. The great killer, however, was the bubonic plague, or Black Death, which first struck Europe in 1348. Since the plague recurred at irregular and unpredictable intervals, and killed off the young as well as the old, it disrupted marriage and family life and made it impossible for many years for Europe to regain the former level of population. In some places whole villages disappeared. Cultivated fields were abandoned for want of able-bodied men and women to work them. The towns were especially vulnerable, since the plague bacillus was carried by rats, which infested the dark houses crowded within town walls. Trade and exchange were obstructed; prices, wages, and incomes moved erratically; famine made its victims more susceptible to disease, and deaths from the plague contributed to famine. The living were preoccupied with the burial of the dead and with fears for their own future.

There were immediate social and political repercussions. For the survivors, at least, there were some advantages in that labor became scarce and so could expect higher wages. On the other hand, in the general disorganization, and with landowners and urban employers decimated also, many of the poor could find no work, or took to vagabondage and begging. The upper classes, acting through governments, attempted to control wages and prices, as in the English Statute of Laborers of 1351. Rebellions of workers broke out in various towns, especially in Flanders. There were massive insurrections of peasants in many parts of Europe. In France these were called "jacqueries" (from "Jacques," a nickname for a peasant), of which the first was in 1358. In England a similar large-scale uprising in 1381 came to be known as Wat Tyler's rebellion. Sometimes the spokesmen for these movements went beyond their immediate grievances to question the whole class structure, asking why some should be rich and others poor. It was in Wat Tyler's rebellion that the famous couplet was coined:

> *When Adam delved and Eve span*
> *Who was then a gentleman?*

Governments and the upper classes replied to this menace with ferocious repression. The peasants generally returned to their usual labors. Yet something was

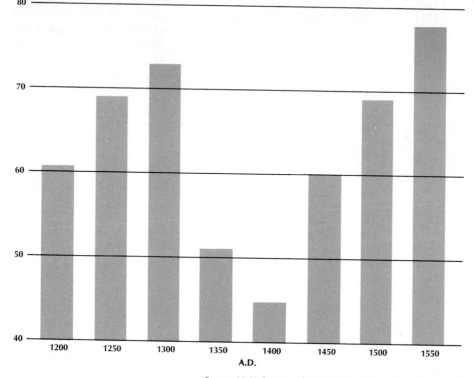

Source: M. K. Bennett, *The World's Food* (New York: Harper, 1954).

ESTIMATED POPULATION OF EUROPE, 1200–1550

The catastrophic drop shown between 1300 and 1400, unparalleled in the history of Europe, was due mainly to the bubonic plague or Black Death, which first appeared in 1348 and raged intermittently thereafter. It is thought that by about A.D. 600, after the collapse of the Roman Empire, the population of Europe may have gradually declined to about twenty million. Then with agricultural improvements, and the end of the Viking attacks and other raids, population grew rapidly, especially after A.D. 1000, reaching a high point in the early fourteenth century. Not until the early sixteenth century was the population of 1300 again attained.

gained for the rural workers, at least in the long run, as underlying economic and demographic forces continued to assert themselves. The landowners, or feudal class, in order to get the work done on their manors, and assure their own incomes, had to offer more favorable terms. These included, for example, the giving of lifetime tenures to peasant families, in return for fixed payment of sums of money. Over the years many of these peasant holdings became hereditary and the value of money decreased, so that payment of a shilling, for example, which in 1400 represented a significant amount, became much less burdensome for the rural worker by 1600. In effect, a class of small peasant property owners began to emerge in much of Europe.

The kings also, who had been building up their position against the church and

subjects. Some frantically performed the Dance of Death in the cemeteries, while others furtively celebrated the Black Mass, parodying religion in a mad desire to appease the devil. The Order of Flagellants grew up; its members went through the streets, two by two, beating each other with chains and whips. It was at this time that the great witchcraft delusion, which was to reach its height in the fifteenth and sixteenth centuries, first became important.

Disaffection with the church, or the thought that it might not be the true or the only way to salvation, spread in all ranks of society. It was not only kings who disputed the claims of the clergy. Obscure parish priests, close to the distress of ordinary people, began to doubt the powers of their ecclesiastical superiors. One of these humble clerics was William Langland, who in his *Piers Plowman*, in the 1360s, contrasted the sufferings of the honest poor with the hypocrisy and corruption in high places. Such unsettling ideas spread very widely; in England those who held them were known as Lollards. Since the actual poor left no records, it is hard to say exactly what their ideas consisted of, but something like them was also expressed by John Wyclif, who taught at Oxford. About 1380, Wyclif was saying that the true church could do without elaborate possessions, and even that an organized church might not be necessary for salvation, since ordinary, devout persons could do without priests and obtain salvation by reading the Bible, which he translated into English. Similar ideas appeared in Bohemia in central Europe, with John Huss as their spokesman. Here they became a national movement, for the Hussites were both a religious party and at the same time a Slavic or Czech party protesting against the supremacy of the Germans who lived in Bohemia. The Hussite wars ravaged central Europe for decades in the fifteenth century. The ideas of the Lollards and of Huss and Wyclif were branded as heresy, or unacceptable deviations from the true doctrine of the church.

Influential and established persons did not yet turn to heresy, and still less to witchcraft or flagellation. Their answer to the needs of the day was to assemble a great Europe-wide or general council of the church, in which reforms could be pressed by the whole body of Christians upon the reluctant and rival popes.

The Conciliar Movement

In 1409 such a church council met at Pisa. All parts of the Latin West were represented. The council declared both reigning popes deposed, and obtained the due election of another, but since the first two refused to resign there were now three. In 1414 an even greater and more fully attended council met at Constance. Its aims were three: to end the now threefold schism, to extirpate heresy, and to reform the church "in head and members," or from top to bottom. Not much was accomplished in reform. To discourage heresy, John Huss was interrogated, condemned, and burned at the stake. The schism was ended. All three popes were at last persuaded or compelled to withdraw, and another, Martin V, was elected. The unity of the church, under the papacy, was at last restored.

The majority at the Council of Constance wished to make general councils part of the permanent apparatus of the church for all time in the future. They regarded the pope as, so to speak, a constitutional monarch, and the council as a representative body for all Christians. Martin V, however, no sooner elected pope, reaffirmed the prerogatives of the papal office. He dissolved the Council of

Constance, and repudiated its decrees. The next thirty years saw a continuing contest of wills between successive popes and successive councils.

In this battle for jurisdiction few reforms could be adopted, and fewer still enforced. Increasingly the life of the church was corrupted by money. No one believed in bribery; but everyone knew that many high churchmen (like many high civil officials of the day) could be bribed. To buy or sell a church office was a crime in the canon law, known as "simony," but it was a crime which in the fifteenth century could not be suppressed. For churchmen to live with mistresses was considered understandable, if unseemly; the standards of laymen in such matters were not high; but for a bishop or other ecclesiastic to give lucrative church positions to his own children (or other relatives) was the abuse known as nepotism, and it, too, could not be eradicated. To sell divine grace for money, all agreed, was not only wrong but impossible. But in 1300 Boniface VIII had given encouragement to the practice of "indulgences." A person, if properly confessed, absolved, and truly repentant, might, by obtaining an indulgence, be spared certain of the temporal punishments of purgatory. One obtained such an indulgence, almost always, in return for a donation of money. The practice proved to be a fatally easy method of fund raising, despite complaints against the sale of indulgences.

Gradually the popes prevailed over the councils. The conciliar movement was greatly weakened for Christendom as a whole when the powerful French element secured its aims by a local national arrangement. In the Pragmatic Sanction of Bourges, in 1438, the Gallican (or French) church affirmed the supremacy of councils over popes, declared its administrative independence from the Holy See, suppressed the payment of annates to Rome, and forbade papal intervention in the appointment of French prelates. The papacy thus lost influence in France, but the conciliarists themselves were divided. In 1449, with the dissolution of the Council of Basel, the conciliar movement came to an end. In 1450 a great Jubilee was held to celebrate the papal triumph.

The papacy, its prestige and freedom of action thus secured, now passed into the hands of a series of cultivated gentlemen, men of the world, men of "modern" outlook in tune with their times—the famous popes of the Renaissance. Some, like Nicholas V (1447–1455) or Pius II (1458–1464), were accomplished scholars and connoisseurs of books. Some were like Innocent VIII (1484–1492), a pleasant man who was the first pope to dine in public with ladies. Alexander VI (1492–1503), of the Spanish Borgia family, exploited his office for the benefit of his relatives, trying to make his son Cesare Borgia the ruler of all Italy, while his daughter, Lucretia Borgia, gathered literary men and artists about her, and developed a perhaps exaggerated reputation for depravity. Alexander VI's successor, Julius II (1503–1513), was a capable general, and Leo X (1513–1521) was a superb patron of architects and painters. But we must now describe the Italian Renaissance, in which worthies of this kind were elevated to the Holy See.

6. THE RENAISSANCE IN ITALY

In Italy in the fifteenth century, and especially at Florence, we observe not merely a decay of medieval certainties but the appearance of a new and constructive attitude toward the world. The Renaissance, a French word meaning "rebirth," first received its name from those who thought of the Middle Ages as a dark time from which the human spirit had to be awakened. It was called a *re*birth in the belief that men now, after a long interruption, took up and resumed a civilization like that of the Greco-Romans. Medieval people had thought of the times of Aristotle or Cicero as not sharply distinct from their own. In the Renaissance, with a new historical sense, arose the conception of "modern" and "ancient" times, separated by a long period with a different life style and appropriately called the Middle Ages.

A few useful distinctions can be made. The basic institutions of Europe, the very languages and nationalities, the great frameworks of collective action in law, government, and economic production, all originated in the Middle Ages. But the Renaissance marked a new era in thought and feeling, by which Europe and its institutions were in the long run to be transformed. The origins of modern natural science can be traced more to the medieval universities than to the Renaissance thinkers. But it was in the Italy of the Quattrocento (as Italians call the fifteenth century) that other fields of thought and expression were first cultivated. The Italian influence in other countries, in these respects, remained very strong for at least 200 years. It pertained to high culture, and hence to a limited number of persons, but extended over the whole area represented by literature and the arts—literature meaning all kinds of writing, and the arts including all products of human skill. The effects of the Italian Renaissance, though much modified with the passage of time, were evident in the books and art galleries of Europe and America, and in the architecture of their cities, until the revolution of "modern" art in the early twentieth century. They involved the whole area of culture which is neither theological nor scientific but concerns essentially moral and civic questions, asking what man ought to be or ought to do, and is reflected in matters of taste, style, propriety, decorum, personal character, and education. In particular, it was in Renaissance Italy that an almost purely secular attitude first appeared, in which life was no longer seen by leading thinkers as a brief preparation for the hereafter.

The Italian Cities and the New Conception of Man

The towns of Italy, so long as trade converged in the Mediterranean, were the biggest and most bustling of all the towns that rose in Europe in the Middle Ages. The crafts of Italy included many refined trades such as those of the goldsmith or stonecarver, which were so zealously pursued that artisanship turned into art, and a delight in the beautiful became common among all classes. Merchants made fortunes in commerce; they lent their money to popes or princes, and so made further fortunes as bankers. They bought the wares of the craftsmen-artists. They rejoiced, not so much in money or the making of money, as in the beautiful things and psychological satisfactions that money could buy; and if they forgot the things that money could not buy, this is only to say again that their outlook was "secular."

The towns were independent city-states. There was no king to build up a government for Italy as a whole, and for several generations the popes were either absent at Avignon or engaged in disputes arising from the Great Schism, so that the influence of Rome was unimportant. The merchant oligarchies, each in its own city, enjoyed an unhampered stage on which to pursue interests other than those of business. In some, as at Milan, they succumbed to or worked with a local prince or despot. In others, as at Florence, Venice, and Genoa, they continued to govern themselves as republics. They had the experience of contending for public office, of suppressing popular revolt or winning popular favor, of producing works of public munificence, of making alliances, hiring armies, outwitting rivals, and conducting affairs of state. In short, Italy offered an environment in which many facets of human personality could be developed.

All this was most especially true in Florence, the chief city of Tuscany. In the fifteenth century it had a population of about 60,000, which made it only moderately large as Italian cities went.[2] Yet, like ancient Athens, Florence produced an extraordinary sequence of gifted men in a short period. From the days of Dante, Petrarch, and Boccaccio, who all died before 1375, to those of Machiavelli, who lived until 1527, an amazing number of the leading figures of the Italian Renaissance were Florentines. Like Athens also, Florence lost its republican liberty as well as its creative powers. Its history can be summarized in that of the Medici family. The founder of the family fortunes was Giovanni (d. 1429), a merchant and banker of Florence. His son, Cosimo de' Medici (1389–1464), allying himself with the popular element against some of the leading families of the republic, soon became unofficial ruler himself. Cosimo's grandson, Lorenzo the Magnificent (1449–1492), also used his great wealth to govern but is chiefly remembered as a poet, connoisseur, and lavish benefactor of art and learning. In the next century Tuscany became a grand duchy, of which the Medici were hereditary grand dukes until the family died out in 1737. Thus established, they furnished numerous cardinals and two popes to the church, and two Medici women became queens of France.

What arose in Italy, in these surroundings, was no less than a new conception of man himself. The world was so exciting that another world need not be thought of. It seemed very doubtful whether a quiet, cloistered, or celibate life was on a higher plane than an active gregarious life, or family life, or even a life of promiscuity and adventure. It was hard to believe that clergy were any better than laity, or that life led to a stern divine judgment in the end. That man's will and intelligence might mislead him seemed a gloomy doctrine. That man was a frail creature, in need of God's grace and salvation, though perhaps said with the lips, was not felt in the heart. Instead, what captivated the Italians of the Renaissance was a sense of man's tremendous powers.

Formerly, the ideal had been seen in renunciation, in a certain disdain for the concerns of this world. Now a life of involvement was also prized. Formerly, poverty had been greatly respected, at least in Christian doctrine. Now voices were heard in praise of a proper enjoyment of wealth. In the past, men had admired a life of contemplation, or meditative withdrawal. Now the humanist Leonardo Bruni could write, in 1433, "The whole glory of man lies in activity." Often, to be sure, the two attitudes existed in the same person. Sometimes they divided different groups within the same city. As always, the old persisted along with the new. The result might be psychological stress and civil conflict.

The new esteem for human activity took both a social and an individualistic turn. In cities maintaining their republican forms, as at Florence in the early fifteenth century, a new civic consciousness or sense of public duty was expressed. For this purpose the writings of Cicero and other ancients were found to be

[2] See the picture essay, pp. 93–103.

highly relevant, since they provided an ethics independent of the Christian and medieval tradition. There was also a kind of cult of the great individual, hardly known to the ancients, and one which gave little attention to collective responsibility. Renaissance individualism put its emphasis on outstanding attainments. The great individual shaped his own destiny in a world governed by fortune. He had *virtù*, the quality of being a man (*vir*, "man"), and although women might also exhibit *virtù*, it was a quality which in the society of the day was more to be expected in the most aggressive adult males. It meant the successful demonstration of human powers. A man of *virtù*, in the arts, in war, or in statecraft, was a man who knew what he was doing, who, from resources within himself, made the best use of his opportunities, hewing his way through the world, and excelling in all that he did. For the arts, such a spirit is preserved in the autobiography of Benvenuto Cellini.

The growing preoccupation with things human can be traced in new forms of painting, sculpture, and architecture that arose in Italy at this time. These arts likewise reflected an increasing this-worldliness, a new sense of reality and a new sense of space, of a kind different from that of the Middle Ages, and which was to underlie European thinking almost to our own time. Space was no longer indeterminate, unknowable, or divine; it was a zone occupied by physical human beings, or one in which human beings might at least imagine themselves moving about. Reality meant visible and tangible persons or objects in this space, "objective" in the sense that they looked or felt the same to all normal persons who perceived them. It was a function of the arts to convey this reality, however idealized or suffused by the artist's individual feeling, in such a way that observers could recognize in the image the identity of the thing portrayed.

Architecture reflected the new tendencies. Though the Gothic cathedral at Milan was built as late as 1386, at Florence and elsewhere architects preferred to adapt Greco-Roman principles of design, such as symmetrical arrangements of doors and windows, the classical column, the arch and the dome. More public buildings of a nonreligious character were built, and more substantial town houses were put up by wealthy merchants, in styles meant to represent grandeur, or civic importance, or availability and convenience for human use. Gardens and terraces were added to many such buildings.

Sculpture, confined in the Middle Ages to the niches and portals of cathedrals, now emerged as an independent and free-standing art. Its favored subjects were human beings, now presented so that the viewer could walk around the object and see it from all directions, thus bringing it securely into his own world. The difference from the religious figures carved on medieval churches was very great. Like the architects, the sculptors in parting from the immediate past found much in the Greek and Roman tradition that was modern and useful to their purpose. They produced portrait busts of eminent contemporaries, or figures of great leaders sometimes on horseback, or statues depicting characters from Greco-Roman history and mythology. The use of the nude, in mythological or allegorical subjects, likewise showed a conception of humanity that was more in keeping with the Greek than with the Christian tradition.

Painting was less influenced by the ancients, since the little of ancient painting that had survived was unknown during the Renaissance. The invention of painting in oils opened new pathways for the art. Merchants, ecclesiastics, and princes provided a mounting demand. In subject matter painting remained conservative, dealing most often with religious themes. It was the conception and presentation that were new. The new feeling for space became evident. With the discovery of the mathematics of perspective, space was presented in exact relation to the beholder's eye. The viewer, in a sense, entered into the world of the painting. A three-dimensional effect was achieved, with careful representation of distance through variation of size, and techniques of shading or chiaroscuro added to the illusion of physical volume. Human figures were often placed in a setting of painted architecture, or against a background of landscape or scenery, showing castles or hills, which though supposedly far away yet closed in the composition with a knowable boundary. In such a painting everything was localized in place and time; a part of the real world was caught and put in the picture. The idea was not to suggest eternity, as in earlier religious painting, nor yet to express private fantasy or the workings of the unconscious, as sometimes in "postmodern" art, but to present a familiar theme in an understandable setting, often with a narrative content, that is, by the telling of a story.

Painters were able also, like the sculptors, by a close study of human anatomy, to show people in distinctive and living attitudes. Faces took on more expression; individual personality was depicted. Differences among men were shown, not merely abstract characteristics that all men or certain kinds of men, such as kings or saints, had in common. Painting became less symbolic, less an intimation of general truths, more a portrayal of concrete realities as they met the eye. In the portrait by Bellini of a *condottiere* the reader can see for himself, though who the man was is not known, how a strong, real, and vivid personality looks out from the canvas.[3] Similarly, the great religious paintings were peopled with human beings. In Leonardo da Vinci's *Last Supper* Christ and his disciples are seen as a group of men each with his own characteristics, Raphael's Madonnas seem to be young Italian women, and in the mighty figures of Michelangelo the attributes of humanity invade heaven itself.

There were always countercurrents that make such generalizations debatable. The main tone of the arts in Renaissance Italy was to take satisfaction in beauty, to present the world as desirable, to be clear-cut, lucid, and finite. But many Florentines were troubled by the worldliness and even paganism that had grown up about them. Their anxieties were expressed in a movement for religious reforms led by the priest Savonarola. As it ran its course it became involved in political questions, until Savonarola was tried and burned at the stake in 1498.

Humanism: The Birth of "Literature"

The literary movement in Renaissance Italy is called humanism because of the rising interest in humane letters, *litterae humaniores*. There had indeed been much writing in the later Middle Ages. Much of it had been of a technical character, as in theology, philosophy, or law; some of it had been meant to convey information, as in chronicles, histories, and cosmographical descriptions of the world. Great hymns had been composed, lively student songs had been heard at the universities, plays had been performed in cathedrals, the old legends of King Arthur and Roland had been written down, and occasionally a monk would try his hand at a long narrative poem. Yet it is hardly too much to say that literature, in the

[3] See p. 63.

modern sense, first appeared in the fourteenth and fifteenth centuries in Italy. There came to be a class of men who looked upon writing as their main life's work, who wrote for each other and for a somewhat larger public, and who used writing to deal with general questions, or to examine their own states of mind, or resolve their own difficulties, or used words to achieve artistic effects, or simply to please and amuse their readers.

The Italian humanists, like their predecessors, wrote a good deal in Latin. They differed from earlier literate persons in that they were not, for the most part, members of the clergy. They complained that Latin had become monkish, barbaric, and "scholastic," a jargon of the schools and universities, and they greatly preferred the classic style of a Cicero or a Livy. In all this there was much that was unfair, much that was merely literary, and something that anticipated the famous twentieth-century problem of the "two cultures," or failure of understanding between persons of humanistic interests and those of more scientific concerns. Medieval Latin was a vigorous living language that used words in new senses, many of which have passed into English and the Romance languages as perfectly normal expressions. Yet in the ancient writers the humanists found qualities that medieval writing did not have. They discovered a new range of interests, a new sensibility, discussion of political and civic questions, a world presented without the overarching framework of religious belief. In addition, the Greeks and Romans unquestionably had style—a sense of form, a taste for the elegant and the epigrammatic. They had often also written for practical ends, in dialogues, orations, or treatises that were designed for purposes of persuasion.

If the humanists therefore made a cult of antiquity it was because they saw kindred spirits in it. They sensed a relevancy for their own time. The classical influence, never wholly absent in the Middle Ages, now reentered as a main force in the higher civilization of Europe. The humanists polished their Latin, and increasingly they learned Greek. They made assiduous searches for classical texts hitherto unknown. Many were found; they had of course been copied and preserved by the monks of preceding times.

But while an especial dignity attached to writing in Latin, known throughout Europe, most of the humanists wrote in Italian also. Or rather, they used the mode of speech current in Florence. This had also been the language of Dante in the *Divine Comedy*. To this vast poem the humanists now added many writings in Florentine or Tuscan prose. The result was that Florentine became the standard form of modern Italian. It was the first time that a European vernacular—that is, the common spoken tongue as opposed to Latin—became thus standardized amid the variety of its dialects and adapted in structure and vocabulary to the more complex requirements of a written language. French and English soon followed, and most of the other European languages somewhat later.

The Florentine exile, Francesco Petrarca, or Petrarch, has been called the first man of letters. The son of a merchant, he spent his life in travel throughout France and Italy. Trained for the law, and ordained to the clergy, he became a somewhat rootless critic of these two esteemed professions, which he denounced for their "scholasticism." He lived in the generation after Dante, dying in 1374, and he anticipated the more fully developed humanism that was to come. His voluminous writings show him to have been the prey of contrary attitudes. He was attracted by life, love, beauty, travel, and connections with men of importance in church and state; he could also spurn all these things as ephemeral and deceptive. He loved Cicero for his common sense and his commitment to political liberty; indeed, he discovered a manuscript of Cicero's letters in 1345. He loved St. Augustine for his otherworldly vision of the City of God. But in Cicero's writings he also found a deep religious concern, and in St. Augustine he esteemed the active man who had been a bishop, a writer heavily engaged in the controversies of his time, and one who taught that for true Christians the world is not evil.

Petrarch wrote sonnets in Italian, an epic in Latin, an introspective study of himself, and a great many letters which he clearly meant to be literary productions. He aspired to literary fame. In all this we see a new kind of writer, who uses language not merely as a practical tool but as a medium of more subtle expression, to commune with himself, to convey moods of discouragement or satisfaction, to clarify doubts, to improve his own understanding of the choices and options that life affords. With Petrarch, in short, literature became a kind of calling, and also a consideration of moral philosophy, still related but no longer subordinate to religion. It was moral philosophy in the widest sense, raising questions of how human beings should adjust to the world, what a good life could be or ought to be, or where the genuine and ultimate rewards of living were to be found.

Petrarch was an indication of things to come. Boccaccio, his contemporary and also a Florentine, wrote the *Decameron* in Italian, a series of tales designed both to entertain and to impart a certain wisdom about human character and behavior. They were followed by the main group of humanists, far more numerous but less well remembered. Men of letters began to take part in public life, to gather pupils and found schools, to serve as secretaries to governing bodies or princes, and even to occupy office themselves. Thus the humanist Coluccio Salutati became chancellor of Florence in 1375. During the following decades Florence was threatened by the expansive ambitions of Milan, where the princely despotism of the Visconti family had established itself. Against such dangers a new and intense civic consciousness asserted itself. Salutati, in addition to the usual duties of chancellor, served the state with his pen, glorifying Florentine liberty, identifying it with the liberties of ancient republican Rome before they were undermined by the Caesars. He was succeeded as chancellor by two other humanists, Bruni and Poggio. Bruni wrote a history of Florence which marked a new achievement in historical writing, when compared with the annals and chronicles of the Middle Ages. He saw the past as clearly past, different from but relevant to the present; and he introduced a new division of historical periods. On the model of such ancient writers as Livy, he adopted a flowing narrative form. And he used history for a practical political purpose, to show that Florence had a long tradition of liberty and possessed values and attainments worth fighting for against menacing neighbors. History took on a utility that it had had for the Greeks and Romans and was to retain in the future in Europe and eventually America: the function of heightening a sentiment, not yet of nationalism, but of collective civic consciousness or group identity. It was meant to arouse men to a life of commitment and participation.

All this literary activity was of a scholarly type, in which authors broadened their understanding as much by reading as by personal experience of the world. And scholarly activity, the habit of attending closely to what a page really said, had consequences that went beyond either pure literature or local patriotism. A new critical attitude developed. Bruni, in his history, showed a new sense of the need for authentic sources. Lorenzo Valla became one of the founders of textual criticism. Gaining a historical sense for the Latin language, he observed that its characteristic words and expressions varied from one time to another. He put this knowledge to the service of the king of Naples in a dispute with the pope. Valla showed, by analysis of the language used in the document, that the Donation of Constantine, on which the papacy then based its temporal claims, could not have been written in Constantine's time in the fourth century, and so was a forgery. Pico della Mirandola and others looked for aspects of truth not revealed in the Christian Scriptures. As men of letters, they put their faith in books, but as men of the Renaissance they were receptive to anything written by men anywhere. A group at the Academy of Florence took a serious interest in the study of Plato. The enthusiastic and very learned young Pico, at the age of twenty-three, in 1486, offered to expatiate publicly on all human knowledge in 900 theses, to be drawn from "the Chaldaic, Arabic, Hebrew, Grecian, Egyptian and Latin sages."

Schooling and Manners

While Italian humanism thus contributed much to literature and scholarship, to classical learning, and to the formation of modern national languages, it also had tangible and lasting effects in education. Here its impact remained in all regions of European civilization until the twentieth century. The medieval universities were essentially places for professional training in theology, medicine, and law. Except in England this continued to be their primary function. What came to be known as secondary education, the preparation of young men either for the universities or for "life," owes more to the Renaissance. The organized education of women came much later.

Medieval schooling had been chaotic and repetitious. Youngsters of all ages sat together with a teacher, each absorbing from the confusion whatever he could of Latin rules and vocabulary. The Renaissance launched the idea of putting different age groups or levels of accomplishment into separate classes, in separate rooms, each with its own teacher, with periodic promotion of the pupil from one level to the next. Latin remained the principal subject, with Greek now added. But many new purposes were seen in the study of Latin. It was intended to give skill in the use of language, including the pupil's native tongue. Rhetoric was the art of using language to influence others. It heightened communication. Knowledge alone was not enough, said the historian and chancellor Bruni, who also wrote a short work on education—"to make effectual use of what we know we must add the power of expression." Nor was Latin merely the necessary professional tool for the priest, the physician, the lawyer, or the government servant. The student learned Latin (and Greek) in order to read the ancient writings— epics, lyrics, orations, letters, histories, dialogues, and philosophical treatises —and these writings, especially at a time when the modern literatures were undeveloped, opened his horizons in all directions. They had a practical application; and at least as late as the American and French revolutions men found useful lessons in the rise and decline of the Roman republic and the troubles of the Greek city-states. The classics were meant also to have a moral impact, to produce a balanced personality, and to form character. Not everyone could be important or gifted, said the humanist Vittorino, but we all face a life of "social duty," and "all are responsible for the personal influence which goes forth from us." These aims built themselves permanently into the educational system of modern Europe.

Young men were trained also for a more civilized deportment in everyday social living. Personal style in the upper classes became somewhat more studied.

Hitherto Europeans had generally acted like big children; they spat, belched, and blew their noses without inhibition, snatched at food with their fingers, bawled at each other when aroused, or sulked when their feelings were offended. It was Italians of the Renaissance who first taught more polite habits. Books of etiquette began to appear, of which the most successful was Castiglione's *Book of the Courtier.* The "courtier" was ancestor to the "gentleman"; "courtesy" was originally the kind of behavior suited to princely courts.

The "courtier," according to Castiglione, should be a man of good birth but is chiefly the product of training. His education in youth, and his efforts in mature years, should be directed toward mixing agreeably in the company of his equals. His clothes should be neat, his movements graceful, his approach to other people perfectly poised. He must converse with facility, be proficient in sports and arms, and know how to dance and appreciate music. He should know Latin and Greek. With literary and other subjects he should show a certain familiarity but never become too engrossed. For the well-bred man speaks with "a certain carelessness, to hide his art, and show that what he says or does comes from him without effort or deliberation." Pedantry and heaviness must yield to a certain air of effortless superiority, so that even if the "courtier" knows or does something seriously, he must treat it lightly as one of many accomplishments. At its best, the code taught a certain considerateness for the feelings of others, and incorporated some of the moral ideas of the humanists, aiming at a creditable life in active society. Castiglione's book was translated into numerous languages, and a hundred editions were printed before 1600. Its ideal was inculcated for centuries by private tutors and in the schools.

Politics and the Italian Renaissance

The Italian Renaissance, for all its accomplishments, produced no institution or great idea by which masses of men living in society could be held together. Indeed, the greatest of Europe's institutions, the Roman church, in which Europeans had lived for centuries, and without which they did not see how they could live at all, fell into sheer neglect under the Renaissance popes. Nor did Italy develop any effectual political institutions. Florence during the fifteenth century passed from a high-spirited republicanism to acceptance of one-man rule. Throughout the peninsula the merchants, bankers, connoisseurs, and courtly classes who controlled the city-states could not fight for themselves, nor arouse their citizens to fight for them. They therefore hired professional fighting men, *condottieri*, private leaders of armed bands, who contracted with the various city-states to carry on warfare, and often raised their price or changed sides during hostilities. Italian politics became a tangled web, a labyrinth of subterfuge and conspiracy, a platform on which great individuals might exhibit their *virtù*. "Italian cunning" became a byword throughout Europe. Dictators rose and fell. The Medici became dukes in Florence, the Sforza in Milan, while in Venice and Genoa, where the republics were kept, narrow oligarchies held the rule. These states, along with the states of the church, jockeyed about like pugilists in a ring, held within an intricate, shifting, and purely local balance of power.

Italy was the despair of its patriots, or of such few as remained. One of these was Niccolò Machiavelli, who, in *The Prince* (1513), wrote the most lasting work of the Italian Renaissance. He dreamed of the day when the citizens of his native

Florence, or indeed of all Italy, should behave like early Romans—show virility in their politics, fight in citizen armies for patriotic causes, and uphold their dignity before Europe. It was outside Italy, in kings Ferdinand of Aragon, Louis XI of France, and Henry VII of England, that Machiavelli was obliged to find his heroes. He admired them because they were successful builders of states. In *The Prince* he produced a handbook of statecraft which he hoped Italy might find useful. He produced also the first purely secular treatise on politics.

Medieval writings on politics, those of Thomas Aquinas or Marsiglio of Padua, for example, had always talked of God's will for the government of men, with such accompanying matters as justice and right, or divine and natural law. All this Machiavelli put aside. He "emancipated" politics from theology and moral philosophy. He undertook to describe simply what rulers actually did, and thus anticipated what was later called the scientific spirit, in which questions of good and bad are excluded, and the observer attempts to discover only what really happens. What really happens, said Machiavelli, is that effective rulers and governments act only in their own political interest. They keep faith or break it, observe treaties or repudiate them, are merciful or ruthless, forthright or sly, peaceable or aggressive, according to their estimates of their political needs. Machiavelli was prepared to admit that such behavior was bad; he only insisted that it was in this way, however regrettably, that successful rulers behaved. He was thought unduly cynical even in an age not characterized by political delicacy. He had nevertheless diagnosed the new era with considerable insight. It was an age when politics was in fact becoming more secular, breaking off from religion, with the building up of states and with state authority emerging as a goal requiring no other justification.

But the most successful states of the time, as Machiavelli saw, were not in Italy. They were what history knows as the New Monarchies, and they owed their strength to something more than princely craft, for they enjoyed a measure of spontaneous loyalty from their own peoples. Italy was politically helpless. Politics in Italy was not about anything vital; it was an affair of *virtù*; and the people of Italy lost interest in politics, as they did in war, becoming "effeminate" in the eyes of outsiders.

So Italy, the sunny land of balmy Mediterranean skies, rich in the busy life of its cities, its moneyed wealth, its gorgeous works of art, lay helplessly open to the depredations of less easygoing peoples, from Spain and the north, who possessed institutions in which men could act together in large numbers. In a new age of rising national monarchies the city-states of Italy were too small to compete. In 1494 a French army crossed the Alps. Italy became a bone of contention between France and Spain. In 1527 a horde of undisciplined Spanish and German mercenaries, joined by foot-loose Italians, fell upon Rome itself. Never, not even from the Goths of the fifth century, had Rome experienced anything so horrible and degrading. The city was sacked, thousands were killed, soldiers milled about for a week in an orgy of rape and loot, the pope was imprisoned, and cardinals were mockingly paraded through the streets facing backward on the backs of mules. By this time religious passions were aroused; we are encroaching on the story of the Reformation.

After the sack of Rome the Renaissance faded away. Politically, for over three hundred years, Italy remained divided, the passive object of the ambitions of outside powers. Meanwhile its culture permeated the rest of Europe.

7. THE RENAISSANCE OUTSIDE ITALY

Outside Italy people were much less conscious of any sudden break with the Middle Ages. Developments north of the Alps, and in Spain, were more an outgrowth of what had gone before. There was indeed a Renaissance in the Italian sense. In some of the innovations in painting the Flemish masters preceded those of Italy. In the north also, as in Italy a little sooner, writers favored a neoclassical Latin, but the modern written languages also began to develop.

But the northern Renaissance was more a blend of the old and the new. In it, above all, the religious element was stronger than in Italy. The most important northern humanists were men like Thomas More in England and the Dutch Erasmus. The French humanism that produced Rabelais also produced John Calvin.

Religious Scholarship and Science

It is customary to distinguish between the "pagan" humanism of Italy and the Christian humanism of the north. In the north, Christian humanists studied the Hebrew and Greek texts of the Bible and read the Church Fathers, both Latin and Greek, in order to deepen their understanding of Christianity and to restore its moral vitality. Among lesser people, too, without pretense to humanistic learning, religion remained a force. Medieval intellectual interests persisted. This is apparent from the continuing foundation of universities. The humanists generally regarded universities as centers of a pedantic, monkish, and "scholastic" learning. Concentrating upon theology, or upon medicine and law, the universities gave little encouragement to experimental science and still less to purely literary studies. In Italy in the fifteenth century no new universities were established. But in Spain, in France, in Scotland, in Scandinavia, and above all in Germany, new universities sprouted up. Between 1386 and 1506 no less than fourteen universities were established in Germany. At one of the newest, Wittenberg, founded in 1502, Martin Luther was to launch the Protestant Reformation.

Germany at this time, on the eve of the great religious upheaval, and before the shift of the commercial artery from central Europe to the Atlantic seaboard, was a main center of European life. Politically, the German-speaking world was an ill-defined and ill-organized region, composed of many diverse parts, from which the Netherlands and Switzerland were not yet differentiated. Parts of it were infested by robber knights, picturesque in legend, but unpleasant for those

PORTRAIT OF A CONDOTTIERE
by Giovanni Bellini (Italian, 1430–1516)

An emphatic portrayal of Renaissance individualism. Note the artist's ability to present a concrete human being, one who is not merely an abstract type. For the "condottieri" see p. 60. The name of this particular "condottiere" is not known. But the hard expression and set features, the firm lines about the mouth and chin, the bull neck and the unflinching gaze suggest an aggressive character of considerable "virtù." The face is thoughtful and intelligent but devoid of spirituality. The man is clearly in the habit of depending on himself alone. The artist has heightened the sense of his subject's independence and self-sufficiency by making him stand out from a dark and entirely vacant background. Courtesy of the National Gallery of Art, Washington, D.C., Samuel H. Kress Collection.

who had to live with them in reality. Economically, nevertheless, western and southern Germany enjoyed a lead; the towns traded busily, and German banking families, like the famous Fugger, controlled more capital than any others in Europe. Technical inventiveness was alive; mining was developing; and it was in the Rhineland, at Mainz, that Gutenberg, about 1450, produced the first books printed with movable type. In painting, the western fringe of the Germanic world produced the Flemish masters, and south Germany gave birth to Dürer and the Holbeins.

Intellectually, Germany shared in the Latin culture of Europe, a fact often obscured by the Latinizing of German names. Regiomontanus (the Latin name of Johann Müller) laid the foundations during his short lifetime (1436–1476) for a mathematical conception of the universe. He was probably the most influential scientific worker of the fifteenth century, especially since Leonardo da Vinci's scientific labors remained unknown. Nicholas of Cusa (1401?–1464), a Rhinelander, was a churchman whose mystical philosophy entered into the later development of mathematics and science. From such a background of mathematical interests came Copernicus (Niklas Koppernigk, 1473–1543), who believed that the earth moved about the sun; he was indeed a Pole, but he originated in the mixed German-Polish region of East Prussia. Fortified by the same mathematical interests, Europe's best-known cartographers were also Germans, such as Behaim and Schöner, whose world maps the reader may see on pages 292–293. Paracelsus (Latin for Hohenheim) undertook to revolutionize medicine at the University of Basel. His wild prophecies made him a mixture of scientist and charlatan; but, in truth, science was not yet clearly distinguished from the occult, with which it shared the idea of control over natural forces. A similar figure, remembered in literature and the arts, was the celebrated Dr. Faustus. In real life, Faust, or Faustus, was perhaps a learned German of the first part of the sixteenth century. He was rumored to have sold his soul to the devil in return for knowledge and power. The Faust story was dramatized in England as early as 1593 by Christopher Marlowe, and, much later, by Goethe in poetry and by Gounod in the opera. In the legend of Faust later generations were to see a symbol of the inordinate striving of modern man. Oswald Spengler published his *Decline of the West* in 1918. Needing a name for the European civilization whose doom he prophesied, he called it "Faustian."

The idea of man's powers to understand and control physical nature, as developed most especially north of the Alps, corresponded in many ways to the more purely Italian and humanistic idea of the infinite richness of human personality. Together, they constituted the new Renaissance spirit, for both emphasized the emancipation of humanity's limitless potentialities. The two ideas constantly interacted; in fact, most of the scientific workers just mentioned—Regiomontanus, Nicholas of Cusa, Copernicus—spent many years in Italy, receiving the stimulus of Italian thought.[4]

Mysticism and Lay Religion

In the north a genuine religious impulse, in addition to religious humanistic scholarship, also remained alive. Where in Italy the religious sense, if not extinct, seemed to pass into the aesthetic, into a joyous and public cult in which God was

---

[4] On da Vinci, Copernicus, and the rise of modern science in general, see Chapter VII.

glorified by works of art, in the north it took on a more mystical and a more so-
berly moral tone. Germany in the fourteenth century produced a series of mystics.
The mystic tendencies of Nicholas of Cusa have been mentioned. More typical
mystics were Meister Eckhart (d. 1327) and Thomas à Kempis (d. 1471), author
of the *Imitation of Christ*. The essence of mysticism lay in the belief, or experience, that the individual soul could in perfect solitude commune directly with
God. The mystic had no need of reason, nor of words, nor of joining with other
people in open worship, nor even of the sacraments administered by the priests—
nor even of the church. The mystics did not rebel against the church; they accepted its pattern of salvation; but at bottom they offered, to those who could follow, a deeper religion in which the church as a social institution had no place. All
social institutions, in fact, were transcended in mysticism by the individual soul;
and on this doctrine, both profound and socially disruptive, Martin Luther was
later to draw.

For the church, it was significant also that religion was felt deeply outside the
clergy. Persons stirred by religion, who in the Middle Ages would have taken holy
orders, now frequently remained laymen. In the past the church had often needed
reform. But in the past, in the bad times of the tenth century, for example, the
clergy had found reformers within their own ranks. The church had thus been repeatedly reformed and renewed without revolution. Now, in the fifteenth and
early sixteenth centuries an ominous line seemed to be increasingly drawn: between the clergy as an established interest, inert and set in its ways, merely living,
and living well, off the church; and groups of people outside the clergy—religious
laymen, religiously inclined humanists and writers, impatient and headstrong
rulers—who were more influential than ever before, and more critical of ecclesiastical abuses.

Lay religion was especially active in the Netherlands. A lay preacher, Gerard
Groote, attracted followers by his sermons on spiritual regeneration. In 1374 he
founded a religious sisterhood, which was followed by establishments for religiously minded men. They called themselves, respectively, the Sisters and the
Brothers of the Common Life, and they eventually received papal approval. They
lived communally, but not as monks and nuns, for they took no vows, wore ordinary clothing, and were free to leave at will. They worked at relieving the poor,
and in teaching. The schools of the Brothers, since some of them came to have as
many as a thousand boys, were the first to be organized in separate classes, each
with its own room and its own teacher, according to the pupil's age or level of advancement. The Sisters maintained similar though less elaborate schools for girls.
Reading and writing were of course taught, but the emphasis was on a Christian
ideal of character and conduct, to instil such qualities as humility, tolerance,
reverence, love of one's neighbor, and conscientiousness in the performance of
duty. This Modern Devotion, as it was called, spread widely in the Netherlands
and adjoining parts of Germany.

Erasmus of Rotterdam

In this atmosphere grew up the greatest of all the northern humanists, and indeed
the most notable figure of the entire humanist movement, Erasmus of Rotterdam
(1466–1536). Like all the humanists, Erasmus chose to write in a "purified" and
usually intricate Latin style. He regarded the Middle Ages as benighted, ridiculed

the scholastic philosophers, and studied deeply the classical writers of antiquity. He had the strength and the limitations of the pure man of letters. To the hard questions of serious philosophy he was largely indifferent; he feared the unenlightened excitability of the common people, and he was almost wholly unpolitical in his outlook. He rarely thought in terms of worldly power or advantage and made too little allowance for those who did. An exact contemporary to the most notorious of the worldly Renaissance popes, Erasmus was keenly aware of the need of a reform of the clergy. He put his faith in education, enlightened discussion, and gradual moral improvement. He led no burning crusade and counseled against all violence or fanaticism. He prepared new Greek and Latin editions of the New Testament. Urging also the reading of the New Testament in the vernacular languages, he hoped that with a better understanding of Christ's teaching people might turn from their evil ways. In his *Praise of Folly* he satirized all worldly pretensions and ambitions, those of the clergy most emphatically. In his *Handbook of a Christian Knight* he showed how a man might take part in the affairs of the world while remaining a devout Christian. Mildness, reasonableness, tolerance, restraint, scholarly understanding, a love of peace, a critical and reforming zeal which, hating nobody, worked through trying to make men think, a subdued and controlled tone from which shouting and bad temper were always excluded—such were the Erasmian virtues.

Erasmus achieved an international eminence such as no one of purely intellectual attainments has ever enjoyed. He corresponded with the great of Europe. He lectured at Cambridge and edited books for a publisher at Basel. The king of Spain named him a councilor, the king of France called him to Paris, Pope Leo X assisted him when he was in trouble. Theologians found fault with Erasmus' ideas (in which, indeed, the supernatural had little importance), but among the chief practical men of the church, the popes and prelates, he had many admirers. Erasmus, it must be noted, attacked only the abuses in the church, the ignorance or sloth of the clergy, the moral or financial corruption of their lives. The essence and principle of the Roman Catholic church he never called into question. Whether the Erasmian spirit, so widely diffused about 1520, would have sufficed to restore the church without the revolutionary impact of Protestantism is one of the many unanswerable questions of history.

8. THE NEW MONARCHIES

Meanwhile, in Europe outside Italy, kings were actively building up the institutions of the modern state. It was these states, more than any other single factor,

ERASMUS OF ROTTERDAM
by Hans Holbein, the Younger (German, 1497–1543)

The classic portrayal of humanism at its best. The portrait was painted in 1523, when Erasmus was fifty-six, and the Lutheran Reformation had already begun in Germany. Holbein has conveyed the mood of tight-lipped calm, or of saddened humanity, felt by a lifelong reforming writer who has lived to see violent revolution. The face, finely delineated, and highlighted against the deeper tones of the cap and cloak, is concentrated upon Erasmus' only weapon, the pen. The picture captures the life of thought; it is a picture of the human mind, as Bellini's "Condottiere" is a picture of the will. Courtesy of the Louvre (Giraudon).

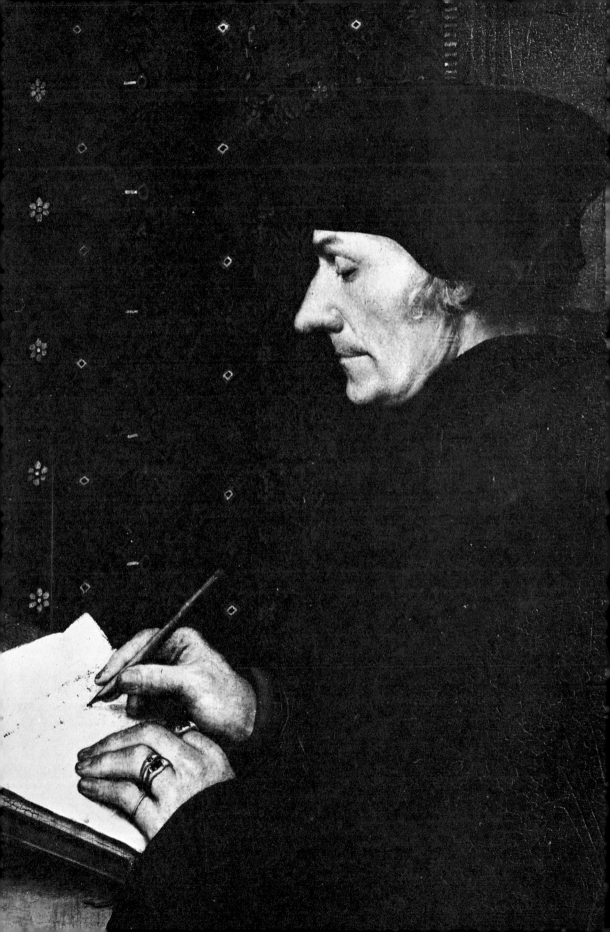

that were to determine the course of the religious revolution. Whether a country turned Protestant, remained Catholic, or divided into separate religious communities was to depend very largely upon political considerations.

War, civil war, class war, feudal rebellion, and plain banditry afflicted a good deal of Europe in the middle of the fifteenth century. In this formless violence central governments had become very weak. Various rulers now tried to impose a kind of civil peace. They have been conveniently called the New Monarchs, but they were not really very new, because they resumed the interrupted labors of kings in the High Middle Ages.[5] They thus laid foundations for the national, or at least territorial, states.

The New Monarchs offered the institution of monarchy as a guarantee of law and order. Arousing latent sentiments of loyalty to the reigning dynasty, they proclaimed that hereditary monarchy was the legitimate form of public power, which all should accept without turmoil or resistance. They especially enlisted the support of middle-class people in the towns, who were tired of the private wars and marauding habits of the feudal nobles. Townspeople were willing to let parliaments be dominated or even ignored by the king, for parliaments had proved too often to be strongholds of unruly barons, or had merely accentuated class conflict. The king, receiving money in taxes, was able to organize armies with which to control the nobles. The use of the pike and the longbow, which enabled the foot soldier to stand against the horseman, was here of great potential value. The king, if only he could get his monarchy sufficiently organized, and his finances into reliable order, could hire large numbers of foot soldiers, who generally came from the endless ranks of plebeians, unlike the knightly horsemen. But to organize his monarchy, the king had to break down the mass of feudal, inherited, customary, or "common" law in which the rights of the feudal classes were entrenched. For this purpose, at least on the Continent, the New Monarch made use of Roman law, which was now actively studied in the universities.[6] He called himself a "sovereign"—it was at this time that kings began to be addressed as "majesty." The king, said the experts in Roman law, incorporated the will and welfare of the people in his own person—and they would cite the principle *salus populi suprema lex*, "the welfare of the people is the highest law." The king, they added, could *make* law, enact it by his own authority, regardless of previous custom or even of historic liberties—and they would quote, *quod principi placuit legis habet vigorem*, or "what pleases the prince has the force of law."

The New Monarchy in England, France, and Spain

The New Monarchy came to England with the dynasty of the Tudors (1485–1603), whose first king, Henry VII (1485–1509), after gaining the throne by force, put an end to the civil turbulence of the Wars of the Roses. In these wars the great English baronial families had seriously weakened each other, to the great convenience of the king and the bulk of the citizenry. Henry VII passed laws against "livery and maintenance," the practice by which great lords maintained private armies wearing their own livery or insignia. Since ordinary procedures had recently failed to give security, with witnesses afraid to testify and juries afraid to offend the mighty, Henry VII used his royal council as a new court

---

[5] See pp. 34–36.
[6] See p. 16.

to deal with property disputes and infractions of the public peace. It met in a room decorated with stars, whence its name, the Star Chamber. It represented the authority of the king and his council, and it dispensed with a jury. Later denounced as an instrument of despotism, it was popular enough at first, because it preserved order and rendered substantial justice. Henry VII, though miserly and unpleasant in person, was accepted as a good ruler. National feeling in England consolidated around the house of Tudor.

In France the New Monarchy was represented by Louis XI (1461–1483), of the Valois line, and his successors. In the five centuries since the first French king had been crowned, the royal domain had steadily expanded from its original small nucleus around Paris through a combination of inheritance, marriage, war, intrigue, and conquest. Louis XI continued to round out the French borders. Internally, he built up a royal army, suppressed brigands, and subdued rebellious nobles. He acquired far greater powers than the English Tudors to raise taxation without parliamentary consent. The Estates General of France met only once in his reign. On that occasion, remembering the anarchy of the past, they requested the king to govern without them in the future. The French monarchy also enlarged its powers over the clergy. We have seen how, by the Pragmatic Sanction of 1438, the Gallican church had won considerable national independence.[7] In 1516 King Francis I reached an agreement with Pope Leo X, the Concordat of Bologna. By this agreement the Pragmatic Sanction was rescinded; the pope received his "annates," or money income, from French ecclesiastics; the king appointed the bishops and abbots. The fact that, after 1516, the kings of France already controlled their own national clergy was one reason why, in later years, they were never tempted to turn Protestant.

Strictly speaking, there was no kingdom of Spain. Various Spanish kingdoms had combined into two, Aragon and Castile. To Aragon, which lay along the Mediterranean side of the peninsula, belonged the Balearic Islands, Sardinia, Sicily, and the south Italian kingdom of Naples. To Castile, after 1492, belonged the newly discovered Americas. The two were joined in a personal union by the marriage of Ferdinand of Aragon and Isabella of Castile in 1469. The union was personal only; that is, both kingdoms recognized the two monarchs, but they had no common political, judicial, or administrative institutions. There was little or no Spanish national feeling; indeed, the Catalans in northern Aragon spoke a language quite different from Castilian Spanish. The common feeling throughout Spain was the sense of belonging to the Spanish Catholic church. The common memory was the memory of the Christian crusade against the Moors. The one common institution, whose officials had equal authority and equal access to all the kingdoms, was a church court, the Inquisition. The church in Spain was in vigorous condition. Cardinal Ximenes, shortly before 1500, managed to rid it of the abuses and the inertia which debilitated the church in the rest of Europe. The *reconquista* was at last completed. In 1492 Granada, the southern tip of Spain, was conquered from the Moors. Its annexation added to the heterogeneous and undigested character of the Spanish dominions.

In these circumstances the New Monarchy in Spain followed a religious bent. Unification took place around the church. The rulers, though they made efforts at political centralization, worked largely through facilities offered by the church, notably the Inquisition. They insisted on religious conformity. National feeling

---

[7] See p. 52.

Habsburg Dominions
Church Lands
Boundary of Holy Roman Empire

SHETLAND I.

THE HEBRIDES

ORKNEY I.

SWEDEN

FINLAND

NORWAY

Bergen

Oslo

Stockholm

Helsingfors

ESTONIA

LIVONIA

Riga

COURLAND

SCOTLAND

Edinburgh

NORTH SEA

BALTIC SEA

DENMARK

Copenhagen

Danzig

PRUSSIA

Vilna

IRELAND

Dublin

York

ENGLAND

WALES

London

Canterbury

DUTCH
NETHERLANDS

Hamburg

BRANDENBURG

Berlin

Warsaw

LITHUANIA

Vistula R.

POLA

Calais
(England)

BELGIAN
NETH.

Münster

Antwerp

Brussels

Rhine

Cologne

Wittenberg

SAXONY

SILESIA

Breslau

Cracow

Lemberg

POLAND

GALICIA

PODOL

ATLANTIC OCEAN

St. Malo

Rouen

Paris

LUX.

Trier

PALA-
TINATE

Metz

Worms

Schmalkalden

Prague

BOHEMIA

MORAVIA

CARPATHIANS

MOLDAV

Orléans

FRANCE

Strasbourg

BAVARIA

Augsburg

Ratisbon

Munich

AUSTRIA

Vienna

Danube R.

HUNGARY

TRANSYLVANIA

Bourges

BURGUNDY

FR.
COMTÉ

Basel

SWISS
CONFEDERATION

Geneva

TYROL

Budapest

Angoulême

Bordeaux

SAVOY

Milan

Trent

Venice

Parma

Mohacs

Belgrade

WALLACHIA

Bucharest

DAUPHINE

Avignon

Genoa

VENETIAN REPUBLIC

DALMATIA

BOSNIA

Danub

OTTOMAN

Marseilles

Florence

PAPAL
STATES

ADRIATIC SEA

MONTENEGRO

Sofia

Santiago

Burgos

Valladolid

NAVARRE

PYRENEES

ARAGON

CATALONIA

Barcelona

CORSICA
(Genoa)

Rome

Adrianop

SPAIN

Escorial

Madrid

CASTILE

Toledo

BALEARIC I.

SARDINIA
(Aragon)

NAPLES

Naples
(Aragon)

ALBANIA

Salonica

AEGEAN
SEA

GREECE

Lepanto

CHIO
(Geno

Valencia

Seville

Granada

GRANADA

Cadiz

MEDITERRANEAN

Palermo

SICILY
(Aragon)

IONIAN I.
(Venice)

MOREA

SEA

(Venice)

Melilla (Spain)

Algiers

Tunis

MALTA (Knights of St. John)

CRETE
(Venice)

SULTANATE
OF FEZ

SULTANATE OF ALGIERS

SULTANATE
OF TUNIS

B A R B A R Y   S T A T E S

orto

UGAL

on

PGAL

Bayonne

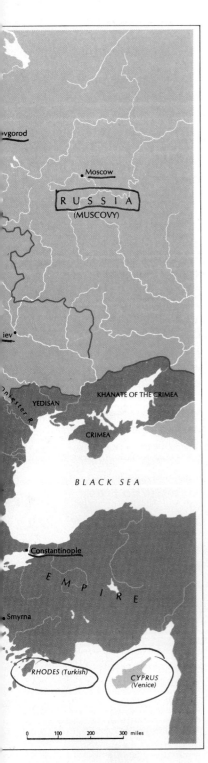

EUROPE, 1526

The main feature of the political map of Europe about 1526 is the predominance of the house of Habsburg. Much of Europe was ruled by the Habsburg Emperor Charles V, who was at the same time King Charles I of Spain. As is explained in this and the following chapter, Charles left his possessions in Austria, Hungary, and Bohemia to his brother, those in Spain, the Netherlands, Italy, and America to his son. He thus established the Austrian and Spanish branches of the Habsburg dynasty. France was nearly encircled by Habsburg dominions and habitually formed alliances with various German princes and with Sweden, Poland, and Turkey. The Habsburgs remained the principal power in Europe until after the Thirty Years' War, which ended in 1648.

was church feeling; the sense of "Spanishness" was a sense of Catholicity. Formerly the Spanish had been among the most tolerant of Europeans; Christians, Muslims, and Jews had managed to live together. But in the wave of national (or religious) excitement that accompanied the conquest of Granada both the Jews and the Moors were expelled. The expulsion of the Jews by a decree of 1492 was actually a sign of former toleration in Spain, for the Jews had been similarly expelled from England in 1290 and from France in 1306. They were not again legally allowed in England until the mid-seventeenth century, nor in France (with great exceptions) until the French Revolution. It would appear that in the history of many European peoples the attainment of a certain degree of national consciousness brought a feeling against Jews as "outsiders."[8]

All persons in Spain were now supposed to be Christians. In fact, however, Spain was the one country in Europe where a person's Christianity could not be taken for granted, because many Spanish families had been Jewish or Muslim for centuries, and had only accepted Christianity to avoid expulsion. Hence arose a fear of false Christians, of an unassimilated element secretly hostile to the foundations of Spanish life. It was feared that Moriscos (Christians of Moorish background) and Marranos (Christians of Jewish background) retained a clandestine sympathy for the religion of their forebears. A distaste for eating pork, or an inclination not to work on Saturday, was enough to arouse suspicion. Thousands of such persons were haled before the Inquisition, where, as in the civil courts under Roman procedure, torture could be employed to extort confessions. Spanish life became rigidly and ostentatiously orthodox. It was safest to be profuse in one's external devotions. It was the way of proving oneself to be a good Spaniard. The national and the Catholic were fused.

The life of Spain remained a great crusade, a crusade within Spain against Moriscos and Marranos, a crusade carried against the Moors into Africa itself, which the Spanish invaded immediately after the conquest of Granada. The crusade crossed the ocean into the Americas, where the Spanish church set about gathering the Indians into the fold. And it was soon to spread to Europe also. Spain was ready, before Protestantism ever appeared, to play its role in the Reformation, to be the avenging angel to extirpate heresy, and the stern apostle demanding Catholic reform.

The Holy Roman Empire and the Habsburg Supremacy

Ideas of the New Monarchy were at work even in Germany, which is to say, in the Holy Roman Empire. There were three kinds of states in the Empire. There were the princely states—duchies, margraviates, etc.—each a little hereditary dynastic monarchy in itself, such as Saxony, Brandenburg, or Bavaria. There were ecclesiastical states—bishoprics, abbacies, etc.—in which the bishop or abbot, whose rule was of course not hereditary, conducted the government. A large portion of the area of the Empire consisted in these church-states, as may be seen from the map on pages 70–71. Third, there were the imperial free cities,

---

[8] The Jews who left Spain (the Sephardic Jews) went to North Africa and the Near East, and in smaller numbers to the Dutch Netherlands and even to southwestern France (one of the exceptions noted above). Those who left England two centuries earlier generally went to Germany, the great center of Ashkenazic Jewry in the Middle Ages. Driven from Germany in the fourteenth century they concentrated in Poland, which remained the great center of European Jewry until the Nazi massacres of the 1940s. See map, p. 819 below.

some fifty in number; their collective area was not large, but they dominated the commercial and financial life of the country. There was in truth also a fourth category, made up of some thousands of imperial knights, noblemen of minor consequence who possessed a few manors, but who belonged to no state, recognizing the supremacy of none but the emperor.

The states, over the centuries, had prevented the emperor from infringing upon their local liberties. They had taken care to keep the emperorship an elective office, so that with each election local liberties could be reaffirmed. After 1356 the right of electing an emperor was vested in seven electors—namely, four of the princely lords, the Count Palatine, Duke of Saxony, Margrave of Brandenburg, and King of Bohemia (the one king in the Empire), and in three ecclesiastical lords, the archbishops of Mainz, Trier, and Cologne. In 1452 the electors chose the Archduke of Austria to be emperor. His family name was Habsburg. The Habsburgs, by using the resources of their hereditary possessions in Austria (and later elsewhere) and by delicately balancing and bribing the numerous political forces within Germany, managed to get themselves consistently reelected to the Holy Roman Emperorship in every generation, with one exception, from 1452 until 1806.

The principles of New Monarchy were successful mainly in the hereditary princely states of reasonable size. Here the rulers went through the familiar process of quelling their own feudal subordinates, increasing their revenues, enforcing local peace, and letting their own parliamentary bodies fall into abeyance. Thus Brandenburg, Saxony, Bavaria, Württemberg, and a few others, though small, began to take on the semblance of modern states.

The Habsburg emperors also tried to introduce the centralizing principles of the New Monarchy in the Empire as a whole. Under Maximilian I (1493–1519) there seemed to be progress in this direction: the Empire was divided into administrative "circles," and an Imperial Chamber and Council were created, but they were all doomed to failure before the immovable obstacle of states' rights. Maximilian was the author of the Habsburg family fortunes in a quite different way. *Bella gerunt alii; tu, felix Austria, nubes*—"where others have to fight wars, you, fortunate Austria, marry!" Maximilian himself married the heiress of the dukes of Burgundy, who, over the past century, had acquired a number of provinces in the western extremities of the Empire—the Netherlands and the Free County of Burgundy, which bordered upon France. Maximilian by this marriage had a son Philip, whom he married to Joanna, heiress to Ferdinand and Isabella of Spain. Philip and Joanna produced a son Charles. Charles combined the inheritances of his four grandparents: Austria from Maximilian, the Netherlands and Free County from Mary of Burgundy, Castile and Spanish America from Isabella, Aragon and its Mediterranean and Italian possessions from Ferdinand. In addition, in 1519, he was elected Holy Roman Emperor and so became the symbolic head of all Germany.

Charles V of the Empire (he was known as Charles I in Spain) was thus beyond all comparison the most powerful ruler of his day. But still other fortunes awaited the house of Habsburg. The Turks, who had occupied Constantinople in 1453, were at this time pushing through Hungary and menacing central Europe. In 1526 they defeated the Hungarians at the battle of Mohacs. The parliaments of Hungary, and of the adjoining kingdom of Bohemia, hoping to gain allies in the face of the Turkish peril, thereupon elected Charles V's brother Ferdinand as their king. The Habsburg family was now entrenched in central Europe, in the Netherlands, in Spain, in the Mediterranean, in south Italy, in America. No one since Charlemagne had stood so far above all rivals. Contemporaries cried that Europe was threatened with "universal monarchy," with a kind of world-state in which no people could preserve its independence.

The reader who wishes to understand the religious revolution, and consequent emergence of Protestantism, to which we shall now turn, must bear in mind the extraordinarily intricate interplay of the factors that have now been outlined: the decline of the church, the growth of secular and humanistic feeling, the spread of lay religion outside the official clergy, the rise of monarchs who wished to control everything in their kingdoms, including the church, the resistance of feudal elements to these same monarchs, the lassitude of the popes and their fear of church councils, the atomistic division of Germany, the Turkish peril, the zeal of Spain, the preeminence of Charles V, and the fears felt in the rest of Europe, especially in France, of absorption or suffocation by the amazing empire of the Habsburgs.

9. THE PROTESTANT REFORMATION

Three streams contributed to the religious upheaval of the sixteenth century. First, among simple people, or the laboring poor, who might find their spokesmen among local priests, there was an endemic dissatisfaction with all the grand apparatus of the church, or a belief that its bishops and abbots were part of a wealthy and oppressive ruling class. For such people, religious ideas were mixed with protest against the whole social order. They found expression in the great peasant rebellion in Germany in the 1520s. The sects which emerged are known historically as Anabaptists, and the modern Baptists, Mennonites, and Moravian Brothers are among their descendants. Second, and forming a group generally more educated and with broader views of the world, were the middle classes of various European cities, especially of cities that were almost like autonomous little republics, as in Germany, Switzerland, and the Netherlands. They might wish to manage their own religious affairs as they did their other business, believing that the church hierarchy was too much embedded in a feudal, baronial, and monarchical system with which they had little in common. The modern churches of Calvinist origin came in large part from this stream. Third, there were the kings and ruling princes, who had long disputed with the church on matters of property, taxes, legal jurisdiction, and political influence. Each such ruler wanted to be master in his own territory. In the end it was the power of such rulers that determined which form of religion should officially prevail. The Lutheran and Anglican churches were in this tradition, and to some extent the Gallican church, as the French branch of the Roman Catholic church was called. As it turned out, by 1600, the second and third streams had won many successes, but the first was suppressed. Socio-religious radicalism was reduced to an undercurrent in countries where Anglican, Lutheran, Calvinist, or Roman Catholic churches were established.

Since northern Europe became Protestant while the south remained Catholic, it may look as if the north had broken off in a body from a once solid Roman church. The reality was not so simple. Let us for a moment put aside the term

"Protestant," and think of the adherents of the new religion as religious revolutionaries.[9] Their ideas were revolutionary because they held, not merely that
"abuses" in the church must be corrected, but that the Roman church itself was
wrong in principle. Even so, there were many who hoped, for years, that old and
new ideas of the church might be combined. Many deplored the extremes but
gradually in the heat of struggle had to choose one side or the other. The issues
became drawn, and each side aspired to destroy its adversary. For over a century
the revolutionaries maintained the hope that "popery" would everywhere fall.
For over a century the upholders of the old order worked to annihilate or recon-
vert "heretics." Only slowly did Catholics and Protestants come to accept each
other's existence as an established fact of European society. Though the religious
frontier that was to prove permanent appeared as early as 1560, it was not generally accepted until after the Thirty Years' War, which closed in 1648.

Luther and Lutheranism

The first who successfully defied the older church authorities was Martin Luther.
He was a monk, and an earnest one, until he was almost forty years old. A vehement and spiritually uneasy man, with many dark and introspective recesses in his
personality, Luther was terrified by the thought of the awful omnipotence of God,
distressed by his own littleness, apprehensive of the devil, and suffering from the
chronic conviction that he was damned. The means offered by the church to allay
such spiritual anguish—the sacraments, prayer, attendance at Mass—gave him no
satisfaction. From a reading and pondering of St. Paul (Romans i, 17)—"the just
shall live by faith"—there dawned upon him a new realization and sense of peace.
He developed the doctrine of justification by faith alone. This held that what
"justifies" a man is not what the church knew as "works" (prayer, alms, the sacraments, holy living) but "faith alone," an inward bent of spirit given to each soul
directly by God. Good works, Luther thought, were the consequence and external evidence of this inner grace, but in no way its cause. A man did not "earn"
grace by doing good; he did the good because he possessed the grace of God. With
this idea Luther for some years lived content. Even years later some high-placed
churchmen believed that in Luther's doctrine of justification by faith there was
nothing contrary to the teachings of the Catholic church.

Luther, now a professor at Wittenberg, was brought out of seclusion by an incident of 1517. A friar named Tetzel was traveling through Germany distributing
indulgences, authorized by the pope to finance the building of St. Peter's in
Rome.[10] In return for them the faithful paid certain stipulated sums of money.
Luther thought that people were being deluded, that no one could in this way obtain grace for himself, or ease the pains of relatives in purgatory, as was officially
claimed. In the usual academic manner of the day, he posted ninety-five theses on
the door of the castle church at Wittenberg. In them he reviewed the Catholic
sacrament of penance. Luther held that, after confession, the sinner is freed of his
burden not by the priest's absolution, but by inner grace and faith alone. Increas-

---

[9] The word "Protestant" arose as an incident in the struggle, at first denoting certain Lutherans who drew up a
formal protest against an action of the diet of the Empire in 1529. Only very gradually did the various groups of
anti-Roman reformers think of themselves as collectively Protestant.
[10] On indulgences see p. 52.

ingly, it seemed that the priesthood performed no necessary function in the relation between man and God.

Luther at first appealed to the pope, Leo X, to correct the abuse of indulgences in Germany. When the pope refused action Luther (like many before him) urged the assembly of a general church council as an authority higher even than the pope. He was obliged, however, to admit in public debate that even the decision of a general council might be mistaken. The Council of Constance, he said, had in fact erred in its condemnation of John Huss. But if neither the pope, nor yet a council, had authority to define true Christian belief, where was such authority to be found? Luther's answer was, in effect: There is no such authority. He held that each individual might read the Bible and freely make his own interpretation according to his own conscience. This idea was as revolutionary, for the church, as would be the assertion today that neither the Supreme Court nor any other body may authoritatively interpret or enforce the Constitution of the United States, since each citizen may interpret the Constitution in his own way.

From his first public appearance Luther won ardent supporters, for there was a good deal of resentment in Germany against Rome. In 1519 and 1520 he rallied public opinion in a series of tracts, setting forth his main beliefs. He declared that the claim of the clergy to be different from the laity was an imposture. He urged people to find Christian truth in the Bible for themselves, and in the Bible only. He denounced the reliance on fasts, pilgrimages, saints, and Masses. He rejected the belief in purgatory. He reduced the seven sacraments to two—baptism and the communion, as he called the Mass. In the latter he repudiated the new and "modern" doctrine of transubstantiation, while affirming that God was still somehow mysteriously present in the bread and wine.[11] He declared that the clergy should marry, upbraided the prelates for their luxury, and demanded that monasticism be eliminated. To drive through such reforms, while depriving the clergy of their pretensions, he called upon the temporal power, the princes of Germany. He thus issued an invitation to the state to assume control over religion, an invitation which, in the days of the New Monarchy, a good many rulers were enthusiastically willing to accept.

Threatened by a papal bull with excommunication unless he recanted, Luther solemnly and publicly burned the bull. Excommunication followed. To the emperor, Charles V, now fell the duty of apprehending the heretic and repressing the heresy. Luther was summoned to appear before a diet of the Empire, held at Worms in the Rhineland. He declared that he could be convinced only by Scripture or right reason; otherwise—"I neither can nor will recant anything, since it is neither right nor safe to act against conscience. God help me! Amen." He was placed under the ban of the Empire. But the Elector of Saxony and other north German princes took him under their protection. In safe seclusion, he began to translate the Bible into German.

Luther's excitable obstinacy, intemperate language, and sweeping repudiation of existing authorities antagonized many who had at first looked upon him with favor, and who still hoped for a reform of the church without revolution. Among these was Erasmus, who, as often happens to those who find themselves in the middle, was in his last years looked upon by both sides, Lutheran and Catholic, as a meddlesome friend of the opposition.

---

[11] See pp. 39, 41.

Lutheranism, or at least anti-Romanism, swept over Germany, assuming the proportions of a national upheaval. It became mixed with all sorts of political and social revolution. A league of imperial knights, adopting Lutheranism, attacked their neighbors, the church-states of the Rhineland, hoping by annexations to enlarge their own meager territories. In 1524 the peasants of a large part of Germany revolted. They were stirred by new religious ideas, worked upon by preachers who went beyond Luther in asserting that anyone could see for himself what was right. Their aims, however, were social and economic; they demanded a regulation of rents and security of common village rights and complained of exorbitant exactions and oppressive rule by their manorial overlords. Luther repudiated all connection with the peasants, called them filthy swine, and urged the princes to suppress them by the sword. The peasants were unmercifully put down, but popular unrest continued to stir the country, expressing itself, in a religious age, in various forms of extreme religious frenzy. Various leaders had various followings, known collectively as Anabaptists. Some said that all the world needed was love, some that Christ would soon come again, some that they were saints and could do no wrong, and some that infant baptism was useless, immersion of full-grown adults being required, as described in the Bible. The roads of Germany were alive with obscure zealots, of whom some tens of thousands converged in 1534 on the city of Münster. There they proclaimed the reign of the saints, abolished property, and introduced polygamy as authorized in the Old Testament. A Dutch tailor, John of Leyden, claimed authority from God himself, and, hemmed in by besieging armies, ruled Münster by a revolutionary terror. Luther advised his followers to join even with Catholics to repress such an appalling menace. After a full year Münster was relieved. The "saints" were pitilessly rooted out; John of Leyden died in torture.

Luther, horrified at the way in which religious revolution became confused with social revolution, defined his own position more conservatively. He restricted, while never denying, the right of private judgment in matters of conscience, and he made a larger place for an established clergy, Lutheranized, to be sure, but still established as teachers over the laity. Always well disposed to temporal rulers, having called upon the princes to act as religious reformers, he was thrown by the peasant and Anabaptist uprisings into an even closer alliance with them. Lutheranism took on a character of submissiveness to the state. Christian liberty, Luther insisted, was an internal freedom, purely spiritual, known only to God. In worldly matters, he said, the good Christian owed perfect obedience to established authority. Lutheranism, more than Catholicism and more than the Calvinism which soon arose, came to hold the state in a kind of religious awe as an institution almost sacred in its own right.

In the revolution that was rocking Germany it was not the uprising of imperial knights, nor that of peasants or tailors and journeymen, that was successful, but the rebellion of the higher orders of the Empire against the emperor. Charles V, as Holy Roman Emperor, was bound to uphold Catholicism because only in a Catholic world did the Holy Empire have any meaning. The states of the Empire, always fearing the loss of local liberty, saw in Charles' efforts to repress Luther a threat to their own freedom. Many imperial free cities, and most of the dynastic states of north Germany, now insisted on adding to their other rights and liberties the right, or liberty, to determine their own religion. The *ius reformandi*, they said, the right or power to reform, belonged to member states, not to the Empire itself. They became Lutheran, locally, introducing Lutheran bishops, doctrines, and forms of worship. Where a state turned Lutheran it usually "secularized" (i.e., confiscated) the church properties within its borders, a process which considerably enriched some of the Lutheran princes and gave them a strong material interest in the success of the Lutheran movement. In most of the church-states, since the Catholic archbishop or bishop was himself the government, Catholicism prevailed. But a few church-states turned Lutheran. A good example of the secularization of a church-state was afforded in East Prussia, just outside the Empire. This territory belonged to the Teutonic Order, a Catholic organization of which the grand commander, an elective official, was at this time Albert of Brandenburg. In 1525 Albert declared for Luther and converted East Prussia into a secular duchy, of which he and his descendants became hereditary dukes.

Against the emperor, a group of Lutheran princes and free cities formed the League of Schmalkald. The king of France, Francis I, though a Catholic in good standing, allied with and supported the League. Political interests overrode religious ones. Against the "universal monarchy" of the swollen Habsburgs the French found alliances where they could, allying with the Turks as with the Lutherans, building up a balance of power against their mighty foe. It became the studied policy of Catholic France to maintain the religious division of Germany.

Charles V strove to find some basis of agreement by which the permanent religious division of Germany could be avoided. He was at war with France over certain disputed territories and with the Turks, who in 1529 besieged Vienna itself. Though the Lutheran princes did render a little help at the last moment, it seemed on the whole that the infidels might overrun Germany before the German states would yield their liberties to their own emperor.

Charles appealed to the pope, urging him to assemble a Europe-wide council in which all disputed matters could be considered, the Protestants heard, compromises effected, and church unity and German unity (such as it was) restored. The king of France schemed at Rome to prevent the pope from calling any such council. The kings of both France and England urged national councils instead, in which religious questions could be settled on a national basis. Pope after pope delayed. The papacy feared that a council of all Latin Christendom might get out of control, since Catholics as much as Protestants demanded reform. At the very rumor of a council the price of salable offices in Rome abruptly fell. To the papacy, remembering the Council of Constance, nothing was more upsetting than the thought of a council, not even the Protestants, not even the Turks. So the popes procrastinated, no council met, years passed, and a new generation grew up in Lutheranism. Desperately, in 1548, Charles tried to settle matters himself, issuing the *Interim*, to guide religion in all Germany until a general church council could complete its work. The *Interim* upheld the main Catholic doctrines, but, to attract the Protestants, allowed marriage of the clergy and one or two other minor concessions. Neither side would accept it: Protestants found that it gave too little, and Catholics refused to have their religion tampered with by the temporal power.

Meanwhile the Schmalkaldic League, allied with France, had actually gone to war with the emperor in 1546. Germany fell into an anarchy of civil struggle between Catholic and Protestant states, the latter aided by France. The war was ended by the Peace of Augsburg of 1555.

The terms set at Augsburg signified a complete victory for the cause of Lutheranism and states' rights. Each state of the Empire received the liberty to be either

Lutheran or Catholic as it chose—*cuius regio eius religio*, "whose the region, his the religion." No individual freedom of religion was permitted; if a ruler or a free city decided for Lutheranism, then all persons had to be Lutheran. Similarly in Catholic states all had to be Catholic. The Peace of Augsburg provided also, by the so-called Ecclesiastical Reservation, that any Catholic bishop or other church-man who turned Lutheran in the future (or who had turned Lutheran as recently as 1552) should not carry his territory with him, but should turn Lutheran as an individual and move away, leaving his land and its inhabitants Catholic. Since the issues in Germany were still far from stabilized, this proviso was often disre-garded in later years.

The Peace of Augsburg was thus, in religion, a great victory for Protestantism, and at the same time, in German politics and constitutional matters, a step in the disintegration of Germany into a mosaic of increasingly separate states. Luther-anism prevailed in the north, and in the south in the duchy of Württemberg and various detached islands formed by Lutheranized free cities. Catholicism pre-vailed in the south (except in Württemberg and certain cities), in the Rhine val-ley, and in the direct possessions of the house of Habsburg, which in 1555 reached as far north as the Netherlands. The Germans, because of conditions in the Holy Roman Empire, were the one large European people to emerge from the religious conflict almost evenly divided between Catholic and Protestant.

No rights were granted by the Peace of Augsburg to another group of religious revolutionaries which neither Lutherans nor Catholics were willing to tolerate, namely, the followers of John Calvin.

Lutheranism, it must be pointed out, was adopted by the kings of Denmark and Sweden as early as the 1520s. Since Denmark controlled Norway, and Swe-den ruled Finland and the eastern Baltic, all Scandinavia and the Baltic regions became, like north Germany, Lutheran. Beyond this area Lutheranism failed to take root. Like Anglicanism in England (to be described shortly) Lutheranism was too closely associated with established states to spread easily as an interna-tional movement. The most successful international form of the Protestant move-ment was Calvinism.

Calvin and Calvinism

John Calvin was a Frenchman, born Jean Cauvin, who called himself Calvinus in Latin. Born in 1509, he was a full generation younger than Luther. He was trained both as a priest and as a lawyer, and had a humanist's knowledge of Latin and Greek, as well as Hebrew. At the age of twenty-four, experiencing a sudden con-version, or fresh insight into the meaning of Christianity, he joined forces with the religious revolutionaries of whom the best known was then Luther. Three years later, in 1536, he published, in the international language, Latin, his *Insti-tutes of the Christian Religion*. Where Luther had aimed much of his writing either at the existing rulers of Germany, or at the German national feeling against Rome, Calvin addressed his *Institutes* to all the world. He seemed to appeal to human reason itself; he wrote in the severe, logical style of the trained lawyer; he dealt firmly, lucidly, and convincingly with the most basic issues. In the *Institutes* people in all countries, if dissatisfied with the existing Roman church, could find cogent expression of universal propositions, which they could apply to their own local circumstances as they required.

With Luther's criticisms of the Roman church, and with most of Luther's fundamental religious ideas, such as justification by faith and not by works, Calvin agreed. In what they retained of the Catholic Mass, the communion or Lord's Supper as they called it, Luther and Calvin developed certain doctrinal differences. Both rejected transubstantiation, but where Luther insisted that God was somehow actually present in the bread and wine used in the service ("consubstantiation"), Calvin and his followers tended more to regard it as a pious act of symbolic or commemorative character.

The chief differences between Calvin and Luther were two. Calvin made far more of the idea of predestination. Both, drawing heavily on St. Augustine, held that man by his own actions could earn no merit in the sight of divine justice, that any grace which anyone possessed came from the free action of God alone. God, being Almighty, knew and willed in advance all things that happened, including the way in which every life would turn out. He knew and willed, from all eternity, that some were saved and some were damned. Calvin, a severe critic of human nature, felt that those who had grace were relatively few. They were the "elect," the "godly," the little band chosen without merit of their own, from all eternity, for salvation. A person could feel in his own mind that he was among the saved, God's chosen few, if throughout all trials and temptations he persisted in a saintly life. Thus the idea of predestination, of God's omnipotence, instead of turning to fatalism and resignation, became a challenge to unrelenting effort, a sense of burning conviction, a conviction of being on the side of that Almighty Power which must in the end be everlastingly triumphant. It was the most resolute spirits that were attracted to Calvinism. Calvinists, in all countries, were militant, uncompromising, perfectionist—or Puritan, as they were called first in England and later in America.

The second way in which Calvinism differed from Lutheranism was in its attitude to society and to the state. Calvinists refused to recognize the subordination of church to state, or the right of any government—king, parliament, or civic magistracy—to lay down laws for religion. On the contrary, they insisted that true Christians, the elect or godly, should Christianize the state. They wished to remake society itself into the image of a religious community. They rejected the institution of bishops (which both the Lutheran and Anglican churches retained), and provided instead that the church should be governed by presbyteries, elected bodies made up of ministers and devout laymen. By thus bringing an element of lay control into church affairs, they broke the monopoly of priestly power and so promoted secularization. On the other hand, they were the reverse of secular, for they wished to Christianize all society.

Calvin, called in by earlier reformers who had driven out their bishop, was able to set up his model Christian community at Geneva in Switzerland. A body of ministers ruled the church; a consistory of ministers and elders ruled the town. The rule was strict; all loose, light, or frivolous living was suppressed; disaffected persons were driven into exile. The form of worship was severe, and favored the intellectual rather than the emotional or the aesthetic. The service was devoted largely to long sermons elucidating Christian doctrine, and all appeals to the senses—color, music, incense—were rigidly subdued. The black gown of Geneva replaced brighter clerical vestments. Images, representing the saints, Mary, or Christ, were taken down and destroyed. Candles went the way of incense. Chanting was replaced by the singing of hymns. Instrumental music was frowned upon, and many Calvinists thought even bells to be a survival of "popery." In all things Calvin undertook to regulate his church by the Bible. Nor was he more willing than Luther to countenance any doctrine more radical than his own. When a Spanish refugee, Michael Servetus, who denied the Trinity, i.e., the divinity of Christ, sought asylum at Geneva, Calvin pronounced him a heretic and burned him at the stake.

To Geneva flocked reformers of all nationalities, Englishmen, Scots, French-men, Netherlanders, Germans, Poles, and Hungarians, to see and study a true scriptural community so that they might reproduce it in their own countries. Geneva became the Protestant Rome, the one great international center of Re-formed doctrine. Everywhere Calvinists made their teachings heard (even in Spain and Italy in isolated cases), and everywhere, or almost everywhere, little groups which had locally and spontaneously broken with the old church found in Calvin's *Institutes* a reasoned statement of doctrine and a suggested method of organization. Thus Calvinism spread, or was adopted, very widely. In Hungary and Bohemia large elements turned Protestant, and usually Calvinist, partly as a way of opposing the Habsburg rule. In Poland there were many Calvinists, along with less organized Anabaptists and Unitarians, or Socinians, as those who denied the Trinity were then called. Calvinists spread in Germany, where, opposing both Lutheran and Catholic churches as ungodly impositions of worldly power, they were disliked equally by both. In France the Huguenots were Calvinist, as were the Protestants of the Netherlands. John Knox in the 1550s brought Calvin-ism to Scotland, where Presbyterianism became and remained the established religion. At the same time Calvinism began to penetrate England, from which it was later to reach British America, giving birth to the Presbyterian and Congre-gationalist churches of the United States.

Calvinism was far from democratic in any modern sense, being rather of an al-most aristocratic outlook, in that those who sensed themselves to be God's chosen few felt free to dictate to the common run of mankind. Yet in many ways Calvin-ism entered into the development of what became democracy. For one thing, Calvinists never venerated the state; they always held that the sphere of the state and of public life was subject to moral judgment. For another, the Calvinist doc-trine of the "calling" taught that a man's labor had a religious dignity, and that any form of honest work was pleasing in the sight of God. In the conduct of their own affairs Calvinists developed a type of self-government. They formed "cove-nants" with one another, and devised machinery for the election of presbyteries. They refused to believe that authority was transmitted downward through bish-ops or through kings. They were inclined also to a democratic outlook by the cir-cumstance that in most countries they remained an unofficial minority. Only at Geneva, in the Dutch Netherlands, in Scotland, and in New England (and for a few years in England in the seventeenth century) were Calvinists ever able to pre-scribe the mode of life and religion of a whole country. In England, France, and Germany, Calvinists remained in opposition to the established authorities of church and state and hence were disposed to favor limitations upon established power. In Poland and Hungary many Calvinists were nobles who disliked royal authority.

The Reformation in England

England was peculiar in that its government broke with the Roman church be-fore adopting any Protestant principles. Henry VIII (1509–1547) in fact prided himself on his orthodoxy. When a few obscure persons, about 1520, began to whisper Luther's ideas in England, Henry himself wrote a *Defense of the Seven Sacraments* in refutation, for which a grateful pope conferred upon him the title of "Defender of the Faith." But the king had no male heir. Recalling the anarchy from which the Tudor dynasty had extricated England, and determined as a New Monarch to build up a durable monarchy, he felt, or said, that before all else he must have a son. In order to remarry, he requested the pope to annul his existing marriage to Catherine of Aragon. Popes in the past had obliged monarchs similarly pressed. The pope now, however, was embarrassed by the fact that Catherine, who objected, was the aunt of the Emperor Charles V, whom the pope was in no position to offend. Henry, not a patient man, drove matters forward. He put in a new archbishop of Canterbury, repudiated the Roman connection, and married the youthful Anne Boleyn. The fact that only three years later he put to death the unfortunate Anne, and thereafter in quick succession married four more wives, for a total of six, threw considerable doubt on the original character of his motives.

Henry acted through Parliament, believing, as he said, that a king was never stronger than when united with representatives of his kingdom. In 1534 Parliament passed the Act of Supremacy, which declared the English king to be the "Protector and Only Supreme Head of the Church and Clergy of England." All subjects were required, if asked, to take the oath of supremacy acknowledging the religious headship of Henry and rejecting that of the pope. For refusing this oath Sir Thomas More, a statesman and humanist best known as the author of *Utopia*, was executed for treason. He received a somewhat delayed reward four centuries later when the Roman church pronounced him to be a saint. Henry, in the next few years, closed all the monasteries in England. The extensive monastic lands, accumulated by never-dying corporations from gifts made over the centuries, were seized by the king, who passed them out to numerous followers, thus strengthening and reconstituting a landed aristocracy which had been seriously weakened in the Wars of the Roses. The new landed gentry remained firm supporters of the house of Tudor and the English national church, whatever its doctrines.

It was Henry's intent not to change the doctrines at all. He simply wished to be the supreme head of an English Catholic church. On the one hand, in 1536, he forcibly suppressed a predominantly Catholic rebellion, and, on the other, in 1539, through the Six Articles, required everybody to believe in transubstantiation, the celibacy of the clergy, the need of confession, and a few other test items of Catholic faith and practice. But it proved impossible to maintain this position, for a great many people in England began to favor one or another of the ideas of Continental Reformers, and a small minority were willing to accept the entire Protestant position.

For three decades the government veered about. Henry died in 1547 and was succeeded by his ten-year-old son, Edward VI, under whom the Protestant party came to the fore. But Edward died in 1553 and was succeeded by his much older sister, Mary, the daughter of Catherine of Aragon and a devout Roman Catholic whose whole life had been embittered by the break with Rome. Mary tried to re-Catholicize England, but she actually made Catholicism more unpopular with the English. In 1554 she married Philip of Spain, who became king of England, though only nominally. The English did not like Philip, nor the Spanish, nor the intense Spanish Catholicism that Philip represented. Under Mary, moreover, some three hundred persons were burned at the stake, as heretics, in public mass executions. It was the first (and last) time that such a thing had happened in

England, and it set up a wave of horror. In any event, Mary did not live long. She was succeeded in 1558 by Henry's younger daughter, Elizabeth, the child of Anne Boleyn. Whatever Elizabeth's real views in religion might be (she concealed them successfully and was rumored to have none), she could not be a Roman Catholic. For Catholics she was illegitimate and so unable to be queen.

Under Elizabeth the English became Protestant, gradually and in their own way. The Church of England took on a form of its own. Organizationally, it resembled a Lutheran church. It was a state church, for its existence and doctrines were determined by the temporal power, in this case the monarch acting through Parliament. All English subjects were obliged to belong to it, and laws were passed against "recusants," a term used to cover both the Roman Catholics and the more advanced Calvinists who refused to acknowledge it. With the exception of monasteries and certain other church foundations, the Church of England retained the physical possessions, buildings, and internal organization of the medieval church —the bishops and the archbishops, who continued to sit in the House of Lords, the episcopal courts with their jurisdiction over marriage and wills, the tithes or church taxes paid by all landowners, the parish structure, the universities of Oxford and Cambridge. In religious practice, the Church of England was definitely Protestant: English replaced Latin as the language of the liturgy, there was no cult of the saints, and the clergy married, though Elizabeth confessed to some embarrassment at the thought of an archbishop having a wife. In doctrine, it was Elizabeth's policy to make the dogmas broad and ambiguous, so that persons of all shades of belief could be more readily accommodated. The Thirty-nine Articles (1563), composed by a committee of bishops, defined the creed of the Anglican church. In the light of the burning issues of the day many of the articles were evasive, though Protestant in tone. All but one of the Anglican bishops had been newly appointed by Elizabeth at her accession; many had lived in exile among Continental Protestants in the reign of Mary Tudor; and except on the matter of church government through bishops (known as episcopacy) a strong Calvinist impress was set upon Anglican belief in the time of Elizabeth. Anglicans, for a century or more, generally considered themselves closer to Geneva than to Rome, the seat of "popery," and regarded Lutherans as "semi-papist." There remained, however, a High Church element, emphasizing the Catholic rather than the Protestant character of Anglicanism.

The same ecclesiastical settlement was prescribed for Ireland, where English or rather Anglo-Norman conquerors had settled since the twelfth century, shortly after the Norman conquest of England. A replica of the Church of England was now established, called the Church of Ireland, which took over the properties and position of the Roman church in the lesser island. The native Irish remained almost solidly Roman Catholic. As in Hungary or Bohemia people who resented the Habsburgs were likely to turn Protestant rather than share in the ruler's religion, so in Ireland the fact that the ruling English were Protestant only confirmed the Irish in their attachment to the Roman church. The Catholic priests, deprived of status, income, and church buildings, and often in hiding, became national leaders of a discontented people.

The Religious Situation by 1560

Neither in England, nor in Germany, nor in a Europe at large penetrated by international Calvinism were the issues regarded as settled in 1560. Nor had the

Roman church accepted the new situation. But by 1560 the chief Protestant doctrines had been affirmed, and geographically Protestantism had made many conquests. The unity of Latin Christendom had been broken. Christendom was disintegrating into a purely intangible ideal. A world of separate states and nations was taking its place.

Protestants differed with one another, yet there was much that all had in common. All rejected the papal authority. None participated in any effective international organization; the ascendancy of Geneva was spiritual only and proved to be temporary. All Protestants rejected the special, sacerdotal, or supernatural character of the priesthood; indeed, the movement was perhaps most fundamentally a revolt against the medieval position of the clergy. Protestants generally called their clergy ministers, not priests. All Protestant clergy could marry. There were no Protestant monks, nuns, or friars. All Protestant churches replaced Latin

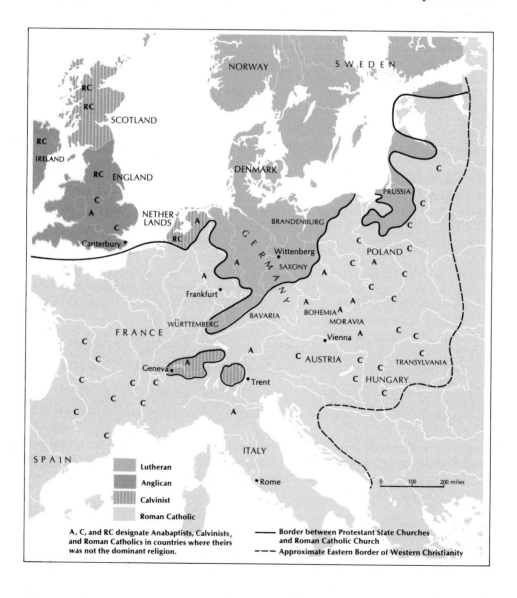

Lutheran

Anglican

Calvinist

Roman Catholic

A, C, and RC designate Anabaptists, Calvinists, and Roman Catholics in countries where theirs was not the dominant religion.

——— Border between Protestant State Churches and Roman Catholic Church

--- Approximate Eastern Border of Western Christianity

with the vernacular in religious services—English, French, German, Czech, as the case might be. All Protestants reduced the number of sacraments, usually to two or three; such sacraments as they retained they regarded more as symbols than as actual carriers of divine grace; all believed, in one way or another, in justification by faith. All denied transubstantiation, or the miracle of the Mass. All gave up the obligatory confessional, and with it priestly absolution. All gave up the idea of purgatory as a kind of temporal zone between heaven and hell and hence abandoned the practice of saying prayers and Masses for the dead. It need hardly be added that nothing like indulgences remained. All gave up the cult of the saints and of the Virgin Mary, whose intercession in heaven was no longer expected. All declared that the one true source of Christian belief was the Holy Scripture. And while all established Protestant churches, in the sixteenth century, insisted on conformity to their own doctrines, allowing no individual freedom, all Protestants still had some small spark of the spirit first ignited by Luther, so that none flatly repudiated the right of private judgment in matters of conscience.

It has sometimes been maintained that one of the motivations in Protestantism was economic—that a new acquisitive, aggressive, dynamic, progressive, capitalistic impulse shook off the restrictions imposed by medieval religion. The fact that Protestant England and Holland soon underwent a rapid capitalistic development gives added likelihood to this idea. The alacrity with which Protestant governments confiscated church lands shows a keen material interest; but in truth, both before and after the Reformation, governments confiscated church properties without breaking with the Roman church. That profound economic changes were occurring at the time will become apparent in the following chapter. Yet it seems that economic conditions were far less decisive than religious convictions and political circumstances. Calvinism won followers not only in cities, but in agrarian countries such as Scotland, Poland, and Hungary. Lutheranism spread more successfully in the economically retarded north Germany than in the busy south. The English were for years no more inclined to Protestantism than the French, and in France, while many lords and peasants turned Protestant, Paris

STATE RELIGIONS IN EUROPE ABOUT 1560

It is not possible to draw an accurate religious map of Europe during the Reformation, because in many countries persons of different religions were intermixed. What the map shows is the legally authorized, established or territorial churches about 1560. Many Catholics lived north of the heavy line, and many Protestants south of it. Most widely dispersed were the Calvinists and the more radical Protestants or Anabaptists. Calvinism was established in various Swiss cantons, the Dutch provinces, and Scotland, but there were many Calvinist congregations elsewhere, especially in southern France and in Poland and Hungary. Radical Protestants, who rejected the principle of the state church, could be found in both Protestant and Catholic countries; they were most numerous in parts of Germany and in Bohemia-Moravia, but included the American Pilgrim Fathers. In Germany, under the Holy Roman Empire, each principality and free city chose its own religion; hence, the Germans were the only large European nationality to emerge from the Reformation almost evenly divided between Catholics and Protestants. In other large countries in the century after 1560 one side or the other, Protestant or Catholic, was reduced to a small minority. Such minorities were either persecuted, barely tolerated, or at least out of favor with their respective governments until the French Revolution.

and many other towns remained as steadfastly Catholic. It is possible that Protestantism, by casting a glow of religious righteousness over a man's daily business and material prosperity, later contributed to the economic success of Protestant peoples, but it does not seem that economic forces were of any distinctive importance in the first stages of Protestantism.

10. CATHOLICISM REFORMED AND REORGANIZED

The Catholic movement corresponding to the rise of Protestantism is known as the Catholic Reformation or the Counter Reformation, the former term being preferred by Catholics, the latter by Protestants. Both are applicable. On the one hand the Catholic church underwent a genuine reform, which might have worked itself out in one way or another even if the stimulus of revolutionary Protestantism had been absent. On the other hand the character of the reform, the decisions made, and the measures adopted were shaped by the need of responding explicitly to the Protestant challenge; and certainly, also, there was a good deal of purely "counter" activity aimed at the elimination of Protestantism as such.

The demand for reform was as old as the abuses against which it was directed. Characteristically, it had expressed itself in the demand for a general or ecumenical church council. The conciliar movement, defeated by the popes about 1450, showed signs of revival after 1500.[12] But it was almost as hard, even then, to assemble a general council as it is today to create an international body possessing any effective authority.

Several years before Luther had been heard of, Europe's two most important secular rulers, the king of France and the Holy Roman Emperor, jointly convened on their own authority a council at Pisa in 1511. It was their purpose to force reforms upon Pope Julius II, and if necessary depose him. But no delegates from other countries attended; the five cardinals and handful of bishops who came to Pisa were regarded as minions of the two rulers who sent them. The council thus lacked moral authority, no one listened to it, and it accomplished nothing, never even attaining historically the name of a council. The pope, however, to ward off the danger of a council under secular auspices, himself assembled the Fifth Lateran Council at Rome in 1512. It was supposed to be general, ecumenical, Europe-wide, representing that "spiritual unity" sometimes imagined to have existed in Europe before Luther. In fact, few took it seriously, because it was composed mainly of Italian prelates, who began by denouncing the doctrines of the Council of Constance and ended by making a few tame resolutions on miscellaneous topics.

Then came the Lutheran upheaval, and the attempts of Charles V, in the interests of German unity, to persuade the pope to assemble a true and adequately empowered council, so that removal of abuses in the church, which no one really defended, would take away the grounds upon which many Germans were turning to Lutheranism. But meanwhile the king of France found reason to favor the pope and to oppose the emperor. The French king, Francis I (1515–1547), could support the pope because he had obtained from the papacy what he wanted, namely, control over the Gallican church, as acquired in the Concordat of

---

[12] On the conciliar movement see pp. 51–52.

Bologna of 1516.[13] And he had reason to oppose Charles V, because Charles V ruled not only in Germany but in the Netherlands, Spain, and much of Italy, thus encircling France and threatening Europe with what contemporaries called "universal monarchy." Francis I therefore actively encouraged the Protestants of Germany, as a means of maintaining dissension there, and used his influence at Rome against the calling of a council by which the troubles of the Catholic world might be relieved.

Gradually, in the curia, there arose a party of reforming cardinals who concluded that the need of reform was so urgent that all dangers of a council must be risked. The pope summoned a council to meet in 1537, but the wars between France and the Empire forced its abandonment. Then a council was called for 1542, but no one came except a few Italians so that it had to be suspended. Finally, in 1545, a council did assemble and begin operations. It met at Trent, on the Alpine borders of Germany and Italy. The Council of Trent, which shaped the destiny of modern Catholicism, sat at irregular intervals for almost twenty years—in 1545–1547, 1551–1552, and 1562–1563. It was not until the Second Vatican Council in the 1960s that some of the main decisions made at Trent were substantially modified.

The Council of Trent

The council was beset by difficulties of a political nature, which seemed to show that under troubled conditions an international council was no longer a suitable means of regulating Catholic affairs. For one thing, it was poorly attended. Whereas at the Fourth Lateran Council of 1215, and at Constance in 1415, some five hundred prelates had assembled, the attendance at Trent was never nearly so great; it sometimes fell as low as twenty or thirty, and the important decree on "justification," the prime issue raised by Luther, and one on which some good Catholics had until then believed a compromise to be possible, was passed at a session where only sixty prelates were present. The most regular in attendance were the Italians and Spanish; the French and Germans came erratically and in smaller numbers. Even with the small attendance, the old conciliar issue was raised. A party of bishops believed that the bishops of the Catholic church, when assembled in council from all parts of the Catholic world, collectively constituted an authority superior to that of the pope. To stave off this "episcopal" movement was one of the chief duties of the cardinal legates deputed by the pope to preside over the sessions.

The popes managed successfully to resist the idea of limiting the papal power. In the end they triumphed, through a final ruling, voted by the council, that no act of the council should be valid unless accepted by the Holy See. It is possible that had the conciliar theory won out, the Catholic church might have become as disunited in modern times as the Protestant. It was clear, at Trent, that the various bishops tended to see matters in a national way, in the light of their own problems at home, and to be frequently under strong influence from their respective secular monarchs. In any case, the papal party prevailed, which is to say that the centralizing element, not the national, triumphed. The Council of Trent in fact marked an important step in the movement which issued, three hundred

[13] See p. 69.

years later, in the promulgation of the infallibility of the pope when speaking *ex cathedra* on matters of faith and morals. After 1563 no council met at all until the Vatican Council of 1870 at which this papal infallibility was proclaimed.[14] The Council of Trent thus preserved the papacy as a center of unity for the Catholic church and helped prevent the very real threat of its dissolution into state churches. Even so, the council's success was not immediate, for in every important country the secular rulers at first accepted only what they chose of its work, and only gradually did its influence prevail.

Questions of national politics and of church politics apart, the Council of Trent addressed itself to two kinds of labors—to a statement of Catholic doctrine and to a reform of abuses in the church. When the council began to meet, in 1545, the Protestant movement had already gone so far that any reconciliation was probably impossible: Protestants, especially Calvinists, simply did not wish to belong to the church of Rome under any conditions. In any case, the Council of Trent made no concessions.

It declared justification to be by works and faith combined. It enumerated and defined the seven sacraments, which were held to be vehicles of grace independent of the spiritual state of those who received them.[15] The priesthood was declared to be a special estate set apart from the laity by the sacrament of holy orders. The procedures of the confessional and of absolution were clarified. Transubstantiation was reaffirmed. As sources of Catholic faith, the council put Scripture and tradition on an equal footing. It thus rejected the Protestant claim to find true faith in the Bible alone and reasserted the validity of church development since New Testament times. The Vulgate, a translation of the Bible into Latin made by St. Jerome in the fourth century, was declared to be the only version on which authoritative teaching could be based. The right of individuals to believe that their own interpretation of Scripture was more true than that of church authorities (private judgment) was denied. Latin, as against the national languages, was prescribed as the language of religious worship—a requirement abolished by the Second Vatican Council in the 1960s. Celibacy of the clergy was maintained. Monasticism was upheld. The existence of purgatory was reaffirmed. The theory and correct practice of indulgences were restated. The veneration of saints, the cult of the Virgin, and the use of images, relics, and pilgrimages were approved as spiritually useful and pious actions.

It was easier for a council to define doctrines than to reform abuses, since the latter consisted in the rooted habits of thousands and millions of people's lives. The council decreed, however, a drastic reform of the monastic orders. It acted against the abuse of indulgences while upholding the principle. It ruled that bishops should reside habitually in their dioceses and attend more carefully to their proper duties. It gave bishops more administrative control over clergy in their own dioceses, such as mendicant friars, who in the past had been exempt from episcopal jurisdiction, and whose presence had often caused disturbance, or indeed scandal, among the local people. The abuse by which one man had held numerous church offices at the same time (pluralism) was checked, and steps were taken to assure that church officials should be competent. To provide an educated clergy, the council ordered that a seminary should be set up in each diocese for the training of priests.

[14] See p. 600.
[15] See p. 39.

The Counter Crusade

As laws in general have little force unless sustained by opinion, so the reform decrees of the Council of Trent would have remained ineffectual had not a renewed sense of religious seriousness been growing at the same time. Herein lay the inner force of the Catholic Reform. In Italy, as the Renaissance became more undeniably pagan, and as the sack of Rome, in 1527, showed the depths of hatred felt even by Catholics toward the Roman clergy, the voices of severer moralists began to be heeded. The line of Renaissance popes was succeeded by a line of reforming popes, of whom the first was Paul III (1534–1549). The reforming popes insisted on the primacy of the papal office, but they regarded this office, unlike their predecessors, as a moral and religious force. In many dioceses the bishops began on their own initiative to be more strict. The new Catholic religious sense, more than the Protestant, centered in a reverence for the sacraments and a mystical awe for the church itself as a divine institution. Both men and women founded many new religious orders, of which the Jesuits became the most famous. Others were the Oratorians for men and the Ursulines for women. The new orders dedicated themselves to a variety of educational and philanthropic activities. Missionary fervor for a long time was more characteristic of Catholics than of Protestants. It reached into Asia and the Americas, and in Europe expressed itself as an intense desire for the reconversion of Protestants. It showed itself, too, in missions among the poor, as in the work of St. Vincent de Paul among the human wreckage of Paris, for which the established Protestant churches failed to produce anything comparable. In America, as colonies developed in the sixteenth and seventeenth centuries, the Protestant clergy tended to take the layman's view of the Indians, while Catholic clergy labored to convert and preserve them; and the Catholic church generally worked to mitigate the brutality of Negro slavery, to which the pastors in English and Dutch colonies, perhaps because they were more dependent upon the laity, remained largely indifferent.

We have seen how in Spain, where the Renaissance had never taken much hold, the very life of the country was a boundless Christian crusade.[16] It was in Spain that much of the new Catholic feeling first developed, and from Spain that much of the missionary spirit first went out. It was Spain that gave birth to St. Ignatius Loyola (1491–1556). A soldier in youth, he too, like Luther and Calvin, had a religious "experience" or "conversion," which occurred in 1521, before he had heard of Luther, and while Calvin was still a boy. Loyola resolved to become a soldier of the church, a militant crusader for the pope and the Holy See. On this principle he established the Society of Jesus, commonly known as the Jesuits. Authorized by Paul III in 1540, the Jesuits constituted a monastic order of a new type, less attached to the cloister, more directed toward active participation in the affairs of the world. Only men of proven strength of character and intellectual force were admitted. Each Jesuit had to undergo an arduous and even horrifying mystical training, set forth by Loyola in his *Spiritual Exercises.* The order was ruled by an iron discipline, which required each member to see in his immediate superior the infallibility of Holy Church. If, said Loyola, the church teaches to be black what the eye sees as white, the mind will believe it to be black. Aside from demanding absolute submission in matters of faith, the Jesuits generally favored rationality and a measure of liberty in the religious life. For two hundred

[16] See pp. 69–72.

years they were the most famous schoolmasters of Catholic Europe, eventually conducting some five hundred schools for boys of the upper and middle classes. In them they taught, besides the faith, the principles of gentlemanly deportment (their teaching of dancing and dramatics became a scandal to more puritanical Catholics), and they carried over the Renaissance and humanist idea of the Latin classics as the main substance of adolescent education. The Jesuits made a specialty of work among the ruling classes. They became confessors to kings and hence involved in political intrigue. In an age when Protestants subordinated the organized church either to the state or to the individual conscience, and when even Catholics frequently thought of the church within a national framework, the Jesuits seemed almost to worship the church itself as a divine institution, the Church Militant and the Church Universal, internationally organized and governed by the Roman pontiff. All full-fledged Jesuits took a special vow of obedience to the pope. Jesuits in the later sessions of the Council of Trent fought obstinately, and successfully, to uphold the position of Rome against that of the national bishops. The high papalism of the Jesuits (later called "ultramontanism") for centuries made them as obnoxious to many Catholics as they were to the Protestants.

By 1560 the Catholic church, renewed by a deepening of its religious life, and by an uncompromising restatement of its dogmas and discipline, had devised also the practical machinery for a counteroffensive against Protestantism. The Jesuits acted as an international missionary force. They recruited members from all countries, including those in which the governments had turned Protestant. English Catholics, for example, trained as Jesuits on the Continent, returned to England to overthrow the heretic usurper, Elizabeth, seeing in the universal church a higher cause than national independence in religion. Jesuits poured also into the most hotly disputed regions where the issue still swayed in the balance—France, Germany, Bohemia, Poland, Hungary. As after every great revolution, many people after an initial burst of Protestantism were inclined to turn back to the old order, especially as the more crying evils within the Catholic church were corrected. The Jesuits reconverted many who thus hesitated.

For the more recalcitrant other machinery was provided. All countries censored books; Protestant authorities labored to keep "papist" works from the eyes of the faithful, and Catholic authorities took the same pains to suppress all knowledge of "heretics." All bishops, Anglican, Lutheran, and Catholic, regulated reading matter within their dioceses. In the Catholic world, with the trend toward centralization under the pope, a special importance attached to the list published by the bishop of Rome, the papal Index of Prohibited Books. Only with special permission, granted to reliable persons for special study, could Catholics read books listed on the Index, on which most of the significant works written in Europe since the Reformation have been included.

All countries, Protestant and Catholic, also set up judicial and police machinery to enforce conformity to the accepted church. In England, for example, Elizabeth established the High Commission to bring "recusants" into the Church of England. All bishops, Protestant and Catholic, likewise possessed machinery of enforcement in their episcopal courts. But no court made itself so dreaded as the Inquisition. In reality two distinct organizations went under this name, the word itself being simply an old term of the Roman law, signifying a court of inquest or inquiry. One was the Spanish Inquisition, established originally, about 1480, to ferret out Jewish and Muslim survivals in Spain. It was then introduced into all countries ruled by the Spanish crown and employed against Protestantism, particularly in the Spanish Netherlands, which was an important center of Calvinism. The other was the Roman or papal Inquisition, established at Rome in 1542 under a permanent committee of cardinals called the Holy Office; it was in a sense a revival of the famous medieval tribunal established in the thirteenth century for the detection and repression of heresy. Both the Spanish and the Roman Inquisition employed torture, for heresy was regarded as the supreme crime, and all persons charged with crime could be tortured, in civil as well as ecclesiastical courts, under the existing laws. In the use of torture, as in the imposition of the harshest sentence, burning alive, the Roman Inquisition was milder than the Spanish. With the growth of papal centralization the Roman Inquisition in principle offered a court to protect purity of faith in all parts of the Catholic world. But the national resistance of Catholic countries proved too strong; few Catholics wished the agents of Rome inquiring locally into their opinions; and the Roman Inquisition never functioned for any length of time outside of Italy. In France no form of the Inquisition was admitted either then or later.

In the "machinery" of enforcing religious belief, however, no engine was to be so powerful as the apparatus of state, of political sovereignty. Where Protestants won control of government, people became Protestant. Where Catholics retained control of governments, Protestants became in time small minorities. And it was in the clash of governments, which is to say in war, for about a century after 1560, that the fate of European religion was worked out. In 1560 the strongest powers of Europe—Spain, France, Austria—were all officially Catholic. The Protestant states were all small or at most middle-sized. The Lutheran states of Germany, like all German states, were individually of little weight. The Scandinavian monarchies were far away. England, the most considerable of Protestant kingdoms, was a country of only four million people, with an independent and hostile Scotland to the north, and with no sign of colonial empire yet in existence. In the precedence of monarchs, as arranged in the earlier part of the century, the king of England ranked just below the king of Portugal, and next above the king of Sicily. Clearly, had a great combined Catholic crusade ever developed, Protestantism could have been wiped out. To launch such a crusade was the dream of the king of Spain. It never succeeded; why, will be seen in the next chapter.

The Florence of the Renaissance

The supreme site of the Italian Renaissance, Florence was both a city lying on either side of the river Arno and an independent republic, with a territory extending, by 1500, for about fifty miles in most directions from Florence itself. The city had grown wealthy in the later Middle Ages from the production of woolens. It developed also an intense civic spirit in its conflicts with other Italian cities. It became a home of merchant princes, of whom the Medici were the most famous. Such families, enriched in earlier generations by the woolen trade, then passing into banking, emerged as an urban patriciate or governing class, the more easily because there was no royalty to overshadow them, and the feudal nobility in the surrounding country was very weak.

Patricians were sometimes opposed by the populace, and sometimes, like the early Medici, they had popular followings of their own. Outbursts of factionalism were therefore very common, compounded by the rivalry with other Italian cities, and by the increasing involvement of the Holy Roman Emperor, the king of France, and the pope. The Medici became dominant in the fifteenth century, were expelled in 1494, restored in 1512, expelled again in 1527, then again restored in 1530, this time permanently, since they remained as hereditary grand dukes of Tuscany until 1737. The following pages suggest something of the wealth, the civic life, and the political crises of Florence until the end of the republic in the 1530s.

More interesting to outsiders than the civil turmoil were Florentine literature and works of art. Writers of a new kind, the humanists, abounded in the city. Reflecting the new interests of the Renaissance, they rejected the church-centered and university-oriented learning of the Middle Ages, and they brought a new spirit to the study of the Latin and Greek classics, in which they found a keen significance for their own times. Of these writers, the best remembered is Machiavelli, who worked to strengthen Florentine republicanism during the period of the Medici exile from 1494 to 1512.

Also born in Florence, either in the city or in the republic, were Michelangelo, Leonardo da Vinci, Masaccio, Donatello, Brunelleschi, Botticelli, and Benvenuto Cellini, to name only the most eminent painters and sculptors, in addition to such lesser lights as the historian Guicciardini and the explorer Amerigo Vespucci, Latinized as Americus Vespucius, after whom America was named. Never since ancient Athens had so much talent appeared in so small a place within the short span of three or four generations. Patronage by the ruling elite was reinforced by a high degree of literacy in the general population; a chronicler reports that as early as 1338 there were 8,000 boys and girls in the schools. Such conditions promoted a degree of taste and understanding in which architecture, painting, sculpture, literature, and intellectual discussion could flourish.

This view of Florence shows the river Arno bisecting it and flowing on into the Tuscan plain. In the right center is the Duomo, or cathedral, dominating the city. The scene, painted by Vasari, shows the situation in 1530, when the city was besieged by the Holy Roman Emperor, Charles V. The defenses were strong, and Michelangelo himself served as one of nine citizens in charge of engineering and fortifications. The Imperial army, shown encamped outside the walls, eventually overcame the resistance and restored the exiled Medici to power.

At the extreme left is the sign of the wool guild of Florence, in which a sheep is appropriately displayed. The near left shows the modest establishment of a fifteenth-century banker, engaged in the actual counting or changing of money.

Above, Lorenzo de' Medici, the "Magnificent," examines a model for a villa built for him about 1480 on the outskirts of the city. The Medici town house, or "palace," appears on the last page of the present essay.

At the left is a part of a huge fresco executed for the chapel of the Medici town house by Benozzo Gozzoli in 1469. It is called the Procession of the Three Kings to Bethlehem, but what it really represents is the important personages of Florence at their most resplendent. The presence of an African servant in Italy at this early date is to be noted. He wears his hair in African style and carries a bow. To the right of him is Cosimo de' Medici on a white horse, followed by a throng whose varied complexions and miscellaneous headgear, including the miter of a Greek patriarch, suggest the cosmopolitanism of the city.

98

The three figures at the left are from a painting by Domenico Ghirlandaio, done about 1490 for a chapel in memory of a woman who had died in childbirth. The theme is "Zacharias in the Temple," but the three heads are actually portraits of contemporary Florentine humanists. The painting thus illustrates, like the one by Gozzoli on the preceding pages, the use of religious themes to convey secular subjects, or of everyday observation to convey religious ideas.

Above, the governing council, or "signoria," deliberates on going to war against the neighboring city of Pisa, during the period of republican revival after expulsion of the Medici in 1494. A Nemesis floats over the councilors' heads.

99

Valse el c° della lana a o contanty 26 ŷ 13 ß 4 ₰ di ₰

Upper left: Detail of the fall of Troy, enacted in Florentine costume in the streets of Florence. The building at the left is the Medici palace (see the next page). At the right, the African warrior wielding a large bow is Memnon, King of the Ethiopians, who according to an ancient legend fought at Troy on the side of the Trojans.

Lower left: Two wool merchants with their goods, from a book of 1492 on arithmetic. Arabic numerals are visible above, but the bags of wool are marked "CLX" or 160 in Roman numerals.

Above: The Piazza della Signoria showing the burning of Savonarola. The dome of the cathedral is half in view at the left. The arcade at the right is the "loggia dei lanzi," built about 1380 as an open but sheltered place for public assemblies. The "palazzo della signoria," or town hall, the large square building, very dark in this picture, dates from 1298 and so reflects the medieval fortress-like style, with small windows, crenelated roof lines, and high towers that characterized this part of Italy before the classicizing features of Renaissance architecture were adopted.

These are town houses, or "palazzi," of Florentine patricians. At the right is the Palazzo Medici, built for Cosimo de' Medici in the 1440s. At the left is the slightly later Palazzo Rucellai. Architects such as Brunelleschi transformed the old fortress-like dwellings of an earlier day into these massive and elegant residences. The new style is evident in the horizontal composition, the long rows of wide, closely spaced, identical windows, the pilasters, and the cornices under the overhanging roof. The interiors were often even more classical, with arches and columns enclosing an open courtyard.

It was in the Medici Palace that Lorenzo the Magnificent received his following of artists and humanists, and that Pope Leo X (born 1475; pope, 1513–1521) and Catherine de' Medici (born 1519; queen of France, 1547–1559; queen mother, 1559–1589) spent their youth.

III.
Economic Renewal and Wars of Religion, 1560-1648

I t is convenient to think of the period of about a century following 1560 as the age of the Wars of Religion, which may be said to have ended with the Peace of Westphalia in 1648. France, England, the Netherlands, and the Holy Roman Empire fell into internal struggles in which religion was the most burning issue, but in which political, constitutional, economic, and social questions were also involved. They, and other powers, also fought in international wars in which the conflict between Catholics and Protestants was a main source of contention but in which other interests were at work too. Often the ideological lines became blurred, as Catholics lent aid to Protestants, or vice versa, somewhat as ideological issues in our own day tend to be confused.

The time of the long, drawn-out Wars of Religion was also a time of economic renewal. From the beginning of the sixteenth century society was transformed by contacts with a newly discovered overseas world, by expanded trade routes, an emergent capitalism, and the formation of new social classes. The effects of these profound changes, however, were obscured and delayed by the politico-religious struggles. In the present chapter we must first examine the geographical discoveries, then survey the broad new economic and social developments under way, and

Chapter Emblem: A mariner's, or simplified, astrolabe that could be taken to sea and used in determination of latitude.

finally trace the impact of the religious wars on various parts of Europe. The wars, as we shall see, left Spain and Germany very much weakened, and opened the way for the English, Dutch, and French to profit from the economic changes and play leading roles in the drama of early modern times.

11. THE OPENING OF THE ATLANTIC

Always until about 1500 the Atlantic Ocean had been a barrier, an end. About 1500 it became a bridge, a starting place. In the Middle Ages, and even in Roman times, small craft had groped from port to port on Europe's Atlantic coast. Vikings settled Iceland in the ninth century, and even touched North America soon thereafter. In 1317 the Venetians established the Flanders galleys, commercial flotillas which regularly made the passage between the Adriatic and the North Sea. In the fifteenth century, with further improvements in shipbuilding, in the rigging and manipulation of sails, and with the adoption of the mariner's compass, it became feasible to sail in the open ocean out of sight of land. It was the Portuguese who first made use of this opportunity. They were perhaps mainly drawn by the simple lure of exploration, but they were certainly tempted, on the material level, by the thought of trading directly with Asia.

For centuries Asia had been a source for Europe of many highly valued commodities, partly manufactures in which Europe could not compete, such as silk and cotton fabrics, rugs, jewelry, porcelains, and fine steel, and partly raw or semimanufactured drugs and foodstuffs, such as sugar and above all spices. The latter—pepper, cinnamon, cloves, ginger, nutmeg, and many less common ones—were of more importance then than now. They were used in pharmacy and in the preservation of meat, as in the making of sausages. They added palatability to fresh meats and other foods, which easily spoiled in the absence of refrigeration. Europeans had never themselves gone to the sources of supply of Eastern goods. Somewhere, east of Suez, barely known to Europeans, was another world of other merchants, who moved the wares of China, India, and the East Indies Spice Islands by caravan over land and by boat through the Red Sea or Persian Gulf to the markets of the eastern Mediterranean. Traders of the two worlds met and did business at such thriving centers as Alexandria or Beirut or Constantinople.

The Portuguese in the East

For some time the Portuguese royal house had sponsored and encouraged exploration of the Atlantic. In 1498 the Portuguese navigator Vasco da Gama, having rounded Africa in the wake of other intrepid explorers, found himself in the midst of the unknown world of Arab commerce. He landed on the Malabar Coast (the southwest coast of India), where he found a busy commercial population of heterogeneous religious background. These people knew at least as much about Europe as Europeans did about India (one Jew was able to act as da Gama's interpreter) and they realized that the coming of the Portuguese would disturb their established channels of commerce. Da Gama, playing upon local rivalries, was able to load his ships with the coveted wares, but on his second voyage, in 1502, he came better prepared, bringing a fighting fleet of no less than twenty-one vessels. A ferocious war broke out between the Portuguese and Arab mer-

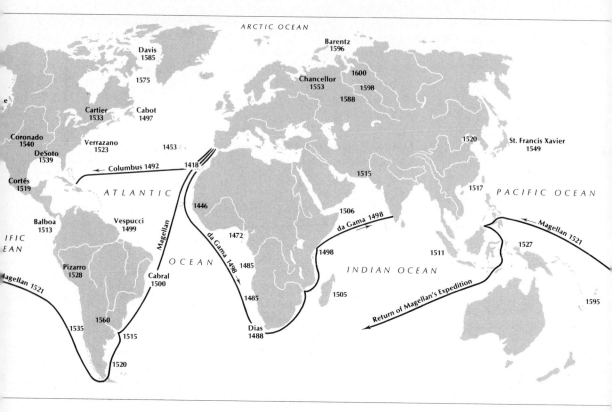

EUROPEAN DISCOVERIES, 1450–1600

Since very remote times the human race has occupied all the continents—except Antarctica —and most of the islands, and between A.D. 1000 and 1450 Norsemen reached Greenland and North America, various Europeans traveled overland to China, and Genoese sailors visited the Azores and the Canary Islands. "Discovery," however, means the bringing of newly found countries within the habitual knowledge of the society from which the discoverer comes. It was the Europeans who thus "discovered" the rest of the world between about 1450 and 1600. They did so by using maritime skills and geographical knowledge developed in the Mediterranean; hence many of the first discoverers—Columbus, Cabot, Vespucci, Verrazano—were Italians, though in the service respectively of Spain, England, Portugal, and France. Two of the greatest, however, da Gama and Magellan, were Portuguese. Dates on the map show the years of first significant European arrival at the points indicated. With a few exceptions, as for Coronado and the Russian penetration of Siberia, these dates mark the explorers' arrival by sea across the open ocean. Still unknown to Europeans in 1600 were most of the interior of both Americas and of Africa, northeastern Asia, and the very existence of Australia and New Zealand. (See also maps on pp. 292–293, and the picture essay, pp. 147–155.)

chants, the latter supported in one way or another by the Egyptians, the Turks, and even the distant Venetians, all of whom had an interest in maintaining the old routes of trade. For the Portuguese, trained like the Spaniards in long wars against the Moors at home, no atrocities were too horrible to commit against the infidel competitors whom they found at the end of their heroic quest. Cities were devastated, ships burned at their docks, prisoners butchered and their dismembered hands, noses, and ears sent back as derisive trophies. One Brahmin, muti-lated in this way, was left alive to bear them to his people. Such, unfortunately, was India's introduction to the West.

In the following years, under the first governor general, Albuquerque, the Por-tuguese built permanent fortified stations at Goa on the Malabar Coast, at Aden near the mouth of the Red Sea, at Ormuz near the mouth of the Persian Gulf, and in East Africa. In 1509 they reached Malacca, near the modern Singapore, from which they passed northward into China itself, and eastward to Amboina, the heart of the Spice Islands, just west of New Guinea. Thus an empire was created, the first of Europe's commercial-colonial empires, maintained by superiority of firearms and sea power and with trade alternating with war and plunder. Albu-querque died in 1515, dreaming grandiose and preposterous dreams—to deflect the course of the Nile and so destroy Egypt and Egyptian commerce, and to capture Mecca and exchange it for the Holy Land. It should be added that bold Jesuits soon arrived, led by St. Francis Xavier, who, by 1550, had baptized thousands of souls in India, Indonesia, and even Japan.

By the new route the cost of Eastern goods for Europeans was much reduced, for the old route had involved many transshipments, unloadings, and reloadings, movements by sea and by land, through the hands of many merchants. In 1504 spices could be bought in Lisbon for only a fifth of the price demanded in Venice. The Venetians (who in their desperation even talked of digging a Suez canal) were hopelessly undersold; their trade thereafter was confined to products of the Near East itself. As for the Portuguese, never was a commercial monopoly built so fast. The lower prices added enormously to European demand and consumption. Beginning in 1504, only five years after da Gama's first return, an average of twelve ships a year left Lisbon for the East.

The Discovery of America

Meanwhile, as every American schoolchild can tell, the same quest for a route to the East had led to the somewhat disappointing discovery of America. Like most such discoveries, this was no chance hit of a queer or isolated genius. Behaim's globe, constructed in 1492,[1] the very year of Columbus' first voyage, could hardly fail to suggest the idea of sailing westward. Nevertheless, it was Christopher Co-lumbus who had the persistence and daring to undertake the unprecedented westward voyage. Before the invention of sufficiently accurate clocks (in the eighteenth century) mariners had no way of determining longitude, i.e., their east-west position, and learned geographers, as may be seen from Behaim's map, greatly underestimated the probable distance from Europe westward to Asia. When Columbus struck land, he naturally supposed it to be an outlying part of the Indies. The people were soon called Indians, and the islands where Columbus landed, the West Indies.

Columbus had sailed with the backing of Queen Isabella of Castile, and the new lands became part of the composite dominions of the crown of Spain. The Spaniards, hoping to beat the Portuguese to the East (which da Gama had not yet reached), received Columbus' first reports with enthusiasm. For his second voy-age they gave him 17 ships, filled with 1,500 workmen and artisans. Columbus

[1] See p. 292.

himself, until his death in 1506, kept probing about in the Caribbean, baffled and frustrated, hoping to find something that looked like the fabulous East. Others were more willing to accept the new land for what it was. Churchmen, powerful in Spain, regarded it as a new field for crusading and conversion. The government saw it as a source of gold and silver for the royal exchequer. Foot-loose gentry of warlike habits, left idle by the end of war with the Moors, turned to it to make their fortunes. The *conquistadores* fell upon the new lands. Cortés conquered the Aztecs in Mexico, Pizarro the Incas in Peru. They despoiled the native empires. Mines for precious metals were opened almost immediately. The Indians were put to forced labor, in which many died. The attempts of the church to protect its Indian converts, and restrictions set by the royal authorities on their exploitation, led almost immediately to the importation of African slaves, of whom, it was estimated, 100,000 had been brought to America by 1560.

Explorers began to feel their way along the vast dim bulk that barred them from Asia. A Spanish expedition, led by Magellan, found a southwestern passage in 1520, sailed from the Atlantic into the Pacific, crossed the Pacific, discovered the Philippine Islands, and fought its way through hostile Portuguese across the Indian Ocean back to Spain. The globe was thus circumnavigated for the first time, and an idea of the true size and interconnection of the oceans was brought back to Europe. Geographical experts immediately incorporated the new knowledge, as in the map drawn by Schöner in 1523.[2] Meanwhile others sailing for Spain, the Cabots sailing for England, Jacques Cartier for France, began the long and fruitless search for a northwest passage. An English expedition, looking for a northeast passage, discovered the White Sea in 1553. English merchants immediately began to take the ocean route to Russia. Archangel became an ocean port.

For a century it was only the Spanish and Portuguese who followed up the new ocean routes to America and the East. These two peoples, in a treaty of 1494, divided the globe between them. The Philippines, because of Magellan's discovery, went to Spain; Brazil, because it had been discovered by Cabral in 1500, to Portugal. Otherwise Spain received all America, and Portugal all rights of trade in Asia and the East Indies.

The Spanish Empire in America

In the populous and civilized East the Portuguese were never more than a handful of outsiders who could not impose their language, their religion, or their way of life. In America, after the first fiendishness of the *conquista*, the Spanish estab-

[2] See p. 292.

THE GEOGRAPHER
by Jan Vermeer (Dutch, 1632–1675)

The impact on Europe of the opening of the Atlantic may be seen in this painting and the following one. For the first time in human history it became possible to conceive, with some accuracy, of the relationships of the oceans and continents throughout the globe. The wonder aroused by the Age of Discovery is evident in this painting by Vermeer. By the seventeenth century the Dutch had built up a large ocean-going trade, and many of the leading instrument makers and cartographers lived in the Netherlands. For Vermeer and Dutch painting see below, p. 160. Courtesy of the Städelsches Kunstinstitut, Frankfurt.

lished their own civilization. In Protestant countries, and also in France, as the years went on there arose an extremely unfavorable idea of the Spanish regime in America, where, it was noted, the Inquisition was presently established and the native peoples were reduced to servitude by the conquerors. The Spanish themselves came to dismiss this grim picture as a Black Legend concocted by their rivals. The true character of the Spanish empire in America is not easy to portray. The Spanish government (like the home governments of all colonial empires until the American Revolution, and even later) regarded its empire as existing for the benefit of the mother country. The Indians were put into servitude, to work in mines or in agriculture. The government introduced the encomienda, a kind of distant analogue to the European manor. The "lord" of the encomienda controlled the labor of his Indians, but according to law he could not deprive Indians of their own parcels of land, and he must make Indians work for him no more than four days a week, leaving them two days to work on their parcels. Such conditions corresponded very closely to those in which the white masses of eastern Europe lived until the nineteenth century. How much the royal regulations were enforced in remote encomiendas is another question, on which answers vary. Negro slavery never assumed the importance in Spanish America that it later assumed in the Dutch, French, and English colonies. The white population remained small. Castilian Spaniards looked down on American-born whites, or creoles. Since few women emigrated from Spain, there arose a large class of mestizos, of mixed white and Indian descent.

The mestizos, along with many pure Indians, adopted to a considerable degree the Spanish language and the faith of the Spanish church. The Indians, while unfree, had usually been unfree under their own tribal chiefs; they were spared from tribal war; and the rigors of the Inquisition were mild compared with the sheer physical cruelty of the Aztecs or Incas. The printing press was brought to Mexico in 1544. By the middle of the sixteenth century Spanish America consisted of two great viceroyalties, those of Mexico and Peru, with twenty-two bishoprics, and with a university in each viceroyalty, the University of Lima established in 1551, that of Mexico in 1553. When Harvard College was founded in New England (in 1636) there were five universities on the European model in Spanish America.

In 1545 a great discovery was made, the prodigiously rich silver deposits at Potosí in Peru. (It is now in Bolivia.) Almost simultaneously, better methods of extracting silver from the ore by the use of mercury were developed. American

STUDY OF TWO BLACK HEADS
by Rembrandt van Rijn (Dutch, 1606–1669)

One consequence of the new intercontinental travel was the mass transportation to the Americas of black Africans as slaves. Some appeared also in Europe, where they attracted a great deal of personal curiosity and produced much speculation on the diversity of human races. Rembrandt, though he never traveled more than twenty miles from his native Leyden, painted all types of persons who streamed into the Netherlands. The greatest of the Dutch painters, and a profound observer of human beings, he was no doubt fascinated by the dark color tones, rugged features, and secret inner feelings of these two men in the strange world into which they had been cast. Courtesy of the Mauritshuis, The Hague (A. Dingjan).

production of precious metals shot up suddenly and portentously. For years, after the mid-century, half a million pounds of silver flowed annually from America to Spain, and ten thousand pounds of gold. The riches of Potosí financed the European projects of the king of Spain. Peruvian ores, Indian labor, and Spanish management combined to make possible the militant and anti-Protestant phase of the Counter Reformation.

The opening of the Atlantic reoriented Europe. In an age of oceanic communications Europe became a center from which America, Africa, and Asia could all be reached. In Europe itself, the Atlantic coast enjoyed great advantages over the center. No sooner did the Portuguese begin to bring spices from the East Indies than Antwerp began to flourish as the point of redistribution for northern Europe. But for a century after the great discoveries the northern peoples did not take to the oceans. French corsairs did indeed put out from Bayonne or Saint-Malo, and Dutch prowlers and English "sea dogs" followed at the close of the century, all bent upon plundering the Iberian treasure ships. Still the Spanish and Portuguese kept their monopoly. No organized effort, backed by governments, came from the north until about 1600. For it is by no means geography alone that determines economic development, and the English, Dutch, and French could not make use of the opportunities with which the opening of the Atlantic provided them until they had cleared up domestic troubles at home and survived the perils and hazards of the Wars of Religion.

12. THE COMMERCIAL REVOLUTION

In the great economic readjustment that was taking place in Europe, the opening of ocean trade routes was important, but it was by no means the only factor. Two others were the growth of population and a long, gradual rise in prices, or a slow inflation.

European population again grew rapidly, as in the High Middle Ages, reaching about 90 million in 1600, of which 20 million represented the growth during the sixteenth century. The increase took place in all countries, though it is well to remember that distribution was quite different from what we have known in more recent times. England in 1600 had no more than five million inhabitants. France had almost four times as many, and the German states altogether about as many as France. Italy and Spain had fewer than France, and distant Russia, within its then boundaries, may have had no more than ten million people. Some cities grew substantially, with London and Paris approaching 200,000; Antwerp, Lisbon, and Seville, thanks to the ocean trade, jumped to 100,000 by 1600. But smaller towns remained much the same; Europe as a whole was probably no more urbanized than in the later Middle Ages. Most of the population growth represented increasing density in the rural regions.[3]

The steady rise in prices, which is to say the steady decline in value of a given unit of money (such as a shilling), constituted a gradual inflation. It has been called a "price revolution," but it was so slow as to be hardly comparable to the kinds of inflation known in the twentieth century. One cause seems to have lain in the growth of population itself, which set up an increasing demand for food. This

---

[3] See Appendix III for estimates of population of certain cities and countries at various dates.

meant that new land was brought under cultivation, land that was less fertile, more inaccessible or more difficult to work than the fields that had been cultivated previously. With increasing costs of production, agricultural prices rose; in England, for example, they about quadrupled during the sixteenth century. Prices were also pushed upward by the increase in the volume of money. The royal habit of debasing the currency brought a larger amount of money into circulation, since larger numbers of florins, *reals*, or *livres* were obtained from the same amount of bullion. The flow of gold and silver from America also made money more plentiful, but the impact of Peruvian and Mexican mines can easily be exaggerated. Even before the discovery of America, the development of gold and silver mines had augmented the European money supply. In any case, an increase of money supply is inflationary only if it runs ahead of the volume of monetary transactions. The expansion of both population and commerce thus checked the inflationary forces. Nevertheless, the long trend of prices was upward. It affected all prices, including rents and other payments that were set in money values, but it seems that the price of hired labor, i.e., wages, rose the least. The price changes thus had different effects on the well-being of social classes.

Commercial undertakings were favored by rising prices and growing population. Merchants could count on increasing numbers of customers, new men could enter trade with hope of success, stocks of goods rose in value with the passage of time, and borrowed money could more easily be repaid. Governments benefited also, so far as kings could count on having more taxpayers and more soldiers.

The economic changes in Europe in the early modern period have been called the "Commercial Revolution," which in general signifies the rise of a capitalistic economy and the transition from a town-centered to a nation-centered economic system. This "revolution" was an exceptionally slow and protracted one, for it began at least as early as the fourteenth century and lasted until machine industry began to overshadow commerce.

Changes in Commerce and Production

In the Middle Ages the town and its adjoining country formed an economic unit.[4] Craftsmen, organized in guilds, produced common articles for local use. Peasants and lords sold their agricultural products to the local town, from which they bought what the craftsmen produced. The town protected itself by its own tariffs and regulations. In the workshop the master both owned his "capital"—his house, workbench, tools, and materials—and acted as a workman himself along with half a dozen journeymen and apprentices. The masters owned a modest capital, but they were hardly capitalists. They produced only upon order, or at least for customers whose tastes and number were known in advance. There was little profit, little risk of loss, and not much innovation.

All this changed with the widening of the trading area, or market. Even in the Middle Ages, as we have seen, there was a certain amount of long-distance trading in articles that could not be produced as well in one place as in another. Gradually more articles came within this category. Where goods were produced to be sold at some time in the future, in faraway places, to persons unknown, the local guildmaster could not manage the operation. He lacked the money (or "capital")

4 See pp. 32–33.

to tie up in stocks of unsold wares; he lacked the knowledge of what distant customers wanted, or where, in what quantities, and at what price people would buy. In this type of business a new type of man developed. Economists call him the "enterpriser," or *entrepreneur*. He usually started out as a merchant working in an extensive market, and ended up as a banker. The Italian Medici family has been mentioned.[5] Equally typical were the German Fuggers.

The first of this family, Johann Fugger, a small-town weaver, came to Augsburg in 1368. He established a business in a new kind of cloth, called fustian, in which cotton was mixed, and which had certain advantages over the woolens and linens in which people then clothed themselves. He thus enjoyed a more than local market, and made trips to Venice to obtain the cotton imported from the Near East. Gradually the family began to deal also in spices, silks, and other Eastern goods obtained at Venice. They made large profits, which were invested in other enterprises, notably mining. They lent money to the Renaissance popes. They lent Charles V the money which he spent to obtain election as Holy Roman Emperor in 1519. They became bankers to the Habsburgs in both Germany and Spain. Together with other German and Flemish bankers, the Fuggers financed the Portuguese trade with Asia, either by outright loans or by providing in advance, on credit, the cargoes which the Portuguese traded for spices. The wealth of the Fuggers became proverbial and declined only through repeated Habsburg bankruptcies and with the general economic decline that beset Germany in the sixteenth century.

Other dealers in cloth, less spectacular than the first Fugger, broke away from the town-and-guild framework in other ways. England until the fifteenth century was an exporter of raw wool and an importer of finished woolens from Flanders. In the fifteenth century certain Englishmen began to develop the spinning, weaving, and dyeing of wool in England. To avoid the restrictive practices of the towns and guilds they "put out" the work to people in the country, providing them with looms and other equipment for the purpose, of which they generally retained the ownership themselves. This "putting out" or "domestic" system spread very widely. In France the cloth dealers of Rouen, feeling the competition of the new silk trade, developed a lighter, cheaper, and more simply made type of woolen cloth. Various guild regulations in Rouen, to protect the workers there, prohibited the manufacture of this cheaper cloth. The Rouen dealers, in 1496, took the industry into the country, installed looms in peasant cottages, and farmed out the work to the peasants.

Capital and Labor

This domestic system, or system of rural household industry, remained typical of production in many lines (cloth, hardware, etc.) in western Europe until the introduction of factories in the late eighteenth century. It signified a new divergence between capital and labor.[6] On the one hand were the workers, people who worked as the employer needed them, received wages for what they did, and had no interest in or knowledge of more than their own task. Living both by agriculture and by cottage industry, they formed an expansible labor force, available when labor was needed, left to live by farming or local charity when times were

---

[5] See pp. 54, 102.
[6] On capitalism, see also pp. 248–249, 259–263.

bad. On the other hand was the man who managed the whole affair. He had no personal acquaintance with the workers. Estimating how much of his product, let us say woolens, he could sell in a national or even international market, he purchased the needed raw materials, passed out wool to be spun by one group of peasants, took the yarn to another group for weaving, collected the cloth and took it still elsewhere to be dyed, paying wages on all sides for services rendered, while retaining ownership of the materials and the equipment and keeping the coordination and management of the whole enterprise in his own head. Much larger business enterprises could be established in this way than within the municipal framework of guild and town. Indeed, the very master weavers of the guilds often sank to the status of subcontractors, hardly different from wage employees, of the great "clothiers" and "drapers" by whom the business was dominated. The latter, with the widening market, became personages of national or even international repute. And, of course, the bigger the business the more of a capital investment it represented.

Certain other industries, new or virtually new in the fifteenth and sixteenth centuries, could by their nature never fit into a town-centered system and were capitalistic from the start, in that they required a large initial outlay before any income could be received. One such was mining. Another was printing and the book trade. Books had a national and even international market, being mainly in Latin; and no ordinary craftsman could afford the outlay required for a printing press, for fonts of type, supplies of paper, and stocks of books on hand. Printers therefore borrowed from capitalists, or shared with them an interest in business. Shipbuilding was so stimulated by the shift to the oceans as almost to be a new industry, and still another was the manufacture of cannons and muskets. For the latter the chief demand came from the state, from the New Monarchies which were organizing national armies. In the rise of capitalism the needs of the military were in fact fundamentally important. Armies, which started out by requiring thousands of weapons, in the seventeenth century required thousands of uniforms, and in the eighteenth century many solidly built barracks and fortifications. These were the first demands for mass production; and where governments themselves did not take the initiative, private organizers stepped in as middlemen between these huge requirements and the myriads of small handicraft workers by whom, before the industrial age, the actual product was still manufactured.

The new sea route to the East and the discovery of America brought a vast increase in trade not only of luxury items but of bulk commodities like rice, sugar, tea, and other consumer goods. Older commercial activities were transformed by the widening of markets. Spain increasingly drew cereals from Sicily. The Netherlands were fed from Poland, the French wine districts lived on food brought from northern France. With the growth of shipping, the timber, tar, pitch, and other "naval stores" of Russia and the Baltic came upon the commercial scene. There was thus an ever growing movement of heavy staple commodities, in which again only men controlling large funds of capital could normally take part.

Not all capital was invested; some was simply lent, either to the church, or to governments, or to impecunious nobles, or, though perhaps this was the least common type of lending in the sixteenth century, to persons engaged in trade and commerce. Bankers and others who lent money expected to receive back, after a time, a larger sum than that of the loan. They expected "interest"; and they sometimes received as much as 30 percent a year. In the Middle Ages the taking of interest had been frowned upon as usury, denounced as avarice, and forbidden in the canon law. It was still frowned upon in the sixteenth century by almost all but the lenders themselves. The Catholic church maintained its prohibitions. The theologians of the University of Paris ruled against it in 1530. Luther, who hated "Fuggerism," continued to preach against usury. Calvin made allowances, but as late as 1640, in capitalist Holland itself, the stricter Calvinist ministers still denounced lending at interest. Nothing could stop the practice. Borrowers compounded with lenders to evade prohibitions, and theologians of all churches began to distinguish between "usury" and a "legitimate return." Gradually, as interest rates fell, as banking became more established, and as loans were made for economically productive uses rather than to sustain ecclesiastics, princes, and nobles in their personal habits, the feeling against a "reasonable" interest died down, and interest became an accepted feature of capitalism. The Bank of Amsterdam, in the seventeenth century, because depositors knew that their money was safe and could be withdrawn at will, was able to attract deposits from all countries by offering a very low rate of interest, which enabled it in turn to make loans, at a low rate, to finance commercial activities.

The net effect of all these developments was a "commercialization of industry." The great man of business was the merchant. Industry, the actual processes of production, still in an essentially handicraft stage, was subordinate to the buyers and sellers. Producers—weavers, hatters, metalworkers, gunsmiths, glassworkers, etc.—worked to fill the orders of the merchants, and often with capital which the merchants supplied and owned. The man who knew where the article could be sold prevailed over the man who simply knew how to produce it. This commercial capitalism remained the typical form of capitalism until after 1800, when, with the introduction of power machinery, it yielded to industrial capitalism, and merchants became dependent on industrialists, who owned, understood, and organized the machines.

Mercantilism

There was still another aspect of the commercial revolution, namely, the various government policies that go historically under the name of "mercantilism." Rulers, as we have seen, were hard pressed for money, and needed more of it as it fell in value. The desire of kings and their advisers to force gold and silver to flow into their own kingdoms was one of the first impulses leading to mercantilist regulation. Gradually this "bullionist" idea was replaced by the more general idea of building up a strong and self-sufficient economy. The means adopted, in either case, was to "set the poor on work," as they said in England, to turn the country into a hive of industry, to discourage idleness, begging, vagabondage, and unemployment. New crafts and manufactures were introduced, and favors were given to merchants who provided work for "the poor" and who sold the country's products abroad. It was thought desirable to raise the export of finished goods and reduce the export of unprocessed raw materials, to curtail all imports except of needed raw materials, and thus obtain a "favorable" balance of trade so that other countries would have to pay their debts in bullion. Since all this was done by a royal or nationwide system of regulations, mercantilism became in the economic sphere what the state building of the New Monarchies was in the political, signifying the transition from town to national units of social living.[7]

Mercantilists frowned upon the localistic and conservative outlook of the guilds. In England the guilds ceased to have any importance. Parliament, in the time of Elizabeth, did on a national scale what guilds had once done locally when it enacted the Statute of Artificers of 1563, regulating the admission to apprenticeship and level of wages in various trades. In France the royal government kept the guilds in being, because they were convenient bodies to tax, but it deprived them of most of their old independence and used them as organizations through which royal control of industry could be enforced. In both countries the government assisted merchants who wished to set up domestic or cottage industry in the country, against the protests of the town guilds, which in their heyday had forbidden rural people to engage in crafts. Governments generally tried to suppress idleness. The famous English Poor Law of 1601 (which remained in effect, with amendments, until 1834) was designed both to force people to work and to relieve absolute destitution.

Governments likewise took steps to introduce new industries. The silk industry was brought from Italy to France under royal protection, to the dismay of French woolen and linen interests. The English government assisted in turning England from a producer of raw wool into a producer of finished woolens, supervising the immigration of skilled Flemish weavers, and even fetching from faraway Turkey, about 1582, two youths who understood the more advanced dyeing arts of the Near East. Generally, under mercantilism, governments fought to steal skilled workers from each other while prohibiting or discouraging the emigration of their own skilled workers, who might take their trade secrets and "mysteries" to foreign parts.

By such means governments helped to create a national market and an industrious nationwide labor supply for their great merchants. Without such government support the great merchants, such as the drapers or clothiers, could never have risen and prospered. The same help was given to merchants operating in foreign markets. Henry VII of England in 1496 negotiated a commercial treaty with Flanders, known as the Intercursus Magnus; and in the next century the kings of France signed a number of treaties with the Ottoman Empire by which French merchants obtained privileges in the Near East. A merchant backed by a national monarchy was in a much stronger position than one backed merely by a city, such as Augsburg or Venice. This backing on a national scale was again given when national governments subsidized exports, paying bounties for goods whose production they wished to encourage, or when they erected tariff barriers against imports to protect their own producers from competition. Thus a national tariff system was superimposed on the old network of provincial and municipal tariffs. These latter were now thought of as "internal tariffs," and mercantilists usually wished to abolish them, in order to create an area of free trade within the state as a whole. But local interests were so strong, and a sense of interprovincial and intertown unity was so slow to develop, that for centuries they were unable to get rid of local tariffs except in England.

In wild or distant parts of the world, or in exotic regions nearer home, such as

[7] On the New Monarchies, see pp. 66–74.

the Muslim Near East or Russia, it was not possible for individual merchants to act by merely private initiative. Merchants trading with such countries needed a good deal of capital, they often had to obtain special privileges and protection from native rulers, and they had to arm their ships against Barbary or Malay pirates or against hostile Europeans. Merchants and their respective governments came together to found official companies for the transocean trade. In England, soon after the English discovery of the White Sea in 1553, a Russia Company was established. A Turkey Company soon followed. Shortly after 1600 a great many such companies were operating out of England, Holland, and France. The most famous of all were the East India Companies, which the English founded in 1600, the Dutch in 1602, the French not until 1664. Each of these companies was a state-supported organization, with special rights. Each was a monopoly in that only merchants who belonged to the company could legally engage in trade in the region for which the company had a charter. Each was expected to find markets for the national manufactures, and most of them were expected to bring home gold or silver. With these companies the northern peoples began to encroach on the Spanish and Portuguese monopoly in America and the East. With them new commercial-colonial empires were to be launched. But, as has been already observed, before this could happen it was necessary for certain domestic and purely European conflicts and controversies to be settled.

13. CHANGING SOCIAL STRUCTURES

Social structure, for present purposes, refers to the composition, functions, and interrelationships of social classes. Because changes in social structure are slow, they are hard to identify with any particular period of time. In general, however, with the effects of the commercial revolution, population growth, and the falling value of money, the classes of Europe, broadly defined, took on forms that were to last until the industrial era of the nineteenth and twentieth centuries. These classes were the landed aristocracy, the peasantry or mass of agricultural workers, the miscellaneous middle classes, and the urban poor.

While all prices rose in the sixteenth century, it was agricultural prices that rose the most. Anyone who had agricultural products to sell was likely to benefit. Among such beneficiaries were peasants who held bits of land in return for payments to a manorial lord set in unchangeable sums of money, in the old values of the fourteenth or even thirteenth century. Such peasants in effect paid much less to the lord than in the past. Other rural workers, however, either held no land of their own or produced only at a subsistence level with nothing to sell in the market. Such peasants, and hired hands dependent on wages, found their situation worsened. Village life became less equalitarian than it had been in the Middle Ages. In England a class of small freeholders (the "yeomanry") developed between the landed gentry and the rural poor. On the Continent, at least in France, western Germany, and the Netherlands, some peasants acquired more secure property rights, resembling those of small freeholders in England. But both in England and on the Continent a large class of unpropertied rural workers remained in poverty.

Land rents went up as agricultural prices rose, and inflation and population growth drove up rentals for housing in the towns. Owners of real property (i.e., land and buildings) were favored by such changes, but within the former class of feudal lords the effects were mixed. If one's great-grandfather had let out land in earlier times in exchange for fixed sums of money, the income received had actually declined. But those who received payments in kind from their tenants, for example, in bushels of wheat or barley, or who managed their estates themselves, could sell their actual agricultural products at current prices and so increase their money income.

Basic Social Classes

The former feudal class, or nobles, thus turned into a more modern kind of aristocracy. If income from their estates declined, they sought service in the king's army or government or appointment to the more prestigious offices in the church. If landed income increased, they were more wealthy. In either case they became more concerned with civilian pursuits, and were likely to develop more refined tastes and pay more attention to the education of their children. Like the peasants, the landowning class became more heterogeneous, ranging from the small gentry to the great peers of England, and from small or impoverished nobles to the *grands seigneurs* of France. Some led a life of leisure; others were eager to work in the higher reaches of organized government. The most impoverished nobles sometimes had the longest pedigrees. As their social functions changed, and as persons of more recent family background competed for education, government employment, and even military service, there came to be an increasing importance set upon ancestry as a badge of status. Among the upper class, there was more insistence on high birth and distinguished forebears in the seventeenth and eighteenth centuries than there had been before.

Below the aristocracy were the "middle classes," or "bourgeoisie." *Bourgeois* was a French word, which, like the English "burgher," originally meant a person living in a chartered town or borough and enjoying its liberties. The bourgeoisie was the whole social class made up of individual bourgeois. In a much later sense of the word, derived from Karl Marx, the term "bourgeoisie" was applied to the class of owners of capital. This sense must be kept distinct from the earlier meaning, which is usually adopted in this book. In this latter sense, the word refers to the middle levels of society between the aristocracy on the one hand, which drew its income from land, and the laboring poor on the other, who depended on wages or charity, or who often went hungry. Class lines tended to blur as aristocratic families formed the habit of living in towns, and middle-class burghers began to buy land in the country. Some bourgeois thus came to live on landed rents, while some of the gentry and aristocracy, most notably in England, bought shares in the great overseas trading companies or engaged in other forms of business enterprise. Aristocrats possessing large agricultural estates, timberlands, or mines increasingly brought their products to market to be sold at a profit. But even when aristocrat and bourgeois became economically more alike, a consciousness of social difference between them remained.

The middle class became more numerous in the sixteenth century, and increasingly so thereafter. It was an indefinite category, since the countries of Europe were very different in the size and importance of their middle classes, in the kinds of persons that made them up, and in the types of occupations pursued. Near the top were the urban elites who governed the towns; they might draw their incomes from rural property, from commerce, or from the emoluments of government itself, and they sometimes intermarried with persons of noble status. Especially where the towns were strong or broad royal government was lacking, as in the Netherlands, the German free cities, or north Italy, such urban patriciates formed virtual aristocracies in themselves. But in a larger perspective the families of merchants, bankers, and shipowners were middle-class, as were those of the traditional learned professions, law and medicine. So in general were judges, tax officials, and other employees of governments, except in the highest ranks. In the professions and in government service the younger sons of the aristocracy might be found alongside the offspring of the middle classes, most commonly in England, less so in France, and even less as one moved into Germany or Spain. The clergy was drawn from all classes; there were poor parish priests, who might be the sons of peasants, and noblemen among the bishops and abbots; but the bulk of the clergy was recruited from middle-class families. In Protestant countries, where the clergy married, their sons and daughters became an important element in the middle class. Members of trade guilds were middle-class, though the guilds differed widely in social status, from those of the great wholesale merchants or the goldsmiths, down through the guilds of such humble occupations as the tanners and barrel makers. At the bottom the middle class faded into the world of small retail shopkeepers, innkeepers, owners of workshops in which ordinary articles were manufactured by hand, the lesser skilled tradespeople and their employees, journeymen, and apprentices.

The mass of the population in all countries was composed of the working poor. These included not only the unskilled wage laborers but the unemployed, unemployable, and paupers, with a large fringe that turned to vagabondage and begging. They were unable to read or write, and were often given to irregular habits which distressed both middle-class persons and government officials. The efforts of mercantilist governments to put the poor to work, or make them contribute to the wealth of the country, have already been mentioned. Charitable relief also developed toward the end of the sixteenth century, as shown in the English Poor Law of 1601 and in similar efforts on the Continent. The idea gained ground that begging was a public nuisance, and that the poor should be segregated in workhouses or hospices from the rest of society. Most of the poor were of course not recipients of such relief. They were the people who tilled the fields, tended the livestock, dug in the mines, went to sea as fishermen or common sailors, found work in the towns as casual laborers, porters, water carriers, or removers of excrement, or entered the domestic service of noble and upper middle-class families, whose rising standard of living required a growing number of chambermaids, washerwomen, footmen, lackeys, coachmen, and stable boys. It has already been remarked that wages rose less than prices in the sixteenth century. The poor, if not positively worse off than in former times, gained the least from the great developments with which much history is concerned. The very growth of social differentiation, the fact that the middle and upper classes made such advances, left the condition of the poor correspondingly worse.[8]

Social Roles of Education and Government

Education in the latter part of the sixteenth century took on an altogether new importance for the social system. One consequence of the Reformation, in both

---

[8] See pp. 242–247.

Protestant and Catholic countries, was the attempt to put a serious and effective pastor in each parish. This set up a demand for a more educated clergy. The growth of commerce made it necessary to have literate clerks and agents. Governments wanted men from both the noble and middle classes who could cooperate in large organizations, be reliable, understand finance, keep records, and draft proposals. There was also a widespread need for lawyers.

The new demand for education was met by an outburst of philanthropy, which reached a high point in both England and France between about 1580 and 1640. Many endowed scholarships were established. At what would now be called a secondary level, hundreds of "grammar schools" were founded at this time in England. In France the *collèges* combined the work of the English grammar school with what corresponded to the first year or two of university work at Oxford or Cambridge. Of the 167 most important French colleges still existing at the time of the Revolution in 1789, only 36 had been founded in the centuries before 1560, and 92 were established in the years between 1560 and 1650. Provision for girls' schools was more sporadic, but the Ursuline sisters, for example, founded in Italy in 1535, by the year 1700 had about 350 convents in Catholic Europe and even in Canada, in most of which the education of girls was a principal occupation of the sisters. Mme. de Maintenon, the morganatic wife of Louis XIV, founded and closely supervised a school for the daughters of the French gentry and lesser nobility.

Dutch and Swiss Protestants founded the universities of Leyden and Geneva. New universities, both Protestant and Catholic, appeared in Germany. In Spain the multiplication of universities was phenomenal. Castile, with only two universities dating from the Middle Ages, had twenty by the early seventeenth century; Salamanca was enrolling over 5,000 students a year. Five universities also existed in Spanish America by 1600. In England, new colleges were founded at Oxford and Cambridge, and it was especially in these years that some of the Oxford and Cambridge colleges became very wealthy. Annual freshman admissions at Oxford, barely 100 in 1550, rose to over 500 in the 1630s, a figure not exceeded, or even equaled, during the following two hundred years. If this fivefold increase seems small, compared with figures for Spain or other countries, it must be remembered that England was not very populous, that English grammar schools did some of the teaching offered by universities elsewhere, and that the study of law, important in Continental universities, was carried on in England outside the universities, at the Inns of Court.

The schools, colleges, and universities drew their students from a wide range of social classes. For girls less organized schooling was offered, but an intelligent and lucky boy of poor family had perhaps a better chance for education than at any time in Europe until very recently. In Spain most of the students seem to have been nobles, or "hidalgos," aspiring to positions in the church or the royal government; but hidalgos were very numerous in Spain, overlapping with what might be called the middle class in other countries. The French colleges, including those operated by the Jesuits, recruited their students very widely, taking in the sons of nobles, merchants, shopkeepers, artisans, and even, more rarely, of peasants. English grammar schools did likewise; it was in later times that a few of them, like Eton and Harrow, became more exclusive Public Schools. As for universities, we have detailed knowledge for Oxford, which recorded the status of its students at matriculation, classifying them as "esquires," "gentlemen," "clergy," and "plebeians." From 1560 to 1660 about half of the Oxford students were "plebeians," which in the language of that time could embrace the whole middle class from big merchants down to quite modest levels. It seems certain that Oxford and Cambridge were more widely representative of the English people in 1660 than in 1900.

Social classes were formed not only by economic forces, and not only by education, but also by the action of governments. Government could inhibit economic growth, as in Spain, or promote it, as in England. Kings contributed to the rise of capitalism and a business class by granting monopolies, borrowing from bankers, and issuing charters to trading companies. In many countries, and notably in France, many families owed their middle-class position to the holding of government offices, some of which might become a form of inheritable property. It might also be the action of governments, as much as economic conditions, that kept alive a distinction between nobles and commoners, or "privileged" and "unprivileged" classes, of which more will be heard.[9] Where peasants suffered heavily from royal taxes, it was more from political than from economic causes. The king, by "making" nobles—that is, by conferring titles of nobility on persons who did not inherit them—could raise a few in the middle class to higher status. Tax exemption could be a sign of high social standing. The king was also the fountain of honor, at the top of "society" in the more frivolous sense of the word. The royal court formed the apex of a pyramid of social rank, in which each class looked up to or down upon the others. Those favored with the royal presence disdained the plain country nobility, who sniffed at the middle classes, who patronized or disparaged the hired servants, day laborers, and the poor. Looking upward, people were expected to show deference for their betters.

Eastern and Western Europe

One other remark may be made on social structure. It was in the sixteenth century that a great difference developed between eastern and western Europe. In the west, the commercial revolution and the declining value of money were advantageous to the middle class and to many of the peasantry for whom the old burdens of the manorial system were lightened. In eastern Europe, it was the lords who benefited from rising prices and the growing market for grain and forest products. Here too the institution of the manor existed; but the peasants' land tenures were more precarious than in the west, more dependent on accidents of death or on the wishes of the lord, and the lord worked a larger part of the manor with his own work force for his own use or profit.

The rise of prices and expansion of Baltic shipping gave the lord the incentive to increase his output. In northeast Germany (where such lords were called Junkers), in Poland, and as time went on in Russia, Bohemia, and Hungary, beginning in the sixteenth century and continuing into the eighteenth, a vast process set in by which the mass of the peasantry sank into serfdom. It was hastened in many regions by the violence and insecurity engendered by the religious wars. Typically, peasants lost their individual parcels of land, or received them back on condition that they render unpaid labor services to the lord. Usually peasants owed three or four days a week of such forced labor (called *robot* in Bohemia and adjoining territories), remaining free to work during the remainder of the week on their own parcels. Often the number of days of *robot* exacted by the lord was

[9] See pp. 182, 352, 357.

greater, since in eastern Europe, where central monarchy was weak and central-ized legal systems almost unknown, the lord himself was the final court of appeal for his people. His people were in fact his "subjects." Serfdom in Germany was not called serfdom, an ill-sounding word, but "hereditary subjection." By what-ever name they were known throughout eastern Europe, serfs, or hereditary sub-jects of the manorial lord, could not leave the manor, marry, or learn a trade without the lord's express permission. The lord, drawing on this large reserve of compulsory labor, using most of it for agriculture but teaching some quick-minded youths the various handicrafts that were needed on the estate, worked the land as his own venture, sold the produce, and retained the profit.

Thus, in eastern Europe at the beginning of modern times, the rural masses lost personal freedom and lived in a poverty unknown among the peasants to the west, poor as the latter were. In western Europe there were peasants who were already on the way to becoming small proprietors. They were free people under the law. They could migrate, marry, and learn trades as opportunity offered. Those who held land could defend it in the royal courts, and raise crops and take part in the market economy on their own account. They owed the lord no forced labor—or virtually none, for the ten days a year of corvée still found in parts of France hardly compared with the almost full-time *robot* of the peasant of eastern Europe.

The landlord in the east, from the sixteenth century onward, was solidly en-trenched in his own domain, monarch of all he surveyed, with no troublesome bourgeoisie to annoy him (for towns were few), and with kings and territorial rulers solicitous of his wishes. Travelers from the west were impressed with the lavishness of great Polish and Lithuanian magnates, with their palatial homes, private art galleries, well-stocked libraries, collections of jewels, swarms of serv-ants, trains of dependent lesser gentry, gargantuan dinners, and barbaric hospi-tality. The Junkers of northeast Germany lived more modestly, but enjoyed the same kind of independence and social superiority. The importance of all this will become evident when, in later chapters, we turn to Prussia, Poland, Russia, and the Austrian lands.

But meanwhile, with all the economic growth and social development that has been sketched in the preceding pages, Europe was torn by the destructive ferocity of the Wars of Religion.

14. THE CRUSADE OF CATHOLIC SPAIN: THE DUTCH AND ENGLISH

The Ambitions of Philip II

Charles V, having tried in vain for thirty-five years to preserve religious unity in Germany, abdicated his many crowns and retired to a monastery in 1556, the year after the Peace of Augsburg.[10] He left Austria, Bohemia, and Hungary (or the small part of it not occupied by the Turks) to his brother Ferdinand, who was soon elected Holy Roman Emperor.[11] All his other possessions Charles left to his son Philip, who became Philip II of Spain. The Habsburg dynasty remained

[10] See p. 79.
[11] See map, pp. 70–71.

thereafter divided into two branches, the Austrian and the Spanish. The two cooperated in European affairs. The Spanish branch for a century was the more important. Philip II (1556–1598) not only possessed the Spanish kingdoms but in 1580 inherited Portugal, so that the whole Iberian peninsula was brought under his rule. He possessed the seventeen provinces of the Netherlands and the Free County of Burgundy, which were member states of the Holy Roman Empire, lying on its western border, adjacent to France. Milan in north Italy and Naples in the south belonged to Philip, and since he also held the chief islands, as well as Tunis, he enjoyed a naval ascendancy in the western Mediterranean which was threatened only by the Turks. For five years, until 1558, he was titular king of England, and in 1589, in the name of his daughter, he laid claim to the throne of France. All America belonged to Philip II, and after 1580 all the Portuguese empire as well, so that except for a few nautical daredevils all ships plying the open ocean were the Spanish king's.

Philip II therefore naturally regarded himself as an international figure, and the more so because he thought in terms not of nationality but of religion. Before all else he was a Catholic, fervid and fanatical, committed to upholding the sway of the universal church, within which all nations were no more than minorities and all heretics no more than rebels. A grave and sober man, of abstemious personal habits, sharing in the moral severity of the Catholic Reform, and in the dark, brooding, and tormented inner world of the Spanish mystics, he took upon himself the headship of a far-flung Catholic counteroffensive, into which he was willing to pour with grim persistence the blood and treasure of all his kingdoms. To economic and material interests he gave no thought, and in such matters Spanish society began to deteriorate in his reign; but for all material problems the wealth of Potosí provided a facile solution, and meanwhile Spain entered upon the Golden Age of its culture.

In this period, the *siglo de oro*, running in round dates from 1550 to 1650, Cervantes wrote his *Don Quixote* and Lope de Vega his seven hundred dramas, while El Greco, Murillo, and Velázquez painted their pictures, and the Jesuit Suarez composed works on philosophy and law that were read even in Protestant countries. But the essence of Spanish life was its peculiarly intensive Catholicism. The church was vitally present at every social level, from the archbishop of Toledo, who ranked above grandees and could address the king as an equal, down to a host of penniless and mendicant friars, who mixed with the poorest and most disinherited of the people. It is said that about 1600 a third of the population of Spain was in one way or another in the service of the church. Spain, whose whole history had been a crusade, was ideally suited to be Philip's instrument in the re-Catholicizing of Europe.[12]

Philip II built himself a new royal residence ("palace" is hardly the word), the Escorial, which well expressed in solid stone its creator's inner spirit. Madrid itself was a new town, merely a government center, far from the worldly distractions of Toledo or Valladolid. But it was thirty miles from Madrid, on the bleak arid plateau of central Castile, overlooked by the jagged Sierra, that Philip chose to erect the Escorial. He built it in honor of St. Lawrence, on whose feast day he had won a battle against the French. The great pile of connecting buildings was laid out in the shape of a grill, since, according to martyrologists, St. Lawrence,

[12] See pp. 69–72.

in the year 258, had been roasted alive on a grill over burning coals. Somber and vast, angular and unrelieved, made of blocks of granite meant to last forever, and with its highest spire rising three hundred feet from the ground, the Escorial was designed not only as a palace but as a monastery and a mausoleum. The monks moved in before the king, who, when he installed himself, brought with him eight coffins, those of his father, his dead wives, and his children, to remind him of his own. Here, in an atmosphere that could be painted only by El Greco, the king of Spain worked and lived, a slim figure dressed almost like a monk himself, always industrious, avid for detail, dispatching his couriers to Mexico, to Manila, to Vienna, to Milan, his troops and his bars of bullion to Italy and the Netherlands, his diplomats to all courts, and his spies to all countries, wholly and utterly absorbed in his one consuming project.

Let us try to see the events of the time internationally, for though it may be confusing to try to see all nations together, it is distorting to look at only one of them alone. The first years of Philip's reign were also the first years of Elizabeth's reign in England, where the religious issue was still in flux; they were years in which Calvinism agitated the Netherlands, and when France, ruled by teen-aged boys, fell apart into implacable civil war. Religious loyalties that knew no frontiers overlapped all political boundaries. Everywhere there were people who looked for guidance outside their own countries. Calvinists in England, France, and the Netherlands felt closer to one another than to their own monarchs or their own neighbors. Zealous Catholics, in all three countries, welcomed the support of international Catholic forces—the Jesuits, the king of Spain, the pope. National unity threatened to dissolve or was not yet formed. The sense of mutual trust between people who lived side by side was eaten away; and people who lived not only in the same country, but in the same town, on the same street, or even in the same house, turned against each other in the name of a higher cause.

For about five years, beginning in 1567, it seemed that the Catholic cause might prevail. The great crusade took the offensive on all fronts. In 1567 Philip sent a new and firmer governor general to the Netherlands, the Duke of Alva, with 20,000 Spanish soldiers; the duke proceeded to suppress religious and political dissidents by establishing a Council of Troubles. In 1569 Philip put down a revolt of the Moriscos in Spain. In the same year the Catholics of northern England, led by the Duke of Norfolk, and sewing the cross of crusaders on their garments, rose in armed rebellion against their heretic queen. In the next year, 1570, the pope excommunicated Elizabeth, and absolved her subjects from allegiance to her, so that English Catholics, if they wished, could henceforth in good conscience conspire to overthrow her. In 1571 the Spanish won a great naval battle against the Turks, at Lepanto off the coast of Greece; on their sails they wove the same cross that had been raised at the other corner of Europe, by the Duke of Norfolk in England; and they themselves believed that they were carrying on the crusades of the Middle Ages. In the next year, 1572, the Catholic leaders of France, with the advice of the pope and of Philip II, decided to make an end of the Huguenots, or French Protestants. Over three thousand were seized and put to death on the eve of St. Bartholomew's Day in Paris alone; and this massacre was followed by lesser liquidations throughout the provinces.

But none of these victories proved enduring. The Turkish power was not seriously damaged at Lepanto. In fact, the Turks took Tunis from Philip two years later. The Moriscos were not assimilated. The English Catholic rebellion was stamped out; eight hundred persons were put to death by Elizabeth's government. The revolt in the Netherlands remained very much alive, as did the French Huguenots. Twenty years later England was Protestant, the Dutch were winning independence, a Huguenot had become king of France, and the Spanish fleet had gone to ruin in northern waters. Let us see how these events came to pass.

The Revolt of the Netherlands

The Netherlands, or Low Countries (they had no other name), roughly comprised the area of the modern kingdoms of the Netherlands and Belgium and the grand duchy of Luxembourg. They consisted of seventeen provinces, which in the fifteenth century, one by one, had been inherited, purchased, or conquered by the dukes of Burgundy, from whom they were inherited by Charles V and his son, Philip II. In the mid-sixteenth century neither a Dutch nor a Belgian nationality yet existed. In the northern provinces the people spoke German dialects; in the southern provinces they spoke dialects of French; but neither here, nor elsewhere in Europe, was it felt that language boundaries had anything to do with political borders. The southern provinces had for centuries been busy commercial centers, and we have seen how Antwerp, having once flourished on trade with Venice, now flourished on trade with Lisbon. The northern provinces, or rather the two of them which were most open to the sea, the counties of Holland and Zeeland, had developed rapidly in the fifteenth century. They had a popular literature of their own, written in their own kind of German, which came to be called Dutch. The lay piety of the Brothers of the Common Life had originated in this region, and here Erasmus of Rotterdam had been born. The wealth of the northern provinces was drawn from deep-sea fishing. Amsterdam was said to be built on herring bones, and the Dutch, when they added trading to fishing, still lived by the sea.

The northern provinces felt no tie with each other and no sense of difference from the southern. Each of the seventeen provinces was a small state or country in itself. Each province enjoyed typical medieval liberties, privileges, and immunities, including the right to preserve its own law and consent to its own taxes. This constitution of the Netherlands, for such it was, went under the name of the *Joyeuse Entrée*, from the "joyous entry" made by the reigning duke into Brussels in 1355 after a solemn promise to recognize the liberties of the province of Brabant. The common bond of all seventeen provinces was simply that beginning with the dukes of Burgundy they had the same ruler; but since they had the same ruler they were called upon from time to time to send delegates to an estates general, and so developed an embryonic sense of federal collaboration. The feeling of Netherlandish identity was heightened with the accession of Philip II, for Philip, unlike his father, was thought of as foreign, a Spaniard who lived in Spain; and after 1560 Spanish governors general, Spanish officials, and Spanish troops were seen more frequently in the Netherlands. Moreover, since the Netherlands was the crossroads of Europe, with a tradition of earnestness in religion, Protestant ideas took root very early, and after 1560, when the religious wars began in France, a great many French Calvinists fled across the borders. At first, there were probably more Calvinists in the southern provinces than in the northern, more among the people that we now call Belgians than among those that we now call Dutch.

The revolt against Philip II was inextricably political and religious at the same time, and it became increasingly an economic struggle as the years went by. It began in 1566, when some 200 nobles of the various provinces founded a league to check the "foreign" or Spanish influence in the Netherlands. The league, to which both Catholic and Protestant nobles belonged, petitioned Philip II not to employ the Spanish Inquisition in the Netherlands. They feared the trouble it would stir up; they feared it as a foreign court; they feared that in the enforcement of its rulings the liberties of their provinces would be crushed. Philip's agents in the Netherlands refused the petition. A mass revolt now broke out. Within a week fanatical Calvinists pillaged 400 churches, pulling down images, breaking stained-glass windows, defacing paintings and tapestries, making off with gold chalices, destroying with a fierce contempt the symbols of "popery" and "idolatry." The fury spread from town to town, to Antwerp, to Amsterdam, to Armentières (now in France, but then in the Netherlands); it was chiefly journeymen wage earners, numerous in the industrial Netherlands, and aroused by social and economic grievances as well as religious belief, who formed the rank and file for these anti-Catholic and anti-Spanish demonstrations. Before such vandalism many of the petitioning nobles recoiled; the Catholics among them, as well as less militant Protestants, unable to control their revolutionary followers, began to look upon the Spanish authorities with less disfavor.

Philip II, appalled at the sacrilege, forthwith sent in the Inquisition, the Duke of Alva, and reinforcements of Spanish troops. Alva's Council of Troubles, nicknamed the Council of Blood, sentenced some thousands to death, levied new taxes, and confiscated the estates of a number of important nobles. These measures united people of all classes in opposition. What might have been primarily a class conflict took on the character of a national opposition. At its head emerged one of the noblemen whose estates had been confiscated, William of Orange (called

THE LOW COUNTRIES, 1648

This group of towns and provinces, along the lower reaches of the Rhine, Meuse, and Scheldt rivers, originated in the Middle Ages as part of the Holy Roman Empire. The northern or Dutch provinces were recognized as independent of the Empire in 1648. Early in the seventeenth century a political frontier emerged between the "Dutch" and "Belgian" parts, but the word "Belgium" was not used until much later, the southern or Habsburg provinces being called the Spanish Netherlands in the seventeenth century and the Austrian Netherlands in the eighteenth. The large bishopric of Liège remained a separate church-state until the French Revolution. The language frontier, then as now, ran roughly east and west somewhat south of Brussels, with French to the south and Flemish (a form of Dutch, and hence Germanic) to the north of the line.

William the Silent), Philip II's "stadholder" or lieutenant in the County of Holland. Beginning to claim the authority of a sovereign, he issued letters of marque, or authorizations to ship captains—Dutch, Danes, Scots, English—to make war at sea. Fishing crews, "sea dogs," and downright pirates began to raid the small port towns of the Netherlands and France, descending upon them without warning, desecrating the churches, looting, torturing, and killing, in a wild combination of religious rage, political hatred, and lust for booty. The Spanish reciprocated by renewing their confiscations, their inquisitorial tortures, and their burnings and hangings. The Netherlands was torn by anarchy, revolution, and civil war. No lines were clear, either political or religious. But in 1576 the anti-Spanish feeling prevailed over religious difference. Representatives of all seventeen provinces, putting aside the religious question, formed a union to drive out the Spanish at any cost.

The Involvement of England

But the Netherlands revolution, though it was a national revolution with political independence as its first aim, was only part of the international politico-religious struggle. All sorts of other interests became involved in it. Queen Elizabeth of England lent aid to the Netherlands, though for many years surreptitiously, not wishing to provoke a war with Spain, in which it was feared that English Catholics might side with the Spaniards. Elizabeth was troubled by having on her hands an unwanted guest, Mary Queen of Scots, a Catholic who had been queen of France until her husband's premature death, and queen of Scotland until driven out by irate Calvinist lords, and who—if the pope, the king of Spain, the Society of Jesus, and many English Catholics were to have their way—would also be queen of England instead of the usurper Elizabeth.[13] Elizabeth under these circumstances kept Mary Stuart imprisoned. Many intrigues were afoot to put Mary on the English throne, some with, and some without, Mary's knowledge.

In 1576 Don Juan, hero of Lepanto, and half-brother of Philip II, became governor general of the embattled Netherlands. It was his grandiose idea, formed after consultations in Rome, not merely to subdue the Netherlands but to use that country as a base for an invasion of England, and after overthrowing Elizabeth with Spanish troops, to put Mary Stuart on the throne, marry her himself, and so become king of a re-Catholicized England. Thus the security of Elizabethan and Protestant England was coming to depend on the outcome of fighting in the Netherlands. Elizabeth signed an alliance with the Netherlands patriots.

Don Juan died in 1578 and was succeeded as governor general of the Netherlands by the prince of Parma. A diplomat as well as a soldier, Parma broke the solid front of the seventeen provinces by a mixture of force and persuasion. He promised that the historic liberties of the *Joyeuse Entrée* would be respected, and he appealed not only to the more zealous Catholics but to moderates who were wearying of the struggle and repelled by mob violence and religious vandalism. On this basis he rallied the southernmost provinces to his side. The seven northern provinces, led by Holland and Zeeland, responded by forming the Union of Utrecht in 1579. In 1581 they formally declared their independence from the king of Spain, calling themselves the United Provinces of the Netherlands. Thus originated what was more commonly called the Dutch Republic, or simply "Holland"

---

[13] Mary Stuart, a great-granddaughter of Henry VII, was the next lawful heir to the English throne after Elizabeth, since Elizabeth had no children.

in view of the predominance of that county among the seven. The great Flemish towns—Antwerp, Ghent, and Bruges—at first sided with the Union.

Where formerly all had been turmoil, a geographical line was now drawn. The south rallying to Philip II now faced a still rebellious north. But neither side accepted any such partition. Parma still fought to reconquer the north, and the Dutch, led by William the Silent, still struggled to clear the Spanish out of all seventeen provinces. Meanwhile the two sides fought to capture the intermediate Flemish cities. When Parma moved upon Antwerp, still the leading port of the North Sea, and one from which an invasion of England could best be mounted, Elizabeth at last openly entered the war on the side of the rebels, sending 6,000 English troops to the Netherlands under the Earl of Leicester in 1585.

England was now clearly emerging as the chief bulwark of Protestantism and of anti-Spanish feeling in northwestern Europe. In England itself, the popular fears of Spain, the popular resentment against Catholic plots revolving about Mary Stuart, and the popular indignation at "foreign" and "outside" meddling in English matters produced an unprecedented sense of national solidarity. The country rallied to Protestantism and to Elizabeth, and even the Catholic minority for the most part disowned the conspiracies against her. The English were now openly and defiantly allied with the Protestant Dutch. Not only were they fighting together in the Netherlands, but both English and Dutch sea raiders fell upon Spanish shipping, captured the treasure ships, and even pillaged the Spanish Main, the mainland coast of northern South America. The Dutch were beginning to penetrate East Indian waters. Elizabeth was negotiating with Scotland, with German Calvinists and French Huguenots. At the Escorial it was said that the Netherlands could only be rewon by an invasion of England, that the queen of the heretics must be at last dethroned, that in any case it was cheaper to launch a gigantic attack upon England than to pay the cost of protecting Spanish galleons, year after year, against the depredations of piratical sea dogs.

Philip II therefore prepared to invade England. The English retorted with vigor. Mary Stuart, after almost twenty years' imprisonment, was executed in 1587; an aroused Parliament, more than Elizabeth herself, demanded her life on the eve of foreign attack. Sir Francis Drake, most spectacular of the sea dogs, sailed into the port of Cádiz and burnt the very ships assembling there to join the Armada. This was jocosely described as singeing the beard of the king of Spain.

The great Armada, the *armada católica*, was ready early in 1588. With crosses on the sails and banners bearing the image of the Holy Virgin, it went forth as to a new Lepanto against the Turks of the north. It consisted of 130 ships, weighing 58,000 tons, carrying 30,000 men and 2,400 pieces of artillery—the most prodigious assemblage of naval power that the world had ever seen. In Spain only the pessimistic observed that its commander was no seaman, that some of its ships were too cumbersome, and some too frail, to weather the gales of the north, that orders had to be issued to its crews in six languages, and the antagonisms of Portuguese, Catalans, Castilians, Irishmen, and émigré English Catholics somehow appeased. The plan was for the fleet to sail to the Netherlands, from which it was to escort the prince of Parma's army across the straits to the English coast. In the Channel the Armada was met by some two hundred English vessels, with Sir Francis Drake as vice-admiral under Lord Howard of Effingham. The English craft—lighter, smaller, and faster, though well furnished with guns—harried the lumbering mass of the Armada, broke up its formations, attacked its great vessels one by one. It found no refuge at Calais, where English fireships drove it out again to sea. Then arose a great storm, the famous "Protestant wind," which blew the broken Armada northward, into seas that to southerners seemed almost polar, around the tip of Scotland, the Orkneys, the Hebrides, and northern Ireland, forbidding coasts which the Spaniards had to skirt without charts or pilots, and which they strewed with their wreckage and their bones.

The Results of the Struggle

The war went on for several years. Philip died in 1598, after a long and horrible illness, a frustrated and broken man. In the wars with Spain the English had, above all else, assured their national independence. They had acquired an intense national spirit, a love of "this other Eden, demi-paradise," "this precious stone set in the silver sea," as Shakespeare wrote; and they had become more solidly Protestant, almost unanimously set against "popery." With the ruin of the Armada, they were more free to take to the sea; we have seen how the English East India Company was founded in 1600.[14]

In the Netherlands, the battle lines swayed back and forth until 1609. In that year a Twelve Years' Truce was agreed to. By this truce the Netherlands were partitioned. The line of partition ran somewhat farther north than it had in Parma's time, for the Spaniards had retaken Antwerp and other cities in the middle zone. The seven provinces north of the line, those that had formed the Union of Utrecht in 1579, were henceforth known as Dutch. The ten provinces south of the line were known as the Spanish Netherlands. Protestants in the south either became Catholics or fled to the north, so that the south (the modern Belgium) became solidly Catholic, while the number of Protestants in the north was increased. Even so, the Dutch were not a completely Protestant people, for probably as many as a third of them remained Catholic. Calvinism was the religion of most Dutch burghers and the religion favored by the state; but in the face of an exceptionally large religious minority the Dutch Netherlands adopted a policy of toleration. The southern Netherlands were ruined by almost forty years of war. The Dutch, moreover, occupied the mouth of the Scheldt and refused to allow ocean-going vessels to proceed upstream to Antwerp or to Ghent. The Scheldt remained "closed" for two centuries, and the Flemish cities never recovered their old position. Amsterdam became the commercial and financial center of northern Europe; it retained its commercial supremacy for a century and its financial supremacy for two centuries. For the Dutch, as for the English, the weakening of Spanish naval power opened the way to the sea. The Dutch East India Company was organized in 1602. Both Dutch and English began to found overseas colonies. The English settled in Virginia in 1607, the Dutch at New York in 1612.

As for Spain, while it remained the most formidable military power of Europe for another half-century, its internal decline had already begun. At the death of Philip II the monarchy was living from hand to mouth, habitually depending on the next arrival of treasure from the Indies. The productive forces of the country were weakened by inflation, by taxation, by emigration, by depopulation. At Seville, for example, only 400 looms were in operation in 1621, where there had been 16,000 a century earlier. Spain suffered from the very circumstances that made it great. The qualities most useful in leading the Counter Reformation were not those on which a modern society could most easily be built. The generations of crusading against infidels, heathen, and heretics had produced an exceptionally large number of minor aristocrats, chevaliers, dons, and hidalgos, who as a class were contemptuous of work, and who were numerous enough and close enough to the common people to impress their haughty indifference upon the country as a whole. With the extreme concentration on religion the ablest men entered the church, and so great was the popular admiration for saints and mystics, missionaries and crusaders, theologians, archbishops, ascetics, and begging friars, that more secular activities offered little psychological satisfaction or reward.

The very unity accomplished under Ferdinand and Isabella threatened to dissolve. After more than a century of the Inquisition people were still afraid of false Christians and crypto-Muslims. The question of the Moriscos rose again in 1608.[15] The Moriscos included some of the best farmers and most skilled artisans in the country. They lived in almost all parts of Spain and were in no sense a "foreign" element, since they were simply the descendants of those Spaniards who, in the Muslim period, which had begun 900 years before, had adopted the Muslim religion and Arabic language and culture. They were now supposedly Christian, but the true and pure Christians accused them of preserving in secret the rites of Islam and of sympathy for the Barbary pirates. They were thought to be clannish, marrying among themselves; and they were so efficient, sober, and hard working that they outdistanced other Spaniards in competition. In 1609 some 150,000 Moriscos were driven out of Valencia; in 1610 some 64,000 were driven from Aragon; in 1611 an unknown number were expelled from Castile. All were simply put on boats and sent off with what they could carry. Spain, whose total population was rapidly falling in any case, thus lost one of the most socially valuable, if not religiously orthodox, of all its minorities.

Nor could the Christian kingdoms hold peaceably together. In 1640 Portugal, which had been joined to the Spanish crown since 1580 when its own ruling line had run out, reestablished its independence. That same year Catalonia rose in open rebellion. The Catalan war, in which the French streamed across the Pyrenees to aid the rebels, lasted for almost twenty years. Catalonia was at last reconquered, but it managed to preserve its old privileges and separate identity. Catalan and Castilian viewed each other with increased repugnance. The Spanish kingdoms were almost as disunited, in spirit and in institutions, as in the days of Isabella and Ferdinand. They suffered, too, during the seventeenth century from a line of kings whose mental peculiarities reached the point of positive imbecility. Meanwhile, however, the might of Spain was still to be felt in both Germany and France.

15. THE DISINTEGRATION AND RECONSTRUCTION OF FRANCE

Both France and Germany, in the so-called Wars of Religion, fell into an advanced state of decomposition, France in almost forty years of civil war between 1562 and 1598, Germany in a long period of civil troubles culminating in the Thirty Years' War between 1618 and 1648. From this decomposition France recovered in the seventeenth century, but Germany did not.

---

[15] See p. 72.

Political and Religious Disunity

The Wars of Religion in France, despite the religious savagery shown by partisans of both sides, were no more religious than they were political and were essentially a new form of the old phenomenon of feudal rebellion against a higher central authority. "Feudal," in this postmedieval sense, generally refers not to nobles only, but to all sorts of component groups having rights within the state, and so includes towns and provinces, and even craft guilds and courts of law, in addition to the church and the noble class. It remained to be seen whether all these elements could be welded into one body politic.

In France the New Monarchy, resuming the work of medieval kings, had imposed a certain unity on the country.[16] Normally, or apart from civil war, the country acted as a unit in foreign affairs. The king alone made treaties, and in war his subjects all fought on his side, if they fought at all. Internally, the royal centralization was largely administrative; that is, the king and those who worked for him dealt with subordinate bodies of all kinds, while these subordinate bodies remained in existence with their own functions and personnel. France by the ideas of the time was a very large country. It was three times as large as England and five times as populous. At a time when the traveler could move hardly thirty miles a day it took three weeks of steady plodding to cross the kingdom. Local influence was therefore very strong. Beneath the platform of royalty there was almost as little substantial unity in France as in the Holy Roman Empire. Where the Empire had three hundred "states," France had some three hundred areas with their own legal systems. Where the Empire had free cities, France had *bonnes villes*, the king's "good towns," each with its stubbornly defended corporate rights. Where the Empire had middle-sized states like Bavaria, France had provinces as great as some European kingdoms—Brittany, Burgundy, Provence, Languedoc—each ruled by the French king, to be sure, but each with its own identity, autonomy, laws, courts, tariffs, taxes, and parliament or provincial estates. To all this diversity, in France as in Germany, was now added diversity of religion. Calvin himself was by birth and upbringing a Frenchman. Calvinism spread in France very rapidly.

Nor was France much attached to a papal, Rome-centered, or international Catholicism. The French clergy had long struggled for its national or Gallican liberties; the French kings had dealt rudely with popes, ignored the Council of Trent, and allied for political reasons with both the Lutherans and the Turks. Since 1516 the king of France had the right to nominate the French bishops.[17] The fact that both the monarchy and the clergy felt already independent of Rome held them back from the revolutionary solutions of Protestantism. The Protestantism which did spread in France was of the most clear-cut and radical kind, namely, Calvinism, which preached at kings, attacked bishops, and smashed religious images and desecrated the churches. Even in countries that became Protestant—England, north Germany, even the Netherlands—this extreme Protestantism was the doctrine of a minority. In France there was no middle-of-the-road Protestantism, no broad and comfortable Anglicanism, no halfway Lutheranism inspired by governments, and in the long run, as will be seen, the middle of the road was occupied by Catholics.

[16] See p. 69.
[17] See above, pp. 52, 69, 91.

At first, however, the Huguenots, as the French Calvinists were called, though always a minority, were neither a small one nor modest in their demands. In a class analysis, it is clear that it was chiefly the nobility that was attracted to Protestantism, though of course it does not follow that most French Protestants were nobles, since the nobility was a small class. More than a third, and possibly almost a half, of the French nobility was Protestant in the 1560s or 1570s. Frequently the seigneur, or lord of one or more manors, believed that he should have the *ius reformandi*, or right to regulate religion on his own estates, as the princes of Germany decided the religion of their own territories. It thus happened that a lord might defy the local bishop, put a Calvinist minister in his village church, throw out the images, simplify the sacraments, and have the service conducted in French. In this way peasants also became Huguenots. Occasionally peasants turned Huguenot without encouragement by the lord. It was chiefly in southwestern France that Protestantism spread as a general movement affecting whole areas. But in all parts of the country, north as well as south, many towns converted to Protestantism. Usually this meant that the bourgeois oligarchy, into whose hands town government had generally fallen, went over to Calvinism and thereupon banned Catholic services, of which the sequel might be either that the journeymen wage earners followed along, or that, estranged by the class differences whose development has been described above, they remained attached to their old priests.[18] In general, the unskilled laboring mass probably remained the least touched of all classes by Calvinist doctrine.

Both Francis I and Henry II opposed the spread of Calvinism—as did Lutheran and Anglican rulers—for Calvinism, a kind of grassroots movement in religion, rising spontaneously among laity and reforming ministers, seemed to threaten not only the powers of monarchy but the very idea of a nationally established church. The fact that in France the nobility, a traditionally ungovernable class, figured prominently in the movement only made it look the more like political or feudal rebellion. Persecution of Huguenots, with burnings at the stake, began in the 1550s.

Then in 1559 King Henry II was accidentally killed in a tournament. He left three sons, of whom the eldest in 1559 was only fifteen. Their mother, Henry's widow, was Catherine de' Medici, an Italian woman who brought to France some of the polish of Renaissance Italy, along with some of its taste for political intrigue, with which she attempted to govern a distracted country for her royal sons. (Their names were Francis II, who died in 1560, Charles IX, who died in 1574, and Henry III, who lasted until 1589.) The trouble was that, with no firm hand in control of the monarchy, the country fell apart, and that in the ensuing chaos various powerful factions tried to get control of the youthful monarchs for their own purposes. Among these factions were both Huguenots and Catholics. The Huguenots, under persecution, were too strong a minority to go into hiding. Counting among their number a third or more of the professional warrior class, the nobles, they took naturally and aggressively to arms.

The Civil and Religious Wars

Exact history distinguishes no less than nine civil wars in the concluding four decades of the sixteenth century in France, but in this history they will be telescoped

---

[18] See pp. 118–123.

together. They were not civil wars of the kind where one region of a country takes up arms against another, each retaining some apparatus of government, as in the American Civil War or the civil wars of the seventeenth century in England. They were civil wars of the kind fought in the absence of government. Roving bands of armed men, without territorial base or regular means of subsistence, wandered about the country, fighting and plundering, joining or separating from other similar bands, in shifting hosts that were quickly formed or quickly dissolved. The underlying social conditions detached many people from their old routines and threw them into a life of adventure. The more prominent leaders could thus easily obtain followers, and at the coming of such cohorts the peasants usually took to the woods, while bourgeois would lock the gates of their cities. Or else peasants would form protective leagues, like vigilantes; and even small towns maintained diminutive armies.

The Huguenots were led by various personages of rank, such as Admiral de Coligny and Henry of Bourbon, king of Navarre, a small independent kingdom at the foot of the Pyrenees between Spain and France. A pronounced Catholic party arose under the Guise family, headed by the Duke of Guise and the Cardinal of Lorraine. Catherine de' Medici was left in the middle, opposed like all monarchs to Calvinism, but unwilling to fall under the domination of the Guises. While the Guises wished to extirpate heresy they wished even more to govern France. Among the Huguenots some fought for local liberties in religion, while the more ardent spirits hoped to drive "idolatry" and "popery" out of all France, and indeed out of the world itself. Catherine de' Medici for a time tried to play the two parties against each other. But in 1572, fearing the growing influence of Coligny over the king, and taking advantage of a great concourse of leading Huguenots in Paris to celebrate the marriage of Henry of Navarre, she decided to rid herself of the heads of the Huguenot party at a single blow. In the resulting massacre of St. Bartholomew's Day some thousands of Huguenots were dragged from their beds after midnight and unceremoniously murdered. Coligny was killed; Henry of Navarre escaped by temporarily changing his religion.

This outrage only aroused Huguenot fury and led to a renewal of civil war, with mounting atrocities committed by both sides. The armed bands slaughtered each other and terrorized noncombatants. Both parties hired companies of mercenary soldiers, mainly from Germany. Spanish troops invaded France at the invitation of the Guises. Protestant towns, like Rouen and La Rochelle, appealed to Elizabeth of England, reminding her that kings of England had once reigned over their parts of France, inviting English invasion and a renewal of the horrors of the Hundred Years' War; but Elizabeth was too preoccupied with her own problems to give more than very sporadic and insignificant assistance. Neither side could subdue the other, and hence there were numerous truces, during which fighting still flared up, since no one had the power to impose peace. The truces usually acknowledged the status quo, allowing Protestant worship locally in places where it was actually going on; but the Protestants felt no security in such terms, nor were Catholics satisfied at such recognition of heresy, so that each truce expired in further war.

Gradually, mainly among the more perfunctory Catholics, but also among moderate Protestants, there developed still another group, who thought of themselves as the "politicals" or *politiques*. The *politiques* were men who concluded that too much was being made of religion, that no doctrine was important enough to justify everlasting war, that perhaps after all there might be room for two churches, and that what the country needed above all else was civil order. Theirs was the secular not the religious view. They believed that men lived primarily in the state, not in the church. They were willing to overlook a man's ideas if only he would obey the king and go peaceably about his business. To escape anarchy they put their hopes in the institution of monarchy. Henry of Navarre, now again a Protestant, was at heart a *politique*. Another was the political philosopher Jean Bodin (1530–1596), the first thinker to develop the modern theory of sovereignty. He held that in every society there must be one power strong enough to give law to all others, with their consent if possible, without their consent if necessary. Thus from the disorders of the religious wars in France was germinated the idea of royal absolutism and of the sovereign state.

The End of the Wars: Reconstruction under Henry IV

In 1589 both Henry III, the reigning king, and Henry of Guise, the Catholic party chief who was trying to depose him, were assassinated, each by a partisan of the other. The throne now came by legal inheritance to the third of the three Henrys, Henry of Navarre, the Huguenot chieftain. He reigned as Henry IV. Most popular and most amiably remembered of all French kings, except for medieval St. Louis, he was the first of the Bourbon dynasty, which was to last until the French Revolution.

The civil wars did not end with the accession of Henry IV. The Catholic party refused to recognize him, set up a pretender against him, and called in the Spaniards. Henry, the *politique*, sensed that the majority of the French people were still Catholic, and that the Huguenots were not only a minority but after thirty years of civil strife an increasingly unpopular minority kept going as a political party by obstinate nobles. Paris especially, Catholic throughout the wars, refused to admit the heretic king within its gates. Supposedly remarking that "Paris is well worth a Mass," Henry IV in 1593 abjured the Calvinist faith, and subjected himself to the elaborate processes of papal absolution. Thereupon the *politiques* and less excitable Catholics consented to work with him. The Huguenots, at first elated that their leader should become king, were now not only outraged by Henry's abjuration but alarmed for their own safety. They demanded not only religious liberty, but positive guarantees.

Henry IV in 1598 responded by issuing the Edict of Nantes. The Edict granted to every seigneur, or noble who was also a manorial lord, the right to hold Protestant services in his own household. It allowed Protestantism in towns where it was in fact the prevailing form of worship, and in any case in one town of each *baillage* (a unit corresponding somewhat to the English shire) throughout the country; but it barred it from Catholic episcopal towns and from a zone surrounding and including the city of Paris. It promised that Protestants should enjoy the same civil rights as Catholics, the same chance for public office, and access to the Catholic universities. In certain of the superior law courts it created "mixed chambers" of both Protestants and Catholics—somewhat as if a stated minority representation were to be legally required in United States federal courts today. The Edict also gave Protestants their own means of defense, granting them about 100 fortified towns to be held by Protestant garrisons under Protestant command.

The Huguenot minority, reassured by the Edict of Nantes, became less of a rebellious element within the state. The majority of the French people viewed the Edict with suspicion. The parlements, or supreme law courts, of Paris, Bordeaux, Toulouse, Aix, and Rennes all refused to recognize it as the law of the land. It was the king who forced toleration upon the country. He silenced the parlements, and subdued Catholic opposition by doing favors for the Jesuits. France's chief minority was thus protected by the central government, not by popular wishes. Where in England the Catholic minority had no rights at all, and in Germany the religious question was settled only by cutting the country into small and hostile fragments, in France a compromise was effected, by which the Protestant minority had both individual and territorial rights. A considerable number of French statesmen, generals, and other important persons in the seventeenth century were Protestants.

Henry IV, having appeased the religious controversy, did everything that he could to let the country gradually recover, to replant, rebuild, transact business, and rediscover the arts of peace. His ideal, as he breezily put it, was a "chicken in the pot" for every Frenchman. He worked also to put the ruined government back together, to collect taxes, pay officials, discipline the army, and supervise the administration of justice. Roads and bridges were repaired and new manufactures were introduced under mercantilist principles. Never throughout his reign of twenty-one years did he summon the Estates General. A country that had just hacked itself to pieces in civil war was scarcely able to govern itself, and so, under Henry IV, the foundations of the later royal absolutism of the Bourbons were laid down.

Henry IV was assassinated in 1610 by a crazed fanatic who believed him a menace to the Catholic church. Under his widow, Marie de' Medici, the nobility and upper Catholic clergy again grew restless and forced the summoning of the Estates General, in which so many conflicting and mutually distrustful interests were represented that no program could be adopted, and Marie dismissed them in 1615 to the general relief of all concerned. No Estates General of the kingdom as a whole thereafter met until the French Revolution. National government was to be conducted by and through the king.

Cardinal Richelieu

In the name of Marie de' Medici and her young son, Louis XIII, the control of affairs gradually came into the hands of an ecclesiastic, Cardinal Richelieu. In the preceding generation Richelieu might have been called a *politique*. It was the state, not the church, whose interests he worked to further. He tried to strengthen the state economically by mercantilist edicts. He attempted to draw impoverished gentlemen into trade by allowing them to engage in maritime commerce without loss of noble status. For wholesale merchants, as an incentive, he made it possible to become nobles, in return for payments into the royal exchequer. He founded and supported many commercial companies on the Anglo-Dutch model.

For a time it seemed that civil war might break out again. Nobles still feuded with each other and evaded the royal jurisdiction. Richelieu prohibited private warfare and ordered the destruction of all fortified castles not manned and needed by the king himself. He even prohibited dueling, a custom much favored by the d'Artagnans of the day, but regarded by Richelieu as a mere remnant of private war. The Huguenots, too, with their own towns and their own armed forces under the Edict of Nantes, had become something of a state within the state. In 1627 the Duke of Rohan led a Huguenot rebellion, based on the city of La Rochelle, which received military support from the English. Richelieu after a year suppressed the rebellion, and in 1629, by the Peace of Alais, amended the Edict of Nantes. For this highly secularized cardinal of the Catholic church it was agreeable for the Protestants to keep their religion, but not for them to share in the instruments of political power. The Huguenots lost, in 1629, their fortified cities, their Protestant armies, and all their military and territorial rights, but in their religious and civil rights they were not officially molested for another fifty years.

The French monarchy no sooner reestablished itself after the civil wars than it began to recur to the old foreign policy of Francis I, who had opposed on every front the European supremacy of the house of Habsburg.[19] The Spanish power still encircled France at the Pyrenees, in the Mediterranean, in the Free County of Burgundy (the Franche-Comté), and in Belgium. The Austrian branch had pretensions to supremacy in Germany and all central Europe. Richelieu found his opportunity to assail the Habsburgs in the civil struggles which now began to afflict Germany.

16. THE THIRTY YEARS' WAR, 1618–1648: THE DISINTEGRATION OF GERMANY

The Holy Roman Empire extended from France on the west to Poland and Hungary on the east. It included the Czechs of Bohemia, and sizable French-speaking populations in what are now Belgium, Lorraine, eastern Burgundy, and western Switzerland; but with these exceptions the Empire was made up of Germans.[20] Language, however, was far less important than religion as the tie which people felt to be basic to a community; and in religion the Empire was almost evenly divided. Where in England, after stabilization set in, Roman Catholics sank to a minority of some 3 percent, and in France the Huguenots fell to not much over 5 percent, in Germany there was no true minority, and hence no majority, and religion gave no ground for national concentration. Possibly there were more Protestants than Catholics in the Empire in 1600, for not only was Protestantism the state religion in many of the 300 states, but individual Protestants were exceedingly numerous in the legally Catholic states of the Austrian Habsburgs. Bohemia had a Protestant majority, rooted in the Czech people, and even in Austria, in meetings of the estates, the Protestants sometimes prevailed. Farther east, outside the Holy Roman Empire, the Hungarian nobles were mainly Protestant, and Transylvania, in the elbow of the Carpathian Mountains, was an active center of Calvinism.

In 1500 Germany had led in the life of Europe, but in 1600 it showed evidences of backwardness and provincialism. Literature had declined, and the language itself became barbarized and ungainly. Where both Catholics and Calvinists recognized international affiliations and read with interest books written in other countries, Lutherans were suspicious of the world outside the Lutheran states of Germany and Scandinavia, and hence suffered from a cultural isolation. The German universities, both Lutheran and Catholic, attracted fewer students than

[19] See map, pp. 70–71; and p. 78.
[20] See maps, pp. 70–71, 142–143.

formerly, and their intellectual effort was consumed in combative dogmatics, each side demonstrating the truth of its own ideas. More witches were burned in Germany than in the west, the popular fairy tales were more gruesome, and the educated were more fascinated by astrology. The commerce of south Germany and the Rhineland was in decay, both because of the shift of trade to the Atlantic and because the Dutch controlled the mouth of the Rhine in their own interests. German bankers, such as the Fuggers, were of slight importance after 1600. It was now in the West that capital was being formed.

Background of the Thirty Years' War

The Peace of Augsburg in 1555, with its principle of *cuius regio eius religio*, had provided that in each state the government could prescribe the religion of its subjects.[21] In some states a bishop himself constituted the government. In these cases, whenever an incumbent died, there was a race to name his successor, to secure the territory as Lutheran or Catholic. In 1593 a small war was fought for the control of Aachen, in 1600 another for the control of Cologne. In general, in the decades following the Peace of Augsburg, the Lutherans made considerable gains, putting Lutheran administrators into the church states, or "secularizing" them and converting them into lay principalities. The Catholics did not accept this constant attrition, which violated the Ecclesiastical Reservation of the Peace of Augsburg. In addition, Calvinism spread into Germany. Though Calvinists had no rights under the Peace of Augsburg, a number of states became Calvinist. One of these was the Palatinate, important because it was strategically placed across the middle Rhine, and because its ruler, the Elector Palatine, was one of the seven persons who elected the Holy Roman Emperor. In 1608 the Protestant states, urged on by the Elector Palatine, formed a Protestant union to defend their gains. To obtain support, they negotiated with the Dutch, with the English, and with Henry IV of France. In 1609 a league of Catholic German states was organized by Bavaria. It looked for help from Spain.

The Germans were thus falling apart, or rather coming together, into two parties in anticipation of a religious war, and each party solicited foreign assistance against the other. Other issues were also maturing. The Twelve Years' Truce between Spain and the Dutch, signed in 1609, was due to expire in 1621. The Spanish (whose military power was still unaffected by internal decline) were again preparing to crush the Dutch Republic, or, at the very least, to open the mouth of the Scheldt and to get Dutch traders out of the East Indies. Since the Dutch insisted on independence, and were in any case unwilling to leave the Indies or to remove their stranglehold on the port of Antwerp, a renewal of the Dutch-Spanish war appeared to be inevitable. The Spanish also wished to consolidate the Habsburg position in central Europe. From Milan in north Italy they proposed to build up a fork of territory, one of whose prongs would lead through the easternmost of the Swiss cantons directly to Habsburg Austria, the other through the westernmost Swiss cantons to the valley of the Rhine. There, on and near the Rhine, if they could conquer a few states like the Calvinistic Palatinate, they might join the Netherlands and Franche-Comté (the Free County of Burgundy, ruled by Spain) into a large and continuous territorial block.[22] These Spanish

---

[21] See pp. 78–79.
[22] See map, pp. 142–143.

designs in the Rhineland and Switzerland naturally aroused the opposition of France. Moreover, the Austrian branch of the Habsburg family was slowly bestirring itself to eradicate Protestantism in its own domains and even to turn the Holy Roman Empire into a more modern and national type of state. The idea of a strong power in Germany was abhorrent to the French. France, through opposition to the Habsburgs, was again put in the position of chief protector of Protestantism. France, as we have observed, was a giant of Europe, five times as populous as England, over ten times as populous as Sweden or the Dutch Republic, incomparably more populous than any single German state. And France after 1600 was at last unified within—at least relatively. As a French writer has observed, speaking of these years, the appearance of the fleur-de-lis upon the Rhine would tumble to the ground the vast projects of the Counter Reformation.

The Thirty Years' War, resulting from all these pressures, was therefore exceedingly complex. It was a German civil war fought over the Catholic-Protestant issue. It was also a German civil war fought over constitutional issues, between the emperor striving to build up the central power of the Empire and the member states struggling to maintain independence. These two civil wars by no means coincided, for Catholic and Protestant states were alike in objecting to imperial control. It was also an international war, between France and the Habsburgs, between Spain and the Dutch, with the kings of Denmark and Sweden and the prince of Transylvania becoming involved, and with all these outsiders finding allies within Germany, on whose soil most of the battles were fought. The wars were further complicated by the fact that many of the generals were soldiers of fortune, who aspired to create principalities of their own, and who fought or refused to fight to suit their own convenience.

The Four Phases of the War

The fighting began in Bohemia. It is in fact customary to divide the war into four phases, the Bohemian (1618–1625), the Danish (1625–1629), the Swedish (1630–1635), and the Swedish-French (1635–1648).

In 1618 the Bohemians, or Czechs, fearing the loss of their Protestant liberties, dealt with two emissaries from the Habsburg Holy Roman Emperor, Matthias (who was also their king), by a method occasionally used in that country—throwing them out of the window. After this "defenestration of Prague" the king-emperor sent troops to restore his authority, whereupon the Bohemians deposed him and elected a new king. In order to obtain Protestant assistance, they chose the Calvinist Elector Palatine, the head of the Protestant Union. This young man proceeded to Bohemia, where he assumed the title of Frederick V. He brought aid to the Bohemians from the Protestant Union, the Dutch sent money, and the prince of Transylvania harried the Habsburg rear. The Emperor Ferdinand, Matthias' successor, assisted by money from the pope, Spanish troops sent up from Milan, and the forces of Catholic Bavaria, managed to overwhelm the Bohemians at the battle of the White Mountain in 1620. Frederick fled, jeered or pitied as the "winter king." His ancestral domains in the Palatinate were overrun by the Spaniards.

Two facts emerged in consequence of the Bohemian war. First, the Spaniards were entrenching themselves in the Rhineland, building up their position against the French and the Dutch. Second, Bohemia was reconquered and revolutionized by the Habsburgs. Ferdinand got himself elected again as king. He confiscated the estates of almost half the Bohemian nobles. He granted these lands as endowments for Catholic churches, orders, and monasteries, or gave them out to a swarm of adventurers of all nationalities who had entered his service, and who now became the new landed aristocracy of Bohemia. Jesuits streamed in, and through missions and schools, as well as court proceedings and executions, the re-Catholicization of Bohemia began. In Austria also, which had at first joined Bohemia in rebellion, Protestantism was stamped out.

With Protestant fortunes at a low ebb, and the Protestant Union itself dissolved in 1621, the lead in Protestant affairs was now taken by the king of Denmark, who was also Duke of Holstein, a state of the Holy Roman Empire. His aims were well mixed with politics, for he hoped by acquiring a few bishoprics in Germany to construct a kingdom for his younger son. With a little aid from the Dutch and English, and with promises from Richelieu, he entered the fray. Against him the Emperor Ferdinand raised another army, or, rather, commissioned Albert of Wallenstein to raise one on his own private initiative. Wallenstein assembled a force of professional fighters, of all nationalities, who lived by pillage rather than by pay. His army was his personal instrument, not the emperor's, and he therefore followed a policy of his own, which was so tortuous and well concealed that the name of Wallenstein has always remained an enigma. Possibly he dreamed of a united empire and a revived Germany from which foreigners should be expelled; certainly he dreamed of creating a sizable principality for himself. Wallenstein and other imperial generals soon defeated the king of Denmark, reached the Baltic coast, and even invaded the Danish peninsula.

The full tide of the Counter Reformation now flowed over Germany. Not only was Catholicism again seeping into the Palatinate, and again flooding Bohemia, but it rolled northward into the inner recesses of the Lutheran states. By the Edict of Restitution, in 1629, the emperor declared all church territories secularized since 1552 automatically restored to the Catholic church. Two archbishoprics, twelve bishoprics, and over a hundred small territories formerly belonging to monasteries and religious orders were involved. Some, like the bishopric of Lübeck, were as far north as the Baltic. Some had been Protestant since the oldest person could remember. Terror swept over Protestant Germany. It seemed that the whole Protestant Reformation, now a century old, might be undone.

Among those to be alarmed were the French and the Swedes. Richelieu, however, was still putting down fractious nobles and Huguenots. He had not yet consolidated France to his satisfaction and believed that France, without fighting itself, could counter the Habsburg ambitions through the use of allies. He sent diplomats to help extricate the king of Sweden from a war with Poland, and he promised him financial assistance, which soon rose to a million livres a year in return for the maintenance in Germany of 40,000 Swedish troops. The Dutch subsidized the Swedes with some 50,000 florins a month.

The king of Sweden was Gustavus Adolphus, a ruler of superlative ability, who had conciliated all parties in Sweden and thus created a base from which he could safely conduct overseas operations. He had extended Swedish holdings on the east shore of the Baltic. Using Dutch and other military experts, he had created the most modern army of the times, noted for its firm discipline, high courage, and mobile cannon. Himself a religious man, he had his troops march to battle singing Lutheran hymns. He was ideally suited to be the Protestant champion, a role he now willingly took up, landing in Germany in 1630. Richelieu, besides giving financial help, negotiated with the Catholic states of Germany, playing on their fears of imperial centralization and so sowing discord among German Catholics and isolating the emperor, against whom the Swedish war machine was now hurled.

The Swedes, with military aid from Saxony, won a number of spectacular victories, at Breitenfeld in 1631 and Lützen in 1632, where, however, Gustavus Adolphus was killed. His chancellor, Oxenstierna, carried on. The Swedish army penetrated into Bohemia, and as far south as the Danube. What those in the higher counsels of Sweden were aiming at is not clear. Perhaps they dreamed of a great federal Protestant empire, to include Scandinavia and north Germany, a Lutheran empire confronting a Catholic and Habsburg empire in the south. But the brilliant Swedish victories came to little. Both sides were weakened by disagreement. Wallenstein, who disliked the Spanish influence in Germany, virtually ceased to fight the Swedes and Saxons, with whom he even entered into private talks, hoping to create an independent position for himself. He was finally disgraced by the emperor and assassinated by one of his own staff. On the Swedish-Saxon side, the Saxons decided to make a separate peace. Saxony therefore signed with the emperor the Peace of Prague of 1635. The other German Protestant states concurred in it and withdrew their support from the Swedes. The emperor, by largely annulling the Edict of Restitution, allayed Protestant apprehensions. The Swedes were left isolated in Germany. It seemed that the German states were coming together, that the religious wars might be nearing an end. But, in fact, in 1635, the Thirty Years' War was only well begun. Neither France nor Spain wished peace or reconciliation in Germany.

Richelieu renewed his assurances to the Swedes, paid subsidies even to the wealthy Dutch, hired a German princeling, Bernard of Saxe-Weimar, to maintain an army of Germans in the French service, and, cardinal of the Roman church though he was, at last came out openly and plainly in favor of the German Protestants.

So the fleur-de-lis at last moved toward the Rhine, though not at first with the success for which Frenchmen or Protestants might hope. The Spanish, from their bases in Belgium and Franche-Comté, drove instead deep into France. Champagne and Burgundy were ravaged, and Paris itself was seized with panic. The Spanish also raided the south. The French had a taste of the plunder, murder, burnings, and stealing of cattle by which Germany had been afflicted. But the French soon turned the tables. When Portugal and Catalonia rebelled against Philip IV, France immediately recognized the independence of Portugal under the new royal house of Braganza—as did England, Holland, and Sweden with equal alacrity. French troops streamed over the Pyrenees into Catalonia, spreading the usual devastation. Richelieu even recognized a Catalan republic.

In Germany the last or Swedish-French phase of the war was not so much a civil war among Germans as an international struggle on German soil. Few German states now sided with the French and Swedes. A feeling of national resentment against foreign invasion even seemed to develop.

The Peace of Westphalia, 1648

Peace talks began in 1644 in Westphalia, at the two towns of Münster and Osnabrück. The German states were crying for peace, for a final religious settlement,

Austrian Habsburgs
Spanish Habsburgs
Swedish Dominions
Brandenburg-Prussia
Church Lands
Boundary of the Holy Roman Empire

100   200   300 miles

SHETLAND I.

ORKNEY I.

NORWAY

Bergen

Helsingfors

STOCKHOLM

S W E D E N

FINLA

ESTON

B A L T I C   S E A

KINGDOM OF
DENMARK AND NORWAY

SCOTLAND

Edinburgh

LIVO

Riga

Belfast

N O R T H   S E A

DENMARK
(TO SWEDEN, 1658)
Copenhagen

COURLAND

IRELAND

Dublin   Liverpool

ENGLAND
(COMMONWEALTH 1649-1660
UNITED KINGDOM 1707)

SCHLESWIG

HOLSTEIN

SWEDISH
POMERANIA

Stralsund

Lübeck

Hamburg

BRANDENBURG-PRUSSIA

POMERALIA

Danzig

DUCHY
OF
PRUSSIA

LI

Bristol

London

UNITED
PROVINCES

Amsterdam
Ryswick
Utrecht

Bremen
HANOVER
Verden
Osnabrück
Münster

Elbe R.

BRANDENBURG
Berlin
Magdeburg

Vistula R.

GREAT
POLAND

Warsaw

P

E N G L I S H   C H A N N E L

Brussels

SPANISH
NETH.

MINOR
GERMAN STATES

Cologne

Leipzig
SAXONY

Dresden

Oder R.

Breslau
SILESIA

LITTLE
POLAND

Cracow

Lemberg

GALICIA

A T L A N T I C   O C E A N

Rouen

Paris

Rennes

Nantes

Orléans

Trier
Metz
LORRAINE
ALSACE

Mainz
PALATINATE

Strassbourg

Prague
BOHEMIA

MORAVIA

C A R P A T H

FRANCE

Bordeaux

Lyons

FRANCHE
COMTÉ

SWISS CANTONS

SAVOY

PIEDMONT

BAVARIA
Augsburg

AUSTRIA

Vienna

KINGDOM   OF   HUNGARY

Budapest

H U N G A R Y

O T T O M

TRA

LaCoruña

León

Valladolid

Oporto

NAVARRE

PYRENEES

Montauban

Avignon

Marseilles

Milan

Parma

Genoa

Venice

REPUBLIC   OF   VENICE

A D R I A T I C   S E A

Zara

SLAVONIA

BOSNIA

Belgrade

SERBIA

MONTENEGRO

PORTUGAL
(TO SPAIN
1580-1640)

Lisbon

SPAIN

Escorial   Madrid

CASTILE

Mérida   Toledo

ARAGON

CATALONIA

Saragossa

Barcelona

Valencia

Florence

TUSCANY

CORSICA
(Genoa)

PAPAL
STATES

Aquila

Rome

Bari

ALBANIA

Salonica

GREECE

Cadiz

Seville

Malaga

Murcia

BALEARIC   I.

MINORCA

MAJORCA

SARDINIA

Naples

NAPLES

KINGDOM OF THE
TWO SICILIES

IONIAN I.
(Venice)

Tangier
(Portugal)   Ceuta

M E D I T E R R A N E A N

Palermo

SICILY

S E A

Oran (Spain)

Algiers

Tunis

MALTA
(Knights of St. John)

ND MOROCCO

ALGERIA

TUNISIA

B A R B A R Y   S T A T E S

NGRIA

•Moscow

R U S S I A

nsk •

L U A N I A

A N D

•Kiev

LIA

MOLD AVIA YEDISAN

NIA

BESSARABIA CRIMEA

HIA DOBRUJA

arest• BLACK SEA

R.

ube

ARIA

LIA

•Constantinople

E M P I R E

EAN

EA

•Smyrna

ens

RHODES
(Turkish)

CYPRUS
(Turkish)

RETE
nice)

EUROPE, 1648

The map shows the European states at the time of the Peace of
Westphalia. The main feature of the Peace of Westphalia was
that the threat of domination of Europe by the Catholic Habsburgs was averted. A plurality of independent sovereign states
was henceforth considered normal. The plurality of religions
was also henceforth taken for granted for Europe as a whole,
though each state continued to require, or at least to favor,
religious uniformity within its own borders. By weakening the
Habsburgs, and furthering the disintegration of Germany,
the Peace of Westphalia opened the way for the political
ascendancy of France.

and for "reform" of the Holy Roman Empire. France and Sweden insisted that the German states should individually take part in the negotiations, a disintegrating principle that the German princes eagerly welcomed and which the emperor vainly resisted. To Westphalia, therefore, hundreds of diplomats and negotiators now repaired, representing the Empire, its member states, Spain, France, Sweden, the Dutch, the Swiss, the Portuguese, the Venetians, many other Italians, and the pope. There had been no such European congress since the Council of Constance, and the fact that a European assemblage had in 1415 dealt with affairs of the church, and now in the 1640s dealt with affairs of state, war, and power, was a measure of the secularization that had come over Europe. The papal nuncio, it may be remarked, was barely listened to at Westphalia, and the pope never signed the treaties.

The negotiations dragged on, because the armies were still fighting, and after each battle one side or the other raised its terms. France and Spain refused to make peace with each other at all and in fact remained at war until 1659. But for the Holy Roman Empire a settlement was agreed to, incorporated in 1648 in the two treaties of Münster and Osnabrück, and commonly known as the Peace of Westphalia.

The Peace of Westphalia represented a general checkmate to the Counter Reformation in Germany. It not only renewed the terms of the Peace of Augsburg, granting each German state the right to determine its own religion, but it added Calvinism to Lutheranism and Catholicism as an acceptable faith. On the controversial issue of church territories secularized after 1552 the Protestants won a complete victory.

The dissolution of the Holy Roman Empire, which had been advanced by the drawing of internal religious frontiers in the days of Luther, was now confirmed in politics and international law. Borderlands of the Empire fell away. The Dutch and Swiss ceased to belong to it, both the United Provinces and Swiss cantons (or Helvetic Body) being recognized as sovereign and independent. The Dutch, in addition, were confirmed in their conquest of both banks of the lower Scheldt, the closure of that river to ocean-going vessels, and hence the commercial destruction of Antwerp. They likewise received, from Portugal, the right to have outposts in Brazil and Indonesia.

From the disintegrating western frontier of the Holy Empire the French cut off small pieces, receiving sovereignty over three Lorraine bishoprics, which they had occupied for a century, and certain rights in Alsace which were so confused that they later led to trouble. The king of Sweden received the bishoprics of Bremen and Verden and the western half of Pomerania, including the city of Stettin. Sweden thus added to its trans-Baltic possessions. The mouths of the German rivers were now controlled by non-Germans, the Oder, Elbe, and Weser by Sweden, the Rhine and the Scheldt by the Dutch. In the interior of the Empire Brandenburg received eastern Pomerania, the large archbishopric of Magdeburg, and two smaller bishoprics, while Bavaria also increased its stature, obtaining part of the Palatinate and a seat in the electoral college, so that the Empire now had eight electors.

It was in the new constitution of the Empire itself, not in territorial changes, that the greatest victory of the French and their Swedish and Dutch allies was to be found. The German states, over three hundred in number, became virtually sovereign. Each received the right to conduct diplomacy and make treaties with foreign powers. The Peace of Westphalia further stipulated that no laws could be made by the Empire, no taxes raised, no soldiers recruited, no war declared or peace terms ratified except with the consent of the imperial estates, the 300-odd princes, ecclesiastics, and free cities in the Reichstag assembled. Since it was well known that agreement on any such matters was impossible, the principle of self-government, or of medieval constitutional liberties, was used to destroy the Empire itself as an effective political entity. While most other European countries were consolidating under royal absolutism, Germany sank back into "feudal chaos."

Not only did the Peace of Westphalia block the Counter Reformation, and not only did it frustrate the Austrian Habsburgs and forestall for almost two centuries any movement toward German national unification, but it also marked the advent in international law of the modern European *Staatensystem*, or system of sovereign states. The diplomats who assembled at Westphalia represented independent powers which recognized no superior or common tie. No one any longer pretended that Europe had any significant unity, religious, political, or other. Statesmen delighted in the absence of any such unity, in which they sensed the menace of "universal monarchy." Europe was understood to consist in a large number of unconnected sovereignties, free and detached atoms, or states, which acted according to their own laws, following their own political interests, forming and dissolving alliances, exchanging embassies and legations, alternating between war and peace, shifting position with a shifting balance of power.

Physically Germany was wrecked by the Thirty Years' War. Cities were sacked by mercenary soldiers with a rapacity that their commanders could not control; or the commanders themselves, drawing no supplies from their home governments, systematically looted whole areas to maintain their armies. Magdeburg was besieged ten times, Leipzig five. In one woolen town of Bohemia, with a population of 6,000 before the wars, the citizens fled and disappeared, the houses collapsed, and eight years after the peace only 850 persons were found there. On the site of another small town Swedish cavalry found nothing but wolves. The peasants, murdered, put to flight, or tortured by soldiers to reveal their few valuables, ceased to give attention to farming; agriculture was ruined, so that starvation followed, and with it came pestilence. Even revised modern estimates allow that in many extensive parts of Germany as much as a third of the population may have perished. The effects of fire, disease, undernourishment, homelessness, and exposure in the seventeenth century were the more terrible because of the lack of means to combat them. The horrors of modern war are not wholly different from horrors that men and women have experienced in the past.

Germany as such, physically wrecked and politically cut into small pieces, ceased for a long time to play any part in European affairs. A kind of political and cultural vacuum existed in central Europe. On the one hand, the western or Atlantic peoples—French, English, Dutch—began in the seventeenth century to take the lead in European affairs. On the other hand, in eastern Germany, around Berlin and Vienna, new and only half-German power complexes began to form. These themes will be traced in the two following chapters.

With the close of the Thirty Years' War the Wars of Religion came to an end.

While in some later conflicts, as in Hungary or in Ireland and Scotland, religion remained an issue, it was never again an important issue in the political affairs of Europe as a whole. In general, by the close of the seventeenth century, the division between Protestant and Catholic had become stabilized. Neither side any longer expected to make territorial gains at the expense of the other. Both the Protestant and the Catholic reformations were accomplished facts.

The World Overseas

With the Age of Discovery, Europe entered into habitual communication with the "Indies," as Asia, Africa, and America were at first vaguely and collectively called.

Europeans found some peoples in these countries less civilized than themselves, and others whom they considered equally civilized or more so, as in India and China. From Asia, while the Europeans at first sought for spices, they soon imported manufactures of a more refined kind than Europe could then produce, such as Indian cottons and Chinese porcelains. In Asia, as in Africa, the Europeans were transients—traders, sailors, missionaries, and officials sent to govern small outposts. There was no settlement of European families except at the Cape of Good Hope. The interior of Africa remained unknown. The Mogul empire in India until after 1700, and the Ming empire in China, succeeded by the Ch'ing or Manchu empire about 1650, long commanded the awe and respect of Europeans. China exerted a special fascination. During the European Enlightenment, in the eighteenth century, China was admired as a huge empire that had no clergy, and was governed by an enlightened literary class, the mandarins, recruited by competitive examination rather than by noble birth.

The aboriginal Americans and the black Africans were regarded by the Europeans as savages, who in any case could not defend themselves against European organization and weapons. The American Indians were either killed off, subjugated or pushed aside. America was valuable to Europeans for its natural resources, whose exploitation required masses of labor which was supplied from Africa. In the ensuing slave trade, the number of Africans who were taken to America, including the two continents and the West Indies, was far greater than the number of Europeans who settled there before 1800. A few Spanish emigrated permanently to New Spain, and a few Portuguese to Brazil, but by the time of the American Revolution the most purely "European" region was the Atlantic coast of North America, where about two million whites lived with half a million blacks and a very few Indians.

Europe itself was transformed by these overseas ventures. A wealthy commercial class grew up in northwestern Europe. Naval power became decisive. The inflow of American gold and silver affected currency values and hence the relationship between social classes. Population grew with the adoption of the American potato. Men took increasing pride in their understanding of the world. There was much speculation on the diversity of human races and cultures, which sometimes led to a new kind of race consciousness on the part of Europeans, and sometimes to a cultural relativism in which European ways were seen as only one variant of human behavior as a whole.

Right: "Our Lady of the Navigators," painted about 1535 by Alejo Fernandez for the Casa de Contratacion, or Trade House, at Seville. The figures to whom the Virgin extends her protection, with their sharply individualized features, are thought to represent various actual explorers; the one to the left may be Columbus. The picture evokes the combination of religious spirit with adventure and gold-seeking that motivated the early expeditions.

The Spaniards stamped out much of the Indian religion as idolatrous, yet it is to Spanish priests that we owe the preservation of much of our knowledge of the pre-Conquest culture. The page at the above right is from a book in which a Spaniard wrote down the Aztec language in the Latin alphabet. A human sacrifice is also depicted.

At the above left is a page from a book published in England, translated from the Dutch. The author, Johannes Nieuhoff, spent three years in Java and nine in Brazil, where the Dutch had a settlement in the 1640s. He was thus well qualified to write on the "West and East Indies," whose wonders are suggested by palms, parasols, and elephants. The aerial creature is probably a "flying squirrel" of a kind that is common in Indonesia.

148

"An Episode in the Conquest of America," by Jan Mostaert of Haarlem in Holland. An early visualization of the New World by a painter who died in 1555. The multitude of busy small figures suggests the style of the Flemish Breughel, and the placid livestock is Dutch. The American Indians are seen as naked, helpless, and confused—and very different from Europeans.

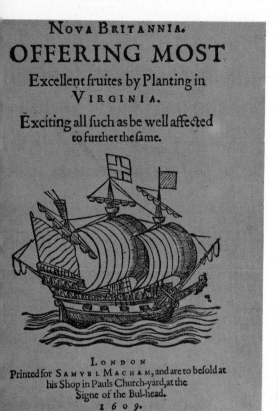

Opposite, above: Europeans negotiate with an African chief and his council on the Guinea coast. The Europeans have guns, the Africans only spears, but the Africans, in contrast to the American Indians on the preceding page, are fully clothed and seated with dignity in an organized situation. They may be discussing the sale of slaves.

Above, center: Black slaves are stooped over in a diamond-processing operation in Brazil, while overseers watch with whips. The slaves seem to be sifting material in water made to flow through the little compartments.

Above, left: An early advertisement to attract European immigration to what eventually became the United States. This one was published in London two years after the founding of Jamestown, the first permanent English settlement in America. "Planting" meant settling in the seventeenth century.

Right: The headquarters of the Dutch East India Company in 1665 in Bengal, long before the British predominance there. It is wholly walled off from the Indian life around it, with offices, living quarters, and spacious gardens for the employees of the Company. A large Dutch flag flies at the corner of the enclosure, and others can be seen on the ships in the Hooghly River (in the Ganges delta); these ships kept the Dutch traders in continual touch with Holland, though the voyage took almost a year.

152

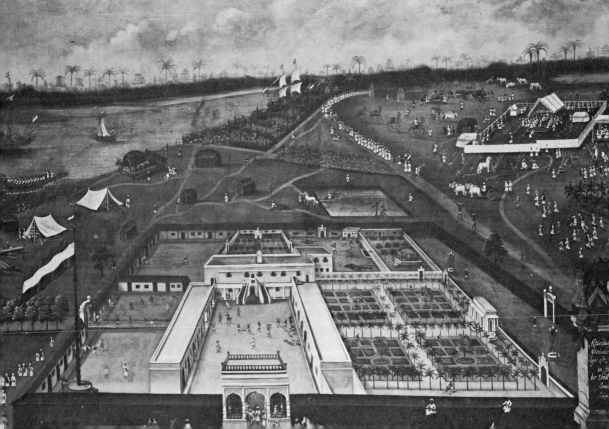

These two prints suggest some results of three centuries of European experience with the world overseas. In China, no Europeans had as yet any territorial foothold. China was seen by Europe as a kind of counterpart civilization to itself. Confucius is shown here in a library of suspiciously European appearance, but holding a book in which Chinese characters are represented. He symbolized for Europeans the great teacher of virtue and wisdom, of social harmony and civic duty, far removed from the theological bickering of European religions.

Meanwhile the settlement at Jamestown had grown into a string of populous colonies. Above, we see Boston Common in 1768. The town seems rural, but has substantial houses with fences and rows of planted trees. British troops have just moved in, because of rising political troubles. They have pitched their tents on the common, where they march and drill in full sight of the citizens. The first fighting of the American Revolution was soon to begin here.

IV.
The Establishment of West-European Leadership

I f the reader were to take a map of Europe, set a compass on the city of Paris, and draw a circle with a radius of five hundred miles, a zone would be marked out from which much of modern or "Western" civilization has radiated since about 1650. It was within this zone that a secular society, modern natural science, a developed capitalism, the modern state, parliamentary government, democratic ideas, machine industry, and much else either originated or received their first full expression. The extreme western parts of Europe—Ireland, Portugal, and Spain—were mainly outside the circle. But within it were England, southern Scotland, France, the Low Countries, Switzerland, western and central Germany, and northern Italy. This area, for over two hundred years beginning in the seventeenth century, was the earth's principal center of what anthropologists might call cultural diffusion. Western Europe, as a dynamic cultural area, was to have a tremendous impact on the rest of Europe, the Americas, and ultimately the whole world.

This leadership of western Europe became established in the half-century following the Peace of Westphalia. The fading out of the Italian Renaissance, the subsiding of religious wars, the ruin of the Holy Roman Empire, and the decay of Spain all cleared the stage on which the Dutch, English, and French were to be the

Chapter Emblem: A commemorative medal, in which Louis XIV receives the homage of Tournai and Courtrai, Flemish towns temporarily annexed in 1667.

principal actors. But the Dutch were few in number, and the English during most of the seventeenth century were weakened by domestic discord. It was France that for a time played the most imposing role. The whole half-century following the Peace of Westphalia is in fact often called the Age of Louis XIV.

17. THE *GRAND MONARQUE* AND THE BALANCE OF POWER

This king of France inherited his throne in 1643 at the age of five, assumed the personal direction of affairs in 1661 at the age of twenty-three, and reigned for seventy-two years until his death in 1715. No one else in modern history has held so powerful a position for so long a time. Louis XIV was more than a figurehead. For over half a century, during his whole adult life, he was the actual and working head of the French government. Inheriting the achievement of Richelieu,[1] he made France the strongest country in Europe. Using French money, by bribes or other inducements, he built up a pro-French interest in virtually every country from England to Turkey. His policies and the counter-policies that others adopted against him set the pace of public events, and his methods of government and administration, war and diplomacy, became a model for other rulers to copy. During this time the French language, French thought and literature, French architecture and landscape gardens, French styles in clothes, cooking, and etiquette became the accepted standard for Europe. France seemed to be the land of light, and Louis XIV was called by his fascinated admirers Louis the Great, the *Grand Monarque*, and the Sun King. To the internal achievements of France we shall shortly return.

Internationally, the consuming political question of the last decades of the seventeenth century (at least in western Europe—eastern Europe we shall reserve for the next chapter) was the fate of the still vast possessions of the Spanish crown. Spain was what Turkey was later called, "the sick man of Europe." To its social and economic decline[2] was added hereditary physical deterioration of its rulers. In 1665 the Spanish throne was inherited by Charles II, an unfortunate afflicted by many ills of mind and body, impotent, even imbecile, the pitiable product of generations of inbreeding in the Habsburg house. His rule was irresolute and feeble. It was known from the moment of his accession that he could have no children, and that the Spanish branch of the Habsburg family would die out with his own death. The whole future not only of Spain but of the Spanish Netherlands, the Spanish holdings in Italy, and all Spanish America was therefore in question. Charles II dragged out his miserable days until 1700, the object of jealousy and outright assault during his lifetime, and precipitating a new European war by his death.

Louis XIV, who in his youth married a sister of Charles II, intended to benefit from the debility of his royal brother-in-law. His expansionist policies followed two main lines. One was to push the French borders eastward to the Rhine, annexing the Spanish Netherlands (or Belgium) and the Franche-Comté or Free County of Burgundy, a French-speaking region lying between ducal Burgundy and Switzerland.[3] Such a policy involved the further dismemberment of the Holy

[1] See pp. 136–137.
[2] See pp. 130–131.
[3] See map, pp. 142–143.

Roman Empire. The other line of Louis XIV's ambitions, increasingly clear as time went on, was his hope of obtaining the entire Spanish inheritance for himself. By combining the resources of France and Spain he would make France supreme in Europe, in America, and on the sea. To promote these ends Louis XIV intrigued with the smaller and middle-sized powers of Europe. He took various princes of Germany, and for a time a king of England, into his pay. He supported, with complete disregard of ideology, the republicans in Holland against their prince, and the royalists in England against the parliamentary opposition, knowing that in Holland it was the republicans, and in England the partisans of high monarchy, who were most dependent on foreign assistance.

Were Louis XIV to succeed in his aims, he would create the "universal monarchy" dreaded by diplomats, that is to say, a political situation in which one state might subordinate all others to its will. The technique used against universal monarchy was the balance of power. Universal monarchy had formerly been almost achieved by the Austro-Spanish Habsburgs. The Habsburg supremacy had been blocked mainly by a balance of power headed by France, of which the Thirty Years' War and the Peace of Westphalia were the outstanding triumphs. Now the danger of universal monarchy came from France, and it was against France that the balance of power was directed.

The Idea of the Balance of Power

It will be useful to explain what a balance of power was and was not meant to be. The phrase itself, which came into general use at this time, has been employed ever since in different though related senses. In one sense it refers to a condition of equilibrium, or of even balance, in which power is distributed among many separate states. The second sense arises when this equilibrium is disturbed. If one state preponderates, and if others then form a coalition against it, then the coalition itself may be called the "balance," though it is actually the counterweight by which balance or equilibrium is to be restored. In a third sense one speaks of "holding" or "controlling" the balance of power; here the balance refers to that decisive increment of weight or power which one state may bring to bear. Thus if a state is a vitally necessary member of a coalition, more needed by its allies than it is in need of them, it may be said to "hold" the balance. Or if it belongs to no coalition at all, but tries to keep all other states in a condition of equilibrium, so that its own intervention on one side or the other would be decisive, it may also be said to "hold" the balance, although strictly speaking not participating in the balance at all.

The aim of statesmen pursuing policies of balance of power in the seventeenth and eighteenth centuries was generally to preserve their own independence of action to the utmost. Hence the basic rule was to ally against any state threatening domination. If one state seemed to dictate too much, others would shun alliance with it unless they were willing (from ideological sympathy or other reasons) to become its puppets. They would seek alliance with the other weaker states instead. They would thus create a balance or counterweight, or "restore the balance," against the state whose ascendancy they feared. Another more subtle reason for preferring alliance with the weak rather than with the strong was that in such an alliance each member could feel his own contribution to be necessary and valued, hence could preserve his own dignity and prestige, and by threatening to withdraw his support could win consideration of his own policies. Indeed, the balance of power may be defined as a system in which each state tends to throw its weight where it is most needed, so that its own importance may be enhanced.

The purpose of balance-of-power politics was not to preserve peace, but to preserve the sovereignty and independence of the states of Europe, or the "liberties of Europe," as they were called, against potential aggressors. The system was effective as a means to this end in the seventeenth and eighteenth centuries. Combinations were intricate, and alliances were readily made and unmade to deal with emerging situations. One reason for the effectiveness of the system lay in the great number of states capable of pursuing an independent foreign policy. These included not only the greater and middle-sized states of Austria, Spain, France, England, Holland, Sweden, and Bavaria, but a great number of small independent states, such as Denmark, the German principalities, Portugal after 1640, and Savoy, Venice, Genoa, and Tuscany. States moved easily from one alliance to another, or from one side of the balance to another. They were held back by no ideologies or sympathies, especially after the religious wars subsided, but could freely choose or reject allies, aiming only to protect their own independence or enlarge their own interests. Moreover, owing to the military technology of the day, small states might count as important military partners in an alliance. By controlling a strategic location, like the king of Denmark, or by making a contribution of ships or money, like the Dutch Republic, they might add just enough strength to an alliance to balance and overbalance the opposing great power and its allies.

As the ambitions of Louis XIV became bolder, and as the capacity of Spain to resist them withered away, the prevention of universal monarchy under France depended increasingly on combining the states of Europe into a balance of power against him. The balance against Louis XIV was engineered mainly by the Dutch. The most tireless of his enemies, and the man who did more than any other to checkmate him, was the Dutchman William III, the prince of Orange, who in his later years was king of England and Scotland as well.

Let us, after first surveying the Dutch in the seventeenth century, turn to the British Isles, where a momentous conflict occurred between Parliament and king. We shall then examine the French absolute monarchy under Louis XIV and conclude the present chapter with the wars of Louis XIV, particularly the War of the Spanish Succession, in which the great international issues of the time conflicted and were resolved.

18. THE DUTCH REPUBLIC

Dutch Civilization and Government

The ambassadors of kings, strolling beside a canal at The Hague, might on occasion observe a number of burghers in plain black garments step out of a boat and proceed to make a meal of cheese and herring on the lawn, and they would recognize in these portly figures Their High Mightinesses the Estates General of the United Provinces, as the Dutch government was known in the diplomatic language of the day. Though noblemen lived in the country, the Dutch were the most bourgeois of all peoples. They were not the only republicans in Europe, since the Swiss cantons, Venice, Genoa, and even England for a few years were republics, but of all republics the United Provinces was by far the most wealthy, the most flourishing, and the most preeminently civilized.

The Dutch acquired a nationality of their own in the long struggle against Spain, and with it a pride in their own freedom and independence. In the later phases of the war with Spain, notably during the Thirty Years' War, they were able to rely more on their wealth, ready money, shipping, and diplomacy than on actual fighting, so that during the whole seventeenth century they enjoyed a degree of comfort, and of intellectual, artistic, and commercial achievement unexcelled in Europe. The classic Dutch poets and dramatists wrote at this time, making a literary language of what had formerly been a dialect of Low German. Hugo Grotius produced, in his *Law of War and Peace*, a pioneering treatise on international law. Baruch Spinoza, of a family of refugee Portuguese Jews, quietly turned out works of philosophy, examining the fundamentals of reality, of human conduct, and of church and state. Spinoza made his living by grinding lenses; there were many other lens grinders in Holland; some of them developed the microscope, and some of these, in turn—Leeuwenhoek, Swammerdam, and others —peering through their microscopes and beholding for the first time the world of microscopic life, became founders of modern biological science. The greatest Dutch scientist was Christian Huyghens (1629–1695), who worked mainly in physics and mathematics; he improved the telescope (a Dutch invention), made clocks move with pendulums, discovered the rings of Saturn, and launched the wave theory of light. A less famous writer, Balthasar Bekker, in his *World Bewitched* (1691) delivered a decisive blow against the expiring superstition of witchcraft.

But the most eternally fresh of the Dutch creations, suffering from no barrier of time or language, were the superb canvases of the painters. Frans Hals produced bluff portraits of the common people. Jan Vermeer threw a spell of magic and quiet dignity over men, and especially women, of the burgher class. Rembrandt conveyed the mystery of human consciousness itself. In Rembrandt's *Masters of the Cloth Hall* (see illustration) we face a group of men who seem about to speak from the canvas, inclined slightly forward, as intent on their business as judges on the proceedings in a courtroom; men of the kind who conducted the affairs of Holland, in both commerce and government; intelligent men, calculating but not cunning, honest but determined to drive a hard bargain, stern rather than mild; and the sober black cloaks, with the clean white collars, set against the carved woodwork and rich table covering of the Cloth Hall, seem to suggest that personal vanity must yield to collective undertakings, and personal simplicity be maintained in the midst of material opulence. And in Vermeer's *Geographer*, painted in 1669 (also reproduced in this book—see p. 109), there appears not only an immaculately scrubbed and dusted Dutch interior, but something of a symbol of the modern world in its youth—the pale northern sunlight streaming through the window, the globe and the map, the dividers in the scholar's right hand, instrument of science and mathematics, the tapestry flung over the table (or is it an Oriental rug brought from the East?), the head lifted in thought and eyes resting on an invisible world of fresh discoveries and opening horizons.

In religion, after initial disputes, the Dutch Republic adopted toleration. Early in the seventeenth century the Dutch Calvinists divided. One group favored a modification of Calvinism, with a toning down of the doctrine of absolute and unconditional predestination; it drew its main support from the comfortable

THE MASTERS OF THE CLOTH HALL
by Rembrandt van Rijn (Dutch, 1606–1669)

This painting was done on commission for the Cloth Hall of Amsterdam, that is, the guild
of "clothiers" or "drapers" such as are described on pp. 114–115 in connection with the
Commercial Revolution. The men shown are the heads of the guild. Over a period of forty
years Rembrandt produced some 600 paintings, in addition to etchings and drawings,
in which he conveyed all types of experience, from the commercial practicality of the
present group to the deeply mystical and religious. The vitality of Dutch culture in the
seventeenth century is shown also in the pictures on pp. 109, 111, and 282. Courtesy of the
Rijksmuseum, Amsterdam.

burghers and its doctrines from a theologian of Leyden named Arminius. To deal with this Arminian heresy a great international Calvinist synod met in 1618 at Dordrecht in Holland. Of the hundred delegates almost a third came from Scotland, England, Germany, Switzerland, and France. The orthodox party won out at the synod; one old man was put to death; the philosopher Grotius fled to France for safety. But beginning in 1632 the Arminians were tolerated. Rights were granted to the large Catholic minority. Jews had long been welcomed in the republic; and Christian sects despised everywhere else, such as the Mennonites, found a refuge in it. Although none of these people had as many political or economic rights as the Calvinists, the resulting mixture stimulated both the intellectual life and the commercial enterprise of the country.

The Dutch as early as 1600 had 10,000 ships, and throughout the seventeenth century they owned most of the shipping of northern Europe. They were the carriers between Spain, France, England, and the Baltic. Much coastwise shipping between ports of France was in Dutch hands. They settled in Bordeaux to buy wines, lent money to vintners, and soon owned many vineyards in France itself. They sailed on every sea. They explored the waters around Spitzbergen and almost monopolized Arctic whaling. They entered the Pacific by way of South America, where they rounded Cape Horn and named it after Hoorn in Holland. Organized in the East India Company of 1602, their merchants increasingly replaced the Portuguese in India and the Far East. In Java, in 1619, they founded the city of Batavia—the Latin name for Holland. (It is now called Jakarta.) Finding some Englishmen in 1623 at Amboina, in the midst of the Spice Islands, they tortured and killed them. The English did not return until the days of Napoleon. Not long after 1600 the Dutch reached Japan. But the Japanese, fearing the political consequences of Christian penetration, in 1641 expelled all other Europeans and confined the Dutch to limited operations on an island near Nagasaki. The Dutch remained for over two centuries the sole link of the West with Japan. In 1612 the Dutch founded their first settlement on Manhattan Island, and in 1621 they established a Dutch West India Company to exploit the loosely held riches of Spanish and Portuguese America. They founded colonies at Pernambuco and Bahia in Brazil (lost soon thereafter) and at Caracas, Curaçao, and in Guiana in the Caribbean. In 1652 the Dutch captured the Cape of Good Hope in South Africa from the Portuguese. Dutch settlers soon appeared—men, women, and children. From these settlers and from French Huguenots and others have come the modern Afrikaner people, whose language and religion still reflect their mainly Dutch origins.

In 1609 the Dutch founded the Bank of Amsterdam. European money was a chaos; coins were minted not only by great monarchs but by small states and cities in Germany and Italy, and even by private persons. In addition, under inflationary pressures, kings and others habitually debased their coins by adding more alloy, while leaving the old coins in circulation along with the new. Anyone handling money thus accumulated a miscellany of uncertain value. The Bank of Amsterdam accepted deposits of such mixed money from all persons and from all countries, assessed the gold and silver content, and, at rates of exchange fixed by itself, allowed depositors to withdraw equivalent values in gold florins minted by the Bank of Amsterdam. These were of known and unchanging weight and purity. They thus became an internationally sought money, an international measure of value, acceptable everywhere. Depositors were also allowed to draw checks against their accounts. These conveniences, plus a safety of deposits guaranteed by the Dutch government, attracted capital from all quarters and made possible loans for a wide range of purposes. Amsterdam remained the financial center of Europe until the French Revolution.

Under their republican government the Dutch enjoyed great freedom, but it can hardly be said that their form of government met all the requirements of a state. Their High Mightinesses (the *Hooge Moogende*), who made up the Estates General, were only delegates from their respective seven provinces and could act only as the estates of the provinces gave instructions. The seven provinces, like the states of the Holy Roman Empire in which they had originated, were jealous of their own independence. Each province had, as its executive, an elected stadholder, but there was no stadholder for the United Provinces as a whole. This difficulty was overcome by the fact that most of the various provinces usually elected the same man as stadholder. The stadholder in most provinces was usually the head of the house of Orange, which since the days of William the Silent and the wars for independence had enjoyed exceptional prestige in the republic. The prince of Orange, apart from being stadholder, was simply one of the feudal noblemen of the country. But the noble class had been outdistanced by the commercial, and affairs were generally managed by the burghers. The burghers, intent on making money and enjoying comfort, rarely worried over military questions and hated taxes.

Politics in the Dutch Republic was a seesaw between the burghers, pacifistic and absorbed with business, and the princes of Orange, to whom the country owed most of its military security. When foreigners threatened invasion, the power of the stadholder increased. When all was calm, the stadholder could do little. The Peace of Westphalia produced a mood of confidence in the burghers, followed by a constitutional crisis, in the course of which the stadholder William II died, in 1650. No new stadholder was elected for twenty-two years. The burgher, civilian, and decentralizing tendencies prevailed.

In 1650, eight days after his father's death, was born the third William of the house of Orange, seemingly fated never to be stadholder and to pass his life as a private nobleman on his own estates. William III grew up to be a grave and reserved young man, small and rather stocky, with thin compressed lips and a determined spirit. He learned to speak Dutch, German, English, and French with equal facility, and to understand Italian, Spanish, and Latin. He observed the requirements of his religion, which was Dutch Calvinism, with sober regularity. He had a strong dislike, Dutch and Calvinistic, for everything magnificent or pompous; he lived plainly, hated flattery, and took no pleasure in social conversation. In these respects he was the opposite of his life-long enemy the Sun King, whom he resembled only in his diligent preoccupation with affairs. In 1677 he married the king of England's niece, Mary.

Foreign Affairs: Conflict with the English and French

Meanwhile matters were not going favorably for the Dutch Republic. In 1651 the revolutionary government then ruling England passed a Navigation Act. This act may be considered the first of a long series of political measures by which the British colonial empire was built up. It was aimed against the Dutch carrying trade. It provided that goods imported into England and its dependencies must be brought in English ships, or in ships belonging to the country exporting the goods.

Since the Dutch were too small a people to be great producers and exporters themselves, and lived largely by carrying the goods of others, they saw in the new English policy a threat to their economic existence. The English likewise, claiming sovereignty of the "narrow seas," demanded that Dutch ships salute the English flag in the Channel. Three wars between the Dutch and English followed, running with interruptions from 1652 to 1674 and generally indecisive, though the English annexed New York.

While thus assaulted at sea by the English, the Dutch were menaced on land by the French. Louis XIV made his first aggressive move in 1667, claiming the Spanish Netherlands and Franche-Comté by alleging certain rights of his Spanish wife, and overrunning the Spanish Netherlands with his army. The Dutch, to whom the Spanish Netherlands were a buffer against France, set into motion the mechanism of the balance of power. Dropping temporarily their disputes with the English, they allied with them instead; and since they were able also to secure the adherence of Sweden, the resulting Triple Alliance was sufficient to give pause to Louis XIV, who withdrew from the Spanish Netherlands. But in 1672 Louis XIV again rapidly crossed the Spanish Netherlands, attacked with forces five times as large as the Dutch, and occupied three of the seven Dutch provinces.

A popular clamor now arose among the Dutch for William of Orange, demanding that the young prince, who was now twenty-two years of age, be installed in the old office of stadholder, in which his ancestors had defended them against Spain. He was duly elected stadholder in six provinces. In 1673 these six provinces voted to make the stadholderate hereditary in the house of Orange. William, during his whole tenure or "reign" in the Netherlands, attempted to centralize and consolidate his government, put down the feudal liberties of the provinces, and free himself from constitutional checks, moving generally in the direction of absolute monarchy, which by the tests of power and under French example was the successful form of government at the time. He was unable, however, to go far in this course, and the United Provinces remained a decentralized patrician republic until 1795. Meanwhile, to stave off the immediate menace of Louis XIV, William resorted to a new manipulation of the balance of power. He formed an alliance this time with the minor powers of Denmark and Brandenburg (the German margraviate around Berlin) and with the Austrian and Spanish Habsburgs. Nothing could indicate more clearly the new balance of power precipitated by the rise of France than this coming over of the Dutch to the Habsburg side. The alliance was successful to the extent at least of wearying Louis XIV of the war. Peace was signed in 1678 (treaty of Nimwegen), but only at the expense of Spain and the Holy Roman Empire, from which Louis XIV took the long coveted Franche-Comté, together with another batch of towns in Flanders. The Dutch preserved their territory intact.

In the next ten years came the great windfall of William's life. In 1689 he became king of England. He was now able to bring the British Isles into his perpetual combinations against France. Since the real impact of France was yet to be felt, and the real bid of Louis XIV for universal monarchy was yet to be made, and since the English at this time were rapidly gaining in strength, the entrance of England was a decisive addition to the balance formed against French expansion. In this way the constitutional troubles of England, by bringing a determined Dutchman to the English throne, entered into the general stream of European affairs and helped to assure that western Europe and its overseas offshoots should not be dominated totally by France.

19. BRITAIN: THE PURITAN REVOLUTION

After the defeat of the Spanish Armada and recession of the Spanish threat the English were for a time less closely involved with the affairs of the Continent. They played no significant part in the Thirty Years' War, and were almost the only European people, west of Poland, who were not represented at the Congress of Westphalia. At the time of the Westphalia negotiations in the 1640s they were in fact engaged in a civil war of their own. This English civil war was a milder variant of the Wars of Religion which desolated France, Germany, and the Netherlands. It was fought not between Protestants and Catholics as on the Continent, but between the more extreme or Calvinistic Protestants called Puritans and the more moderate Protestants, or Anglicans, adhering to the established Church of England. As in the wars on the Continent, religious differences were mixed indistinguishably with political and constitutional issues. As the Huguenots represented to some extent feudal rebelliousness against the French monarchy, as German Protestants fought for states' rights against imperial centralization, and the Calvinists of the Netherlands for provincial liberties against the king of Spain, so the Puritans asserted the rights of Parliament against the mounting claims of royalty in England.

The civil war in England was relatively so mild that England itself can be said to have escaped the horrors of the Wars of Religion. The same was not true of the British Isles as a whole. After 1603 the kingdoms of England and Scotland, while otherwise separate, were ruled by the same king; the kingdom of Ireland remained, as before, a dependency of the English crown. Between England and Presbyterian Scotland there was constant friction, but the worst trouble was between England and Catholic Ireland, which was the scene of religious warfare as savage as that on the Continent.

England in the Seventeenth Century

For the English the seventeenth century was an age of great achievement, during which they made their debut as one of the chief peoples of modern Europe. In 1600 only four or five million persons, in England and Lowland Scotland, spoke the English language. The number did not rise rapidly for another century and a half. But the population began to spread. Religious discontents, reinforced by economic pressures, led to considerable emigration. Twenty thousand Puritans settled in New England between 1630 and 1640, and about the same number went to Barbados and other West India islands during the same years. A third stream, again roughly of the same size, but made up mainly of Scottish Presbyterians, settled in northern Ireland under government auspices, driving away or expropriating the native Celts. English Catholics were allowed by the home government to settle in Maryland. A great many Anglicans went to Virginia in the mid-century, adding to the small settlement made at Jamestown in 1607. Except for the movement to northern Ireland, called the "plantation of Ulster," these migrations took place without much attention on the part of the government, through private initiative organized in commercial companies. After the middle of the century the government began deliberately to build an empire. New York was conquered from the Dutch, Jamaica from the Spanish, and Pennsylvania and the Carolinas were established. All the Thirteen Colonies except Georgia were founded before 1700, and there were at that time perhaps half a million people in

British North America. Relative to the home population, it was as if the United States should in three generations build up a distant colonial appendage with fifteen million inhabitants.

The English also, like the Dutch, French, and Spanish at the time, were creating their national culture. Throughout western Europe the national languages, encroaching upon international Latin on the one hand and local dialects on the other, were becoming adequate vehicles for the expression of thought and feeling. Shakespeare and Milton projected their mighty conceptions with overwhelming power of words, not since equaled in English or in any other tongue. The English classical literature, rugged in form but deep in content, vigorous yet subtle in insight, majestic, abundant, and sonorous in expression, was almost the reverse of French classical writing, with its virtues of order, economy, propriety, and graceful precision. The English could never thereafter quite yield to French standards, nor be dazzled or dumbfounded, as some peoples were, by the cultural glories of the Age of Louis XIV. There were no painters at all comparable to those on the Continent, but in music it was the age of Campion and Purcell, and in architecture the century closed with the great buildings of Christopher Wren.

Economically the English were enterprising and affluent, though in 1600 far outdistanced by the Dutch. They had a larger and more productive country than the Dutch, and were therefore not as limited to purely mercantile and seafaring occupations. Coal was mined around Newcastle, and was increasingly used, but was not yet a leading source of English wealth. The great industry was the growing of sheep and manufacture of woolens, which were the main export. Weaving was done to a large extent in the country, under the putting-out system, and organized by merchants according to the methods of commercial capitalism.[4] Since 1553 the English had traded with Russia by way of the White Sea; they were increasingly active in the Baltic and eastern Mediterranean; and with the founding of the East India Company, in 1600, they competed with the Dutch in assaulting the old Portuguese monopoly in India and the Far East. But profitable as such overseas operations were, the main wealth of England was still in the land. The richest men were not merchants but landlords, and the landed aristocracy formed the richest class.

Background to the Civil War: Parliament and the Stuart Kings

In England, as elsewhere in the seventeenth century, the kings clashed with their old medieval representative bodies. In England the old body, Parliament, won out against the king. But this was not the unique feature in the English development. In Germany the estates of the Holy Roman Empire triumphed against the emperor, and much the same thing, as will be seen, occurred in Poland. But on the Continent the triumph of the old representative bodies generally meant political dissolution or even anarchy. Successful governments were generally those in which kingly powers increased; this was the strong tendency of the time, evident even in the Dutch Republic after 1672 under William of Orange. The unique thing about England was that Parliament, in defeating the king, arrived at a workable form of government. Government remained strong but came under parliamentary control. This determined the character of modern England and launched into

[4] See p. 115.

the history of Europe and of the world the great movement of liberalism and representative institutions.

What happened was somewhat as follows. In 1603, on the death of Queen Elizabeth, the English crown was inherited by the son of Mary Stuart, James VI of Scotland, who became king of England also, taking there the title of James I. James was a philosopher of royal absolutism. He had even written a book on the subject, *The True Law of Free Monarchy.* By a "free" monarchy James meant a monarchy free from control by Parliament, churchmen, or laws and customs of the past. It was a monarchy in which the king, as father to his people, looked after their welfare as he saw fit, standing above all parties, private interests, and pressure groups. He even declared that kings drew their authority from God, and were responsible to God alone. The doctrine which he represented is known as the divine right of kings.[5]

Probably any ruler succeeding Elizabeth would have had trouble with Parliament, which had shown signs of restlessness in the last years of her reign, but had deferred to her as an aging woman and a national symbol. She had maintained peace within the country and fought off the Spaniards, but these very accomplishments persuaded many people that they could safely bring their grievances into the open. James I was a foreigner, a Scot, who lacked the touch for dealing with the English, and who was moreover a royal pedant, the "wisest fool in Christendom," as he was uncharitably called. Not content with the actualities of control, as Elizabeth had been, he read the Parliament tiresome lectures on the royal rights. He also was in constant need of money. The wars against Spain had left a considerable debt. James was far from economical, and, in any case, in an age of rising prices, he could not live within the fixed and customary revenues of the English crown. These were of a medieval character, increasingly quaint under the new conditions—rights of wardship and marriage, escheats, franc-fiefs and fees for the distraint of knighthood, together with "tunnage and poundage," or rights given to the king by Parliament at his accession (and normally unchanged during his reign) to collect specified duties on exports and imports, according to quantity, not value, and hence not rising in proportion to prices.

Neither to James I nor to his son Charles I, who succeeded him in 1625, would Parliament grant adequate revenue, because it distrusted them both. Many members of Parliament were Puritans, dissatisfied with the organization and doctrine of the Church of England.[6] Elizabeth had tried to hush up religious troubles, but James threatened to "harry the Puritans out of the land," and Charles supported the Anglican hierarchy which, under Archbishop Laud, sought to enforce religious conformity. Many members of Parliament were also lawyers, who feared that the common law of England, the historic or customary law, was in danger. They disliked the prerogative courts, the Star Chamber set up by Henry VII, the High Commission set up by Elizabeth.[7] They heard with trepidation the modern doctrine that the sovereign king could make laws and decide cases at his own discretion.[8] Last but not least, practically all members of Parliament were property owners. Landowners, supported by the merchants, feared that if the king suc-

[5] See p. 180.
[6] See pp. 79–81.
[7] See pp. 68–69, 90.
[8] See p. 68.

ceeded in raising taxes on his own authority their wealth would be insecure. Hence there were strong grounds for resistance.

In England the Parliament was so organized as to make resistance effective.[9] There was only one Parliament for the whole country. There were no provincial or local estates, as in the Dutch Republic, Spain, France, Germany, and Poland. Hence all parliamentary opposition was concentrated in one place. In this one place, the one and only Parliament, there were only two houses, the House of Lords and the House of Commons. The landed interest dominated in both houses, the noblemen in the Lords and the gentry in the Commons. In the Commons the gentry, who formed the bulk of the aristocracy, mixed with representatives of the merchants and the towns. Indeed the towns frequently chose country gentlemen to represent them. Hence the houses of Parliament did not accentuate, as did the estates on the Continent, the class division within the country. Nor was the church present in Parliament as a separate force. Before Henry VIII's break with Rome the bishops and abbots together had formed a large majority in the House of Lords. Now there were no abbots left, for there were no monasteries. The House of Lords was now predominantly secular; in the first Parliament of James I there were eighty-two lay peers and twenty-six bishops. The great landowners had captured the House of Lords. The smaller landowners of the Commons had been enriched by receiving former monastic lands and had prospered by raising wool. The merchants had likewise grown up under mercantilistic protection. Parliament was strong not only in organization but in the social interests and wealth that it represented. No king could long govern against its will.

In 1629 king and Parliament came to a deadlock. Charles I attempted to rule without Parliament, which could legally meet only at the royal summons. He intended to give England a good and efficient government. Had he succeeded, the course of English constitutional development would have paralleled that of France. But by certain reforms in Ireland he antagonized the English landlords who had interests in that country. By supporting the High Anglicans he made enemies of the Puritans. By attempting to modernize the navy with funds raised without parliamentary consent (called "ship money") he alarmed all property owners, whose opposition was typified in the famous lawsuit of a country gentleman, John Hampden, in 1637.

The ship-money case illustrates the best arguments of both sides. It was the old custom in England for coastal towns to provide ships for the king's service in time of war. More recently, these coastal towns had provided money instead. Charles I wished to maintain a navy in time of peace and to have ship money paid by the country as a whole, including the inland counties. In the old or medieval view it was the function of the towns which were directly affected to maintain a fleet. In the new view, sponsored by the king, the whole nation was the unit on which a navy should be based. The country gentlemen whom Parliament mainly represented, and most of whom lived in inland counties, had less interest in the navy, and in any case were unwilling to pay for it unless they could control the foreign policies for which a navy might be used. The parliamentary class represented the idea, derived from the Middle Ages, that taxes should be authorized by Parliament. The king represented the newer ideas of monarchy that were developing on the Continent. John Hampden lost his case in court, but he won the sympathy of

---

[9] See pp. 35–36.

the politically significant classes of the country. Until the king could govern with the confidence of Parliament, or until Parliament itself was willing, not merely to keep down taxes, but to assume the responsibilities of government under modern conditions, neither a navy nor any effectual government could be maintained.

The Scots were the first to rebel. In 1637 they rioted in Edinburgh against attempts to impose the Anglican religion in Scotland. Charles, to raise funds to put down the Scottish rebellion, convoked the English Parliament in 1640, for the first time in eleven years. When it proved hostile to him he dissolved it and called for new elections. The same men were returned. The resulting body, since it sat theoretically for twenty years without new elections, from 1640 to 1660, is known historically as the Long Parliament. Its principal leaders—men like John Hampden, John Pym, and Oliver Cromwell—were small or moderately well-to-do landowning gentry. The merchant class, while furnishing no leaders, lent its support.

The Long Parliament, far from assisting the king against the Scots, used the Scottish rebellion as a means of pressing its own demands. These were revolutionary from the outset. Parliament insisted that the chief royal advisers be not merely removed but impeached and put to death. It abolished the Star Chamber and the High Commission. The most extreme Calvinist element, the "root and branch" men or "radicals," drove through a bill for the abolition of bishops, revolutionizing the Anglican church. In 1642 Parliament and king came to open war, the king drawing followers mainly from the north and west, the Parliament from the commercially and agriculturally more advanced counties of the south and east. During the war, as the price of support from the Scottish army, Parliament adopted the Solemn League and Covenant. This prescribed that religion in England, Scotland, and Ireland should be made uniform "according to the word of God and the example of the best reformed churches." Thus Presbyterianism became the established legal religion of the three kingdoms.

The Emergence of Cromwell

The parliamentary forces, called Roundheads from the close haircuts favored by Puritans, gradually defeated the royalists. The wars brought a hitherto unknown gentleman named Oliver Cromwell to the foreground. A devout Puritan, he organized a new and more effective military force, the Ironsides, in which extreme Protestant exaltation provided the basis for morale, discipline, and the will to fight. Parliament had no sooner defeated the king than it fell out with its own army. The army, in which a more popular class was represented than in the Parliament, became the center of advanced democratic ideas. Many of the soldiers objected to Presbyterianism as much as to Anglicanism. They favored a free toleration for all "godly" forms of religion, with no superior church organization above local groups of like-minded spirits.

Cromwell concluded that the defeated king, Charles I, could not be trusted, that "ungodly" persons of all kinds put their hopes in him (what later ages would call counterrevolution), and that he must be put to death. Since Parliament hesitated, Cromwell with the support of the army broke Parliament up. The Long Parliament, having started in 1640 with some 500 members, had sunk by 1649 to about 150 (for this revolution, like others, was pushed through by a minority); of these Cromwell now drove out almost 100, leaving a Rump of 50 or 60. This operation was called Pride's Purge, after the Colonel Pride who commanded the soldiers by whom Parliament was intimidated; and in subsequent revolutions such excisions have been commonly known as purges, and the residues, sometimes, as rumps. The Rump put King Charles to death on the scaffold in 1649.

England, or rather the whole British Isles, was now declared a republic. It was named the Commonwealth. Cromwell tried to govern as best he could. Religious toleration was decreed except for Unitarians and atheists on the one hand, and except for Roman Catholics and the most obstinate Anglicans on the other—a considerable exception. Cromwell had to subdue both Scotland and Ireland by force. In Scotland the execution of the king, violating the ancient national Scottish monarchy of the Stuarts, had swung the country back into the royalist camp. Cromwell crushed the Scots in 1650. Meanwhile the Protestant and Calvinist fury swept over Ireland. A massacre of newly settled Protestants in Ulster in 1641 had left bitter memories which were now avenged. The Irish garrisons of Drogheda and Wexford were defeated and massacred. Thousands of Catholics were killed; priests were put to the sword, and women and small children dispatched in cold blood. Where formerly, in the "plantation" of Ulster, a whole Protestant population had been settled in northern Ireland, bodily replacing the native Irish, now Protestant landlords were scattered over the country as a whole, replacing the Catholic landlords and retaining the Catholic peasantry as their tenants. What now happened in Ireland was a close parallel to what had happened thirty years before in Bohemia, except that Protestant and Catholic roles were reversed.[10] For the Irish, as for the Czechs, the native religion and clergy were driven underground, a foreign and detested church was established, and a new and foreign landed aristocracy, originally recruited in large measure from military adventurers, was settled upon the country, in which, as soon as it assured the payment of its rents, it soon ceased to reside.

In England itself Cromwell ruled with great difficulty. In external affairs his regime was successful enough, for he not only completed the subjugation of Ireland, but in the Navigation Act of 1651[11] he opened the English attack on the Dutch maritime supremacy, and in a war with Spain, in which the English acquired Jamaica, he opened the English bidding for the inheritance of the Spanish Habsburgs. But he failed to gain the support of a majority of the English. The Puritan Revolution, like others, produced its extremists. It failed to satisfy the most ardent and could not win over the truly conservative, so that Cromwell found himself reluctantly more autocratic, and more alone.

A party arose called the Levellers, who were in fact what later times would call advanced political democrats. They were numerous in the Puritan army, though their chief spokesman, John Lilburne, was a civilian. Appealing to natural rights and to the rights of Englishmen, they asked for a nearly universal manhood suffrage, equality of representation, a written constitution, and subordination of Parliament to a reformed body of voters. They thus anticipated many ideas of the American and French revolutions over a century later. There were others in whom religious and social radicalism were indistinguishably mixed. George Fox, going beyond Calvinism or Presbyterianism, founded the Society of Friends, or "Quakers," who caused consternation by rejecting various social amenities in the name of the Spirit. A more ephemeral group, the "Diggers," proceeded to occupy and cultivate common lands, or lands privately owned, in a general repudiation

[10] See pp. 139–140, 218.
[11] See pp. 163–164.

of property. The Fifth Monarchy Men were a millennial group who felt that the end of the world was at hand. They were so called from their belief, as they read the Bible, that history had seen four empires, those of Assyria, Persia, Alexander, and Caesar; and that the existing world was still "Caesar's" but would soon give way to the fifth monarchy, of Christ, in which justice would at last rule.

Cromwell opposed such movements, by which all established persons in society felt threatened. As a regicide and a Puritan, however, he could not turn to the royalist and Anglican interests. Unable to agree even with the Rump, he abolished it also in 1653, and thereafter vainly attempted to govern, as Lord Protector, through representative bodies devised by himself and his followers, under a written constitution, the Instrument of Government. Actually, he was driven to place England under military rule, the regime of the "major generals." These officials, each in his district, repressed malcontents, vagabonds, and "bandits," closed ale houses, and prohibited cockfighting, in a mixture of moral puritanism and political dictatorship. Cromwell died in 1658; and his son was unable to maintain the Protectorate. Two years later, with all but universal assent, royalty was restored. Charles II, son of the dead Charles I, became king of England and of Scotland.

Cromwell, by beheading a king and keeping his successor off the throne for eleven years, had left a lesson which was not forgotten. Though he favored constitutional and parliamentary government and had granted a measure of religious toleration, he had in fact ruled as a dictator in behalf of a stern Puritan minority. The English people now began to blot from their memories the fact that they had ever had a real revolution. The fervid dream of a "godly" England was dissipated forever. What was remembered was a nightmare of standing armies and major generals, of grim Puritans and overwrought religious enthusiasts. The English lower classes ceased to have any political consciousness for over a century, except in sporadic rioting over food shortages or outbursts against the dangers of "popery." Democratic ideas were generally rejected as "levelling." They were generally abandoned in England after 1660 or were cherished by obscure individuals who could not make themselves heard. Such ideas, indeed, had a more continuous history in the English colonies in America, where some leaders of the discredited revolution took refuge.

20. BRITAIN: THE TRIUMPH OF PARLIAMENT

The Restoration, 1660–1688: The Later Stuarts

What was restored in 1660 was not only the monarchy, in the person of Charles II, but also the Church of England and the Parliament. Everything, legally, was supposed to be as it had been in 1640. The difference was that Charles II, knowing the fate of his father, was careful not to provoke Parliament to extremes, and that the classes represented in Parliament, frightened by the disturbances of the past twenty years, were for some time more warmly loyal to the king than they had been before 1640 and more willing to uphold the established church.

Parliament during the Restoration enacted some far-reaching legislation. It changed the legal basis of land tenure, abolishing certain old feudal payments owed by landholders to the king. The possession of land thus came to resemble private property of modern type, and the landowning class became more definitely a propertied aristocracy. In place of the feudal dues to the king, which had been automatically payable, Parliament arranged for the king to receive income in the form of taxation, which Parliament could raise or reduce in amount. This gave a new power to Parliament and a new flexibility to government. The aristocracy, in short, cleared their property of customary restrictions and obligations and at the same time undertook to support the state by imposing taxes on themselves. The English aristocracy proved more willing than the corresponding classes on the Continent to pay a large share of the expenses of government. Its reward was that, for a century and a half, it virtually ran the government to the exclusion of everyone else. Landowners in this period directed not only national affairs through Parliament, but also local affairs as justices of the peace. The justices, drawn from the gentry of each county, decided small lawsuits, punished misdemeanors, and supervised the parish officials charged with poor relief and care of the roads. The regime of the landlord-justices came to be called the "squirearchy."

Other classes drew less immediate advantage from the Restoration. The Navigation Act of 1651 was renewed and even added to, so that commercial, shipping, and manufacturing interests were well protected. But in other ways the landed classes now in power showed themselves unsympathetic to the business classes of the towns. Many people in the towns were Dissenters, of the element formerly called Puritan, and now refusing to accept the restored Church of England. Parliament excluded Dissenters from the town "corporations," or governing bodies, forbade any dissenting clergymen to teach school or come within five miles of an incorporated town, and prohibited all religious meetings, called "conventicles," not held according to the forms and by the authority of the Church of England. The effect was that many middle-class townspeople found it difficult or impossible to follow their preferred religion, to obtain an education for their children, either elementary or advanced (for Oxford and Cambridge were a part of the established church), to take part in local affairs through the town corporations, or to sit in the House of Commons, since the corporations in many cases chose the burgesses who represented the towns. The lowest classes, the very poor, were discouraged by the same laws from following sectarian and visionary preachers. Another enactment fell upon them alone, the Act of Settlement of 1662, which decentralized the administration of the Poor Law, making each parish responsible only for its own paupers. Poor people, who were very numerous, were condemned to remain in the parishes where they lived. A large section of the English population was immobilized.

But it was not long after the Restoration that Parliament and king were again at odds. The issue was again religion. There was at this time a tendency throughout Europe for Protestants to return voluntarily to Roman Catholicism, a tendency naturally dreaded by the Protestant churches. It was most conspicuously illustrated when the daughter of Gustavus Adolphus himself, Queen Christina of Sweden, to the consternation of the Protestant world, abdicated her throne and was received into the Roman church. In England the national feeling was excitedly anti-Catholic. No measures were more popular than those against "popery"; and the squires in Parliament, stiffly loyal to the Church of England, dreaded papists even more than Dissenters. The king, Charles II, was personally inclined to Catholicism. He admired the magnificent monarchy of Louis XIV, which he would have liked to duplicate, so far as possible, in England. At odds with his Parliament,

Charles II made overtures to Louis XIV. The secret treaty of Dover of 1670 was the outcome. Charles thereby agreed to join Louis XIV in his expected war against the Dutch; and Louis agreed to pay the king of England three million livres a year during the war. He hoped also that Charles II would soon find it opportune to rejoin the Roman church.

While these arrangements were unknown in detail in England, it was known that Charles II was well disposed to the French and to Roman Catholicism. England went to war again with the Dutch. The king's brother and heir, James, Duke of York, publicly announced his conversion to Rome. Charles II, in a "declaration of indulgence," announced the nonenforcement of laws against Dissenters. The king declared that he favored general toleration, but it was rightly feared that his real aim was to promote Roman Catholicism in England, and that his policy might be the opening wedge for the Counter Reformation, which had already swept Protestantism out of Bohemia and Poland and was at this very moment menacing it in France. Parliament retorted in 1673 by passing the Test Act, which required all officeholders to take communion in the Church of England. The Test Act renewed the legislation against Dissenters and also made it impossible for Catholics to serve in the government or in the army and navy. The Test Act remained on the statute books until 1828.

While Charles' pro-French and pro-Catholic policies were extremely unpopular, both among the country gentry who disliked Frenchmen from prejudice, and the merchants who found in them increasingly pressing competitors, still the situation might not have come to a head except for the avowed Catholicism and French orientation of Charles' brother James, due to be the next king since Charles had no legitimate children. A strong movement developed in Parliament to exclude James by law from the throne. The exclusionists—and those generally who were most suspicious of the king, Catholics, and Frenchmen—received the nickname of Whigs. The king's supporters were popularly called Tories. The Whigs, while backed by the middle class and merchants of London, drew their main strength from the upper aristocracy, especially certain great noblemen who might expect, if the king's power were weakened, to play a prominent part in ruling the country themselves. The Tories were the party of the lesser aristocracy and gentry, those who were suspicious of the "moneyed interest" of London, and felt a strong loyalty to church and king. These two parties became permanently established in English public life. But all the Whigs and Tories together, at this time, did not number more than a few thousand persons.

The Revolution of 1688

James II, despite Whig vexation, became king in 1685. He soon antagonized even the Tories. The Tories were strong Anglicans or Church of England men. As landowners they appointed most of the parish clergy, who imparted Tory sentiments to the rural population, and from their ranks were drawn the bishops, archdeacons, university functionaries, and other higher personnel of the church. The laws keeping Dissenters and Catholics from office had given Anglicans a monopoly in local and national government and in the army and navy. James II acted as if there were no Test Act, claiming the right to suspend its operation in individual cases, and appointed a good many Catholics to influential and lucrative positions. He offered a program, as his brother had done, of general religious toleration, to allow Protestant Dissenters as well as Roman Catholics to participate in public life. Such a program, whether frankly meant as a secularizing of politics or indirectly intended as favoritism to Catholics, was equally repugnant to the Church of England. Seven bishops refused to endorse it. They were prosecuted for disobedience to the king but were acquitted by the jury. James, by these actions, violated the liberties of the established church, threatened the Anglican monopoly of church and state, and aroused the popular terrors of "popery." He was also forced to take the position philosophically set forth by his grandfather James I, that a king of England could make and unmake the law by his own will. The Tories joined the Whigs in opposition. In 1688, a son was born to James II and baptized into the Catholic faith. The prospect now opened up of an indefinite line of Catholic rulers in England. Leading men of both parties thereupon abandoned James II. They offered the throne to his grown daughter Mary, born and brought up a Protestant before her father's conversion to Rome.

Mary was the wife of William of Orange. William, it will be recalled, had spent his adult life in blocking the ambitions of the king of France, who, it should be recalled likewise, threatened Europe with a "universal monarchy" by absorbing or inheriting the world of Spain. To William III it would be a mere distraction to be husband to a queen of England, or even to be king in his own name, unless England could be brought to serve his own purposes. He was immutably Dutch; his purpose was to save Holland and hence to ruin Louis XIV. His chief interest in England was to bring the English into his balance of power against France. Since the English were generally anti-French, and had chafed under the pro-French tendencies of their kings, William without difficulty reached an understanding with the discontented Whigs and Tories. Protected by a written invitation from prominent Englishmen, he invaded England with a considerable army. James II fled, and William was proclaimed co-ruler with Mary over England and Scotland. In the next year, 1690, at the Boyne River in Ireland, a motley army of Dutchmen, Germans, Scots, and French Huguenots under William III defeated a French and Irish force led by James II. Thus the liberties of England were saved. James II fled to France.

Louis XIV of course refused to recognize his inveterate enemy as ruler of England. He maintained James at the French court with all the honors due the English king. It was thereafter one of his principal war aims to restore the Catholic and Stuart dynasty across the Channel. The English, contrariwise, had added reason to fight the French. French victory would mean counterrevolution and royal absolutism in England. The whole Revolution of 1688 was at stake in the French wars.

In 1689, Parliament enacted a Bill of Rights, stipulating that no law could be suspended by the king (as the Test Act had been), no taxes raised or army maintained except by parliamentary consent, and no subject (however poor) arrested and detained without legal process. William III accepted these articles as conditions to receiving the crown. Thereafter the relation between king and people was a kind of contract. It was further provided, by the Act of Settlement of 1701, that no Catholic could be king of England; this excluded the descendants of James II, known in the following century as the Pretenders. Parliament also passed the Toleration Act of 1689, which allowed Protestant Dissenters to practice their religion but still excluded them from political life and public service. Since ways of evading these restrictions were soon found, and since even Catholics were not molested unless they supported the Pretenders, there was thereafter no serious trouble over religion in England and Lowland Scotland.

The English Parliament could make no laws for Scotland, and it was to be feared that James II might some day be restored in his northern kingdom. The securing of the parliamentary revolution in England, and of the island's defenses against France, required that the two kingdoms be organically joined. There was little sentiment in Scotland, however, for a merger with the English. The English tempted the Scots with economic advantages. The Scots still had no rights in the English East India Company, nor in the English colonies, nor within the English system of mercantilism and Navigation Acts. They obtained such rights by consenting to a union. In 1707 the United Kingdom of Great Britain was created. The Scots retained their own legal system and established Presbyterian church, but their government and parliament were merged with those of England. The term "British" came into use to refer to both English and Scots.

As for Ireland, it was now feared as a center of Stuart and French intrigue. The Revolution of 1688 marked the climax of a long record of trouble. Ireland had never been simply "conquered" by England, though certain English or rather Anglo-Norman families had carved out estates there since the twelfth century. By the end of the Middle Ages Ireland was organized as a separate kingdom with its own parliament, subordinate to the English crown. During the Reformation the Irish remained Catholic while England turned Protestant, but the monasteries were dissolved in Ireland as in England; and the organized church as such, the established Church of Ireland, with its apparatus of bishoprics, parishes, and tithes, became an Anglican communion in which the mass of native Irish had no interest. Next came the plantation of Ulster, already mentioned, in which a mass of newcomers, mainly Scottish and Presbyterian, settled in the northern part of the island.[12] Then in Cromwell's time, as just seen, English landlords spread through the rest of the country; or rather, a new Anglo-Irish upper class developed, in which English landowning families, residing most often in England, added the income from Irish estates to their miscellaneous revenues. Ireland therefore by the close of the seventeenth century was a very mixed country. Probably two-thirds of its population was Catholic, of generally Celtic ethnic background; perhaps a fifth was Presbyterian, with recent Scottish connections; the small remainder was made up of Anglicans, largely Anglo-Irish of recent or distant origin in England, who controlled most of the land, manned the official church, and were influential in the Irish parliament. It was essentially a landlord and peasant society, in which the Presbyterian as well as the Catholic mass was overwhelmingly agricultural; towns were small, and the middle class scarcely developed.

After the Revolution of 1688, in which the final overthrow of James II took place at the Boyne River, the English feared Ireland as a source of danger to the postrevolutionary arrangements in England. Resistance of the subjugated Catholics had also to be prevented. Hence to the burden of an alien church and absentee landlordism was now added the "penal code." Catholic clergy were banished, and Catholics were forbidden to vote or to sit in the Irish parliament. Catholic teachers were forbidden to teach, and Catholic parents were forbidden to send children overseas to be educated in Catholic schools. No Catholic could take a

[12] See pp. 83, 165, 170.

degree from Dublin University. Catholic Irishmen were forbidden to purchase land, to lease it for more than thirty-one years, to inherit it from a Protestant, or to own a horse worth more than £5. A Catholic whose son turned Protestant found his own property rights limited in his son's favor. Catholics were forbidden to be attorneys, to serve as constables, or, in most trades, to have more than two apprentices. Some disabilities fell on the Protestant Irish also. Thus Irish shipping was excluded from the British colonies, nor could the Irish import colonial goods except through England. Export of Irish woolens and glass manufactures was prohibited. No import tariff on English manufactures could be levied by the Irish parliament. About all that was left to the Irish, in international trade, was the export of agricultural produce; and the foreign exchange acquired in this way went very largely to pay the rents of absentee landlords.

The purpose of the penal code was in part strategic, to weaken Ireland as a potentially hostile country during a long period of wars with France. In part it was commercial, to favor English manufactures by removing Irish competition. And in part it was social, to confirm the position of the Anglican interest, or "ascendancy" as it came to be called. Parts of the code were removed piecemeal in the following decades, and a Catholic merchant class grew up in the eighteenth century; but much remained in effect for a long time, so that, for example, a Catholic could not vote for members of the Irish parliament until 1793, and even then could not be elected to it. In general, the Irish emerged from the seventeenth century as the most repressed people of western Europe.

England, immediately after the expulsion of James II, joined William III's coalition against France. To the alliance England brought a highly competent naval force, together with very considerable wealth. William's government, to finance the war, borrowed £1,200,000 from a syndicate of private lenders, who in return for holding government bonds were given the privilege of operating a bank. Thus originated, in 1694, both the Bank of England and the British national debt. Owners of liquid assets, merchants of London and Whig aristocrats with fat rent rolls, having lent their money to the new regime, had a compelling reason to defend it against the French and James II. And having at last a government whose policies they could control, they were willing to entrust it with money in large amounts. The national debt rapidly rose, while the credit of the government held consistently good; and for many years the Continent was astonished at the wealth that the British government could tap at will, and the quantities of money that it could pour into the wars of Europe.

The events of 1688 came to be known to the English as the Glorious Revolution. The Revolution was considered to have vindicated the principles of parliamentary government, the rule of law, and even the right of rebellion against tyranny. It has often been depicted as the climax in the growth of English constitutional self-government. Political writers like John Locke, shortly after the events, helped to give wide currency to these ideas.[13] There was in truth some justification for these views even though in more recent times some writers have "deglorified" the Revolution of 1688. They point out that it was a class movement, promoted and maintained by the landed aristocracy. The Parliament which boldly asserted itself against the king was at the same time closing itself to large segments of the people. Where in the Middle Ages members of the House of Commons had usually

---

[13] On John Locke and the philosophy of the Glorious Revolution see pp. 299–301.

received pay for their services, this custom disappeared in the seventeenth century, so that thereafter only men with independent incomes could sit. After the parliamentary triumph of 1688 this tendency became a matter of law. An act of 1710 required members of the House of Commons to possess private incomes at such a level that only a few thousand persons could legally qualify. This income had to come from the ownership of land. England from 1688 to 1832 was the best example in modern times of a true aristocracy, i.e., of a country in which the aristocratic landowning class not only enjoyed privileges but also conducted the government. But the landowning interest was then the only class sufficiently wealthy, numerous, educated, and self-conscious to stand on its own feet. The rule of the "gentlemen of England" was within its limits a regime of political liberty.

21. THE FRANCE OF LOUIS XIV, 1643–1715: THE TRIUMPH OF ABSOLUTISM

French Civilization in the Seventeenth Century

Having traveled in the outer orbits of the European political system, we come now to its radiant and mighty center, the domain of the Sun King himself, the France against which the rest of Europe felt obliged to combine, and on whose push and pull depended the course of the lesser bodies—the future of the Spanish possessions, the independence of Holland, the maintenance in England of the parliamentary revolution. The France of Louis XIV owed much of its ascendancy to the quantity and quality of its people. Population was stabilized or possibly even falling in the seventeenth century, the last century in which France was seriously disturbed by famine, pestilence, and peasant rebellion. With 19 million inhabitants in 1700 France was still over three times as populous as England and twice as populous as Spain. Its fertile soil, in an agricultural age, made it a wealthy country, though the wealth was very unevenly distributed. France was big enough to harbor many contradictions. Millions of its people lived in poverty, yet the number in comfortable or even luxurious circumstances was very large. There were both modest country nobles and cosmopolitan *grands seigneurs*. The middle class included an inordinate number of lawyers, officeholders, and bureaucrats, and the country was less commercial than Holland or England, yet in sheer numbers there may have been more merchants in France than in either of the other two countries. Protestants were a declining minority, yet in the mid-seventeenth century there were still more French Huguenots than Dutch Calvinists. It was a self-sufficient country, yet the French in this century began trading in India and Madagascar, founded Canada, penetrated the Great Lakes and the Mississippi valley, set up plantations in the West Indies, expanded their ancient commerce with the Levant, enlarged their mercantile marine, and for a time had the leading navy of Europe.

The dominance of France meant the dominance not merely of power, but of a people generally admitted to be in the forefront of civilization. They carried over the versatility of the Italy of the Renaissance. In Poussin and Claude Lorrain they produced a notable school of painters, their architecture was emulated throughout Europe, and they excelled in military fortification and general engineering. Much of their literature, though often written by bourgeois writers, was designed for an aristocratic and courtly audience, which had put aside the uncouth manners of an earlier day and prided itself on the refinement of its tastes and perceptions. Corneille and Racine wrote austere tragedies on the fundamental situations of human life. Molière, in his comedies, ridiculed bumbling doctors, new-rich bourgeois, and foppish aristocrats, making the word "marquis" almost a joke in the French language. La Fontaine gave the world his animal fables, and La Rochefoucauld, in his witty and sardonic maxims, a great nobleman's candid judgment on human nature. In Descartes the French produced a great mathematician and scientific thinker, in Pascal a scientist who was also a profound spokesman for Christianity, in Bayle the father of modern skeptics. It was French thought and the French language, not merely the armies of Louis XIV, which in the seventeenth century were sweeping the European world.

The Development of Absolutism in France

This ascendancy of French culture went along with a regime in which political liberties were at a discount. It was an embellishment to the absolute monarchy of Louis XIV. France had a tradition of political freedom in the feudal sense. It had the same kind of background of feudal liberties as did the other countries of Europe. It had an Estates General, which had not met since 1615 but was not legally abolished. In some regions Provincial Estates, still meeting frequently, retained a measure of self-government and of power over taxation. There were about a dozen bodies known as parlements,[14] which, unlike the English Parliament, had developed as courts of law, each being the supreme court for a certain area of the country. The parlements upheld certain "fundamental laws" which they said the king could not overstep, and they often refused to enforce royal edicts which they declared to be unconstitutional. We have already observed how France, beneath the surface, was almost as composite as Germany.[15] French towns had won charters of acknowledged rights, and many of the great provinces enjoyed liberties written into old agreements with the crown. These local liberties were the main reason for a good deal of institutional complication. There were some 300 "customs" or regional systems of law; it was observed that a traveler sometimes changed laws more often than he changed horses. Internal tariffs ran along the old provincial borders. Tolls were levied by manorial lords. The king's taxes fell less heavily on some regions than on others. Neither coinage nor weights and measures were uniform throughout the country. France was a bundle of territories held together by allegiance to the king.

This older kind of freedom discredited itself in France at the very time when by triumphing in Germany it pulled the Holy Roman Empire to pieces, and when in England it successfully made the transition to a more modern form of political liberty, embodied in the parliamentary though aristocratic state. In France the old medieval, feudal, or local type of liberty became associated with disorder. It has already been related how after the disorders of the sixteenth-century religious wars people had turned with relief to the monarchy and how Henry IV and then Richelieu had begun to make the monarchy strong.[16] The troubles of the Fronde provided additional incentive for absolutism in France.

[14] Spelled *parlements* in French, to distinguish from the English Parliament.
[15] See p. 132 and map, p. 183.
[16] See pp. 135–137.

The Fronde broke out immediately after the Peace of Westphalia, while Louis XIV was still a child, and was directed against Cardinal Mazarin, who was governing in his name. It was an abortive revolution, led by the same elements, the parlements and the nobility, which were to precipitate the great French Revolution in 1789. The parlements, especially the Parlement of Paris, insisted in 1648 on their right to pronounce certain edicts unconstitutional. Barricades were thrown up and street fighting broke out in Paris. The nobility rebelled, as it had often in the past. Leadership was assumed by certain prominent noblemen who, roughly like the great Whigs of England, had enough wealth and influence to believe that, if the king's power were kept down, they might govern the country themselves. The nobility demanded a calling of the Estates General, expecting to dominate over the bourgeoisie and the clergy in that body. Armed bands of soldiers, unemployed since the Peace of Westphalia and led by nobles, roamed about the country terrorizing the peasants. If the nobles had their way, it was probable that the manorial system would fall on the peasants more heavily, as in eastern Europe, where triumphant lords were at this very time exacting increased labor services from the peasants. Finally the rebellious nobles called in Spanish troops, though France was at war with Spain. By this time the bourgeoisie, represented in the parlements, had withdrawn support from the rebellious nobles. The agitation subsided in total failure, because bourgeoisie and aristocracy could not work together, because the nobles outraged the loyalty of many Frenchmen by joining with a power with which France was at war, and because the *frondeurs*, especially after the parlements deserted them, had no systematic or constructive program, aiming only at the overthrow of the unpopular Cardinal Mazarin and at obtaining offices and favors for themselves.

After the Fronde, as after the religious wars, the bourgeoisie and peasantry of France, to protect themselves against the claims of the aristocracy, were in a mood to welcome the exercise of strong power by the kings. And in the young Louis XIV they had a man more than willing to grasp all the power he could get. Louis, on Mazarin's death in 1661, announced that he would govern the country himself. He was the third king of the Bourbon line. It was the Bourbon tradition, established by Henry IV and by Richelieu, to draw the teeth from the feudal aristocrats, and this tradition Louis XIV followed. He was not a man of any transcendent abilities, though he had the capacity, often found among successful executives, of learning a good deal from conversation with experts. His education was not very good, having been made purposely easy; but he had the ability to see and stick to definite lines of policy, and he was extremely methodical and industrious in his daily habits, scrupulously loading himself with administrative business throughout his reign. He was extremely fond of himself and his position of kingship, with an insatiable appetite for admiration and flattery; he loved magnificent display and elaborate etiquette, though to some extent he simply adopted them as instruments of policy rather than as a personal whim.

With the reign of Louis XIV the "state" in its modern form took a long step forward. The state in the abstract has always seemed theoretical to the English-speaking world. Let us say, for simplicity, that the state represents a fusion of justice and power. A sovereign state possesses, within its territory, a monopoly over the administration of justice and the use of force. Private persons neither pass legal judgments on others nor control private armies of their own. For private and unauthorized persons to do so, in an orderly state, constitutes rebellion. This was in contrast to the older feudal practice, by which feudal lords maintained manorial courts and led their own followers into battle. Against these feudal practices Louis XIV energetically worked, though not with complete success, claiming to possess in his own person, as sovereign ruler, a monopoly over the lawmaking processes and the armed forces of the kingdom. This is the deeper meaning of his reputed boast, *L'état, c'est moi*—"the state is myself." In the France of the seventeenth century, divided by classes and by regions, there was in fact no means of consolidating the powers of state except in a single man.

The state, however, while representing law and order within its borders, has generally stood in a lawless and disorderly relation to other states, since no higher monopoly of law and force has existed. Louis XIV, personifying the French state, had no particular regard for the claims of other states or rulers. He was constantly either at war or preparing for war with his neighbors. The modern state, indeed, was created by the needs of peace at home and war abroad. Machinery of government, as devised by Louis XIV and others, was a means of giving order and security within the territory of the state, and of raising, supporting, and controlling armies for use against other states.

The idea that law and force within a country should be monopolized by the lawful king was the essence of the seventeenth-century doctrine of absolutism. Its principal theorist in the time of Louis XIV was Bishop Bossuet. Bossuet advanced the old Christian teaching that all power comes from God, and that all who hold power are responsible to God for the way they use it. He held that kings were God's representatives in the political affairs of earth. Royal power, according to Bossuet, was absolute but not arbitrary: not arbitrary because it must be reasonable and just, like the will of God which it reflected; absolute in that it was free from dictation by parlements, estates, or other subordinate elements within the country. Law, therefore, was the will of the sovereign king, so long as it conformed to the higher law which was the will of God. This doctrine, affirming the divine right of kings, was popularly held in France at the time and was taught in the churches. "Absolutism" and "absolute monarchy" became the prevailing forms of government on the European continent in the seventeenth and eighteenth centuries. It must be remembered, however, that these terms, if not historians' clichés, referred more to legal principle than to facts. A ruler was "absolute" because he was not legally bound by any other persons or institutions in the country. In reality he became dependent upon a host of advisers and bureaucrats, he often had to compromise with vested interests, and he could be thwarted by the sheer weight of local custom, or meet resistance from lawyers, ecclesiastics, nobles, grandees, hereditary officeholders, and miscellaneous dignitaries.

Government and Administration

Possibly the most fundamental step taken by Louis XIV was to assure himself of control of the army. Armed forces had formerly been almost a private enterprise. Specialists in fighting, leading their own troops, worked for governments more or less as they chose, either in return for money or to pursue political aims of their own. This was especially common in central Europe, but even in France great noblemen had strong private influence over the troops, and in times of disorder nobles led armed retainers about the country. Colonels were virtually on their own. Provided with a general commission and with funds by some government, they recruited, trained, and equipped their own regiments, and likewise fed and supplied them, often by preying upon bourgeois and peasants in the vicinity. In these circumstances it was often difficult to say on whose side soldiers were fighting. It was hard for governments to set armies into motion and equally hard to make them stop fighting, for commanders fought for their own interests and on their own momentum. War was not a "continuation of policy"; it was not an act of the state; it easily degenerated, as in the Thirty Years' War, into a kind of aimless and perpetual violence.

Louis XIV made war an activity of state. He saw to it that all armed persons in France fought only for him. This produced peace and order in France, while strengthening the fighting power of France against other states. Under the older conditions there was also little integration among different units and arms of the army. Infantry regiments and troops of horse went largely their own way, and the artillery was supplied by civilian technicians under contract. Louis XIV created a stronger unity of control, put the artillery organically into the army, systematized the military ranks and grades, and clarified the chain of command, placing himself at the top. The government supervised recruiting, required colonels to prove that they were maintaining the proper number of soldiers, and assumed most of the responsibility for equipping, provisioning, clothing, and housing the troops. Higher officers, thus becoming dependent on the government, could be subjected to discipline. The soldiers were put into uniforms, taught to march in step, and housed in barracks; thus they too became more susceptible to discipline and control. Armed forces became less of a terror to their own people and a more effective weapon in the hands of government. They were employed usually against other governments but sometimes to suppress rebellion at home. Louis XIV also increased the French army in size, raising it from about 100,000 to about 400,000. These changes, both in size and in degree of government control, were made possible by the growth of a large civilian administration. The heads of this administration under Louis XIV were civilians. They were in effect the first ministers of war, and their assistants, officials, inspectors, and clerks constituted the first organized war ministry.

Louis XIV was not only a vain man, but made it a political principle to overawe the country with his own grandeur. He built himself a whole new city at the old village of Versailles about ten miles from Paris. Where the Escorial had the atmosphere of a monastery, Versailles was a monument to worldly splendor. Tremendous in size alone, fitted out with polished mirrors, gleaming chandeliers, and magnificent tapestries, opening on to a formal park with fountains and shaded walks, the palace of Versailles was the marvel of Europe and the envy of lesser kings. It was virtually a public building, much of it used for government offices, and with nobles, churchmen, notable bourgeois, and servants milling about on the king's affairs. The more exclusive honors of the château were reserved for the higher aristocrats. The king surrounded his daily routine of rising, eating, and going to bed (known as the *lever, dîner,* and *coucher*) with an infinite series of ceremonial acts, so minute and so formalized that there were, for example, six different entries of persons at the *lever,* and a certain gentleman at a specified moment held the right sleeve of the king's nightshirt as he took it off. The most exalted persons thought themselves the greater for thus waiting on so august a being. In this way, and by more material favors, many great lords were induced to live habitually at court. Here, under the royal eye, they might engage in palace intrigue but were kept away from real political mischief. Versailles had a debilitating effect on the French aristocracy. The king himself was one of the few who could proceed through such rounds of elaborate living and still be able to attend regularly to public affairs. Neither the nobles whom he kept about him nor his own successors, Louis XV and Louis XVI, were able to carry the burden.

For positions in the government, as distinguished from his personal entourage, Louis XIV preferred to use men whose upper-class status was recent. Such men, unlike the greatest nobles, could aspire to no independent political influence of their own. He never called the Estates General, which in any case no one except some of the nobility wanted. Some of the Provincial Estates, because of local and aristocratic pressures, he allowed to remain functioning. He temporarily destroyed the independence of the parlements, commanding them to accept his orders, as Henry IV had commanded them to accept the Edict of Nantes.[17] He stifled the old liberties of the towns, turning their civic offices into empty and purchasable honors and likewise regulating the operation of the guilds. He developed a strong system of administrative coordination, centering in a number of councils of state, which he attended in person, and in "intendants" who represented these councils throughout the country. Councilors of state and intendants were generally of bourgeois origin or newly ennobled. Each intendant, within his district, embodied all aspects of the royal government, supervising the flow of taxes and recruiting of soldiers, keeping an eye on the local nobility, dealing with towns and guilds, controlling the more or less hereditary officeholders, stamping out bandits, smugglers, and wolves, policing the marketplaces, relieving famine, watching the local law courts, and often deciding cases himself. In this way a firm and uniform administration was superimposed upon the heterogeneous mass of the old France. In contrast to England, all local questions were handled by agents of the central government, usually honest and often efficient, but essentially bureaucrats constantly instructed by, and referring back to, their superiors at Versailles.

Economic and Financial Policies: Colbert

To support the reorganized and enlarged army, the panoply of Versailles, and the growing civil administration, the king needed a good deal of money. Finance was always the weak spot in the French monarchy. Methods of collecting taxes were costly and inefficient. Direct taxes passed through the hands of many intermediate officials; indirect taxes were collected by private concessionaries called tax farmers, who made a substantial profit. The state always received far less than what the taxpayers actually paid. But the main weakness arose from an old bargain between the French crown and nobility; the king might raise taxes without consent if only he refrained from taxing the nobles. Only the "unprivileged" classes paid direct taxes, and these came almost to mean the peasants only, since many bourgeois in one way or another obtained exemptions. The system was outrageously unjust in throwing the tax burden on the poor and helpless. It was ruinous to the government, since the government could never raise enough money, however hard it taxed the poor, being unable to tap the real source of ready wealth, namely, the wealthier people. It was ruinous also to the French nobility,

---

[17] See pp. 135–136.

who in paying no direct taxes lost their hold over the government, lacked incentive to interest themselves in public affairs, and were unable to assume leadership of the bulk of the population. Louis XIV was willing enough to tax the nobles but was unwilling to fall under their control, and only toward the close of his reign, under extreme stress of war, was he able, for the first time in French history, to impose direct taxes on the aristocratic elements of the population. This was a great step toward equality before the law and toward sound public finance, but so many concessions and exemptions were won by nobles and bourgeois that the reform lost much of its value.

Like his predecessors, Louis resorted to all manner of expedients to increase his revenues. He raised the tax rates, always with disappointing results. He devalued the currency. He sold patents of nobility to ambitious bourgeois. He sold government offices, judgeships, and commissions in the army and navy. For both financial and political reasons the king used his sovereign authority to annul the town charters, then sell back reduced rights at a price; this produced a little income but demoralized local government and civic spirit. The need for money, arising from the fundamental inability to tax the wealthy, which in turn reflected the weakness of absolutism, of a government which would not or could not share its rule with the propertied classes, corrupted much of the public life and political aptitude of the French people.

Louis XIV wished, if only for his own purposes, to make France economically powerful. His great minister Colbert worked for twenty years to do so. Colbert went beyond Richelieu in the application of mercantilism, aiming to make

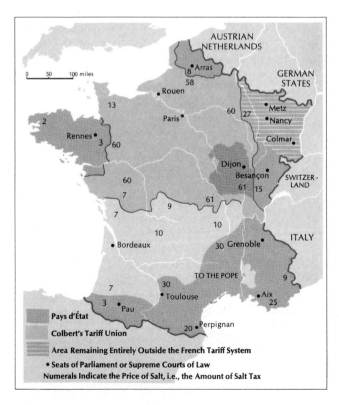

Pays d'État

Colbert's Tariff Union

Area Remaining Entirely Outside the French Tariff System

• Seats of Parliament or Supreme Courts of Law

Numerals Indicate the Price of Salt, i.e., the Amount of Salt Tax

FRANCE FROM THE LAST YEARS OF LOUIS XIV TO THE REVOLUTION OF 1789

The map gives an idea of the diversity of law and administration before the Revolution. Dark areas are "pays d'état," provinces in which representative bodies ("estates") continued to meet. Cities named are the seats of what the French called parliaments (see p. 178). The key indicates Colbert's tariff union, the Five Great Farms (see p. 184). The area marked with hatching remained outside the French tariff system entirely; it continued to trade with the states of the Holy Roman Empire (from which it had been annexed) without interference by the French government. Numerals indicate the price of salt, i.e., the amount of the salt tax, in various regions. In general, it will be seen that regions farthest from Paris enjoyed the most "privileges" or "liberties," preserving their legal and judicial identity, Provincial Estates, local tariffs, and a favored position in national taxation.

France a self-sufficing economic unit and to increase the wealth from which taxes were drawn.[18] He managed to abolish local tariffs in a large part of central France, where he set up a tariff union oddly entitled the Five Great Farms (since the remaining tolls were collected by tax farmers); and although vested interests and provincial liberties remained too strong for him to do away with all internal tariffs, the area of the Five Great Farms was in itself one of the largest free-trade areas in Europe, being about the size of England. For the convenience of businessmen Colbert promulgated a Commercial Code, replacing much of the local customary law, and long a model of business practice and business regulation. He improved communications by building roads and canals, of which the most famous was one joining the Bay of Biscay with the Mediterranean. Working through the guilds, he required the handicraft manufacturers to produce goods of specified kind and quality, believing that foreigners, if assured of quality by the government, would purchase French products more freely. He gave subsidies, tax exemptions, and other privileges to expand the manufacture of silks, tapestries, glassware, and woolens. He helped to found colonies, built up the navy, and established the French East India Company. Export of some goods, notably foodstuffs, was forbidden, for the government wished to keep the populace quiet by holding down the price of bread. Export of other goods, mainly manufactures, was encouraged, partly as a means of bringing money into the country, where it could be funneled into the royal treasury. The growth of the army, and the fact that under Louis XIV the government clothed and equipped the soldiers, and hence placed unprecedentedly large orders for uniforms, overcoats, weapons, and ammunition, greatly stimulated the employment of weavers, tailors, and gunsmiths and advanced the commercial capitalism by which such labors were organized. In general, trade and manufacture developed in France under more direct government guidance than in England. They long gave the English an extremely brisk competition. Not until the age of iron and coal did France begin economically to lag.

Religion: The Revocation of the Edict of Nantes, 1685

The consolidation of France under Louis XIV reached its high point in his policies toward religion. Toward Rome Louis backed the old claims of the Gallican church to enjoy a certain national independence of policy. He repressed the movement known as Jansenism, a kind of Calvinism within the Catholic church, which persisted for almost two centuries. But it was the Protestants who suffered most.

France, in the early years of Louis XIV's reign, still allowed more religious toleration than any other large state in Europe. The Huguenots had lost their separate political status under Richelieu, but they continued to live in relative security and contentment, protected by the Edict of Nantes of 1598.[19] From the beginning, however, toleration had been a royal rather than a popular policy, and under Louis XIV the royal policy changed. The fate of Catholics at the hands of a triumphant Parliament in England suggests that the Protestants in France would have been no better off under more popular institutions.

Bending all else to his will, Louis XIV resented the presence of heretics among his subjects. He considered religious unity necessary to the strength and dignity of

[18] On mercantilism in general, see pp. 116–118.
[19] See pp. 135–137.

his rule. He perhaps envied the right claimed by most governments at the time, Protestant as well as Catholic, to determine the religion of their respective peoples. He fell under the influence of certain Catholic advisers, who, not content with the attrition by which some Protestants were turning back to Catholicism in any case, wished to hasten the process to the greater glory of themselves. Systematic conversion of Huguenots was begun. Life for Protestant families was gradually made unbearable. Finally they were literally "dragooned," mounted infantrymen being quartered in Huguenot homes to reinforce the persuasions of missionaries. In 1685 Louis revoked the Edict of Nantes. During the persecutions a good many Protestants left France, migrating to Holland, Germany, and America. Their loss was a blow to French economic life, for although Protestants were found in all levels of French society, those of the commercial and industrial classes were the most mobile. With the revocation of the Edict of Nantes France embarked on a century of official intolerance (slowly mitigated in practice), under which Protestants in France were in much the same position as Catholics in the British Isles. The fact that a hundred years later, when Protestants were again tolerated, many of them were found to be both commercially prosperous and politically loyal indicates that they fared far better than the Catholic Irish.

All things considered, the reign of Louis XIV brought considerable advantages to the French middle and lower classes. His most bitter critics, with the natural exception of Protestants, were disgruntled nobles such as the duke of Saint-Simon, who thought that he showed too many favors to persons of inferior social rank. Since Protestants were an unpopular minority, his repression of them won much approval. Colbert's system of economic regulation, and perpetuation of the guilds, meant that innovation and private enterprise developed less fully than in England, but France was economically stronger in 1700 than in 1650. Peasants were heavily taxed, but they did not sink into the serfdom that was rising in eastern Europe. Compared to later times, France was still a hodgepodge of competing jurisdictions, special privilege, and bureaucratic ineptitude. The king was in truth far from "absolute," but France was nevertheless the best organized of the large monarchies on the Continent. Louis XIV, in turning both high and low into dutiful subjects, put an end to civil war and even advanced the cause of civil equality. For a long time he was generally popular. What finally turned his people against him in his last years was the strain of his incessant wars.

22. THE WARS OF LOUIS XIV: THE PEACE OF UTRECHT, 1713

Before 1700

From the outset of his reign Louis pursued a vigorous foreign policy. The quarrel between the house of France and the house of Habsburg had gone on for more than a century. The Austrian branch of the Habsburgs had been checkmated at the Peace of Westphalia. With the Spanish branch the French remained at war for another decade, until the Peace of the Pyrenees in 1659. When, two years later, Louis XIV assumed his personal rule, Spanish territories still faced France on three sides, northeast, east, and south; but so weakened was Spain that this fact was no longer a menace to France so much as a temptation to French expansion. Louis XIV could count on popular national feeling to support him, for the dream of a frontier on the Rhine and the Alps was captivating to Frenchmen. He struck in 1667. (The war was called the "War of Devolution," from a legal term used in the preliminary demands.) He was blocked, as noted above, by a Triple Alliance engineered by the Dutch.[20] With strength renewed by reforms at home, and in alliance with Charles II of England, he struck again in 1672 (the "Dutch War"), invading the Dutch provinces on the lower Rhine, and this time raising up his great adversary and inveterate enemy, the prince of Orange.[21] William III, bringing the Austrian and Spanish Habsburgs, Brandenburg, and Denmark into alliance with the Dutch Republic, forced Louis to sign the treaty of Nimwegen in 1678. The French gave up their ambitions against Holland but took from Spain the rich province of Franche-Comté, which outflanked Alsace on the south, and brought French power to the borders of Switzerland.

In the very next year, 1679, Louis further infiltrated the dissolving frontier of the Holy Roman Empire, this time in Lorraine and Alsace. By the Peace of Westphalia the French king had rights in this region, but the terms of that treaty were so ambiguous, and the local feudal law so confusing, that claims could be made in contrary directions. Louis XIV now set up *chambres de réunion*, as he called them, law courts in which French judges examined the claims to various parcels of territory and pronounced in favor of the king of France. French troops thereupon moved in. In 1681 French troops occupied the city of Strasbourg, which, as a free city of the Holy Roman Empire, regarded itself as an independent little republic. A protest went up throughout Germany against this undeclared invasion. But Germany was not a political unity. Since 1648 each German state conducted its own foreign policy, and at this very moment, in 1681, Louis XIV had an ally in the Elector of Brandenburg (forerunner of the kings of Prussia); and the electors of the Rhineland church-states—the archbishops of Cologne, Trier, and Mainz— were on the French payroll, receiving "subsidies" from the French king. The diet of the Holy Roman Empire was divided between an anti-French and a pro-French party. The emperor, Leopold I, was distracted by developments in the East. The Hungarians, incited and financed by Louis XIV, were again rebelling against the Habsburgs. They appealed to the Turks, and the Turks in 1683 moved up the Danube and actually besieged Vienna—as in 1529. Louis XIV, if he did not on this occasion positively assist the Turks, ostentatiously declined to join the proposed crusade against them.

The emperor, with Polish assistance, succeeded in getting the Turkish host out of Austria.[22] Returning to western problems, observing the western border of the Empire constantly crumbling, Franche-Comté already lost, the Spanish Netherlands constantly threatened, Lorraine and Alsace absorbed bit by bit, and the Rhineland archbishops reduced to the status of French puppets, and not forgetting that Louis XIV had designs on the whole of Habsburg Spain, the Emperor Leopold gathered the Catholic powers into a combination against the French. The Protestant states at the same time, aroused by Louis' revocation of the Edict of Nantes in 1685 and by Huguenot émigrés who called down the wrath of God on the perfidious Sun King, began to ally the more readily with William of Orange. Catholic and Protestant enemies of Louis XIV came together in 1686 in the League of Augsburg, which comprised the Holy Roman Emperor, the kings of

[20] See p. 164.
[21] See pp. 164, 174.
[22] See pp. 215–216.

Spain and of Sweden, the electors of Bavaria, Saxony, and the Palatinate, and the Dutch Republic. In 1686 the king of England was still a protégé of France, but three years later, when William became king in England, that country too joined the League.

The War of the League of Augsburg broke out in 1688. The French armies won battles but could not drive so many enemies from the field. The French navy could not overpower the combined fleets of the Dutch and English. Louis XIV found himself badly strained (it was at this time that he first imposed direct taxes on the French nobles) and finally made peace at Ryswick in the Netherlands in 1697. The Peace of Ryswick, terminating the long "War of the League of Augsburg," left matters about where they had been when the war began.

In all the warring and negotiating, in the plans of the Augsburg allies and in the maneuvers of Louis XIV, the question had not been merely the fate of this or that piece of territory, nor even the French thrust to the east, but the eventual disposition of the whole empire of Spain. The Spanish king, Charles II, prematurely senile, momentarily expected to die, yet lived on year after year. He was still alive at the time of the Peace of Ryswick. The greatest diplomatic issue of the day was still unsettled.

The War of the Spanish Succession

The War of the Spanish Succession lasted eleven years, from 1702 to 1713. It was less destructive than the Thirty Years' War, for armies were now supplied in more orderly fashion, subject to more orderly discipline and command, and could be stopped from fighting at the will of their governments. Except for the effects of civil war in Spain and of starvation in France, the civilian populations were generally spared, and in this respect the war foreshadowed the typical warfare of the eighteenth century, fought by professional armies rather than by whole peoples. Among wars of the largest scale, the War of the Spanish Succession was the first in which religion counted for little, the first in which commerce and sea power were the principal stakes, the first in which English money was liberally used in Continental politics, and the first that can be called a "world war," because it involved the overseas world together with the leading powers of Europe.

The struggle had long been foreseen. The two main aspirants to the Spanish inheritance were the king of France and the Holy Roman Emperor, each of whom had married a sister of the perpetually moribund Charles II, and each of whom could hope to place a younger member of his family on the throne of Spain. During the last decades of the seventeenth century the powers had made various treaties agreeing to "partition" the Spanish possessions. The idea was, by dividing the Spanish heritage between the two claimants, to preserve the balance of power in Europe.[23] But when Charles II finally died, in 1700, it was found that he had made a will, in which he stipulated that the world of Spain should be kept intact, that all Spanish territories without exception should go to the grandson of Louis XIV, and that if Louis XIV refused to accept in the name of his seventeen-year-old grandson, the entire inheritance should pass to the son of the Habsburg emperor in Vienna. Louis XIV decided to accept. With Bourbons reigning in Versailles and Madrid, even if the two thrones were never united, French influence

---

[23] On the idea of the balance of power see pp. 158–159.

would run from Belgium to the Straits of Gibraltar, and from Milan to Mexico and Manila. At Versailles the word went out: "The Pyrenees exist no longer."

Never, at least in almost two centuries, had the political balance within Europe been so threatened. Never had the other states faced such a prospect of relegation to the sidelines. William III acted at once; he gathered the stunned or hesitant diplomats into the last of his coalitions, the Grand Alliance of 1701. He died the next year, before hostilities began, and with Louis XIV at the seeming apex of his grandeur, but he had in fact launched the engine that was to crush the Sun King. The Grand Alliance included England, Holland, and the emperor, supported by Brandenburg and eventually by Portugal and the Italian duchy of Savoy. Louis XIV could count on Spain, which was generally loyal to the late king's will. Otherwise his only ally was Bavaria, whose rivalry with Austria made it a habitual satellite of France. The Bavarian alliance gave the French armies an advanced position toward Vienna and maintained that internal division, balance of power, or cancellation of forces within Germany which was fundamental to the politics of the time, and of a long time to come.

The war was long, mainly because each side no sooner gained a temporary advantage than it raised its demands on the other. The English, though they sent relatively few troops to the Continent, produced in John Churchill, Duke of Marlborough, a preeminent military commander for the Allied forces. The Austrians were led by Prince Eugene of Savoy. The Allies won notable battles at Blenheim in Bavaria (1704), and at Ramillies (1706), Oudenarde (1708), and Malplaquet (1709) in the Spanish Netherlands. The French were routed; Louis XIV asked for peace but would not agree to it because the Allied terms were so enormous. Louis fought to hold the two crowns, to conquer Belgium, to get French merchants into Spanish America, and at the worst in self-defense. After minor successes in 1710 he again insisted on controlling the crown of Spain. The Spanish fought to uphold the will of the deceased king, the unity of the Spanish possessions, and even the integrity of Spain itself—for the English moved in at Gibraltar and made a menacing treaty with Portugal, while the Austrians landed at Barcelona and invaded Catalonia, which (as in 1640) again rose in rebellion, recognizing the Austrian claimant, so that all Spain fell into civil war.

The Austrians fought to keep Spain in the Habsburg family, to crush Bavaria, and to carry Austrian influence across the Alps into Italy. The Dutch fought as always for their security, to keep the French out of Belgium, and to close the river Scheldt. The English fought for these same reasons and also to keep the French-supported Catholic Stuarts out of England and preserve the Revolution of 1688. It was to be expected that the Stuarts, if they returned, would ruin the Bank of England and repudiate the National Debt. Both maritime powers, England and Holland, fought to keep French merchants out of Spanish America and to advance their own commercial position in America and the Mediterranean. These being the war aims, the Whigs were the implacable war party in England, the vaguely pro-Stuart and anticommercial Tories being quite willing to make peace at an early date. As for the minor allies, Brandenburg and Savoy, their rulers had simply entered the alliance to gain such advantages as might turn up.

The Peace of Utrecht

Peace was finally made at the treaties of Utrecht and Rastadt of 1713 and 1714. So fierce was the Whig war spirit in England that ratification of the treaty of

Utrecht incidentally marked a step in English constitutional history. The Whigs thought the treaty insufficiently favorable to England. The Tories, pledged to peace, had won the House of Commons in 1710, but the Whigs continued to control the House of Lords. Queen Anne, at the request of Tory leaders and in the interests of peace, raised twelve Tory commoners to the peerage, the number required to give a Tory majority in the Lords and hence to obtain ratification of the treaty. This established itself as a precedent; it became an unwritten article of the British constitution that when the Lords blocked the Commons on an issue of fundamental importance, enough new Lords of appropriate views would be created to make a majority in that House.[24]

The treaty of Utrecht, with its allied instruments, in fact partitioned the world of Spain. But it did not divide it between the two legal claimants only. The British remained at Gibraltar, to the great irritation of the Spaniards, and likewise annexed the island of Minorca. The Duke of Savoy was granted the former Spanish island of Sardinia in return for his contribution to the Allied cause.[25] The rest of the Spanish Mediterranean holdings—Milan, Naples, and Sicily—passed to the Austrian Habsburgs, as did the Spanish Netherlands (or Belgium), subsequently referred to as the Austrian Netherlands—except that the tiny region of Spanish Guelderland was handed over to the Elector of Brandenburg for his pains. In Spain itself, shorn of its European possessions but retaining America, the grandson of Louis XIV was confirmed as king (Philip V of Spain), on the understanding that the French and Spanish thrones should never be inherited by the same person. The Bourbons reigned in Spain, with interruptions, from Philip V to the republican revolution of 1931. French influence was strong in the eighteenth century, for a good many French courtiers, advisers, administrators, and businessmen crossed the Pyrenees with Philip V. They helped somewhat to revive the Spanish monarchy by applying the methods of Louis XIV, and they passed a swelling volume of French manufactures through Seville into Spanish America.

The old objective of William III, to prevent domination by France, was realized at last. The war itself was the main cause of French loss of strength. It produced poverty, misery, and depopulation, exposed Louis XIV to severe criticism at home, and led to a revival of aristocratic and parliamentary opposition. By the peace treaties the French abandoned, for the time being, their efforts to conquer Belgium. They ceased to recognize the Stuart pretender as king of Great Britain. They surrendered to the British two of their colonies, Newfoundland and Nova Scotia (called Acadia), and recognized British sovereignty in the disputed American northwest, known as the Hudson Bay territory. But the French were only checked, not downed. They retained the conquests of Louis XIV in Alsace and the Franche-Comté. Their influence was strong in Spain. Their deeper strength and capacity for recovery were soon evident in renewed economic expansion. Their language and civilization continued to spread throughout Europe.

The Dutch received guarantees of their security. They were granted the right to garrison the "Dutch Barrier," a string of forts in Belgium on the side toward

---

[24] The precedent was invoked in 1832 and 1911, but never since 1713 have the Lords allowed themselves to be swamped by newcomers. They have yielded at the threat.

[25] By the terms of 1713 Sardinia was awarded to Austria and Sicily to Savoy, but Sardinia and Sicily were exchanged in 1720. The kingdom of the Two Sicilies (Naples and Sicily) was thereby reconstituted. Savoy was originally a small region in the high Alps, whose ruler acquired the lowland area around Turin in the Middle Ages, with the title of Duke of Savoy. His domains were thereafter also called Piedmont because some of them lay at the foot of the Alps. After 1720 the Duke of Savoy became the King of Sardinia, because that island, though the least important of his possessions, provided a less controversial basis for a royal title. See the map on p. 317.

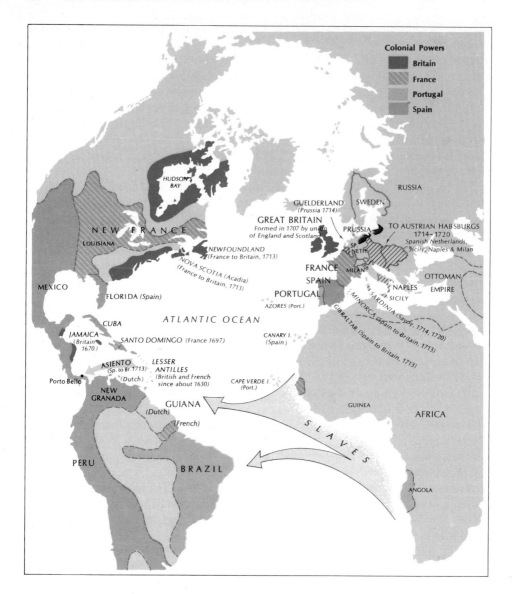

THE ATLANTIC WORLD AFTER THE PEACE OF UTRECHT, 1713

The map shows the partitioning of the Spanish empire and the rise of the British. Spain
and its American possessions went to the Bourbon Philip V; the European possessions of
Spain—the Netherlands, Milan, Naples, and Sicily—went to the Habsburgs. Britain meanwhile was strengthened by the union of England and Scotland, the acquisition of Minorca,
Gibraltar, and the commercial privilege of the "asiento" from Spain, and of Newfoundland
and Nova Scotia from France. (See also map, p. 317.)

France. With Belgium transferred to Austria, which was not expected to stimulate Belgian commerce, and with the closure of the river Scheldt reconfirmed at Utrecht, the Dutch could comfortably expect a minimum of competition from their southern neighbors. But the Dutch, strained by the war and outdistanced by England, never again played a primary role in European political affairs. Two other small states ascended over the diplomatic horizon, Savoy and Brandenburg. The rulers of both, for having sided with the victors, were recognized as "kings" by the treaty of Utrecht. Savoy came to be known as "Sardinia," and Brandenburg as "Prussia." More is said of Prussia in the next chapter.

The greatest winners were the British. Great Britain made its appearance as a great power. Union of England and Scotland had taken place during the war. Based at Gibraltar and Minorca, Britain was now a power in the Mediterranean. Belgium, the "pistol pointed at the heart of England," was in the innocuous hands of the Austrians. The Austrians had not especially wanted Belgium because it was too distant from Vienna and too likely to embroil them with France. They had taken it largely at the instigation of the maritime states, Britain and Holland, which saw in transfer to Austria a good solution to the problem. The British added to their American holdings at the expense of France. Far more valuable than Newfoundland or Nova Scotia, won from France, was the *asiento* extorted from Spain. The *asiento* granted the lucrative privilege (which the French had sought) of providing Spanish America with African slaves. Much of the wealth of Bristol and Liverpool in the following decades was to be built upon the slave trade. The *asiento*, by permitting one shipload of British goods to be brought each year to Porto Bello in Panama, also provided opportunities for illicit trade in nonhuman cargoes. The Spanish empire was pried open, and British merchants entered on an era of wholesale smuggling into Spanish America, competing strenuously with the French, who because of their favored position in Spain were usually able to go through more legal channels. Moreover, the British, by defeating France, assured themselves of a line of Protestant kings and of the maintenance of constitutional and parliamentary government. The landed aristocracy and their merchant allies could now govern as they saw fit. The result was a rapid increase of wealth in England, precipitating within a few generations a veritable Industrial Revolution.

Except for the addition of England, the same powers were parties to the treaty of Utrecht in 1713 as to the Peace of Westphalia in 1648, and they now confirmed the system of international relations established by Westphalia. The powers accepted each other as members of the European system, recognized each other as sovereign states connected only by free negotiation, war, and treaty, and adjusted their differences through rather facile exchanges of territory, made in the interests of a balance of power, and without regard to the nationality or presumed wishes of the peoples affected. With Germany still in its "feudal chaos," Italy negligible, and Spain subordinated to France, the treaty of Utrecht left France and Great Britain as the two most vigorous powers of Europe and as the two principal carriers and exporters of the type of civilization most characteristic of the modern world. In the next chapter we turn to central and eastern Europe, to see how these regions developed along lines of their own, though under strong influence from the West.

The Age of Grandeur

The seventeenth century was an age of high monarchy, or royal absolutism, of which the great exemplar was France. A style of life that developed first in Italy during the Renaissance, and which set high value on patronage of the arts, courtly manners, elaborate clothing, and elegant speech, was taken over in France (with some influence from the two Medici queens), and from France was diffused throughout much of Europe. It was especially suited to monarchies, since the kings, with their increasingly organized governments, could afford the necessary expense and even required a palatial atmosphere in which to impress their often unruly subjects. The same applies in a way to the papal monarchy of the church, and the new ideas came as much from papal Rome as from republican Florence. The result is best illustrated by architecture, to which the following pages are devoted.

It was an architecture derived from classical elements of design, but it soon went beyond the Greeks and Romans. The baroque, as it is called, delighted in arches and colonnades, domes and entablatures, and ornamented windows and cornices. Indoors and outdoors flowed together in complexes of façades, staircases, terraces, balustrades, gardens, fountains, and formal vistas. Statuary was distributed inside and out. Mirrors, paintings, and tapestries adorned the interiors. Great halls were built for state receptions, and paved courtyards for troops of soldiers, throngs of retainers, the arrival of coaches, or simply to provide open views.

Architecture passed over into city planning. Versailles was a new city; the plan of modern Paris also dates from Louis XIV; and Washington, D.C., planned by a Frenchman, with its diagonal streets and circles, punctuated by statues, still reflects these traditions of neoclassical monumentality. On the other hand it was the kings who initiated a movement to the suburbs. Versailles was built ten miles from Paris, away from the clamor and restlessness of the city, and where the king already owned enough land for a new spacious development. When other monarchs imitated Louis XIV they often did likewise. The Habsburgs built Schönbrunn outside Vienna, and the Hohenzollern Frederick II built Sans Souci at Potsdam about twenty miles from Berlin.

The Russian tsars, in their new city of St. Petersburg, and the kings of Sweden, in their new royal palace at Stockholm, joined the host of German princes in emulating the royal grandeur of France. It was different where royalty counted for less. The Dutch had no king and cared little for public magnificence. Sans Souci was hardly more than a wealthy gentleman's home. The English, with their antimonarchical revolutions, built no grandiose royal palaces at this time. But they built Blenheim Palace and presented it to John Churchill, the first Duke of Marlborough, as a reward for his services in the last great war against the *Grand Monarque*.

194

Above: The Emperor Constantine (d. 337) discusses with Pope Julius II (d. 1513) the building of a new church of St. Peter's in Rome. An older church, of which parts went back to Constantine's time, was torn down to make room for the new one.

The new St. Peter's, seen here in a seventeenth-century print, required a century and a half for completion. The great dome of the church is the work of Michelangelo. The pair of immense semicircular arcades, each four columns thick, was built about a hundred years later by Bernini, one of the great masters of the baroque.

The château of Versailles was mainly built by Louis XIV in the 1670s, on a site used by his predecessor as a hunting lodge. Thirty thousand workmen were employed at one time in the building operations, which are shown in a painting of the period at the left above. The painting below shows the château and its adjacent buildings about a hundred years later, shortly before the Revolution. The twin structures in the foreground, left and right of the vast court, were assigned to government offices. The château proper is in the middle distance, with the gardens invisible behind it, except that the long rectangular basin of the Grand Canal can be seen reaching to the horizon.

At Versailles, for thirty years, the Sun King received visitors from all countries in overwhelming splendor. The memorable arrival in 1684 of ambassadors from far-off Siam (now Thailand) is recorded in the print below.

Louis XIV gave sponsorship and subsidies to cultural activities of many kinds, usually organized as academies. At the left, he appears on a visit to the Academy of Sciences, founded in 1666. A scientific gentleman is explaining the "philosophical apparatus" to the king.

AMBASSADEURS DE SIAM

198

The opera developed as an art form in the seventeenth century and was characteristic of the baroque in its simultaneous use of different arts, its ostentation, and general staginess. At the left, below, Lully's "Alceste" is performed for Louis XIV in the courtyard of a lesser palace before the building of Versailles.

Left, above: Frederick the Great's Sans Souci. The young Frederick had been disciplined by his drill sergeant father for writing poetry and corresponding with Frenchmen, but after becoming king, in 1740, at the age of twenty-eight, he gave full rein to his French tastes, and after the first Silesian War built this residence, whose name means "carefree." Here he met with Voltaire and other intellectual companions.

Above: There were many buildings in St. Petersburg, now Leningrad, on the model of European palaces of the day, but here we have signs of the Western influences penetrating to Moscow. If the structures seem dreamy and evanescent, it is because they are only temporary pavilions set up in 1775 to celebrate the end of a victorious war with Turkey.

At the left: Schönbrunn Palace, near Vienna. The Habsburg monarchs, as the Turkish menace receded, planned this great edifice to compete with their Bourbon rivals. The plan was never completed, partly because the sensible Maria Theresa (1740–1780) thought that what is seen here was enough. It was here that the six-year-old Mozart astonished the court with his precocious virtuosity.

At the right: Blenheim Palace in Oxfordshire, presented to the Duke of Marlborough for his victories over Louis XIV. Built in the 1720s with funds voted by Parliament, a monument in a way to England's rising greatness, it has always been thought by the English to be a little exaggerated. The architect, Vanbrugh, left everyone dissatisfied. He sacrificed interiors to external splendor, putting the kitchen 400 yards from the dining room. Voltaire said that if only the rooms were as wide as the walls were thick, it would be a convenient little château.

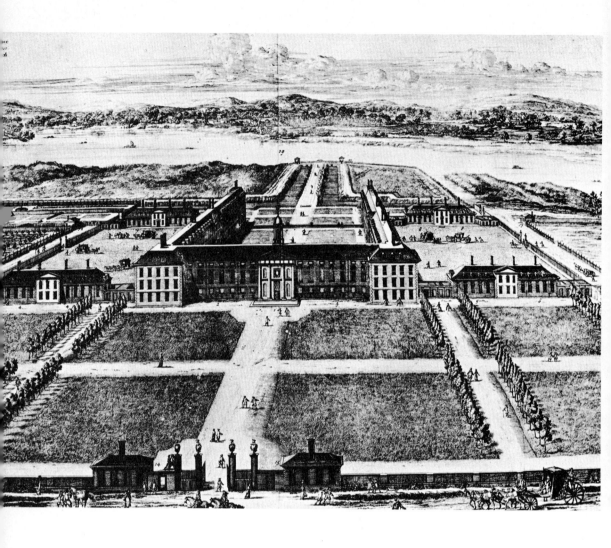

These two buildings were built at the same time for the same purpose, as homes for old and retired soldiers. It was a sign of the growth of royal government to have professional standing armies, in which men might spend their whole lives apart from the civilian population.

At the left is Chelsea Royal Hospital, founded by Charles II; at the right, the Invalides, founded by Louis XIV. The much greater size and imposing dome of the French establishment contrast with the simplicity of the English, and reflect the far greater power of France at that time. The broad avenues radiating beyond the Invalides, then in open country, are now boulevards of central Paris.

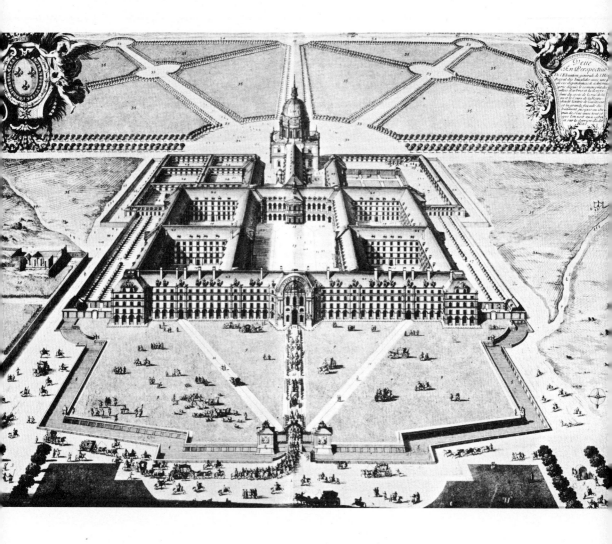

V.
The
Transformation of
Eastern Europe,
1648-1740

I n Eastern Europe, in the century after the Peace of Westphalia of 1648, it became apparent that political systems that failed to become more "modern" might be in danger of going out of existence. In the mid-seventeenth century most parts of Eastern Europe belonged to one or another of three old-fashioned political organizations—the Holy Roman Empire, the Republic of Poland, and the empire of the Ottoman Turks.[1] All three were loose, sprawling, and increasingly ineffective. They were pushed aside and superseded by three new and stronger powers, Prussia, Austria, and Russia. These three, by overrunning the intermediate ground of Poland, came to adjoin one another and cover all Eastern Europe except the Balkans. It was in this same period that Russia expanded territorially, adopted some of the technical and administrative apparatus of Western Europe, and became an active participant in European affairs.

East and West are of course relative terms. For the Russians Germany and even Poland were "western." But for Europe as a whole a real though indefinite line ran along the Elbe and the Bohemian mountains to the head of the Adriatic Sea. East of this line towns were fewer than in the West, human labor less productive, the middle classes less strong. Above all, the peasants were governed by their landlords.[2] From the sixteenth to the eighteenth century, in eastern Europe in

[1] See maps, pp. 206 and 210.
[2] See pp. 122–123.

Chapter Emblem: A Russian medal commemorating the capture of Narva from the Swedes in 1704, and hence the establishment of Russian power on the Baltic.

contrast to what happened in the West, the peasant mass increasingly lost its freedom. The commercial revolution and widening of the market, which in the West raised up a strong merchant class and tended to turn working people into a legally free and mobile labor force, in eastern Europe strengthened the great landlords who produced for export, and who secured their labor force by the institutions of serfdom and "hereditary subjection." The main social unit was the agricultural estate, which the lord exploited with uncompensated compulsory labor (or *robot*) furnished by his people, who could neither migrate, marry, nor learn a trade except as he permitted, and who, until the eighteenth century, had no legal protector or court of appeal other than himself. In the East, therefore, the landlords were exceedingly powerful. They were the only significant political class. And the three new states that grew up—Prussia, Austria, Russia—were alike in being landlord states.

23. THREE AGING EMPIRES

In 1648 the whole mainland of Europe from the French border almost to Moscow was occupied by the three large and loosely built structures that have been mentioned—the Holy Roman Empire, the Republic of Poland, and the empire of the Ottoman Turks.[3] The Turkish power reached to about fifty miles from Vienna, extended over what is now Rumania, and prevailed over the Tartars on the north shore of the Black Sea. Even so, its European holdings were but a projection from the main mass in Asia and Africa. Poland extended roughly from a hundred miles east of Berlin to a hundred miles west of Moscow, and virtually from "sea to sea" in the old phrase of its patriots, from the Baltic around Riga almost to the Black Sea coast, which, however, was held by Tartar Khans under the overlordship of the Turkish sultan at Constantinople. The Holy Roman Empire extended from Poland and Hungary to the North Sea.

These three empires were by no means alike. The Holy Empire bore some of the oldest traditions of Christendom. Poland too had old connections with the West. Turkey was a Muslim power, strange to Europe and contemptuous of it. Yet in some ways the three resembled each other. In all of them central authority had become weak, consisting largely of understandings between a nominal head and outlying dignitaries or potentates. All lacked efficient systems of administration and government. All were being put out of date by newer types of state of which France was the leading example. All, but especially Poland and Turkey, were made up of diverse ethnic or language groups.[4] None of these peoples, nor any combination of them—neither the dominant Germans, Poles, and Turks, nor the submerged Lithuanians, White Russians, Ukrainians, Czechs, Slovaks, Rumanians, Croats, Magyars, Serbs, Bulgars, or Greeks—had been formed into a compact organization. The whole immense area was politically soft. It was malleable in the hands of whoever might become a little stronger than his neighbor. We must try to see in what this softness consisted, and then how newer and harder "state forms" (as the Germans would say) were created.

[3] For the origins of the Holy Roman and Ottoman Empires, see pp. 29 and 46.
[4] For language groups, see map in Chapter XI, section 53.

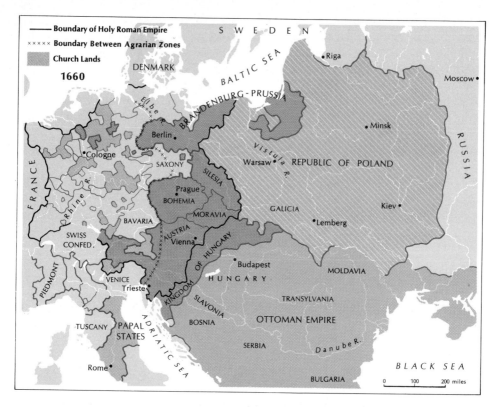

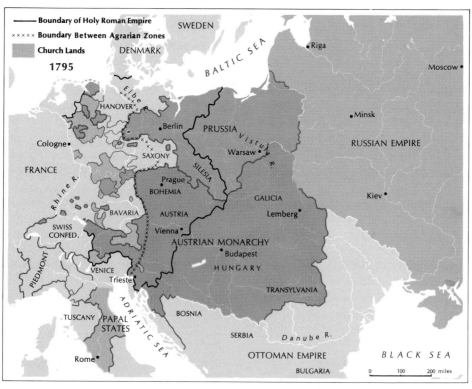

The Holy Roman Empire after 1648

With the Holy Roman Empire the reader is already familiar.[5] It was an empire, especially after the Peace of Westphalia, with next to no army, revenues, or working organs of government. Voltaire called it neither holy, Roman, nor an empire. As the seventeenth-century German jurist Pufendorf put it, it was somewhat of an abortion and a monstrosity. Created in the Middle Ages, it was Roman in that it was then believed to continue the imperial sway of the Rome of antiquity, and it was holy in being the secular counterpart to the spiritual empire of the pope. It had been ruined by the Reformation, which left the Germans divided almost evenly between Protestant and Catholic, with each side thereafter demanding special safeguards against the other. The Empire continued, however, to be universal in principle, having no relation to nationality, and theoretically being a form of government suitable to all peoples, although it had never made good this theoretical claim and had shown no expansionist tendency since the Middle Ages. In actuality, the Empire was very roughly coterminous with the German states and the region of the German language, except that it excluded after 1648 the Dutch and Swiss, who no longer considered themselves German; and it likewise excluded those Germans who since the fourteenth century had settled along the eastern shores of the Baltic.

Large parts of the Empire had suffered repeatedly from the Thirty Years' War. Yet the war, and the peace terms which followed it, only accentuated a situation which had long been unfavorable. Postwar revival was difficult; the breakup of commercial connections and the wartime losses of savings and capital were hard to overcome. Germany fell increasingly out of step with western Europe. The burgher class, its ambitions blocked, lost much of its old vitality. No overseas colonies could be founded, for want of strong enough government backing, as was shown when a colonial venture of Brandenburg came to nothing. There was no stock exchange in Germany until one was established at Vienna in 1771, half a century after those of London, Paris, and Amsterdam. Laws, tariffs, tolls, and coinage were more variegated than in France. Even the calendar varied. It varied, indeed, throughout Europe as a whole, since Protestant states long declined to accept the corrected calendar issued by Pope Gregory XIII in 1582, but in parts of divided Germany the holidays, the date of the month, and the day of the week changed every few miles. The arts and letters, flourishing in western Europe as never before, were at a low ebb in Germany in the seventeenth century. In science the Germans during and after the Thirty Years' War did less than the English, Dutch, French, or Italians, despite the great mathematician and philosopher

[5] See pp. 25, 29, 37, 72–74, 141–145.

CENTRAL AND EASTERN EUROPE, 1660–1795

This complex area is shown in simplified form on p. 210. The upper panel of the present map indicates boundaries as of 1660, the lower panel those of 1795. Both panels show the border between the eastern and western agrarian zones, running from the mouth of the Elbe River into central Germany and down to Trieste. East of this line, from the sixteenth to the eighteenth centuries, the mass of people sank into a kind of serfdom in which they rendered forced labor to their lords on large farms. West of the line the peasants owed little or no forced labor and tilled small farms which they owned or rented. This line is one of the most important sociological boundaries in the history of modern Europe.

Leibniz, one of the great minds of the age. Only in music, as in the work of the Bach family, did the Germans at this time excel. But music was not then much heard beyond the place of its origin. Germany for the rest of the world was a mute country, a byway in the higher civilization of Europe.

After the Thirty Years' War each German state had sovereign rights. These "states" numbered some 300 or 2,000, depending on how they were counted. The higher figure included the "knights of the Empire," found in south Germany and the Rhineland. They were persons who acknowledged no overlordship except that of the emperor himself. The knights had tiny estates of their own, averaging not over a hundred acres apiece, consisting of a castle and a manor or two, enclosed by the territory of a larger state but not forming a part of it. These free knights had arisen in various ways; in Württemberg, for example, the lords simply ceased to attend the diet, won exemption from the duke's jurisdiction, and retired to their own domains, leaving the surface of Württemberg pockmarked with small units politically independent of it. It was as if, in England, the peers had lost interest in the House of Lords and had set up independently, each on his own estates. Since the emperor, whom the knights regarded as their only superior, had in fact no authority, the knights were in effect private persons enjoying sovereign status—the last anomaly of bizarre neofeudalism and distorted freedom.

But even without the knights there were about three hundred states capable of some independence of action—free cities, abbots without subjects, archbishops and bishops ruling with temporal power, landgraves, margraves and dukes, and one king, the king of Bohemia. The highest ranking were called electors, who had the privilege of electing the emperor. By the Golden Bull of 1356 there were seven electors—three ecclesiastics (the archbishops of Cologne, Mainz, and Trier) and four laymen, the Count Palatine of the Rhine, the Duke of Saxony, the Margrave of Brandenburg, and the King of Bohemia. Bavaria was made an electorate at the Peace of Westphalia, and Hanover at the end of the century, so that finally there were nine electors. The fact that nearly half the electors were Protestants after the Reformation, whereas the Holy Empire had meaning only in a Catholic world, added to the internal confusion and general oddity of the system.

All these states were intent on preserving what were called the "Germanic liberties." They were gladly assisted by outside powers, notably but not exclusively France. The Germanic liberties meant freedom of the member states from control by emperor or Empire. The electors, at each election of an emperor, required the candidate to accept certain "capitulations," in which he promised to safeguard all the privileges and immunities of the states. The Habsburgs, though consistently elected after 1438, had none of the advantages of hereditary rulers, each having to bargain away in turn any gains made by his predecessor. The elective principle meant that imperial power could not be accumulated and transmitted from one generation to the next. It opened the doors to foreign intrigue, since the electors were willing to consider whichever candidate would promise them most. The French repeatedly supported a rival candidate to the Habsburgs. After 1648 they had a party in the electoral college, Bavaria and Cologne being the most consistently pro-French. Cardinal Mazarin in 1658 even entertained the thought of making the young Louis XIV Holy Roman Emperor. He had to accept election of a Habsburg, despite liberal use of French money, but the new emperor, Leopold I, undertook not to engage the Empire in any war supporting the Spanish Habsburgs against France. In 1742 the French obtained the elevation of their Bavarian ally to the imperial throne. The office of emperor became the political football of Germans and non-Germans working together.

Nor would the German states, after the Thirty Years' War, allow any authority to the imperial diet. The diet possessed the power to raise troops and taxes for the whole Empire, but the power remained unused. On matters affecting religion, after 1648, either Protestants or Catholics could demand the *ius eundi in partes*, or "right of sitting apart." Each religious group then constituted itself as a chamber, Protestant or Catholic, and since agreement of the two was required, each possessed a veto. The deliberations of the diet became notorious for their wordiness and futility. Many sessions were spent, for example, in attempts to fix for all Germany a common date for Easter, on which the whole calendar depended. In 1663 a diet met to consider measures against a new Turkish advance on the Danube. It was the last diet ever to be convoked, for it lasted "forever," i.e., until the end of the Holy Empire in 1806. It became the "perpetual diet" of Regensburg, never dismissed or renewed, unresponsive to events or issues, the states simply replacing their representatives individually, generation after generation, as at an endless congress of diplomats.

The states which insisted with such obstinacy on their liberties from the Empire gave few liberties to their subjects. The free cities were closed oligarchies, as indeed were most cities in other countries, but in Germany the burgher oligarchs of the free cities were virtually sovereign also. Most of the other states, large or small, developed in the direction of absolutism. Absolutism was checked for Germany as a whole, only to reappear in miniature in hundreds of different places. Each ruler thought himself a little Louis XIV, each court a small Versailles. Subjects became attached by ties of sentiment to their rulers, who almost always lived in the neighborhood and could be readily seen by passers-by. People liked the little courts, the toy armies, the gossipy politics, and the familiar officials of their tiny states.

The Empire, for all its faults, had the merit of holding this conglomeration of states in a lawful relation to one another. It was a kind of miniature league of nations. For a century and a half after the Peace of Westphalia infinitesimally small states existed alongside larger ones, or often totally enclosed within them, without serious fear for their security and without losing their independence. Only in power politics and in European or world affairs was the Empire a shadow. For the Germans it was a reality, a world in itself, which no one for a long time dreamed of violating or even reforming, for its existence assured a way of life which most Germans were glad to keep.

Yet there were many ambitious rulers in Germany after the Peace of Westphalia. They had won recognition of their sovereignty in 1648. They were busily building absolutist monarchies over their subjects. They aspired also to extend their dominions and cut a greater figure in the world. There were other ways of doing this than by devouring their smaller neighbors outright. One was by marriage and inheritance. The Empire in this respect was a paradise of fortune hunters; the variety of possible marriages was enormous because of the great number of ruling families. Another outlet for ambition lay in the high politics of the Empire. The Wittelsbach family, which ruled in Bavaria, managed to win an electorate in the Thirty Years' War; they consistently placed members of the family as archbishop of Cologne and in the other great Rhineland sees, and with the interest thus built up were able to sell their influence to France, which in turn backed them against the Habsburgs. The Guelph family, ruling in Hanover, schemed for years to obtain an electorate, which they finally extorted from the emperor in 1692; in 1714 they inherited the throne of Great Britain, preferred by the British as Protestants to their Catholic Stuart cousins. Two electors of Saxony in these years got themselves crowned king of Poland. The Hohenzollerns, electors of Brandenburg, were extremely fortunate in the seventeenth century in inheriting territories as far apart as the Rhine and the Vistula. The Habsburgs, hereditary rulers in Austria, a mere archduchy, were confirmed by the Peace of Westphalia as hereditary kings of Bohemia, where they had formerly depended on election.

The half-century after the Peace of Westphalia was a highly critical period in central Europe. The situation in Germany was fluid. No one could tell which, if any, of the half-dozen chief German states would emerge in the lead. Nothing was crystallized; anything might happen. Two states definitely came forward after 1700, built by the skill and persistence of their rulers—Austria and Prussia. It is a curious and revealing fact that neither really had a name of its own. They were for a long time known most commonly as "houses"—the house of Austria or Habsburg and the house of Brandenburg or Hohenzollern. Each house put together a certain combination of territories. Each would have been as willing to

AGING EMPIRES AND NEW POWERS

The left panel shows the "three aging empires" which occupied much of central and eastern Europe in the seventeenth century. (See pp. 205–214.) Though maintaining themselves with growing difficulty under modern conditions, the Polish Republic lasted until 1795, the Holy Roman Empire until 1806, the Ottoman Empire until 1923. Meanwhile, beginning in the seventeenth century, the political leadership in this area was assumed by three states of more modern type, organized around the institutions of monarchy, the standing army, and the professional bureaucracy or civil service—the reorganized Austrian Empire of the Habsburgs, the Hohenzollern kingdom of Prussia, and the Russian empire of the Romanovs. These are shown in the right panel. All three figured prominently in the affairs of Europe for over two hundred years; all perished in the First World War, 1914–1918.

possess any other combination had the course of events been different. By extension of meaning, one came to be called "Austria," which for centuries had been simply an archduchy on the upper Danube, and the other "Prussia," which for centuries had meant only a certain stretch of the Baltic coast. To the development of these two states we shall shortly turn.

The Republic of Poland about 1650

Running almost a thousand miles eastward from the Holy Roman Empire in the middle of the seventeenth century lay the vast tract of the Republic of Poland, called a republic because its king was elected, and because the political classes took pride in their constitutional liberties. Its vast size was one cause of its internal peculiarities. No administrative system could have kept up with the expansion of its frontiers, so that a large degree of freedom had always been left to outlying lords. In addition, the population was heterogeneous.

The Polish state was a far more recent and less substantial creation than the Holy Roman Empire. It was made up of two main parts, Poland proper in the west and the Grand Duchy of Lithuania in the east, the two having been joined by a union of their crowns.[6] Only in the extreme west, in the valley of the Vistula River, was there a mass of Polish population. The Duchy of Prussia, a fief of the Polish crown, was peopled by Germans. Further east a White Russian and Ukrainian peasantry was presided over by a scattering of Polish and Lithuanian landlords. Even in Poland itself the urban population was not generally Polish, the townspeople being largely Germans and Jews. The latter spoke Yiddish, a dialect basically German, and were very numerous because a king of Poland, in the later Middle Ages, had welcomed Jewish settlers fleeing from Germany.[7] The Jews did not adopt the Polish language. Tending at first to live in separate communities because of their religion, they were later confined to compulsory ghettos, islands of Orthodox Jewish life in the Gentile ocean. The Germans too held aloof, resisting assimilation to their less advanced surroundings. An unsurpassable barrier thus existed between town and country. There was no national middle class. The official and political language was Latin. Roman Catholicism was the leading religion.

Poland is interesting as the region in which the landed aristocracy won over all other groups in the country, neither allowing the consolidation of the state on absolutist lines, nor yet creating an effective constitutional or parliamentary government. The Polish aristocracy, or *szlachta*, made up some 8 percent of the population, a far higher proportion than the aristocracy of any country of western Europe. On this ground the old Polish kingdom has sometimes been considered, especially by later Polish nationalists, as the possessor of an early form of democracy. The aristocracy were sticklers for their liberties, called the "Polish liberties," which resembled the German liberties in consisting largely of a fierce suspicion of central authority and in being a perpetual invitation to foreign interference. As in the Holy Roman Empire, the monarchy was elective, and the king upon election had to accept certain contractual agreements, which, like the German "capitulations," made impossible the accumulation of authority by the crown. As in the Empire, the royal elections were a cockpit of foreign influence, bribery, and

---

[6] See maps, pp. 206 and 210.
[7] See p. 72, note.

intrigue. The Poles were too factious to accept one of their own number as king. They were divided into pro-French, pro-Swedish, pro-Russian, and other parties. From 1572 to the extinction of Poland over two centuries later there were only two native Polish kings who reigned for any length of time, and one of these was the discarded lover of a Russian empress. The other was the national hero John Sobieski, whose decisive action against the Turks is noted below.

As in Germany, also, the central diet was ineffective and the nuclei of political action were local. The aristocracy met in fifty or sixty regional diets, turbulent assemblages of warlike gentry, in which the great lords used the little ones for their own purposes. The central diet, from which the towns were excluded, was a periodic meeting of emissaries, under binding instructions, from the regional diets. It came to be recognized, as one of the liberties of the country, that the central diet could take no action to which any member objected. Any member, by stating his unalterable opposition, could oblige a diet to disband. This was the famous *liberum veto*, the free veto, and to use it to break up a diet was called "exploding" the diet. The first diet was exploded in 1652. Of fifty-five diets held from that year to 1764, forty-eight were exploded.

Government became a fiasco. The monopoly of law and force, characteristic of the modern state, failed to develop in Poland. The king of Poland had practically no army, no law courts, no officials, and no income. The nobility paid no taxes. By 1750 the revenues of the king of Poland were about one-thirteenth those of the tsar of Russia and one seventy-fifth those of the king of France. Armed force was in the hands of a dozen or so aristocratic leaders, who also conducted their own individual foreign policies, pursuing their own adventures against the Turks, or bringing in Russians, French, or Swedes to help them against other Poles. The landlords became local monarchs on their manorial estates, and the mass of the rural population fell deeper into a serfdom scarcely different from slavery, bound to compulsory labor on estates resembling plantations, with police and disciplinary powers in the hands of the lords, and with no outside legal or administrative system to set the limits of exploitation. Some Polish aristocrats, hiring architects or buying libraries from Germany and western Europe, traveling with trains of servants to Italy or France, masters of many languages and habitually associating with the great, became among the most accomplished and cosmopolitan people in Europe. A great Polish nobleman could boast of more territory and subjects, and of more international consideration, than many a sovereign princeling of Germany. But the mass of the aristocracy became an unruly body of decayed gentry, dependent on their connections with the powerful families, and indifferent to western Europe.

The huge expanse comprised under the name of Poland was, in short, a power vacuum, an area of low political pressure; and as centers of higher pressure developed, notably around Berlin and Moscow, the push against the Polish frontiers became steadily stronger. It was facilitated by the centrifugal habits of the Poles themselves. As early as 1660 the East Prussian fief became independent of the Polish crown. As early as 1667 the Muscovites reconquered Smolensk and Kiev. Already there was confidential talk of partitioning Poland, which, however, was deferred for a century. The history of the world would have been different had the Poland of the seventeenth century held together. There would have been no kingdom of Prussia and no Prussian influence in Germany; nor would Russia have become the chief Slavic power or reached so far into central Europe.

The Ottoman Empire about 1650

The Ottoman state, the third of the three empires which together spread over so much of Europe, was larger than either of the others, and in the seventeenth century was more solidly organized. In 1529 the Turks had attacked Vienna and seemed about to burst into Germany.[8] To the Christian world the Turks were a mystery as well as a terror. They were in truth among the rougher of the Muslim peoples, who had erupted from central Asia only a few centuries before and owed most of their higher civilization to the Arabs and the Persians. Their dominions extended, about 1650, from the Hungarian plain and the south Russian steppes as far as Algeria, the upper Nile, and the Persian Gulf. The empire was based to a large degree on military proficiency. Long before Europe the Turks had a standing army, of which the main striking force was the janissaries. The janissaries were originally recruited from Christian children taken from their families in early childhood, brought up as Muslims, reared in military surroundings, and forbidden to marry; without background or ties, interests, or ambition outside the military organization to which they belonged, they were an ideal fighting material in the hands of political leaders. The Turkish forces were long as well equipped as the Christian, being especially strong in heavy artillery. But by the mid-seventeenth century they were falling behind. They had changed little, or for the worse, since the days of Suleiman the Magnificent a century before, whereas in the better organized Christian states discipline and military administration had been improved, and firearms, land mines, and siegecraft had become more effective.

The Turks cared little about assimilating subject peoples to their language or institutions. Law was religious law derived from the Koran. Law courts and judges were hard to distinguish from religious authorities, for there was no separation between religious and secular spheres. The sultan was also the caliph, the commander of the faithful, and while on the one hand there was no clergy in the European sense, on the other hand religious influences affected all aspects of life. The Turks, for the most part, applied the Muslim law only to Muslims.

The Ottoman government left its non-Muslim subjects to settle their own affairs in their own way, not according to nationality, which was generally indistinguishable, but according to religious groupings. The Greek Orthodox church, to which most Christians in the empire belonged, thus became an almost autonomous intermediary between the sultan and a large fraction of its subjects. Armenian Christians and Jews formed other separate bodies. Except in the western Balkans (Albania and Bosnia) there was no general conversion of Christians to Islam during the Turkish rule, although there were many individual cases of Christians turning Muslim to obtain the privileges of the ruling faith. North of the Danube the Christian princes of Transylvania, Wallachia, and Moldavia (later combined in the modern Rumania) continued to rule over Christian subjects. They were kept in office for that purpose by the sultan, to whom they paid tribute. In general, since their subjects were more profitable to them as Christians, the Turks were not eager to proselytize for Islam.

The Ottoman Empire was therefore a relatively tolerant empire, far more so than the states of Europe. Christians in the Turkish empire fared better than Muslims would have fared in Christendom or than the Moors had in fact fared in

---

[8] See pp. 45, 73–74, and 78.

Spain. Christians were less disturbed in Turkey than were Protestants in France, after 1685, or Catholics in Ireland. The empire was tolerant because it was composite, an aggregation of peoples, religions, and laws, having no drive, as did the Western states, toward internal unity and complete legal sovereignty. The same was evident in the attitude toward foreign merchants.

The king of France had had treaty arrangements with Turkey since 1535, and many traders from Marseilles had spread over the port towns of the Near East. They were exempted by treaty from the laws of the Ottoman Empire and were liable to trial only by their own judges, who though residing in Turkey were appointed by the king of France. They were free to exercise their Roman Catholic religion, and if disputes with Muslims arose, they appeared in special courts where the word of an infidel received equal weight with that of a follower of the prophet. Similar rights in Turkey were obtained by other European states. Thus began "extraterritorial" privileges of the kind obtained by Europeans in later centuries in China and elsewhere, wherever the local laws were regarded as backward. To the Turks of the seventeenth century there was nothing exceptional about such arrangements. Only much later, under Western influence, did the Turks learn to resent these "capitulations" as impairments of their own sovereignty.

Yet the Turkish rule was oppressive, and the "terrible Turk" was with reason the nightmare of eastern Europe. Ottoman rule was oppressive to Christians if only because it relegated them to a despised position, and because everything they held holy was viewed by the Turks with violent contempt. But it was oppressive also in that it was arbitrary and brutal even by the none too sensitive standards of Europeans. It was worse in these respects in the seventeenth century than formerly, for the central authority of the sultans had become corrupt, and the outlying governors, or pashas, had a virtually free hand with their subjects.

Those parts of the Ottoman Empire which adjoined the Christian states were among the least firmly attached to Constantinople. The Tartar Khans of south Russia, like the Christian princes of the Danubian principalities, were simply protégés who paid tribute. Hungary was occupied but was more a battlefield than a province. These regions were disputed by Germans, Poles, and Russians. It seemed in the middle of the seventeenth century as if the grip of the Turks might be relaxing. But a dynasty of unusually capable grand viziers, the Kiuprilis, came to power and retained it contrary to Turkish customs for fifty years. Under them the empire again put forth a mighty effort. By 1663 the janissaries were again mobilizing in Hungary. Tartar horsemen were on the move. Central Europe again felt the old terror. The pope feared that the dreaded enemy might break into Italy. Throughout Germany by the emperor's order special "Turk bells" sounded the alarm. The states of the Empire assembled in 1663 as a diet at Regensburg. They voted to raise a small imperial army. The Holy Roman Empire, even in its senility, bestirred itself temporarily against the historic enemy of the Christians. But it was not the Empire, but the house of Austria, under whose auspices the Turks were to be repelled.

24. THE FORMATION OF AN AUSTRIAN MONARCHY

Having now surveyed the three very different empires whose occupancy of most of Europe from France to Muscovy kept the whole area politically malleable and soft, we turn to the three new states which consolidated themselves in this region, namely, Austria, Prussia, and Russia.

The Recovery and Growth of Habsburg Power, 1648–1740

The Austria which appeared by 1700 was in truth a new creation, though not as obviously so as the two others. The Austrian Habsburgs had long enjoyed an eminent role. Formerly their position had rested on their headship of the Holy Roman Empire and on their family connection with the more wealthy Habsburgs of Spain. In the seventeenth century these two supports collapsed. The hope for an effective Habsburg empire in Germany disappeared in the Thirty Years' War. The connection with Spain lost its value as Spain declined, and vanished when in 1700 Spain passed to the house of France. The Austrian family in the latter half of the seventeenth century stood at the great turning point of its fortunes. It successfully made a difficult transition, emerging from the husk of the Holy Empire and building an empire of its own. At the same time the Habsburgs continued to be Holy Roman Emperors and remained active in German affairs, using resources drawn from outside Germany to maintain their influence over the German princes. The relation of Austria to the rest of Germany became a political conundrum, forcibly solved by Bismarck in 1866 by the exclusion of Austria, only to be raised again by Adolf Hitler in the twentieth century.

The dominions considered by the house of Austria to be its own direct possessions were in three parts. The oldest were the "hereditary provinces"—Upper and Lower Austria, with the adjoining Tyrol, Styria, Carinthia, and Carniola. Second, there was the kingdom of Bohemia—Bohemia, Moravia, and Silesia joined under the crown of St. Wenceslas. Third, there was the kingdom of Hungary—Hungary, Transylvania, and Croatia joined under the crown of St. Stephen. Nothing held all these regions together except the fact that the Austrian Habsburg dynasty, in the seventeenth century, reaffirmed its grip upon them all. During the Thirty Years' War the dynasty rooted Protestantism and feudal rebelliousness out of Austria and the hereditary provinces, and reconquered and re-Catholicized Bohemia. And in the following decades it conquered Hungary also.

Since 1526 most of Hungary had been occupied by the Turks. For generations the Hungarian plain was a theater of intermittent warfare between the armies of Vienna and Constantinople. The struggle flared up again in 1663, when the Kiuprili vizier started Turkish armies moving up the Danube. A mixed force, assembled from the Empire and from all Christendom, obliged the Turks in 1664 to accept a twenty-year truce. But Louis XIV, who in these years was busily dismembering the western frontier of the Empire, stood to profit greatly from a diversion on the Danube. He incited the Turks (old allies of France through common hostility to the Habsburgs) to resume their assaults, which they did as the twenty-year truce came to a close.

In 1683 a vast Turkish host reached the city of Vienna and besieged it. The Turks again, as in 1529, peered into the very inner chambers of Europe. The garrison and people of Vienna, greatly outnumbered, held off the besiegers for two months, enough time for a defending force to arrive. Both sides showed the composite or "international" character of the conflict. The Turkish army included some Christians—Rumanian and Hungarian—the latter being in rebellion against Habsburg rule in Hungary. The Christian force was composed mainly of Poles, Austrian dynastic troops, and Germans from various states of the Empire. It was

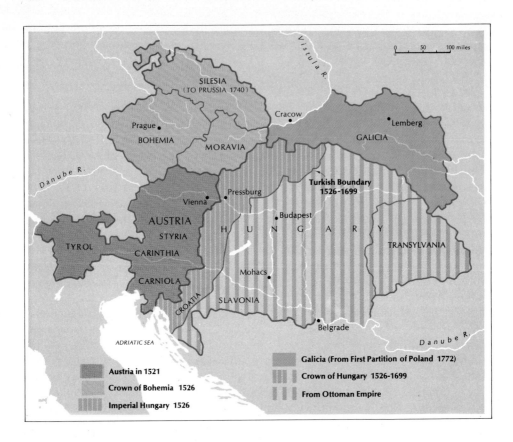

THE GROWTH OF THE AUSTRIAN MONARCHY, 1521–1772

The map shows the main body of the Austrian monarchy as it came to be in the eighteenth century and continued until the collapse of the empire in 1918. There were three main parts: (1) a nucleus, composed of Austria and adjoining duchies, often called the "hereditary provinces"; (2) the lands of the Bohemian crown, which became Habsburg in 1526 and where the Habsburgs reasserted their power during the Bohemian phase of the Thirty Years' War; and (3) the lands of the Hungarian crown, where at first the Habsburgs held only the segment called Imperial Hungary, the rest remaining Turkish until reconquered by the Habsburgs in 1699. In the first partition of Poland the Habsburgs annexed Galicia. Silesia was lost to Prussia in 1740. Outlying parts of the empire in the eighteenth century, not shown on the map, were most of what is now Belgium (then the Austrian Netherlands) and the duchy of Milan in Italy. The Italian duchy of Tuscany, where the Medici family died out in 1737, was thereafter ruled as a separate state by a Habsburg archduke.

financed largely by Pope Innocent XI; it was commanded in the field by the Habsburg general, Duke Charles of Lorraine, who hoped to protect his inheritance from annexation by France; and its higher command was entrusted to John Sobieski, king of Poland. Sobieski contributed greatly to the relief of Vienna, and his bold action represented the last great military effort of the moribund Republic of Poland. When the Turks abandoned the siege, a general anti-Turkish counteroffensive developed. Forces of the pope, Poland, Russia, and the republic of Venice joined with the Habsburgs. It was in this war, in fighting between Turks and

Venetians, that the Parthenon at Athens, which had survived for two thousand years but was now used as an ammunition dump by the Turks, was blown to ruins.

The Habsburgs had the good fortune to obtain the services of a man of remarkable talent, Prince Eugene of Savoy. Eugene, like many other servants of the Austrian house, was not Austrian at all; he was in fact French by origin and education but like many of the aristocratic class of the time was an international personage. More than anyone else he was the founder of the modern Austrian state. Distinguished both as a military administrator and as a commander in the field, he reformed the supply, equipment, training, and command of the Habsburg forces, along lines laid out by Louis XIV, and in 1697 he won the battle of Zenta, driving the Turks out of Hungary. At the Peace of Karlowitz (1699) the Turks yielded most of Hungary, together with Transylvania and Croatia, to the Habsburg house.

The Habsburgs were now free to pursue their designs in the west. They entered the War of the Spanish Succession to win the Spanish crown, but although an Austrian archduke campaigned in Spain for years, assisted by the English, they had to content themselves at the treaty of Rastadt in 1714 with the annexation of the old Spanish Netherlands and with Milan and Naples. Prince Eugene, freed now in the west, again turned eastward. Never before or afterward were the Austrians so brilliantly successful. Eugene captured Belgrade and pushed through the Iron Gate into Wallachia. But the Turks were not yet helpless; and by the Peace of Belgrade (1739) a frontier was drawn which on the Austrian side remained unchanged until the twentieth century. The Turks continued to hold Rumania and the whole Balkan peninsula except Catholic Croatia, which, incorporated in the Habsburg empire, was again faced toward Europe. The Habsburg government, to open a window on the Mediterranean, developed a seaport at Trieste.

The Austrian Monarchy by 1740

Thus the house of Austria, in two or three generations after its humiliation at the Peace of Westphalia, acquired a new empire of very considerable proportions. Though installed in Belgium and Italy, it was essentially an empire of the middle Danube, with its headquarters at Vienna in Austria proper, but possessing the sizable kingdoms of Hungary and Bohemia, and so filling the basin enclosed by the Alpine, Bohemian, and Carpathian mountain systems. Though German influence was strong, the empire was international or nonnational. At the Habsburg court, and in the Habsburg government and army, the names of Czech, Hungarian, Croatian, and Italian noblemen were very common. It is hard today to see this empire as it was, because it is hard to see it except through the eyes of its enemies. It made enemies of all Protestants. Democrats came to hate it. When the nationalistic movement swept over Europe in the nineteenth century, the empire was denounced as tyrannical by Hungarians, Croats, Serbs, Rumanians, Czechs, Poles, Italians, and even some Germans, whose national ambitions were blocked by its existence. Later, disillusioned by nationalism in central and eastern Europe, some tended to romanticize unduly the old Danubian monarchy, noting that it had at least the merit of holding many discordant peoples together.

The empire was from the first international, based on a cosmopolitan aristocracy of landowners who felt closer to each other, despite difference of language, than to the laboring masses who worked on their estates. Not for many years, until after 1848, did the Habsburg government really touch these rural masses; it dealt with the landed class and with the relatively few cities, and left the landlords to control the peasants. The old diets remained in being in Bohemia, Hungary, and the Austrian provinces. No diet was created for the empire as a whole. The diets were essentially assemblages of landlords; and though they no longer enjoyed their medieval freedom, they retained certain powers over taxation and administration and a sense of constitutional liberty against the crown, like the Provincial Estates in France. So long as they produced taxes and soldiers as needed, and accepted the wars and foreign policy of the ruling house, no questions were asked at Vienna. The peasants remained in, or reverted to, serfdom.[9]

The Habsburgs were determined to make their new empire unmistakably hereditary and Catholic. The first to feel the blow had been Bohemia. The Czech rebellion had been crushed, as we have seen, at the battle of the White Mountain in 1620.[10] This ended, until 1918, the national independence of a people who had greatly prospered in the Middle Ages. The reigning Habsburg, Ferdinand II, abrogated the elective Bohemian monarchy and declared the kingdom hereditary. He poured Catholic missionaries into the country. He confiscated the estates of the rebel nobles and granted them to a host of adventurers of many nationalities, mostly colonels and generals of the Thirty Years' War. A few of these were Czechs, but most were ignorant of the languages and customs of the people, and they owed their position entirely to the Habsburgs. Bohemia remained an entirely separate kingdom. Its new aristocracy, while remaining apart from the native peasantry and the towns, soon developed a sense of Bohemian autonomy and a desire to be let alone by the central government at Vienna.

Somewhat the same happened in Hungary after its reconquest from the Turks in 1699. Protestantism was widespread in Hungary, where it formed part of the famous Hungarian liberties. Every Hungarian magnate, like princes of the Holy Roman Empire, possessed the *ius reformandi*, or right to reform religion on his own estates. There was thus religious disorder, and religion and politics were mixed. The Turks, during their occupation, favored the Protestants, knowing that Protestants would have no longing for a Catholic Habsburg king. In Hungary, therefore, as in Bohemia, the first step following the reconquest was to repress Protestantism, which was not only detested as heretical but feared as pro-Turkish. The elective monarchy was done away with; the crown of St. Stephen[11] became the hereditary possession of the Habsburgs. The Hungarian nobles lost their constitutional right of armed rebellion. German veterans were settled in the country, the Croats given privileges, and even Serbs imported from across the Danube, all to weaken the grip of the Magyar aristocracy; the effect was to scramble the nationalities in an already heterogeneous region. Hardly had Eugene's armies entered Turkish Hungary when a rebellion against the Habsburgs broke out in 1703, led by Prince Francis Rakoczy, who received help from Louis XIV but was finally crushed by 1711 and spent the rest of his life in France and Turkey. The Hungarians, proud and stubborn, became nationalistic before the era of nationalism. And for all that the Habsburgs could do, Hungary remained a distinct kingdom, and the magnates of Hungary remained the most free-handed aristocracy in Europe, except for the Poles.

[9] See pp. 122–123.
[10] See pp. 139–140.
[11] See p. 26.

Thus, despite the efforts of the Habsburgs, the Austrian monarchy remained a collection of territories held together by a personal union. Inhabitants of Austria proper considered their ruler as archduke, Bohemians saw in him the king of Bohemia, Magyars the apostolic king of Hungary. Each country retained its own law, diet, and political life. No feeling in the people held these regions together, and even the several aristocracies were joined only by common service to the house. For the empire to exist, all crowns had to be inherited by the same person.

After the reconquest of Hungary the king-archduke, Charles VI (1711–1740), devised a form of insurance to guarantee such an undivided succession. This took the form of a document called the Pragmatic Sanction, first issued in 1713. By it every diet in the empire and the various archdukes of the Habsburg family were to agree to regard the Habsburg territories as indivisible and to recognize only one specified line of heirs. The matter became urgent when it developed that Charles would have no children except a daughter, Maria Theresa, and that the direct male line of the Austrian Habsburgs, as of the Spanish a few years before, was about to become extinct. Charles VI gradually won acceptance of the Pragmatic Sanction by all parts of his empire and all members of his family. He then set about having foreign powers guarantee it, knowing that Bavaria, Prussia, or others might well put in claims for this or that part of the inheritance. This process took years, and was accomplished at the cost of many damaging concessions. Charles VI had attempted, for example, to revive Belgium commercially by founding an overseas trading company at Ostend. The British government, before agreeing to guarantee the Pragmatic Sanction, demanded and obtained the abandonment of this commercial project. Finally all powers signed. Charles VI died in 1740, having done all that could be done, by domestic law and international treaty, to assure the continuation of the Austrian empire.

He was scarcely dead when armed "heirs" presented themselves. A great war broke out to partition the Austrian empire, as the Spanish empire had been partitioned shortly before. Bohemia threw off its allegiance. Hungary almost did the same. But these events belong later in the story.[12] At the moment it is enough to know that by 1740 a populous empire, of great military strength, had been founded on the Danube.

25. THE FORMATION OF PRUSSIA

It was characteristic of the seventeenth century that very small states were able to play an influential part in European affairs, seemingly out of all proportion to their size. The main reason why small states could act as great powers was that armies were small and weapons simple. Difficulties of supply and communications, the poor state of the roads, the lack of maps, the absence of general staffs, together with many other administrative and technical difficulties, held down the number of soldiers who could be successfully managed in a campaign. The battles of the Thirty Years' War, on the average, were fought by armies of less than 20,000 men. And while Louis XIV, by the last years of his reign, built up a military establishment aggregating some 400,000, the actual field armies in the wars of Louis XIV did not exceed, on the average, 40,000. Armies of this size were well within the reach of smaller powers. If especially well trained, disciplined, and

---

[12] See pp. 264–275.

equipped, and if ably commanded and economically employed, the armies of small powers could defeat those of much larger neighbors. On this fact, fundamentally, the German state of Prussia was to be built. But Prussia was not the first to exploit the opportunity with spectacular consequences. The first, it may be said, was Sweden.

Sweden's Short-Lived Empire

Sweden almost, but not quite, formed an empire out of the malleable matter of central and eastern Europe in the seventeenth century. The population of Sweden at the time was not over a million; it was smaller than that of the Dutch Republic. But the Swedes produced a line of extraordinary rulers, ranging from genius in Gustavus Adolphus (1611–1632) through the brilliantly erratic Queen Christina (1632–1654) to the amazing military exploits of Charles XII (1697–1718). The elective Swedish kingship was made definitely hereditary, the royal power freed from control by the estates, craftsmen and experts brought from the west, notably Holland, war industries subsidized by the government, and an army created with many novel features in weapons, organization, and tactics.

With this army Gustavus Adolphus crossed the Baltic in the Thirty Years' War, made alliances with Protestant German princes, cut through the yielding mass of the Holy Roman Empire, and helped to ward off unification of Germany by the Habsburgs.[13] The Swedish crown, by the Peace of Westphalia, received certain coastal regions of Germany—western Pomerania, including the city of Stettin, and the former bishoprics of Bremen and Verden on the North Sea. Subsequently, in a confused series of wars, in which a Polish king claimed to be king of Sweden, and a Swedish king claimed to be king of Poland, the Swedes won control of virtually all the shores and cities of the Baltic. Only Denmark at the mouth of that sea and the territories of the house of Brandenburg, which had almost no ports, remained independent. For a time the Baltic was a Swedish lake. The Russians were shut off from it, and the Poles and even the Germans, who lived on its shores, could reach it only on Swedish terms.

The final Swedish effort was made by the meteoric Charles XII. As a young man he found his dominions attacked by Denmark, Poland, and Russia; he won victories over them but would not make peace; he then led an army back and forth across the East European plain, only to be ruined by the Russians, and spend more long years as a guest and protégé of the Turks.[14] With the death of Charles XII in 1718 the Swedish sphere contracted to Sweden itself, except that Finland and reduced holdings in northern Germany remained Swedish for a century more. The Swedes in time proved themselves exceptional among European peoples in not harping on their former greatness. They successfully and peaceably made the transition from the role of a great power to that of a small one.

The Territorial Growth of Brandenburg-Prussia

In the long run it was to be Prussia that dominated this part of Europe. Prussia also became famous for its "militarism," which may be said to exist when military

---

[13] See pp. 140–144.
[14] See p. 233.

needs and military values permeate all other spheres of life. Through its influence on Germany over a period of two centuries it played a momentous part in the modern world. The south coast of the Baltic, where Prussia was to arise, was an unpromising site for the creation of a strong political power. It was an uninviting country, thinly populated, with poor soil and without mineral resources, more backward than Saxony or Bohemia, not to mention the busy centers of south Germany and western Europe. It was a flat open plain, merging imperceptibly into Poland, without prominent physical features or natural frontiers.[15] The coastal region directly south from Sweden was known as Pomerania. Inland from it, shut off from the sea, was the electoral margraviate of Brandenburg, centering about Berlin. In 1415 the Hohenzollern family had come to rule Brandenburg, which was to be the nucleus of modern Prussia. Brandenburg had been founded in the Middle Ages as a "mark" or "march" of the Holy Roman Empire, to fight the battles of the Holy Empire against the then heathen Slavs. All Germany east of the Elbe represented a medieval conquest by the German-speaking peoples—the German *Drang nach Osten*, or drive to the East. From the Elbe to Poland, German conquerors and settlers had replaced the primitive Slavs, eliminating them or absorbing them by intermarriage.

Extending eastward from Brandenburg and Pomerania, and outside the Holy Roman Empire, stretched a region inhabited by Slavic peoples and known historically as Pomerelia. Next to the east came "Prussia," which eventually was to give its name to all territories of the Hohenzollern monarchy. This original Prussia formed part of the lands of the Teutonic Knights, a military crusading order which had conquered and Christianized the native peoples in the thirteenth century.[16] Except for its seacoast along the Baltic, the duchy of Prussia was totally enclosed by the Polish kingdom. To the north, along the Baltic, as far as the Gulf of Finland, German minorities lived among undeveloped Lithuanians, Latvians (or Letts), and Estonians. The towns were German, founded as German commercial colonies in the Middle Ages, and many of the landlords were German also, descendants of the Teutonic Knights, and later known as the "Baltic barons." These Germans at that time, since nationalist sentiment scarcely existed, felt no affiliation with the main block of Germans farther west, but they retained their German language and traditions.

Modern Prussia began to appear in the seventeenth century when a number of territories came together in the hands of the Hohenzollerns of Brandenburg, who, we have noted, had ruled in Brandenburg since 1415. In 1618 the Elector of Brandenburg inherited the duchy of Prussia. Another important development occurred when the old ruling line in Pomerania expired during the Thirty Years' War. Although the Swedes succeeded in taking the better part of Pomerania, including the city of Stettin, the Elector of Brandenburg received at the Peace of Westphalia eastern or Farther Pomerania. Barren, rural, and harborless though it was, it at least had the advantage of connecting Brandenburg with the Baltic. The Hohenzollerns no sooner obtained it than they began to dream of joining it to the duchy of Prussia, a task which required the absorption of the intermediate and predominantly Slavic Pomerelia, which was part of Poland. (This task was accomplished in 1772. The Hohenzollern administrators then called the old duchy "East Prussia" and the old Pomerelia "West Prussia"; but by that time, in a

---

[15] See maps, pp. 6–7, 142–143, 206, 210.
[16] See p. 44.

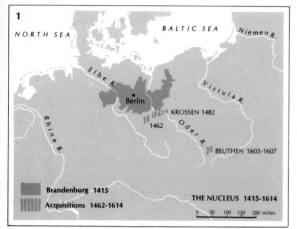

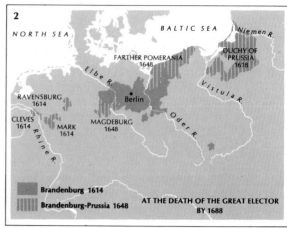

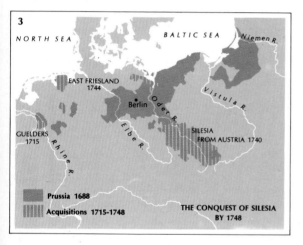

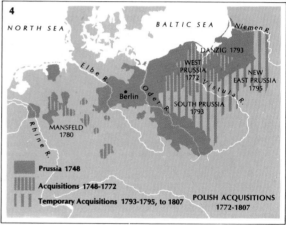

THE GROWTH OF PRUSSIA, 1415–1918

The maps shown here give a conspectus of Prussian history from the time when Brandenburg began to expand in the seventeenth century. One may see, by looking at all the panels
together, how Prussia was really an east-European state until 1815; its center of gravity
shifted westward, in significant degree, only in the nineteenth century. Panel 2 shows the
early formation of three unconnected masses; Panel 3, the huge bulk of Silesia relative to
the small kingdom that annexed it (pp. 265–268); Panel 4, the fruits of the partitions of
Poland (p. 328); Panel 5, Napoleon pared Prussia down (pp. 395–396). The main crisis at
the Congress of Vienna, and its resolution, are shown in Panels 6 and 7 (pp. 422–423). Bismarck's enlargement of Prussia appears in Panel 8 (pp. 523–524). The boundaries established by Bismarck remained unchanged until the fall of the Prussian monarchy in 1918.

general confusion of nomenclature, "Prussia" also referred to all the Hohenzollern
provinces taken together.)

Had the duchy of Prussia and Farther Pomerania been the only acquisitions of
the Hohenzollerns, their state would have been oriented almost exclusively
toward eastern Europe. But at the Peace of Westphalia they received, in addition
to Farther Pomerania, the large bishopric of Halberstadt and the still larger arch-

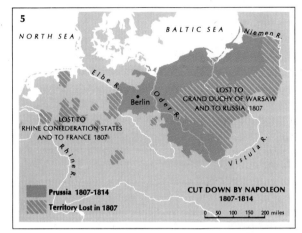

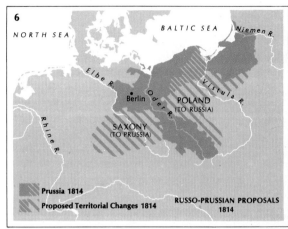

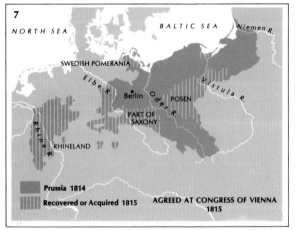

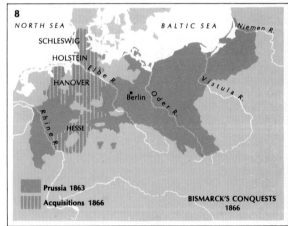

bishopric of Magdeburg, which lay on the west bank of the Elbe. Moreover, through the play of inheritance so common in the Holy Roman Empire, the Hohenzollerns had earlier fallen heir, in 1614, to the small state of Cleves on the Rhine at the Dutch border and a few other small territories also in western Germany. These were separated from the main mass around Brandenburg by many intermediate German principalities. But they gave the Hohenzollerns a direct contact with the more advanced regions of western Europe, and a base from which larger holdings in the Rhineland were eventually to be built up.

In the seventeenth century, meanwhile, the dominions of the house of Brandenburg were in three disconnected masses. The main mass was Brandenburg, with the adjoining Pomerania and Elbe bishoprics. There was a detached eastern mass in ducal Prussia and a small detached western mass on and near the Rhine. The middle and western masses were within the Holy Roman Empire. The eastern mass was outside the Empire, and until 1660, a fief of Poland. To connect and unify the three masses became the underlying long-range policy of the Brandenburg house.

In the midst of the Thirty Years' War, in 1640, a young man of twenty, named

Frederick William, succeeded to these diverse possessions. Known later as the Great Elector, he was the first of the men who made modern Prussia. He had grown up under trying conditions. Brandenburg was one of the parts of Germany to suffer most heavily from the war. Its location made it the stamping ground of Swedish and Habsburg armies. In 1640, in the twenty-two years since the beginning of the war, the population of Berlin had fallen from about 14,000 to about 6,000. Hundreds of villages had been wiped out. Wolves roamed over the countryside.

Frederick William concluded that in his position, ruling a small and open territory, without natural frontiers or possibility of defense in depth, he must put his main reliance on a competent army. With an effective army, even if small, he could oblige the stronger states to take him into their calculations and so could enter with some hope of advantage into the politics of the balance of power. This long remained the program of the Brandenburgers—to have an army but not to use it, to conserve it with loving and even miserly care, to keep an "army in being," and to gain their ends by diplomatic maneuver. They did so by siding with France against the Habsburgs, or with Sweden against Poland. They aspired also to the title not merely of margrave or elector, but king. The opportunity came in 1701, when the Habsburg emperor was preparing to enter the War of the Spanish Succession. He wanted the support of 8,000 Brandenburg troops. The elector named his price: recognition of himself, by the emperor, as king "in Prussia." The emperor yielded; the title, at first explicitly limited to the less honorable king *in* Prussia, soon became king *of* Prussia. Another rent was made in the old fabric of the Holy Empire. There was now a German king above all the other German princes.

The Prussian Military State

The preoccupation of Prussia with its army was unquestionably defensive in origin, arising from the horrors of the Thirty Years' War. But it outlasted its cause, and became the settled habit and character of the country. Prussia was not unique, in a world of Bourbons and Habsburgs, Swedes, Russians, Turks, and the growing British navy, in the attention it paid to its armed forces. The unique thing about Prussia was the disproportion between the size of the army and the size of the resources on which the army was based. The government, to maintain the army, had to direct and plan the life of the country for this purpose. Nor was Prussia the originator of the "standing" army, kept active in time of peace, and always preparing for war. Most governments imitated Louis XIV in establishing standing armies, not merely to promote foreign ambitions but to keep armed forces out of the hands of nobles and military adventurers, and under control by the state.

But Prussia was unique in that, more than in any other country, the army developed a life of its own, almost independent of the life of the state. It was older than the Prussian state. In 1657 the Great Elector fought a great battle at Warsaw with soldiers from all parts of his dominions. It was the first time that men from Cleves, Brandenburg, and ducal Prussia had ever done anything together. The army was the first "all Prussian" institution. Institutions of civilian government developed later and largely to meet the needs of the army. And in later generations the army proved more durable than the state. When Prussia collapsed before Napoleon in 1806, the spirit and morale of the Prussian army carried on; and when the Hohenzollern empire finally crashed in 1918, the army still maintained its life and traditions on into the Republic, which again it survived.[17]

In all countries, to some extent, the machinery of the modern state developed as a means of supporting armed forces, but in Prussia the process was exceptionally clear and simple. In Prussia the rulers drew roughly half their income from the crown domain and only about half from taxes. The crown domain, consisting of manors and other productive enterprises owned directly by the ruler as lord, was in effect a kind of government property, for the Prussian rulers used their income almost entirely for state purposes, being personally men of simple and even Spartan habits. The rulers of Prussia, until a century after the accession of the Great Elector, were able to pay the whole cost of their civil government from their own income, the proceeds of the crown domain. But to maintain an army they had to make the domain more productive, and also find a new income derived from taxes. To develop the domain and account for and transfer the funds, they created a large body of civilian officials. The domain bulked so large that much of the economy of the country was not in private hands but consisted of enterprises owned and administered by the state. For additional income the Great Elector introduced taxes of the kind used in France, such as excise taxes on consumers' goods and a government monopoly on the sale of salt. These taxes, together with the old land tax, began to be collected during the disorders of the Thirty Years' War by war commissioners, later organized into a general commissariat. In effect, the army itself collected the taxes and determined the purposes for which the funds should be spent. All taxes, for a century after the accession of the Great Elector, were levied for the use of the army.

Economic life grew up under government sponsorship, rather than by the enterprise of a venturesome business class. This was because, for a rural country to maintain an organized army, productive and technical skills had to be imported, mainly from the West. The Great Elector in his youth spent a number of years in Holland, where he was impressed by the wealth and prosperity that he saw. After becoming elector he settled Swiss and Frisians in Brandenburg (the Frisians were almost Dutch); he welcomed Jews from Poland; and when Louis XIV began to persecute the French Protestants, he provided funds and special officials to assist the immigration of 20,000 Huguenots to Brandenburg. Frenchmen for a time formed a sixth of the population of Berlin and were the most advanced element of that comparatively primitive city. The government, as in France under Colbert, initiated and helped to finance various industries; but the importance of such government participation was greater than in France, because the amount of privately owned capital available for investment was incomparably less. Military needs, more than elsewhere, dominated the market for goods, because civilian demand, in so poor a country, was relatively low; so that the army, in its requirements for food, uniforms, and weapons, was a strong force in shaping the economic growth of the country.

The army had a profound effect also on the social development and class structure of Prussia. The civilian middle class remained submissive, and it became the policy of the rulers to absorb practically the whole landed aristocracy, the Junkers, into military service. They used the army, with conscious purpose, as a means

---

[17] See pp. 412–414, 682–683, 747.

of implanting an "all Prussian" psychology in the landed families of Cleves, Brandenburg, Pomerania, and the former dominions of the Teutonic Knights. The sense of service to the king or state was exalted as the supreme human virtue. The fact that Prussia was a very recent and artificial combination of territories, so that loyalty to it was not at first a natural sentiment, made it all the more necessary to instill it by obvious and martial means. Emphasis fell on duty, obedience, service, and sacrifice. That military virtues became characteristic of the whole Prussian aristocracy was also due, like so much else, to the small size of the population. In France, for example, with perhaps 50,000 male adult nobles, only a small minority served habitually as army officers. In Prussia there were few Junker families that did not have some of their members in uniform.

Moreover, the Great Elector and his successors, like all absolutist rulers, repressed the estates or parliamentary assemblages in which the landed aristocracy was the main element. To mollify the squires, the rulers promised commissions in the army to men of their class. They promised them also a free hand over their peasants. The Prussian monarchy was largely based on an understanding between the ruler and the landlord gentry—the latter agreed to accept the ruler's government and to serve in his army, in return for holding their own peasants in hereditary subjection. Serfdom spread in Prussia as elsewhere in eastern Europe.[18] In East Prussia the condition of the peasants became as deplorable as in Poland.

The Prussian rulers believed that the Junkers made better army officers because they were brought up in the habit of commanding their own peasants. Bourgeois officers, a minority in all armies, were of the utmost rarity in Prussia. To preserve the officer class, legislation forbade the sale of "noble" lands, i.e., manors, to persons not noble. In France, again by way of contrast, where manorial rights had become simply a form of property, bourgeois and even peasants could legally acquire manors and enjoy a lordly or "seigneurial" income. In Prussia this was not possible; classes were frozen by owning nonexchangeable forms of property. It was thus harder for middle-class persons to enter the aristocracy by setting up as landed gentry. The bourgeois class in any case had little spirit of independence. Few of the old towns of Germany were in Prussia. The Prussian middle class was not wealthy. It was not strong by the possession of private property. The typical middle-class man was an official, who worked for the government as an employee or leaseholder of the large crown domain, or in an enterprise subsidized by the state. The civil service in Prussia, from the days of the Great Elector, became notable for its honesty and efficiency. But the middle class, more than elsewhere, deferred to the nobles, served the state, and stood in awe of the army.

These peculiar features of Prussia developed especially under Frederick William I, who was king from 1713 to 1740. He was an earthy, uncouth man, who, were the matter less serious, might almost be regarded as a comical character. He disdained whatever savored of "culture," to which his father and grandfather (the Great Elector) and also his son (Frederick the Great) were all strongly attracted. He begrudged every penny not spent on the army. He cut the expense of the royal household by three-fourths. On his coronation journey to Königsberg he spent 2,547 thalers, where his father had spent five million. He ruled the country in a fatherly German way, supervising it like a private estate, prowling the streets of Berlin in an old seedy uniform, and disciplining negligent citizens with blows of

---

[18] See pp. 122–123, 204–205, 212, 218, 228.

his walking stick. He worked all the time, and expected everyone else to do likewise. He loved the army, which all his policies were designed to serve. He was the first Prussian king to appear always in uniform. He rearranged the order of courtly precedence, pushing army officers up and civilians down. His love of tall soldiers is famous; he collected a special unit, men between six and seven feet high, from all over Europe, and indeed Peter the Great sent him some from Asia. He devised new forms of discipline and maneuver, founded a cadet corps to train the sons of the Junkers, and invented a new system of recruiting (the canton system, long the most effective in Europe), by which each regiment had a particular district or canton assigned to it as a source of soldiers. He raised the size of the army from 40,000 at his accession to 83,000 at his death. During his reign Berlin grew to be a city of 100,000, of whom 20,000 were soldiers, a proportion probably matched in no other city of Europe. He likewise left to his successor (for he fought practically no wars himself) a war chest of 7,000,000 thalers.

With this army and war chest Frederick II, later called the Great, who became king in 1740, startled Europe. Charles VI of Austria had just died. His daughter Maria Theresa entered upon her manifold inheritance. All Europe was hedging on its guarantee of the Pragmatic Sanction. While others waited, Frederick struck. Serving no notice, he moved his forces into Silesia, to which the Hohenzollerns had an old though doubtful claim. Silesia was a part of the kingdom of Bohemia on the side toward Poland, lying in the upper valley of the Oder River, and adjoining Brandenburg on the north. The addition of Silesia to the kingdom of Prussia almost doubled the population and added valuable industries, so that Prussia now, with 6,000,000 people and an army which Frederick raised to 200,000, at last established itself as a great power. It must be added that, judged simply as a human accomplishment, Prussia was a remarkable creation, a state made on a shoestring, a triumph of work and duty.

26. THE "WESTERNIZING" OF RUSSIA

The affairs of central and eastern Europe, from Sweden to Turkey and from Germany to the Caspian Sea, were profoundly interconnected. The underlying theme of the present chapter, it may be recalled, is that this whole great area was fluid, occupied by the flabby bodies of the Holy Roman Empire, Poland, and Turkey, and that in this fluid area three harder masses developed—the modern Austrian monarchy, the kingdom of Prussia, and the Russian empire. All, too, in varying degree, were modernized by borrowings from the West.

In the century after 1650 the old tsardom of Muscovy turned into modern Russia. Moving out from the region around Moscow, the Russians not only established themselves across northern Asia, reaching the Bering Sea about 1700, but also entered into closer relations with Europe, undergoing especially in the time of Tsar Peter the Great (1682–1725) a rapid process of Europeanization. To what extent Russia became truly European has always been an open question, disputed both by western Europeans and by Russians themselves. In some ways the Russians have been European from as far back as Europe itself can be said to have existed, i.e., from the early Middle Ages. Ancient Russia had been colonized by Vikings, and the Russians had become Christians long before the Swedes, the Lithuanians, or the Finns. But Russia had not been part of the general development of Europe for a number of reasons. For one thing, Russia had been converted to the Greek Orthodox branch of Christianity; therefore, the religious and cultural influence of Constantinople, not of Rome, had predominated. Second, the Mongol invasions and conquest about 1240 had kept Russia under Asiatic domination for about two hundred and fifty years, until 1480 when a grand duke of Muscovy, Ivan III (1462–1505), was able to throw off the Mongol overlordship and cease payment of tribute.[19] Last, Russian geography, especially the lack of warm-water or ice-free seaports, had made commerce and communication with the West difficult. For these reasons Russia had not shared in the general European development after about 1100, and the changes that took place in the seventeenth and eighteenth centuries may accurately be called Europeanization, or at least a wholesale borrowing of the apparatus of civilization from the West. The Europeanizing or westernizing of Russia was by no means a unique thing. It was a step in the expansion of the European type of civilization and hence in the formation of the modern world as we have known it in the last three hundred years.

In some ways the new Russian empire resembled the new kingdom of Prussia. Both took form in the great plain which runs uninterruptedly from the North Sea into inner Asia. Both lacked natural frontiers and grew by addition of territories to an original nucleus. In both countries the state arose primarily as a means of supporting a modern army. In both the government developed autocratically, in conjunction with a landlord class which was impressed into state service and which in turn held the peasantry in serfdom. Neither Russia nor Prussia had a native commercial class of any political importance. In neither country could the modern state and army have been created without the importation of skills from western Europe. Yet Prussia, with its German connections, its Protestant religion, its universities, and its nearness to the busy commercial artery of the Baltic, was far more "European" than Russia, and the Europeanization of Russia may perhaps better be compared with the later westernization of Japan.[20] In the Russia of 1700, as in the Japan of 1870, the main purpose of the westernizers was to obtain scientific, technical, and military knowledge from the West, in part with a view to strengthening their own countries against penetration or conquest by Europeans. Yet here too the parallel must not be pushed too far. Russia became more fully Europeanized than did the peoples of Asia. In time, its upper classes intermarried with Europeans, and Russian music and literature became part of the culture of Europe. Russia developed a unique blend of European and non-European traits.

Russia before Peter the Great

The Russians in the seventeenth century, as today, were a medley of peoples distinguished by their language, which was of the Slavic family, of the great Indo-European language group.[21] The Great Russians or Muscovites lived around Moscow. Moving out from that area, they had penetrated the northern forests and had also settled in the southern steppes and along the Volga, where they had assimilated various Asiatic peoples known as Tartars. After two centuries of expansion, from roughly 1450 to 1650, the Russians had almost but not quite reached

---

[19] See pp. 27, 45.
[20] See pp. 543–549.
[21] See p. 13, and the language map in Chapter XI, section 53.

the Baltic and the Black seas. The Baltic shore was held by Sweden. The Black Sea coast was still held by Tartar Khans under the protection of Turkey. In the rough borderlands between Tartar and Russian lived the semi-independent cowboy-like Cossacks, largely recruited from migratory Russians. West of Muscovy were the White Russians (or Byelorussians) and southwest of Muscovy the Little Russians (or Ruthenians or Ukrainians), both in the seventeenth century under the rule of Poland, which was then the leading Slavic power.

The energies of the Great Russians were directed principally eastward. They conquered the Volga Tartars in the sixteenth century, thus reaching the Ural Mountains, which they immediately crossed. Muscovite pioneers, settlers, and townbuilders streamed along the river systems of Siberia, felling timber and trading in furs as they went. In the 1630s, while the English founded Boston and the Dutch New York, the Russians were establishing towns in the vast Asiatic stretches of Siberia, reaching to the Pacific itself. A whole string of settlements, remote, small, and isolated—Tomsk and Tobolsk, Irkutsk and Yakutsk—extended for 5,000 miles across northern Asia.

It was toward the vast heartland of central Asia that Muscovy really faced, looking out upon Persia and China across the deserts. The bazaars of Moscow and Astrakhan were frequented by Persians, Afghans, Kirkhiz, Indians, and Chinese. The Caspian Sea, into which flowed the Volga, the greatest of Russian rivers, was better known than was the Baltic. Europe as sensed from Moscow was in the rear. During most of the seventeenth century even Smolensk and Kiev belonged to Poland. Yet the Russians were not totally shut off from Europe. In 1552, when Ivan the Terrible conquered Kazan from the Tartars, he had a German engineer in his army. In the next year, 1553, Richard Chancellor arrived in Moscow from England by the roundabout way of Archangel on the White Sea.[22] Thereafter trade between England and Muscovy was continuous. The tsars valued Archangel as their only inlet from the West, through which military materials could be imported. The English valued it as a means of reaching the wares of Persia.

Russia in the seventeenth century reflected its long estrangement from Europe and its long association with the peoples of Asia. Women of the upper classes were secluded and often wore veils. Men wore beards and skirted garments that seemed exotic to Europeans. Customs were crude, wild drunkenness and revelry alternating with spasms of repentance and religious prostration. Dwarfs and fools, no longer the fashion in the West, still amused the tsar and his retainers. Superstition infected the highest classes of church and state. Life counted for little; murder, kidnapping, torture, and elaborate physical cruelty were common. The Russian church supported no such educational or charitable institutions as did the Catholic and Protestant churches of Europe and had developed no such respect for learning or sentiments of humanity. Churchmen feared the incipient Western influences. "Abhorred of God," declared a Russian bishop, "is any who loves geometry; it is a spiritual sin." Even arithmetic was hardly understood in Russia. Arabic numerals were not used, and merchants computed with the abacus. The calendar was dated from the creation of the world. Ability to predict an eclipse seemed a form of magic. Clocks, brought in by Europeans, seemed as wonderful in Russia as they did in China, where they were brought in by Jesuits at about the same time.

[22] See p. 108.

Yet this great barbarous Russia, which fronted on inner Asia, was European in some of its fundamental social institutions. It possessed a variant of the manorial and feudal systems. It felt the same wave of constitutional crises that was sweeping over Europe at the same time. Russia had a duma or council of retainers and advisers to the tsar, and the rudiments of a national assembly corresponding to meetings of the estates in western Europe. In Russia as in Europe the question was whether power should remain in the hands of these bodies or become concentrated in the hands of the ruler. Ivan the Terrible, who ruled from 1533 to 1584 and was the first grand duke of Muscovy to assume the title of tsar,[23] was a shrewd observer of contemporary events in Poland. He saw the dissolution that was overtaking the Polish state and was determined to avoid it in Muscovy. His ferocity toward those who opposed him made him literally terrible, but though his methods were not used in Europe, his aims were the aims of his European contemporaries. Not long after his death Russia passed into a period known as the Time of Troubles (1604–1613), during which the Russian nobles elected a series of tsars and demanded certain assurances of their own liberties. But the country was racked by contending factions and civil war, like the religious wars in France or the Thirty Years' War in central Europe.

In 1613 a national assembly, hoping to settle the troubles, elected a seventeen-year-old boy as tsar, or emperor, believing him young enough to have no connection with any of the warring factions. The new boy tsar was Michael Romanov, of a gentry family, related by marriage to the old line of Ivan the Terrible. Thus was established, by vote of the political classes of the day, the Romanov dynasty which ruled in Russia until 1917. The early Romanovs, aware of the fate of elective monarchy in Poland and elsewhere, soon began to repress the representative institutions of Russia and set up as absolute monarchs. Here again, though they were more lawless and violent than any European king, they followed the general pattern of contemporary Europe.

Nor can it be said that the main social development of the seventeenth century in Russia, the sinking of the peasantry into an abyss of helpless serfdom, was exclusively a Russian phenomenon. The same generally took place in eastern Europe.[24] Serfdom had long been overtaking the older free peasantry of Russia. In Russia, as in the American colonies, land was abundant and labor scarce. The natural tendency of labor was to migrate over the great plain, to run off to the Cossacks, or to go to Siberia. In the Time of Troubles, especially, there was a good deal of moving about. The landlords wished to assure themselves of their labor force. To this end they obtained the support of the Romanov tsars. The manor, or what corresponded to it in Russia, came to resemble the slave plantation of the New World.[25] Laws against fugitive serfs were strengthened; lords won the right to recover fugitives up to fifteen years after their flight, and finally the time limit was abolished altogether. Peasants came to be so little regarded that a law of 1625 authorized anyone killing another man's peasant simply to give him another peasant in return. Lords exercised police and judicial powers. By a law of 1646 landowners were required to enter the names of all their peasants in government registers;

---

[23] The Slavic word *tsar*, like the German *Kaiser*, derives from *Caesar*, a title used as a synonym for *emperor* in the Roman, the Holy Roman, and the Byzantine (or Eastern Roman) empires. The spelling *czar*, also common in English, reveals the etymology and the current English-language pronunciation, *zar*.

[24] See pp. 122–123, 204–205, 226–227.

[25] See pp. 251–252.

peasants once so entered, together with their descendants, were regarded as attached to the estate on which they were registered. Thus the peasant lost the freedom to move at his own will. For a time he was supposed to have secure tenure of his land; but a law of 1675 allowed the lords to sell peasants without the land, and thus to move peasants like chattels at the will of the owner. This sale of serfs without land, which made their condition more like slavery as practiced in America, became indeed a distinctive feature of serfdom in Russia, since in Poland, Prussia, Bohemia, and other regions of serfdom, the serf was generally regarded as "bound to the soil," inseparable from the land.

Against the loss of their freedom the rural population of Russia protested as best it could, murdering landlords, fleeing to the Cossacks, taking refuge in a vagrant existence, countered by wholesale government-organized manhunts and by renewed and more stringent legislation. A tremendous uprising was led in 1667 by Stephen Razin, who gathered a host of fugitive serfs, Cossacks, and adventurers, outfitted a fleet on the Caspian Sea, plundered Russian vessels, defeated a Persian squadron, and invaded Persia itself. He then turned back, ascended the Volga, killing and burning as he went and proclaiming a war against landlords, nobles, and priests. Cities opened their gates to him; an army sent against him went over to his side. He was caught and put to death in 1671. The consequence of the rebellion, for over a century, was that serfdom was clamped on the country more firmly than ever.

Even from the church the increasingly wretched rural people drew little comfort. The Russian Orthodox church at this same time went through a great internal crisis, and ended up as hardly more than a department of the tsardom, useful to the government in instilling a superstitious reverence for Holy Russia. The Russian church had historically looked to the Patriarch of Constantinople as its head. But the conquest of Constantinople by the Turks made the head of the Greek Orthodox church a merely tolerated inferior to the Muslim sultan-caliph, so that the Russians in 1589 set up an independent Russian patriarch of their own. In the following generations the Russian patriarchate first became dependent on, then was destroyed by, the tsarist government.

In the 1650s the Russian patriarch undertook certain church reforms, mainly to correct mistranslations in Russian versions of the Bible and other sacred writings. The changes aroused the horror and indignation of the general body of believers. Superstitiously attached to the mere form of the written word, believing the faith itself to depend on the customary spelling of the name of Jesus, the malcontents saw in the reformers a band of cunning Greek scholars perpetrating the work of Antichrist and the devil. The patriarch and higher church officials forced through the reforms but only with the help of the government and the army. Those who rejected the reforms came to be called Old Believers. More ignorant and fanatical than the established church, agitated by visionary preachers, dividing into innumerable sects, the Old Believers became very numerous, especially among the peasants. Old Believers were active in Stephen Razin's rebellion and in all the sporadic peasant uprisings that followed. The peasants, already put by serfdom outside the protection of law, were also largely estranged from the established religion. A distrust of all organized authority settled over the Russian masses, to whom both church and government seemed mere engines of repression.

But while willing enough to modernize to the extent of correcting mistranslations from the Greek, the church officials resisted the kind of modernization that was coming in from western Europe. They therefore opposed Peter the Great at the end of the century. After 1700 no new patriarch was appointed. Peter put the church under a committee of bishops called the Holy Synod, and to the Synod he attached a civil official called the Procurator of the Holy Synod, who was not a churchman but head of a government bureau, and whose task was to see that the church did nothing displeasing to the tsar. Peter thus secularized the church, making himself in effect its head. But while the consequences were more extreme in Russia than elsewhere, it must again be noted that this action of Peter's followed the general pattern of Europe. Secular supervision of religion had become the rule almost everywhere, especially in Protestant countries. Indeed an Englishman of the time thought that Peter the Great, in doing away with the patriarchate and putting the church under his own control, was wisely imitating England, which he visited in his youth.

Peter the Great: Foreign Affairs and Territorial Expansion

The Russia in which Peter the Great became tsar, in 1682, was in short European in some ways and had in any case been in contact with Westerners for over a century. Without Peter, Russia would have developed its European connections more gradually. Peter, by his tempo and methods, made the process a social revolution.

Peter obtained his first knowledge of the West in Moscow itself, where a part of the city known as the German quarter was inhabited by Europeans of various nationalities, whom Peter often visited as a boy. Peter also in his early years mixed with Westerners at Archangel, still Russia's only port, for he was fascinated by the sea and took lessons in navigation on the White Sea from Dutch and English ship captains. Like the Great Elector of Brandenburg, Peter as a young man spent over a year in western Europe, especially Holland and England, where he was profoundly impressed with the backwardness of his own country. He had considerable talents as a mechanic and organizer. He labored with his own hands as a ship's carpenter in Amsterdam and talked with political and business leaders on means of introducing Western organization and technology into Russia. He visited workshops, mines, commercial offices, art galleries, hospitals, and forts. Europeans saw in him a barbarian of genius, a giant of a man standing a head above most others, bursting with physical vitality and plying all he met with interminable questions on their manner of working and living. He had neither the refinement nor the pretension of Western monarchs; he mixed easily with workmen and technical people, dressed cheaply and carelessly, loved horseplay and crude practical jokes, and dismayed his hosts by the squalid disorder in which he and his companions left the rooms put at their disposal. A man of acute practical mind, he was as little troubled by appearances as by moral scruples.

Peter on his visit to Europe in 1697–1698 recruited almost 1,000 experts for service in Russia, and many more followed later. He cared nothing for the civilization of Europe except as a means to an end, and this end was to create an army and a state which could stand against those of the West. His aim from the beginning was in part defensive, to ward off the Poles, Swedes, and Turks who had long pushed against Russia; and in part expansionist, to obtain seaports or "windows on the West," warm-water ports on the Baltic and Black seas, free from the shortcomings of Archangel, which was frozen a good part of the year and in any case offered only a roundabout route to Europe. For all but two years of his long reign Peter was at war.

The Poles were a receding danger. A Polish prince had indeed been elected tsar of Muscovy during the Time of Troubles, and for a while the Poles aspired to conquer and Catholicize the Great Russians, but in 1667 the Russians had regained Smolensk and Kiev, and the growing anarchy in Poland made that country no longer a menace, except as the Swedes or others might install themselves in it. The Turks and their feudatories the Tartars, though no longer expanding, were still obstinate foes. Peter before going to Europe managed in 1696 to capture Azov at the mouth of the Don, but he was unable to hold any of the Black Sea coast and learned in these campaigns to know the inferiority of the Russian army. The Swedes were the main enemy of Russia. Their army, for its size, was still probably the best in Europe. By occupying Finland, Karelia, and Livonia they controlled the whole eastern shore of the Baltic including the Gulf of Finland. In 1697, the Swedish king having died, Peter entered into an alliance with Poland and Denmark to partition the overseas possessions of the Swedish house.

The new king of Sweden, the youthful Charles XII, though descended from civilized enough forebears, was in some ways as crude as Peter (as an adolescent he had sheep driven into his rooms in the palace in order to enjoy the warlike pleasure of killing them), but he proved also to have remarkable aptitude as a general. In 1700, at the battle of Narva, with an army of 8,000 men, he routed Peter's 40,000 Russians. The tsar thus learned another lesson on the need of westernizing his state and army. Fortunately for the Russians Charles XII, instead of immediately pressing his advantage in Russia, spent the following years in furthering Swedish interests in Poland, where he forced the Poles to elect the Swedish candidate as their king. Peter meanwhile, with his imported officers and technicians, reformed the training, discipline, and weapons of the Russian army. Finally Charles XII invaded Russia with a large and well-prepared force. Peter used against him the strategy later used by the Russians against Napoleon and Adolf Hitler; he drew the Swedes into the endless plains, exposing them to the Russian winter, which happened to be an exceptionally severe one, and in 1709, at Poltava in south Russia, he met and overwhelmed the demoralized remainder. The entire Swedish army was destroyed at Poltava, only the king and a few hundred fugitives managing to escape across the Turkish frontier. Peter in the next years conquered Livonia and part of eastern Finland. He landed troops near Stockholm itself. He campaigned in Pomerania almost as far west as the Elbe. Never before had Russian influence reached so deeply into Europe. The imperial day of Sweden was now over, terminated by Russia. Peter had won for Russia a piece of the Baltic shore and with it warm-water outlets. These significant developments ending the great Northern War (1709–1721) were confirmed in the treaty of Nystadt in 1721.

War is surely not the father of all things, as has been sometimes claimed, but these wars did a good deal to father imperial Russia. The army was transformed from an Asiatic horde into a professional force of the kind maintained by Sweden, France, or Prussia. The elite of the old army had been the *streltsi*, a kind of Moscow guard, composed of nobles and constantly active in politics. A rebellion of the *streltsi* in 1698 had cut short Peter's tour of Europe; he had returned and quelled the mutiny by ferocious use of torture and execution, killing five of the rebels with his own hands. The *streltsi* were liquidated only two years before the

THE GROWTH OF RUSSIA IN THE WEST

At the accession of Peter the Great in 1682 the Russian empire, expanding from the old grand duchy of Muscovy, had almost but not quite reached the Black and Baltic seas. Most of Peter's conquests were in the Baltic region where he pushed back the Swedes and built St. Petersburg. Under Catherine the Great (1762–1796) Russia took part in the three partitions of Poland and also reached the Black Sea. Tsar Alexander I (1801–1825), thanks largely to the Napoleonic wars, was able to acquire still more of Poland and annex Finland and Bessarabia; he also made conquests in the Caucasus. In the nineteenth century the western boundary of Russia remained stabilized but additional gains were made in the Caucasus. Russia also spread over northern Asia in the seventeenth century, first reaching the Pacific as early as 1630. (See also map, pp. 720–721.)

great Russian defeat at Narva. Peter then rebuilt the army from the ground up. He employed European officers of many nationalities, paying them half again as much as native Russians of the same grades. He filled his ranks with soldiers supplied by districts on a territorial basis, somewhat as in Prussia. He put the troops into uniforms resembling those of the West and organized them in regiments of standardized composition. He armed them with muskets and artillery of the kind used in Europe and tried to create a service of supply. With this army he had not only driven the Swedes back into Sweden, but also dominated Russia itself. At the very time of the Swedish invasion large parts of the country were in rebellion, as in the days of Stephen Razin, for the whole middle and lower Volga, together with the Cossacks of the Don and Dnieper, rose against the tsar and rallied be-

hind slogans of class war and hatred of the tsar's foreign experts. Peter crushed these disturbances with the usual ruthlessness. The Russian empire, loose and heterogeneous, was held together by military might.

While the war was still in progress, even before the decisive battle of Poltava, Peter laid the foundations of a wholly new city in territory conquered from the Swedes and inhabited not by Russians but by various Baltic peoples. This city is now called Leningrad. Peter named it St. Petersburg after himself and his patron saint. From the beginning it was more truly a city than Louis' spectacular creation at Versailles established at almost the same time. Standing at the head of the Gulf of Finland, it was Peter's chief window on the West. Here he established the offices of government, required noblemen to build town houses, and gave favorable terms to foreign merchants and craftsmen to settle. Peter meant to make St. Petersburg a symbol of the new Russia, a new city facing toward Europe and drawing the minds of the Russians westward, replacing the old capital, Moscow, which faced toward Asia and was the stronghold of opposition to his westernizing program. St. Petersburg soon became one of the leading cities of northern Europe. It remained the capital of Russia until the Revolution of 1917 when Moscow resumed its old place.

Internal Changes under Peter the Great

The new army, the new city, the new and expanding government offices all required money, which in Russia was very scarce. Taxes were imposed on an inconceivable variety of objects—on heads, as poll taxes; on land; on inns, mills, hats, leather, cellars, and coffins; on the right to marry, sell meat, wear a beard, or be an Old Believer. The tax burden fell mainly on the peasants; and to assure the payment of taxes the mobility of peasants was further restricted, and borderline individuals were classified as peasants in the government records, so that serfdom became both more onerous and more nearly universal. To raise government revenues and to stimulate production Peter adopted the mercantilist policies exemplified by Colbert in France. He encouraged exports, built a fleet on the Baltic, and developed mining, metallurgy, and textiles, which were indispensable to the army. He organized mixed groups of Russians and foreigners into commercial companies, provided them with capital from government funds (little private capital being available), and gave them a labor supply by assigning them the use of serfs in a given locality. Serfdom, in origin mainly an agricultural institution, began to spread in Russia as an industrial institution also. The fact that serf owners obtained the right to sell serfs without land, or to move them from landed estates into mines or towns, made it easier for industry in Russia to develop on the basis of unfree labor. Nor were the employers of serfs, in these government enterprises, free to modify or abandon their projects at will. They too were simply in the tsar's service. The economic system rested largely on impressment of both management and labor, not on private profit and wages as in the increasingly capitalistic West. In this way Peter's efforts to force Russia to a European level of material productivity widened the gap between Russia and western Europe.

To oversee and operate this system of tax collecting, recruiting, economic controls, serf hunting, and repression of internal rebellion Peter created a new administrative system. The old organs of local self-government wasted away. The duma and the national assembly, decadent anyway in that they could not function without disorder, disappeared. In their place Peter put a "senate" dependent on himself, and ten territorial areas called "governments," or *gubernii*—the very words were not Slavic but Latin and showed imitation of the West. The church he ruled through his Procurator of the Holy Synod.[26] At the top of the whole structure was himself, an absolute ruler, tsar, and autocrat of all the Russias. Before his death, dissatisfied with his son, he abolished the rule of hereditary succession to the tsardom, claiming the right for each tsar to name his own successor. Transmission of supreme power was thus put outside the domain of law, and in the following century the accession of tsars and tsarinas was marked by strife, conspiracy, and assassination. The whole system of centralized absolutism, while in form resembling that of the West, notably France, was in fact significantly different, for it lacked legal regularity, was handicapped by the insuperable ignorance of many officials, and was imposed on a turbulent and largely unwilling population. The empire of the Romanovs has been called a state without a people.

Peter, to assure the success of his westernizing program, developed what was called "state service," which had been begun by his predecessors. Virtually all landowning and serf-owning aristocrats were required to serve in the army or civil administration. Offices were multiplied to provide places for all. In the state service birth counted for nothing. Peter used men of all classes; Prince Dolgoruky was of the most ancient nobility, Prince Menshikov had been a cook, the tax administrator Kurbatov was an ex-serf, and many others were foreigners of unknown background. Status in Peter's Russia depended not on inherited rank

[26] See p. 232.

which Peter could not control, but on rank in his state service, civilian grades being equated with military, and all persons in the first eight grades being considered gentry. "History," wrote a Scot serving in Peter's army, "scarcely affords an example where so many people of low birth have been raised to such dignities as in tsar Peter's reign, or where so many of the highest birth and fortune have been leveled to the lowest ranks of life." In this respect especially, Peter's program resembled a true social revolution. It created a new governing element in place of the old, almost what in modern parlance would be called a party, a body of men working zealously for the new system with a personal interest in its preservation. These men, during Peter's lifetime and after his death, were the bulwarks against an anti-Western reaction, the main agents in making Peter's revolution stick. In time the new families became hereditary themselves. The priority of state service over personal position was abandoned a generation after Peter's death. Offices in the army and government were filled by men of property and birth. After Peter's revolution, as after some others, the new upper class became merged with the old.

Revolutionary also, suggesting the great French Revolution or the Russian Revolution of 1917, were Peter's unconcealed contempt for everything reminiscent of the old Russia and his zeal to reeducate his people in the new ways. He required all gentry to put their sons in school. He sent many abroad to study. He simplified the Russian alphabet. He edited the first newspaper to appear in Russia. He ordered the preparation of the first Russian book of etiquette, teaching his subjects not to spit on the floor, scratch themselves, or gnaw bones at dinner, to mix socially with women, take off their hats, converse pleasantly, and look at people while talking. The beard he took as a symbol of Muscovite backwardness; he forbade it in Russia, and himself shaved a number of men at his court. He forced people to attend evening parties to teach them manners. He had no respect for hereditary aristocracy, torturing or executing the highborn as readily as the peasants. As for religion, we are told that he was a pious man and enjoyed singing in church, but he was contemptuous of ecclesiastical dignity, and in one wild revel paraded publicly with drunken companions clothed in religious vestments and mocking the priests. Like most great revolutionists since his time he was aggressively secular.

The Results of Peter's Revolution

Peter's tactics provoked a strong reaction. Some adhered strictly to the old ways, others simply thought that Peter was moving too fast and too indiscriminately toward the new. Many Russians resented the inescapable presence of foreigners, who often looked down on Russians as savages, and who enjoyed special privileges such as the right of free exit from Russia and higher pay for similar employments. One center around which malcontents rallied was the church. Another was Peter's son Alexis, who declared that when he became tsar he would put a stop to the innovations and restore respect for the customs of old Russia. Peter, after some hesitation, finally put his own son to death. He ruled that each tsar should choose his own successor. He would stop at nothing to remake Russia in his own fashion.

Peter died in 1725, proclaimed "the Great" in his own lifetime by his admiring Senate. Few men in all history have exerted so strong an individual influence, which has indirectly become more far-reaching as the stature of Russia itself has

grown. Though the years after Peter's death were years of turmoil and vacilla-
tion, his revolutionary changes held firm against those who would undo them. It
is not simply that he Europeanized Russia and conquered a place on the Baltic;
these developments might have come about in any case. It is by the methods he
used, his impatient forcing of a new culture on Russia, that he set the future character of his empire. His methods fastened autocracy, serfdom, and bureaucracy
more firmly upon the country. Yet he was able to reach only the upper classes.
Many of these became more Europeanized than he could dream, habitually
speaking French and living spiritually in France or in Italy. But as time went on
many upper-class Russians, because of their very knowledge of Europe, became
impatient of the stolid immovability of the peasants around them, sensed themselves as strangers in their own country, or were troubled by a guilty feeling that
their position rested on the degradation and enslavement of human beings. Russian psychology, always mysterious to the West, could be explained in part by the
violent paradoxes set up by rapid Europeanization. As for the peasant masses,
they remained outside the system, egregiously exploited, estranged except by force
of habit from their rulers and their social superiors, regarded by them as brutes or
children, never sharing in any comparable way in their Europeanized civilization. These facts worked themselves out in later times. As for Peter's own time,
Russia by his efforts came clearly out of its isolation, its vast bulk was now organized to play a part in international affairs, and its history thenceforward was a
part of the history of Europe and increasingly of the world. Russia, like Prussia
and the Austrian monarchy, was to be counted among the powers of Europe.

27. THE PARTITIONS OF POLAND

The fate of Poland in the eighteenth century reaches beyond the time limits of the
present chapter, but it illustrates and brings together many of the strands traced
in the preceding pages, so that a few words on it at this point may be useful. Poland in the eighteenth century, if Russia is considered non-European, was still by
far the largest European state. It still reached from the Baltic almost to the Black
Sea and extended eastward for 800 miles across the north-European plain. But it
was the classic example, along with the Holy Roman Empire, of an older political
structure which failed to develop modern organs of government.[27] It fell into ever
deeper anarchy and confusion. Without army, revenues, or administration, internally divided among parties forever at cross-purposes, with many Poles more
willing to bargain with foreigners than to work with each other, the country was
a perpetual theater for diplomatic maneuvering and was finally absorbed by its
growing neighbors.

The Polish royal elections in the eighteenth century were as usual the subject of
international interference. The election of 1733 precipitated a European war
known as the War of the Polish Succession. Two Polish kings in these years were
in fact Germans. Stanislas I, a native Pole, was twice dethroned, but since he was
supported by France, and was in fact the father of Louis XV's wife, he was set up
for his own lifetime as duke of Lorraine. The former duke of Lorraine, by the facile play of the balance of power, became grand duke of Tuscany and the husband

---

[27] See pp. 211–212, and maps, pp. 206 and 210.

of the Habsburg Maria Theresa. After these troubles of the 1730s a reforming movement began to gather strength in Poland. Polish patriots hoped to do away with the *liberum veto* and other elements in the constitution that made government impossible.[28] Their efforts were repeatedly frustrated by foreign influence, notably that of Catherine II, tsarina of Russia (1762–1796), who preferred a Poland in which she could intervene at will. In 1763 she strengthened her hold over the country by obtaining the election of another Russian puppet, a Polish nobleman named Stanislas Poniatowski, her former lover, as king. She declared herself protector of the Polish liberties. It was to the Russian advantage to maintain the existing state of affairs in Poland, which enabled Russian influence to pervade the whole country, rather than to divide the country with neighbors who might exclude Russian influence from their own spheres. The Prussians, however, long awaiting the day when they might join the old duchy of Prussia with Brandenburg-Pomerania in one continuous territory, were more willing to entertain the prospect of a partition of Poland.

The opportunity presented itself in 1772 in connection with a war between Russia and Turkey, which threw the whole situation in eastern Europe into question.[29] The Turkish empire was at last showing unmistakable signs of weakness. Russian victories were so overwhelming that both Austrians and Prussians feared for the balance of power in that part of Europe. The Prussians therefore came forward with a proposal. It was a proposal to prevent an Austro-Russian war and to preserve the balance in eastern Europe by leaving the Ottoman Empire more or less intact, while having all three European powers annex territory from Poland instead. The proposition was accepted by the three parties.

The Russians called off their war with Turkey and withdrew their armies. By the treaty of Kuchuk Kainarji, a village in Rumania, the sultan renounced his sovereignty over the Black Sea Tartars, admitted Russian shipping to the Black Sea and the Straits, and recognized the Russian government as the "protector" of Christian interests in Constantinople. The Russians soon used their advantage to absorb the north coast of the Black Sea, and to send Russian naval vessels into the Mediterranean for the first time.

Poland was meanwhile sacrificed.[30] By the first partition, in 1772, its outer territories were cut away. Russia took an eastern slice, around the city of Vitebsk. Austria took a southern slice, the region known as Galicia. Prussia took the Pomerelian borderland in West Prussia. The Prussians thus at last realized their old ambition. Prussia now reached continuously as a solid block from the Elbe to the borders of Lithuania.[31] The partition sobered the Poles, who renewed their efforts at a national revival, hoping to create an effective sovereignty which could secure the country against outsiders. But the Polish movement lacked deeper strength, for it was confined mainly to the nobles, who had themselves brought the country to ruin. The mass of the serf population, and the numerous Jews, did not care whether they were governed by Poles, Russians, or Germans. In addition, the Polish national revival was persistently blocked by the three neighboring powers. In 1792, when Europe was again at war in consequence of the great French Revolution, the three Eastern monarchies seized the opportunity to finish with Poland.

[28] See p. 212.
[29] See p. 327.
[30] For the partitions see map, p. 328.
[31] See map, panel 4, p. 222.

By the second and third partitions, in 1793 and 1795, they absorbed all the remaining Polish territory.

Russia, Prussia, and Austria thereby became contiguous, covering the whole of eastern Europe north of the Balkans; and they continued to do so, except for a few years in the time of Napoleon, until they all collapsed in the First World War, when Poland and the Baltic provinces of Russia reemerged.

VI.
The Struggle
for Wealth
and Empire

I n the preceding chapters we saw how western Europe, and especially England and France, by about the year 1700, came to occupy a position of leadership in Europe as a whole. We have traced the political history of western Europe through the War of the Spanish Succession, terminated in 1713–1714 by the treaties of Utrecht and Rastadt. Affairs of central Europe and Germany have been carried to 1740. In that year a new kingdom of Prussia and a new or renovated Austrian monarchy, each passing into the hands of a new ruler, stood on the eve of a struggle for ascendancy in central Europe. As for eastern Europe, we have observed the Europeanizing and expansion of the Russian empire, and seen how the vast area called Poland ceased to form an independent state.

More important in the long run than these political events, and going on through the seventeenth and eighteenth centuries, was the cumulative increase of all forms of knowledge, to which we turn in the two chapters that follow. Equally important was the growing wealth of Europe, or at least of the Atlantic region north of Spain. The new wealth, in the widest sense, meaning conveniences of every kind, resulted from new technical and scientific knowledge, which in turn it helped to produce; and the two together, more wealth and more knowledge, helped to form one of the most far-reaching ideas of modern times, the idea of progress, which retained its force well into the twentieth century.

The new wealth of Europe was not like the age-old wealth of the gorgeous East, said by Milton to "shower on her kings barbaric pearl and gold." It consisted of gold, to be sure, but even more of bank deposits and facilities for credit, of more and better devices for mining coal, casting iron, and spinning thread, more

Chapter Emblem: A Spanish doubloon or gold coin minted in 1790, showing Charles IV as King of Spain and the Indies.

productive agriculture, better and more comfortable houses, a wider variety of diet on the table, more and improved sailing ships, warehouses, and docks; more books, more newspapers, more medical instruments, more scientific equipment; greater government revenues, larger armies, and more numerous government employees. In the wealthy European countries, and because of the growing wealth, more people were freed from the necessity of toiling for food, clothing, and shelter, and were enabled to devote themselves to all sorts of specialized callings in government, management, finance, war, teaching, writing, inventing, exploring, and researching, and in producing the amenities rather than the barest necessities of life.

28. ELITE AND POPULAR CULTURES

The accumulation of wealth and knowledge was not evenly distributed among the various social classes.[1] There had always been differences between rich and poor, with many gradations between the extremes, but at the time we are now considering, as the seventeenth century turned into the eighteenth, there came to be a more obvious distinction between elite and popular cultures. The terms are hard to define. The elite culture was not exactly the culture of the rich and well-to-do, nor was the popular culture limited to the general run of the people. The word "elite" suggests a minority within a given range of interests; thus there are elites not only of wealth, but of social position and of power; elites of fashion, of patronage and connoisseurship in the arts, and of artists themselves; elites of education, of special training as in medicine and law, and of discovery and accomplishment in technology and the sciences. In general, persons taking part in an elite culture could share at will in the popular culture, by attending public amusements or simply by talking familiarly with their servants. But the relation was asymmetric. Those born in popular culture could not share in the culture of the elites, at least not without transforming themselves, through education or marriage, which could occur only in exceptional cases.

A main difference was simply one of language. At the popular level people generally used a local form of speech, varying from one place to another, with a distinctive accent, and full of words that had become obsolete elsewhere, or that might not be understood even a few miles away. In the Middle Ages this variety had been overcome by the use of Latin. Since the invention of printing and the rise of national literatures, and with the spreading influence of schools, of which we have seen that many were founded between 1550 and 1650, there came to be standard forms of English, French, Italian, and other languages employed by all educated persons. Grammar and spelling became regularized. Virtually all printing was in a national language when it was not in Latin. Since only a minority were able to get the necessary education, the mass of the people continued to speak as they did before. Their way of talking was now considered a dialect, a peasant language, or what was called *patois* in French or *Volkssprache* in German. And while it may be true, as some scientific philologists have said, that no form of speech is "better" than another, it is also true that facility in the national language was a sign of elite culture until the spread of universal elementary

[1] See pp. 119–122.

schooling in the nineteenth century. It gave access to at least certain segments of the elite culture, as it continues to do today.

The elite culture was transmitted largely by way of books, although acquired also by word of mouth within favored families and social circles. The popular culture was predominantly oral, although also expressed in cheaply printed almanacs, chapbooks, woodcuts, and broadsides. Since it was so largely oral, and left so few written records, popular culture is difficult for historians to reconstruct, although it made up the daily lives, interests, and activities of the great majority in all countries. It must always be remembered that what we read as history, in this as in most other books, is mostly an account of the work of minorities, either of power-wielders, decision-makers, and innovators whose actions nevertheless affected whole peoples, or of writers and thinkers whose ideas appealed to a limited audience. Persons who were illiterate or barely literate changed their ideas more slowly than the more mobile and more informed members of the elite. Great movements initiated by minorities spread slowly, generation after generation, to wider social classes, so that what was characteristic of popular culture at a given moment, such as a belief in magic, had often been common to all classes a century or two before.

The humanism of the Renaissance, being transmitted so largely through books and the study of Greek and Latin, remained limited to the elite culture. The strength of the Protestant Reformation lay in combining the efforts of highly educated persons, such as Luther and Calvin, with the anger, distress, disillusionment, and hopes of many very ordinary people. The rise of science and the ensuing Enlightenment, to be considered in the two following chapters, were originated by small numbers of experimenters and writers but slowly reshaped the thinking of others. The process of diffusion might be slow and uncertain. Astrology, for example, was in the Middle Ages a branch of scientific inquiry; in the seventeenth century astrologers were still consulted by emperors and kings; then divination by the stars was denounced by both the clergy and secular thinkers as a superstition, and astrology was expelled from astronomy, but horoscopes are still to be found in American and European newspapers in our own time.

The differences of wealth, if not wholly decisive, were of great importance. Culture in the broader or anthropologist's sense of the word includes material circumstances of food, drink, and shelter. In some respects the lot of the poor in the seventeenth century was worse than in the Middle Ages. Less meat was eaten in Europe, because as population grew there was less land available for the raising of livestock. With the growth of a market economy many peasants raised wheat, but ate bread made of rye, barley, or oats, or even looked for acorns and roots in times of famine. The consumption of bread by working people in France in the eighteenth century was about a pound per day per person, because little else except cabbages and beans was eaten on ordinary days; after 1750 the use of white bread became more usual. Meanwhile the rich, or the merely affluent, developed more delicate menus prepared by professional cooks, one of whom is said to have committed suicide when his soufflé fell.

In the towns the poor lived in crowded and unwholesome buildings, and in the country in dark and shabby cabins where stoves only gradually replaced holes in the roof for the escape of smoke. The poor had no glass in their windows, the middle classes had some, and the rich had glass windows and mirrors in profusion. In humble homes the dishes were wooden bowls, slowly replaced by pewter, while china plates began to appear on the tables of the more well-to-do. Table forks, with one for each diner, originating in Italy, were brought to France by Catherine de Medici along with other items of Italian culture, and soon spread among those able to afford them, though Louis XIV still preferred to use his fingers. Silver bowls and pitchers were ancient, but became more elaborate and more often seen in upper-class circles. The poor had no furniture, or only a few benches and a mat to sleep on; the middle classes had chairs and beds; the rich not only had substantial furniture but were becoming more conscious of style. Among persons of adequate income it became usual to have houses with specialized rooms, such as separate bedrooms, and a dining room. The prominent and the fashionable fitted out rooms for social receptions and entertainments, called salons in France, with walls of wood paneling, lighted by chandeliers reflected in mirrors, and provided with sofas and armchairs, which the invention of upholstery made more comfortable. The poor, after dark, huddled on chests or on the floor by a single candle.

In the use of beverages the seventeenth century saw progress, if that is the right word. Coffee and tea, along with sugar and tobacco, all imported from overseas, were exotic rarities in 1600, more widely enjoyed in 1700, and available to all but the very destitute by the time of the French Revolution. Coffee shops developed, and taverns multiplied. Cheap wines became more plentiful in southern Europe, as did beer in the north. The distillation of alcohol had been developed in the Middle Ages, when brandy, a distilled wine, was used as a medicine; by the seventeenth century it was a familiar drink. Whisky and gin also came into use at about this time. The taverns and coffee shops offered a place for neighborly gatherings for the middling and lower sorts of the population, but drunkenness also became more of a social problem, especially for the working classes that could not drink in domestic privacy, and so made themselves visible in the streets, as shown by Hogarth's pictures of "Gin Lane" in London about 1750. Arising from all this poverty and disorganization, especially in the large cities, was an increase in illegitimacy and abandonment of children. It was calculated that in Paris in 1780 there were 7,000 abandoned children for 30,000 births, but many of these infants were brought from the country to be deposited in the foundling hospitals of the city, which were overwhelmed.

There was much that persons of all classes and cultures shared. Most important, in principle, was religion. The refined and the rude, the learned and the untutored, heard the same sermons in church, were baptized, married, and buried by the same sacraments, often by the same priest, and were subject to religious and moral obligations that transcended the boundaries of social class. Such was most likely to be the case in small communities of unmixed religion, or where the lord and lady of the manor attended the same church as the villagers. Where different churches existed in fact, whether or not officially tolerated, religion played less of a role in social cohesion. In England, for example, the Nonconformists, who succeeded the old Puritans after the Stuart Restoration, developed a kind of middle-class culture that was noticeably different from the culture of the Anglican gentry. Rich families in both Protestant and Catholic countries might have their own private chaplains and build chapels of their own. In towns that were big enough for neighborhood diversification some churches became fashionable and others merely popular. In any case some people in the seventeenth century were not very good Christians at all; these would include those in inaccessible rural areas as well as some of the poorest in the larger towns, who were often up-rooted and homeless migrants from an overcrowded countryside. Reforming bish-ops, especially in France, undertook to ameliorate the situation, so that the seven-teenth century was a great age of internal missionary work, and it may be that in the following century, as skepticism began to pervade the elite culture, the popu-lar culture was more Christianized than it had been in the past.

Rich and poor were also subject to the same diseases, the same dangers of tainted food and polluted water, and the same smells and filth in noisy streets lit-tered with horse droppings, puddles, and garbage. Not of course equally: in the elite culture people called on the service of doctors, who had been trained in the universities, while ordinary sufferers sought out popular healers, who were often women; and it made a difference whether one rode through the streets in a coach, as the affluent did, or picked one's way on foot with the common people. Conges-tion was worst in rapidly growing cities, such as London, Paris, Amsterdam, and Naples, where the differences between wealth and poverty were both more ex-treme and more shockingly visible. There were recurrent fears of shortage of food, as crop failure or local famine struck this or that region, in which case some starved and some ate less, while those able to do so simply paid higher prices. In some towns charitable organizations developed, often on the initiative of upper-class women, to finance and assist religious sisters in relief of the poor. Hunger and the fear of hunger sometimes produced riots, which however had little politi-cal significance except insofar as upper-class people tried to make use of them for their own purposes.

It was also in less material aspects that the elite and popular cultures increas-ingly diverged. The upper strata set a new importance on polite manners, in which the French now set the tone, with much bowing, doffing of hats, and ex-change of compliments, beside which the manners of ordinary people now seemed uncouth.[2] The etiquette of princely courts became more formal, the court fools and jesters disappeared, and royalty surrounded itself not with rough retainers but with ladies and gentlemen. About 1600 the plays of Shakespeare were staged in public theaters where all classes mixed and enjoyed the same performance, but in the following century it became usual for the upper classes to have private theaters, of the kind shown on p. 198 above. People of higher social position took to stylish dancing, which their children had to learn from dancing teachers, while plain people continued to cavort more spontaneously in country dances and jigs. For evening parties, the polite world met in salons to engage in bright conversa-tion, while working people, especially in the country, met in a neighbor's house after the day's labors were over, and there, while the men mended their imple-ments and the women mended the clothes, engaged in local gossip, or listened to storytellers, or sat by while someone read aloud from one of the cheaply printed books that were now widely circulated.

Enough of these books have survived, along with popular almanacs, to make it possible to form some ideas of the mental horizons of the nonliterate and inartic-ulate classes. They were often written by printers or their employees or by others who were in effect intermediaries between the elite and popular cultures, and who purposely addressed themselves to what they knew of popular interests. The almanacs purveyed astrological observations, advice on the weather, proverbs,

---

[2] On etiquette see pp. 59–60 and 181–182.

and scraps of what had once been science but was now offered as occult wisdom. Other little books undertook to teach the ABCs, or told how to behave in church, how to approach persons of the other sex, how to show respect for superiors, or how to compose a proper letter of love, thanks, or condolence, or have such a letter written by the professional letter writers to whose services illiterate persons resorted. Still others put into print the stories that had long circulated in the oral tradition, fairy tales, saints' lives, or accounts of the doings of outlaws such as Robin Hood. Miracles, prodigies, witches, ogres, angels, and the devil figured prominently in such narratives. It is a curious fact that where educated persons were now schooled in Greek mythology and admired the heroes of ancient Rome, the plain people were still engrossed by tales of medieval chivalry, knights errant, and holy hermits that had once been avidly listened to in baronial halls. Memories of the times of King Arthur and Charlemagne lingered in the popular consciousness. There were many long and complex tales of the exploits of Roland and other paladins who had fought for Christianity against the infidels, all set in a world of faraway adventure without definite location in time or place. Saracens, Moors, Turks, and Muslims in general, along with Jews, were generally seen in such stories as a menace.

Belief in witchcraft and magic was to be found in 1600 in all social classes. The witches in *Macbeth* were perfectly believable to Shakespeare's audience. Learned books were still written on these subjects, and indeed it may be that learned writers, and the judges in law courts, had stirred up more anxiety about witches and magicians than ordinary people would otherwise have felt. By 1700 a great change was evident; witches, magicians, and miscellaneous enchantments were disappearing from the elite culture, but still figured in the popular mind. Unaffected as yet by either science or doubt, ordinary people inclined to think that there was something true about magic, which they distinguished as good and bad. Good magic unlocked the "secrets" of nature; popular writings on alchemy told of famous sages of the past who knew how to turn base metals into gold; there were special formulas that added to the efficacy of prayer; there were old women who had a secret knowledge of medicinal herbs, in which indeed there might be some pragmatic value, but which was blended with the mysterious and the occult. Bad magic was used to cause harm; it taught the black arts; it gave force to curses; it often involved a compact with the devil; it was what made witches so fearsome. By 1700 such ideas were subsiding. Judges no longer believed that such powers existed, and so would no longer preside at witchcraft trials. The same may be said of belief in prophecies and oracles; in the elite culture only those recorded in the Old Testament retained any credibility, but there was still a popular acceptance of recent prophecies and foretellings of the future.

Popular culture continued to express itself also in fairs and carnivals. For men and women who lived limited lives these were exciting events that occurred only at certain times of the year, and to which people flocked from miles around. At the fairs one could buy things that local shops and wandering peddlers could not supply. There would be puppet shows, jugglers, and acrobats. There were conjurers who refused to admit like modern magicians that they were using merely natural means. A mountebank was someone who mounted a platform (*banco* in Italian) where he sold questionable remedies for various ills, while keeping up a patter of jokes and stories, often accompanied by a clown. Blind singers and traveling musicians entertained the throngs, and for the tougher minded there were cockfights and bear baiting. In such a hubbub itinerant preachers might denounce the vanities of this world, or throw doubt on the wisdom of bishops and lawyers.

Carnival went on for several weeks preceding Lent. The word itself, from the Italian *carne vale*, meant "farewell to meat," from which good Christians were to abstain during the forty-day Lenten fast; in France it climaxed in the Mardi Gras ("fat Tuesday"). It persisted in Protestant countries also. It was a time for big eating and heavy drinking, and for general merrymaking and foolery. Comical processions marched through the streets. Farces were performed, and mock sermons delivered. Young men showed their strength in tugs-of-war, footraces, and a rough-and-tumble kind of football. A common theme was what was called in England "the world turned upside down." Men and women put on each other's clothing. Horses were made to move backward with the rider facing the tail. Little street dramas showed the servant giving orders to the master, the judge sitting in the stocks, the pupil beating the teacher, or the husband holding the baby while the wife clutched a gun. In general, the carnival was a time for defying custom and ridiculing authority. It is hard to know how much such outbursts were expressions of genuine resentments, and how much they were only a form of play. They could, indeed, be both.

In 1600 people of all classes took part in these festive activities. In the following century, as both the Protestant and the Catholic reformations extended their influences, the clergy undertook to purge such public events of what they considered excesses, and with the growth of the state the civil authorities began to frown on them as incitements to subversion. By 1700 the people of elite culture, the wealthy, the fashionable, and the educated, were more inclined to stay away, or attended only as spectators to be amused at the simple pleasures of the common people. In the eighteenth century, as the various elites took to more formal manners and to neoclassicism in literature and the arts, the gulf between the elite and popular cultures widened. The clergy campaigned against necromancy and tried to restrain the faithful in the matter of pilgrimages and veneration of dubious local saints. As the medical profession developed, the popular healers and venders of nostrums were seen as charlatans and quacks. As scientific and other knowledge increased, those who lacked it appeared simply as ignorant. It may be said both that the elites withdrew from the popular culture, and that the people as a whole had not yet been brought into the pale of higher civilization. In any case, class distinctions became sharper than ever. But nothing ever stands still, and before the year 1800 there were persons in the elite culture who were beginning to "rediscover" the people, to collect ballads and fairy tales, and lay a foundation for what in the nineteenth century was called "folklore."[3]

29. THE GLOBAL ECONOMY OF THE EIGHTEENTH CENTURY

The opening of the Atlantic in the sixteenth century, it will be recalled, had reoriented Europe. In an age of oceanic communications western Europe became a center from which America, Asia, and Africa could all be reached. A global economy had been created. The first to profit from it had been the Portuguese and Spanish, and they retained their monopoly through most of the sixteenth century,

---

[3] See pp. 410–411 and 440–442.

but the decline of the Portuguese and Spanish paved the way for the triumph of the British, the French, and the Dutch. In the eighteenth century the outstanding economic development was the expansion of the global economy and the fact that Europe became incomparably wealthier than any other part of the world.

Commerce and Industry in the Eighteenth Century

The increase of wealth was brought about by the methods of commercial capitalism and handicraft industry. Though the Industrial Revolution in England is usually dated from 1760 or 1780, it was not until the nineteenth century that the use of steam engines and power-driven machinery, and the growth of large factories and great manufacturing cities, brought about the conditions of modern industrialism. The economic system of the eighteenth century, while it contained within itself the seeds of later industrialism, represented the flowering of the older merchant capitalism, domestic industry, and mercantilist government policies which had grown up since the sixteenth century and which have been already described.[4]

Most people in the eighteenth century lived in the country. Agriculture was the greatest single industry and source of wealth. Cities remained small. London and Paris, the largest of Europe, each had a population of 600,000 or 700,000, but the next largest cities did not much exceed 200,000, and in all Europe at the time of the French Revolution (in 1789) there were only fifty cities with as many as 50,000 people. Urbanization, however, was no sign of economic advancement. Spain, Italy, and even the Balkan peninsula, according to an estimate made in the 1780s, each had more large cities (over 50,000) than did Great Britain. Urbanization did not equate with industry because most industry was carried on in the country, by peasants and part-time agricultural workers who worked for the merchant capitalists of the towns. Thus, while it is true to say that most people still lived in the country, it would be false to say that their lives and labors were devoted to agriculture exclusively. One English estimate, made in 1739, held that there were 4,250,000 persons "engaged in manufactures" in the British Isles, a figure that included women and children, and comprised almost half the entire population. These people worked characteristically in their own cottages, employed as wage earners by merchant capitalists under the "domestic" system.[5] Almost half of them, about 1,500,000, were engaged in the weaving and processing of woolens. Others were in the copper, iron, lead, and tin manufactures; others in leather goods; much smaller were the paper, glass, porcelain, silk, and linen trades; and smallest of all, in 1739, was the manufacture of cotton cloth, which accounted for only about 100,000 workers. The list suggests the importance of nonagricultural occupations in the preindustrial age.

England, even with half its population engaged at least part of the time in manufactures, was not yet the unrivaled manufacturing country that it was to become after 1800. England in the eighteenth century produced no more iron than Russia and no more manufactures than France. The population of England was still small; it began to grow rapidly about 1760, but as late as 1800 France was still twice as populous as England and Scotland together. France, though less

[4] See pp. 112–118.
[5] See p. 114.

intensively developed than England, with probably far less than half its people "engaged in manufactures," nevertheless, because of its greater size, remained the chief industrial center of Europe.

Although foreign and colonial trade grew rapidly in the eighteenth century, it is probable that, in both Great Britain and France, the domestic or internal trade was greater in volume and occupied more people. Great Britain, with no internal tariffs, with an insignificant guild system, and with no monopolies allowed within the country except to inventors, was the largest area of internal free trade in Europe. France, or at least Colbert's Five Great Farms,[6] offered a free-trading internal market hardly less great. A great deal of economic activity was therefore domestic, consisting of exchange between town and town or between region and region. The proportions between domestic and international trade cannot be known. But foreign trade was important in that the largest enterprises were active in it, the greatest commercial fortunes were made in it, and the most capital was accumulated from it. And it was the foreign trade that led to international rivalry and war.

The World Economy: The Dutch, British, and French

On the international economic scene a great part was still played by the Dutch. After the Peace of Utrecht the Dutch ceased to be a great political power, but their role in commerce, shipping, and finance remained undiminished, or diminished only relatively by the continuing commercial growth of France and Great Britain. They were still the middlemen and common carriers for other peoples. Their freight rates remained the lowest of Europe. They continued to grow rich on imports from the East Indies. To a large extent also, in the eighteenth century, the Dutch simply lived on their investments. The capital they had accumulated over two hundred years they now lent out to French or British or other entrepreneurs. Dutch capital was to be found in every large commercial venture of Europe and was lent to governments far and wide. A third of the capital of the Bank of England in the mid–eighteenth century belonged to Dutch shareholders. The Bank of Amsterdam remained the chief clearing house and financial center of Europe. Its supremacy ended only with the invasion of Holland by a French Revolutionary army in 1795.

The Atlantic trade routes, leading to America, to Africa, and to Asia, tempted the merchants of many nationalities in Europe. A great many East India companies were established—usually to do business in America as well as the East, for the "Indies" at the beginning of the eighteenth century was still a general term for the vast regions overseas. Both the English and the French East India companies were reorganized, with an increased investment of capital, shortly after 1700. A number of others were established—by the Scots, the Swedes, the Danes, the imperial free city of Hamburg, the republic of Venice, Prussia, and the Austrian monarchy. But, with the exception of the Danish company which lasted some sixty years, they all failed after only a few years, either for insufficiency of capital or because they lacked strong diplomatic, military, and naval support. Their failure showed that, in the transocean trade, unassisted business enterprise was not enough. Merchants to succeed in this sphere needed strong national backing. Nei-

---

[6] See p. 184.

ther free city, nor small kingdom, nor tiny republic, nor the amorphous Austrian empire provided a firm enough base.

It was the British and French who won out in the commercial rivalry of the eighteenth century. Britain and France were alike in having, besides a high level of industrial production at home, governments organized on a national scale and able to protect and advance, under mercantilist principles, the interests of their merchants in distant countries. For both peoples the eighteenth century—or the three-quarters of a century between the end of the War of the Spanish Succession in 1713 and the beginning of the French Revolution in 1789—was an age of spectacular enrichment and commercial expansion.

Although the trade figures are difficult to arrive at, French foreign and colonial trade may well have grown even more rapidly than the British in the years between the 1720s and the 1780s. In any event, by the 1780s, the two countries were about equal in their total foreign and colonial trade. The British in the 1780s enjoyed proportionately more of the trade with America and Asia, the French more of the trade with the rest of Europe and the Near East. The contest for markets played an important part in the colonial and commercial wars between Britain and France all through the eighteenth century and on into the final and climactic struggle, and British triumph, in the time of Napoleon.

Asia, America, and Africa in the Global Economy

In the expanding global economy of the eighteenth century each continent played its special part. The trade with Asia was subject to an ancient limitation. Asia was almost useless as a market for European manufactures. There was much that Europeans wanted from Asia, but almost nothing that Asians wanted from Europe. The peoples of Chinese, Indian, and Malay culture had elaborate civilizations with which they were content; they lacked the dynamic restlessness of Europeans, and the masses were so impoverished (more so even than in Europe) that they could buy nothing anyway. Europeans found that they could send little to Asia except gold. The drain of gold from Europe to Asia had gone on since ancient times and, accumulating over the centuries, was one source of the fabulous treasures of Oriental princes. To finance the swelling demand for Asian products it was necessary for Europeans constantly to replenish their stocks of gold. The British found an important new supply in Africa along the Gulf of Guinea, where one region (the present Ghana) was long called the Gold Coast. The word "guinea" became the name of a gold coin minted in England from 1663 to 1813 and long remained a fashionable way of saying twenty-one shillings.

What Europeans sought from Asia was still in part spices—pepper and ginger, cinnamon and cloves—now brought in mainly by the Dutch from their East India islands. But they wanted manufactured goods also. Asia was still in some lines superior to Europe in technical skill. It is enough to mention rugs, chinaware, and cotton cloth. The very names by which cotton fabrics are known in English and other European languages reveal the places from which they were thought to come. "Madras" and "calico" refer to the Indian cities of Madras and Calicut, "muslin" to the Arabic city of Mosul. "Gingham" comes from a Malay word meaning "striped"; "chintz" from a Hindustani word meaning "spotted." Most of the Eastern manufactures were increasingly imitated in the eighteenth century in Europe. Axminster and Aubusson carpets competed with Oriental rugs. In 1709 a

German named Boettcher discovered a formula for making a vitreous and trans-
lucent substance comparable to the porcelain of China; this European "china,"
made at Sèvres, Dresden, and in England, soon competed successfully with the
imported original. Cotton fabrics were never produced in Europe at a price to
compete with India until after the introduction of power machinery, which began in England about 1780. Before that date the demand for Indian cotton goods
was so heavy that the woolen, linen, and silk interests became alarmed. They
could produce nothing like the sheer muslins and bright calico prints which
caught the public fancy, and many governments, to protect the jobs and capital
involved in the old European textile industries, simply forbade the import of Indian cottons altogether. But it was a time of many laws and little enforcement,
the forbidden fabrics continued to come in, and Daniel Defoe observed in 1708
that, despite the laws, cottons were not only sought as clothing by all classes, but
"crept into our houses, our closets and bedchambers; curtains, cushions, chairs
and at last beds themselves were nothing but calicoes or Indian stuffs." Gradually,
in the face of tariff protection for "infant industries" in Europe, and the rapid
growth of European cotton manufactures, import of cottons and other manufactures from Asia declined. After about 1770 most of the imports of the British East
India Company consisted of tea, which was brought from China.

America in the eighteenth century bulked larger than Asia in the trade of western Europe. The American trade was based mainly on one commodity—sugar.
Sugar had long been known in the East, and in the European Middle Ages little
bits of it had trickled through to delight the palates of lords and prelates. About
1650 sugar cane was brought in quantities from the East and planted in the West
Indies by Europeans. A whole new economic system arose in a few decades. It
was based on the "plantation." A plantation was an economic unit consisting of a
considerable tract of land, a sizable investment of capital, often owned by ab-
sentees in France or England, and a force of impressed labor, supplied by blacks
brought from Africa as slaves. Sugar, produced in quantity with cheap labor at
low cost, proved to have an inexhaustible market. The eighteenth century was the
golden age, economically speaking, of the West Indies. From its own islands
alone, during the eighty years from 1713 to 1792, Great Britain imported a total
of £162,000,000 worth of goods, almost all sugar; imports from India and China,
in the same eighty years, amounted to only £104,000,000. The little islands of Jamaica, Barbados, St. Kitts, and others, as suppliers of Europe, not only dwarfed
the whole mainland of British America but the whole mainland of Asia as well.
For France, less well established than Britain on the American mainland and in
Asia, the same holds with greater force. The richest of all the sugar colonies, San
Domingo, now called Haiti, belonged to France.

The plantation economy, first established in sugar, and later in cotton (after
1800), brought Africa into the foreground. Slaves had been obtained from Black
Africa from time immemorial, both by the Roman Empire and by the Muslim
world, both of which, however, enslaved blacks and whites indiscriminately.
After the European discovery of America, blacks were taken across the Atlantic
by the Spanish and Portuguese. Dutch traders landed them in Virginia in 1619, a
year before the arrival of the Pilgrim Fathers in Massachusetts. But slavery in the
Americas before 1650 may be described as occasional. With the rise of the plantation economy after 1650, and especially after 1700, it became a fundamental economic institution. Slavery now formed the labor supply of a very substantial and

heavily capitalized branch of world production. About 610,000 blacks were landed from Africa in the island of Jamaica alone between 1700 and 1786. Total figures are hard to give, but it is certain that, until well after 1800, far more Africans than Europeans made the voyage to the Americas. The transatlantic slave trade in the eighteenth century was conducted mainly by English-speaking interests, principally in England but also in New England, followed as closely as they could manage it by the French. Yearly export of merchandise from Great Britain to Africa, used chiefly in exchange for slaves, increased tenfold between 1713 and 1792. As for merchandise coming into Britain from the British West Indies, virtually all produced by slaves, in 1790 it constituted almost a fourth of all British imports. If we add British imports from the American mainland, including what in 1776 became the United States, the importance of black labor to the British economic system will appear still greater, since a great part of exports from the mainland consisted of agricultural products, such as tobacco and indigo, produced partly by slaves. It can scarcely be denied that the phenomenal rise of British capitalism in the eighteenth century was based to a considerable extent on the enslavement of Africans. The town of Liverpool, an insignificant place on the Irish Sea in 1700, built itself up by the slave trade and the trade in slave-produced wares to a busy transatlantic commercial center, which in turn, as will be seen later, stimulated the "industrial revolution" in Manchester and other neighboring towns.[7]

The west-European merchants, British, French, and Dutch, sold the products of America and Asia to their own peoples and those of central and eastern Europe. Trade with Germany and Italy was fairly stable. With Russia it enormously increased. To cite the British record only, Britain imported fifteen times as much goods from Russia in 1790 as in 1700, and sold the Russians six times as much. The Russian landlords, as they became Europeanized, desired Western manufactures and the colonial products such as sugar, tobacco, and tea which could be purchased only from western Europeans. They had grain, timber, and naval stores to offer in return. Similarly, landlords of Poland and north Germany, in the seventeenth and eighteenth centuries, found themselves increasingly able to move their agricultural products out through the Baltic and hence increasingly able to buy the products of western Europe, America, and Asia in return. Landlords of eastern Europe thus had an incentive to make their estates more productive. "Big" agriculture spread, developing in eastern Europe a system not unlike the plantation economy of the New World. It had many effects. It contributed, along with political causes, to reducing the bulk of the east-European population to serfdom. It helped to civilize and refine, in a word to "Europeanize," the upper classes. And it helped to enrich the merchants of western Europe.[8]

The Wealth of Western Europe: Social Consequences

The wealth which accumulated along the Atlantic seaboard of Europe was, in short, by no means produced by the efforts of western Europeans only. All the world contributed to its formation. The natural resources of the Americas, the resources and skills of Asia, the gold and manpower of Africa, all alike went into producing the vastly increased volume of goods moving in world commerce.

[7] See p. 431.
[8] See pp. 122–123.

Europeans directed the movement. They supplied capital; they contributed technical and organizing abilities; and it was the demand of Europeans, at home in Europe and as traders abroad, that set increasing numbers of Indians to spinning cotton, Chinese to raising tea, Malays to gathering spices, and Africans to the tending of sugar cane. A few non-Europeans might benefit in the process—Indian or Chinese merchants "subsidized" by the East India companies, African chiefs who captured slaves from neighboring tribes and sold them to Europeans. But the profits of the world economy really went to Europe. The new wealth, over and above what was necessary to keep the far-flung and polyglot labor force in being, and to pay other expenses, piled up in Britain, Holland, and France.

Here it was owned by private persons. It accumulated within the system of private property and as part of the institutions of private enterprise or private capitalism. Governments were dependent on these private owners of property, for governments, in western Europe, had almost no source of revenue except loans and taxes derived from their peoples. When the wealth owners gave their support, the government was strong and successful, as in England. When they withdrew support, the government collapsed, as it was to collapse in France in the Revolution of 1789.

In a technical sense there were many "capitalists" in western Europe, persons who had a little savings which they used to buy a parcel of land or a loom or entrusted to some other person to invest at interest. And in a general sense the new wealth was widely distributed; the standard of living rose in western Europe in the eighteenth century. Tea, for example, which cost as much as £10 a pound when introduced into England about 1650, was an article of common consumption a hundred years later. But wealth used to produce more wealth, i.e., capital, was owned or controlled in significant amounts by relatively few persons. In the eighteenth century some people became unprecedentedly rich (including some who started quite poor, for it was a time of open opportunity); the great intermediate layers of society became noticeably more comfortable; and the people at the bottom, such as the serfs of eastern Europe, the Irish peasantry, the dispossessed farm workers in England, the poorest peasants and workmen of France, were worse off than they had been before. The poor continued to live in hovels. The prosperous created for themselves that pleasant world of the eighteenth century that is still admired, a world of well-ordered Georgian homes, closely cropped lawns and shrubs, furniture by Chippendale or à la Louis XV, coaches-and-four, family portraits, high chandeliers, books bound in morocco, and a staff of servants "below stairs."

Families enriched by commerce, and especially the daughters, mixed and intermarried with the old families which owned land. The merchant in England or France no sooner became prosperous than he bought himself a landed estate. In France he might also purchase a government office or patent of nobility. Contrariwise, the landowning gentleman, especially in England, no sooner increased his landed income than he invested the proceeds in commercial enterprise or government bonds. The two forms of property, bourgeois and aristocratic, tended to merge. Until toward the end of the century the various propertied interests worked harmoniously together, and the unpropertied classes, the vast majority, could influence the government only by riot and tumult. On the whole the period, though one of commercial expansion, was an age of considerable social stability in western Europe.

The foregoing might be illustrated from the lives of thousands of men and women. Two examples are enough, one English and one French. They show the working of the world economic system, the rise of the commercial class in western Europe, and the role of that class in the political life of the Western countries.

Thomas Pitt, called "Diamond" Pitt, was born in 1653, the son of a parish clergyman in the Church of England. He went to India in 1674. Here he operated as an "interloper," trading in defiance of the legal monopoly of the East India Company. Returning to England, he was prosecuted by the company and fined £400 but was rich enough to buy the manor of Stratford and with it the borough of Old Sarum, a rotten borough which gave him a seat in the House of Commons without the trouble of an election. He soon returned to India, again as an interloper, where he competed so successfully with the company that it finally took him into its own employment. He traded on his own account, as well as for the company, sent back some new chintzes to England, and defended Madras against the nawab of the Carnatic, buying off the nawab with money. In 1702, though his salary was only £300 a year, he purchased a 410-carat uncut diamond for £20,400. He bought it from an Indian merchant who had himself bought it from an English skipper, who in turn had stolen it from the slave who had found it in the mines and who had concealed it in a wound in his leg. Back in Europe, Pitt had his diamond cut at Amsterdam and sold it in 1717 to the regent of France for £135,000. The regent put it in the French crown; it was appraised at the time of the French Revolution at £480,000. A daughter of "Diamond" Pitt became the Countess of Stanhope, one of his sons the Earl of Londonderry. Another son became father to the William Pitt who guided Britain through the Seven Years' War with France, and who was raised to the peerage as the Earl of Chatham. After this Pitt the city of Pittsburgh was named, so that a fortune gained in the East gave its name to a frontier settlement in the interior of America. Chatham's younger son, the second William Pitt, became prime minister at twenty-four. The younger Pitt guided Britain through another and greater war with France, until his death in 1806 during the high tide of the Napoleonic empire.

Jean Joseph Laborde was born in 1724, of a bourgeois family of southern France. He went to work for an uncle who had a business at Bayonne trading with Spain and the East. From the profits he built up vast plantations and slave-holdings in San Domingo. His ships brought sugar to Europe, and returned with prefabricated building materials, each piece carefully numbered, for his plantations and refineries in the West Indies. He became one of the leading bankers in Paris. His daughter became the Countess de Noailles. He himself received the title of marquis, which he did not use. He bought a number of manors and châteaux near Paris. As a real estate operator he developed that part of Paris, then suburban, now called the Chaussée d'Antin. During the Seven Years' War he was sent by the French government to borrow money in Spain, where he was told that Spain would lend nothing to Louis XV, but would gladly lend him personally 20,000,000 reals. In the War of American Independence he raised 12,000,000 livres in gold for the government, to help pay the French army and navy, thus contributing to the success of the American Revolution. He acted as investment agent for Voltaire, gave 24,000 livres a year to charity, and subscribed 400,000 livres in 1788 toward building new hospitals in Paris. In July 1789 he helped to finance the insurrection which led to the fall of the Bastille and the Revolution. His son, in June 1789, took the Oath of the Tennis Court, swearing to write a constitution for France. He himself was guillotined in 1794. His children turned to scholarship and the arts.

30. WESTERN EUROPE AFTER UTRECHT, 1713–1740

The Peace of Utrecht registered the defeat of French ambitions in the wars of Louis XIV. The French move toward "universal monarchy" had been blocked. The European state system had been preserved. Europe was to consist of a number of independent and sovereign states, all legally free and equal, continuously entering or leaving alliances along the principles of the balance of power. More specifically, the peace settlement of 1713–1714 placed the Bourbon Philip V on the Spanish throne but partitioned the Spanish empire.[9] Spain itself, with Spanish America and the Philippines, went to Philip V. Of the remaining Spanish possessions, Belgium, Milan, and Naples-Sicily went to the Austrian Habsburgs, Sardinia ultimately to the Duke of Savoy, Minorca and Gibraltar to Great Britain. Britain likewise took from France Newfoundland, Nova Scotia, and the Hudson Bay region. Great Britain, consolidated during the wars as a combined kingdom of England and Scotland, installed as a naval power in the Mediterranean, winning territory from France and Spain, and receiving trading rights within the hitherto closed domain of Spanish America, emerged as the most dynamic of the Atlantic powers.

Men in authority turned to repairing the damages of war. Spain was somewhat rejuvenated by the French influence under its new Bourbon house. The drift and decadence that had set in under the last Habsburgs were at least halted. The Spanish monarchy was administratively strengthened. Its officials followed the absolutist government of Louis XIV as a model. The estates of the east-Spanish kingdoms, Aragon and Valencia, ceased to meet, going like the Estates General of France into the limbo of obsolete institutions. They had chosen the losing side in the Spanish civil war that accompanied the War of the Spanish Succession, and their disappearance in the reign of Philip V removed a source of the localism and cross-purposes which afflicted Spain. On the whole the French influence in eighteenth-century Spain was intangible. Nothing was changed in substance, but the old machinery functioned with more precision. Administrators were better trained and took a more constructive attitude toward government work; they became more aware of the world north of the Pyrenees, and recovered confidence in their country's future. They tried also to tighten up the administration of their American empire. More revenue officers and coast guards were introduced in the Caribbean, whose zeal led to repeated clashes with smugglers, mainly British. Friction on the Spanish Main, reinforced by Spanish dislike for British occupation of Gibraltar, kept Spain and Britain in a continual ferment of potential hostility.

The Dutch after Utrecht receded from the political stage, though their alliance was always sought because of the huge shipping and financial resources they controlled. The Swiss also became important in banking and financial circles. The Belgians founded an overseas trading company in 1723 on the authority of their new Austrian ruler; this "Ostend Company" sent out six voyages to China, which were highly profitable, but the commercial jealousy of the Dutch and British

---

[9] See pp. 189–191 and maps, pp. 190 and 317.

obliged the Austrian emperor to withdraw his support, so that the enterprise soon came to an end. The Scots began at about this time to play their remarkable role of energizing business affairs in many countries. Union with England gave them access to the British empire and to the numerous commercial advantages won by the English. John Law, the financial wizard of France, was a Scot, as was William Paterson, one of the chief founders of the Bank of England.

France and Britain after 1713

Our main attention falls on Britain and France. Though one was the victor and the other the vanquished in the wars ended in 1713, and though one stood for absolutism and the other for constitutionalism in government, their development in the years after Utrecht was in some ways surprisingly parallel. In both countries for some years the king was personally ineffective, and in both the various propertied interests therefore gained many advantages. Both enjoyed the commercial expansion described above. Both went through a short period of financial experimentation and frantic speculation in stocks, the bubble bursting in each case in 1720. Each was thereafter governed by a statesman, Cardinal Fleury in France and Robert Walpole in England, whose policy was to keep peace abroad and conciliate all interests at home. Fleury and Walpole held office for about two decades, toward the end of which the two countries again went to war. But the differences are at least as instructive as the parallels.

In France the new king was a child, Louis XV, the great-grandson of Louis XIV, and only five years old when he began to reign in 1715. The government was entrusted to a regent, the Duke of Orleans, an elder cousin of the young king. Orleans, lacking the authority of a monarch, had to admit the aristocracy to a share in power. Most of the nobles had never liked the absolutism of Louis XIV, and there was much dissatisfaction with absolutism among all classes, because of the ruin and suffering brought by Louis XIV's wars.

The higher nobles, ousted by Louis XIV, now reappeared in the government. For a time Orleans worked through committees of noblemen, roughly corresponding to ministries, a system lauded by its backers as a revival of political freedom; but the committees proved so incompetent that they were soon abandoned. The old parlements of France,[10] and especially the Parlement of Paris, which Louis XIV had reduced to silence, vigorously reasserted themselves after his death. The parlements were primarily law courts, originally composed of bourgeois judges; but Louis XIV and his predecessors, to raise money, had made the judgeships into salable offices, to which they attached titles of nobility to increase the price. Hence in the time of the Regency the judges of the parlements had bought or inherited their seats, and were almost all nobles. Because they had property rights in their offices, they could not be removed by the king. The Regent conceded much influence to the Parlement of Paris, utilizing it to modify the will of Louis XIV. The parlements broadened their position, claiming the right to assent to legislation and taxes, through refusing to enforce what they considered contrary to the unwritten constitution or fundamental laws of France. They managed to exercise this right, off and on, from the days of the Regency until the great Revolution of 1789. The eighteenth century, for France, was a period of absolutism checked and balanced by organized privileged groups. It was an age of aristo-

[10] See pp. 178–179, 182.

cratic resurgence, in which the nobles won back many powers of which Louis XIV had tried to deprive them.

In Great Britain the Parliament was very different from the French parlements, and the British aristocracy was more politically competent than the *noblesse* of France. Parliament proved an effective machine for the conduct of public business. The House of Lords was hereditary, with the large exception of the bishops, who were appointed by the government and made up about a quarter of the active members of the upper house. The House of Commons was not at all representative of the country according to modern ideas. Only the wealthy, or those patronized by the wealthy, could sit in it,[11] and they were chosen by diverse and eccentric methods, in counties and towns, almost without regard to the size or wishes of the population. Some boroughs were owned outright, like the Old Sarum of the Pitt family. But through the machinations of bosses, or purchase of seats, all kinds of interests managed to get representatives into the Commons. Some members spoke for the "landed interest," others for the "funded interest" (mainly government creditors), others for the "London interest," the "West India interest," the "East India interest," and others. All politically significant groups could expect to have their desires heeded in Parliament, and all therefore were willing to go through parliamentary channels. Parliament was corrupt, slow, and expensive, but it was effective. For Parliament was not only a roughly representative body; it could also act, having acquired, in practice, a sovereign power of legislation.

Queen Anne, the last reigning Stuart, died in 1714. She was succeeded by George I, Elector of Hanover, as provided for by Parliament in the Act of Settlement of 1701.[12] George I was the nearest relative of the Stuarts who was also a Protestant. A heavy middle-aged German who spoke no English, he continued to spend much of his time in Germany, and he brought with him to England a retinue of German ministers and favorites and two ungainly mistresses, dubbed in England the "Elephant and the Maypole." He was never popular in England, where he was regarded as at best a political convenience. He was in no position to play a strong hand in English public life, and during his reign Parliament gained much independence from the crown.

The main problem was still whether the principles of the Revolution of 1688 should be maintained.[13] The agreement of parties which had made that revolution relatively bloodless proved to be temporary. The Whigs, who considered the revolution as their work, long remained a minority made up of a few great landowning noblemen, wealthy London merchants, lesser business people, and Nonconformists in religion. The Whigs generally controlled the House of Lords, but the House of Commons was more uncertain; at the time of the Peace of Utrecht its majority was Tory. We have already noted the significance for English constitutional development of the conflict at that time between the prowar Whig majority in the House of Lords and the Tory majority in Commons, and how the conflict was resolved to help establish the primacy of the House of Commons.[14] After 1714 the two parties tended to dissolve, and the terms "Whig" and "Tory" ceased to have much definite meaning. In general the government, and the Angli-

[11] See pp. 176–177.
[12] See p. 174.
[13] See pp. 174–176.
[14] See p. 189.

can bishops who were close to the government, remained "Whig." Men who were remote from the central government, or suspicious of its activities, formed a kind of country party quite different from the earlier Tories. Gentry and yeomen of the shires and byways were easily aroused against the great noblemen and men of money who led the Whigs. In the established church the lesser clergy were sometimes critical of the Whig bishops. Outside the official church were a group of Anglican clergy who refused the oath of loyalty after 1688 and were called Non-Jurors; they kept alive a shadow church until 1805. In Scotland also, the ancestral home of the Stuarts, many were disaffected with the new regime.

Tories, Non-Jurors, and Scots made up a milieu after 1688 in which what would now be called counterrevolution might develop. Never enthusiastic for the "Whig wars" against France,[15] critical of the mounting national debt which the wars created, distrustful of the business and moneyed interests, they began to look wistfully to the exiled Stuarts. After 1701, when James II died in France, the Stuart claims devolved upon his son, who lived until 1766, scheming time and again to make himself king of England. His partisans were known as Jacobites, from *Jacobus*, the Latin for James; they regarded him as "James III," where others called him the Pretender. The Jacobites felt that if he would give up his Catholic religion, he should be accepted as Britain's rightful king. To strengthen his claims they kept agitating the theory of divine right.

The Whigs could not tolerate a return of the Stuarts. The restoration of "James III" and his divine-right partisans would undo the principles of the Glorious Revolution—limited monarchy, constitutionalism, parliamentary supremacy, the rule of law, the toleration of dissenting Protestants, in short all that was summarized and defended in the writings of John Locke.[16] Moreover, those who held stock in the Bank of England or who had lent their money to the government would be ruined, since "James III" would surely repudiate a debt contracted by his foes. The Whigs were bound to support the Hanoverian George I. And George I was bound to look for support in a strange country among the Whigs.

George lacked personal appeal even for his English friends. To his enemies he was ridiculous and repulsive. The successful establishment of his dynasty would ruin the hopes of Tories and Jacobites. In 1715 the Pretender landed in Scotland, gathered followers from the Highlands, and proclaimed a rebellion against George I. Civil war seemed to threaten. But the Jacobite leaders bungled, and many of their followers proved to be undecided. They were willing enough to toast the "king over the water" in protest against the Whigs but not willing in a showdown to see the Stuarts, with all that went with them, again in possession of the crown of England. The Fifteen, as the revolt came to be called, petered out. But thirty years later came the Forty-five. In 1745, during war with France, the Pretender's son, "Bonnie Prince Charlie" or the "Young Pretender," again landed in Scotland and again proclaimed rebellion. This time, though almost no one in England rallied, the uprising was more successful. A Scottish force penetrated to within eighty miles of London and was driven back and crushed with the help of Hanoverian regiments rushed over from Germany. The government set out to destroy Jacobitism in the Highlands. The social system of the Highlands was wiped out; the clans were broken up; McDuffs and McDougals were forcibly reorganized according to modern notions of property and of landlord and tenant.[17]

[15] See pp. 174, 176, 188–191.
[16] See pp. 173, 299–301.
[17] See pp. 338–339.

The Jacobite uprisings confirmed the old reputation of England in the eyes of Europe, namely, as Voltaire said, that its government was as stormy as the seas which surrounded it. To partisans of monarchy on the Continent they illustrated the weaknesses of parliamentary government. But their ignominious collapse actually strengthened the parliamentary regime in England. They left little permanent mark and soon passed into an atmosphere of romantic legend.

The "Bubbles"

Meanwhile, immediately after the Peace of Utrecht, the problem of dealing with a postwar economic situation had to be faced in both England and France. In both countries it meant finding a way to carry the greatly swollen government debt. Organized permanent public debt was new at the time. The possibilities and limitations of large-scale banking, paper money, and credit were not clearly seen. In France there was much amazement at the way in which England and Holland, though smaller and less wealthy than France, had been able to maximize their resources through banking and credit and even to finance the alliance which had eclipsed the Sun King. In addition there was much private demand for both lending and borrowing money. Private persons all over western Europe were looking for enterprises in which to invest their savings. And promoters and organizers, anticipating a profit in this or that line of business, were looking for capital with which to work. Out of this whole situation grew the "South Sea bubble" in England and the "Mississippi bubble" in France. Both bubbles broke in 1720, and both had important long-range effects.

A close tie between government finance and private enterprise was usual at the time, under mercantilist ideas of government guidance of trade. In England, for example, a good deal of the government debt was held by companies organized for that purpose. The government would charter a company, strengthen it with a monopoly in a given line of business, and then receive from the company, after the stockholders had bought up the shares, a large sum of cash as a loan. Much of the British debt, contracted in the wars from 1689 to 1713, was held in this way by the Bank of England, founded in 1694;[18] by the East India Company, reorganized in 1708 in such a way as to provide funds for the government; and by the South Sea Company, founded in 1711. The Bank enjoyed a legal monopoly over certain banking operations in London, the East India Company over trade with the East, the South Sea Company for exploiting the *asiento*[19] and other commercial privileges extorted from Spain. The companies were owned by private investors. Savings drawn from trade and agriculture, put into shares in these companies, became available both for economic reinvestment and for use of the government in defraying the costs of war.

In 1716 the Prince Regent of France was attracted to a Scottish financier, John Law, reputedly by Law's remarkable mathematical system in gambling at cards. Law founded a much needed French central bank. In the next year, 1717, he organized a *Compagnie d'Occident*, popularly called the Mississippi Company, which obtained a monopoly of trade with Louisiana, where it founded New Orleans in 1718. This company, under Law's management, soon absorbed the French East India, China, Senegal, and African companies. It now enjoyed a legal monopoly of all French colonial trade. Law then proposed, and was author-

[18] See p. 176.
[19] See p. 191.

ized by the Regent, to assume the entire government debt. The company received from individuals their certificates of royal indebtedness or "bonds," and gave them shares of company stock in return. It proposed to pay dividends on these shares and to extinguish the debt from profits in the colonial trade and from a monopoly over the collection of all indirect taxes in France. The project carried with it a plan for drastic reform of the whole taxation system, to make taxes both more fair to the taxpayer and more lucrative to the government. Shares in the Mississippi Company were gobbled up by the public. There was a frenzy of speculation, a wild fear of not buying soon enough. Quotations rose to 18,000 livres a share. But the company rested only on unrealized projects. Shareholders began to fear for their money. They began to unload. The market broke sharply. Many found their life savings gone. Others lost ancestral estates on which they had borrowed in the hope of getting rich. Those, however, who had owned shares in the company before the rise, and who had resisted the speculative fever, lost nothing by the bursting of inflated prices, and later enjoyed a gilt-edged commercial investment.

Much the same thing happened in England, where it was thought by many that Law was about to provide a panacea for France. The South Sea Company, outbidding the Bank of England, took over a large fraction of the public debt by receiving government "bonds" from their owners in return for shares of its stock. The size and speed of profits to be made in Spanish America were greatly exaggerated, and the market value of South Sea shares rose rapidly for a time, reaching £1,050 for a share of £100 par value. Other schemes abounded in the passion for easy money. Promoters organized mining and textile companies, as well as others of more fanciful or bolder design: a company to bring live fish to market in tanks, an insurance company to insure female chastity, a company "for an undertaking which shall in due time be revealed." Shares in such enterprises were snatched at mounting prices. But in September 1720 the South Sea stockholders began to sell, doubting whether operations would pay dividends commensurate to £1,000 a share. They dragged down the whole unstable structure. As in France, many people found that their savings or their inheritances had disappeared.

Indignation in both countries was extreme. Both governments were implicated in the scandal. John Law fled to Brussels. The Regent was discredited; he resigned in 1723, and French affairs were afterward conducted by Cardinal Fleury. In

M. BACHELIER, DIRECTOR OF THE LYONS FARMS
by Jean-Baptiste Oudry (French, 1686–1755)

The "farms" of which M. Bachelier was a director were the semiprivate syndicates to which the French monarchy delegated or "farmed" the collection of its indirect taxes. The government received a definite sum in advance from the farmers, who then engaged in the more uncertain but profitable business of actual collection. Tax farmers were generally hated, and many became very rich. Nothing is known of the man in this picture. He may have been one of the wealthy persons who advanced money to the government, or only one of their high-level employees. In any case, he is shown writing at a table as a man of business, but he is not looking at his work; and with his head turned toward the spectator, his huge wig, his lace cuffs, and his left hand politely extended, he typifies the ruling elite at the close of the reign of Louis XIV. Courtesy of the University of Michigan Museum of Art, Ann Arbor.

England there was a change of ministers. Robert Walpole, a country gentleman of Whig persuasion, who had long sat in the Commons, and who had warned against the South Sea scheme from the beginning, became the principal minister to George I.

Britain recovered from the crisis more successfully than France. Law's bank, a useful institution, was dissolved in the reaction against him. France lacked an adequate banking system during the rest of the century. French investors developed a morbid fear of paper securities and a marked preference for putting their savings into land. Commercial capitalism and the growth of credit institutions in France were retarded. In England the same fears were felt. Parliament passed the "Bubble Act," forbidding all companies except those specifically chartered by the government to raise capital by the sale of stock. In both countries the development of joint-stock financing along the lines of the modern corporation was slowed down for over a century. Business enterprises continued to be typically owned by individuals and partnerships, which expanded by reinvestment of their own profits, and so had another reason to keep profits up and wages down. But in England Walpole managed to save the South Sea Company, the East India Company, and the Bank, all of which were temporarily discredited in the eyes of the public. England continued to perfect its financial machinery.

The credit of the two governments was also shaken by the "bubbles." Much of the French war debt was repudiated in one way or another. Repudiation was in many cases morally justifiable, for many government creditors were unscrupulous war profiteers, but financially it was disastrous, for it discouraged honest people from lending their money to the state. Nor was much accomplished toward reform of the taxes. The nobles continued to evade the taxes imposed on them by Louis XIV, John Law's plans for taxation evaporated with the rest of his project, and when in 1726 a finance minister tried to levy a 2 percent tax on all property, the vested interests, led by the Parlement of Paris, annihilated this proposal also. Lacking an adequate revenue, and repudiating its debts, the French monarchy had little credit. The conception of public or national debt hardly developed in France in the eighteenth century. The debt was considered to be the king's debt, for which no one except a few ministers felt any responsibility. The Bourbon government in fact often borrowed through the church, the Provincial Estates, or the city of Paris, which lenders considered to be better financial risks than the king himself. The government was severely handicapped in its foreign policy and its wars. It could not fully tap the wealth of its own subjects.

In England none of the debt was repudiated. Walpole managed to launch and keep going the system of the sinking fund, by which the government regularly set aside the wherewithal to pay interest and principal on its obligations. The credit of the British government became absolutely firm. The debt was considered a national debt, for which the British people itself assumed the responsibility. Parliamentary government made this development possible. In France no one could tell what the king or his ministers might do, and hence everyone was reluctant to trust them with his money. In England the people who had the money could also, through Parliament, determine the policies of state, decide what the money should be spent for, and levy enough taxes to maintain confidence in the debt. Similarities to France there were; the landowners who controlled the British Parliament, like those who controlled the Parlement of Paris, resisted direct taxation, so that the British government drew two-thirds or more of its revenues from indirect taxes paid by the mass of the population. Yet landowners, even dukes, did pay important amounts of taxes. There were no exemptions by class or rank, as in France. All propertied interests had a stake in the government. The wealth of the country stood behind the national debt. The national credit seemed inexhaustible. This was the supreme trump card of the British in their wars with France from the founding of the Bank of England in 1694 to the fall of Napoleon 120 years later. And it was the political freedom of England that gave it its economic strength.

Fleury in France; Walpole in England

Fleury was seventy-three years old when he took office, and ninety when he left it. He was not one to initiate programs for the distant future. Louis XV, as he came of age, proved to be indolent and selfish. Public affairs drifted, while France grew privately more wealthy, especially the commercial and bourgeois classes. Walpole likewise kept out of controversies. His motto was *quieta non movere*, "let sleeping dogs lie." It was to win over the Tory squires to the Hanoverian and Whig regime that Walpole kept down the land taxes; this policy was successful, and Jacobitism quieted down. Walpole supported the Bank, the trading companies, and the financial interests, and they in turn supported him. It was a time of political calm, in which the lower classes were quiet and the upper classes not quarreling, favorable therefore to the development of parliamentary institutions.

Walpole has been called the first prime minister and the architect of cabinet government, a system in which the ministers, or executives, are also members of the legislative body. He saw to it, by careful rigging, that a majority in the Commons always supported him. He avoided issues on which his majority might be lost. He thus began to acknowledge the principle of cabinet responsibility to a majority in Parliament, which was to become an important characteristic of cabinet government. And by selecting colleagues who agreed with him, and getting rid of those who did not, he advanced the idea of the cabinet as a body of ministers bound to each other and to the prime minister, obligated to follow the same policies and to stand or fall as a group. Thus Parliament was not only a representative or deliberative body like the diets and estates on the Continent, but one that developed an effective executive organ, without which neither representative government nor any government could survive.

To assure peace and quiet in domestic politics the best means was to avoid raising taxes. And the best way to avoid taxes was to avoid war. Fleury and Walpole both tried to keep at peace. They were not in the long run successful. Fleury was drawn into the War of the Polish Succession in 1733. Walpole kept England out of war until 1739. He always had a war party to contend with, and the most bellicose were those interested in the American trade—the slave trade, the sugar plantations, and the illicit sale of goods in the Spanish empire. The British official figures show that while trade with Europe, in the eighteenth century, was always less in war than in peace, trade with America always increased during war, except, indeed, during the War of American Independence.

In the 1730s there were constant complaints of indignities suffered by sturdy Britons on the Spanish Main. The war party produced a Captain Jenkins, who carried with him a small box containing a withered ear, which he said had been cut from his head by the outrageous Spaniards. Testifying in the House of Commons, where he "commended his soul to God and his cause to his country," he stirred up a commotion which led to war. So in 1739, after twenty-five years of peace, England plunged with wild enthusiasm into the War of Jenkins' Ear. "They are ringing the bells now," said Walpole; "they will soon be wringing their hands." The war soon became merged in a conflict involving Europeans and others in all parts of the world.

31. THE GREAT WAR OF THE MID–EIGHTEENTH CENTURY: THE PEACE OF PARIS, 1763

The fighting lasted until 1763, with an uneasy interlude between 1748 and 1756. It went by many names. The opening hostilities between England and Spain were called, by the English, the War of Jenkins' Ear. The Prussians spoke of three "Silesian" wars. The struggle on the Continent in the 1740s was often known as the War of the Pragmatic Sanction. British colonials in America called the fighting of the 1740s King George's War, or used the term "French and Indian Wars," for the whole sporadic conflict. Disorganized and nameless struggles at the same time shook the peoples of India. The names finally adopted by history were the War of the Austrian Succession for operations between 1740 and 1748 and the Seven Years' War for those between 1756 and 1763. The two wars were really one. They involved the same two principal issues, the duel of Britain and France for colonies, trade, and sea power, and the duel of Prussia and Austria for territory and military power in central Europe.

Eighteenth-Century Warfare

Warfare at the time was in a kind of classical phase, which strongly affected the development of events. It was somewhat slow, formal, elaborate, and indecisive. The enlisted ranks of armies and navies were filled with men considered economically useless, picked up by recruiting officers among unwary loungers in taverns or on the wharves. All governments protected their productive population, peasants, mechanics, and bourgeois, preferring to keep them at home, at work, and paying taxes. Soldiers were a class apart, enlisted for long terms, paid wages, professional in their outlook, and highly trained. They lived in barracks or great forts, and were dressed in bright uniforms (like the British "redcoats"), which, since camouflage was unnecessary, they wore even in battle. Weapons were not destructive; infantry was predominant and was armed with the smooth-bore musket, to which the bayonet could be attached. In war the troops depended on great supply depots built up beforehand, which were practically immovable with the transportation available, so that armies, at least in central and western Europe, rarely operated more than a few days' march from their bases. Soldiers fought methodically for pay. Generals hesitated to risk their troops, which took years to train and equip, and were very expensive. Strategy took the form not of seeking out the enemy's main force to destroy it in battle, but of maneuvering for advantages of position, applying a cumulative and subtle pressure somewhat as in a game of chess.

There was little national feeling, or feeling of any kind. The Prussian army recruited half or more of its enlisted personnel outside Prussia; the British army was largely made up of Hanoverian or other German regiments; even the French army had German units incorporated in it. Deserters from one side were enlisted by the other. War was between governments, or between the oligarchies and aristocracies which governments represented, not between whole peoples. It was fought for power, prestige, or calculated practical interests, not for ideologies, moral principles, world conquest, national survival, or ways of life. Popular nationalism had developed farthest in England, where "Rule Britannia" and "God Save the King," both breathing a low opinion of foreigners, became popular songs during these mid–eighteenth-century wars.

Civilians were little affected, except in India or the American wilderness where European conditions did not prevail. In Europe, a government aspiring to conquer a neighboring province did not wish to ruin or antagonize it beforehand. The fact that the west-European struggle was largely naval kept it well outside civilian experience. Never had war been so harmless, certainly not in the religious wars of earlier times, or in the national wars initiated later. This was one reason why governments went to war so lightly. On the other hand governments also withdrew from war much more readily than in later times. Their treasuries might be exhausted, their trained soldiers used up; only practical or rational questions were at stake; there was no war hysteria or pressure of mass opinion; the enemy of today might be the ally of tomorrow. Peace was almost as easy to make as war. Peace treaties were negotiated, not imposed. So the eighteenth century saw a series of wars and treaties, more wars, treaties, and rearrangements of alliances, all arising over much the same issues, and with exactly the same powers present at the end as at the beginning.

The War of the Austrian Succession, 1740–1748

The War of the Austrian Succession was started by the king of Prussia. Frederick II, or the "Great," was a young man of twenty-eight when he became king in 1740. His youth had not been happy; he was temperamentally incompatible with his father. His tastes as a prince had run to playing the flute, corresponding with French men of letters, and writing prose and verse in the French language. His father, the sober Frederick William I,[20] thought him frivolous and effeminate, and dealt with him so clumsily that at the age of eighteen he tried to escape from the kingdom. Caught and brought back, he was forced to witness the execution, by his father's order, of the friend and companion who had shared in his attempted flight. Frederick changed as the years passed from a jaunty youth to an aged cynic, equally undeceived by himself, his friends, or his enemies, and seeing no reason to expect much from human nature. Though his greatest reputation was made as a soldier, he retained his literary interests all his life, became a historian of merit, and is perhaps of all modern monarchs the only one who would have a respectable standing if considered only as a writer. An unabashed freethinker, like many others of his day, he considered all religions ridiculous and laughed at the divine right of kings; but he would have no nonsense about the rights of the house of Brandenburg, and he took a solemn view of the majesty of the state.

Frederick, in 1740, lost no time in showing a boldness which his father would have surely dreaded. He decided to conquer Silesia,[21] and on December 16, 1740,

[20] See pp. 226–227.
[21] See map, p. 222, panel 3.

he invaded that province, a region adjoining Prussia, lying in the upper valley of the Oder, and belonging to the kingdom of Bohemia and hence to the Danubian empire of the Habsburgs. The Pragmatic Sanction, a general agreement signed by the European powers, including Prussia, had stipulated that all domains of the Austrian Habsburgs should be inherited integrally by the new heiress, Maria Theresa.[22] The issue was between law and force. Frederick in attacking Silesia could invoke nothing better than "reason of state," the welfare and expansion of the state of which he was ruler. But he was not mistaken in the belief that if he did not attack the Austrians someone else soon would.

The Pragmatic Sanction was universally disregarded. All turned against Maria Theresa. Bavaria and Saxony put in claims. Spain, still hoping to revise the Peace of Utrecht, saw another chance to win back former Spanish holdings in Italy. The decisive intervention was that of France. It was the fate of France to be torn between ambitions on the European continent and ambitions on the sea and beyond the seas. Economic and commercial advantage might dictate concentration on the impending struggle with Britain. But the French nobles were less interested than the British aristocrats in commercial considerations. They were influential because they furnished practically all the army officers and diplomats. They saw in Austria the traditional enemy, in Europe the traditional field of valor, and in Belgium, which now belonged to the Austrians, the traditional object for annexation to France. Cardinal Fleury, much against his will and judgment, found himself forced into war against the Habsburgs.

Maria Theresa was at this time a young woman of twenty-three. She proved to be one of the most capable rulers ever produced by the house of Habsburg. She bore ten children, and set a model of conscientious family living at a time of much indifference to such matters among the upper classes. She was as devout and as earnest as Frederick of Prussia was irreligious and seemingly flip. She dominated her husband and her grown sons as she did her kingdoms and her duchies. With a good deal of practical sense, she reconstructed her empire without having any doctrinaire program, and she accomplished more in her methodical way than more brilliant contemporaries with more spectacular projects of reform.

She was pregnant when Frederick invaded Silesia, giving birth to her first son, the future emperor Joseph II, in March 1741. She was preoccupied at the same time by the political crisis. Her dominions were assailed by half a dozen outside powers, and were also quaking within, for her two kingdoms of Hungary and Bohemia (both of which had accepted the Pragmatic Sanction) were slow to see which way their advantage lay. She betook herself to Hungary to be crowned with the crown of St. Stephen—and to rally support. The Hungarians were still in a grumbling frame of mind, as in the days of the Rakoczy rebellion forty years before.[23] She made a carefully arranged and dramatic appearance before them, implored them to defend her, and swore to uphold the liberties of the Hungarian nobles and the separate constitution of the kingdom of Hungary. All Europe told how the beautiful young queen, by raising aloft the infant Joseph at a session of the Hungarian parliament, had thrown the dour Magyars into paroxysms of chivalrous resolve. The story was not quite true, but it is true that she made an eloquent address to the Magyars, and that she took her baby with her and proudly exhibited him. The Hungarian magnates pledged their "blood and life," and delivered a hundred thousand soldiers.

[22] See p. 219.
[23] See pp. 218–219.

The war, as it worked out in Europe, was reminiscent of the struggles of the time of Louis XIV, or even of the Thirty Years' War now a century in the past. It was, again, a kind of civil struggle within the Holy Roman Empire, in which a league of German princes banded together against the monarchy of Vienna. This time they included the new kingdom of Prussia. It was, again, a collision of Bourbons and Habsburgs, in which the French pursued their old policy of maintaining division in Germany, by supporting the German princes against the Habsburgs. The basic aim of French policy, according to instructions given by the French foreign office to its ambassador in Vienna in 1725, was to keep the Empire divided by the principles of the Peace of Westphalia,[24] preventing the union of German powers into "one and the same body, which would in fact become formidable to all the other powers of Europe." This time the Bourbons had Spain on their side. Maria Theresa was supported only by Britain and Holland, which subsidized her financially, but which had inadequate land forces. The Franco-German-Spanish combination was highly successful. In 1742 Maria Theresa, hard pressed, accepted the proposals of Frederick for a separate peace. She temporarily granted him Silesia, and he temporarily slipped out of the war which he had been the first to enter. The French and Bavarians moved into Bohemia and almost organized a puppet kingdom with the aid of Bohemian nobles. The French obtained the election of their Bavarian satellite as Holy Roman Emperor, Charles VII. In 1745 the French won the battle of Fontenoy in Belgium, the greatest battle of the war; they dominated Belgium, which neither the Dutch nor British were able to defend. In the same year they fomented the Jacobite rebellion in Scotland.

But the situation overseas offset the situation in Europe. It was America that tilted the balance. The French fortress of Louisburg on Cape Breton Island was captured by an expedition of New Englanders in conjunction with the British navy. British warships drove French and Spanish shipping from the seas. The French West Indies were blockaded. The French government, in danger of losing the wealth and taxes drawn from the sugar and slave trades, announced its willingness to negotiate.

Peace was made at Aix-la-Chapelle in 1748. It was based on an Anglo-French agreement in which Maria Theresa was obliged to concur. Britain and France arranged their differences by a return to the *status quo ante bellum*. The British returned Louisburg despite the protests of the Americans and relaxed their stranglehold on the Caribbean. The French returned Madras, which they had captured, and gave up their hold on Belgium. The Atlantic powers recognized Frederick's annexation of Silesia and required Maria Theresa to cede some Italian duchies—Parma and Piacenza—to a Spanish Bourbon. Belgium was returned to Maria Theresa at the especial insistence of Britain and the Dutch. She and her ministers were very dissatisfied. They would infinitely have preferred to lose Belgium and keep Silesia. They were required, in the interest of a European or even intercontinental balance of power, to give up Silesia and to hold Belgium for the benefit of the Dutch against the French.

The war had been more decisive than the few readjustments of the map seemed to show. It proved the weakness of the French position, straddled as it was between Europe and the overseas world. Maintaining a huge army for use in Europe, the French could not, like Britain, concentrate upon the sea. On the other hand, because vulnerable on the sea, they could not hold their gains in Europe or

[24] See pp. 141–146.

conquer Belgium. The Austrians, though bitter, had reason for satisfaction. The war had been a war to partition the Habsburg empire. The Habsburg empire still stood. Hungary had thrown in its lot with Vienna, a fact of much subsequent importance. Bohemia was won back. In 1745, when Charles VII died, Maria Theresa got her husband elected Holy Roman Emperor, a position for which she could not qualify because she was a woman. But the loss of Silesia was momentous. Silesia was as populous as the Dutch Republic, heavily German, and industrially the most advanced region east of the Elbe. Prussia by acquiring it doubled its population and more than doubled its resources. Prussia with Silesia was unquestionably a great power. Since Austria was still a great power there were henceforth two great powers in the vague world known as "Germany," a situation which came to be known as the German dualism. But the transfer of Silesia, which doubled the number of Germans ruled by the king of Prussia, made the Habsburg empire less German, more Slavic and Hungarian, more Danubian and international. Silesia was the keystone of Germany. Frederick was determined to hold it, and Maria Theresa to win it back. A new war was therefore foreseeable in central Europe. As for Britain and France, the peace of Aix-la-Chapelle was clearly only a truce.

The next years passed in a busy diplomacy, leading to what is known as the "reversal of alliances" and Diplomatic Revolution of 1756. The Austrians set themselves to nipping off the growth of Prussia. Maria Theresa's foreign minister, Count Kaunitz, perhaps the most artful diplomat of the century, concluded that the time had come to abandon ideas that were centuries old. The rise of Prussia had revolutionized the balance of power. Kaunitz, reversing traditional policy, proposed an alliance between Austria and France—between the Habsburgs and the Bourbons. He encouraged French aspirations for Belgium in return for French support in the destruction of Prussia. The overtures between Austria and France obliged Britain, Austria's former ally, to reconsider its position in Europe; the British had Hanover to protect, and were favorably impressed by the Prussian army. An alliance of Great Britain and Prussia was concluded in January 1756. Meanwhile Kaunitz consummated his alliance with France. One consequence was to marry the future Louis XVI to one of Maria Theresa's daughters, Marie Antoinette, the "Austrian woman" of Revolutionary fame. The Austrian alliance was never popular in France. Some Frenchmen thought that the ruin of Prussia would only enhance the Austrian control of Germany and so undo the fundamental "Westphalia system." The French progressive thinkers, known as "philosophes," believed Austria to be priest-ridden and backward, and were for ideological reasons admirers of the freethinking Frederick II. Dissatisfaction with its foreign policy was one reason for the growth of a revolutionary attitude toward the Bourbon government.

In any case, when the Seven Years' War broke out in 1756, though it was a continuation of the preceding war in that Prussia fought Austria, and Britain France, the belligerents had all changed partners. Great Britain and Prussia were now allies, as were, more remarkably, the Habsburgs and the Bourbons. In addition, Austria had concluded a treaty with the Russian empire for the annihilation of Prussia.

The Seven Years' War, 1756–1763: In Europe and America

The Seven Years' War began in America. Let us turn, however, to Europe first. Here the war was another war of "partition." As a league of powers had but recently attempted to partition the empire of Maria Theresa, and a generation before had in fact partitioned the empires of Sweden and Spain, so now Austria, Russia, and France set out to partition the newly created kingdom of Prussia. Their aim was to relegate the Hohenzollerns to the margraviate of Brandenburg. Prussia, even with Silesia, had less than 6,000,000 people; each of its three principal enemies had 20,000,000 or more. But war was less an affair of peoples than of states and standing armies, and the Prussian state and Prussian army were the most efficient in Europe. Frederick fought brilliant campaigns, won victories as at Rossbach in 1757, moved rapidly along interior lines, eluded, surprised, and reattacked the badly coordinated armies opposed to him. He proved himself the great military genius of his day. But genius was scarcely enough. Against three such powers, reinforced by Sweden and the German states, and with no ally except Great Britain (and Hanover) whose aid was almost entirely financial, the kingdom of Prussia by any reasonable estimate had no chance of survival. There were times when Frederick believed all to be lost, yet he went on fighting, and his strength of character in these years of adversity, as much as his ultimate triumph, later made him a hero and symbol for the Germans. His subjects, Junkers and even serfs, advanced in patriotic spirit under pressure. The coalition tended to fall apart. The French lacked enthusiasm; they were fighting Britain, the Austrian alliance was unpopular, and Kaunitz would not plainly promise them Belgium. The Russians found that the more they moved westward the more they alarmed their Austrian allies. Frederick was left to deal only with the implacable Austrians, for whom he was more than a match. By the peace of Hubertusburg in 1763 not only did he lose nothing; he retained Silesia.

For the rest, the Seven Years' War was a phase in the long dispute between France and Great Britain. Its stakes were supremacy in the growing world economy, control of colonies, and command of the sea. The two empires had been left unchanged in 1748 by the peace of Aix-la-Chapelle. Both held possessions in India, in the West Indies, and on the American mainland.[25] In India both British and French possessed only disconnected commercial establishments on the coast, infinitesimal specks on the giant body of India. Both also traded with China at Canton. Both occupied way stations on the route to Asia, the British in St. Helena and Ascension Island in the south Atlantic, the French in the much better islands of Mauritius and Reunion in the Indian Ocean. Frenchmen were active also on the coasts of Madagascar. The greatest way station, the Cape of Good Hope, belonged to the Dutch. In the West Indies the British plantations were mainly in Jamaica, Barbados, and some of the Leeward Islands; the French in San Domingo, Guadeloupe, and Martinique. All were supported by the booming slave trade in Africa.

On the American mainland the French had more territory, the British more people. In the British colonies from Georgia to Nova Scotia lived perhaps two million whites, predominantly English but with strong infusions of Scots-Irish, Dutch, Germans, French, and Swedes. Philadelphia, with some 40,000 people, was as large as any city in England except London. The colonies, in population, bulked about a quarter as large as the mother country. But they were provincial, locally minded, incapable of concerted action. In 1754 the British government called a congress at Albany in New York, hoping that the colonies would assume some collective responsibility for the coming war. The congress adopted an

25 See maps, pp. 190, 274.

"Albany plan of union" drawn up by Benjamin Franklin, but the colonial legislatures declined to accept it, through fear of losing their independence. The colonials were willing, in a politically immature way, to rely on Britain for military action against France.

The French were still in possession of Louisburg on Cape Breton Island, a stronghold begun by Louis XIV, located in the Gulf of St. Lawrence. It was designed for naval domination of the American side of the north Atlantic, and to control access to the St. Lawrence River, the Great Lakes, and the vast region now called the Middle West. Through all this tract of country Frenchmen constantly came and went, but there were sizable French settlements only around New Orleans in the south and Quebec in the north. One source of French strength was that the French were more successful than the British in gaining the support of the Indians. This was probably because the French, being few in numbers, did not threaten to expropriate the Indians from their lands, and also because Catholics at this time were incomparably more active than Protestants in Christian missions among non-European peoples.

Both empires, French and British, were held together by mercantilist regulations framed mainly in the interest of the home countries. In some ways the British empire was more liberal than the French; it allowed local self-government and permitted immigration from all parts of Europe. In other ways the British system was more strict. British subjects, for example, were required by the Navigation Acts to use empire ships and seamen—English, Scottish, or colonial—whereas the French were more free to use the carrying services of other nations. British sugar planters had to ship raw sugar to the home country, there to be refined and sold to Europe, whereas French planters were free to refine their sugar in the islands. The mainland British colonials were forbidden to manufacture ironware and numerous other articles for sale; they were expected to buy such objects from England. Since the British sold little to the West Indies, where the slave population had no income with which to buy, the mainland colonies, though less valued as a source of wealth, were a far more important market for British goods. The colonials, though they had prospered under the restrictive system, were beginning to find much of it irksome at the time of the Seven Years' War, and indeed evaded it when they could.

Fighting was endemic even in the years of peace in Europe. Nova Scotia was a trouble spot. French in population, it had been annexed by Britain at the Peace of Utrecht. Its proximity to Louisburg made it a scene of perpetual agitation. The British government in 1755, foreseeing war with France, bodily removed about 7,000 of its people, who called themselves Acadians, scattering them in small numbers through the other mainland colonies. But the great disputed area was the Alleghenies. British colonials were beginning to feel their way westward through the mountains. French traders, soldiers, and empire builders were moving eastward toward the same mountains from points on the Mississippi and the Great Lakes. In 1749, at the request of Virginia and London capitalists, the British government chartered a land-exploitation company, the Ohio Company, to operate in territory claimed also by the French. The French threw up a fort at the point where the Ohio River is formed by the junction of two smaller rivers—Fort Duquesne, later called Pittsburgh. A force of colonials and British regular troops, under General Braddock, started through the wilderness to dislodge the French. It was defeated in July 1755, perhaps through its commander's unwillingness to take advice from the colonial officers, of whom one was George Washington.

A year later France and Britain declared war. The British were brilliantly led by William Pitt, subsequently the Earl of Chatham, a man of wide vision and superb confidence. "I know that I can save the country," he said, "and I know that no one else can." He concentrated British effort on the navy and colonies, while subsidizing Frederick of Prussia to fight in Europe, so that England, as he put it, might win an empire on the plains of Germany. Only the enormous credit of the British government made such a policy feasible. In 1758 British forces successfully took Fort Duquesne. Louisburg fell again in the same year. Gaining entry to the St. Lawrence, the British moved upstream to Quebec, and in 1759 a force under General Wolfe, stealthily scaling the heights, appeared by surprise on the Plains of Abraham outside the fortress, forcing the garrison to accept a battle, which the British won. With the fall of Quebec no further French resistance was possible on the American mainland. The British also, with superior naval power, occupied Guadeloupe and Martinique and the French slave stations in Africa.

The Seven Years' War, 1756–1763: In India

Both British and French interests were meanwhile profiting from disturbed conditions in India. As large as Europe without Russia, India was a congested country of impoverished masses, speaking hundreds of languages and following many religions and subreligions, the two greatest being the Hindu and the Muslim. Waves of invasion through the northwest frontier since the Christian year A.D. 1001 had produced a Muslim empire, whose capital was at Delhi and which for a short time held jurisdiction over most of the country. These Muslim emperors were known as Great Moguls. The greatest was Akbar, who ruled from 1556 to 1605, built roads, reformed the taxes, patronized the arts, and attempted to minimize religious differences among his peoples. The Muslim artistic culture flourished for a time after Akbar. One of his successors, Shah Jehan (1628–1658), built the beautiful Taj Mahal near Agra, and at Delhi the delicately carved alabaster palace of the Moguls, in which he placed the Peacock Throne, made of solid gold and studded with gems.

But meanwhile there was restlessness among the Hindus. The Sikhs, who had originated in the fifteenth century as a reform movement in Hinduism, went to war with the Mogul emperor in the seventeenth century. They became one of the most ferociously warlike of Indian peoples. Hindu princes in central India formed a "Mahratta confederacy" against the Muslim emperor at Delhi. Matters were made worse when Aurungzeb, the last significant Mogul emperor (1658–1707), adopted repressive measures against the Hindus. After Aurungzeb, India fell into political dissolution. Many of the modern princely states originated or became autonomous at this time. Hindu princes rebelled against the Mogul. Muslims, beginning as governors or commanders under the Mogul, set up as rulers in their own right. Thus originated Hyderabad, which included the fabulous diamond mines of Golconda, and whose ruler long was called the wealthiest man in the world. Princes and would-be princes fought with each other and with the emperor. New Muslim invaders also poured across the northwest frontier. In 1739 a Persian force occupied Delhi, slaughtered thirty thousand people and departed with the Peacock Throne. Between 1747 and 1761 came a series of forays from Afghanistan, which again resulted in the looting of Delhi and the massacre of uncounted thousands.

The situation in India resembled, on a larger and more frightful scale, what had happened in Europe in the Holy Roman Empire, where also irreconcilable religious differences (of Catholics and Protestants) had torn the country asunder, ambitious princes and city-states had won a chaotic independence, and foreign armies appeared repeatedly as invaders. India, like central Europe, suffered chronically from war, intrigue, and rival pretensions to territory; and in India, as in the Holy Roman Empire, outsiders and ambitious insiders benefited together.

The half-unknown horrors in the interior had repercussions on the coasts. Here handfuls of Europeans were established in the coastal cities. By the troubles in the interior the Indian authorities along the coasts were reduced, so to speak, to a size with which the Europeans could deal. The Europeans—British and French—were agents of their respective East India companies. The companies built forts, maintained soldiers, coined money, and entered into treaties with surrounding Indian powers, under charter of their home governments, and with no one in India to deny them the exercise of such sovereign rights. Agents of the companies, like Indians themselves, ignored or respected the Mogul emperor as suited their own purpose. They were, at first, only one of the many elements in the flux and reflux of Indian affairs.

Neither the British nor the French government, during the Seven Years' War, had any intention of territorial conquest in India, their policy in this respect differing radically from policy toward America. Nor were the two companies imperialistic. The company directors, in London and Paris, disapproved of fantastic schemes of intervention in Indian politics, insisted that their agents should attend to business only, and resented every penny and every sou not spent to bring in commercial profit. But it took a year or more to exchange messages between Europe and India, and company representatives in India, caught up in the Indian vortex, and overcome by the chance to make personal fortunes or by dreams of empire, acted very much on their own, committing their home offices without compunction. Involvement in Indian affairs was not exactly new. We have seen how "Diamond" Pitt, in 1702, purchased the good will of the nawab of the Carnatic, when the nawab threatened, by military force, to reduce the English traders at Madras to submission.[26] But the first European to exploit the possibilities of the situation was the Frenchman Dupleix. Dupleix felt that the funds sent out by the company in Paris, to finance trade in India, were insufficient. His idea seems to have been not empire-building, but to make the company into a local territorial power, in order that, from taxes and other political revenues, it might have more capital for its commercial operations. In any case, during the years of peace in Europe after 1748, Dupleix found himself with about 2,000 French troops in the Carnatic, the east coast around Madras. He lent them out to neighboring native rulers in return for territorial concessions. The first to drill native Indians by European methods, he was the originator of the "sepoys." Following a program of backing claimants to various Indian thrones, he built up a clientele of native rulers under obligation to himself. He was very successful, for a few European troops or sepoys could overcome hordes of purely Indian forces in pitched battle. But he was recalled to France in 1754, after the company became apprehensive of war with Britain and other trouble; and he died in disgrace.

When war came in 1756, British interests in India were advanced chiefly by

[26] See p. 254.

Robert Clive. He had come out many years before as a clerk for the company but had shown military talents and an ability to comprehend Indian politics. He had maneuvered, with little success, against Dupleix in the Carnatic in the 1740s. In 1756, on hearing the news of war in Europe, he shifted his attention to Bengal, hoping to drive the French from their trading stations there. The French were favored in Bengal by the local Muslim ruler, Suraja Dowla, who proceeded to anticipate Clive's arrival by expelling the British from Calcutta. Capturing the city, he shut up 146 Englishmen in a small room without windows (soon known as the "Black Hole of Calcutta") and kept them there all night, during which most of them died of suffocation. Clive, soon appearing with a small force of British and sepoys, routed Suraja Dowla at the battle of Plassey in 1757. He put his own puppet on the Bengal throne and extorted huge reparations both for the company and for himself. Back in England he was received with mixed feelings, and again, in India, strove to purify the almost incredible corruption of company employees there, men normal enough but demoralized by irresistible chances for easy riches. Finally he committed suicide in 1774.

It was British sea power, more fundamentally than Clive's tactics, that assured the triumph of British over French ambitions in the East. The British government still had no intention of conquest in India, but it could not see its East India Company forced out by agents of the French company in collaboration with Indian princes. Naval forces were therefore dispatched to the Indian Ocean, and they not only allowed Clive to shift from Madras to Calcutta at will, but gradually cut off the French posts in India from Europe and from each other. By the end of the war all the French establishments in India, as in Africa and America, were at the mercy of the British. The French overseas lay prostrate, and France itself was again detached from the overseas world on which much of its economy rested. In 1761 France made an alliance with Spain, which was alarmed for the safety of its own American empire after the British victories at Quebec and in the Caribbean. But the British also defeated Spain.

The Peace Settlement of 1763

The British armed forces had been spectacularly successful. Yet the peace treaty, signed at Paris in February 1763, five days before the Austro-Prussian peace of Hubertusburg, was by no means unfavorable to the defeated. The French Duke of Choiseul was a skillful and single-minded negotiator. The British, Pitt having fallen from office in 1761, were represented by a confused group of parliamentary favorites of the new king, George III. France ceded to Britain all French territory on the North American mainland east of the Mississippi. Canada thereby became British, and the colonials of the Thirteen Colonies were relieved of the French presence beyond the Alleghenies. To Spain, in return for aid in the last days of the war, France ceded all holdings west of the Mississippi and at its mouth. France thereby abandoned the North American continent. But these almost empty regions were of minor commercial importance, and the French, in return for surrendering them, retained many economically more valuable establishments elsewhere. In the West Indies the British planters, and in England the powerful "West India interest," feared competition from the French sugar islands, which produced more cheaply, and wanted them left outside the protected economic system of the British empire. France therefore received back Guadeloupe and

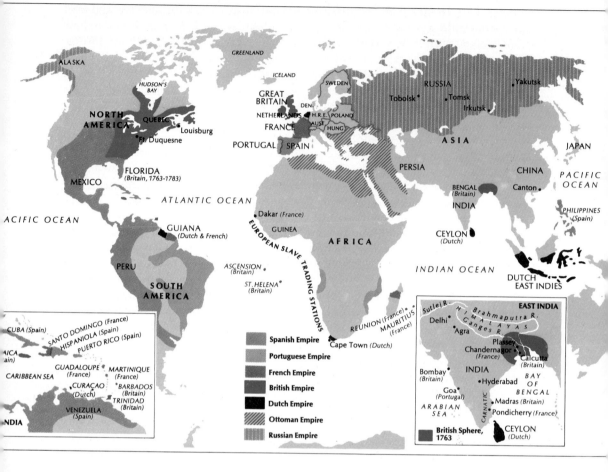

THE WORLD IN 1763

At the Peace of Paris of 1763 the British overseas empire triumphed over the French. The French ceded their holdings on the North American mainland east of the Mississippi to Britain, those west of the Mississippi to Spain. Britain also took Florida from Spain in 1763, but lost it, returning it to Spain in 1783, at the close of the War of American Independence. The French retained their sugar islands in the West Indies and their trading stations in India; they were stopped from empire-building but did not greatly suffer commercially from the Seven Years' War. The British proceeded to build their empire in India. (See also map, p. 317.)

(See also map, p. 317.)

Martinique, as well as most of its slave stations in Africa. In India, the French remained in possession of their commercial installations—offices, warehouses, and docks—at Pondicherry and other towns. They were forbidden to erect fortifications or pursue political ambitions among Indian princes—a practice which neither the French nor the British government had hitherto much favored in any case.

The treaties of Paris and Hubertusburg, closing the prolonged war of the mid-century, made the year 1763 a memorable turning point. Prussia was to continue in being. The dualism of Germany was to be lasting; Austria and Prussia eyed each other as rivals. Frederick's aggression of 1740 was legalized and even moralized by the heroic defense that had proved necessary to retain the plunder. Frederick himself, from 1763 until his death in 1786, was a man of peace, philosophical and even benign. But the German crucible had boiled, and out of it had come a Prussia harder and more metallic than ever, more disposed, by its escape from annihilation, to glorify its army as the steel framework of its life.

The Anglo-French settlement was far-reaching and rather curious. Although the war was won overwhelmingly by the British, it resulted in no commercial calamity to the French. French trade with America and the East grew as rapidly after the Seven Years' War as before it, and in 1785 was double what it had been in 1755. For England the war opened up new commercial channels. British trade with America and the East probably tripled between 1755 and 1785.[27] But the outstanding British gains were imperial and strategic. The European balance of power was preserved, the French had been kept out of Belgium, British subjects in North America seemed secure, and Britain had again vindicated its command of the sea. British sea power implied, in turn, that British seaborne commerce was safe in peace or war, while the seaborne commerce of the French, or of any others, depended ultimately on the political requirements of the British. But the French still had a few cards to play, and were to play them in the American and French Revolutions.

For America and India the peace of 1763 was decisive. America north of Mexico was to become part of an English-speaking world. In India the British government was drawn increasingly into a policy of territorial occupation; a British "paramount power" eventually emerged in place of the empire of the Moguls. British political rule in India stimulated British business there, until in the greatest days of British prosperity India was one of the main pillars of the British economic system, and the road to India became in a real sense the lifeline of the British empire. But in 1763 this state of affairs was still in the future and was to be reached by many intermediate steps.

[27] See pp. 250–252.

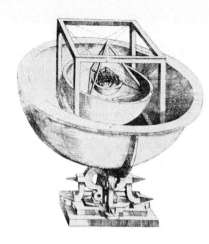

VII.
The Scientific View of the World

The seventeenth century has been called the century of genius. One reason is that it was the age when science became "modern." It was the great age of Galileo and Sir Isaac Newton, whose combined lifetimes spanned the century, with Galileo dying and Newton being born in the same year, 1642. When Galileo was young those who probed into the secrets of nature still labored largely in the dark, isolated from one another and from the general public, working oftentimes by methods of trial and error, not altogether clear on what they were trying to do, with their thinking still complicated by ideas not nowadays considered scientific. They had nevertheless accomplished a good deal. Discoveries had been made, and ideas developed, without which the intellectual revolution of the seventeenth century would not have occurred. But in a way all scientific investigators before Galileo seem to be precursors, patient workers destined never to enter into the world toward which they labored. In 1727, when Newton died, all was changed. Scientific men were in continual touch with one another, and science was recognized as one of the principal enterprises of European society. Scientific methods of inquiry had been defined. The store of factual knowledge had become very large. The first modern scientific synthesis, or coherent theory of the physical universe, had been presented by Newton. Scientific knowledge was applied increasingly to navigation, mining, agriculture, and many branches of manufacture. Science and invention were joining hands. Science was accepted as the main force in the advancement of civilization and progress. And science was becoming popularized; many people who were not themselves scien-

Chapter Emblem: A Copernican globe designed by Kepler in 1596 to illustrate movement of the planets about the sun.

tists "believed" in science and attempted to apply scientific habits of thought to diverse problems of man and society.

The history of science is too great a story to be told in this book, but there are a few ideas about it which even a book of this kind must attempt to make clear. First, science, purely as a form of thought, is one of the supreme achievements of the human mind, and to have a humanistic understanding of man's powers one must sense the importance of science, as of philosophy, literature, or the arts. Second, science has increasingly affected practical affairs, entering into the health, wealth, and happiness of humankind. It has changed the size of populations and the use of raw materials, revolutionized methods of production, transport, business, and war, and so helped to relieve some human problems while aggravating others. This is especially true of modern civilization since the seventeenth century. Third, in the modern world ideas have had a way of passing over from science into other domains of thought. Many people today, for example, in their notions of themselves, their neighbors, or the meaning of life, are influenced by ideas which they believe to be those of Freud or Einstein—they talk of repressions or relativity without necessarily knowing much about them. Ideas derived from biology and from Darwin—such as evolution and the struggle for existence—have likewise spread far and wide. Similarly the scientific revolution of the seventeenth century had repercussions far beyond the realm of pure science. It changed ideas of religion and of God and man. And it helped to spread certain very deep-seated beliefs, such as that the physical universe in which man finds himself is essentially orderly and harmonious, that the human reason is capable of understanding and dealing with it, and that man can conduct his own affairs by methods of peaceable exchange of ideas and rational agreement. Thus was laid a foundation for belief in free and democratic institutions.

The purpose of this chapter is to sketch the rise of modern science in the seventeenth century and the emergence of the scientific view of the world and of human affairs. The chapter that follows will describe the popularization and application of these ideas in the eighteenth century, in the era generally known as the Age of Enlightenment.

32. PROPHETS OF A SCIENTIFIC CIVILIZATION: BACON AND DESCARTES

Science before the Seventeenth Century

The scientific view became characteristic of European society about the middle of the seventeenth century. There had, indeed, been a few in earlier times who caught glimpses of a whole civilization reared upon science. To us today the most famous of these is Leonardo da Vinci (1452–1519), the universal genius of the Italian Renaissance, who had been artist, engineer, and scientific thinker all in one. Leonardo, by actual dissection of dead bodies, had obtained an accurate knowledge of human anatomy; he had conceived of the circulation of the blood and the movement of the earth about the sun; and he had drawn designs for submarines and airplanes and speculated on the use of parachutes and poison gases. But Leonardo had not published his scientific ideas. He was known almost exclusively as an artist. His work in science remained outside the stream of scientific thought, without influence on its course. It was not even known until the discovery of his private notebooks in recent years. Leonardo thus figures in the history of science as an isolated genius, a man of brilliant insights and audacious theories, which died with their author's death, whereas science depends on a transmission of ideas in which investigators build upon one another's discoveries, test one another's experiments, and fill in the gaps in one another's knowledge.

A century after the death of Leonardo da Vinci educated Europeans were by no means scientifically minded. Among thoughtful persons many currents were stirring. On the one hand there was a great deal of skepticism, a constantly doubting frame of mind, which held that no certain knowledge is possible for human beings at all, that all beliefs are essentially only customs, that some people believe one thing and some another, and that there is no sound way of choosing between them. This attitude was best expressed by the French essayist Montaigne (1533–1592), whose thought distilled itself into an eternal question, *Que sais-je?* "What do I know?" with the always implied answer, "Nothing." Montaigne's philosophy led to a tolerant, humane, and broad-minded outlook; but as a system of thought it was not otherwise very constructive. On the other hand, there was also a tendency to over-belief, arising from the same inability to distinguish between true and false. There was no accepted line between chemistry and alchemy, or between astronomy and astrology; all alike were regarded as ways of penetrating the "secrets" of nature. The sixteenth century had been a great age of charlatans, such as Nostradamus and Paracelsus, some of whom, notably Paracelsus, mixed magic and valid science in a way hardly understandable to us today.[1] As late as the seventeenth century, especially in central Europe where the Thirty Years' War produced chaos and terror, kings and generals kept private astrologers to divine the future. The two centuries from about 1450 to about 1650 were also the period when fear of witches was at its height. The witchcraft panic lasted longest in Germany and central Europe, probably kept alive by the insecurities engendered by the Thirty Years' War. But about twenty persons were hanged as witches in Massachusetts as late as 1692, for the English colonies, as a remote and outlying part of the European world, were among the last to feel some of the waves originating in Europe. It was in Scotland, another outlying region of Europe, that the last known execution for witchcraft took place, in 1722.

It was by no means clear, in the early part of the seventeenth century, which way Europe was going to develop. It might conceivably have fallen into a kind of chaos, as India did at about this time. We have seen that much of Europe was racked by chronic and marauding violence, to which an end was put by the consolidation of the modern state and the conversion of armed bands into organized and disciplined armies. Similarly, in things of the mind, there was no settled order. Doubt went with superstition, indifference with persecution. Science in time provided Europe with a new faith in itself. The rise of science in the seventeenth century possibly saved European civilization from petering out in a long post-medieval afterglow, or from wandering off into the diverse paths of a genial skepticism, ineffectual philosophizing, desultory magic, or mad fear of the unknown.

Bacon and Descartes

Two men stand out as prophets of a world reconstructed by science. One was the Englishman Francis Bacon (1561–1626), the other the Frenchman René Descartes

[1] See p. 64.

(1596–1650). Both published their most influential books between 1620 and 1640. Both addressed themselves to the problem of knowledge. Both asked themselves how it is possible for human beings to know anything with certainty or to have a reliable, truthful, and usable knowledge of the world of nature. Both shared in the doubts of their day. They branded virtually all beliefs of preceding generations (outside religion) as worthless. Both ridiculed the tendency to put faith in ancient books, to cite the writings of Aristotle or others, on questions having to do with the workings of nature. Both attacked earlier methods of seeking knowledge; they rejected the methods of the "schoolmen" or "scholastics," the thinkers in the academic tradition of the universities founded in the Middle Ages. On the whole, medieval philosophy had been rationalistic and deductive.[2] That is, its characteristic procedure was to start with definitions and general propositions and then discover what further knowledge could be logically deduced from the definitions thus accepted. Or it proceeded by affirming the nature of an object to be such-and-such (e.g., that "man is a political animal") and then describing how objects of such a nature do or should behave. These methods, which owed much to Aristotle and other ancient codifiers of human thought, had generally ceased to be fruitful in discovery of knowledge of nature. Bacon and Descartes held that the medieval (or Aristotelian) methods were backward. They held that truth is not something that we postulate at the beginning and then explore in all its ramifications, but that it is something which we find at the end, after a long process of investigation, experiment, or intermediate thought.

Bacon and Descartes thus went beyond mere doubt. They offered a constructive program, and though their programs were different, they both became heralds or philosophers of a scientific view. They maintained that there was a true and reliable method of knowledge. And they maintained in addition that once this true method was known and practiced, once the real workings of nature were understood, men would be able to use this knowledge for their own purposes, control nature in their own interests, make undreamed of useful inventions, improve their mechanical arts, and add generally to their wealth and comfort. Bacon and Descartes thus announced the advent of a scientific civilization.

Francis Bacon planned a great work in many volumes, to be known as the *Instauratio Magna* or "Great Renewal," calling for a complete new start in science and civilization. He completed only two parts. One, published in 1620, was the *Novum Organum* or new method of acquiring knowledge. Here he insisted on *inductive* method. In the inductive method we proceed from the particular to the general, from the concrete to the abstract. For example, in the study of leaves, if we examine millions of actual leaves, of all sizes and shapes, and if we assemble, observe, and compare them with minute scrutiny, we are using an *inductive* method in the sense meant by Bacon; if successful, we may arrive at a knowledge, based on observed facts, of the general nature of a leaf as such. If, on the other hand, we begin with a general idea of what we think all leaves are like, i.e., all leaves have stems, and then proceed to describe an individual leaf on that basis, we are following the *deductive* method; we draw logical implications from what we already know, but we learn no more of the nature of a leaf than what we knew or thought we knew at the beginning. Bacon advised men to put aside all traditional ideas, to rid themselves of prejudices and preconceptions, to look at the world with fresh eyes, to observe and study the innumerable things that are

[2] See pp. 39–43.

actually perceived by the senses. Men before Bacon used the inductive method, but he formalized it as a method and became a leading philosopher of empiricism. This philosophy, the founding of knowledge on observation and experience, has always proved a useful safeguard against fitting facts into preconceived patterns. It demands that we let the patterns of our thought be shaped by actual facts as we observe them.

The other completed part of Bacon's great work, published in 1623, was called in its English translation *The Advancement of Learning*. Here Bacon developed the same ideas and especially insisted that true knowledge was useful knowledge. In *The New Atlantis* (1627), he portrayed a scientific utopia in which men enjoyed a perfect society through their knowledge and command of nature. The usefulness of knowledge became the other main element in the Baconian tradition. In this view there was no sharp difference between pure science and applied science or between the work of the purely scientific investigator and that of the mechanic or inventor who in his own way probed into nature and devised instruments or machines for putting natural forces to work. The fact that knowledge could be used for practical purposes became a sign or proof that it was true knowledge. For example, the fact that men could aim their cannon and hit their targets more accurately in the seventeenth century became a proof of the theory of ballistics which had been scientifically worked out. Enthusiastic Baconians believed that knowledge was power. True knowledge could be put to work, if not immediately at least in the long run, after more knowledge was discovered. It was useful to mankind, unlike the "delicate learning" of the misguided scholastics. In this coming together of knowledge and power arose the far-reaching modern idea of progress. And in it arose many of the problems of modern men, since the power given by scientific knowledge can be either bad or good.

But Bacon, though a force in redirecting the European mind, never had much influence on the development of actual science. Kept busy as Lord Chancellor of England and in other government duties, he was not even fully abreast of the most advanced scientific thought of his day. Like the public generally of his lifetime, he was undisturbed by the new theories of astronomers who held that the earth moved about the sun. Bacon's greatest weakness was his failure to understand the role of mathematics. Mathematics, dealing with pure abstractions and proceeding deductively from axioms to theorems, was not an empirical or inductive method of thought such as Bacon demanded. Yet science in the seventeenth century went forward most successfully in subjects where mathematics could be applied. Even today the degree to which a subject is truly scientific depends on the degree to which it can be made mathematical. We have pure science where we have formulas and equations, and the scientific method itself is both inductive and deductive.

Descartes was a great mathematician in his own right. He is considered the inventor of coordinate geometry. He showed that by use of coordinates (or graph paper, in simple language) any algebraic formula could be plotted as a curve in space, and contrariwise that any curve in space, however complex, could be converted into algebraic terms and thus dealt with by methods of calculation. And one effect of his general philosophy was to create belief in a vast world of nature that could be reduced to mathematical form.

Descartes set forth his ideas in his *Discourse on Method*, in 1637, and in many more technical writings. He advanced the principle of systematic doubt. He began by trying to doubt everything that could reasonably be doubted, thus sweeping away past ideas and clearing the ground for his own "great renewal," to use Bacon's phrase. He held that he could not doubt his own existence as a thinking and doubting being (*cogito ergo sum*, "I think, therefore I exist"); he then deduced, by systematic reasoning, the existence of God and much else. He arrived at a philosophy of dualism, the famous "Cartesian dualism," which held that God has created two kinds of fundamental reality in the universe. One was "thinking substance"—mind, spirit, consciousness, subjective experience. The other was "extended substance"—everything outside the mind and hence objective. Of everything except the mind itself the most fundamental and universal quality was that it occupied a portion of space, minute or vast. Space itself was conceived as infinite, and everywhere geometric.

This philosophy had profound and long-lasting effects. For one thing, the seemingly most real elements in human experience, color and sound, joy and grief, seemed somehow to be shadowy and unreal, or at least illusive, with no existence outside the mind itself. But all else was quantitative, measurable, reducible to formulas or equations. Over all else, over the whole universe or half-universe of "extended substance," the most powerful instrument available to the human understanding, namely, mathematics, reigned supreme. "Give me motion and extension," said Descartes, "and I will build you the world."

Descartes also, with French genius, expressed the Baconian idea. Instead of the "speculative philosophy of the schools," he wrote in the *Discourse on Method*, men might discover a "practical philosophy by which, understanding the forces and action of fire, water, air, the stars and heavens and all other bodies that surround us, as distinctly as we understand the mechanical arts of our craftsmen, we can use these forces in the same way for all purposes for which they are appropriate, and so make ourselves the masters and possessors of nature. And this is desirable not only for the invention of innumerable devices by which we may enjoy without trouble the fruits of the earth and the conveniences it affords, but mainly also for the preservation of health, which is undoubtedly the principal good and foundation of all other good things in this life."

33. THE ROAD TO NEWTON: THE LAW OF UNIVERSAL GRAVITATION

Scientific Advances

Meanwhile actual scientific discovery was advancing on many fronts. It did not advance on all with equal speed. Some of the sciences were, and long remained, dependent mainly on the collection of specimens. Botany was one of these; Europe's knowledge of plants expanded enormously with the explorations overseas, and botanical gardens and herb collections in Europe became far more extensive than ever before, bringing important enlargements in the stock of medicinal drugs. Other sciences drew their impetus from intensive and open-minded observation. The Flemish Vesalius, by a book published in 1543, *The Structure of the Human Body*, renewed and modernized the study of anatomy. Formerly anatomists had generally held that the writings of Galen, dating from the second century A.D., contained an authoritative description of all human muscles and tissues. They had indeed dissected cadavers but had dismissed those not conforming

to Galen's description as somehow abnormal or not typical. Vesalius put Galen behind him and based his general description of the human frame on actual bodies as he found them. In physiology also, dealing with the functioning rather than the structure of living bodies, there was considerable progress. Here the method of laboratory experiment could be profitably used. William Harvey, after years of laboratory work, including the vivisection of animals, published in 1628 a book *On the Movement of the Heart and Blood.* Here he set forth the doctrine, confirmed by evidence, of the continual circulation of the blood through arteries and veins. The Italian Malpighi, using the newly invented microscope, confirmed Harvey's findings by the discovery of capillaries in 1661. The Dutch Leeuwenhoek, also by use of the microscope, was the first to see blood corpuscles, spermatozoa, and bacteria, of which he left published drawings.

These sciences, and also chemistry, although work in them went continually on, did not come fully into their own until after 1800. They were long overshadowed by astronomy and physics. Here mathematics could be most fully applied, and mathematics underwent a rapid development in the seventeenth century. Decimals came into use to express fractions, the symbols used in algebra were improved and standardized, and in 1614 logarithms were invented by the Scot John Napier. Coordinate geometry was mapped out by Descartes, the theory of probabilities developed by Pascal, and calculus invented simultaneously in England by Newton and in Germany by Leibniz. These advances made it more generally possible to think about nature in purely quantitative terms, to measure with greater precision, and to perform complex and laborious computations. Physics and astronomy were remarkably stimulated, and it was in this field that the most astonishing scientific revolution of the seventeenth century took place.

The Scientific Revolution: Copernicus to Galileo

From time immemorial, since the Greek Ptolemy had codified ancient astronomy in the second century A.D.,[3] educated Europeans had held a conception of the cosmos which we call Ptolemaic. The cosmos in this view was a group of concentric spheres, a series of balls within balls each having the same center. The innermost ball was the earth, made up of hard, solid, earthy substance such as men were familiar with underfoot. The other spheres, encompassing the earth in series, were all transparent. They were the "crystalline spheres" made known to us by the

[3] See p. 15.

A SCHOLAR HOLDING A THESIS ON BOTANY
by Willem Moreelse (Dutch, before 1630–1666)

The Netherlands became a great intellectual center in the seventeenth century, with five universities founded during the years of struggle against Spain. The most famous was at Leyden, but the present scholar may be a new doctor of the University of Utrecht, where the little-known painter Willem Moreelse worked. Crowned with laurel, the successful candidate proudly displays his thesis, on which the Latin words announce that "any plant shows the presence of God." The bringing of hitherto unknown plants from the rest of the world to Europe contributed strongly not only to science but to medicine, food supply, and the pleasures of chocolate, tea, and coffee. Courtesy of The Toledo Museum of Art, Gift of Edward Drummond Libbey, 1962.

poets; their harmony was the "music of the spheres." These spheres all revolved about the earth, each sphere containing, set in it as a jewel, a luminous heavenly body or orb which moved about the earth with the movement of its transparent sphere. Nearest to the earth was the sphere of the moon; then, in turn, the spheres of Mercury and Venus, then the sphere of the sun, then those of the outer planets. Last came the outermost sphere containing all the fixed stars studded in it, all moving majestically about the earth in daily motion, but motionless with respect to each other because held firmly in the same sphere. Beyond the sphere of the fixed stars, in general belief, lay the "empyrean," the home of angels and immortal spirits; but this was not a matter of natural science.

A person standing on the earth, and looking up into the sky, thus felt himself to be enclosed by a dome of which his own position was the center. In the blue sky of day he could literally see the crystalline spheres; in the stars at night he could behold the orbs which these spheres carried with them. All revolved about him, presumably at no very alarming distance. The celestial bodies were commonly supposed to be of different material and quality from the earth. The earth was of heavy dross; the stars and planets and the sun and moon seemed made of pure and gleaming light, or at least of a bright ethereal substance almost as tenuous as the crystal spheres in which they moved. The cosmos was a hierarchy of ascending perfection. The heavens were purer than the earth.

This system corresponded to actual appearances, and except for scientific knowledge would be highly believable today. It was formulated also in rigorous mathematical terms. Ever since the Greeks, and becoming increasingly intricate in the Middle Ages, a complex geometry had grown up to explain the observed motion of the heavenly bodies. The Ptolemaic system was a mathematical system. And it was for purely mathematical reasons that it first came to be reconsidered. There was a marked revival of mathematical interest at the close of the Middle Ages, in the fourteenth and fifteenth centuries, a renewed concentration on the philosophical traditions of Pythagoras and Plato. In these philosophies could be found the doctrine that numbers might be the final key to the mysteries of nature. With them went a metaphysical belief that simplicity was more likely to be a sign of truth than complication, and that a simpler mathematical formulation was better than a more complex one.

These ideas motivated Nicholas Copernicus, born in Poland of German and Polish background, who, after study in Italy, wrote his epochal work *On the Revolutions of the Heavenly Orbs.* In this book, published in 1543 after his death, he held the sun to be the center of the solar system and fixed stars, and the earth to be one of the planets revolving in space around it. This view had been entertained by a few isolated thinkers before. Copernicus gave a mathematical demonstration. To him it was a purely mathematical problem. With increasingly detailed knowledge of the actual movement of the heavenly bodies it had become necessary to make the Ptolemaic system more intricate by the addition of new "cycles" and "epicycles," until, as John Milton expressed it later, the cosmos was

> *With Centric and Concentric scribbled o'er,*
> *Cycle and Epicycle, Orb in Orb.*

Copernicus needed fewer such hypothetical constructions to explain the known movements of the heavenly bodies. The heliocentric or sun-centered theory was mathematically a little simpler than the geocentric or earth-centered theory hitherto held.

The Copernican doctrine long remained a hypothesis known only to experts. Most astronomers for a time hesitated to accept it, seeing no need, from the evidence yet produced, of so overwhelming a readjustment of current ideas. Tycho Brahe (1546–1601), the greatest authority on the actual positions and movements of the heavenly bodies in the generations immediately after Copernicus, never accepted the Copernican system in full. But his assistant and follower, John Kepler (1571–1630), not only accepted the Copernican theory but carried it further.

Kepler, a German, was a kind of mathematical mystic, part-time astrologer, and scientific genius. He felt ecstasy at the mysterious harmonies of mathematical forms. He built upon the exact observations of Tycho Brahe. Copernicus had believed the orbits of the planets about the sun to be perfect circles. Tycho showed that this belief did not fit the observable facts. Kepler discovered that the orbits of the planets were ellipses. The ellipse, like the circle, is an abstract mathematical figure with knowable properties. Kepler demonstrated that, as a planet moves in its elliptical path about the sun, the straight line connecting it with the sun sweeps through an area of space proportional to the time taken by the planet's motion; that is, that a planet sweeps equal areas in equal times; or, more simply, that the closer a planet is to the sun in its elliptical orbit, the faster it moves. Kepler further showed that the length of time in which the several planets revolve about the sun varies proportionately with their distance from the sun: the square of the time is proportional to the cube of the distance.

It is not possible for most people to understand the mathematics involved, but it is possible to realize the astounding implications of Kepler's laws of planetary motion. Kepler showed that the actual world of stubborn facts, as observed by Tycho, and the purely rational world of mathematical harmony, as surmised by Copernicus, were not really in any discrepancy with each other; that they really corresponded exactly. Why they should he did not know; it was the mystery of numbers. He digested an overwhelming amount of hitherto unexplained information into a few brief statements. He showed a cosmic mathematical relationship between space and time. And he described the movement of the planets in explicit formulas, which any competent person could verify at will.

The next step was taken by Galileo (1564–1642). So far the question of what the heavenly bodies were made of had hardly been affected. Indeed, they were not thought of as bodies at all, but rather as orbs. Only the sun and moon had any dimension; stars and planets were only points of light; and the theories of Copernicus and Kepler, like those of Ptolemy, might apply to insubstantial luminous objects in motion. In 1609 Galileo built a telescope. Turning it to the sky, he perceived that the moon had a rough and apparently mountainous surface, as if made of the same kind of material as the earth. Seeing clearly the dark part of the moon in its various phases, and noting that in every position it only reflected the light of the sun, he concluded that the moon was not itself a luminous object, another indication that it might be made of earth-like substance. He saw spots on the sun, as if the sun were not pure and perfect. He found that the planets had visible breadth when seen in the telescope, but that the fixed stars remained only points of light, as if incalculably further away. He discovered also that Jupiter had satellites, moons moving around it like the moon around the earth. These discoveries reassured him of the validity of the Copernican theory, which he had in any case already accepted. They suggested also that the heavenly bodies might be of the same substance as the earth, masses of matter moving in space. Contrariwise, it became easier to think of the earth as itself a kind of heavenly body revolving about the sun. The difference between the earth and the heavens was disappearing. This struck a terrifying blow at all earlier philosophy and theology. Some professors were afraid to look through the telescope, and Galileo was condemned and forced to an ostensible recantation by his church.

Moreover, where Kepler had found mathematical laws describing the movement of planets, Galileo found mathematical laws describing the movement of bodies on the earth. Formerly it had been thought that some bodies were by nature heavier than others, and that heavier bodies fell to the ground faster than light ones. Galileo in 1591, according to the story, dropped a ten-pound and a one-pound weight simultaneously from the top of the Leaning Tower of Pisa. The truth of this story has been questioned, but in any case Galileo showed that despite all previous speculation on the subject two bodies of different weights, when allowance was made for differences in air resistance due to differences of size or shape, struck the ground at the same time. His further work in dynamics, or the science of the motion of bodies, took many years to accomplish. He had to devise more refined means for measuring small intervals of time, find means of estimating the air resistance, friction, and other impediments which always occur in nature, and conceive of pure or absolute motion, and of force and velocity, in abstract mathematical terms. He made use of a new conception of inertia, in which only *change* in motion, not the origination of motion, had to be explained. This dispensed with the need of an Unmoved Mover felt in the older philosophy. Of bodies moving on the earth, Galileo discovered that when falling freely they fall with a velocity that increases according to mathematical formula.

The Achievement of Newton: The Promise of Science

It was the supreme achievement of Newton to bring Kepler and Galileo together, that is, to show that Kepler's laws of planetary motion and Galileo's laws of terrestrial motion were two aspects of the same laws. Galileo's findings, holding that moving bodies move uniformly in a straight line unless deflected by a definite force, made it necessary to explain why the planets, instead of flying off in straight lines, tend to fall toward the sun, the result being their elliptical orbits—and why the moon, similarly, tends to fall toward the earth. Newton seems early to have suspected that the answer would be related to Galileo's laws of falling bodies —that is, that gravity, or the pull of the earth upon objects on earth, might be a form of a universal gravitation, or similar pull, characterizing all bodies in the solar system. Great technical difficulties stood in the way, but finally, after inventing calculus, and using a new measurement of the size of the earth made by a Frenchman and experiments with circular motion made by the Dutch Huyghens on the pendulum, Newton was able to bring his calculations to fruition, and to publish, in 1687, his *Mathematical Principles of Natural Philosophy.*

This stupendous book showed that all motion that could then be timed and measured, whether on the earth or in the solar system, could be described by the same mathematical formulas. All matter moved as if every particle attracted every other particle with a force proportional to the product of the two masses, and inversely proportional to the square of the distance between them. This "force" was universal gravitation. What it was Newton did not pretend to explain. For two hundred years the law stood unshaken, always verified by every new relevant discovery. Only in the last century have its limitations been found; it does not hold good in the infinitesimal world of subatomic structure or in the macrocosm of the whole physical universe as now conceived.

With Newton's work (which affected other fields than are here mentioned) the promise of science seemed fulfilled. Even in purely practical affairs conveniences followed, as anticipated by the Baconians. The tides could now be understood and predicted by the gravitational interplay of earth, moon, and sun. Exact mathematical knowledge of the solar system was of great help to navigation. In the eighteenth century chronometers were developed, making possible the finding of precise longitude at sea. Merchant ships and naval squadrons could thus operate with more assurance. Better determination of longitude, at sea and on land, was of great value to cartography, the science of map making, since it is by differences of longitude that more accurate east-west distances are ascertained. Eighteenth-century Europeans were the first human beings to have a fairly accurate idea of the shapes and sizes of continents and oceans. Or again, mathematical advance, including the development of calculus, which allowed an exact treatment of curves and trajectories, reinforced by technical discoveries in the working of metals, led to an increased use of artillery. Armies in 1750 used twice as many cannon per soldier as in 1650. Naval ordnance also improved. These were items making armed forces more expensive to maintain, requiring governments to increase their taxes, and hence producing constitutional crises. Improved firearms likewise heightened the advantage of armies over insurrectionists or private fighting bands, thus strengthening the sovereignty of the state. They gave Europeans the military advantage over other peoples, in America, India, or elsewhere, on which the world ascendancy of Europe in the European age was built. This example, chosen somewhat at random, suggests the almost inconceivable ramifications of the practical consequences of science.

The instance of the steam engine may also be cited. Steam power was eventually almost literally to move the world. In 1700 it was a cloud no bigger than a man's hand. Yet it was in sight on the horizon. A Frenchman, Denis Papin, in 1681 invented a device in which steam moved a piston, but it produced so little power that it was used only in cooking. British scientists turned their minds to it. Robert Boyle, discoverer of "Boyle's law" on the pressure of gases, studied the problem; scientists, mechanics, and instrument makers collaborated. In 1702 Thomas Newcomen, a man without scientific training but associated with scientists, produced the steam engine known thereafter as Newcomen's engine, from which, as will be seen, James Watt developed the steam engine as we know it. Newcomen's engine was primitive according to later ideas. It burnt so much fuel that it could be used only in coal mines. But it was used. Not long after 1700 it was widely employed to pump water from the coal pits. It saved labor, cheapened production, and opened hitherto unusable deposits to exploitation. It was the first application of steam to an economic purpose.

The faith in natural knowledge was becoming institutionalized. Organized bodies of men, possessing equipment and funds, were engaged in scientific study. Most notable of these were the Royal Society of London, founded in 1662, and the Academy of Sciences in France, founded in 1666. Both originated when earlier and informal groups, usually gentlemen of the landed classes, received charters from their governments to pursue scientific interests. Scientific periodicals began to be published. Scientific societies provided the medium for prompt interchange of ideas indispensable to the growth of scientific knowledge. They published articles not only on the natural sciences and mathematics, but also on paleography, numismatics, chronology, legal history, and natural law. The work of the learned had not yet yielded to specialization. All felt a common interest in the advance of all fronts of knowledge. It is to be noted also how the scientific movement was an international one, shared in by all central and western Europe except Portugal and Spain. Men of many nationalities constantly made use of each other's hypotheses or discoveries. Many or even most of the books written in this age were first published in Latin, still the international language of science and learning, and many articles in the new scientific journals were written in Latin also.

The Scientific Revolution and the World of Thought

It was perhaps in the world of thought that the revolution accomplished from Copernicus to Newton was most profound. It has been called the greatest spiritual readjustment that human beings have been required to make. The old heavens were exploded. Man was no longer the center of creation. The luminaries of the sky no longer shone to light his way or to give him beauty. The sky itself was an illusion, its color a thing in the mind only, for when a man now looked upward he was really looking only into the darkness of endless space. The old cosmos, comfortably enclosed and ranked in an ascending order of purity, gave way to a new cosmos which seemed to consist in an infinite emptiness through which particles of matter were distributed. Man was the puny denizen of a material object swinging in space along with other very distant material objects of the same kind. About the physical universe there was nothing especially Christian, nothing that the God portrayed in the Bible would be likely to have made. The gap between Christianity and natural science, always present yet always bridged in the Middle Ages, now opened wider than ever. It was felt with anguish by some in the seventeenth century, notably by the Frenchman Blaise Pascal, a considerable scientist, preeminent mathematician, and deep and troubled Christian believer. He left a record of his state of mind in his *Pensées*, or *Thoughts*, jottings from which he hoped some day to write a great book on the Christian faith. "I am terrified," he said in one of these jottings, "by the eternal silence of these infinite spaces."

But on the whole the reaction was more optimistic. Man might be merely a reed, as Pascal said, but Pascal added, "a thinking reed." Man might be no longer the physical center of the world. But it was the human mind that had penetrated the world's laws. The Newtonian system, as it became popularized, a process which took about fifty years, led to a great intellectual complacency. Never had confidence in human powers been so high. As Alexander Pope put it,

> Nature and nature's laws lay hid in night;
> God said, "Let Newton be," and all was light.

Or, according to another epigram on the subject, there was only one universe to discover, and this universe had been discovered by Newton. Everything seemed possible to the human reason. The old feeling of dependency upon God lost much of its force, or became something to be discussed by clergymen in church on

Sunday. Man was not really a little creature, a wayfarer in a world that was alien to him, yearning for the reunion with God that would bring him peace. Man was a dignified creature, one of great capacity in his own right, living in a world that was understandable and manageable by him, and in which he might install himself with quite adequate comfort. These ideas contributed greatly to the secularizing of European society, pushing religion and churches to the sidelines.

The scientific discoveries also reinforced the old philosophy of natural law. This philosophy, developed by the Greeks and renewed in the Middle Ages, held that the universe is fundamentally orderly, and that there is a natural rightness or justice, universally the same for all people, and knowable by reason. It was very important in political theory, where it stood out against arbitrariness and the mere claims of power. The laws of nature as discovered by science were somewhat different, but they taught the same lesson, namely, the orderliness and minute regularity of the world. It was reassuring to feel that everywhere throughout an infinite space, whether or not yet discovered and probed by man, every particle of matter was quietly attracting every other particle by a force proportionate to the product of the masses and inversely proportional to the square of the distance. The physical universe laid bare by science—orderly, rational, balanced, smoothly running, without strife or rivalry or contention—became a model on which many thinkers, as time went on, hoped to refashion human society. They hoped to make society also fulfill the rule of law.

In some ways it would be possible to exaggerate the impact of pure science. Scientists themselves did not usually apply their scientific ideas to religion and society. Few suffered the spiritual torment of Pascal. Both Descartes and Newton wrote placid tractates arguing for the truth of certain ecclesiastical doctrines. Bacon and Harvey were conservative politically, upholders of king against Parliament. The Englishman Joseph Glanvill, in the 1660s, used the Cartesian dualism to demonstrate the probable existence of witches. Descartes, despite his systematic doubt, held that the customs of one's country were to be accepted without question. Natural science, in the pure sense, was not inherently revolutionary or even upsetting. If Europeans in the seventeenth century began to waver in many old beliefs it was not only because of the stimulus of pure science, but also because of an increasing knowledge and study of humanity itself.

34. NEW KNOWLEDGE OF MAN AND SOCIETY

Here one of the most potent forces at work was the discovery and exploration of the world overseas. Europe was already becoming part of the world as a whole, and could henceforth understand itself only by comparison with non-European regions. Great reciprocal influences were at work. The influences of European expansion on other parts of the world are easily seen: the Indian societies of America were modified or extinguished, the indigenous societies of Africa were dislocated and many of their members enslaved and transported; in the long run even the ancient societies of Asia were to be undermined. From the beginning the counterinfluence of the rest of the world upon Europe was equally great. It took the form not only of new medicines, new diseases, new foods, new and exotic manufactures brought to Europe, and the growth of material wealth in west-European countries. It affected European thinking also. It undermined the old

Europe and its ideas, just as Europe was undermining the old cultures beyond the oceans. Vast new horizons opened before Europeans in the sixteenth and seventeenth centuries. Europeans of this period were the first people to whom it was given to know the globe as a whole, or to realize the variety of the human race and its multifarious manners and customs.

The Current of Skepticism

This realization was very unsettling. The realization of human differences had the effect, in Europe, of breaking what anthropologists call the "cake of custom." A new sense of the relative nature of social institutions developed. It became harder to believe in any absolute rightness of one's own ways. Montaigne, already mentioned, expressed the relativist outlook clearly, and nowhere more clearly than in his famous essay on cannibals. The cannibals, he said humorously, did in fact eat human flesh; that was their custom, and they have their customs as we have ours; they would think some of our ways odd or inhuman; peoples differ, and who are we to judge? Travelers' books spread the same message increasingly through the seventeenth century. As one of them observed (whether or not rightly), in Turkey it was the custom to shave the hair and wear the beard, in Europe to shave the beard and wear the hair; what difference does it really make? That the ways of non-Europeans might be good ways was emphasized by Jesuit missionaries. Writing from the depths of the Mississippi Valley or from China, the Jesuit fathers often dwelt on the natural goodness and mental alertness of the native peoples they encountered, perhaps hoping in this way to gain support in Europe for their missionary labors. Sometimes strange people appeared in Europe itself. In 1684 a delegation of aristocratic Siamese arrived in Paris, followed by another in 1686. The Parisians went through a fad for Siam; they recounted how the king of Siam, when asked by a missionary to turn Christian, replied that divine Providence, had it wished a single religion to prevail in the world, could easily have so arranged it. The Siamese seemed civilized, wise, philosophic; they allowed Christians to preach in their own country, whereas it was well known what would happen to a Siamese missionary who undertook to preach in Paris. China also was seen through an ideal glow. By 1700 there were even professors of Arabic, at Paris, Oxford, and Utrecht, who said that Islam was a religion to be respected, as good for Muslims as Christianity was for Christians.

Thus was created a strong current of skepticism, holding that all beliefs are relative, varying with time and place. Its greatest spokesman at the end of the century was Pierre Bayle (1647–1706). Bayle was influenced by the scientific discoveries also; not exactly that he understood them, for he was an almost purely literary scholar, but he realized that many popular beliefs were without foundation. Between 1680 and 1682 a number of comets were seen. The one of 1682 was studied by a friend of Newton's, Edmund Halley, the first man to predict the return of a comet. He identified the one of 1682 with the one observed in 1302, 1456, 1531, and 1607, and predicted its reappearance in 1757 (it appeared in 1759); it was seen again in 1910 and the 1980s and is still called Halley's Comet. In the 1680s people were talking of comets excitedly. Some said that comets emitted poisonous exhalations, others that they were supernatural omens of future events. Bayle, in his *Thoughts on the Comet*, argued at great length that there was no basis for any such beliefs except human credulity. In 1697 he published his *Historical and Critical Dictionary*, a tremendous repository of miscellaneous lore, conveying the message that what is called truth is often mere opinion, that most people are amazingly gullible, that many things firmly believed are really ridiculous, and that it is very foolish to hold too strongly to one's own views. Bayle's *Dictionary* remained a reservoir on which skeptical writers continued to draw for generations. Bayle himself, having no firm basis in his own mind for settled judgment, mixed skepticism with an impulse to faith. Born a Protestant, he was converted to Rome, then returned to his Calvinist background. In any case his views made for toleration in religion. For Bayle, as for Montaigne, no opinion was worth burning your neighbor for.

The New Sense of Evidence

But in the study of humankind, as in the study of physical nature, Europeans of the seventeenth century were not generally content with skepticism. They were not possessed by a mere negative and doubting mood, important and salutary as such an attitude was. In the subjects collectively called the humanities, as in pure science, they were looking not for disbelief but for understanding. They wanted new means of telling the true from the false, a new method for arriving at some degree of certainty of conviction. And here, too, a kind of scientific view of the world arose, if that term be understood in a general sense. It took the form of a new sense of evidence. Evidence is that which allows one to believe a thing to be true, or at least truer than something else for which the evidence is weaker. And if to believe without evidence is the sign of primitive or irrational thinking, to require evidence before believing is in a way to be scientific, or at least to trust and use the power of human intelligence.

The new sense of evidence, and of the need of evidence, revealed itself in many ways. One of the clearest was in the law. The English law of evidence, for example, began to take on its modern form at the close of the seventeenth century. Previously the belief had been that the more atrocious the crime the less evidence should be necessary in arriving at a verdict of guilty; this was thought necessary to protect society from the more hideous offenses. From the end of the seventeenth century, in English law, the judge lost his power of discretion in deciding what should constitute evidence, and the same rules of evidence were applied in all forms of accusation, the essential question being recognized as always the same— did such-and-such a fact (however outrageous) occur or did it not? After 1650 mere hearsay evidence, long vaguely distrusted, was ruled definitely out of court. After 1696 even persons charged with felony were allowed legal counsel.

The new sense of evidence was probably the main force in putting an end to the delusions of witchcraft. What made witchcraft so credible and so fearsome was that many persons confessed themselves to be witches, admitting to supernatural powers and to evil designs upon their neighbors.[4] Many or most such confessions were extracted under torture. Reformers urged that confessions obtained under torture were not evidence, that people would say anything to escape unbearable pain, so that no quantity of such confessions offered the slightest ground for believing in witches. As for the voluntary confessions, and even the boastings of some people of their diabolical powers, it was noted that such statements often came from half-demented old women, or from persons who would today be called hysterical or psychotic. Witches came to be regarded as self-deluded. Their ideas of

---

[4] See pp. 51, 246.

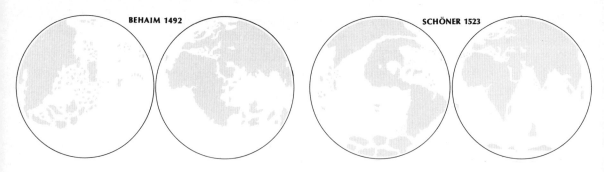

THE GROWTH OF GEOGRAPHICAL KNOWLEDGE

The four maps show the best scientific knowledge at their respective dates. Behaim has no inkling of the existence of America and has filled in the hemisphere opposite to Europe with a mass of islands, representing what he has heard of the East Indies and Japan. He knows pretty well the limits of Africa. Schöner in 1523 fills in America and even distinguishes two American continents. He knows of the Gulf of Mexico but fails to realize the narrowness of the Isthmus of Panama. He knows of the Straits of Magellan (but not Cape Horn) and hopefully fills in a corresponding Northwest Passage in the

themselves were no longer accepted as evidence. But it must be added that, except in England, the use of legal torture lasted on through most of the eighteenth century, in criminal cases in which the judge believed the accused to be guilty.

History and Historical Scholarship

What are called the historical sciences also developed rapidly at this time. History, like the law, depends on the finding and using of evidence. The historian and the judge must answer the same kind of question—did such-and-such a fact really occur? All knowledge of history, so far as it disengages itself from legend and wishful thinking, rests ultimately on pieces of evidence, written records, and other works of man created in the past and surviving in some form or other in the present. On this mass of material the vast picture of the past is built, and without it men would be ignorant of their own antecedents or would have only folk tales and tribal traditions.

There was much skepticism about history in the seventeenth century. Some said that history was not a form of true knowledge because it was not mathematical. Others said that it was useless because Adam, the perfect man, had neither had nor needed any history. Many felt that what passed for history was only a mass of fables. History was distrusted also because historians were often pretentious, claiming to be high-flying men of letters, writing for rhetorical or inspirational appeal or for argumentative reasons, disdaining the hard labor of actual study. History was losing the confidence of thinking people. How was it possible, they asked, to feel even a modicum of certainty about alleged events that had happened long before any living person had been born?

This doubting attitude itself arose from a stricter sense of evidence, or from a realization that there was really no proof for much of what was said about the past. But scholars set to work to assemble what evidence there was. They hoped to create a new history, one that should contain only reliable statements. Europe was littered with old papers and parchments. Abbeys, manor houses, royal archives

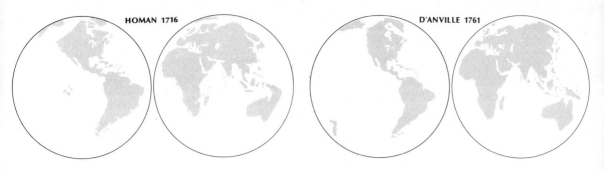

HOMAN 1716   D'ANVILLE 1761

north. His conception of the Indian Ocean is quite accurate. To Homan, two centuries later, the size and shapes of oceans and continents are well known, but he believes New Guinea joined to Australia and is frankly ignorant of the northwest coast of North America, representing it by a straight line. The Great Lakes and the interior of North America have become known to Europe. D'Anville in 1761 has no island of Tasmania, does not understand that Alaska is a peninsula, and believes the American polar regions to be impassable by sea. Otherwise his map is indistinguishable from one on the same scale today.

were full of written documents, many of them of unknown age or unknown origin, often written in a handwriting which people could no longer read. Learned and laborious enthusiasts set to work to explore this accumulation. They added so much to the efforts of their predecessors as virtually to create modern critical scholarship and erudition. The French Benedictine monk Jean Mabillon, in 1681, in his book *On Diplomatics* (referring to ancient charters and "diplomas") established the science of paleography, which deals with the deciphering, reading, dating, and authentication of manuscripts. The Frenchman DuCange in 1678 published a dictionary of medieval Latin which is still used. Others, like the Italian Muratori, spent whole lifetimes exploring archives, collecting, editing, or publishing masses of documents, comparing manuscript copies of the same text and trying to discover what the author had really said, rejecting some as fabrications or forgeries, pronouncing others to be genuine pieces of historical evidence. Others made themselves experts in ancient coins, many of which were far more ancient than the oldest manuscripts; they founded the science of numismatics. Still others, or indeed the same ones, turned to a critical examination of the inscriptions on old buildings and ruins.

Another important but little-known historical "science," namely, chronology, was greatly stimulated also. Chronology deals with the age of the world and with finding a common denominator between the dating systems of various peoples. Probably it is not natural for the human mind to think in terms of dates at all. For simple people it is enough to know that some things happened "long ago." In the seventeenth century the new interest in numbers, evident in physical science, turned also to the human past. Archbishop James Usher, an Anglican prelate of Ireland, after much study of the Bible, announced the date of 4004 B.C. as that of the creation of the world. His chronological system was later printed in the margins of the Authorized Version of the English Bible, and is still adhered to by some fundamentalists as if part of the Bible itself. But Usher's system was not accepted by scholars even in his own time. Geographical knowledge was revealing China and its dynasties to Europe; historical knowledge was beginning to discover ancient Egypt. The Chinese and Egyptian records claimed a greater antiquity for their countries than the Old Testament seemed to allow for the human race. There was much erudite conjecture; one scholar about 1700 counted seventy estimates of the age of the world, ranging as high as 170,000 years, a figure which then seemed fantastic and appalling.

The difficulty was not only in the language of the Old Testament. It was in finding the correspondence between the chronological systems of different peoples. A Chinese system of dating by dynasties might be coherent within itself, but how could it be equated with the European system of dating from the birth of Christ, a date as unknown to the Chinese as the date of Wu Wang was to Europeans? Even European records presented the same difficulty; the Romans counted by consulships, or from the supposed year of the founding of Rome; many medieval documents told only the year of some obscure ruler's reign. Only infinite patience, interminable research, and endless calculation could reduce such a jumble to the simple system of modern textbooks. This is of more importance than may be at first thought. A common system of dating is a great aid to thinking of human history as an interconnected whole. An overall conception of the human race is made easier by the dating of all events according to the Christian era. This itself, it may be pointed out, is an arbitrary and conventional scale, since Christ is now thought to have been born not in A.D. 1, but in 4 B.C.

Common dating was of importance in practical affairs as well as in historical knowledge. Europe was disunited even on the Christian calendar. Protestant and some Orthodox countries followed the old or Julian calendar, Catholic countries the corrected or Gregorian calendar, issued in the sixteenth century under authority of Pope Gregory XIII. The two calendars varied in the seventeenth century by ten days. Only gradually was the Gregorian calendar accepted, by England in 1752, by Russia in 1918. Most other peoples today, in China, India, the Arabic world, and elsewhere, use or recognize the Gregorian calendar. Without a uniform way of specifying days and years it would be less easy to transact international affairs, hold international conferences, make plans, or pay and receive money. This common dating, easily taken for granted, was a consequence of the predominance of Europe in modern times. It is a sign of growing unity in world civilization.

The Questioning of Traditional Beliefs

The historical sciences provided a foundation on which a knowledge of human activities in the past could be built, and the growing geographical knowledge spread a panorama of man's diverse activities and peculiarities in the present. This new knowledge of man shared with natural science, and probably derived from it, or from philosophers of science like Descartes and Bacon, the view that many traditional ideas were erroneous, but that much could be known by a disciplined use of the human mind. The humanities and the sciences were alike in demanding evidence for belief and in trusting to the power of reason. In their impact on the old certainties of European life, the studies of man exerted possibly a greater direct force than those of nature. Pascal, in his attempt to defend the Christian faith, feared the spirit of Montaigne, the mood of skepticism and denial, which he felt himself, more than he feared the findings of mathematical and physical science. And the movement of historical thought, with its insistence on textual criticism, threw doubt on much of the Christian religion, or at least on the sacred history related in the Bible, which was considered to be part and parcel of religion itself.

In 1678 a French priest, Richard Simon, published a pioneering work in Biblical criticism, his *Critical History of the Old Testament*. Though his book was condemned both by the church and by the government of Louis XIV, Richard Simon always felt himself to be orthodox; Catholic faith, he insisted, depended more on church tradition than on the literal statements of the Bible. He simply applied to the Old Testament the methods of textual criticism which others were applying to secular documents. He concluded that the Old Testament, as known, rested on medieval manuscripts many of which were of unknown or doubtful origin, that monkish copyists had brought in errors and corruptions, and that the books thought to have been written by Moses could not have been written by him, since they contained obvious contradictions and matter clearly inserted after his death. Others went further, questioning not merely the evidence of the Biblical text, but the very possibility of some events that it related. From the scientific idea of the absolute regularity of nature on the one hand, and from a strong sense of human credulity on the other, they denied that miracles had ever occurred and looked upon oracles and prophecies among either the Greeks or the Hebrews with a dubious eye.

The most profoundly disturbing of all thinkers of the time was Baruch Spinoza (1632–1677), the lens grinder of Amsterdam, a Jew who was excommunicated by his own synagogue and who refused a professorship at the University of Heidelberg, craving only the quiet to think in peace. Spinoza drew on both the scientific and humanistic thought of his day. He arrived at a philosophy holding that God had no existence apart from the world, that everything was itself an aspect of God, a philosophy technically called pantheism but considered by many to be really atheistic. He denied the inspiration of the Bible, disbelieved in miracles and the supernatural, rejected all revelation and revealed religion, Jewish or Christian, and held that few if any governments of the day were really just. He taught a pure, stern, and intellectual ethical code, and one which had few consolations for the average man. His name became a byword for impiety and horrendous unbelief. People were literally afraid to read his works, even when they could find them, which was not often because of the censorship. His influence spread slowly, through the mediation of other writers.

More widely read, less abstruse, more reassuring, dwelling on the merits of common sense, were the writings of the Englishman John Locke (1632–1704), who summarized many of the intellectual trends of his lifetime and exerted a strong influence for the following hundred years. He combined practical experience and theoretical interests. Educated in medicine, he kept in touch with the sciences and was acquainted with Newton. He was associated with the great Whig noblemen who were the main authors of the English revolution in 1688. For political reasons he spent several years in the 1680s in the Netherlands, where he became familiar with thought on the Continent. He wrote on many subjects— finance, economics, education, religious policy, political theory, general philosophy—always with an engaging directness and sober air of the sensible man of the world. In his *Letter on Toleration* (1689) he advocated an established church, but with toleration of all except Roman Catholics and atheists; these he held to be dangerous to society, the former because of a foreign allegiance, the latter because they lacked a basis of moral responsibility. In his *Reasonableness of Christianity* he argued that Christianity, rightly considered, is after all a reasonable form of religion; this softened the friction between religion and natural knowledge but tended to shut out the supernatural and merge religious feeling into an unruffled common sense.

Locke's deepest book was his *Essay Concerning the Human Understanding* (1690). Here he faced the great problem of the day, the problem of knowledge; he asked what it was possible for men to know with certainty, and how certain knowledge was arrived at. His answer was that true or certain knowledge is derived from experience—from perceptions of the sense organs and reflection of the mind on these perceptions. Locke at the end of the century thus echoed Bacon at the beginning; they became the two great pillars of empirical philosophy, insisting on experience and observation as the source of truth. Locke denied Descartes' doctrine of innate ideas, or inevitable disposition of the human mind to think in certain ways. He held that the mind at birth is a blank tablet or *tabula rasa*, and that what a person comes to think or believe depends on the environment in which he lives. Locke's environmentalist philosophy became fundamental to liberal and reforming thought in later years. It seemed that false ideas or superstitions were the result of bad environment and bad education. It seemed that the evil in human actions was due to bad social institutions, and that an improvement in human society would improve human behavior. This philosophy, whether or not wholly true in the final analysis, was largely true with respect to many practical conditions. It gave confidence in the possibility of social progress and turned attention to a sphere in which planned and constructive action was possible, namely, the sphere of government, public policy, and legislation. Here we touch on political theory, to which Locke contributed *Two Treatises of Government*. These are discussed below.

35. POLITICAL THEORY: THE SCHOOL OF NATURAL LAW

Political theory can never be strictly scientific. Science deals with what does exist or has existed. It does not tell what ought to exist. To tell what society and government ought to be like, in view of man's nature and his capacity to be miserable or contented, is a main purpose of political theory. Political theory is in a sense more practical than science. It is the scientists and scholars who are most content to observe facts as they are. Practical people, and scientists and scholars so far as they have practical interests, must always ask themselves what ought to be done, what policies ought to be adopted, what measures taken, what state of affairs maintained or brought about. Conservatives and radicals, traditionalists and innovators, are alike in this respect. It is impossible in human affairs to escape the word "ought."

But political theory was affected by the scientific view. The Renaissance Italian, Niccolò Machiavelli (1469–1527), had opened the way in this direction.[5] Machiavelli too had his "ought"; he preferred a republican form of government in which citizens felt a patriotic attachment to their state. But in his book, *The Prince*, he disregarded the question of the best form of government, a favorite question of Christian and scholastic philosophers of the Middle Ages. He sepa-

[5] See pp. 60–61.

rated the study of politics from theology and moral philosophy. He undertook to describe how governments and rulers actually behaved. He observed that successful rulers behaved as if holding or increasing power were their only object, that they regarded all else as means to this end. Princes, said Machiavelli, kept their promises or broke them, they told the truth or distorted or colored it, they sought popularity or ignored it, they advanced public welfare or disrupted it, they conciliated their neighbors or destroyed them, depending merely on which course of action seemed the best means of advancing their political interests. All this was bad, said Machiavelli; but that was not the question, for the question was to find out what rulers really did. Machiavelli, in *The Prince*, chose to be nonmoral in order to be scientific. To most readers he seemed to be simply immoral. Nor was it possible to draw the line between *The Prince* as a scientific description of fact and *The Prince* as a book of maxims of conduct. In telling how successful rulers obtained their successes, Machiavelli also suggested how rulers *ought* to proceed. And though governments did in fact continue to behave for the most part as Machiavelli said, most people refused to admit that they ought to.

Natural Right and Natural Law

Political theory in the seventeenth century did not embrace the cynicism attributed to Machiavelli. Nor did it fall into the skepticism of those who said that the customs of one's country should be passively accepted, or that one form of government was about as good as another. It directly faced the question, What is right? The seventeenth century was the classic age of the philosophy of natural right or of natural law.

The idea of natural law has underlain a good deal of modern democratic development, and its decline in the last century has been closely connected with many of the troubles of recent times. It is not easy to say in what the philosophy of natural law essentially consisted. It held that there is, somehow, in the structure of the world, a law that distinguishes right from wrong. It held that right is "natural," not a mere human invention. This right is not determined, for any country, by its heritage, tradition, or customs, nor yet by its actual laws (called "positive" laws) of the kind that are enforced in the law courts. All these may be unfair or unjust. We detect unfairness or injustice in them by comparing them with natural law as we understand it; thus we have a basis for saying that cannibalism is bad, or that a law requiring forced labor from orphan children is unjust. Nor is natural law, or the real rightness of a thing, determined by the authority of any person or people. No king can make right that which is wrong. No people, by its will as a people, can make just that which is unjust. Right and law, in the ultimate sense, exist outside and above all peoples. They are universal, the same for all. No one can make them up to suit himself. A good king, or a just people, is a king or people whose actions correspond to the objective standard. But how, if we cannot trust our own positive laws or customs, or our leaders, or even our collective selves, can we know what is naturally right? How do we discover natural law? The answer, in the natural law philosophy, is that we discover it by reason. Man is considered to be a rational animal. And all men are assumed to have, at least potentially and when better enlightened, the same powers of reason and understanding—Germans or English, Siamese or Europeans. This view favored a cosmopolitan outlook and made international agreement and general world progress seem realizable goals. As time went on, the premises of this philosophy came to be questioned. By the twentieth century it was widely thought that man was not an especially rational being but was motivated by drives or urges or instincts, and that human differences were so fundamental that men of different nationalities or classes could never expect to see things in the same way. When this happened the older philosophy of natural law lost its hold on many minds.

In the seventeenth and eighteenth centuries it was generally accepted. Some, carrying over the philosophy of the Middle Ages, thought of natural law as an aspect of the law of God. Others, more secular in spirit, held that the natural law stood of itself. These included even some churchmen; a group of theologians, mainly Jesuits, were condemned by the pope in 1690 for holding that universal right and wrong might exist by reason only, whether God existed or not. The idea of natural law and the faith in human reason went side by side, and both were fundamental in the thought of the time. They were to be found everywhere in Europe, in their religious or their secular form.

On the basis of natural law some thinkers tried to create an international law or "law of nations," to bring order into the maze of sovereign territorial states, great and small, that was developing in Europe. Hugo Grotius, in 1625, published the first great book devoted exclusively to this subject, his *Law of War and Peace*. Samuel Pufendorf followed with his *Law of Nature and of Nations* in 1672. Both held that sovereign states, though bound by no positive law or authority, should work together for the common good, that there was a community of nations as of individuals, and that in the absence of a higher international sovereignty they were all still subordinate to natural reason and justice. Certain concrete doctrines, such as the freedom of the seas or the immunity of ambassadors, were put forward. The principles of international law remained those of natural law. The content came to include specific agreements between governments, certain kinds of admiralty and maritime law, and the terms of treaties such as the treaties of Westphalia, Utrecht, and others. The means of enforcement, to be sure, remained weak or nonexistent in crises.

Hobbes and Locke

In domestic affairs the philosophy of natural law, though it rather favored constitutionalism, was used to justify both constitutional and absolutist governments. Right itself was held to be in the nature of things, beyond human power to change. But forms of government were held to be means to an end. No philosopher at the time thought the state to have an absolute value in itself. The state had to be "justified," made acceptable to the moral consciousness or the reason. There were, indeed, important competing philosophies. On the side of absolutism was the doctrine of the divine right of kings. On the side of constitutionalism were arguments based on heritage or custom, emphasizing the charters, bulls, or compacts of former times and the historic powers of parliaments and estates. But neither the supernatural argument of the divine right of kings, nor the historical argument pointing back to liberties of the Middle Ages, was entirely satisfactory in the scientific atmosphere of the seventeenth century. Neither carried complete conviction to the reason or moral sense of the most acute thinkers. Both were reinforced by arguments of natural law. Two Englishmen stand out above all others in this connection. Absolutism was philosophically justified by Thomas Hobbes, constitutionalism by John Locke.

Hobbes (1588–1679) followed the scientific and mathematical discoveries of his time with more than an amateur interest. In philosophy he held to a materialistic and even atheistic system. In English politics he sided with king against Parliament; he disliked the disorder and violence of the civil war of the 1640s and the unstable conditions of the English republic of the 1650s.[6] He concluded that men have no capacity for self-government. His opinion of human nature was low; he held that men in the "state of nature," or as imagined to exist without government, were quarrelsome and turbulent, forever locked in a war of all against all. In his famous phrase, life in the state of nature was "solitary, poor, nasty, brutish and short." From fear of each other, to obtain order, and enjoy the advantages of law and right, men came to a kind of agreement or "contract" by which they surrendered their freedom of action into the hands of a ruler. It was necessary for this ruler to have unrestricted or absolute power. Only thus could he maintain order. It was intolerably dangerous, according to Hobbes, for anyone to question the actions of government, for such questioning might reopen the way to chaos. Government must in fact be a kind of Leviathan (the monster mentioned in the Bible, Job 41); and it was by the word *Leviathan* that Hobbes entitled his principal book, published in 1651, two years after the execution of King Charles I.

By this book Hobbes became the leading secular exponent of absolutism and one of the principal theorists of the unlimited sovereignty of the state. His influence on later thinkers was very great. He accustomed political theorists to the use of purely natural arguments. He quoted freely from the Bible, but the Bible had no influence on his thought. After Hobbes, all advanced political theorists regarded government as a thing created by human purpose. It was no longer considered, except popularly and except by professional theologians, as part of a divine dispensation of God to man. Hobbes also affected later theorists by his arguments for a sovereign authority, and, more negatively, by obliging them to refute his idea of an unlimited personal sovereign. But he was never a popular writer. In England the cause which he favored was lost. In those Continental countries where royal absolutism prevailed his arguments were received with secret gratification, but his irreligion was too dangerous to make public, and the absolutist argument, on the popular level, remained that of the divine right of kings. In any case Hobbes's arguments were in some ways insufficient for real monarchs. Hobbes abhorred struggle and violence. His case for absolutism required absolutism to produce civil peace, individual security, and a rule of law. He also held that absolute power depended on, or had at least originated in, a free and rational agreement by which people accepted it. An absolute monarchy that flagrantly violated these conditions could with difficulty be justified even by the doctrines of Hobbes. It is in these respects that Hobbes differs from totalitarian theorists of recent times. For Hobbes, in the final analysis, absolute power was an expedient to promote individual welfare. It was a means necessary to the realization of natural law.

John Locke (1632–1704), as has been seen, also stood in the main current of scientific thought and discovery. But in his political philosophy he carried over many ideas of the Middle Ages, as formulated in the thirteenth century by St. Thomas Aquinas[7] and kept alive in England by successive thinkers of the Anglican church. Medieval philosophy had never favored an absolute power. With Hobbes, Locke shared the idea that good government is an expedient of human purpose, neither provided by divine Providence nor inherited by a national tradition. He

[6] See pp. 169–171.
[7] See pp. 41–43.

held, too, like Hobbes and the whole school of natural law, that government was based on a kind of contract, or rational and conscious agreement upon which authority was based. In contrast to Hobbes, he sided with Parliament against king in the practical struggles of politics. About 1680, in the course of these disputes, he wrote *Two Treatises of Government*, which however were not published until shortly after the parliamentary revolution of 1688–1689.[8]

Locke took a more genial view of human nature than Hobbes. As he showed in his other books, he believed that a moderate religion was a good thing, and above all that men could learn from experience and hence could be educated to an enlightened way of life. These ideas favored a belief in self-government. Locke declared (in contradiction to Hobbes) that men in the "state of nature" were reasonable and well disposed, willing to get along with one another though handicapped by the absence of public authority. Men likewise had a moral sense, quite independently of government; and they also possessed by nature certain rights, quite apart from the state. These rights were the rights to life, liberty, and property. Locke threw very heavy emphasis on the right of property, by which he usually meant the possession of land. His philosophy can in fact be regarded as an expression of the landed classes of England in their claims against the king; it should be noted that land ownership in England was more widespread in 1690 than it later became. Men, as individuals in the state of nature, are not altogether able, according to Locke, to win general respect for their individual natural rights. They cannot by their own efforts protect what is "proper" to them, i.e., their property. They agree to set up government to enforce observance of the rights of all. Government is thus created by a contract, but the contract is not unconditional, as claimed by Hobbes. It imposes mutual obligations. The people must be reasonable; only rational beings can be politically free. Liberty is not an anarchy of undisciplined will; it is the freedom to act without compulsion by another. Only rational and responsible creatures can exercise true freedom; but adult human beings, according to Locke, are or can be educated to be rational and responsible. They therefore can and should be free. On government, also, certain conditions and obligations are imposed. If a government breaks the contract, if it threatens the natural rights which it is the sole purpose of government to protect, if, for example, it takes away a man's property without his consent, then the governed have a right to reconsider what they have done in creating the government and may even in the last extremity rebel against it. The right to resist government, Locke admits, is very dangerous, but it is less dangerous than its opposite, which would lead to enslavement; and in any case we are talking about reasonable and responsible people.

If Locke's ideas seem familiar, especially to Americans, it is because of the wide popularizing of his philosophy in the century after his death. Nowhere was his influence greater than in the British colonies. The authors of the American Declaration of Independence and of the Constitution of the United States knew the writings of Locke very thoroughly. Some phrases of the Declaration of Independence echo his very language. In Great Britain also, and in France and elsewhere, in the course of time, Locke's influence was immense.

What Locke did was to convert an episode in English history into an event of universal meaning. In England, in 1688, certain great lords, winning the support

[8] See pp. 173–177.

of the established church, gentry, and merchants, put out one king and brought in another. On the new king they imposed certain obligations—specified in the Bill of Rights of 1689, and all dealing with legal or technical interpretations of the English constitution. The Revolution of 1688 was a very English affair. England in 1688 was still little known to the rest of Europe. The proceedings in England, so far as known, might seem no different from a rebellion of the magnates of Hungary. Locke, in arguing that Parliament had done right to eject James II, put the whole affair on a level of reason, natural right, and human nature. It thus came to have meaning for everyone. At the same time, Locke made the English revolution a sign of progress rather than reaction. The new and modern form of government in 1690 was royal absolutism, with its professional bureaucracy and corps of paid officials. Almost everywhere there was resistance to the kings, led by landed interests and harking back to earlier freedoms. Such resistance seemed to many Europeans to be feudal and medieval. Locke made the form taken by such resistance in England, namely, the Revolution of 1688 against James II, into a modern and forward-looking move. He checked the prestige of absolutism. He gave new prestige to constitutional principles. He carried over, in modified form, many ideas from the scholastic philosophers of the Middle Ages, who had generally maintained that kings had only a relative and restricted power and were responsible to their peoples. To these ideas he added the force of the newer scientific view of the world. He did not rest his case on supernatural or providential arguments. He did not say that constitutional government was the will of God. He said that it rested on experience and observation of human nature, on recognition of certain individual rights and especially the right of property, and on the existence of a purely natural law of reason and justice. He was an almost entirely secular thinker.

One must not claim too much for Locke, or for any writer. England was in fact, in 1688, more modern in many ways than other countries in Europe. The Glorious Revolution was in fact not exactly like uprisings of the landed and propertied classes elsewhere. England in the following century did in fact create a form of parliamentary government that was unique. But facts go together with the theories that give them an understandable meaning. Events in England, as explained by Locke, and as seen in other countries and even in England and its colonies through Locke's eyes, launched into the mainstream of modern history the superb tradition of constitutional government, which has been one of the principal themes in the history of the modern world ever since.

By 1700, at the close of the "century of genius," some beliefs that were to be characteristic of modern times had clearly taken form, notably a faith in science, in human reason, in natural human rights, and in progress. The following period, generally known as the Age of Enlightenment, was to be a time of clarifying and popularizing ideas which the more creative seventeenth century had produced. These ideas were eventually to revolutionize Europe, America, and the world. They were also in subsequent years to be modified, amended, challenged, and even denied. But they are still very much alive today.

VIII.
The Age of Enlightenment

The eighteenth century, or at least the years of that century preceding the French Revolution of 1789, is commonly known as the Age of Enlightenment, and though that name raises more than the usual difficulties, still there is no other that describes so many features of the time so well. People strongly felt that theirs was an enlightened age, and it is from their own evaluation of themselves that our term Age of Enlightenment is derived. Everywhere there was a feeling that Europeans had at last emerged from a long twilight. The past was regarded as a time of barbarism and darkness. The sense of progress was all but universal among the educated classes. It was the belief both of the forward-looking thinkers and writers known as the philosophes and of the forward-looking kings and empresses, the "enlightened despots," together with their ministers and officials.

36. THE PHILOSOPHES—AND OTHERS

The Spirit of Progress and Improvement

The spirit of the eighteenth-century Enlightenment was drawn from the scientific and intellectual revolution of the seventeenth century. The Enlightenment carried over and popularized the ideas of Bacon and Descartes, of Bayle and Spinoza, and, above all, of Locke and Newton. It carried over the philosophy of natural

Chapter Emblem: A French snuffbox showing miniature portraits on tortoise shell of three famous philosophers, Voltaire, Rousseau, and Benjamin Franklin.

law and of natural right. Never was there an age so skeptical toward tradition, so confident in the powers of human reason and of science, so firmly convinced of the regularity and harmony of nature, and so deeply imbued with the sense of civilization's advance and progress.

The idea of progress is often said to have been the dominant or characteristic idea of European civilization from the seventeenth century to the twentieth. It is a belief, a kind of nonreligious faith, that the conditions of human life become better as time goes on, that in general each generation is better off than its predecessors and will contribute by its labor to an even better life for generations to come, and that in the long run all mankind will share in the same advance. All the elements of this belief had been present by 1700. It was after 1700, however, that the idea of progress became explicit. In the seventeenth century it had shown itself in a more rudimentary way, in a sporadic dispute, among men of letters in England and France, known as the quarrel of Ancients and Moderns. The An- cients held that the works of the Greeks and Romans had never been surpassed. The Moderns, pointing to science, art, literature, and invention, declared that their own time was the best, that it was natural for men of their time to do better than the ancients because they came later and built upon their predecessors' achievements. The quarrel was never exactly settled, but a great many people in 1700 were Moderns.

Far-reaching also was the faith of the age in the natural faculties of the human mind. Pure skepticism, the negation of reason, was overcome. Nor were the edu- cated, after 1700, likely to be superstitious, terrified by the unknown, or addicted to magic. The witchcraft mania abruptly died. Indeed all sense of the supernatu- ral became dim. "Modern" people not only ceased to fear the devil; they ceased also to fear God. They thought of God less as a Father than as a First Cause of the physical universe. There was less sense of a personal God, or of the inscrutable imminence of divine Providence, or of man's need for saving grace. God was less the God of Love; He was the inconceivably intelligent being who had made the amazing universe now discovered by human reason. The great symbol of the Christian God was the Cross, on which a divine being had suffered in human form. The symbol which occurred to people of scientific view was the Watch- maker. The intricacies of the physical universe were compared to the intricacies of a watch, and it was argued that just as a watch could not exist without a watchmaker, so the universe as discovered by Newton could not exist without a God who created it and set it moving by its mathematical law. It was almighty intelligence that was thought divine.

Of course not everyone was primarily moved by such ideas. The first half of the eighteenth century was in fact also a time of continuing religious fervor. Isaac Watts wrote many hymns that are still familiar in English-speaking churches; the great church music of J. S. Bach was composed mainly in the 1720s; Handel's ora- torio, *The Messiah*, was first performed in 1741; and it was at about this time that congregations first sang the *Adeste fideles* ("O Come, All Ye Faithful"), originally Catholic in inspiration but soon adopted by Protestants also. The Lutherans of Germany were stirred by the movement known as Pietism, which stressed the inner experience of ordinary persons as distinct from the doctrines taught and de- bated in theological faculties. The quest for an "inner light," or illumination of the soul rather than of the reason, was somewhat contrary to the main thrust of the Age of Enlightenment, and a religious urge for improvement of the individual rather than of social institutions was hardly central to the idea of progress, but such ideas were by no means merely conservative, for they were in general highly critical of the existing order.

Within the Church of England John Wesley, while a student at Oxford, joined a group of like-minded young men for prayer and meditation. They engaged in good works to relieve the sufferings of prisoners and the poor, to whom they distributed food and clothing, while also teaching them how to read. Going outside the restrictive system of parishes, Wesley and others took to "itinerant" preaching, often to immense crowds in open fields. Wesley is said to have traveled 250,000 miles within Great Britain over a period of fifty years. He and the similarly inclined George Whitfield preached also in the English American colonies, where they helped to arouse the Great Awakening of the 1740s. Such movements had a kind of democratizing effect in stressing individual worth and spiritual consciousness independently of the established religious authorities. Indeed, the spokesmen for older churches dismissed such movements as "enthusiasm," which was then a word of reproach. By the end of his long life (he died in 1791), Wesley had about half a million followers in what were called Methodist societies. Wesley himself tried to keep them within the Church of England, but separate Methodist churches were already founded in England and the United States.

In a way these expressions of religious feeling reflected differences between the popular and elite cultures such as have already been described. While some of the elite joined in the new movements, it was on the whole those of the least comfortable classes who did so. The official churches, Anglican, Lutheran, Catholic, did not wish to be disturbed by religious revivalism. Bishops were cultivated gentlemen of the age. But the most vehement intellectual leaders pushed all churches aside.

Oddly enough, in this age of reason, there was also a taste for mystification. A Swiss pastor, J. C. Lavater, attracted attention with his supposed science of "physiognomy," by which character could be read in the play of the facial features. An Austrian physician, A. F. Mesmer, created a stir in Paris by arranging seances where people were touched by a wand, or sat in tubs, to receive "animal magnetism" in the hope of curing various ills. His "mesmerism" was an early stage in the discovery of hypnosis, but it is significant that a committee of the Royal Academy of Sciences, after investigation, concluded that Mesmer's own theories to explain these strange phenomena were without foundation. There was a somewhat gullible vogue for popular science in the 1780s, shared in by a few who soon became famous in the Revolution, such as Marat and Brissot. Popular science simply exaggerated the claims of real science for the control of nature by human manipulation.

More in the mainstream was Freemasonry, which took form in England and soon spread to the Continent. The Masons were generally men of typical Enlightenment views, well disposed toward reason, progress, toleration, and humane reforms, and respectful toward God as architect of the universe, but they met secretly in lodges, in an atmosphere of mysterious rituals and occult knowledge. Men of all walks of life, nobles, clergy, and middle classes, belonged to the lodges, which had the effect of bringing persons of different social classes together, somewhat harmlessly for self-improvement and the improvement of others. Masonry, however, aroused suspicion because of its secrecy, and a small deviant offshoot, the Illuminati of south Germany, was considered so dangerous that the Bavarian government suppressed it in 1786. There were later some who insisted that the French Revolution had been caused by a conspiracy of Illuminati, philosophes, and other clandestine plotters, but this idea was never any more than the belief of a few frightened conservatives. The word Illuminati meant "the enlightened ones," but the notion of secrecy was foreign to the Enlightenment, which relied above all else on publicity.

The Philosophes

Philosophe is simply French for philosopher, but to be "philosophical" in the eighteenth century meant to approach any subject in a critical and inquiring spirit. The French word is used in English to denote a group of writers who were not philosophers in the sense of treating ultimate questions of existence. They were men of letters, popularizers and publicists. Though often learned, they wrote to gain attention, and it was through the philosophes that the ideas of the Enlightenment spread. Formerly authors had generally been gentlemen of leisure, or talented protégés of aristocratic or royal patrons, or professors or clerics supported by the income from religious foundations. In the Age of Enlightenment a great many were free-lancers, grub-streeters, or journalists. They wrote for "the publick."

The reading public had greatly expanded. The educated middle class, commercial and professional, was much larger than ever before. Country gentlemen were putting off their rustic habits, and even noblemen wished to keep informed. Newspapers and magazines multiplied, and people who could not read them at home could read them in coffeehouses or in reading rooms organized for that purpose. There was a great demand also for dictionaries, encyclopedias, and surveys of all fields of knowledge. The new readers wanted matters made interesting and clear. They appreciated wit and lightness of touch. From such a public, literature itself greatly benefited. The style of the eighteenth century became admirably fluent, clear, and exact, neither ponderous on the one hand nor frothy on the other. And from writings of this kind the readers benefited also, from the interior of Europe to the America of Benjamin Franklin. The bourgeois middle class was becoming not only educated but thoughtful. But the movement was not a class movement only.

There was another way in which writings of the day were affected by social conditions. They were all written under censorship. The theory of censorship was to protect people from harmful ideas as they were protected from shoddy merchandise or dishonest weights and measures. In England the censorship was so mild as to have little effect. Other countries, such as Spain, had a powerful censorship but few original writers. France, the center of the Enlightenment, had both a complicated censorship and a large reading and writing public. The church, the Parlement of Paris, the royal officials, and the printers' guilds all had a hand in the censoring of books. French censorship, however, was very loosely administered, and after 1750 writers were disturbed by it very little. It cannot be compared to censorship in some countries in the twentieth century. Yet in one way it had an unfavorable effect on French thought and letters. It discouraged writers from addressing themselves, in a common-sense way, to a serious consideration of concrete public questions. Legally forbidden to criticize church or state, they threw their criticisms on an abstract level. Debarred from attacking things in particular, they tended to attack things in general. Or they talked of the customs of the Persians and the Iroquois but not the French. Their works became full of double meanings, sly digs, innuendoes, and jokes, by which an author, if questioned, could declare that he did not mean what all the world knew he did mean. As for readers, they developed a taste for forbidden books, which were always easy enough to obtain through illicit channels.

Paris was the heart of the movement. Here, in the town houses of the well-to-do, there occurred a coming together of literary and social celebrities such as had hardly ever before been seen. It might even happen, though rarely, that a notable philosophe was also wealthy; such was the case of Helvetius, who not only wrote books *On the Mind* and *On Man*, but also gave grand entertainments at which such matters were discussed. Mainly, however, this mingling of people and ideas went on in salons conducted by women who became famous as hostesses. Mme. de Geoffrin, for example, for a period of twenty-five years beginning about 1750, entertained artists and writers at dinner, sometimes helped them financially, and introduced them to persons of influence in high society or in government. She welcomed visiting foreigners also, such as Horace Walpole and David Hume from England, and young Stanislas Poniatowski before he became king of Poland. Since other women held similar salons, philosophes and other writers had frequent opportunity to meet and exchange ideas. Salons of this kind survived the Revolution. In 1795, after the Terror, the widows of two eminent philosophes, Helvetius and Condorcet, opened or reopened their salons in Paris for people of moderate republican or liberal sentiments. Sophie Condorcet became a writer herself and a translator of Adam Smith. Her salon remained a center of liberal opposition during the years of Napoleon. More short-lived was the salon of the even more famous Mme. de Staël, who also wrote widely read books and who, among her many other ideas, deplored the subordination of women to men that the Revolution had done little to change. In these post-Revolutionary salons much of the French liberalism of the nineteenth century was born.

In Paris also, in the mid–eighteenth century, was published the most serious of all philosophe enterprises, the *Encyclopédie,* edited by Denis Diderot in seventeen large volumes and completed over the years 1751 to 1772. It was a great compendium of scientific, technical, and historical knowledge, carrying a strong undertone of criticism of existing society and institutions and epitomizing the skeptical, rational, and scientific spirit of the age. It was not the first encyclopedia, but it was the first to have a distinguished list of contributors or to be conceived as a positive force for social progress. Virtually all the French philosophes contributed—Voltaire, Montesquieu, Rousseau, d'Alembert (who assisted in the editing), Buffon, Turgot, Quesnay, and many others, all sometimes collectively called the Encyclopedists. But although edited in Paris the *Encyclopédie* became very widely known and read. About 25,000 multivolumed sets were sold before the Revolution, about half of them outside of France, since French had become an international language understood by educated persons all over Europe. Within France itself the *Encyclopédie* was read in all parts of the country and in the most influential ranks of society. At Besançon, for example, a city of about 28,000 inhabitants, 137 sets were sold to local residents, of whom 15 were members of the clergy, 53 were of the nobility, and 69 were lawyers, doctors, merchants, government officials, or others of what was called the Third Estate. The privileged groups of whom the Encyclopedists were the most critical, that is, the clergy and the nobility, read it or at least purchased it far out of proportion to their numbers in the population as a whole.

Men and women who considered themselves philosophes, or close to the philosophes in spirit, were found all over Europe. Frederick the Great was an eminent philosophe; not only was he the friend of Voltaire and host to a circle of literary and scientific men at Potsdam, but he himself wrote epigrams, satires, dissertations, and histories, as well as works on military science, and he had a gift of wit, a sharp tongue, and a certain impishness toward the traditional and the pompous. Catherine the Great, empress of Russia, was also a philosophe for much the same reason. Maria Theresa, of Austria, was not a philosophe; she was too religious and too little concerned with general ideas. Her son Joseph, on the other hand, as we shall see, proved to be a philosophe enthroned. In England Bishop Warburton was considered by some of his friends as a philosophe; he held that the Church of England of his day, as a social institution, was exactly what pure reason would have invented. The Scottish skeptical philosopher David Hume counted as a philosophe, as did Edward Gibbon, who shocked the pious by his attacks on Christianity in his famous *Decline and Fall of the Roman Empire.* Dr. Samuel Johnson was not a philosophe; he worried over the supernatural, adhered to the established church, deflated pretentious authors, and even declared that Voltaire and Rousseau were bad men who should be sent "to the plantations." There were also Italian and German philosophes, like the Marquis di Beccaria who sought to humanize the criminal law, or Baron Grimm who sent a literary newsletter from Paris to his many subscribers.

Montesquieu, Voltaire, and Rousseau

Most famous of all philosophes were the French trio, Montesquieu (1689–1755), Voltaire (1694–1778), and Rousseau (1712–1778). They differed vehemently with each other. All were hailed as literary geniuses in their own day. All turned from pure literature to works of political commentary and social analysis. All thought that the existing state of society could be improved.

Montesquieu, twice a baron, was a landed aristocrat, a seigneur or manorial lord of southern France. He inherited from his uncle a seat in the Parlement of Bordeaux and sat actively in that parlement in the days of the Regency.[1] He was part of the noble resurgence which followed the death of Louis XIV and continued on through the eighteenth century. Although he shared many of the ideas in the stream of aristocratic and antiabsolutist thought, he went beyond a mere self-centered class philosophy. In his great work, *The Spirit of Laws*, published in 1748, he developed two principal ideas. One was that forms of government varied according to climate and circumstances, for example, that despotism was suited only to large empires in hot climates, and that democracy would work only in small city-states. His other great doctrine, aimed against royal absolutism in France (which he called "despotism"), was the separation and balance of powers. In France he believed that power should be divided between the king and a great many "intermediate bodies"—parlements, provincial estates, organized nobility, chartered towns, and even the church. It was natural for him, a judge in parlement, a provincial and a nobleman, to favor the first three and reasonable for

[1] See pp. 256–257.

him to recognize the position of the bourgeoisie of the towns; as for the church, he observed that, while he took no stock in its teachings, he thought it useful as an offset to undue centralization of government. He greatly admired the English constitution as he understood it, believing that England carried over, more successfully than any other country, the feudal liberties of the early Middle Ages. He thought that in England the necessary separation and balance of powers was obtained by an ingenious mixture of monarchy, aristocracy, and democracy (king, lords, and commons), and by a separation of the functions of the executive, legislature, and judiciary. This doctrine had a wide influence and was well known to the Americans who in 1787 wrote the Constitution of the United States. Montesquieu's own philosophe friends thought him too conservative and even tried to dissuade him from publishing his ideas. He was, indeed, technically a reactionary, favoring a scheme of things that antedated Louis XIV, and he was unusual among contemporaries in his admiration of the "barbarous" Middle Ages.

Voltaire was born in 1694 into a comfortable bourgeois family and christened François-Marie Arouet; "Voltaire," an invented word, is simply the most famous of all pen names. Until he was over forty he was known only as a smart writer of epigrams, tragedies in verse, and an epic. Thereafter he turned increasingly to philosophical and public questions. His strength throughout lay in the facility of his pen. He is the easiest of all great writers to read. He was always trenchant, logical, and incisive, sometimes scurrilous; mocking and sarcastic when he wished, equally a master of deft irony and of withering ridicule. However serious in his purpose, he achieved it by creating a laugh.

In his youth Voltaire spent eleven months in the Bastille for what was considered to be impertinence to the Regent, who, however, in the next year rewarded him with a pension for one of his dramas. He was again arrested after a fracas with a nobleman, the Chevalier de Rohan. He remained an incorrigible bourgeois, while never deeply objecting to the aristocracy on principle. Through his admirer Mme. de Pompadour (another bourgeois, though the king's favorite) he became a gentleman of the bedchamber and royal historian to Louis XV. These functions he fulfilled *in absentia*, when at all, for Paris and Versailles were too hot for him. He was the personal friend of Frederick the Great, with whom he lived for about two years at Potsdam. The two finally quarreled, for no stage was big enough to hold two such prima donnas for very long. Voltaire made a fortune from his writings, pensions, speculations, and practical business sense. In his later years he purchased a manor at Ferney near the Swiss frontier. Here he became, as he said, the "hotel keeper of Europe," receiving the streams of distinguished admirers, favor hunters, and distressed persons who came to seek him out. He died at Paris in 1778, at the age of eighty-four, by far the most famous man of letters in Europe. His collected writings fill over seventy volumes.

Voltaire was mainly interested in the freedom of thought. Like Montesquieu, he was an admirer of England. He spent three years in that country, where, in 1727, he witnessed the state funeral accorded to Sir Isaac Newton and his burial in Westminster Abbey. Voltaire's *Philosophical Letters on the English* (1733) and *Elements of the Philosophy of Newton* (1738) not only brought England increasingly before the consciousness of the rest of Europe, but also popularized the new scientific ideas—the inductive philosophy of Bacon, the physics of Newton, and the sensationalist psychology of Locke,[2] whose doctrine that all true ideas arose

---

[2] See pp. 295–296.

from sense experience undercut the authority of religious belief. What Voltaire mainly admired in England was its religious liberty, its relative freedom of the press, and the high regard paid to men of letters like himself. Political liberty concerned him much less than it did Montesquieu. Louis XIV, a villain for Montesquieu and the neoaristocratic school, was a hero for Voltaire, who wrote a laudatory *Age of Louis XIV* (1751) praising the Sun King for the splendor of art and literature in his reign. Voltaire likewise continued to esteem Frederick the Great, though he quarreled with him personally. Frederick was in fact almost his ideal of the enlightened ruler, a man who sponsored the arts and sciences, recognized no religious authority, and granted toleration to all creeds, welcoming Protestants and Catholics on equal terms if only they would be socially useful.

After about 1740 Voltaire became more definitely the crusader, preaching the cause of religious toleration. He fought to clear the memory of Jean Calas, a Protestant put to death on the charge of murdering a son to prevent his conversion to Rome. He wrote also to exonerate a youth named La Barre, who had been executed for defiling a wayside cross. *Écrasez l'infâme!* became the famous Voltairean war cry—"crush the infamous thing!" The *infâme* for him was bigotry, intolerance, and superstition, and behind these the power of an organized clergy. He assaulted not only the Catholic church but the whole traditional Christian view of the world. He argued for "natural religion" and "natural morality," holding that belief in God and the difference between good and evil arose from reason itself. This doctrine had in fact long been taught by the Catholic church. But Voltaire insisted that no supernatural revelation in addition to reason was desirable or necessary, or rather, that belief in a special supernatural revelation made men intolerant, stupid, and cruel. He was the first to present a purely secular conception of world history. In his *Essai sur les moeurs*, or "Universal History," he began with ancient China and surveyed the great civilizations in turn. Earlier writers of world history had put human events within a Christian framework. Following the Bible, they began with the Creation, proceeded to the Fall, recounted the rise of Israel, and so on. Voltaire put Judeo-Christian history within a sociological framework. He represented Christianity and all other organized religions as social phenomena or mere human opinions. Spinoza had said as much; Voltaire spread these ideas through Europe.

In matters of politics and self-government Voltaire was neither a liberal nor a democrat. His opinion of the human race was about as low as his friend Frederick's. If only a government was enlightened he did not care how powerful it was. By an enlightened government he meant one that fought against sloth and stupidity, kept the clergy in a subordinate place, allowed freedom of thought and religion, and advanced the cause of material and technical progress. He had no developed political theory, but his ideal for large civilized countries approached that of enlightened or rational despotism. Believing that only a few could be enlightened, he thought that these few, a king and his advisers, should have the power to carry their program against all opposition. To overcome ignorance, habit, credulity, and priestcraft it was necessary for the state to be strong. It may be said that what Voltaire most desired was liberty for the enlightened.

Jean-Jacques Rousseau was very different. Born in Geneva in 1712, he was a Swiss, a Protestant, and almost of lower-class origin. He never felt at ease in France or in Paris society. Neglected as a child, a runaway at sixteen, he lived for years by odd jobs, such as copying music, and not until the age of forty did he have any success as a writer. He was always the little man, the outsider. In addition, his sex life was unsatisfactory; he finally settled down with an uneducated girl named Thérèse Levasseur, and with her mother, who kept interfering with his affairs. By Thérèse he had five children, whom he deposited at an orphanage. He had no social status, no money, and no sense of money, and after he became famous he lived largely by the generosity of his friends. He was pathetically and painfully maladjusted. He came to feel that he could trust no one, that those who tried to befriend him were deriding or betraying him behind his back. He suffered from what would now be termed complexes; possibly he was paranoiac. He talked endlessly of his own virtue and innocence and complained bitterly that he was misunderstood.

But unbalanced though he was, he was possibly the most profound writer of the age and was certainly the most permanently influential. Rousseau felt, from his own experience, that in society as it existed a good person could not be happy. He therefore attacked society, declaring that it was artificial and corrupt. He even attacked reason, calling it a false guide when followed alone. He felt doubts on all the progress which gave satisfaction to his contemporaries. In two "discourses," one on the *Arts and Sciences* (1750), the other on the *Origin of Inequality Among Men* (1753), he argued that civilization was the source of much evil, and that life in a "state of nature," were it only possible, would be much better. As Voltaire said, when Rousseau sent him a copy of his second discourse (Voltaire who relished civilization in every form), it made him "feel like going on all fours." To Rousseau the best traits of human character, such as kindness, unselfishness, honesty, and true understanding, were products of nature. Deep below reason, he sensed the presence of feeling. He delighted in the warmth of sympathy, the quick flash of intuition, the clear message of conscience. He was religious by temperament, for though he believed in no church, no clergy, and no revelation he had a respect for the Bible, a reverent awe toward the cosmos, a love of solitary meditation, and a belief in a God who was not merely a "first cause" but also a God of love and beauty. Rousseau thus made it easier for serious-minded people to slip away from orthodoxy and all forms of churchly discipline. He was feared by the churches as the most dangerous of all "infidels" and was condemned both in Catholic France and at Protestant Geneva.

In general, in most of his books, Rousseau, unlike so many of his contemporaries, gave the impression that impulse is more reliable than considered judgment, spontaneous feeling more to be trusted than critical thought. Mystical insights were for him more truthful than rational or clear ideas. He became the "man of feeling," the "child of nature," the forerunner of the coming age of romanticism, and an important source of all modern emphasis on the nonrational and the subconscious.

In the *Social Contract* (1762) Rousseau seemed to contradict all this. In it he held, somewhat like Hobbes,[3] that the "state of nature" was a brutish condition without law or morality. In other works he had held that the badness of men was due to the evils of society. He now held that good men could be produced only by an improved society. Earlier thinkers, such as John Locke, for example, had thought of the "contract" as an agreement between a ruler and a people. Rousseau thought of it as an agreement among the people themselves. It was a social, not merely a political, contract. Organized civil society, i.e., the community,

---

[3] See p. 299.

rested upon it. It was an understanding by which all individuals surrendered their natural liberty to each other, fused their individual wills into a combined General Will, and agreed to accept the rulings of this General Will as final. This General Will was the sovereign; and true sovereign power, rightly understood, was "absolute," "sacred," and "inviolable." Government was secondary; kings, officials, or elected representatives were only delegates of a sovereign people. Rousseau devoted many difficult and abstruse pages to explaining how the *real* General Will could be known. It was not necessarily determined by vote of a majority. "What generalizes the will," he said, "is not the number of voices but the common interest that unites them." He said little of the mechanism of government and had no admiration for parliamentary institutions. He was concerned with something deeper. Maladjusted outsider that he was, he craved a commonwealth in which every person could feel that he belonged. He wished a state in which all persons had a sense of membership and participation.

By these ideas Rousseau made himself the prophet of both democracy and nationalism. Indeed, in his *Considerations on Poland*, written at the request of Poles who were fighting against the partitions, Rousseau applied the ideas of the *Social Contract* in more concrete form and became the first systematic theorist of a conscious and calculated nationalism.[4] In writing the *Social Contract* he had in mind a small city-state like his native Geneva. But what he did, in effect, was to generalize and make applicable to large territories the psychology of small city republics—the sense of membership, of community and fellowship, of responsible citizenship and intimate participation in public affairs—in short, of common will. All modern states, democratic or undemocratic, strive to impart this sense of moral solidarity to their peoples. Whereas in democratic states the General Will can in some way be identified with the sovereignty of the people, in dictatorships it becomes possible for individuals (or parties) to arrogate to themselves the right to serve as spokesmen and interpreters of the General Will. Both totalitarians and democrats have regarded Rousseau as one of their prophets.

The *Social Contract* was little read and almost unknown in its own time. Rousseau's influence on his contemporaries was spread by his other writings and especially his novels, *Émile* (1762) and the *Nouvelle Héloïse* (1760). The novels were widely read in all literate classes of society, especially by the women, who made a kind of cult of Jean-Jacques, while he was living and after his death, which occurred in 1778. He was a literary master, able to evoke shades of thought and feeling that few writers had touched before, and by his literary writings he spread in the highest circles a new respect for the common man, a love of common things, an impulse of human pity and compassion, a sense of artifice and superficiality in aristocratic life. Women took to nursing their own babies. Even men spoke of the delicacy of their sentiments. Tears became the fashion. The queen, Marie Antoinette, built herself a village in the gardens at Versailles where she pretended to be a simple milkmaid. In all this there was much that was ridiculous or shallow. Yet it was the wellspring of modern humanitarianism, the force leading to a new sense of human equality. Rousseau estranged the French upper classes from their own mode of life. He made many of them lose faith in their own superiority. That was his main direct contribution to the French Revolution.

4 See pp. 238–240.

Political Economists

In France, somewhat apart from the philosophes, were the Physiocrats, whom their critics called "economists," a word originally thought to be mildly insulting. Many of the Physiocrats, unlike the philosophes, were close to the government as administrators or advisers. Quesnay was physician to Louis XV, Turgot was an experienced official who became minister to Louis XVI, and Dupont de Nemours, an associate of Turgot's, became the founder of the industrial family of the Du Ponts in the United States. Such men concerned themselves with fiscal and tax reform, and with measures to increase the national wealth of France. They opposed guild regulations and price controls as impediments to the production and circulation of goods, and so were the first to use the term *laissez faire* ("let them do as they see fit") as a principle of economic activity. They favored strong government, however, relying on it to overcome traditional obstructions and to provide inducements for the establishment of new industries.

Economics, or what was long called political economy, arose from these activities of the Physiocrats, from the somewhat similar work of "cameralists" in the German states, and from the collection and analysis of quantitative data, that is, the birth of statistics. A good example of the latter was Sir William Petty's *Political Arithmetic*, published in 1690. Economic thinking flourished especially in Great Britain, where Adam Smith's *Enquiry into the nature and causes of the wealth of nations* appeared in 1776. By 1800 the *Wealth of Nations* had been translated into every West European language except Portuguese.

Adam Smith's purpose, like that of the French Physiocrats, was to increase the national wealth by the reduction of barriers that hindered its growth. He undercut the premises of what we have called "the struggle for wealth and empire" in Chapter VI, since he argued that to build up a nation's wealth it was unnecessary to have an empire. He attacked most of the program of mercantilism that had obtained since the sixteenth century, and he expected that Britain's American colonies would soon become independent without loss to British trade. Where others looked to planning by an enlightened government, Adam Smith preferred to limit the functions of government to defense, internal security, and the provision of reasonable laws and fair law courts by which private differences could be adjudicated. For innovation and enterprise he counted more on private persons than on the state. He became the philosopher of the free market, the prophet of free trade. If there was a shortage of a given commodity its price would rise, and so stimulate producers to produce more, while also attracting new persons into that line of production. If there was an excess, if more was produced than purchasers would buy, both capital and labor would withdraw and gradually move into another area where demand was stronger. Demand would increase with lower prices, which depended on lower costs, which in turn depended on the specialization of labor. His most famous example was that of the pin factory of his time, where each of a dozen workers engaged in only one part of the process of manufacture, so that together they produced far more pins than if each man produced whole pins; the price of pins then fell, and more pins could be used by more people. The same principle held in international trade; some countries or climates could produce an article more cheaply than others, so that if each specialized and then exchanged with the others, all would have more. The motivation for all such production and exchange was to be the self-interest of the participants. As he said, we rely for our meat not on the good will of the butcher but on his concern for his own income. To those who might object that this was a system of selfishness Adam Smith would reply (being a professor of moral philosophy at the University of Glasgow) that it was at least realistic, describing how people really behaved, and that it was morally justified since it ultimately produced a maximum both of freedom and of abundance. The mutual interaction of the enlightened self-interest of millions of persons would in the end, as if by an "invisible hand," he said, result in the highest welfare of all. Among problems that Smith minimized, or accepted as lesser evils, were the insecurity of individuals and the dangers of excessive dependency of a whole country on imports of essentials, such as food; and if the visible hand of government continued to regulate the price of bread it was not for economic reasons, but to prevent rioting and obtain social peace.

Main Currents of Enlightenment Thought

It is clear that the currents of thought in France and Europe were divergent and inconsistent. There was a general belief in progress, reason, science, and civilization. Rousseau had his doubts and praised the beauties of character. Montesquieu thought the church useful but did not believe in religion; Rousseau believed in religion but saw no need for any church. Montesquieu was concerned over practical political liberty; Voltaire would surrender political liberty in return for guarantees of intellectual freedom; Rousseau wanted emancipation from the trivialities of society and sought the freedom that consists in merging willingly with nature and with one's fellows. Most philosophes were closest to Voltaire. They were concerned also for equality. It was not a very far-reaching equality, but it meant equality of rights for persons of different religions, a reduction of privileges enjoyed by nobles but not by commoners, more equality of status in law courts and in the payment of taxes, and more opportunity for middle-class persons to rise to positions of honor.

France was the main center of the Enlightenment. French philosophes traveled all over Europe. Frederick II and Catherine II invited French thinkers to their courts. French was the language of the academies of St. Petersburg and Berlin. Frederick wrote his own works in the French language. There was a uniform cosmopolitan culture among the upper classes of Europe, and this culture was predominantly French. But England was important also. Hitherto somewhat on the fringes of the European consciousness, England now moved closer to the center. Montesquieu and Voltaire may be said to have "discovered" England for Europe. Through them the ideas of Bacon, Newton, and Locke, and the whole theory of English liberty and parliamentary government became matters for general discussion and comment. We have seen, too, how Adam Smith's *Wealth of Nations* was soon translated into many languages.

The main agency of progress was thought to be the state. Whether in the form of limited monarchy on the English model favored by Montesquieu, or of an enlightened despotism preferred by Voltaire, or of the ideal republican commonwealth portrayed by Rousseau, the rightly ordered government was considered the best guarantee of social welfare. Even the political economists needed the state to shake people out of the habits of ages, sweep away a mass of local regulation, preserve law and order and the enforcement of contracts, and so assure the existence of a free market. But if they relied on the state, they were not nationalists in any later sense of the word. As "universalists," they believed in the unity of mankind under a natural law of right and reason. In this they carried over the classical and Christian outlook in a secular way. They supposed that all peoples would participate eventually in the same progress. No nation was thought to have a peculiar message. French ideas enjoyed a wide currency, but no one thought of them as peculiarly French, arising from a French "national character." It was simply thought that the French at the time were in the vanguard of civilization. Such was the idea of Condorcet, one of the later philosophes, a leading spokesman of the Enlightenment, who became an active figure in the French Revolution, and also one of its victims, and who in 1794, while in hiding from the guillotine, wrote the great testament to the Enlightenment, his *Sketch of the Progress of the Human Mind.*

37. ENLIGHTENED DESPOTISM: FRANCE, AUSTRIA, PRUSSIA

The Meaning of Enlightened Despotism

Enlightened despotism is hard to define, because it grew out of the earlier absolutism represented by Louis XIV or Peter the Great. Characteristically, the enlightened despots drained marshes, built roads and bridges, codified the laws, repressed provincial autonomy and localism, curtailed the independence of church and nobles, and built up a trained and salaried officialdom. All these things had been done by kings before. The typical enlightened despot differed from his "unenlightened" predecessor mainly in attitude and tempo. He said little of a divine right to his throne. He might even not emphasize his hereditary or dynastic family right. He justified his authority on grounds of usefulness to society, calling himself, as Frederick the Great did, the "first servant of the state."

Enlightened despotism was secular; it claimed no mandate from heaven and recognized no especial responsibility to God or church. The typical enlightened despot consequently favored toleration in religion, and this was an important new emphasis after about 1740; but here again there was precedent in the older absolutism, for the rulers of Prussia had been inclined toward toleration long before Frederick, and even the French Bourbons had recognized a degree of religious liberty for almost a century following the Edict of Nantes.[5] The secular outlook of the enlightened governments is again seen in the common front they adopted against the Jesuits. High papalists and ultramontanes,[6] affirming the authority of a universal church, and at the same time intellectually and in other ways the strongest religious order in the Catholic world, the Jesuits were distasteful to the enlightened monarchs and their civil officials and in the 1760s the order was banned in almost all Catholic countries. In 1773 the pope was persuaded to dissolve the Society of Jesus entirely. The various governments concerned, in France, Austria, Spain, Portugal, and Naples, confiscated the Jesuit property and took over the Jesuit schools. Not until 1814 was the order reconstituted.

Enlightened despotism was also rational and reformist. The typical despot set out to reconstruct his state by the use of reason. Sharing the current view of the past as benighted, he was impatient of custom and of all that was imbedded in custom or claimed as a heritage from the past, such as systems of customary law

---

[5] See pp. 135–137, 184–185.
[6] See p. 90.

and the rights and privileges of church, nobles, towns, guilds, provinces, assemblies of estates, or, in France, the judicial bodies called parlements. The complex of such institutions was disparagingly referred to as "feudalism." Monarchs had long struggled against feudalism in this sense, but in the past they had usually compromised. The enlightened despot was less willing to compromise, and herein lay the difference in tempo. The new despot acted abruptly, desiring quicker results.

Enlightened despotism, in short, was an acceleration of the old institution of monarchy, which now put aside the quasi-sacred mantle in which it had clothed itself and undertook to justify itself in the cold light of reason and secular usefulness. In theory even the dynastic claim was awkward, for it rested on inheritance from the past. Under enlightened despotism the idea of the state itself was changing, from the older notion of an estate belonging by a kind of sanctified property right to its ruler, to a newer notion of an abstract and impersonal authority exercised by public officers, of whom the king was simply the highest.

The trend to enlightened despotism after 1740 owed a great deal to writers and philosophes, but it arose also out of a very practical situation, namely, the great war of the mid–eighteenth century.[7] War, in modern history, has usually led to concentration and rationalizing of government power, and the wars of 1740–1748 and 1756–1763 were no exception. Under their impact even governments where the rulers were not considered by philosophes to be enlightened, notably those of Louis XV and Maria Theresa, and even the government of Great Britain, which was certainly not despotic, embarked on programs which all bear features in common. They attempted to augment their revenues, devise new taxes, tax persons or regions hitherto more or less tax-exempt, limit the autonomy of outlying political bodies, and centralize and renovate their respective political systems. The workings of enlightened despotism might be seen in many states, in Habsburg Tuscany under Leopold, in Bourbon Naples and Spain under Charles III, in Portugal under the minister Pombal, in Denmark under Struensee. But it seems best to consider only the more important countries at some length—France and Austria, Prussia and Russia—and then the rather different, yet not wholly different, course of events in the British empire.

The Failure of Enlightened Despotism in France

It was in France that enlightened despotism had the least success. Louis XV, who had inherited the throne in 1715 and lived until 1774, though by no means stupid, was indifferent to most serious questions, absorbed in the daily rounds at Versailles, disinclined to make trouble for people that he saw personally, and interested in government only by fits and starts. His remark, *après moi le déluge*, whether or not he really said it, sufficiently characterizes his personal attitude to conditions in France. Yet the French government was not unenlightened, and many capable officials carried on its affairs all through the century. These men generally knew what the basic trouble was. All the practical difficulties of the French monarchy could be traced to its system of taxation. The most important impost, the taille, a kind of land tax, was generally paid only by the peasants. Nobles were exempt from it on principle, and office-holders and bourgeois, for

[7] See pp. 264–275.

one reason or another, were generally exempt also. In addition, the church, which owned between 5 and 10 percent of the land of the country, insisted that its property was not taxable by the state; it granted to the king a periodic "free gift" which, though sizable, was less than the government might expect from direct taxation. The consequence of the tax exemptions was that, although France itself was wealthy and prosperous, the government was chronically poor, because the social classes which enjoyed most of the wealth and prosperity did not pay taxes corresponding to their incomes. Louis XIV, under pressure of war, had tried to tax everybody alike by creating new levies—the capitation or poll tax and the *dixième* or tenth, both of which were assessed in proportion to income; but these taxes had been widely evaded. A similar effort was made in 1726, but it too had failed. The propertied classes resisted taxation because they thought it degrading. France had succumbed to the appalling principle that to pay direct taxes was the sure mark of inferior status. Nobles, churchmen, and bourgeois also resisted taxation because they were kept out of policymaking functions of government and so had no sense of political responsibility or control. There were good historical reasons for this, but the result was financially ruinous.[8]

In 1748, under pressure of the heavy war costs, and at the prompting of Mme de Pompadour, Louis XV bestirred himself to appoint a controller general of finance who devised a tax to be paid by all persons receiving income from property—land, manorial rights, business investments, and offices such as parlementary judgeships—irrespective of class status, provincial liberties, or previous exemptions of any kind. A clamor arose from the Parlement of Paris, the eleven provincial parlements, the estates of Brittany, and the church. All these were dominated by noblemen and because of the aristocratic resurgence that had begun with the Regency, were politically stronger than in the days of Louis XIV. They could also now cite Montesquieu to justify their opposition to the crown. The Parlement of Paris ruled the new tax unconstitutional, or incompatible with the laws of France and liberties of Frenchmen. The estates of Brittany, and of other *pays d'états*, i.e., provinces having assemblies of estates, declared that their customary and historic liberties were being outraged. The church protested with vehemence. After several years of wrangling, Louis XV decided to push the matter no further; he withdrew his support from his finance minister, and the whole project collapsed.

The 1750s and 1760s saw continued friction between the ministry and the various semiautonomous bodies within the country. Meanwhile came the enormous costs and humiliating reverses of the Seven Years' War. The government renewed its determination to win effective centralized control. It was decided to eliminate

[8] See pp. 69, 182–183, 260.

EUROPE, 1740

Boundaries are as of 1740. There were now three Bourbon monarchies (France, Spain, and the Two Sicilies), while the Austrian monarchy possessed most of what is now Belgium, and in Italy the duchy of Milan and grand duchy of Tuscany, where the Medici family had recently died out. Prussia expanded by acquiring Silesia in the war of the 1740s. The first partition of Poland in 1772 enlarged Prussia, Austria, and Russia (see maps, pp. 216, 222–223, 234–235, 328). France acquired Lorraine in 1766 and Corsica in 1768. Otherwise there were no changes until the Revolutionary-Napoleonic wars of 1792–1814.

Bourbon Dominions

Habsburg Dominions

Boundary of Holy Roman Empire

SWEDEN

NORWAY

St. Petersbur

Stockholm

SCOTLAND

KINGDOM OF
DENMARK AND NORWAY

Edinburgh

Riga

NORTH SEA

DENMARK

Copenhagen

Memel

BALTIC SEA

PRUSSIA

LITHUANIA

IRELAND

GREAT BRITAIN

SCHLESWIG

Danzig

EAST
PRUSSIA

Minsk

Dublin

Liverpool

ENGLAND

Hamburg

Thorn

WALES

UNITED
PROVINCES

Bremen
HANOVER
(Britain)

Elbe R.

BRANDENBURG

Berlin

Warsaw

POLAND

Amsterdam

Utrecht

Magdeburg

London

AUSTRIAN
NETHERLANDS

ATLANTIC OCEAN

Oudenarde

Antwerp

Cologne

Leipzig

SAXONY

SILESIA

Lublin

CHANNEL I.
(Britain)

CAPE
DE LA HOGUE

Malplaquet

Ramillies

MINOR
GERMAN STATES

Dresden

Breslau

Oder R.

Vistula R.

Lemberg

Rouen

RHINE R.

PALATI-
NATE

Frankfurt

Prague

BOHEMIA

Cracow

PODOLI

Quiberon

Reims

Paris

Seine R.

Metz

Strasbourg

Blenheim

MORAVIA

Orléans

LORRAINE
(France 1766)

BAVARIA

AUSTRIA

Vienna

Pressburg

Munkacz

Loire R.

Tours

Besançon

Munich

Budapest

FRANCE

Limoges

Geneva

SWITZERLAND

TYROL

AUSTRIAN MONARCHY

KINGDOM
OF HUNGARY

TRANSYLVANIA

Bordeaux

Lyons

Garonne R.

Rhone R.

SAVOY

PO R.

MILAN

VENETIA

Venice

CROATIA

Save R.

BANAT

Belgrade

WALLACH

Santiago

Turin

PAR-
MA

Genoa

Bologna

BOSNIA

SERBIA

Danube R.

León

Pamplona

Toulouse

Avignon

Marseilles

Toulon

KINGDOM OF SARDINIA

TUSCANY

PAPAL
STATES

DALMATIA
(Venice)

ADRIATIC SEA

OTTOMAN EMPIRE

MONTENEGRO

Sofia

Burgos

Ebro R.

PORTUGAL

SPAIN

ARAGON

CATALONIA

Barcelona

CORSICA
(Genoa)

Rome

ALBANIA

Salonica

Lisbon

Tagus R.

Madrid

Toledo

BALEARIC I.

MINORCA
(Britain)

MAJORCA
(Spain)

SARDINIA

Benevento

Naples

Bari

NAPLES

IONIAN I.
(Venice)

Athens

Almanza

Guadalquivir R.

Seville

Granada

Cagliari

KINGDOM
OF THE TWO SICILIES

MOREA

Cadiz

Gibraltar (Britain)

MEDITERRANEAN

Palermo

Tangier

SICILY

SEA

Algiers

Tunis

MOROCCO
(Independent)

ALGERIA
(Turkish)

TUNISIA
(Turkish)

MALTA (Knights of St. John)

0   100   200   300 miles

the parlements as a political force, and for this purpose, in 1768, Louis XV called to the chancellorship a man named Maupeou, who simply abrogated the old parlements and set up new ones in their place. Maupeou had the sympathy of Voltaire and most of the philosophes. In the "Maupeou parlements" the judges had no property rights in their seats but became salaried officials appointed by the crown with assurances of secure tenure, and they were forbidden to reject government edicts or to pass on their constitutionality, being confined to purely judicial functions. Maupeou likewise proposed to make the laws and judicial procedure more uniform throughout the whole country. Meanwhile, with the old parlements out of the way, another attempt was made to tax the privileged and exempted groups.

But Louis XV died in 1774. His grandson and successor, Louis XVI, though far superior in personal habits to his grandfather, and possessed by a genuine desire to govern well, resembled Louis XV in that he lacked sustained will power and could not bear to offend the people who could get to see him personally. In any case he was only twenty in 1774. The kingdom resounded with outcries against Maupeou and his colleagues as minions of despotism and with demands for the immediate restoration of the old Parlement of Paris and the others. Louis XVI, fearful of beginning his reign as a "despot," therefore recalled the old parlements and abolished those of Maupeou. The abortive Maupeou parlements represented the farthest step taken by enlightened despotism in France. It was arbitrary, highhanded, and despotic for Louis XV to destroy the old parlements, but it was certainly enlightened in the sense then connoted by the word, for the old parlements were strongholds of aristocracy and privilege and had for decades blocked programs of reform.

Louis XVI, in recalling the old parlements in 1774, began his reign by pacifying the privileged classes. At the same time he appointed a reforming ministry. At its head was Turgot, a philosophe and Physiocrat and a widely experienced government administrator. Turgot undertook to suppress the guilds, which were privileged municipal monopolies in their several trades. He allowed greater freedom to the internal commerce in grain. He planned to abolish the royal *corvée* (a requirement that certain peasants labor on the roads a few days each year), replacing it by a money tax which would fall on all classes. He began to review the whole system of taxation and was known even to favor the legal toleration of Protestants. The Parlement of Paris, supported by the Provincial Estates and the church, vociferously opposed him, and in 1776 he resigned. Louis XVI, by recalling the parlements, had made reform impossible. In 1778 France again went to war with Britain. The same cycle was repeated: war costs, debt, deficit, new projects of taxation, resistance from the parlements and other semiautonomous bodies. In the 1780s the clash led to revolution.[9]

Austria: The Reforms of Maria Theresa (1740–1780) and of Joseph (1780–1790)

For Maria Theresa the war of the 1740s proved the extraordinary flimsiness of her empire.[10] Had the Continental allies won a more smashing victory, not only would Silesia have been lost to Prussia, but Belgium would have gone to France, Bohemia

---

[9] See pp. 354–357.
[10] See pp. 265–268.

and Austria to the elector of Bavaria supported by France, and the emperorship of the Holy Roman Empire, long a source of prestige to the Habsburgs, would have passed permanently in all probability to a Bavarian or other pro-French German prince. Maria Theresa would have become queen of Hungary only. Nor did her subjects show much inclination to remain together under her rule. In Breslau, the capital of Silesia, after the Prussian attack of 1740, the citizens stood so stubbornly by their town liberties that they would not admit her army within their walls. In Bohemia almost half the nobles welcomed the invading Franco-Bavarians. In Hungary Maria Theresa won support but only by confirming the historic Hungarian liberties. The empire was only a loose bundle of territories, without common purpose or common will. The Pragmatic Sanction devised by Charles VI, it should be recalled, had been meant not only to guarantee the Habsburg inheritance against foreign attack, but also to secure the assent of the several parts of the empire to remain united under the dynasty.[11]

The war of the 1740s led to internal consolidation. The reign of Maria Theresa set the course of all later development of the Austrian empire and hence of the many peoples who lived within its borders. She was aided by a notable team of ministers, whose origin illustrated the nonnational character of the Habsburg system. Her most trusted adviser in foreign relations, the astute Kaunitz,[12] was a Moravian; her main assistants in domestic affairs were a Silesian and a Bohemian-Czech. They worked smoothly with the German archduchess-queen and with German officials in Vienna. Their aim was primarily to prevent dissolution of the monarchy by enlarging and guaranteeing the flow of taxes and soldiers. This involved breaking the local control of territorial nobles in their several diets, which corresponded somewhat to the French Provincial Estates. Hungary, profoundly separatist, was let alone. But the Bohemian and Austrian provinces were welded together. The kingdom of Bohemia, in 1749, lost the constitutional charter which it had received in 1627.[13] The several Bohemian and Austrian diets lost their right to consent to taxes. The separate offices, or "chancelleries," by which their affairs had been separately handled at Vienna, were abolished. Formerly local affairs, recruiting, and tax collecting had been dominated by committees of the diets, made up of landed noblemen of the neighborhood, gentlemen amateurs who were often negligent or indifferent, and who, since they served without pay, were impervious to official discipline, reprimand, or coordination. They were replaced by salaried administrators. Bureaucracy took the place of local self-government. Officials (following the form of mercantilist doctrine called "cameralism" in central Europe) planned to augment the economic strength of the empire by increasing production. They checked the local guild monopolies, suppressed brigandage on the roads, and in 1775 produced a tariff union of Bohemia, Moravia, and the Austrian duchies. This region became the largest area of free trade on the European continent, since even France was still divided by internal tariffs. Bohemia, industrially the most advanced part of the empire, benefited substantially; one of its cotton manufacturing plants, at the end of Maria Theresa's reign, employed 4,000 persons.

The great social fact, both in the Habsburg lands and in all eastern Europe, was the serfdom into which the rural masses had progressively fallen during the

[11] See pp. 219, 265–266.
[12] See p. 268.
[13] See pp. 139–140, 218.

past 200 years.[14] Serfdom meant that the peasant belonged more to his landlord than to the state. The serf owed labor to his lord, often unspecified in amount or kind. The tendency, so long as the landlords ruled locally through their diets, was for the serf to do six days a week of forced labor on the lord's land. Maria Theresa, from humane motives, and also from a desire to lay hands on the manpower from which her armies were recruited, launched a systematic attack on the institutions of serfdom, which meant also an attack on the landed aristocracy of the empire. With the diets reduced in power, the protests of the nobles were less effective; still, the whole agricultural labor system of her territories was involved, and Maria Theresa proceeded with caution. Laws were passed against abuse of peasants by lords or their overseers. Other laws regularized the labor obligations, requiring that they be publicly registered and usually limiting them to three days a week. The laws were often evaded. But the peasant was to some extent freed from arbitrary exactions of the lord. Maria Theresa accomplished more to alleviate serfdom than any other ruler of the eighteenth century in eastern Europe, with the single exception of her own son, Joseph II.

The great archduchess-queen died in 1780, having reigned for forty years. Her son, who had been co-regent with his mother since 1765, had little patience with her methods. Maria Theresa, though steady enough in aim, had always been content with partial measures. Instead of advertising her purposes by philosophical generalization she disguised or understated them, never carrying matters to the point of arousing an unmanageable reaction or of uniting against her the vested interests that she undermined. She backed and filled, watched and waited. Joseph II would not wait. Though he thought the French philosophes frivolous, and Frederick of Prussia a mere clever cynic, he was himself a pure representative of the Age of Enlightenment, and it is in his brief reign of ten years that the character and the limitations of enlightened despotism can best be seen. He was a solemn, earnest, good man, who sensed the misery and hopelessness of the lowest classes. He believed existing conditions to be bad, and he would not regulate or improve them; he would end them. Right and reason, in his mind, lay with the views which he himself adopted; upholders of the old order were self-seeking or mistaken and to yield to them would be to compromise with evil.

"The state," said Joseph, anticipating the Philosophical Radicals in England, meant "the greatest good for the greatest number." He acted accordingly. His ten years of rule passed in a quick succession of decrees. Maria Theresa had regulated serfdom. Joseph abolished it. His mother had collected taxes from nobles as well as peasants, though not equally. Joseph decreed absolute equality of taxation. He insisted on equal punishment for equal crimes whatever the class status of the offender; an aristocratic army officer, who had stolen 97,000 gulden, was exhibited in the pillory, and Count Podstacky, a forger, was made to sweep the streets of Vienna chained to common convicts. At the same time many legal punishments were made less physically cruel. Joseph granted complete liberty of the press. He ordered toleration of all religions, except for a few popular sects which he thought too ignorant to allow. He granted equal civil rights to the Jews, and equal duties, making Jews liable, for the first time in Europe, to service in the army. He even made Jewish nobles, an amazing phenomenon to those of aristocratic "blood." He clashed openly and rudely with the pope, supporting a movement

[14] See pp. 122–123, 204–205, 217–218, 226.

called Febronianism which urged more national inde
German Catholic prelates, on the model of the French
manded increased powers in the appointment and super
suppressed a good many monasteries, using their propert)
pitals in Vienna, and thus laying the foundations of Vienn⟨
ical center. He attempted also to develop the empire econ
the port of Trieste, where he even established an East In⟨
soon failed for obvious reasons—neither capital nor naval
coming from central Europe. His attempts to reach the sea c⟨
Belgium, like those of his grandfather at the time of the Oste
blocked by the Dutch and British interests.[15]

To force through his program Joseph had to centralize his sta
ers, except that he went farther. Regional diets and aristocrati⟨
fared even worse than under his mother. Where she had alwa)
Hungary go its own way, he applied most of his measures to Hun   ⌣⌣—what
was right must be right everywhere. His ideal was a perfectly uniform and rational empire, with all irregularities smoothed out as if under a steam roller. He
thought it reasonable to have a single language for administration and naturally
chose German; this led to a program of Germanizing the Czechs, Poles, Magyars,
and others, which in turn aroused their nationalistic resistance. Using the German language, pushing the emperor's program against regional and class opposition, was a hard-pressed, constantly growing, and increasingly disciplined body
of officials. Bureaucracy became recognizably modern, with training courses,
promotion schedules, retirement pensions, efficiency reports, and visits by inspectors. The clergy likewise were employed as mouthpieces of the state to explain
new laws to their parishioners and teach due respect for the government. To
watch over the whole structure Joseph created a secret police, whose agents,
soliciting the confidential aid of spies and informers, reported on the performance
of government employees, or on the ideas and actions of nobles, clergy, or others
from whom trouble might be expected. The police state, so infamous to the liberal world, was first systematically built up under Joseph as an instrument of
enlightenment and reform.

Joseph II, the "revolutionary emperor," anticipated much that was done in
France by the Revolution and under Napoleon. He could not abide "feudalism"
or "medievalism"; he personally detested the nobility and the church. But few of
his reforms proved lasting. He died prematurely in 1790, at the age of forty-nine,
disillusioned and broken-hearted. Hungary and the Belgian provinces were in
revolution against him. They held that their old constitutional liberties had been
outraged—that they were being governed without their consent. In Hungary all
the good will won by Maria Theresa seemed to be lost; in Belgium the provinces
stood stubbornly by the same medieval privileges, the old *Joyeuse Entrée*, which
they had vindicated 200 years before against the king of Spain.[16] Noble landlords
throughout the Habsburg empire, having lost their control over labor by the abolition of serfdom, and their caste status by legal and fiscal reforms, naturally were
indignant. The church believed itself to be prostituted and despoiled. The peasants were grateful for their new personal liberty but balked at the official attitude

[15] See p. 219.
[16] See pp. 126–128.

of condescending uplift, and often, in real life, sympathized with their priests and their gentlefolk. The officials were unequal to the task demanded of them. There were too few bourgeois in most parts of the empire to staff the civil service, so that many functionaries were members of the landowning nobility which Joseph humiliated; and in any case they frequently found the directives that flowed from Vienna impossible to enforce or even to understand. Joseph was a revolutionist without a party. He failed because he could not be everywhere and do everything himself. His reign demonstrated the limitations of a merely despotic enlightenment. It showed that a legally absolute ruler could not really do as he pleased. It suggested that drastic and abrupt reform could only come with a true revolution, on a wave of public opinion, and under the leadership of men who shared in a coherent body of ideas.

Joseph was succeeded by his brother Leopold, one of the ablest rulers of the century, who for many years as grand duke of Tuscany had given that country the best government known in Italy for generations. Now, in 1790, Leopold was plagued by outcries from his sister, Marie Antoinette, caught in the toils of a real revolution in France.[17] He refused to interfere in French affairs; in any case, he was busy dealing with the uproar left by Joseph. He abrogated most of Joseph's edicts, but he did not yield entirely. The nobles did not win back full powers in their diets. The peasants were not wholly consigned to the old serfdom; Joseph's efforts to provide them with land and to rid them of forced labor had to be given up, but they remained personally free, in law, to migrate, marry, or choose an occupation at will. Leopold died in 1792 and was followed by his son Francis II. Under Francis the aristocratic and clerical reaction gathered strength, terrified by the memory of Joseph II and by the spectacle of revolutionary France, with which Austria went to war soon after Leopold's death.

Prussia under Frederick the Great (1740–1786)

In Prussia, Frederick the Great continued to reign for twenty-three years after the close of the Seven Years' War. "Old Fritz," as he was called, spent the time peaceably, writing memoirs and histories, rehabilitating his shattered country, promoting agriculture and industry, replenishing his treasury, drilling his army, and assimilating his huge conquest of Silesia, and, after 1772, that part of Poland which fell to him in the first partition. Frederick's fame as one of the most eminent of enlightened despots rests, however, not so much on his actual innovations as on his own intellectual gifts, which were considerable, and on the admiring publicity which he received from such literary friends as Voltaire. "My chief occupation," he wrote to Voltaire, "is to fight ignorance and prejudices in this country. . . . I must enlighten my people, cultivate their manners and morals, and make them as happy as human beings can be, or as happy as the means at my disposal permit." He did not conceive that sweeping changes were necessary to happiness in Prussia. The country was docile, for its Lutheran church had long been subordinate to the state, its relatively few burghers were largely dependents of the crown, and the independence of the Junker landlords, as expressed in provincial diets, had been curtailed by Frederick's predecessors.[18] Frederick

[17] See p. 367.
[18] See pp. 225–226.

simplified and codified the many laws of the kingdom and made the law courts cheaper, more expeditious, and more honest. He kept up a wholesome and energetic tone in his civil service. He gave religious freedom, and he decreed, though he did not realize, a modicum of elementary education for all children of all classes. Prussia under Frederick was attractive enough for some 300,000 immigrants to seek it out.

But society remained stratified in a way hardly known in western Europe. Nobles, peasants, and burghers lived side by side in a kind of segregation. Each group paid different taxes and owed different duties to the state, and no person could buy property of the type pertaining to one of the other two groups. Property was legally classified, as well as persons; there was little passing from one group to another. The basic aim of these policies was military, to preserve, by keeping intact their respective forms of property, a distinct peasant class from which to draw soldiers and a distinct aristocratic class from which to draw officers. The peasants, except in the western extremities of the kingdom, were serfs holding patches of land on precarious terms in return for obligations to labor on the estates of the lords. They were likewise considered the lord's "hereditary subjects" and were not free to leave the lord's estate, to marry, or to learn a trade except with his permission. Frederick in his early years considered steps to relieve the burden of serfdom. He did relieve it on his own manors, those belonging to the Prussian crown domain, which comprised a quarter of the area of the kingdom. But he did nothing for serfs belonging to the private landlords or Junkers. No king of Prussia could fundamentally antagonize the Junker class which commanded the army. On the other hand, even in Prussia, the existence of a monarchical state was of some advantage to the common man; the serf in Prussia was not so badly off as in adjoining areas—Poland, Livonia, Mecklenburg, or Swedish Pomerania—where the will of the landlords was the law of the land, and which therefore have not inaptly been called Junker republics. In these countries cases came to light in which owners sold their serfs as movable property, or gambled or gave them away, breaking up families in the process, as Russian landlords might do with their serfs or American plantation owners with their slaves. Such abuses were unknown in Prussia.

Frederick's system was centralized not merely at Potsdam but in his own head. He himself attended to all business and made all important decisions. None of his ministers or generals ever achieved an independent reputation. As he said of his army, "no one reasons, everyone executes"—that is, no one reasoned except the king himself. Or again, as Frederick put it, if Newton had had to consult with Descartes he would never have discovered the law of universal gravitation. To have to take account of other people's ideas, or to entrust responsibilities to men less capable than himself, seemed to Frederick wasteful and anarchic. He died in 1786, after ruling forty-six years and having trained no successors. Twenty years later Prussia was all but destroyed by Napoleon.[19] It was not surprising that Napoleon should defeat Prussia, but Europe was amazed, in 1806, to see Prussia collapse totally and abruptly. It was then concluded, in Prussia and elsewhere, that government by a mastermind working in lofty and isolated superiority did not offer a viable form of state under modern conditions.

[19] See pp. 412–414, 417–418.

38. ENLIGHTENED DESPOTISM: RUSSIA

The Russian empire has long been out of sight in the preceding pages. There are reasons for its absence, for it played no part in the intellectual revolution of the seventeenth century, and its role in the struggle for wealth and empire, which reached a climax in the Seven Years' War, was somewhat incidental. In the Age of Enlightenment the role of Russia was passive. No Russian thinker was known to Europe. But European thinkers were well known in Russia. The French-dominated cosmopolitan culture of the European upper classes spread to the upper classes of Russia. The Russian court and aristocracy took over French as their common conversational language. With French (German was also known, and sometimes English, for the Russian aristocrats were remarkable linguists) all the ideas boiling up in western Europe streamed into Russia. The Enlightenment, if it did not affect Russia profoundly, yet affected it significantly. It continued the westernization so forcibly pushed forward by Peter and carried further the estrangement of the Russian upper classes from their own people and their own native scene.

Russia after Peter the Great

Peter the Great died in 1725.[20] To secure his revolution he had decreed that each tsar should name his successor, but he himself had named none and had put to death his own son Alexis to prevent social reaction. Peter was succeeded by his wife, a woman of peasant origin, who reigned for two years as Catherine I. Then came the boy Peter II, son of Alexis and grandson of Peter I. Peter II reigned only from 1727 to 1730. He was followed by Anna, 1730–1740; in her reign the old native Russian party tried to surround the tsardom with various constitutional checks. They failed; Anna was followed by Ivan VI, who was tsar for a few months only, during which his mother, a German woman, ran affairs according to the views of the German party in Russia, which was indispensable to the westerniza-tion program and was resented by the Russian nativists. A palace revolution in 1741 brought to the throne Peter the Great's daughter, Elizabeth, who managed to hold power until her death twenty-one years later. In her reign the military power of Russia expanded, and she entered into European diplomacy and joined in the Seven Years' War against Prussia, fearing that the continued growth of Prussia would endanger the new Russian position on the Baltic. Her nephew, Peter III, was almost immediately dethroned, and probably assassinated, by a group acting in the name of his young wife, Catherine. The victorious coterie gave it out that Peter III had been almost a half-wit, who at the age of twenty-four still played with paper soldiers. Catherine was proclaimed the Empress Catherine II and is called "the Great." She enjoyed a long reign from 1762 to 1796, during which she acquired a somewhat exaggerated reputation as an en-lightened despot.

The names of the tsars and tsarinas between Peter I and Catherine II are of slight importance. But their violent and rapid sequence tells a story. With no principle of succession, dynastic or other, the empire fell into a lawless struggle of parties, in which plots against rulers while living alternated with palace

---

[20] See pp. 237–238.

revolutions upon their death. In all the confusion an underlying issue was always how the westernizing program of Peter would turn out. To western Europe Russia still seemed Byzantine and barbaric.

Catherine the Great (1762–1796): Domestic Program

Catherine the Great was a German woman, of a small princely house of the Holy Roman Empire. She had gone to Russia at the age of fifteen to be married. She had immediately cultivated the good will of the Russians, learned the language, and embraced the Orthodox church. Early in her married life, disgusted with her husband, she foresaw the chance of becoming empress herself. She was nothing like her feminine contemporary Maria Theresa, except possibly in having much the same practical sense. Hearty and boisterous, she wore out a long succession of many lovers, mixing them freely with politics and using them in positions of state. When she died at the age of sixty-seven, of a stroke of apoplexy, she was still living with the last of these venturesome paramours. Her intellectual powers were as remarkable as her physical vigor; even after becoming empress she often got up at five in the morning, lighted her own fire, and turned to her books, making a digest, for example, of Blackstone's *Commentaries on the Laws of England*, published in 1765. She corresponded with Voltaire and invited Diderot, editor of the *Encyclopédie*, to visit her at St. Petersburg, where, she reported, he thumped her so hard on the knee in the energy of his conversation that she had to put a table between them. She bought Diderot's library, allowing him to keep it during his lifetime, and in other ways won renown by her benefactions to the philosophes, whom she probably regarded as useful press agents for Russia. Her gifts to them were substantial, though dwarfed by the £12,000,000 she is estimated to have bestowed on her lovers.

When she first came to power she publicized an intention to make certain enlightened reforms. She summoned a great consultative assembly, called a Legislative Commission, which met in the summer of 1767. From its numerous proposals Catherine obtained a good deal of information on conditions in the country and concluded, from the profuse loyalty exhibited by the deputies, that though a usurper and a foreigner she possessed a strong hold upon Russia. The reforms which she subsequently enacted consisted in a measure of legal codification, restrictions on the use of torture, and a certain support of religious toleration, though she would not allow Old Believers to build their own chapels. Such innovations were enough to raise an admiring chorus from the philosophes, who saw in her, as they saw retrospectively in Peter the Great, the standard-bearer of civilization among a backward people. Like other enlightened despots, Catherine turned assiduously to administrative questions also. Consolidating the machinery of state, she replaced Peter's ten *gubernii* with fifty, each subdivided into districts, and all equipped with appropriate sets of governors and officials.

Whatever ideas Catherine may conceivably have had at first, as a thoughtful and progressive young woman, on the fundamental subject of reforming serfdom in Russia, did not last long after she became empress, and dissolved with the great peasant insurrection of 1773, known as Pugachev's rebellion. The condition of the Russian serfs was deteriorating. Serf owners were increasingly selling them apart from land, breaking up families, using them in mines or manufactures, disciplining and punishing them at will, or exiling them to Siberia. The serf population was restless, worked upon by Old Believers and cherishing distorted popular memories of the mighty hero, Stephen Razin, who a century before had led an uprising against the landlords.[21] Class antagonism, though latent, was profound, nor was it made less when the rough muzhik, in some places, heard the lord and his family talking French so as not to be understood by the servants or saw them wearing European clothes, reading European books, and adopting the manners of a foreign and superior way of life.

In 1773 a Don Cossack, Emelian Pugachev, a former soldier, appeared at the head of an insurrection in the Urals. Following an old Russian custom, he announced himself as the true tsar, Peter III (Catherine's deceased husband), now returned after long travels in Egypt and the Holy Land. He surrounded himself with duplicates of the imperial family, courtiers, and even a secretary of state. He issued an imperial manifesto proclaiming the end of serfdom and of taxes and military conscription. Tens and hundreds of thousands, in the Urals and Volga regions, Tartars, Kirghiz, Cossacks, agricultural serfs, servile workers in the Ural mines, fishermen in the rivers and in the Caspian Sea, flocked to Pugachev's banner. The great host surged through eastern Russia, burning and pillaging, killing priests and landlords. The upper classes in Moscow were terrified; 100,000 serfs lived in the city as domestic servants or industrial workers, and their sympathies went out to Pugachev and his horde. Armies were at first unsuccessful. But famine along the Volga in 1774 dispersed the rebels. Pugachev, betrayed by some of his own followers, was brought to Moscow in an iron cage. Catherine forbade the use of torture at his trial, but he was executed by the drawing and quartering of his body, a punishment, it should perhaps be noted, used at the time in western Europe in cases of flagrant treason.

Pugachev's rebellion was the most violent peasant uprising in the history of Russia, and the most formidable mass upheaval in Europe in the century before 1789. Catherine replied to it by repression. She conceded more powers to the landlords. The nobles shook off the last vestiges of the compulsory state service to which Peter had bound them. The peasants were henceforth the only bound or unfree class. As in Prussia, the state came more than ever to rest on an understanding between ruler and gentry, by which the gentry accepted the monarchy, with its laws, officials, army, and foreign policy, and received from it, in return, the assurance of full authority over the rural masses. Government reached down through the aristocracy and the scattered towns, but it stopped short at the manor; there the lord took over and was himself a kind of government in his own person. Under these conditions the number of serfs increased, and the load on each became more heavy. Catherine's reign saw the culmination of Russian serfdom, which now ceased to differ in any important respect from the chattel slavery to which blacks were subject in the Americas. One might read in the Moscow *Gazette* such advertisements as the following: "For sale, two plump coachmen; two girls eighteen and fifteen years, quick at manual work. Two barbers; one, twenty-one, knows how to read and write and play a musical instrument; the other can do ladies' and gentlemen's hair."

Catherine the Great: Foreign Affairs

Territorially Catherine was one of the main builders of Russia. When she became tsarina in 1762 the empire reached to the Pacific and into central Asia, and it

[21] See p. 231.

touched upon the Gulf of Riga and the Gulf of Finland on the Baltic, but westward from Moscow one could go only 200 miles before reaching Poland, and no one standing on Russian soil could see the waters of the Black Sea.[22] Russia was separated from central Europe by a wide band of loosely organized domains, extending from the Baltic to the Black Sea and the Mediterranean and nominally belonging to the Polish and Turkish states. Poland was an old enemy, which had once threatened Muscovy, and in both Poland and the Ottoman Empire there were many Greek Orthodox Christians with whom Russians felt an ideological tie. In western Europe the disposal of the whole Polish-Turkish tract, which stretched through Asia Minor, Syria, and Palestine into Egypt, came to be called the Eastern Question. Though the name went out of use after 1900, the question itself has never ceased to exist.

Catherine's supreme plan was to penetrate the entire area, Polish and Turkish alike. In a war with Turkey in 1768 she developed her "Greek project," in which "Greeks," i.e., members of the Greek Orthodox Church, would replace Muslims as the dominant element throughout the Middle East. She defeated the Turks in the war, but was herself checked by the diplomatic pressures of the European balance of power. The result, as has been explained, was the first partition of Poland.[23] The three eastern monarchs began to divide up the territory between them. Frederick took Pomerelia, which he renamed West Prussia; Catherine took parts of White Russia; Maria Theresa, Galicia. Frederick digested his portion with relish, realizing an old dream of the Brandenburg house; Catherine swallowed hers with somewhat less appetite, since she had satisfactorily controlled the whole of Poland before; to Maria Theresa the dish was distasteful, and even shocking, but she could not see her neighbors go ahead without her, and she shared in the feast by suppressing her moral scruples. "She wept," said Frederick cynically, "but she kept on taking." Catherine, in 1774, signed a peace treaty with the defeated Turks at Kuchuk Kainarji on the Danube. The sultan ceded his rights over the Tartar principalities on the north coast of the Black Sea, where the Russians soon founded the seaport of Odessa.

Catherine had only delayed, not altered, her plans with respect to Turkey. She decided to neutralize the opposition of Austria. She invited Joseph II to visit her in Russia, and the two sovereigns proceeded together on a tour of her newly won Black Sea provinces. Her favorite of the moment, Potemkin, constructed artificial one-street villages along their way and produced throngs of cheering and happy-looking villagers to greet them, all of which enriched mankind with nothing except the phrase "Potemkin villages" to mean bogus evidence of a nonexistent prosperity. At Kherson the two monarchs passed through a gate marked "The Road to Byzantium." "What I want is Silesia," said Joseph II, but the tsarina induced him to join in a war of conquest against Turkey. This war was interrupted by the French Revolution. Both governments reduced their commitments in the Balkans to await developments in western Europe. It became Catherine's policy to incite Austria and Prussia into a war with revolutionary France, in the name of monarchy and civilization, in order that she might have a free hand in the Polish-Turkish sphere.[24] Meanwhile she contributed to killing off the nationalist and reforming movement among the Poles. In 1793 she arranged with Prussia for the

POLAND SINCE THE EIGHTEENTH CENTURY

The top right panel shows, in simplified form, the ethnic composition of the area included in the great Poland of 1772. In addition to languages shown, Yiddish was spoken by the large scattered Jewish population. Note how the line set in 1795 as the western boundary of Russia persists through later transformations. It reappears as the eastern border of Napoleon's Grand Duchy (pp. 398–401), and of Congress Poland (pp. 422–423). After the First World War the victorious Allies contemplated much this same line as Poland's eastern frontier (the dotted line in the fourth panel, known as the Curzon Line); but the Poles in 1920–1921 conquered territory farther east (p. 715). After the Second World War the Russians pushed the Poles back to the same basic line, but compensated Poland with territory taken from Germany, as far west as the river Oder and its tributary, the Neisse. If the reader will compare the position of Warsaw in each panel he will see how Poland has been shoved westward.

second partition, and in 1795, with both Prussia and Austria, for the third. She was the only ruler who lived to take part in all three partitions of Poland.

Many advanced thinkers of the day praised the partitions of Poland as a triumph of enlightened rulers, putting an end to an old nuisance. The three partitioning powers extenuated their conduct on various grounds, and even took pride in it as a diplomatic achievement by which war was prevented between them. What seemed to be robbery was justified by the argument that the gains were equal; this was the diplomatic doctrine of "compensation." It was argued also that the partitions of Poland put an end to an old cause of international rivalry and war, replacing anarchy with solid government in a large area of eastern Europe. It is a fact that Poland had been scarcely more independent before the partitions than after. It is to be noted also, though nationalist arguments were not used at the time, that on national grounds the Poles themselves had no claim to large parts of the old Poland. The regions taken by Russia, in all three partitions, were inhabited overwhelmingly by White Russians and Ukrainians, among whom the Poles were mainly a landlord class. Russia, even in the third partition, reached only to the true ethnic border of Poland. But later, after the fall of Napoleon, by general international agreement, the Russian sphere was extended deep into the territory inhabited by Poles.

The partitions of Poland, however extenuated, were nevertheless a great shock to the old system of Europe. Edmund Burke, in England, prophetically saw in the first partition the crumbling of the old international order. His diagnosis was a shrewd one. The principle of the balance of power had been historically invoked to preserve the independence of European states, to secure weak or small ones against universal monarchy. It was now used to destroy the independence of a weak but ancient kingdom. Not that Poland was the first to be "partitioned"; the Spanish and Swedish empires had been partitioned, and during the eighteenth century there were attempts to partition Prussia and the Austrian empire also. But Poland was the first to be partitioned without war and the first to disappear totally. That Poland was partitioned without war, a source of great satisfaction to the partitioning powers, was still a very unsettling fact. It was alarming for a huge state to vanish simply by cold diplomatic calculation. It seemed that no established rights were safe even in peacetime. The partitions of Poland showed that in a world where great powers had arisen, controlling modern apparatus of state, it was dangerous not to be strong. They suggested that any area failing to develop a sovereign state capable of keeping out foreign infiltration, and so situated as to be reached by the great powers of Europe, was unlikely to retain its independence. In this way they anticipated, for example, the partitions of Africa a century later, when Africa too, lacking strong governments, was almost totally divided, without war, among half a dozen states of Europe.

Moreover the partitions of Poland, while maintaining the balance in eastern Europe, profoundly changed the balance of Europe as a whole. The disappearance of Poland was a blow to France, which had long used Poland, as it had used Hungary and Turkey, as an outpost of French influence in the East. The three Eastern powers expanded their territory, while France enjoyed henceforth no permanent growth. Eastern Europe bulked larger than ever before in the affairs of Europe. Prussia, Russia, and the Austrian empire became contiguous. They had an interest in common, the repression of Polish resistance to their rule. Polish resistance, dating from before the partitions and continuing after them, was the earliest example of modern revolutionary nationalism in Europe. The independence of Poland, and of other submerged nationalities, became in time a cause much favored in western Europe, while the three great monarchies of eastern Europe were drawn together in common opposition to national liberation; and this fact, plus the fact that the eastern monarchies were primarily landlord states, accentuated the characteristic division of Europe, in the nineteenth century, between a West that inclined to be liberal and an East that inclined to be reactionary. But these ideas anticipate a later part of the story.

As for Catherine, her own protestations of enlightenment tempt one to an ironic judgment of her career. Her foreign policy was purely expansionist and unscrupulous, and the net effect of her domestic policy, aside from a few reforms of detail, was to favor the half-Europeanized aristocracy and to extend serfdom among the people. In her defense it may be observed that unscrupulous expansion was the accepted practice of the time, and that, domestically, probably no ruler could have corrected the social evils from which Russia suffered. If there was to be a Russian empire it had to be with the consent of the serf-owning gentry, which was the only politically significant class. As Catherine observed to Diderot on the subject of reforms: "You write only on paper, but I have to write on human skin, which is incomparably more irritable and ticklish." She had reason to know how easily tsars and tsarinas could be unseated and even murdered, and that the danger of overthrow came not from the peasants but from cliques of army officers and landlords.

She remained attuned to the West. She never thought that the peculiar institutions of Russia should become a model for others. She continued to recognize the standards of the Enlightenment at least as standards. In her later years she gave careful attention to her favorite grandson, Alexander, closely supervising his education, which she planned on the Western model. She gave him as a tutor the Swiss philosophe La Harpe, who filled his mind with humane and liberal sentiments on the duties of princes. Trained by Catherine as a kind of ideal ruler, Alexander I was destined to cut a wide circle in the affairs of Europe, to defeat Napoleon Bonaparte, preach peace and freedom, and suffer from the same internal divisions and frustrations by which educated Russians seemed characteristically to be afflicted.

The Limitations of Enlightened Despotism

Enlightened despotism, seen in retrospect, foreshadowed an age of revolution and even signified a preliminary effort to revolutionize society by authoritative action from above. People were told by their own governments that reforms were needed, that many privileges, special liberties, or tax exemptions were bad, that the past was a source of confusion, injustice, or inefficiency in the present. The state rose up as more completely sovereign, whether acting frankly in its own interest or claiming to act in the interest of its people. All old and established rights were brought into question—rights of kingdoms and provinces, orders and classes, legal bodies and corporate groups. Enlightened despotism overrode or exterminated the Society of Jesus, the Parlement of Paris, the autonomy of Bohemia, and the independence of Poland. Customary and common law was pushed aside by authoritative legal codes. Governments, by opposing the special powers of the church and the feudal interests, tended to make all persons into uniform and equal subjects. To this extent enlightened despotism favored equality before the law. But it could go only a certain distance in this direction. The king was after all a hereditary aristocrat himself, and no government can be revolutionary to the point of breaking up its own foundations.

Even before the French Revolution enlightened despotism had run its course. Everywhere the "despots," for reasons of politics if not of principle, had reached a point beyond which they could not go. In France Louis XVI had appeased the privileged classes, in the Austrian empire Joseph's failure to appease them threw them into open revolt, in Prussia and in Russia the brilliant reigns of Frederick and Catherine wound up in an aggravation of landlordism for the mass of the people. Almost everywhere there was an aristocratic and even feudal revival. Religion also was renewing itself in many ways. Many were again saying that kingship was in a sense divine, and a new alliance was forming between "the throne and the altar." The French Revolution, by terrifying the old vested interests, was to accelerate and embitter a reaction which had already begun. Monarchy in Europe, ever since the Middle Ages, had generally been a progressive institution, acting along the line that Europe seemed destined to take, and in any case setting itself against the feudal and ecclesiastical powers. Enlightened despotism was the culmination of the historic institution of monarchy. After the enlightened despots, and after the French Revolution, monarchy became on the whole nostalgic and backward-looking, supported most ardently by the churches and aristocracies that it had once tried to subdue and least of all by those who felt in themselves the surge of the future.

39. NEW STIRRINGS: THE BRITISH REFORM MOVEMENT

It was not only by monarchs and their ministers, however, that the older privileged, feudal, and ecclesiastical interests were threatened. Beginning about 1760 they were challenged also in more popular quarters. Growing out of the Enlightenment, and out of the failure of governments to cope with grave social and fiscal problems, a new era of revolutionary disturbance was about to open. It was marked above all by the great French Revolution of 1789, but the American Revolution of 1776 was also of international importance. In Great Britain, too, the long-drawn-out movement for parliamentary reform which began in the 1760s was in effect revolutionary in character, though nonviolent, since it questioned the foundations of traditional English government and society. In addition, in the last third of the eighteenth century, there was revolutionary agitation in Switzerland, Belgium, and Holland, in Ireland, Poland, Hungary, Italy, and in lesser degree elsewhere. After 1800 revolutionary ferment was increasingly evident in Germany, Spain, and Latin America. This general wave of revolution may be said not to have ended until after the revolutions of 1848.

Onset of an Age of "Democratic Revolution"

For the whole period the term "Atlantic Revolution" has sometimes been used, since countries on both sides of the Atlantic were affected. It has been called also an age of "Democratic Revolution," since in all the diversity of these upheavals, from the American Revolution to those of 1848, certain principles of the modern democratic society were in one way or another affirmed. In this view, the particular revolutions, attempted revolutions, or basic reform movements are seen as aspects of one great revolutionary wave by which virtually the whole area of Western civilization was transformed. The contrary is also maintained, namely, that each country presented a special case, which is misunderstood if viewed only as part of a vague general international turmoil. Thus the American Revolution, it is argued, was essentially a movement for independence, even essentially conservative in its objectives, and thus entirely different from the French Revolution, in which a thorough renovation of all society and ideas were contemplated; and both were utterly different from what happened in England, where there was no revolution at all. There is truth in both contentions, and it need only be affirmed here that the American revolutionaries, the French Jacobins, the United Irish, the Dutch Patriots, and similar groups elsewhere, though differing from each other, yet shared much in common that can only be characterized as revolutionary and as contributing to a revolutionary age.

It is important to see in what ways the movement that began about 1760 was and was not "democratic." It did not generally demand universal suffrage, though a handful of persons in England did so as early as the 1770s and some of the American states practiced an almost universal male suffrage after 1776, as did the more militant French revolutionaries in 1792. It did not aim at a welfare state, nor question the right of property, though there were signs pointing in these directions in the extreme wing of the French Revolution. It was not especially directed against monarchy as such. The quarrel of the Americans was primarily with the British Parliament, not the king; the French proclaimed a republic by default in 1792, three years after their revolution began; the revolutionary Poles after 1788 tried to strengthen their king's position, not weaken it; and revolutionary groups could come into action where no monarchy existed at all, as in the Dutch provinces before the French Revolution, and the Swiss cantons, the Venetian Republic, or again in Holland, under French influence after 1795. Indeed the first revolutionary outbreak of the period occurred in 1768 at Geneva, a very nonmonarchical small city-republic, ruled by a close-knit circle of hereditary patricians. Royal power, where it existed, became the victim of revolutionaries only where it was used to support various privileged social groups.

The revolutionary movement announced itself everywhere as a demand for "liberty and equality." It favored declarations of rights and explicit written constitutions. It proclaimed the sovereignty of the people, or "nation," and it formulated the idea of national citizenship. In this context the "people" were essentially classless; it was a legal term, the obverse of government, signifying the community over which public authority was exercised and from which government itself was in principle derived. To say that citizens were equal meant originally that there was no difference between noble and common. To say that the people were sovereign meant that neither the king, nor the British Parliament, nor any group of nobles, patricians, regents, or other elite possessed power of government in their own right; that all public officers were removable and exercised a delegated authority within limits defined by the constitution. There must be no "magistrate" above the people, no self-perpetuation or cooptation in office, no rank derived from birth and acknowledged in the law. Social distinctions, as the French said in their Declaration of Rights of 1789, were to be based only "on common utility." Elites of talent or function there might be, but none of birth, privilege, or estate. "Aristocracy" in every form must be shunned. In representative bodies, there could be no special representation for special groups; representatives should be elected by frequent elections, not indeed usually by universal suffrage, but by a body of voters, however defined, in which each voter should count for one in a system of equal representation. Representation by numbers, with majority rule, replaced the older idea of representation of social classes, privileged towns, or other corporate groups.

In short, everything associated with absolutism, feudalism, or inherited right (except the right of property) was repudiated. Likewise rejected was any connection between religion and citizenship, or civil rights. The Democratic Revolution undermined the special position of the Catholic church in France, the Anglican in England and Ireland, the Dutch Reformed in the United Provinces; this was also the great period of what has been called Jewish "emancipation." The whole idea that government, or any human authority, was somehow willed by God and protected by religion faded away. A general liberty of opinion on all subjects was countenanced, in the belief that it was necessary to progress. Here again the secularism of the Enlightenment carried on.

On the whole, the Democratic Revolution was a middle-class movement, and indeed the term "bourgeois revolution" was later invented to describe it. Many of its leaders in Europe were in fact nobles who were willing to forgo the historic privileges of nobility; and many of its supporters were of the poorer classes, especially in the great French Revolution. But the middle classes were the great beneficiaries, and it was a kind of middle-class or bourgeois society that emerged. Persons of noble ancestry continued to exist after the storm was over, but the world of noble values was gone; and they either took part in various activities on much the same terms as others or retreated into exclusive drawing rooms to enjoy their aristocratic distinctions in private. The main drive of the working classes was still to come.

The English-Speaking Countries: Parliament and Reform

If the American Revolution was the first act of a larger drama, it must be understood also in connection with the broader British world of which the American colonies formed a part. The British Empire in the middle of the century was decentralized and composite. Thirty-one governments were directly subordinate to Westminster, ranging from the separate kingdom of Ireland through all the crown and charter colonies to the various political establishments maintained in the East by the East India Company. The whole empire, with about 15,000,000 people of all colors in 1750, was less populous than France or the Austrian monarchy. The whole tract of the American mainland from Georgia to Nova Scotia compared in the number of its white population with Ireland or Scotland—or with Brittany or Bohemia—a figure of about 2,000,000 being roughly applicable in each case.

England had its own way of passing through the Age of Enlightenment. There was general contentment with the arrangements that followed the English Revolution of 1688—it has often been remarked that nothing is so conservative as a successful revolution.[25] British thought lacked the asperity of thought on the Con-

[25] See pp. 173–177.

tinent. The writers who most resembled French philosophes, such as Hume and Gibbon, were innocuously moderate in their political ideas. The prevailing mood was one of complacency, a self-satisfaction in the glories of the British constitution, by which Englishmen enjoyed liberties unknown on the Continent.

In Britain, Parliament was supreme, as in most Continental countries, the monarch. It had the power, as one facetious journalist put it, to do all things except change a man into a woman. The British Parliament was as sovereign as any European ruler, and indeed more so, since less that could be called feudalism remained in England than on the Continent. Nor was there any "despotism" in England, enlightened or otherwise. The young George III, who inherited the throne in 1760, did feel himself to be a "patriot king." He did wish to heighten the influence of the crown and to overcome the factionalism of parties.[26] But it was through Parliament that he had to work. He had to descend into the political arena himself, buy up or otherwise control votes in the Commons, grant pensions and favors, and make promises and deals with other parliamentary politicians. What he did in effect was to create a new faction, the "king's friends." This faction was in power during the ministry of Lord North from 1770 to 1782. It is worth noting that all factions were factions of Whigs, that the Tory party was practically defunct, that Britain did not yet have a two-party system, and that the word "Tory," as it came to be used by American revolutionaries, was little more than a term of abuse.

While Parliament was supreme, and constitutional questions apparently settled, there were nevertheless numerous undercurrents of discontent. These were expressed, since the press was freer in England than elsewhere, in many books and pamphlets which were read in the American colonies and helped to form the psychology of the American Revolution. There was, for example, a school of Anglo-Irish Protestant writers, who argued that since Ireland was in any case a separate kingdom, with its own parliament, it ought to be less dependent on the central government at Westminster. The possibility of a similar separate kingdom, remaining within the British Empire, was one of the alternatives considered

[26] See pp. 257–259.

THE HON. MRS. GRAHAM
by Thomas Gainsborough (English, 1727–1788)

This picture and the three following, on pp. 343, 371, and 374, suggest what is meant by the four basic classes of preindustrial society—aristocracy, middle class, urban workers, and peasantry. High social status is very evident in this portrayal of a young gentlewoman, whose title, "The Honorable," is still used in Great Britain for the daughters of viscounts and barons. Wealth is apparent in the brooch, the plumes, the silks, bows and ruffles, and in the pearls which are both worn in strings and sewn on the hat and garments. The meticulous coiffure and complexities of dress suggest the constant attention of lady's maids. The tall stature, delicate hands, refined mouth and haughty expression all reveal high breeding, and the classical colonnade on which the lady so casually rests her arm lends an air of familiarity with magnificent surroundings. Perhaps the aristocrats of the eighteenth century did not often look like this, but this is the way they liked to imagine themselves and to be portrayed for posterity. In Gainsborough, Sir Joshua Reynolds, and Sir Thomas Lawrence, England had an unparalleled group of artists who specialized in painting the upper class. Courtesy of the National Gallery of Scotland.

by Americans before they settled on independence. In England there was the considerable body of Dissenters, or Protestants not accepting the Church of England, who had enjoyed religious toleration since 1689 but continued to labor (until 1828) under various forms of political exclusion. They overlapped with two other amorphous groups, a small number of "commonwealthmen" and a larger and growing number of parliamentary reformers. The commonwealthmen, increasingly eccentric and largely ignored, looked back nostalgically to the Puritan Revolution and the republican era of Oliver Cromwell.[27] They kept alive memories of the Levellers and ideals of equality, well mixed with a pseudo-history of a simple Anglo-Saxon England that had been crushed by the despotism of the Norman Conquest. The commonwealthmen had less influence in England than in the American colonies and especially New England, which had originated in close connection with the Puritan Revolution. The parliamentary reformers were a more diverse and influential group. They were condemned in the eighteenth century to repeated frustration; not until the First Reform Bill of 1832 was anything accomplished.

The very power of Parliament meant that political leaders had to take strong measures to assure its votes. These measures were generally denounced by their critics as "corruption," on the grounds that Parliament, whether or not truly representative, should at least be free. Control of Parliament, and especially of the House of Commons, was assured by various devices, such as patronage or the giving of government jobs (called "places"), or awarding contracts, or having infrequent general elections (every seven years after 1716); or the fact that in many constituencies there were no real elections at all. The distribution of seats in the Commons bore no relation to numbers of inhabitants. A town having the right to send members to Parliament was called a "borough," but no new borough was created after 1688 (or until 1832). Thus localities that had been important in the medieval or Tudor periods were represented, but towns that had grown up recently, such as Manchester and Birmingham, were not. A few boroughs were populous and democratic, but many had few inhabitants or none, so that influential "borough mongers" decided who should represent them in Parliament.

The reform movement began in England before the American Revolution, with which it was closely associated. Since complaints were diverse, it attracted people of different kinds. The first agitation centered about John Wilkes. Having attacked the policies of George III, been vindicated when the courts pronounced the arrest of his publisher illegal, and been expelled by a House of Commons dominated by the king's supporters, Wilkes became a hero and was three times reelected to the House, which, however, refused to seat him. In a whirl of protests and public meetings, reams of petitions supported him against the House. His followers in 1769 founded the Supporters of the Bill of Rights, the first of many societies dedicated to parliamentary reform. His case raised the question of whether the House of Commons should be dependent on the electorate and the propriety of mass agitation "out of doors" on political questions. It was in this connection, also, that debates in Parliament for the first time came to be reported in the London press. Parliament stood on the eve of a long transition, by which it was to be converted from a select body meeting in private to a modern representative institution answerable to the public and its constituents. Wilkes himself, in 1776, introduced

[27] See pp. 169–171.

the first of many reform bills of which none passed for over half a century. Meanwhile Major John Cartwright, called the "father of reform," had begun a long series of pamphlets on the subject; he lived to be eighty-four but not quite long enough to see the Reform Act of 1832. Dissenting intellectuals, such as Richard Price and Joseph Priestley, joined in the movement. Price, a founder of actuarial statistics, announced in 1776 that only 5,723 persons chose half the membership of the House of Commons. Many London merchants favored reform. So did a great many landowners and country gentry, especially in the north of England, led by Christopher Wyvil. These men objected to the fact that four-fifths of the members of the House of Commons sat for the boroughs and only one-fifth for the shires or counties. They rightly thought that the boroughs were more easily manipulated by the government; they thought that county elections were more honest; and they initiated in 1780 a movement of county associations to promote change in the electoral system.

The important Whig leaders, who had previously managed Parliament by much the same methods, began to sense "corruption" after control passed to George III and his "friends." Their most eloquent spokesman was Edmund Burke. Other reformers called for more frequent elections, "annual parliaments," a wider and more equal or even universal male suffrage, with dissolution of some boroughs in which no one was really represented. Burke favored none of these things; in fact he came strenuously to oppose them. A founder of philosophical conservatism, he was yet in his way a reformer. He was more concerned that the House of Commons should be independent and responsible than that it should be mathematically representative. He thought that the landowning interest should govern. But he pleaded for a strong sense of party in opposition to royal encroachments, and he argued that members of Parliament should follow their own best judgment of the country's interests, bound neither by the king on the one hand nor by their own constituents on the other. Like other reformers, he objected to "placemen," or jobholders dependent on their ministerial patrons, and he objected to the use made, for political purposes, of a bewildering array of pensions, sinecures, honorific appointments, and ornamental offices, ranks, and titles. In his Economical Reform of 1782 he got many of these abolished.

The reform movement, though ineffectual, remained strong. Even William Pitt, as prime minister in the 1780s, gave it his sponsorship. It took on new strength at the time of the French Revolution, spreading then to more popular levels, as men of the skilled artisan class were aroused by events in France and demanded a more adequate "representation of the people" in England. They then had upperclass support from Charles James Fox and a minority of the Whigs. But conservatism, satisfaction with the British constitution, patriotism engendered by a new round of French wars, and reaction against the French Revolution all raised an impassable barrier. Reform was delayed for another generation.

After the American Revolution, which in a way was a civil struggle within the English-speaking world, the English reformers generally blamed the trouble with America on King George III. This was less than fair, since Parliament on the American question was never dragooned by the king. The most ardent reformers later argued that if Parliament had been truly representative of the British people, the Americans would not have been driven to independence. This seems unlikely. In any case, reformers of various kinds, from Wilkes to Burke, were sympathetic to the complaints of the American colonials after 1763. There was much busy correspondence across the Atlantic. Wilkes was a hero in Boston as well as London. Burke pleaded for conciliation with the colonies in a famous speech of 1775. His very insistence on the powers and dignity of Parliament, however, made it hard for him to find a workable solution; and after the colonies became independent he showed no interest in the political ideas of the new American states. It was the more radical reformers in England, as in Scotland and Ireland, who most consistently favored the Americans, both before and after independence. They of course had no power. On the American side, for a decade before independence, the increasingly discontented colonials, reading English books and pamphlets and reports of speeches, heard George III denounced for despotism and Parliament accused of incorrigible corruption. All this seemed to confirm what Americans had long been reading anyway in the works of English Dissenters or old commonwealthmen, now on the fringes of English society but sure of a receptive audience in the American colonies. The result was to make Americans suspicious of all actions by the British government, to sense tyranny everywhere, to magnify such things as the Stamp Act into a kind of plot against American liberties.

The real drift in England in the eighteenth century, however, despite the chronic criticism of Parliament, was for Parliament to extend its powers in a general centralization of the empire. The British government faced somewhat the same problems as governments on the Continent. All had to deal with the issues raised by the great war of the mid-century, in its two phases of the Austrian Succession and Seven Years' War. Everywhere the solution adopted by governments was to increase their own central power. We have seen how the French government, in attempting to tap new sources of revenue, tried to encroach on the liberties of Brittany and other provinces and to subordinate the bodies which in France were called parlements. We have likewise seen how the Habsburg government, also in an effort to raise more taxes, repressed local self-government in the empire and even abrogated the constitution of Bohemia.[28] The same tendency showed itself in the British system. The revocation of the charter of Bohemia in 1749 had its parallel in the revocation of the charter of Massachusetts in 1774. The disputes of the French king with the estates of Brittany or Languedoc had their parallel in the disputes of the British Parliament with the provincial assemblies of Virginia or New York.

Scotland, Ireland, India

There were also problems nearer home. Scotland proved a source of weakness in the War of the Austrian Succession. The Lowlanders were loyal enough, but the Highlanders revolted with French assistance in the Jacobite rising of 1745, and by invading England threatened to take the British government in the rear as it was locked in the struggle with France.[29] The Highlands had never really been under any government, even under the old Scottish monarchy before the union of 1707 with England. Social organization, in the Highland fastnesses, followed the primitive principle of physical kinship. Men looked to their chiefs, the heads of the clans, to tell them whom and when to fight. The chiefs had hereditary jurisdiction, often including powers of life and death, over their clansmen. A few leaders could throw the whole region to the Stuarts or the French. The British govern-

[28] See pp. 315–318, 318–319.
[29] See pp. 258–259.

ment, after 1745, proceeded to make its sovereignty effective in the Highlands. Troops were quartered there for years. Roads were pushed across the moors and through the glens. Law courts enforced the law of the Scottish Lowlands. Revenue officers collected funds for the treasury of Great Britain. The chiefs lost their old quasi-feudal jurisdiction. The old system of land tenure was broken up. The holding of land from clannish chiefs was ended. The clansman swayed by his chief was turned into the subject of the crown of Great Britain. He was turned also, in many cases, into an almost landless "crofter," while some of the chiefs, or their sons, emerged as landed gentlemen of the English type. Fighting Highlanders were incorporated into newly formed Highland regiments of the British army, under the usual discipline imposed by the modern state on its fighting forces. For thirty years the Scots were forbidden to wear the kilt or play the bagpipes.

In Ireland the process of centralization worked itself out more slowly. How Ireland was subjected after the battle of the Boyne has already been described.[30] It was a French army that had landed in Ireland, supported James II and been defeated in 1690. The new English constitutional arrangements, the Hanoverian succession, the Protestant ascendancy, the church and the land settlement in Ireland, together with the prosperity of British commerce, were all secured by the subordination of the smaller island. The native or Catholic Irish remained generally pro-French. The Presbyterian Irish disliked both Frenchmen and popery, but they were alienated from England also; many in fact emigrated to America in the generation before the American Revolution. The island remained quiet in the mid-century wars. When the trouble began between the British Parliament and the American colonies the Presbyterian Irish generally took the American side. They were greatly stirred by the example of American independence. Thousands formed themselves into Volunteer Companies; they wore uniforms, armed, and drilled; they demanded both internal reform of the Irish parliament (which was even less representative than the British) and greater autonomy for the Irish parliament as against the central government at Westminster. Faced with these demands, and fearing a French invasion of Ireland during the War of American Independence, the British government made concessions. It allowed an increase of power to the Irish parliament at Dublin. But from this parliament Catholics were still excluded. In the next war between France and Great Britain, which began in 1793, many Irish felt a warm sympathy for the French Revolution. Catholics and Presbyterians, at last combining, formed a network of United Irish societies throughout the whole island. They sought French aid, and the French barely failed to land a sizable army. Even without French military support, the United Irish rose in 1798 to drive out the English and establish an independent republic. The British, suppressing the rebellion, now turned to centralization. The separate kingdom of Ireland, and the Irish parliament, ceased to exist. The Irish were thereafter represented in the imperial Parliament at Westminster. These provisions were incorporated in the Act of Union of 1801, creating the United Kingdom of Great Britain and Ireland, which lasted until 1922.

British establishments in India also felt the hand of Parliament increasingly upon them. At the close of the Seven Years' War the various British posts in and around Bombay, Madras, and Calcutta were unconnected with each other and subordinate only to the board of directors of the East India Company in London.

---

[30] See pp. 175–176.

Company employees interfered at will in the wars and politics of the Indian states and enriched themselves by such means as they could, not excluding graft, trickery, intimidation, rapine, and extortion.[31] In 1773 the ministry of Lord North passed a Regulating Act, of which the main purpose was to regulate, not Indians, but the British subjects in India, whom no Indian government could control. The company was left with its trading activities, but its political activities were brought under parliamentary supervision. The act gathered all the British establishments under a single governor general, set up a new supreme court at Calcutta, and required the company to submit its correspondence on political matters for review by the ministers of His Majesty's Government. Warren Hastings became the first British governor general in India. He was so high-handed with some of the Indian princes, and made so many enemies among jealous Englishmen in Bengal, that he was denounced at home, impeached, and subjected to a trial which dragged on for seven years in the House of Lords. He was finally acquitted. After Clive, he was the main author of British supremacy in India. Meanwhile, in 1784 an India office was created in the British ministry at home. The governor general henceforth ruled the growing British sphere in India almost as an absolute monarch but only as the agent of the ministry and Parliament of Great Britain.

Thus the trend in the British world was to centralization. Despite the flutter of royalism under George III, it was to a centralization of all British territories under authority of the Parliament. What was happening in empire affairs, as in domestic politics in England, was a continuing application of the principles of 1689. The parliamentary sovereignty established in 1689 was now, after the middle of the eighteenth century, being applied to regions where it had heretofore had little effect. And it was against the British Parliament that the Americans primarily rebelled.

40. THE AMERICAN REVOLUTION

Background to the Revolution

The behavior of the Americans in the Seven Years' War left much to be desired.[32] The several colonial legislatures rejected the Albany Plan of Union drafted by Franklin and commended to them by the British officials. During the war it was the British regular army and navy, financed by taxes and loans in Great Britain, that drove the French out of America. The war effort of the Anglo-Americans was desultory at best. After the defeat of the French the colonials had still to reckon with the Indians of the interior, who preferred French rule to that of their new British and British-colonial masters. Many tribes joined in an uprising led by Pontiac, a western chief, and they ravaged as far eastward as the Pennsylvania and Virginia frontiers. Again, the colonials proved unable to deal with a problem vital to their own future, and peace was brought about by officials and army units taking their orders from Great Britain.

The British government tried to make the colonials pay a larger share toward the expenses of the empire. The colonials had hitherto paid only local taxes. They

[31] See pp. 272–273.
[32] See pp. 269–270.

were liable to customs duties, of which the proceeds went in principle to Great Britain; but these duties were levied to enforce the Acts of Trade and Navigation, to direct the flow of commerce, not to raise revenue; and they were seldom paid, because the Acts of Trade and Navigation were persistently ignored. American merchants, for example, commonly imported sugar from the French West Indies, contrary to law, and even shipped in return the iron wares which it was against the law for Americans to manufacture for export. The colonial in practice paid only such taxes as were approved by his own local legislature for local purposes. The Americans in effect enjoyed a degree of tax exemption within the empire, and it was against this form of provincial privilege that Parliament began to move.

By the Revenue Act of 1764 (the "Sugar" Act), the British ministry, while reducing and liberalizing the customs duties payable in America, entered upon a program of actual and systematic collection. In the following year the ministry attempted to extend to British subjects in America a tax peaceably accepted by those in Great Britain and commonplace in most of Europe. This imposed on all uses of paper, as in newspapers and commercial and legal documents, the payment of a fee which was certified by the affixing of a stamp. The Stamp Act aroused violent and concerted resistance in the colonies, especially among the businessmen, lawyers, and editors who were the most articulate class. It therefore was repealed in 1766. In 1767 Parliament, clumsily casting about to find a tax acceptable to the Americans, hit upon the "Townshend duties," which taxed colonial imports of paper, paint, lead, and tea. Another outcry went up, and the Townshend duties were repealed, except the one on tea, which was kept as a token of the sovereign power of Parliament to tax all persons in the empire.

The colonials had proved stubborn, the government pliable but lacking in constructive ideas. The Americans argued that Parliament had no authority to tax them because they were not represented in it. The British replied that Parliament represented America as much as it represented Great Britain. If Philadelphia sent no actually elected deputies to the Commons, so this argument ran, neither did Manchester in England, yet both places enjoyed a "virtual representation," since members of the Commons did not in any case merely speak for local constituencies but made themselves responsible for imperial interests as a whole. To this many Americans retorted that if Manchester was not "really" represented it ought to be, which was of course also the belief of the English reformers. Meanwhile the strictly Anglo-American question subsided after the repeal of the Stamp Act and the Townshend program. There had been no clarification of principle on either side. But in practice the Americans had resisted significant taxation, and Parliament had refrained from making any drastic use of its sovereign power.

The calm was shattered in 1773 by an event which proved, to the more dissatisfied Americans, the disadvantages of belonging to a global economic system in which the main policies were made on the other side of the ocean. The East India Company was in difficulties. It had a great surplus of Chinese tea,[33] and in any case it wanted new commercial privileges in return for the political privileges which it was losing by the Regulating Act of 1773. In the past the company had been required to sell its wares at public auction in London; other merchants had handled distribution from that point on. Now, in 1773, Parliament granted the company the exclusive right to sell tea through its own agents in America to

---

[33] See p. 251.

American local dealers. Tea was a large item of business in the commercial capitalism of the time. The colonial consumer might pay less for it, but the intermediary American merchant would be shut out. The company's tea was boycotted in all American ports. In Boston, to prevent its forcible landing, a party of disguised men invaded the tea ships and dumped the chests into the harbor. To this act of vandalism the British government replied by measures far out of proportion to the offense. It "closed" the port of Boston, thus threatening the city with economic ruin. It virtually rescinded the charter of Massachusetts, forbidding certain local elections and the holding of town meetings.

And at the same time, in 1774, apparently by coincidence, Parliament enacted the Quebec Act. The wisest piece of British legislation in these troubled years, the Quebec Act provided a government for the newly conquered Canadian French, granting them security in their French civil law and Catholic religion, and laying foundations for the British Empire that was to come. But the act defined the boundaries of Quebec somewhat as the French themselves would have defined them, including in them all territory north of the Ohio River—the present states of Wisconsin, Michigan, Illinois, Indiana, and Ohio. These boundaries were perfectly reasonable, since the few white men in the area were French, and since, in the age before canals or railways, the obvious means of reaching the whole region was by way of the St. Lawrence valley and the Lakes. But to the Americans the Quebec Act was a pro-French and pro-Catholic outrage, and at a time when the powers of juries and assemblies in the old colonies were threatened, it was disquieting that the Quebec Act made no mention of such representative institutions for the new northern province. It was lumped with the closing of an American port and the destruction of the Massachusetts government as one of the "Intolerable Acts" to be resisted.

And indeed the implications of parliamentary sovereignty were now apparent. The meaning of centralized planning and authority was now clear. It was no longer merely an affair of taxation. A government that had to take account of the East India Company, the French Canadians, and the British taxpayers, even if more prudent and enlightened than Lord North's ministry of 1774, could not possibly at the same time have satisfied the Americans of the thirteen seaboard colonies. These Americans, since 1763 no longer afraid of the French empire, were less inclined to forgo their own interests in order to remain in the British. British

MRS. ISAAC SMITH
by John Singleton Copley (American, then English, 1737–1815)

Mrs. Smith may be contrasted with the more aristocratic Mrs. Graham, shown on p. 335. The wife of a Boston merchant, she and her husband both had their portraits painted by Copley in 1769. The picture may be taken to typify, in its portrayal of a middle-aged woman, the bourgeois family background from which came much of the leadership of the American and French revolutions. In general, it was a background of substance, comfort and hard work. Mrs. Smith's costume and surroundings, though less elegant than Mrs. Graham's, suggest her high station in New England society. Her expression is between the prim and the pleasant. She clearly represents, and expects from others, a settled standard of behavior and decorum. Copley, troubled by the rising revolutionary agitation, left America in 1774 and spent the rest of his long life in England. Courtesy of the Yale University Art Gallery, Gift of Maitland Fuller Griggs.

343

policies had aroused antagonism in the coastal towns and in the backwoods, among wealthy land speculators and poor squatter frontiersmen, among merchants and the workingmen who depended on the business of merchants. The freedom of Americans to determine their own political life was in question. Yet there were few in 1774, or even later, prepared to face the thought of independence.

The War of American Independence

After the "Intolerable Acts" self-authorized groups met in the several colonies and sent delegates to a "continental congress" in Philadelphia. This body adopted a boycott of British goods, to be enforced on unwilling Americans by local organizers of resistance. Fighting began in the next year, 1775, when the British commander at Boston sent a detachment to seize unauthorized stores of weapons at Concord. On the way, at Lexington, in a brush between soldiers and partisans or "minutemen," someone fired the "shot heard round the world." The Second Continental Congress, meeting a few weeks later, proceeded to raise an American army, dispatched an expedition to force Quebec into the revolutionary union, and entered into overtures with Bourbon France.

The Congress was still reluctant to repudiate the tie with Britain. But passions grew fierce in consequence of the fighting. Radicals convinced moderates that the choice now lay between independence and enslavement. It appeared that the French, naturally uninterested in a reconciliation of British subjects, would give help if the avowed aim of American rebels was to dismember the British Empire. In January 1776 Thomas Paine, in his pamphlet *Common Sense*, made his debut as a kind of international revolutionary; he was to figure in the French Revolution and to work for revolution in England. He had come from England less than two years before, and he detested English society for its injustices to men like himself. Eloquent and vitriolic, *Common Sense* identified the independence of the American colonies with the cause of liberty for all mankind. It pitted freedom against tyranny in the person of "the royal brute of Great Britain." It was "repugnant to reason," said Paine, "to suppose that this Continent can long remain subject to any external power. . . . There is something absurd in supposing a Continent to be perpetually governed by an island." *Common Sense* was read everywhere in the colonies, and its slashing arguments unquestionably spread a sense of proud isolation from the Old World. On July 4, 1776, the Congress adopted the Declaration of Independence, by which the United States assumed its separate and equal station among the powers of the earth.

The War of American Independence thereupon turned into another European struggle for empire. For two more years the French government remained ostensibly noninterventionist but meanwhile poured munitions into the colonies through an especially rigged up commercial concern. Nine-tenths of the arms used by the Americans at the battle of Saratoga came from France. After the American victory in this battle the French government concluded, in 1778, that the insurgents were a good political risk, recognized them, signed an alliance with them, and declared war on Great Britain. Spain soon followed, hoping to drive the British from Gibraltar and deciding that its overseas empire was more threatened by a restoration of British supremacy in North America than by the disturbing example of an independent American republic. The Dutch were drawn into hostilities through trading with the Americans by way of the Dutch

West Indies. Other powers, Russia, Sweden, Denmark, Prussia, Portugal, and Turkey, irked at British employment of blockade and sea power in time of war, formed an "Armed Neutrality" to protect their commerce from dictation by the British fleet. The French, in a brief revival of their own sea power, landed an expeditionary force of 6,000 men in Rhode Island. Since the Americans suffered from the internal differences inseparable from all revolutions and were in any case still unable to govern themselves to any effect, meeting with the old difficulties in raising both troops and money, it was the participation of regiments of the French army, in conjunction with squadrons of the French fleet, which made possible the defeat of the armed forces of the British Empire and so persuaded the British government to recognize the independence of the United States. By the peace treaty of 1783, though the British were still in possession of New York and Savannah, and though the governments befriending the Americans would just as soon have confined them east of the mountains, the new republic obtained territory as far west as the Mississippi. Canada remained British. It received an English-speaking population by the settlement of over 60,000 refugee Americans who remained loyal to Great Britain.

Significance of the Revolution

The upheaval in America was a revolution as well as a war of independence. The cry for liberty against Great Britain raised echoes within the colonies themselves. The Declaration of Independence was more than an announcement of secession from the empire; it was a justification of rebellion against established authority. Curiously, although the American quarrel had been with the Parliament, the Declaration arraigned no one but the king. One reason was that the Congress, not recognizing the authority of Parliament, could separate from Great Britain only by a denunciation of the British crown; another reason was that the cry of "tyrant" made a more popular and flaming issue. Boldly voicing the natural right philosophy of the age, the Declaration held as "self-evident," i.e., as evident to all reasonable people—that "all men are created equal, that they are endowed by their Creator with certain unalienable rights, that among these are life, liberty, and the pursuit of happiness." These electrifying words leaped inward into America, and outward to the world.

In the new states democratic equality made many advances. It was subject, however, to a great limitation, in that it long really applied only to white males of European origin. It was more than a century before women received the vote. American Indians were few in number, but the black population at the time of the Revolution comprised about a fifth of the whole. It was much larger proportionately than it became later, after mass immigration from Europe raised the proportion of whites. Many American whites of the revolutionary generation were indeed troubled by the institution of slavery. It was abolished outright in Massachusetts, and all states north of Maryland took steps toward its gradual extinction. But to apply the principles of liberty and equality without regard to race was beyond the powers of Americans at the time. In the South, all censuses from 1790 to 1850 showed a third of the population to be slaves. In the North, free blacks found that in fact, and often in law, they were debarred from voting, from adequate schooling, and from the widening opportunities in which white Americans saw the essence of their national life and their superiority to Europe.

For the white majority the Revolution had a democratizing effect in many ways. Lawyers, landowners, and businessmen who led the movement against England needed the support of numbers and to obtain it were willing to make promises and concessions to the lower classes. Or the popular elements, workmen and mechanics, farmers and frontiersmen, often dissidents in religion, extorted concessions by force or threats. There was a good deal of violence, as in all revolutions; the new states confiscated property from the counterrevolutionaries, called Tories, some of whom were in addition tarred and feathered by infuriated mobs. The dissolution of the old colonial governments threw open all political questions. In some states more men became qualified to vote. In some, governors and senators were now popularly elected, in addition to the lower houses of the legislatures as in colonial times. The principle was adopted, still unknown to the parliamentary bodies of Europe, that each member of a legislative assembly should represent about the same number of citizens. Primogeniture and entail, which landed families aspiring to an aristocratic mode of life sometimes favored, went down before the demands of democrats and small property owners. Tithes were done away with, and the established churches, Anglican in the South, Congregationalist in New England, lost their privileged position in varying degree. But the Revolution was not socially as profound as the revolution soon to come in France, or as the revolution in Russia in 1917. Property changed hands, but the law of property was modified only in detail. There had been no such thing in British America as a native nobleman or even a bishop; clergy and aristocracy had been incomparably less ingrained in American than in European society, and the rebellion against them was less devastating in its effect.

The main import of the American Revolution remained political and even constitutional in a strict sense. The American leaders were themselves part of the Age of Enlightenment, sharing fully in its humane and secular spirit. But probably the only non-British thinker by whom they were influenced was Montesquieu, and Montesquieu owed his popularity to his philosophizing upon English institutions. The Americans drew heavily on the writings of John Locke, but their cast of mind went back before Locke to the English Puritan movement of the first half of the seventeenth century. Their thought was formed not only by Locke's ideas of human nature and government, but, as already noted, by the dissenting literature and the neo-republican writings that had never quite died out in England. The realities of life for five generations in America had sharpened the old insistence upon personal liberty and equality. When the dispute with Britain came to a head, the Americans found themselves arguing both for the historic and chartered rights of Englishmen and for the timeless and universal rights of man, both of which were held up as barriers against the inroads of parliamentary sovereignty. The Americans came to believe, more than any other people, that government should possess limited powers and operate only within the terms of a fixed and written constitutional document.

All thirteen of the new states lost no time in providing themselves with written constitutions (in Connecticut and Rhode Island merely the old charters reaffirmed), all of which enshrined virtually the same principles. All followed the thought stated in the great Declaration, that it was to protect "unalienable" rights that governments were instituted among men, and that whenever government became destructive to this end the people had a right to "institute new government" for their safety and happiness. All the constitutions undertook to limit government by a separation of governmental powers. All appended a bill of rights, stating the natural rights of the citizens and the things which no government might justly do. None of the constitutions were as yet fully democratic; even the most liberal gave some advantage in public affairs to the owners of property.

Federalism, or the allocation of power between central and outlying governments, went along with the idea of written constitutions as a principal offering of the Americans to the world. Like constitutionalism, federalism developed in the atmosphere of protest against a centralized sovereign power. It was a hard idea for Americans to work out, since the new states carried over the old separatism which had so distracted the British. Until 1789 the states remained banded together in the Articles of Confederation. The United States was a union of thirteen independent republics. Disadvantages in this scheme becoming apparent, a constitutional convention met at Philadelphia in 1787 and drew up the constitution which is today the world's oldest written instrument of government still in operation. In it the United States was conceived not merely as a league of states, but as a union in which individuals were citizens of the United States of America for some purposes and of their particular states for others. Persons, not states, composed the federal republic, and the laws of the United States fell not merely on the states but on the people.

The consequences of the American Revolution can hardly be overstated. By overburdening the French treasury the American war became a direct cause of the French Revolution. Beyond that, it ushered in the age of predominantly liberal or democratic revolution which lasted through the European revolutions of 1848. The American doctrine, like most thought in the Age of Enlightenment, was expressed in universal terms of "man" and "nature." All peoples regardless of their own history could apply it to themselves, because, as Alexander Hamilton once put it in his youth, "the sacred rights of man are not to be rummaged for among old parchments or musty records. They are written, as with a sunbeam, in the whole volume of human nature, by the hand of Divinity itself, and can never be erased or obscured by mortal power." The Americans, in freeing themselves, had done what all men ought to do.

The revolt in America offered a dramatic judgment on the old colonial system, convincing some, in England and elsewhere, that the empires for which they had long been struggling were hardly worth acquiring, since colonies in time, in the words of Turgot, fell away from the mother country "like ripe fruit." The idea spread, since trade between Britain and America continued to prosper, that one could do business with a country without exerting political influence or control, and this idea became fundamental to the coming movement of economic liberalism and free trade. By coincidence, the book that became the gospel of the free trade movement, Adam Smith's *Wealth of Nations*, was published in England in the year 1776. The American example was pointed to by other peoples wishing to throw off colonial status—first by the Latin Americans, then by the peoples of the older British dominions, and, finally, in the twentieth century, by those of Asia and Africa also. In Europe, the American example encouraged the type of nationalism in which subjugated nations aspire to be free. And at home the Revolution did much to determine the spirit and method by which the bulk of the North American continent was to be peopled and the attitudes for which the United States, when it became a leading power a century and a half later, was to stand before the world.

More immediately, the American example was not lost on the many Europeans who sojourned in the new states during and after the war. Of these the Marquis de Lafayette was the most famous, but there were many others: Thomas Paine, who returned to Europe in 1787; the future French revolutionist Brissot; the future Polish national leader Kosciusko; the future marshals of Napoleon, Jourdan and Berthier; the future reformer of the Prussian army Gneisenau. Contrariwise various Americans went to Europe, notably the aging Benjamin Franklin, who in the 1780s was incredibly lionized in the fashionable and literary world of Paris.

The establishment of the United States was taken in Europe to prove that many ideas of the Enlightenment were practicable. Rationalists declared that here was a people, free of past errors and superstitions, who showed how enlightened beings could plan their affairs. Rousseauists saw in America the very paradise of natural equality, unspoiled innocence, and patriotic virtue. But nothing so much impressed Europeans, and especially the French, as the spectacle of the Americans meeting in solemn conclave to draft their state constitutions. These, along with the Declaration of Independence, were translated and published in 1778 by a French nobleman, the Duke de la Rochefoucauld. They were endlessly and excitedly discussed. Constitutionalism, federalism, and limited government were not new ideas in Europe. They came out of the Middle Ages and were currently set forth in many quarters, for example, in Hungary, the Holy Roman Empire, and the Parlement of Paris. But in their prevailing form, and even in the philosophy of Montesquieu, they were associated with feudalism and aristocracy. The American Revolution made such ideas progressive. The American influence, added to the force of developments in Europe, made the thought of the later Enlightenment more democratic. The United States replaced England as the model country of advanced thinkers. On the Continent there was less passive trust in the enlightened despotism of the official state. Confidence in self-government was aroused.

The American constitutions seemed a demonstration of the social contract. They offered a picture of men in a "state of nature," having cast off their old government, deliberately sitting down to contrive a new one, weighing and judging each branch of government on its merits, assigning due powers to legislature, executive, and judiciary, declaring that all government was created by the people and in possession of a merely delegated authority, and listing specifically the inalienable rights of men—inalienable in that they could not conceivably be taken away, since men possessed them even if denied them by force. And these rights were the very same rights that many Europeans wanted secured for themselves—freedom of religion, freedom of press, freedom of assembly, freedom from arbitrary arrest at the discretion of officials. And they were the same for all, on the rigorous principle of equality before the law. The American example crystallized and made tangible the ideas that were strongly blowing in Europe, and the American example was one reason why the French, in 1789, began their revolution with a declaration of human rights and with the drafting of a written constitution.

And more deeply still, America became a kind of mirage or ideal vision for Europe, a land of open opportunity and of new beginnings, free from the load of history and of the past, wistfully addressed by Goethe:

> *America, thou hast it better*
> *Than has our Continent, the old one.*

It is evident that this was only part of the picture. The United States, as its later history was to show, bore a heavy load of inherited burdens and unsolved problems, especially racial. But in a general way, until new revolutionary movements set in a century later, America stood as a kind of utopia of the common man, not only for the millions who emigrated to it but for other millions who stayed at home, who often wished that their own countries might become more like it, and many of whom might even agree with Abraham Lincoln in calling it the last best hope of earth.

IX.
The French
Revolution

In 1789 France fell into revolution, and the world has never since been the same. The French Revolution was by far the most momentous upheaval of the whole revolutionary age. It replaced the "old regime" with "modern society," and at its extreme phase it became very radical, so much so that all later revolutionary movements have looked back to it as a predecessor to themselves. At the time, in the age of the Democratic or Atlantic Revolution from the 1760s to 1848, the role of France was decisive. Even the Americans, without French military intervention, would hardly have won such a clear settlement from England or been so free to set up the new states and new constitutions that have just been described. And while revolutionary disturbances in Ireland and Poland, or among the Dutch, Italians, and others, were by no means caused by the French example, it was the presence or absence of French aid that usually determined whatever successes they enjoyed.

The French Revolution, unlike the Russian or Chinese revolutions of the twentieth century, occurred in what was in many ways the most advanced country of the day. France was the center of the intellectual movement of the Enlightenment.

Chapter Emblem: A cockade worn during the French Revolution, with the famous motto, and the fleur-de-lis of the monarchy embellished by the cap of liberty.

French science then led the world. French books were read everywhere, and the newspapers and political journals which became very numerous after 1789 carried a message which hardly needed translation. French was a kind of international spoken language in the educated and aristocratic circles of many countries. France was also, potentially before 1789 and actually after 1793, the most powerful country in Europe. It may have been the wealthiest, though not per capita. With a population of some 24,000,000 the French were the most numerous of all European peoples under a single government. Even Russia was hardly more populous until after the partitions of Poland. The Germans were divided, the subjects of the Habsburgs were of diverse nationalities, and the English and Scots together numbered only 10,000,000. Paris, though smaller than London, was over twice as large as Vienna or Amsterdam. French exports to Europe were larger than those of Great Britain. It is said that half the goldpieces circulating in Europe were French. Europeans in the eighteenth century were in the habit of taking ideas from France; they were therefore, depending on their position, the more excited, encouraged, alarmed, or horrified when revolution broke out in that country.

41. BACKGROUNDS

The Old Regime: The Three Estates

Some remarks have already been made about the Old Regime, as the prerevolutionary society came to be called after it disappeared, and about the failure of enlightened despotism in France to make any fundamental alteration in it.[1] The essential fact about the Old Regime was that it was still legally aristocratic and in some ways feudal. Everyone belonged legally to an "estate" or "order" of society. The First Estate was the clergy, the Second Estate the nobility, and the Third Estate included everyone else—from the wealthiest business and professional classes to the poorest peasantry and city workers. These categories were important in that the individual's legal rights and personal prestige depended on the category to which he belonged. Politically, they were obsolescent; not since 1614 had the estates assembled in an Estates General of the whole kingdom, though in some provinces they had continued to meet as provincial bodies. Socially, they were obsolescent also, for the threefold division no longer corresponded to the real distribution of interest, influence, property, or productive activity among the French people.

Conditions in the church and the position of the clergy have been much exaggerated as a cause of the French Revolution. The church in France levied a tithe on all agricultural products, but so did the church in England; the French bishops often played a part in government affairs, but so did bishops in England through the House of Lords. The French bishoprics of 1789 were in reality no wealthier than those of the Church of England were found to be when investigated forty years later. In actual numbers, in the secular atmosphere of the Age of Enlightenment, the clergy, especially the monastic orders, had greatly declined, so that by 1789 there were probably not more than 100,000 Catholic clergy of all

---

[1] See pp. 315–318.

types in the entire population. But if the importance of the clergy has often been overemphasized, still it must be said that the church was deeply involved in the prevailing social system. For one thing, church bodies—bishoprics, abbeys, convents, schools, and other religious foundations—owned between 5 and 10 percent of the land of the country, which meant that collectively the church was the greatest of all landowners. Moreover, the income from church properties, like all income, was divided very unequally, and much of it found its way into the hands of the aristocratic occupants of the higher ecclesiastical offices.

The noble order, which in 1789 comprised about 400,000 persons, including women and children, had enjoyed a great resurgence since the death of Louis XIV in 1715.[2] Distinguished government service, higher church offices, army, parlements, and most other public and semipublic honors were almost monopolized by the titled aristocracy in the time of Louis XVI, who, it will be recalled, had mounted the throne in 1774. Repeatedly, through parlements, Provincial Estates, or the assembly of the clergy dominated by the noble bishops, the aristocracy had blocked royal plans for taxation and shown a desire to control the policies of state. At the same time the bourgeoisie, or upper crust of the Third Estate, had never been so influential. The fivefold increase of French foreign trade between 1713 and 1789 suggests the growth of the merchant class and of the legal and governmental classes associated with it. As members of the bourgeoisie became stronger, more widely read, and more self-confident, they resented the distinctions enjoyed by the nobles. Some of these were financial: nobles were exempt on principle from the most important direct tax, the taille, whereas bourgeois obtained exemption with more effort; but so many bourgeois enjoyed tax privileges that purely monetary self-interest was not primary in their psychology. The bourgeois resented the nobleman for his superiority and his arrogance. What had formerly been customary respect was now felt as humiliation. And they felt that they were being shut out from office and honors, and that the nobles were seeking more power in government as a class. The Revolution was the collision of two moving objects, a rising aristocracy and a rising bourgeoisie.

The common people, below the commercial and professional families in the Third Estate, were probably as well off as in most countries. But they were not well off compared with the upper classes. Wage earners had by no means shared in the wave of business prosperity. Between the 1730s and the 1780s the prices of consumers' goods rose about 65 percent, whereas wages rose only 22 percent. Persons dependent on wages were therefore badly pinched, but they were less numerous than today, for in the country there were many small farmers and in the towns many small craftsmen, both of which groups made a living not by wages but by selling the products of their own labor at market prices. Yet in both town and country there was a significant wage-earning or proletarian element, which was to play a decisive part in the Revolution.

The Agrarian System of the Old Regime

Over four-fifths of the people were rural. The agrarian system had developed so that there was no serfdom in France, to be sure, as it was known in eastern Europe.[3] The relation of lord and peasant in France was not the relation of mas-

[2] See pp. 256–257.
[3] See pp. 33–34, 122–123, 204–205.

ter and man. The peasant owed no labor to the lord—except a few token services in some cases. The peasant worked for himself, either on his own land or on rented land; or he worked as a sharecropper (*métayer*); or he hired himself out to the lord or to another peasant.

The manor, however, still retained certain surviving features of the feudal age. The noble owner of a manor enjoyed "hunting rights," or the privilege of keeping game preserves, and of hunting on his own and the peasants' land. He usually had a monopoly over the village mill, bakeshop, or wine press, for the use of which he collected fees, called *banalités*. He possessed certain vestigial powers of jurisdiction in the manorial court and certain local police powers, from which fees and fines were collected. These seigneurial privileges were of course the survivals of a day when the local manor had been a unit of government, and the noble had performed the functions of government, an age that had long passed with the development of the centralized modern state.

There was another special feature to the property system of the Old Regime. Every owner of a manor (there were some bourgeois and even wealthy peasants who had purchased manors) possessed what was called a right of "eminent property" with respect to all land located in the manorial village. This meant that lesser landowners within the manor "owned" their land in that they could freely buy, sell, lease, and bequeath or inherit it; but they owed to the owner of the manor, in recognition of his "eminent property" rights, certain rents, payable annually, as well as transfer fees that were payable whenever the land changed owners by sale or death. Subject to these "eminent property" rights, landownership was fairly widespread. Peasants directly owned about two-fifths of the soil of the country; bourgeois a little under a fifth. The nobility owned perhaps a little over a fifth, and the church somewhat under a tenth, the remainder being crown lands, wastelands, or commons. Finally, it must be noted that all property rights were subject also to certain "collective" rights, by which villagers might cut firewood or run their pigs in the commons, or pasture cattle on land belonging to other owners after the crops were in, there being usually no fences or enclosures.

All this may seem rather complex, but it is important to realize that property is a changing institution. Even today, in industrialized countries, a high proportion of all property is in land, including natural resources in and below the soil. In the eighteenth century property meant land even more than it does today. Even the bourgeois class, whose wealth was so largely in ships, merchandise, or commercial paper, invested heavily in land, and in France in 1789 enjoyed ownership of almost as much land as the nobility, and of more than the church. The Revolution was to revolutionize the law of property by freeing the private ownership of land from all the indirect encumbrances described—manorial fees, eminent property rights, communal village agricultural practices, and church tithes. It also was to abolish other older forms of property, such as property in public office or in masterships in the guilds, which had become useful mainly to closed and privileged groups. In final effect the Revolution established the institutions of private property in the modern sense and benefited, therefore, most especially the landowning peasants and the bourgeoisie.

The peasants not only owned two-fifths of the soil, but occupied almost all of it, working it on their own initiative and risk. That is to say, land owned by the nobility, the church, the bourgeoisie, and the crown was divided up and leased to peasants in small parcels. France was already a country of small farmers. There was no "big agriculture" as in England, eastern Europe, or the plantations of America. The manorial lord performed no economic function. He lived (there were of course exceptions) not by managing an estate and selling his own crops and cattle, but by receiving innumerable dues, quitrents, and fees. During the eighteenth century, in connection with the general aristocratic resurgence, there took place a phenomenon often called the "feudal reaction." Manorial lords, faced with rising living costs and acquiring higher living standards because of the general material progress, collected their dues more rigorously or revived old ones that had fallen into disuse. Leases and sharecropping arrangements also became less favorable to the peasants. The farmers, like the wage earners, were under a steadily increasing pressure. At the same time the peasants resented the "feudal dues" more than ever, because they regarded themselves as in many cases the real owners of the land and the lord as a gentleman of the neighborhood who for no reason enjoyed a special income and a status different from their own. The trouble was that much of the property system no longer bore any relation to real economic usefulness or activity.

The political unity of France, achieved over the centuries by the monarchy, was likewise a fundamental prerequisite, and even a cause, of the Revolution. Whatever social conditions might have existed, they could give rise to nationwide public opinion, nationwide agitation, nationwide policies, and nationwide legislation only in a country already politically unified as a nation. These conditions were lacking in central Europe. In France a French state existed. Reformers did not have to create it but only capture and remodel it. Frenchmen in the eighteenth century already had the sense of membership in a political entity called France. The Revolution saw a tremendous stirring of this sense of membership and of fraternity, turning it into a passion of citizenship, civic rights, voting powers, use and application of the state and its sovereignty for the public advantage. At the very outbreak of the Revolution people saluted each other as *citoyen* or *citoyenne* and shouted *vive la nation!*

42. THE REVOLUTION AND THE REORGANIZATION OF FRANCE

The Financial Crisis

The Revolution was precipitated by a financial collapse of the government. What overloaded the government was by no means the costly magnificence of the court of Versailles. Only 5 percent of public expenditures in 1788 was devoted to the upkeep of the entire royal establishment. What overloaded all governments was war costs, both current upkeep of armies and navies and the burden of public debt, which in all countries was due almost totally to the war costs of the past. In 1788 the French government devoted about a quarter of its annual expenditure to current maintenance of the armed forces and about a half to the payment of its debts. British expenditures showed almost the same distribution. The French debt stood at almost four billion livres. It had been greatly swollen by the War of American Independence. Yet it was only half as great as the national debt of Great Britain, and less than a fifth as heavy per capita. It was less than the debt of the Dutch Republic. It was apparently no greater than the debt left by Louis XIV three-quarters of a century before. At that time the debt had been lightened by repudiation. No responsible French official in the 1780s even considered repudiation, a sure sign of the progress in the interim of the well-to-do classes, who were the main government creditors.

Yet the debt could not be carried, for the simple reason that revenues fell short of necessary expenditures. This in turn was not due to national poverty, but to the tax exemptions and tax evasions of privileged elements, and to complications in the fiscal system, or lack of system, by which much of what taxpayers paid never came into the hands of the treasury. We have already described how the most important tax, the taille, was generally paid only by the peasants—the nobles being exempt by virtue of their class privilege, and office holders and bourgeois obtaining exemption in various ways.[4] The church too insisted that its property was not taxable by the state; and its periodic "free gift" to the king, though substantial, was less than might have been obtained from direct taxation of the church's land. Thus, although the country itself was prosperous, the government treasury was empty. The social classes which enjoyed most of the wealth of the country did not pay taxes corresponding to their income, and, even worse, they resisted taxation as a sign of inferior status.

A long series of responsible persons—Louis XIV himself, John Law, Maupeou, Turgot—had seen the need for taxing the privileged classes. Jacques Necker, a Swiss banker made director of the finances in 1777 by Louis XVI, made moves in the same direction, and, like his predecessors, was dismissed. His successor, Calonne, as the crisis mounted, came to even more revolutionary conclusions. In 1786 he produced a program in which enlightened despotism was tempered by a modest resort to representative institutions. He proposed, in place of the taille, a general tax to fall on all landowners without exemption, a lightening of indirect taxes and abolition of internal tariffs to stimulate economic production, a confiscation of some properties of the church, and the establishment, as a means of interesting the propertied elements in the government, of provincial assemblies in which all landowners, noble, clerical, bourgeois, and peasant, should be represented without regard to estate or order.

This program, if carried out, might have solved the fiscal problem and averted the Revolution. But it struck not only at privileges in taxation—noble, provincial, and others—but at the threefold hierarchic organization of society. Knowing from experience that the Parlement of Paris would never accept it, Calonne in 1787 convened an "assembly of notables," hoping to win its endorsement of his ideas. The notables insisted on concessions in return, for they wished to share in control of the government. A deadlock followed; the king dismissed Calonne and appointed as his successor Loménie de Brienne, the exceedingly worldly-wise archbishop of Toulouse. Brienne tried to push the same program through the Parlement of Paris. The Parlement rejected it, declaring that only the three estates of the realm, assembled in an Estates General, had authority to consent to new taxes. Brienne and Louis XVI at first refused, believing that the Estates General, if convened, would be dominated by the nobility. Like Maupeou and Louis XV, Brienne and Louis XVI tried to break the parlements, replacing them with a modernized judicial system in which the law courts should have no influence over policy. This led to a veritable revolt of the nobles. All the parlements and

Provincial Estates resisted, army officers refused to serve, the intendants hesitated to act, noblemen began to organize political clubs and committees of correspondence. With his government brought to a standstill, and unable to borrow money or collect taxes, Louis XVI on July 5, 1788, promised to call the Estates General for the following May. The various classes were invited to elect representatives and also to draw up lists of their grievances.

From Estates General to National Assembly

Since no Estates General had met in over a century and a half, the king asked all persons to study the subject and make proposals on how such an assembly should be organized under modern conditions. This led to an outburst of public discussion. Hundreds of political pamphlets appeared, many of them demanding that the old system by which the three estates sat in separate chambers, each chamber voting as a unit, be done away with, since under it the chamber of the Third Estate was always outnumbered. But in September 1788 the Parlement of Paris, restored to its functions, ruled that the Estates General should meet and vote as in 1614, in three separate orders.

The nobility, through the Parlement, thus revealed its aim. It had forced the summoning of the Estates General, and in this way the French nobility initiated the Revolution. The Revolution began as another victory in the aristocratic resurgence against the absolutism of the king. The nobles actually had a liberal program: they demanded constitutional government, guarantees of personal liberty for all, freedom of speech and press, freedom from arbitrary arrest and confinement. Many now were even prepared to give up special privileges in taxation; this might have worked itself out in time. But in return they hoped to become the preponderant political element in the state. It was their idea not merely to have the Estates General meet in 1789, but for France to be governed in all the future through the Estates General, a supreme body in three chambers, one for nobles, one for a clergy in which the higher officers were also nobles, and one for the Third Estate.

This was precisely what the Third Estate wished to avoid. Lawyers, bankers, businessmen, government creditors, shopkeepers, artisans, workingmen, and peasants had no desire to be governed by lords temporal and spiritual. Their hopes of a new era, formed by the philosophy of the Enlightenment, stirred by the revolution in America, rose to the utmost excitement when "good king Louis" called the Estates General. The ruling of the Parlement of Paris in September 1788 came to them as a slap in the face—an unprovoked class insult. The whole Third Estate turned on the nobility with detestation and distrust. The Abbé Sieyès in January 1789 launched his famous pamphlet, *What Is the Third Estate?*, declaring that the nobility was a useless caste which could be abolished without loss, that the Third Estate was the one necessary element of society, that it was identical with the nation, and that the nation was absolutely and unqualifiedly sovereign. Through Sieyès the ideas of Rousseau's *Social Contract* entered the thought of the Revolution. At the same time, even before the Estates General actually met, and not from the books of philosophes so much as from the actual events and conditions, nobles and commoners viewed each other with fear and suspicion. The Third Estate, which had at first supported the nobles against the "despotism" of the king's ministers, now ascribed to them the worst possible motives.

Class antagonism poisoned the Revolution at the outset, made peaceful reform impossible, and threw many bourgeois without delay into a radical and destructive mood. And the mutual suspicion between classes, produced by the Old Regime and inflamed by the Revolution, has troubled France ever since.

The Estates General met as planned in May 1789 at Versailles. The Third Estate, most of whose representatives were lawyers, boycotted the organization in three separate chambers. It insisted that deputies of all three orders should sit as a single house and vote as individuals; this procedure would be of advantage to the Third Estate, since the king had granted it as many deputies as the other two orders combined. For six weeks a deadlock was maintained. On June 13 a few priests, leaving the chamber of the First Estate, came over and sat with the Third. They were greeted with jubilation. On June 17 the Third Estate declared itself the "National Assembly." Louis XVI, under pressure from the nobles, closed the hall in which it met. The members found a neighboring indoor tennis court, and there, milling about in a babel of confusion and apprehension, swore and signed the Oath of the Tennis Court on June 20, 1789, affirming that wherever they foregathered the National Assembly was in existence, and that they would not disband until they had drafted a constitution. This was a revolutionary step, for it assumed virtually sovereign power for a body of men who had no legal authority. The king ordered members of the three estates to sit in their separate houses. He now somewhat tardily presented a reforming program of his own, too late to win the confidence of the disaffected, and in any case continuing the organization of French society in legal classes. The self-entitled National Assembly refused to back down. The king faltered, failed to enforce his commands promptly, and allowed the Assembly to remain in being. In the following days, at the end of June, he summoned about 18,000 soldiers to Versailles.

What had happened was that the king of France, in the dispute raging between nobles and commoners, chose the nobles. It was traditional in France for the king to oppose feudalism. For centuries the French monarchy had drawn strength from the bourgeoisie. All through the eighteenth century the royal ministers had carried on the struggle against the privileged interests. Only a year before, Louis XVI had been almost at war with his rebellious aristocracy. In 1789 he failed to assert himself. He lost control over the Estates General, exerted no leadership, offered no program until it was too late, and provided no symbol behind which parties could rally. He failed to make use of the profound loyalty to himself felt by the bourgeoisie and common people, who yearned for nothing so much as a king who would stand up for them, as in days of yore, against an aristocracy of birth and status. He tried instead, at first, to compromise and postpone a crisis; then he found himself in the position of having issued orders which the Third Estate boldly defied; and in this embarrassing predicament he yielded to his wife, Marie Antoinette, to his brothers, and to the court nobles with whom he lived, and who told him that his dignity and authority were outraged and undermined. At the end of June Louis XVI undoubtedly intended to dissolve the Estates General by military force. But what the Third Estate feared was not a return to the old theoretically absolute monarchy. It was a future in which the aristocracy should control the government of the country. There was now no going back; the revolt of the Third Estate had allied Louis XVI with the nobles, and the Third Estate now feared the nobles more than ever, believing with good reason that they now had the king in their hands.

The Lower Classes in Action

The country meanwhile was falling into dissolution. The lower classes, below the bourgeoisie, were out of hand. For them too the convocation of the Estates General had seemed to herald a new era. The grievances of ages, and those which existed equally in other countries than France, rose to the surface. Short-run conditions were bad. The harvest of 1788 had been poor; the price of bread, by July 1789, was higher than at any time since the death of Louis XIV. The year 1789 was also one of depression; the rapid growth of trade since the American war had suddenly halted, so that wages fell and unemployment spread while scarcity drove food prices up. The government, paralyzed at the center, could not take such measures of relief as were customary under the Old Regime. The masses were everywhere restless. Labor trouble broke out; in April a great riot of workingmen devastated a wallpaper factory in Paris. In the rural districts there was much disorder. Peasants declared that they would pay no more manorial dues and were likewise refusing taxes. In the best of times the countryside was troubled by vagrants, beggars, rough characters, and smugglers who flourished along the many tariff frontiers. Now the business depression reduced the income of honest peasants who engaged in weaving or other domestic industries in their homes; unemployment and indigence spread in the country; people were uprooted; and the result was to raise the number of vagrants to terrifying proportions. It was believed, since nothing was too bad to believe of the aristocrats (though it was not true), that they were secretly recruiting these "brigands" for their own purposes to intimidate the Third Estate. The economic and social crises thus became acutely political.

The towns were afraid of being swamped by beggars and desperadoes. This was true even of Paris, the largest city in Europe except London. The Parisians were also alarmed by the concentration of troops about Versailles. They began to arm in self-defense. All classes of the Third Estate took part. The banker Laborde, whose career was noted in an earlier chapter,[5] and whose son sat in the Assembly at Versailles, was one of many to provide funds. Crowds began to look for weapons in arsenals and public buildings. On July 14 they came to the Bastille, a stronghold built in the Middle Ages to overawe the city, like the Tower of London in England. It was used as a place of detention for persons with enough influence to escape the common jails but was otherwise in normal times considered harmless; in fact there had been talk, some years before, of tearing it down to make room for a public park. Now, in the general turbulence, the governor had placed cannon in the embrasures. The crowd requested him to remove his cannon and to furnish them with arms. He refused. Through a series of misunderstandings, reinforced by the vehemence of a few firebrands, the crowd turned into a mob, which assaulted the fortress, and which, when helped by a handful of trained soldiers and five artillery pieces, persuaded the governor to surrender. The mob, enraged by the death of ninety-eight of its members, streamed in and murdered six soldiers of the garrison in cold blood. The governor was murdered while under escort to the Town Hall. The mayor of Paris met the same fate. Their heads were cut off with knives, stuck on the ends of pikes, and paraded about the city. While all this happened the regular army units on the outskirts of Paris did not stir, their reliability being open to question, and the authorities being in any case unaccustomed to firing on the people.

[5] See pp. 254–255.

The capture of the Bastille, though not so intended, had the effect of saving the Assembly at Versailles. The king, not knowing what to do, accepted the new situation in Paris. He recognized a citizens' committee, which had formed there, as the new municipal government. He sent away the troops that he had summoned and commanded the recalcitrants among nobles and clergy to join in the National Assembly. In Paris and other cities a bourgeois or national guard was established to keep order. The Marquis de Lafayette, "the hero of two worlds," received command over the guard in Paris. For insignia he combined the colors of the city of Paris, red and blue, with the white of the house of Bourbon. The French tricolor, emblem of the Revolution, thus originated in a fusion of old and new.

In the rural districts matters went from bad to worse. Vague insecurity rose to the proportions of panic in the Great Fear of 1789, which spread over the country late in July in the wake of travelers, postal couriers, and others. The cry was relayed from point to point that "the brigands were coming," and peasants, armed to protect their homes and crops and gathered together and working upon each other's feelings, often turned their attention to the manor houses, burning them in some cases, and in others simply destroying the manorial archives in which fees and dues were recorded. The Great Fear became part of a general agrarian insurrection, in which peasants, far from being motivated by wild alarms, knew perfectly well what they were doing. They intended to destroy the manorial regime by force.

The Initial Reforms of the National Assembly

The Assembly at Versailles could restore order only by meeting the demands of the peasants. To wipe out all manorial payments would deprive the landed aristocracy of much of its income. Many bourgeois also owned manors. There was therefore much perplexity. A small group of deputies prepared a surprise move in the Assembly, choosing an evening session from which many would be absent. Hence came the "night of August 4." A few liberal noblemen, by prearrangement, arose and surrendered their hunting rights, their *banalités*, their rights in manorial courts, and feudal and seigneurial privileges generally. What was left of serfdom and all personal servitudes was declared ended. Tithes were abolished. Other deputies repudiated the special privileges of their provinces. All personal tax privileges were given up. On the main matter, the dues arising from "eminent property" in the manors, a compromise was adopted. These dues were all abolished, but compensation was to be paid by the peasants to the former owners. The compensation was in most cases never paid. Eventually, in 1793, in the radical phase of the Revolution, the provision for compensation was repealed. In the end French peasant landowners rid themselves of their manorial obligations without cost to themselves. This was in contrast to what later happened in most other countries, where the peasants, when in turn liberated from manorial obligations, either lost part of their land or were burdened with installment payments lasting many years.

In a decree summarizing the resolutions of August 4 the Assembly declared flatly that "feudalism is abolished." With legal privilege replaced by legal equality, it proceeded to map the principles of the new order. On August 26, 1789, it issued the Declaration of the Rights of Man and Citizen.

The Declaration of 1789 was meant to affirm the principles of the new state, which were essentially the rule of law, equal individual citizenship, and collective sovereignty of the people. "Men are born and remain," declared Article I, "free and equal in rights." Man's natural rights were held to be "liberty, property, security, and resistance to oppression." Freedom of thought and religion were guaranteed; no one might be arrested or punished except by process of law; all persons were declared eligible for any public office for which they met the requirements. Liberty was defined as the freedom to do anything not injurious to others, which in turn was to be determined only by law. Law must fall equally upon all persons. Law was the expression of the general will, to be made by all citizens or their representatives. The only sovereign was the nation itself, and all public officials and armed forces acted only in its name. Taxes might be raised only by common consent, all public servants were accountable for their conduct in office, and the powers of government should be separated among different branches. Finally, the state might for public purposes, and under law, confiscate the property of private persons, but only with fair compensation. The Declaration, printed in thousands of leaflets, pamphlets, and books, read aloud in public places, or framed and hung on walls, became the catechism of the Revolution in France. When translated into other languages it soon carried the same message to all of Europe. Thomas Paine's book, *The Rights of Man*, published in 1791 to defend the French Revolution, gave the phrase a powerful impact in English.

The "rights of man" had become a motto or watchword for potentially revolutionary ideas well before 1789. The thinkers of the Enlightenment had used it, and during the American Revolution even Alexander Hamilton had spoken of "the sacred rights of man" with enthusiasm.[6] "Man" in this sense was meant to apply abstractly, regardless of nationality, race, or sex. In French as in English, then as now, the word "man" was used to designate all human beings, and the Declaration of 1789 was not intended to refer to males alone. In German, for example, where a distinction is made between *Mensch* as a human being and *Mann* as an adult male, the "rights of man" was always translated as *Menschenrechte*. Similarly the word "citizen" in its general sense applied to women, as is shown by the frequency of the feminine *citoyenne* during the Revolution, in which a great many women were very active. But when it came to the exercise of particular legal rights the Revolutionaries went no farther than contemporary opinion. Thus they assigned the right to vote and hold office only to men, and in matters of property, family law, and education it was the boys and men who had the advantages. Very few at the time argued for legal equality between the sexes.

One of them, however, was Olympe de Gouges, a woman of some prominence as a writer for the theater, who in 1791 published *The Rights of Woman*. Following the official Declaration in each of its seventeen articles, she applied them to women explicitly in each case, and she asserted also, in addition, the right of women to divorce under certain conditions, to the control of property in marriage, and for equal access with men to higher education and to civilian careers and public employments. Mary Wollstonecraft in England published a similar *Vindication of the Rights of Woman* in 1792. In France some of the secondary figures in the Revolution, and some of the teachers in boys' schools, thought that women should have greater opportunities at least in education. Among the leaders, only Condorcet argued for legal equality of the sexes. Intent on political change, the Revolutionaries thought that politics, government, law, and war

[6] See p. 347.

were a masculine business, for which only boys and young men needed to be educated or prepared.

Shortly after adoption of the Declaration of the Rights of Man the Revolutionary leadership fell apart. In September 1789 the Assembly began the actual planning of the new government. Some wanted a strong veto power for the king and a legislative body in two houses, as in England. Others, the "patriots," wanted only a delaying veto for the king and a legislative body of one chamber. Here again, it was suspicion of the aristocracy that proved decisive. The "patriots" were afraid that an upper chamber would bring back the nobility as a collective force, and they were afraid to make the king constitutionally strong by giving him a full veto, because they believed him to be in sympathy with the nobles. He was, at the moment, hesitating to accept both the August 4th decrees and the Declaration of Rights. His brother, the Count of Artois, followed by many aristocrats, had already emigrated to foreign parts and, along with these other émigrés, was preparing to agitate against the Revolution with all the governments of Europe. The patriot party would concede nothing, the more conservative party could gain nothing. The debate was interrupted again, as in July, by insurrection and violence. On October 4, a crowd of market women and revolutionary militants, followed by the Paris national guard, took the road from Paris to Versailles. Besieging and invading the château, they obliged Louis XVI to take up his residence in Paris, where he could be watched. The National Assembly also shifted itself to Paris, where it too soon fell under the influence of radical elements in the city. The champions of a one-chamber legislative body and of a suspensive veto for the king won out.

The more conservative revolutionaries, if such they may be called, disillusioned in seeing constitutional questions settled by mobs, began to drop out of the Assembly. Men who on June 20 had bravely sworn the Oath of the Tennis Court now felt that the Revolution was falling into unworthy hands. Some even emigrated, forming a second wave of émigrés that would have nothing to do with the first. So the counterrevolution gathered strength.

But those who wanted still to go forward, and they were many, began to organize in clubs. Most important of all was the Society of Friends of the Constitution, called the Jacobin club for short, since it met in an old Jacobin monastery in Paris. The dues were at first so high that only substantial bourgeois belonged; they were later lowered but never enough to include persons of the poorest classes, who therefore formed lesser clubs of their own. The most advanced members of the Assembly were Jacobins and used the club as a caucus in which to discuss their policies and lay their plans. They remained a middle-class group even during the later and more radical phase of the Revolution. Mme. Rosalie Jullien, for example, who was as excited a revolutionary as her husband and son, attended a meeting of the Paris Jacobin club on August 5, 1792. Tell your friends in the provinces, she wrote to her husband, that these Jacobins are "the flower of the Paris bourgeoisie, to judge by the fancy jackets they wear. There were also two or three hundred women present, dressed as if for the theater, who made an impression by their proud attitude and forceful speech."

Constitutional Changes

In the two years from October 1789 to September 1791 the National Assembly (or the Constituent Assembly, as it had come to be called because it was preparing a constitution) continued its work of simultaneously governing the country, devising a written constitution, and destroying in detail the institutions of the Old Regime. The old ministries, the old organization of government bureaus, the old taxes, the old property in office, the old titles of nobility, the old parlements, the hundreds of regional systems of law, the old internal tariffs, the old provinces, and the old urban municipalities—all went into the discard. Contemporaries, like Edmund Burke, were appalled at the thoroughness with which Frenchmen seemed determined to eradicate their national institutions. Why, asked Burke, should the French fanatics cut to pieces the living body of Normandy or Provence? The truth is that the provinces, like everything else, were impacted in the whole system of special privilege and unequal rights. All had to disappear if the hope of equal citizenship under national sovereignty was to be attained. In place of the provinces the Constituent divided France into eighty-three equal "departments." In place of the old towns, with their quaint old magistrates, it introduced a uniform municipal organization, all towns henceforth having the same form of government, varying only according to size. All local officials, even prosecuting attorneys and tax collectors, were elected locally. Administratively the country was decentralized in reaction against the bureaucracy of the Old Regime. No one outside Paris now really acted for the central government, and local communities enforced the national legislation, or declined to enforce it, as they chose. This proved ruinous when the war came, and although the "departments" created by the Constituent Assembly still exist, it was long traditional in France after the Revolution, as it was before, to keep local officials under strong control by ministers in Paris.

Under the constitution that was prepared, sometimes called the Constitution of 1791 because it went into effect at that date, the sovereign power of the nation was to be exercised by a unicameral elected assembly, called the Legislative Assembly. The king was given only a suspensive veto power by which legislation desired by the Assembly could be postponed. In general, the executive branch, i.e., king and ministers, was kept weak, partly in reaction against "ministerial despotism," partly from a well-founded distrust of Louis XVI. In July 1791 Louis attempted, in the "flight to Varennes," to escape from the kingdom, join with émigré noblemen, and seek help from foreign powers. He left behind him a written message in which he explicitly repudiated the Revolution. Arrested at Varennes in Lorraine, he was brought back to Paris and forced to accept his status as a constitutional monarch. The attitude of Louis XVI greatly disoriented the Revolution, for it made impossible the creation of a strong executive power and left the country to be ruled by a debating society which under revolutionary conditions contained more than the usual number of hotheads.

Not all this machinery of state was democratic. In the granting of political rights the abstract principles of the great Declaration were seriously modified for practical reasons. Since most people were illiterate it was thought that they could have no reasonable political views. Since the small man was often a domestic servant or shop assistant, it was thought that in politics he would be a mere dependent of his employer. The Constituent therefore distinguished in the new constitution between "active" and "passive" citizens. Both had the same civil rights, but only active citizens had the right to vote. These active citizens chose "electors," on the basis of one elector for every hundred active citizens. The electors convened in the chief town of their new "department," and there chose deputies to the national legislature as well as certain local officials. Males over twenty-five years of age, and well enough off to pay a small direct tax, qualified as "active" citizens; well over half the adult male population could so qualify. Of these, men paying a somewhat higher tax qualified as "electors"; even so, almost half the adult males qualified for this role. In practice, what limited the number of available electors was that, to function as such, a man had to have enough education, interest, and leisure to attend an electoral assembly, at a distance from home, and remain in attendance for several days. In any case, only about 50,000 persons served as electors in 1790–1791 because a proportion of one for every hundred active citizens yielded that figure.

Economic Policies

Economic policies favored the middle rather than the lowest classes. The public debt had precipitated the Revolution, but the revolutionary leaders, even the most extreme Jacobins, never disowned the debt of the Old Regime. The reason is that the bourgeois class, on the whole, were the people to whom the money was owed. To secure the debt, and to pay current expenses of government, since tax collections had become very sporadic, the Constituent Assembly as early as November 1789 resorted to a device by no means new in Europe, though never before used on so extensive a scale. It confiscated all the property of the church. Against this property, it issued negotiable instruments called assignats, first regarded as bonds and issued only in large denominations, later regarded as currency and issued in small bills. Holders of assignats could use them, or any money, to buy parcels of the former church lands. None of the confiscated land was given away; all was in fact sold, since the interest of the government was fiscal rather than social. The peasants, even when they had the money, could not easily buy land because the lands were sold at distant auctions or in large undivided blocks. The peasants were disgruntled, though they did acquire a good deal of the former church lands through middlemen. Peasant landowners were likewise expected, until 1793, to pay compensation for their old quitrents and many other manorial fees. And the landless peasants were aroused when the government, with its modern ideas, encouraged the dividing up of the village commons and extinction of various collective village rights, in the interest of individual private property.

The revolutionary leadership favored free economic individualism. It had had enough, under the Old Regime, of government regulation over the sale or quality of goods and of privileged companies and other economic monopolies. Reforming economic thought at the time, not only in France but in England, where Adam Smith had published his epoch-making *Wealth of Nations* in 1776, held that organized special interests were bad for society, and that all prices and wages should be determined by free arrangement between the individuals concerned.[7] The more prominent leaders of the French Revolution believed firmly in this freedom from control. The Constituent Assembly abolished the guilds, which were mainly monopolistic organizations of small businessmen or master craftsmen, interested in keeping up prices and averse to new machinery or new methods. There was also, in France, a rather highly organized labor movement. Since the masterships in the guilds were practically hereditary (as a form of property and privilege), the journeymen formed their own associations, or trade unions, called

[7] See pp. 312–313.

compagnonnages, outside the guilds. Many trades were so organized—the carpenters, plasterers, paper workers, hatters, saddlers, cutlers, nail makers, carters, tanners, locksmiths, and glassworkers. Some were organized nationally, some only locally. All these journeymen's unions had been illegal under the Old Regime, but they had flourished nevertheless. They collected dues and maintained officers. They often dealt collectively with the guild masters or other employers, requiring the payment of a stipulated wage or amendment of working conditions. Sometimes they even imposed closed shops. Organized strikes were quite common. The labor troubles of 1789 continued on into the Revolution. Business fell off in the atmosphere of disorder. In 1791 there was another wave of strikes. The Assembly, in the Le Chapelier law of that year, renewed the old prohibitions of the *compagnonnages*. The same law restated the abolition of the guilds and forbade the organization of special economic interests of any kind. All trades, it declared, were free for all to enter. All men, without belonging to any organization, had the right to work at any occupation or business they might choose. All wages were to be settled privately by the workman and his employer. This was not at all what the workingman, at that time or any other, really wanted. Nevertheless the provisions of the Le Chapelier law remained a part of French law for three-quarters of a century. The embryonic trade unions continued to exist secretly, though with more difficulty than under the hit-and-miss law enforcement of the Old Regime.

The Quarrel with the Church

Most fatefully of all, the Constituent Assembly quarreled with the Catholic church. The confiscation of church properties naturally came as a shock to the clergy. The village priests, whose support had made possible the revolt of the Third Estate, now found that the very buildings in which they worshiped with their parishioners on Sunday belonged to the "nation." The loss of income-producing properties undercut the religious orders and ruined the schools, in which thousands of boys had received free education before the Revolution. Yet it was not on the question of material wealth that the church and the Revolution came to blows. Members of the Constituent Assembly took the view of the church that the great monarchies had taken before them. The idea of separation of church and state was far from their minds. They regarded the church as a form of public authority and as such subordinate to the sovereign power. They frankly argued that the poor needed religion if they were to respect the property of the more wealthy. In any case, having deprived the church of its own income, they had to provide for its maintenance. For the schools many generous and democratic projects of state-sponsored education were drawn up, though under the troubled conditions of the time little was accomplished. For the clergy the new program was mapped out in the Civil Constitution of the Clergy of 1790.

This document went far toward setting up a French national church. Under its provisions the parish priests and bishops were elected, the latter by the same 50,000 electors who chose other important officials. Protestants, Jews, and agnostics could legally take part in the elections, purely on the ground of citizenship and property qualifications. Archbishoprics were abolished, and all the borders of existing bishoprics were redrawn. The number of dioceses was reduced from over 130 to 83, so that one would be coterminous with each department. Bishops were allowed merely to notify the pope of their elevation; they were forbidden to acknowledge any papal authority on their assumption of office, and no papal letter or decree was to be published or enforced in France except with government permission. All clergy received salaries from the state, the average income of bishops being somewhat reduced, that of parish clergymen being raised. Sinecures, plural holdings, and other abuses by which noble families had been supported by the church were done away with. The Constituent Assembly (independently of the Civil Constitution) also prohibited the taking of religious vows and dissolved all monastic houses.

Some of all this was not in principle alarmingly new, since before the Revolution the civil authority of the king had designated the French bishops and passed on the admission of papal documents into France. French bishops, in the old spirit of the "Gallican liberties," were traditionally jealous of papal power in France.[8] Many were now willing to accept something like the Civil Constitution if allowed to produce it on their own authority. The Assembly refused to concede so much jurisdiction to the Gallican church and applied instead to the pope, hoping to force its plans upon the French clergy by invoking the authority of the Vatican. But the Vatican pronounced the Civil Constitution a wanton usurpation of power over the Catholic church. Unfortunately, the pope also went further, condemning the whole Revolution and all its works. The Constituent Assembly retorted by requiring all French clergy to swear an oath of loyalty to the constitution, including the Civil Constitution of the Clergy. Half took the oath and half refused it, the latter half including all but seven of the bishops. One of the seven willing to accept the new arrangements was Talleyrand, soon to be famous as foreign minister of numerous French governments.

There were now two churches in France, one clandestine, the other official, one maintained by voluntary offerings or by funds smuggled in from abroad, the other financed and sponsored by the government. The former, comprising the nonjuring, unsworn or "refractory" clergy, turned violently counterrevolutionary. To protect themselves from the Revolution they insisted, with an emphasis quite new in France, on the universal religious supremacy of the Roman pontiff. They denounced the "constitutional" clergy as schismatics who spurned the pope and as mere careerists willing to hold jobs on the government's terms. The constitutional clergy, those taking the oath and upholding the Civil Constitution, considered themselves to be patriots and defenders of the rights of man; and they insisted that the Gallican church had always enjoyed a degree of liberty from Rome. The Catholic laity were terrified and puzzled. Many were sufficiently attached to the Revolution to prefer the constitutional clergy; but to do so meant to defy the pope, and Catholics who persisted in defying the pope were on the whole those least zealous in their religion. The constitutional clergy therefore stood on shaky foundations. Many of their followers, under stress of the times, eventually turned against Christianity itself.

Good Catholics tended to favor the "refractory" clergy. The outstanding example was the king himself. He personally used the services of refractory priests, and thus gave a new reason for the revolutionaries to distrust him. Whatever chance there was that Louis XVI might go along with the Revolution was exploded, for he concluded that he could do so only by endangering his immortal soul. Former

8 See pp. 52, 69, 86–87, 132, 184.

aristocrats also naturally preferred the refractory clergy. They now put aside the Voltairean levities of the Age of Enlightenment, and the "best people" began to exhibit a new piety in religious matters. The peasants, who found little in the Revolution to interest them after their own insurrection of 1789 and the consequent abolition of the manorial regime, also favored the old-fashioned or refractory clergy. Much the same was true of the urban working-class families, where both men and women might shout against priests and yet want to be sure that their marriages were valid and their children properly baptized. The Constituent Assembly, and its successors, were at their wits' end what to do. Sometimes they shut their eyes at the intrigues of refractory clergy; the constitutional clergy then became fearful. Sometimes they hunted out and persecuted the refractories; in that case they only stirred up religious fanaticism.

The Civil Constitution of the Clergy has been called the greatest tactical blunder of the Revolution. Certainly its consequences were unfortunate in the extreme, and they spread to much of Europe. In the nineteenth century the church was to be officially antidemocratic and antiliberal;[9] and democrats and liberals in most cases were to be violently and outspokenly anticlerical. The main beneficiary was the papacy. The French church, which had clung for ages to its Gallican liberties, was thrown by the Revolution into the arms of the pope. Even Napoleon, when he healed the schism a decade later, acknowledged powers in the papacy that had never been acknowledged by the French kings. These were steps in the process, leading through the proclamation of papal infallibility in 1870,[10] by which the affairs of the modern Catholic church became increasingly centralized at the Vatican.

With the proclamation of the constitution in September 1791, the Constituent Assembly disbanded. Before dissolving, it ruled that none of its members might sit in the forthcoming Legislative Assembly. This body was therefore made up of men who still wished to make their mark in the Revolution. The new regime went into effect in October 1791. It was a constitutional monarchy in which a unicameral Legislative Assembly confronted a king unconverted to the new order. Designed as the permanent solution to France's problems, it was to collapse in ten months, in August 1792, as a result of popular insurrection four months after France became involved in war. A group of Jacobins, known as Girondins, for a time became the left or advanced party of the Revolution and in the Legislative Assembly led France into war.

43. THE REVOLUTION AND EUROPE: THE WAR AND THE "SECOND" REVOLUTION, 1792

The International Impact of the Revolution

The European governments were long reluctant to become involved with France. They were under considerable pressure. On the one hand, pro-French and pro-revolutionary groups appeared immediately in many quarters. The doctrines of the French Revolution, as of the American, were highly exportable: they took the form of a universal philosophy, proclaiming the rights of man regardless of time

[9] See pp. 482–483, 598–600.
[10] See p. 600.

or place, race or nation. Moreover, depending on what one was looking for, one might see in the first disturbances in France a revolt of either the nobility, the bourgeoisie, the common people, or the entire nation. In Poland those who were trying to reorganize the country against further partition hailed the French example. The Hungarian landlords pointed to it in their reaction against Joseph II. In England, for a time, those who controlled Parliament complacently believed that the French were attempting to imitate them.

But it was the excluded classes of European society who were most inspired. The hard-pressed Silesian weavers were said to hope that "the French would come." Strikes broke out at Hamburg, and peasants rebelled elsewhere. One English diplomat found that even the Prussian army had "a strong taint of democracy among officers and men." In Belgium, where the privileged elements were already in revolt against the Austrian emperor, a second revolt broke out, inspired by events in France and aimed at the privileged elements. In England the newly developing "radicals," men like Thomas Paine and Dr. Richard Price, who wished a thorough overhauling of Parliament and the established church, entered into correspondence with the Assembly in Paris. Businessmen of importance, including Watt and Boulton, the pioneers of the steam engine, were likewise pro-French since they had no representation in the House of Commons. The Irish too were excited and presently revolted. Everywhere the young were aroused, the young Hegel in Germany, or in England the young Wordsworth, who later recalled the sense of a new era that had captivated so many spirits in 1789:

> Bliss was it in that dawn to be alive,
> But to be young was very heaven!

On the other hand the anti-Revolutionary movement gathered strength. Edmund Burke, frightened by the French proclivities of English radicals, published as early as 1790 his *Reflections on the Revolution in France*. For France, he predicted anarchy and dictatorship. For England, he sternly advised the English to accept a slow adaptation of their own English liberties. For all the world, he denounced a political philosophy that rested on abstract principles of right and wrong, declaring that every people must be shaped by its own national circumstances, national history, and national character. He drew an eloquent reply and a defense of France from Thomas Paine in the *Rights of Man*. Burke soon began to preach the necessity of war, urging a kind of ideological struggle against French barbarism and violence. His *Reflections* was translated and widely read. In the long run his book proved an influential work in the history of thought. In the short run it fell on willing ears. The king of Sweden, Gustavus III, offered to lead a monarchist crusade. In Russia old Catherine was appalled; she forbade further translations of her erstwhile friend Voltaire, she called the French "vile riffraff" and "brutish cannibals," and she packed off to Siberia a Russian named Radishchev, who in his *Voyage from St. Petersburg to Moscow* pointed out the evils of serfdom. It is said that Russians were even forbidden to speak of the "revolutions of the heavenly spheres." The terrors were heightened by plaintive messages from Louis XVI and Marie Antoinette, and by the émigrés who kept bursting out of France, led as early as July 1789 by the king's own brother, the Count of Artois. The émigrés, who at first were nobles, settled in various parts of Europe and began using their international aristocratic connections. They preached a kind of holy war. They bemoaned the sad plight of the king, but what they most wanted was to get back their manorial incomes and other rights. They hinted that Louis XVI himself was a dangerous revolutionary and much preferred his brother, the unyielding Count of Artois.

In short, Europe was soon split by a division that overran all frontiers. The same was true of America also. In the United States the rising party of Jefferson was branded as Jacobin and pro-French, that of Hamilton as reactionary and pro-British; while in colonial Spanish America ideas of independence were strengthened, and the Venezuelan Miranda became a general in the French army. In all countries of the European world, though least of all in eastern and southern Europe, there were revolutionary or pro-French elements that were feared by their own governments. In all countries, including France, there were implacable enemies of the French Revolution. In all countries were people whose loyalties lay abroad. There had been no such situation since the Protestant Reformation, nor was there anything like it again until after the Russian Revolution of the twentieth century.

The Coming of the War, April 1792

Yet the European governments were slow to move. Catherine had no intention of becoming involved in western Europe. She only wished to involve her neighbors. William Pitt, the British prime minister, resisted the war cries of Burke. Son of the Earl of Chatham, prime minister since 1784, chief founder of the new Tory party, Pitt had a reforming program of his own; he had tried and failed to carry a reform of Parliament and was now concentrating on a policy of orderly finance and systematic economy. His program would be ruined by war. He insisted that the domestic affairs of France were of no concern to the British government. The key position was occupied by the Habsburg emperor, Leopold II, brother to the French queen. Leopold at first answered Marie Antoinette's pleas for help by telling her to adjust herself to conditions in France. He resisted the furious demands of the émigrés, whom he understood perfectly, having inherited from Joseph II a fractious aristocracy himself.

Still, the new French government was a disturbing phenomenon. It openly encouraged malcontents all over Europe. It showed a tendency to settle international affairs by unilateral action. For example, it annexed Avignon at the request of local revolutionaries but without the consent of its historic sovereign, the pope. Or again, in Alsace there had been much overlapping jurisdiction between France and Germany ever since the Peace of Westphalia.[11] The Constituent Assembly abolished feudalism and manorial dues in Alsace as elsewhere in France. To German princes who had feudal rights in Alsace the Assembly offered compensation, but it did not ask their consent; and the German princes concerned, deprived by a revolutionary decree of rights guaranteed them by past treaties, appealed to the Holy Roman Emperor to protest the infringement of international understandings. Moreover, after the arrest of Louis XVI at Varennes, after his attempted flight in June 1791, it became impossible to deny that the French king and queen were prisoners of the revolutionaries.

In August Leopold met with the king of Prussia at Pillnitz in Saxony. The

[11] See maps, pp. 142–143, 183, 317.

resulting Declaration of Pillnitz rested on a famous *if:* Leopold would take military steps to restore order in France if all the other powers would join him. Knowing the attitude of Pitt, he believed that the *if* could never materialize. His aim was mainly to rid himself of the French émigrés. These perversely received the Declaration with delight. They used it as an open threat to their enemies in France, announcing that they would soon return alongside the forces of civilized Europe to punish the guilty and right the wrongs that had been done to them.

In France the upholders of the Revolution were alarmed. They were ignorant of what Leopold really meant and took the dire menaces of the émigrés at their face value. The Declaration of Pillnitz, far from cowing the French, enraged them against all the crowned heads of Europe. It gave a political advantage to the then dominant faction of Jacobins, known to history as the Girondins. These included the philosophe Condorcet, the humanitarian lawyer Brissot, and the civil servant Roland and his more famous wife, Mme. Roland, whose house became a kind of headquarters of the group. They attracted many foreigners also, such as Thomas Paine and the German Anacharsis Cloots, the "representative of the human race." In December 1791 a deputation of English radicals, led by James Watt, son of the inventor of the steam engine, received a wild ovation at the Paris Jacobin club.

The Girondins became the party of international revolution. They declared that the Revolution could never be secure in France until it spread to the world. In their view, once war had come, the peoples of states at war with France would not support their own governments. There was reason for this belief, since revolutionary elements antedating the French Revolution already existed in both the Dutch and the Austrian Netherlands, and to a lesser degree in parts of Switzerland, Poland, and elsewhere. Some Girondins therefore contemplated a war in which French armies should enter neighboring countries, unite with local revolutionaries, overthrow the established governments, and set up a federation of republics. War was also favored by a very different group, led by Lafayette, which wished to curb the Revolution by holding it at the line of constitutional monarchy. This group mistakenly believed that war might restore the much damaged popularity of Louis XVI, unite the country under the new government, and make it possible to put down the continuing Jacobin agitation. As the war spirit boiled up in France, the Emperor Leopold II died. He was succeeded by Francis II, a man much more inclined than Leopold to yield to the clamors of the old aristocracy. Francis resumed negotiations with Prussia. In France all who dreaded a return of the Old Regime listened more readily to the Girondins. Among the Jacobins as a whole, only a few, generally a handful of radical democrats, opposed the war. On April 20, 1792, without serious opposition, the Assembly declared war on "the king of Hungary and Bohemia," i.e., the Austrian monarchy.

The "Second" Revolution: August 10, 1792

The war intensified the existing unrest and dissatisfaction of the unpropertied classes. Both peasants and urban workers felt that the Constituent and the Legislative Assembly had served the propertied interests and had done little for them. Peasants were dissatisfied at the inadequate measures taken to facilitate land distribution; workers felt especially the pinch of soaring prices, which by 1792 had greatly risen. Gold had been taken out of the country by the émigrés; paper money, the assignats, was almost the sole currency, and the future of the government was so uncertain that it steadily lost value. Peasants concealed their food products rather than sell them for depreciating paper. Actual scarcity combined with the falling value of money to drive up the cost of living. The lowest income groups suffered the most. But dissatisfied though they were, when the war began they were threatened with a return of the émigrés and a vindictive restoration of the Old Regime, which at least for the peasants would be the worst of all possible eventualities. The working classes—peasants, artisans, mechanics, shopkeepers, wage workers—rallied to the Revolution but not to the revolutionary government in power. The Legislative Assembly and the constitutional monarchy lacked the confidence of large elements of the population.

In addition, the war at first went very unfavorably for the French. Prussia joined immediately with Austria, and by the summer of 1792 the two powers were on the point of invading France. They issued a proclamation to the French people, the Brunswick Manifesto of July 25, declaring that if any harm befell the French king and queen the Austro-Prussian forces, upon their arrival in Paris, would exact the most severe retribution from the inhabitants of that city. Such menaces, compounding the military emergency, only played into the hands of the most violent activists. Masses of the French people, roused and guided by bourgeois Jacobin leaders, notably Robespierre, Danton, and the vitriolic journalist Marat, burst out in a passion of patriotic excitement. They turned against the king because he was identified with powers at war with France, and also because, in France itself, those who still supported him were using the monarchy as a defense against the lower classes. Republicanism in France was partly a rather sudden historical accident, in that France was at war under a king who could not be trusted, and partly a kind of lower-class or quasi-proletarian movement, in which, however, many bourgeois revolutionaries shared.

Feeling ran high during the summer of 1792. Recruits streamed into Paris from all quarters on their way to the frontiers. One detachment, from Marseilles, brought with them a new marching song, known ever since as the *Marseillaise*, a fierce call to war upon tyranny. The transient provincials stirred up the agitation in Paris. On August 10, 1792, the working-class quarters of the city rose in revolt, supported by the recruits from Marseilles and elsewhere. They stormed the Tuileries against resistance by the Swiss Guard, many of whom were massacred, and

A WOMAN OF THE REVOLUTION
by Jacques-Louis David (French, 1748–1825)

Here is something of what historians mean by the "working class," and it may be compared with the representations of aristocracy and of the middle class already shown (see pp. 335, 343). The coarse garments and untended hair, the colorless lips, the lined forehead, and the evidences of suffering in the eyes—all reveal a life of much labor and few amenities. The woman seems to be observing something with an interest mixed with suspicion, and her air of determination and even of defiance suggests the political-mindedness aroused even in the poorest classes in time of revolution. David painted this portrait in 1795, a year after the Terror in France. He was himself an active revolutionary, a member of the Convention and of the Committee of General Security. It is rare to find portraits of people of this class of society done with so much realism, sympathy, and force. Courtesy of the Musée des Beaux-Arts, Lyon (J. Camponogara).

seized and imprisoned the king and the royal family. A revolutionary municipal government, or "Commune," was set up in Paris. Usurping the powers of the Legislative Assembly, it forced the abrogation of the constitution, and the election, by universal male suffrage, of a Constitutional Convention that was to govern France and prepare a new and more democratic constitution. The very word Convention was used in recollection of the American Constitutional Convention in 1787. Meanwhile hysteria, anarchy, and terror reigned in Paris; a handful of insurrectionary volunteers, declaring that they would not fight enemies on the frontiers until they had disposed of enemies in Paris, dragged about 1,100 persons —refractory priests and other counterrevolutionaries—from the prisons of the city and killed them after drumhead trials. These are known as the "September massacres."

For over two and a half years, since October 1789, there had been an abatement of popular violence. Now the coming of the war and the dissatisfaction of the lower classes with the course of events so far had led to new explosions. The insurrection of August 10, 1792, the "second" French Revolution, initiated the most advanced phase of the Revolution.

44. THE EMERGENCY REPUBLIC, 1792–1795: THE TERROR

The National Convention

The National Convention met on September 20, 1792; it was to sit for three years. It immediately proclaimed the Year One of the French Republic. The disorganized French armies, also on September 20, won a great moral victory in the "cannonade of Valmy," a battle that was hardly more than an artillery duel, but which induced the Prussian commander to give up his march on Paris. The French soon occupied Belgium (the Austrian Netherlands), Savoy (which belonged to the king of Sardinia who had joined with the Austrians), and Mainz and other cities on the German Left Bank of the Rhine. Revolutionary sympathizers in these places appealed for French aid. The National Convention decreed assistance to "all peoples wishing to recover their liberty." It also ordered that French generals, in the occupied areas, should dissolve the old governments, confiscate government and church property, abolish tithes, hunting rights, and seigneurial dues, and set up provisional administrations. Thus revolution spread in the wake of the successful French armies.

The British and Dutch prepared to resist. Pitt, still insisting that the French might have any domestic regime that they chose, declared that Great Britain could not tolerate the French occupation of Belgium. The British and Dutch began conversations with Prussia and Austria, and the French declared war on them on February 1, 1793. Within a few weeks the Republic had annexed Savoy and Nice, as well as Belgium, and had much of the German Rhineland under its military government.[12] Meanwhile, in eastern Europe, while denouncing the rapacity of the French savages, the rulers of Russia and Prussia came to an arrangement of their own, each appropriating a portion of Poland in the second

[12] See map, p. 383.

partition in January 1793.[13] The Austrians, excluded from the second partition, became anxious over their interests in eastern Europe. The infant French Republic, now at war with all Europe, was saved by the weakness of the Coalition, for Britain and Holland had no land forces of consequence, and Prussia and Austria were too jealous of each other, and too preoccupied with Poland, to commit the bulk of their armies against France.

In the Convention all the leaders were Jacobins, but the Jacobins were again splitting. The Girondins were no longer the most advanced revolutionary group as they had been in the Legislative Assembly. Beside the Girondins appeared a new group, whose members preferred to sit in the highest seats in the hall, and therefore were dubbed the "Mountain" in the political parlance of the day. The leading Girondins came from the great provincial cities; the leading Montagnards, though mostly of provincial birth, were representatives of the city of Paris and owed most of their political strength to the radical and popular elements in that city.

These popular revolutionists, outside the Convention, proudly called themselves "sans-culottes," since they wore the workingman's long trousers, not the knee breeches or *culottes*, of the middle and upper classes. They were the working class of a pre-industrial age, shopkeepers and shop assistants, skilled artisans in various trades, including some who were owners of small manufacturing or handicraft enterprises. For two years their militancy and their activism pressed the Revolution forward. They demanded an equality that should be meaningful for people like themselves, they called for a mighty effort against foreign powers that presumed to intervene in the French Revolution, and they denounced the now deposed king and queen (correctly enough) for collusion with the Austrian enemy. The sans-culottes feared that the Convention might be too moderate. They favored direct democracy in their neighborhood clubs and assemblies, together with a mass rising if necessary against the Convention itself. The Girondins in the Convention began to dismiss these popular militants as anarchists. The group known as the Mountain was more willing to work with them, so long at least as the emergency lasted.

The Convention put Louis XVI on trial for treason in December 1792. On January 15 it unanimously pronounced him guilty, but on the next day, out of 721 deputies present, only 361 voted for immediate execution, a majority of one. Louis XVI died on the guillotine forthwith. The 361 deputies were henceforth branded for life as regicides; never could they allow, in safety to themselves, a restoration of the Bourbon monarchy in France. The other 360 deputies were not similarly compromised; their rivals called them Girondins, "moderatists," counterrevolutionaries. All who still wanted more from the Revolution, or who feared that the slightest wavering would bring the Allies and the émigrés into France, now looked to the Mountain wing of the Jacobins.

Background to the Terror

In April 1793 the most spectacular French general, Dumouriez, who had won the victories in Belgium five months before, defected to Austria. The Allied armies now drove the French from Belgium and again threatened to invade France.

---

[13] See pp. 327–329.

THE GLEANERS
by Jean-François Millet (French, 1814–1875)

Three women of the poorest of the French peasantry are shown here. They may be compared with the women depicted on pp. 335, 343, and 371. Bowed with labor, reaching out with strong, muscular hands, clutching their few stalks of grain, these women are exercising a legal right, "glanage," by which poor people were allowed to glean the fields after the owners had taken in the harvest. Many of the owners were more affluent peasants. Glanage was one of the collective village rights, originally common to France, England, and most of Europe, which tended to disappear with the spread of modern private-property institutions. When the painting was first exhibited in 1857, it reminded one irate critic of the French Revolution. "Behind these three gleaning-women," he said, "against the leaden horizon, we can see silhouetted the pikes, riots and scaffolds of '93." Courtesy of the Louvre (Giraudon).

Counterrevolutionaries in France exulted. From the revolutionaries went up the cry, "We are betrayed!" Prices continued to rise, the currency fell, food was harder to obtain, and the working classes were increasingly restless. The sans-culottes demanded price controls, currency controls, rationing, legislation against the hoarding of food, and requisitioning to enforce the circulation of goods. They denounced the bourgeoisie as profiteers and exploiters of the people. While the Girondins resisted, the Mountain went along with the sans-culottes, partly from sympathy with their ideas, partly to win mass support for the war, and partly as a maneuver to get rid of the Girondins. On May 31, 1793, the Commune of Paris, under sans-culotte pressure, assembled a host of demonstrators and insurrection-ists who invaded the Convention and forced the arrest of the Girondin leaders. Other Girondins fled to the provinces, including Condorcet, who, while in hiding, and before his death, found occasion to write his famous book on the *Progress of the Human Mind*.[14]

The Mountain now ruled in the Convention, but the Convention itself ruled very little. Not only were the foreign armies and the émigrés at the gates bent on destroying the Convention as a band of regicides and social incendiaries, but the authority of the Convention was widely repudiated in France itself. In the west, in the Vendée, the peasants had revolted against military conscription; they were worked upon by refractory priests, British agents, and royalist emissaries of the Count of Artois. The great provincial cities, Lyons, Bordeaux, Marseilles, and others, had also rebelled, especially after the fugitive Girondins reached them. These "federalist" rebels demanded a more "federal" or decentralized republic. Like the Vendéans, with whom they had no connection, they objected to the ascendancy of Paris, having been accustomed to more regional independence under the Old Regime. These rebellions became counterrevolutionary, since all sorts of foreigners, royalists, émigrés, and clericals streamed in to assist them.

The Convention had to defend itself against extremists of the Left as well. To the genuine mass action of the sans-culottes were now added the voices of even more excited militants called *enragés*. Various organizers, enthusiasts, agitators, and neighborhood politicians declared that parliamentary methods were useless. Generally they were men outside the Convention—and also women, for women were particularly sensitive to the crisis of food shortage and soaring prices, and an organization of Revolutionary Republican Women caused a brief stir in 1793. All such activists worked through units of local government in Paris and elsewhere, and in thousands of "popular societies" and provincial clubs throughout the whole country. They also formed "revolutionary armies," semimilitary bands of men who scoured the rural areas for food, searched the barns of peasants, denounced suspects, and preached revolution.

As for the Convention, while it cannot be said ever to have had any commanding leaders, the progam it followed for about a year was on the whole that of Maximilien Robespierre, himself a Jacobin but not one to go along forever with popular revolution or anarchy. Robespierre is one of the most argued about and least understood men of modern times. Persons accustomed to stable conditions dismiss him with a shudder as a bloodthirsty fanatic, dictator, and demagogue. Others have considered him an idealist, a visionary, and an ardent patriot whose goals and ideals were at least avowedly democratic. All agree on his personal

[14] See p. 314.

honesty and integrity and on his revolutionary zeal. He was by origin a lawyer of northern France, educated with the aid of scholarships in Paris. He had been elected in 1789 to sit for the Third Estate in the Estates General, and in the ensuing Constituent Assembly played a minor role, though calling attention to himself by his views against capital punishment and in favor of universal suffrage. During the time of the Legislative Assembly, in 1791–1792, he continued to agitate for democracy and vainly pleaded against the declaration of war. In the Convention, elected in September 1792, he sat for a Paris constituency. He became a prominent member of the Mountain and welcomed the purge of the Girondins. He had always kept free of the bribery and graft in which some others became involved and for this reason was known as the Incorruptible. He was a great believer in the importance of "virtue." This term had been used in a specialized way among the philosophes: both Montesquieu and Rousseau had held that republics depended upon "virtue," or unselfish public spirit and civic zeal, to which was added, under Rousseauist influence, a somewhat sentimentalized idea of personal uprightness and purity of life. Robespierre was determined, in 1793 and 1794, to bring about a democratic republic made up of good citizens and honest men.

The Program of the Convention, 1793–1794: The Terror

The program of the Convention, which Robespierre helped to form, was to repress anarchy, civil strife, and counterrevolution at home and to win the war by a great national mobilization of the country's people and resources. It would prepare a democratic constitution and initiate legislation for the lower classes, but it would not yield to the Paris Commune and other agencies of direct revolutionary action. To conduct the government, the Convention granted wide powers to a Committee of Public Safety, a group of twelve members of the Convention who were reelected every month. Robespierre was an influential member; others were the youthful St. Just, the partially paralyzed Couthon, and the army officer Carnot, "organizer of victory."

To repress the "counterrevolution," the Convention and the Committee of Public Safety set up what is popularly known as the "Reign of Terror." Revolutionary courts were instituted as an alternative to the lynch law of the September massacres. A Committee of General Security was created as a kind of supreme political police. Designed to protect the Revolutionary Republic from its internal enemies, the Terror struck at those who were in league against the Republic, and at those who were merely suspected of hostile activities. Its victims ranged from Marie Antoinette and other royalists to the former revolutionary colleagues of the Mountain, the Girondin leaders; and before the year 1793–1794 was over, some of the old Jacobins of the Mountain who had helped inaugurate the program also went to the guillotine. The number of persons who lost their lives in the Terror, from the late summer of 1793 to July 1794, has often been exaggerated. By the standards of the twentieth century, in which governments have undertaken to extirpate whole classes or races, the Terror was fairly mild. Yet about 40,000 persons died in it; and additional hundreds of thousands were at one time or another arrested and held in custody. Most executions took place in the Vendée, at Lyons, and in other places in open rebellion, and were directed against persons in insurrection in time of war. The Terror showed no respect for, or interest in, the class origins of its victims. About 8 percent were nobles, but the nobles as a class were not molested unless suspected of political agitation; 14 percent of the victims were classifiable as bourgeois, mainly of the rebellious southern cities; 6 percent were clergy, while no less than 70 percent were of the peasant and laboring classes. A democratic republic, founded on the Declaration of the Rights of Man, was in principle to follow the Terror once the war and the emergency were over, but meanwhile, the Terror was inhuman at best and in some places atrocious, as at Nantes where 2,000 persons were loaded on barges and deliberately drowned. The Terror left long memories in France of antipathy to the Revolution and to republicanism.

To conduct the government in the midst of the war emergency the Committee of Public Safety operated as a joint dictatorship or war cabinet. It prepared and guided legislation through the Convention. It gained control over the "representatives on mission," who were members of the Convention on duty with the armies and in the insurgent areas of France. It established the *Bulletin des loix*, so that all persons might know what laws they were supposed to enforce or to obey. It centralized the administration, converting the swarm of locally elected officials, left over from the Constituent Assembly, and who were royalists in some places, wild extremists in others, into centrally appointed "national agents" named by the Committee of Public Safety.

To win the war the Committee proclaimed the *levée en masse*, calling on all able-bodied men to rally to the colors. It recruited scientific men to work on armaments and munitions. The most prominent French scientists of the day, including Lagrange and Lamarck, worked for or were protected by the government of the Terror, though one, Lavoisier, "father of modern chemistry," was guillotined in 1794 because he had been involved in tax farming before 1789. For military reasons also the Committee instituted economic controls, which at the same time met the demands of the *enragés* and other working-class spokesmen. The assignats ceased to fall during the year of the Terror. Thus the government protected both its own purchasing power and that of the masses. It did so by controlling the export of gold, by confiscating specie and foreign currency from French citizens, to whom it paid assignats in return, and by legislation against hoarding or the withholding of goods from the market. Food and supplies for the armies, and for civilians in the towns, were raised and allocated by a system of requisitions, centralized in a Subsistence Commission under the Committee of Public Safety. A "general maximum" set ceilings for prices and wages. It helped to check inflation during the crisis, but it did not work very well; the Committee believed, on principle, in a free market economy and lacked the technical and administrative machinery to enforce thorough controls. By 1794 it was giving freer rein to private enterprise and to the peasants, in order to encourage production. It tried also to hold down wages and in that respect failed to win the adherence of many working-class leaders.

In June 1793 the Committee produced, and had adopted by the Convention, a republican constitution which provided for universal male suffrage. But the new constitution was suspended indefinitely, and the government was declared "revolutionary until the peace," "revolutionary" meaning extraconstitutional or of an emergency character. In other ways the Committee showed intentions of legislating on behalf of the lower economic classes. The price controls and other economic regulations answered the demands of the sans-culottes. The last of the manorial regime was done away with; the peasants were relieved of having to pay compensation for the obligations that had been abolished at the opening of the Revolution. Purchase of land by the peasants was made somewhat easier. There were even moves, in the Ventôse laws of March 1794, to confiscate the property of suspects (not merely of the church or convicted émigrés), and to give such property gratis to "indigent patriots"; but these laws were drafted in unworkable form, never received much support from the ruling Committee, and came to very little. The Committee busied itself also with social services and measures of public improvement. It issued pamphlets to teach farmers to improve their crops, selected promising youths to receive instruction in useful trades, opened a military school for boys of all classes, even the humblest, and certainly intended to introduce universal elementary education. It was at this time, also, that slavery was abolished in the French colonies, free blacks having already received civic rights.

The Committee of Public Safety wished to concentrate the Revolution in itself. It had no patience with unauthorized revolutionary violence. With a democratic program of its own, it disapproved of the turbulent democracy of popular clubs and local assemblies. In the fall of 1793 it arrested the leading *enragés* and prohibited revolutionary women's organizations at the same time. Extreme revolutionism thereafter took the name of Hébertism, after Hébert, an officer of the Paris Commune. The Hébertists were a large and indefinable group and included many members of the Convention. They indiscriminately denounced merchants and bourgeoisie. They were the party of extreme Terror; an Hébertist brought about the drownings at Nantes. Believing all religion to be counterrevolutionary, they launched the movement of Dechristianization. Even a Republican calendar was adopted by the Convention. Its main purpose was to blot out from men's minds the Christian cycle of Sundays, saints' days, and such holidays as Christmas and Easter. It counted years from the founding of the French Republic, divided each year into new months of thirty days each, and even abolished the week, which it replaced with the *décade*.[15]

Another form taken by Dechristianization was the cult of reason which sprang up all over France at the end of 1793. In Paris the bishop resigned his office, declaring that he had been deluded; and the Commune put on ceremonies in the cathedral of Notre Dame, in which Reason was impersonated by an actress who was the wife of one of the city officials. But Dechristianization was severely frowned upon by Robespierre. He believed that it would alienate the masses from the Republic and ruin such sympathy as was still felt for the Revolution abroad. The Committee of Public Safety, therefore, ordered the toleration of peaceable Catholics, and in June 1794 Robespierre introduced the "Worship of the Supreme Being," a kind of national and naturalistic cult, in which the Republic was declared to recognize the existence of God and the immortality of the soul. Robespierre hoped that both Catholics and agnostic anticlericals could become reconciled on this ground. But Catholics were now beyond reconciliation, and the freethinkers, appealing to the tradition of Voltaire, regarded Robespierre as a reactionary mystery monger and were instrumental in bringing about his fall.

Meanwhile the Committee proceeded relentlessly against the Hébertists, whose

---

[15] Though not adopted until October 1793, the revolutionary calendar dated the Year I of the French Republic from September 22, 1792. The names of the months, in order, were Vendémiaire, Brumaire, Frimaire (autumn); Nivôse, Pluviôse, Ventôse (winter); Germinal, Floréal, Prairial (spring); Messidor, Thermidor, Fructidor (summer).

main champions it sent to the guillotine in March 1794. The paramilitary "revolutionary armies" were repressed. The extreme Terrorists were recalled from the provinces. The revolutionary Paris Commune was destroyed. Robespierre filled the municipal offices of Paris with his own appointees. This Robespierrist commune disapproved of strikes and tried to hold down wages, on the plea of military necessity; it failed to win over the ex-Hébertists and working-class spokesmen, who became disillusioned with the Revolution and dismissed it as a bourgeois movement. Probably to prevent just such a conclusion, and to avoid the appearance of deviation to the right, Robespierre and the Committee, after liquidating the Hébertists, also liquidated certain right-wing members of the Mountain who were known as Dantonists. Danton and his followers were accused of financial dishonesty and of dealing with counterrevolutionaries; the charges contained some truth but were not the main reason for the executions.

By the spring of 1794 the French Republic possessed an army of 800,000 men, the largest ever raised up to that time by a European power. It was a national army, representing a people in arms, commanded by officers who had been promoted rapidly on grounds of merit, and composed of troops who felt themselves to be citizens fighting for their own cause. Its intense political mindedness made it the more formidable and contrasted strongly with the indifference of the opposing troops, some of whom were in fact serfs and none of whom had any sense of membership in their own political systems. The Allied governments, each pursuing its own ends, and still distracted by their ambitions in Poland, where the third partition was impending, could not combine their forces against France. In June 1794 the French won the battle of Fleurus in Belgium. The Republican hosts again streamed into the Low Countries; in six months their cavalry rode into Amsterdam on the ice. A revolutionary Batavian Republic soon replaced the old Dutch provinces.

Military success made the French less willing to put up with the dictatorial rule and economic regimentation of the Terror. Robespierre and the Committee of Public Safety had antagonized all significant parties. The working-class radicals of Paris would no longer support him, and after the death of Danton the National Convention was afraid of its own ruling committee. A group in the Convention obtained the "outlawing" of Robespierre on 9 Thermidor (July 27, 1794); he was guillotined with some of his associates on the following day. Many who turned against Robespierre believed they were pushing the Revolution farther forward, as in destroying the Girondins the year before. Others thought, or said, that they were stopping a dictator and a tyrant. All agreed, to absolve themselves, in heaping all blame upon Robespierre. The idea that Robespierre was an ogre originated more with his former colleagues than with conservatives of the time.

The Thermidorian Reaction

The fall of Robespierre stunned the country, but its effects manifested themselves during the following months as the "Thermidorian reaction." The Terror subsided. The Convention reduced the powers of the Committee of Public Safety, and it closed the Jacobin club. Price control and other regulations were removed. Inflation resumed its course, prices again rose, and the disoriented and leaderless working classes suffered more than ever. Sporadic risings broke out, of which the greatest was the insurrection of Prairial in the Year III (May 1795), when a mob all but dispersed the Convention by force. Troops were called to Paris for the first time since 1789. Insurrectionists in the working-class quarters threw up barricades in the streets. The army prevailed without much bloodshed, but the Convention arrested, imprisoned, or deported ten thousand of the insurgents. A few organizers were guillotined, including one militant black. The affair of Prairial gave a foretaste of modern social revolution.

The triumphant element was the bourgeois class which had guided the Revolution since the Constituent Assembly and had not been really unseated even during the Terror. It was not mainly a bourgeoisie of modern capitalists, eager to make a financial profit by developing new factories or machinery.[16] The political victors after Thermidor were "bourgeois" in an older sense, those who had not been noble or aristocratic before 1789 yet had held a secure position under the Old Regime, many of them lawyers or officeholders, and often drawing income from the ownership of land. To them were now added new elements produced by the Revolution itself, parvenus and *nouveaux riches*, who had made money by wartime government contracts, or had profited by inflation or by buying up former church lands at bargain prices. Such people, often joined by former aristocrats, and in reaction against Robespierrist virtue, set a noisy and ostentatious style of living that gave a bad name to the new order. They also unleashed a "white terror" against Jacobins, in which many were simply murdered.

But the Thermidorians, disreputable though a few of them were, had not lost faith in the Revolution. Democracy they associated with red terror and mob rule, but they still believed in individual legal rights and in a written constitution. Conditions were rather adverse, for the country was still unsettled, and although the Convention made a separate peace with Spain and Prussia, France still remained at war with Great Britain and the Habsburg empire. But the men of the Convention were determined to make another attempt at constitutional government. They set aside the democratic constitution written in 1793 (and never used) and produced the Constitution of the Year III, which went into effect at the end of 1795.

45. THE CONSTITUTIONAL REPUBLIC: THE DIRECTORY, 1795–1799

The Weakness of the Directory

The first formally constituted French Republic, known as the Directory, lasted only four years. Its weakness was that it rested on an extremely narrow social base, and that it presupposed certain military conquests. The new constitution applied not only to France but also to Belgium, which was regarded as incorporated constitutionally into France, though the Habsburgs had not yet ceded these "Austrian Netherlands," nor had the British yielded in their refusal to accept French occupation. The constitution of 1795 thus committed the republic to a program of successful expansion. At the same time it restricted the politically active class. It gave almost all adult males the vote, but voters voted only for "electors," for whom about the same qualifications were set as in the constitution of 1791. Persons chosen as electors were usually men of some means, able to give

---

[16] On the bourgeoisie and capitalism, see pp. 114–116, 119–120, 248–249, 426.

their time and willing to take part in public life; this in effect meant men of the upper middle class, since the old aristocracy was disaffected. The electors chose all important department officials and also the members of the national Legislative Assembly, which this time was divided into two chambers. The lower chamber was called the Council of Five Hundred, the upper, composed of 250 members, the Council of Ancients—"ancients" being men over forty. The chambers chose the executive, which was called the Directory (whence the whole regime got its name) and was made up of five Directors.

The government was thus constitutionally in the hands of substantial property owners, rural and urban, but its real base was narrower still. In the reaction after Thermidor many people began to consider restoring the monarchy. The Convention, to protect its own members, ruled that two-thirds of the men initially elected to the Council of Five Hundred and Council of Ancients must be ex-members of the Convention. This interference with the freedom of the elections provoked serious disturbances in Paris, instigated by persons called royalists; but the Convention, having now accustomed itself to using the army, instructed a young general who happened to be in Paris, named Bonaparte, to put down the royalist mob. He did so with a "whiff of grapeshot." The constitutional republic thus made itself dependent on military protection at the outset.

The regime had enemies to both right and left. On the right, undisguised royalists agitated in Paris and even in the two councils. Their center was the Clichy Club, and they were in continuous touch with the late king's brother, the Count of Provence, whom they regarded as Louis XVIII (Louis XVI's son, who died in prison, being counted as Louis XVII). Louis XVIII had installed himself at Verona in Italy, where he headed a propaganda agency financed largely by British money. The worst obstacle to the resurgence of royalism in France was Louis XVIII himself. In 1795, on assuming the title, he had issued a Declaration of Verona, in which he announced his intention to restore the Old Regime and punish all involved in the Revolution back to 1789. It has been said, correctly enough in this connection, that the Bourbons "learned nothing and forgot nothing." Had Louis XVIII offered in 1795 what he offered in 1814, it is quite conceivable that his partisans in France might have brought about his restoration and terminated the war. As it was, the bulk of the French adhered not exactly to the republic as set up in 1795, but more negatively to any system that would shut out the Bourbons and former nobility, prevent a reimposition of the manorial system, and secure the new landowners, peasant and bourgeois, in the possession of the church properties which they had purchased.

The Left was made up of persons from various levels of society who still favored the more democratic ideas expressed earlier in the Revolution. Some of them thought that the fall of Robespierre had been a great misfortune. A tiny group of extremists formed the Conspiracy of Equals, organized in 1796 by "Gracchus" Babeuf. His intention was to overthrow the Directory and replace it with a dictatorial government which he called "democratic," in which private property would be abolished and equality decreed. For these ideas, and for his activist program, he has been regarded as an interesting precursor to modern communism. The Directory repressed the Conspiracy of Equals without difficulty and guillotined Babeuf and one other. Meanwhile it did nothing to relieve the distress of the lower classes, who showed little inclination to follow Babeuf but did suffer from the ravages of scarcity and inflation.

The Political Crisis of 1797

In March 1797 occurred the first really free election ever held in France under republican auspices. The successful candidates were for the most part constitutional monarchists or at least vaguely royalist. A change of the balance within the Five Hundred and the Ancients, in favor of royalism, seemed to be impending. This was precisely what most of the republicans of 1793, including the regicides, could not endure, even though they had to violate the constitution to prevent it. Nor was it endurable, for other reasons, to General Napoleon Bonaparte.

Bonaparte had been born in 1769 into the minor nobility of Corsica, shortly after the annexation of Corsica to France. He had studied in French military schools and been commissioned in the Bourbon army but would never have reached high rank under the conditions of the Old Regime. In 1793 he was a fervent young Jacobin officer, who had been useful in driving the British from Toulon, and who was consequently made a brigadier general by the government of the Terror. In 1795, as noted, he rendered service to the Convention by breaking up a demonstration of royalists. In 1796 he received command of an army, with which, in two brilliant campaigns, he crossed the Alps and drove the Austrians from north Italy. Like other generals he got out of control of the government in Paris, which was financially too harassed to pay his troops or to supply him. He lived by local requisitions in Italy, became self-supporting and independent, and in fact made the civilian government in Paris dependent on him.

He developed a foreign policy of his own. Many Italians had become dissatisfied with their old governments, so that the arrival of the French republican armies threw north Italy into a turmoil, in which the Venetian cities revolted against Venice, Bologna against the pope, Milan against Austria, and the Piedmontese monarchy was threatened by uprisings of its own subjects. Combining with some of these revolutionaries, while rejecting others, Bonaparte established a "Cisalpine" Republic in the Po valley, modeled on the French system, with Milan as its capital. Where the Directory, on the whole, had originally meant to return Milan to the Austrians in compensation for Austrian recognition of the French conquest of Belgium, Bonaparte insisted that France hold its position in both Belgium and Italy. He therefore needed expansionist republicans in the government in Paris and was perturbed by the elections of 1797.

The Austrians negotiated with Bonaparte because they had been beaten by him in battle. The British also, in conferences with the French at Lille, discussed peace in 1796 and 1797. The war had gone badly for England; a party of Whigs led by Charles James Fox had always openly disapproved it, and the pro-French and republican radicals were so active that the government suspended habeas corpus in 1794, and thereafter imprisoned political agitators at its discretion. In 1795 an assassin fired on George III, breaking the glass in his carriage. Crops were bad, and bread was scarce and costly. England too suffered from inflation, for Pitt at first financed the war by extensive loans, and a good deal of gold was shipped to the Continent to finance the Allied armies. In February 1797 the Bank of England suspended gold payments to private citizens. Famine threatened, the populace was restless, and there were even mutinies in the fleet. Ireland was in rebellion; the French came close to landing a republican army in it, and it could be supposed that the next attempt might be more successful. The Austrians, Britain's only remaining ally, were routed by Bonaparte, and at the moment the British could subsidize them no further. The British had every reason to make peace.

THE FRENCH REPUBLIC AND ITS SATELLITES, 1798–1799

By 1799 the French Republic had annexed Belgium (the Austrian Netherlands) and the small German bishoprics and principalities west of the Rhine, and had created, with the aid of native sympathizers, a string of lesser revolutionary republics in the Dutch Netherlands, Switzerland, and most of Italy. With the treaty of Campo Formio between France and Austria in 1797, the Holy Roman Empire began to disintegrate, for the German princes of the Left Bank of the Rhine, who were dispossessed when their territories went to France, began to be compensated with territory of the church-states of the Holy Roman Empire. These developments were carried further by Napoleon (see map, p. 401).

Many were inclined to settle for colonial conquests, regarding the war as a renewal of the eighteenth-century struggle for empire.

Prospects for peace seemed good in the summer of 1797, but, as always, it would be peace upon certain conditions. It was the royalists in France that were the peace party, since a restored king could easily return the conquests of the republic and would in any case abandon the new republics in Holland and the Po valley. The republicans in the French government could make peace with difficulty, if at all. They were constitutionally bound to retain Belgium. They were losing control of their own generals. Nor could the supreme question be evaded: Was peace dear enough to purchase by a return of the Old Regime, such as Louis XVIII had himself promised?

The coup d'état of Fructidor (September 4, 1797) resolved all these many issues. It was the turning point of the constitutional republic and was decisive for all Europe. The Directory asked for help from Bonaparte, who sent one of his generals, Augereau, to Paris. While Augereau stood by with a force of soldiers, the councils annulled most of the elections of the preceding spring. Two Directors were purged; one of them, Lazare Carnot, "organizer of victory" in the Committee of Public Safety, and now in 1797 a strict constitutionalist, was driven into exile. On the whole, it was the old republicans of the Convention who secured themselves in power. Their justification was that they were defending the Revolution, keeping out Louis XVIII and the Old Regime. But to do so they had violated their own constitution and quashed the first free election ever held in a constitutional French republic. And they had become more than ever dependent on the army.

After the coup d'état the "Fructidorian" government broke off negotiations with England. With Austria it signed the treaty of Campo Formio on October 17, 1797, incorporating Bonaparte's ideas. Peace now prevailed on the Continent, since only France and Great Britain remained at war, but it was a peace full of trouble for the future. By the new treaty Austria recognized the French annexation of Belgium (the former Austrian Netherlands), the French right to incorporate the Left Bank of the Rhine, and the French-dominated Cisalpine Republic in Italy. In return, Bonaparte allowed the Austrians to annex Venice and most of mainland Venetia. The Venetian possessions in the Ionian Islands, off the coast of Greece, went to France.

In the following months, under French auspices, revolutionary republicanism spread through much of Italy. The old patrician republic of Genoa turned into a Ligurian Republic on the French model. At Rome the pope was deposed from his temporal power and a Roman Republic was established. In southern Italy a Neapolitan Republic, also called Parthenopean, was set up. In Switzerland at the same time, Swiss reformers cooperated with the French to create a new Helvetic Republic.

The Left Bank of the Rhine, in the atomistic Holy Roman Empire, was occupied by a great many German princes who now had to vacate. The treaty of Campo Formio provided that they be compensated by church territories in Germany east of the Rhine, and that France have a hand in the redistribution. The German princes turned greedy eyes on the German bishops and abbots, and the almost 1,000-year-old Holy Empire, hardly more than a solemn form since the Peace of Westphalia, sank to the level of a land rush or real estate speculation, while France became involved in the territorial reconstruction of Germany.

The Coup d'État of 1799: Bonaparte

After Fructidor the idea of maintaining the republic as a free or constitutional government was given up. There were more uprisings, more quashed elections, more purgings both to Left and Right. The Directory became a kind of ineffective dictatorship. It repudiated most of the assignats and the debt but failed to restore financial confidence or stability. Guerrilla activity flared up again in the Vendée and other parts of western France. The religious schism became more acute; the Directory took severe measures toward the refractory clergy.

Meanwhile Bonaparte waited for the situation to ripen. Returning from Italy a conquering hero, he was assigned to command the army in training to invade England. He concluded that invasion was premature and decided to strike indirectly at England, by threatening India in a spectacular invasion of Egypt. In 1798, outwitting the British fleet, he landed a French army at the mouth of the Nile. Egypt was part of the Ottoman Empire, and the French occupation of it alarmed the Russians, who had their own designs on the Near East. The Austrians objected to the French rearrangement of Germany. A year and a half after the treaty of Campo Formio, Austria, Russia, and Great Britain formed an alliance known as the Second Coalition. The French Republic was again involved in a general war. And the war went unfavorably, for in August 1798 the British fleet had cut off the French army in Egypt by winning the battle of the Nile (or Aboukir), and in 1799 Russian forces, under Marshal Suvorov, were operating as far west as Switzerland and north Italy, where the Cisalpine Republic went down in ruin.

General Bonaparte's opportunity had come. He left his army in Egypt and, again slipping through the British fleet, reappeared unexpectedly in France. He found that certain civilian leaders in the Directory were planning a change. They included Sieyès, of whom little had been heard since he wrote *What Is the Third Estate?* ten years before, but who had sat in the Convention and voted for the death of Louis XVI. Sieyès' formula was now "confidence from below, authority from above"— what he now wanted of the people was acquiescence, and of the government, power to act. This group was looking about for a general, and their choice fell on the sensational young Bonaparte, who was still only thirty. Dictatorship by an army officer was repugnant to most republicans of the Five Hundred and the Ancients. Bonaparte, Sieyès, and their followers resorted to force, executing the coup d'état of Brumaire (November 9, 1799), in which armed soldiers drove the legislators from the chambers. They proclaimed a new form of the republic, which Bonaparte entitled the Consulate. It was headed by three consuls, with Bonaparte as the First Consul.

46. THE DESPOTIC REPUBLIC: THE CONSULATE, 1799–1804

The next chapter takes up the affairs of Europe as a whole in the time of Napoleon Bonaparte, the purpose at present being only to tell how he closed, in a way, the Revolution in France.

It happened that the French Republic, in falling into the hands of a general, fell also to a man of such remarkable talents as are often denominated genius. Bonaparte was a short dark man, of Mediterranean type, who would never have looked impressive in civilian clothing. His manners were rather coarse; he lost his temper, cheated at cards, and pinched people by the ear in a kind of formidable play—he was no "gentleman." A child of the Enlightenment and the Revolution, he was entirely emancipated not only from customary ideas but from moral scruples as well. He regarded the world as a flux to be formed by his own mind. He had an exalted belief in his own destinies, which became more mystical and exaggerated as the years went on. He claimed to follow his "star." His ideas of the good and the beautiful were rather blunt, but he was a man of extraordinary intellectual capacity, which impressed all with whom he came in contact. "Never speak unless you know you are the ablest man in the room," he once advised his stepson, on making him viceroy of Italy, a maxim which, if he followed it himself, still allowed him to do most of the talking. His interests ran to solid subjects, history, law, military science, public administration. His mind was tenacious and perfectly orderly; he once declared that it was like a chest of drawers, which he could open or close at will, forgetting any subject when its drawer was closed and finding it ready with all necessary detail when its drawer was opened. He had all the masterful qualities associated with leadership; he could dazzle and captivate those who had any inclination to follow him at all. Some of the most humane men of the day, including Goethe and Beethoven in Germany, and Lazare Carnot among the former revolutionary leaders, at first looked on him with high approval. He inspired confidence by his crisp speech, rapid decisions, and quick grasp of complex problems when they were newly presented to him. He was, or seemed, just what many Frenchmen were looking for after ten years of upheaval.

Under the Consulate France reverted to a form of enlightened despotism, and Bonaparte may be thought of as the last and most eminent of the enlightened despots. Despotic the new regime undoubtedly was from the start. Self-government through elected bodies was ruthlessly pushed aside. Bonaparte delighted in affirming the sovereignty of the people; but to his mind the people was a sovereign, like Voltaire's God, who somehow created the world but never thereafter interfered in it. He clearly saw that a government's authority was greater when it was held to represent the entire nation. In the weeks after Brumaire he assured himself of a popular mandate by devising a written constitution and submitting it to a general referendum or "plebiscite." The voters could take it—or nothing. They took it by a majority officially reported as 3,011,007 to 1,562.

The new constitution set up a make-believe of parliamentary institutions. It gave universal male suffrage, but the citizens merely chose "notables"; men on the lists of notables were then appointed by the government itself to public position. The notables had no powers of their own. They were merely available for appointment to office. They might sit in a Legislative Body, where they could neither initiate nor discuss legislation, but only mutely reject or enact it. There was also a Tribunate which discussed and deliberated but had no enacting powers. There was a Conservative Senate, which had rights of appointment of notables to office ("patronage" in American terms), and in which numerous storm-tossed regicides found a haven. The main agency in the new government was the Council of State, imitated from the Old Regime; it prepared the significant legislation, often under the presidency of the First Consul himself, who always gave the impression that he understood everything. The First Consul made all the decisions and ran the state. The regime did not openly represent anybody, and that was its strength, for it provoked the less opposition. In any case, the political machinery just described fell rapidly into disuse.

Bonaparte entrenched himself also by promising and obtaining peace. The military problem, at the close of 1799, was much simplified by the attitude of the Russians, who in effect withdrew from the war with France. In the Italian theater Bonaparte had to deal only with the Austrians, whom he again defeated, by again crossing the Alps, at the battle of Marengo in June 1800. In February 1801 the Austrians signed the treaty of Lunéville, in which the terms of Campo Formio were confirmed. A year later, in March 1802, peace was made even with Britain.

Peace was made also at home. Bonaparte kept internal order, partly by a secret political police, but more especially through a powerful and centralized administrative machine, in which a "prefect," under direct orders of the minister of the interior, ruled firmly over each of the departments created by the Constituent Assembly. The new government put down the guerrillas in the west. Its laws and taxes were imposed on Brittany and the Vendée. Peasants there were no longer terrorized by marauding partisans. A new peace settled down on the factions left by the Revolution. Bonaparte offered a general amnesty and invited back to France, with a few exceptions, exiles of all stripes from the first aristocratic émigrés to the refugees and deportees of the republican coups d'état. Requiring only that they work for him and stop quarreling with each other, he picked reasonable men from all camps. His Second Consul was Cambacérès, a regicide of the Terror, his Third Consul Lebrun, who had been Maupeou's colleague in the days of Louis XV.[17] Fouché emerged as minister of police; he had been an Hébertist and extreme terrorist in 1793 and had done as much as any man to bring about the fall of Robespierre. Before 1789 he had been an obscure bourgeois professor of physics. Talleyrand appeared as minister of foreign affairs; he had spent the Terror in safe seclusion in the United States, and his principles, if he had any, were those of constitutional monarchy. Before 1789 he had been a bishop and was of an aristocratic lineage almost unbearably distinguished—no one who had not known the Old Regime, he once said, could realize how pleasant it had been. Men of this sort were now willing, for a few years beginning in 1800, to forget the past and work in common toward the future.

Disturbers of the new order the First Consul ruthlessly put down. Indeed, he concocted alarms to make himself more welcome as a pillar of order. On Christmas Eve, 1800, on the way to the opera, he was nearly killed by a bomb, or "infernal machine," as people then said. It had been laid by royalists, but Bonaparte represented it as the work of a Jacobin conspiracy, being most afraid at the moment of some of the old republicans; and over a hundred former Jacobins were again deported. Contrariwise, in 1804, he greatly exaggerated certain royalist plots against him, invaded the independent state of Baden, and there arrested the Duke of Enghien, who was related to the Bourbons. Though he knew Enghien to be innocent, he had him shot. His purpose now was to please the old Jacobins by staining his own hands with Bourbon blood; Fouché and the regicides concluded that they were secure so long as Bonaparte was in power.

The Settlement with the Church; Other Reforms

For all but the most convinced royalists and republicans, reconciliation was made easier by the establishment of peace with the church. Bonaparte himself was a pure eighteenth-century rationalist. He regarded religion as a convenience. He

[17] See pp. 315–318.

388   THE FRENCH REVOLUTION388

advertised himself as a Muslim in Egypt, as a Catholic in France, and as a free-thinker among the professors at the Institute in Paris. But a Catholic revival was in full swing, and he saw its importance. The refractory clergy were the spiritual force animating all forms of counterrevolution. "Fifty émigré bishops, paid by England," he once said, "lead the French clergy today. Their influence must be destroyed. For this we need the authority of the pope." Ignoring the horrified out-cries of the old Jacobins, in 1801 he signed a concordat with the Vatican.

Both parties gained from the settlement. The autonomy of the prerevolutionary Gallican church came to an end. The pope received the right to depose French bishops, since before the schism could be healed both constitutional and refrac-tory bishops had to be obliged to resign. The constitutional or pro-revolutionary clergy came under the discipline of the Holy See. Publicity of Catholic worship, in such forms as processions in the streets, was again allowed. Church seminaries were again permitted. But Bonaparte and the heirs of the Revolution gained even more. The pope, by signing the concordat, virtually recognized the Republic. The Vatican agreed to raise no question over the former tithes and the former church lands. The new owners of former church properties thus obtained clear titles. Nor was there any further question of Avignon, an enclave within France, formerly papal, annexed to France in 1791. Nor were the papal negotiators able to undermine religious toleration; all that Bonaparte would concede was a clause that was purely factual, and hence harmless, stating that Catholicism was the religion of the majority of Frenchmen. The clergy, in compensation for loss of their tithes and property, were assured of receiving salaries from the state. But Bonaparte, to dispel the notion of an established church, put Protestant ministers of all denominations on the state payroll also. He thus checkmated the Vatican on important points. At the same time, simply by signing an agreement with Rome, he disarmed the counterrevolution. It could no longer be said that the Republic was godless. Good relations did not, indeed, last very long, for Bonaparte and the papacy were soon at odds. But the terms of the concordat proved lasting.

With peace and order established, the constructive work of the Consulate turned to the fields of law and administration. The First Consul and his advisers combined what they conceived to be the best of the Revolution and of the Old Regime. The modern state took on clearer form. It was the reverse of everything feudal. All public authority was concentrated in paid agents of government, no person was held to be under any legal authority except that of the state, and the authority of government fell on all persons alike. There were no more estates, legal classes, privileges, local liberties, hereditary offices, guilds, or manors. Judges, officials, and army officers received specified salaries. Neither military commissions nor civil offices could be bought and sold. Citizens were to rise in government service purely according to their abilities.

This was the doctrine of "careers open to talent"; it was what the bourgeoisie had wanted before the Revolution, and a few persons of quite humble birth prof-ited also. For sons of the old aristocracy, it meant that pedigree was not enough; they must also show individual capacity to obtain employment. Qualification came to depend increasingly on education, and the secondary and higher schools were reorganized in these years, with a view to preparing young men for govern-ment service and the learned professions. Scholarships were provided, but it was mainly the upper middle class that benefited. Education, in fact, in France and in Europe generally, came to be an important determinant of social standing, with one system for those who could spend a dozen or more years at school, and another for boys who were to enter the work force at the age of twelve or fourteen.

Another deep demand of the French people, deeper than the demand for the vote, was for more reason, order, and economy in public finance and taxation. The Consulate gave these also. There were no tax exemptions because of birth, status, or special arrangement. Everyone was supposed to pay, so that no disgrace attached to payment, and there was less evasion. In principle these changes had been introduced in 1789; after 1799 they began to work. For the first time in ten years the government really collected the taxes that it levied and so could rationally plan its financial affairs. Order was introduced also into expenditure, and accounting methods were improved. There was no longer a haphazard assortment of different "funds," on which various officials drew independently and confidentially as they needed money, but a concentration of financial management in the treasury; and even in a kind of budget. The revolutionary uncertainties over the value of money were also ended. Because the Directory had shouldered the odium of repudiating the paper money and government debt, the Consulate was able to establish a sound currency and public credit. To assist in government financing, one of the banks of the Old Regime was revived and established as the Bank of France.

Like all enlightened despots, Bonaparte codified the laws, and of all law codes since the Romans the Napoleonic codes are the most famous. To the 300 legal systems of the Old Regime, and the mass of royal ordinances, were now added the thousands of laws enacted but seldom implemented by the revolutionary assemblies. Five codes emerged—the Civil Code (often called simply the Code Napoleon), the codes of civil and of criminal procedure, and the commercial and penal codes. The codes made France legally and judicially uniform. They assured legal equality; all French citizens had the same civil rights. They formulated the new law of property and set forth the law of contracts, debts, leases, stock companies, and similar matters in such a way as to create the legal framework for an economy of private enterprise. They repeated the ban of all previous regimes on organized labor unions and were severe with the individual workingman, his word not being acceptable in court against that of his employer—a significant departure from equality before the law. The criminal code was somewhat freer in giving the government the means to detect crime than in granting the individual the means of defending himself against legal charges. As for the family, the codes recognized civil marriage and divorce but left the wife with very restricted powers over property, and the father with extensive authority over minor children. The codes reflected much of French life under the Old Regime. They also set the character of France as it has been ever since, socially bourgeois, legally equalitarian, and administratively bureaucratic.

In France, with the Consulate, the Revolution was over. If its highest hopes had not been accomplished, the worst evils of the Old Regime had at least been cured. The beneficiaries of the Revolution felt secure. Even former aristocrats were rallying. The working-class movement, repeatedly frustrated under all the revolutionary regimes, now vanished from the political scene, to reappear as socialism thirty years later. What the Third Estate had most wanted in 1789 was now both codified and enforced, with the exception of parliamentary government, which after ten years of turmoil many people were temporarily willing to forgo. Moreover, in 1802, the French Republic was at peace with the papacy,

Great Britain, and all Continental powers. It reached to the Rhine and had dependent republics in Holland and Italy. So popular was the First Consul that in
1802, by another plebiscite, he had himself elected consul for life. A new constitution, in 1804, again ratified by plebiscite, declared that "the government of the
republic is entrusted to an emperor." The Consulate became the Empire, and
Bonaparte emerged as Napoleon I, Emperor of the French.

But France, no longer revolutionary at home, was revolutionary outside its
borders. Napoleon became a terror to the patricians of Europe. They called him
the "Jacobin." And the France which he ruled, and used as his arsenal, was an incomparably formidable state. Even before the Revolution it had been the most
populous in Europe, perhaps the most wealthy, in the front rank of scientific
enterprise and intellectual leadership. Now all the old barriers of privilege, tax
exemption, localism, caste exclusiveness, and routine-mindedness had disappeared. The new France could tap the wealth of its citizens and put able men into
position without inquiring into their origins. Every private, boasted Napoleon,
carried a marshal's baton in his knapsack. The French looked with disdain on
their caste-ridden adversaries. The principle of civic equality proved not only to
have the appeal of justice, but also to be politically useful, and the resources of
France were hurled against Europe with a force which for many years nothing
could check.

X.
Napoleonic Europe

T he repercussions of the French Revolution had been felt throughout Europe since the fall of the Bastille, and even more definitely after the outbreak of war in 1792 and the ensuing victories of the republican armies. They became even more evident after the republican General Bonaparte turned into Napoleon I, Emperor of the French, King of Italy, and Protector of the Confederation of the Rhine. Napoleon came nearer than anyone has ever come to imposing a political unity on the European continent. Of his ascendancy of fifteen years two stories are to be told. One is a story of international relations, reflecting the diverse interests of the contending states of Europe. The other is the story of internal development of the European peoples. The French impact, though based on military success, represented more than mere forcible subjugation. Innovations of a kind made in France by revolution were brought to other countries by administrative decree. There were, for several years, Germans, Italians, Dutchmen, and Poles who worked with the French emperor to introduce the changes that he demanded, and which they themselves often desired. In Prussia it was resistance to Napoleon that gave the incentive to internal reorganization. Whether by collaboration or resistance, Europe was transformed.

It is convenient to think of the fighting from 1792 to 1814 as a "world war," as indeed it was, affecting not only all of Europe but places as remote as Spanish

Chapter Emblem: An Italian cameo of 1810, showing the idealized head of Napoleon crowned with laurels as lawgiver and culture hero.

America, where the wars of independence began, or the interior of North America, where the United States purchased Louisiana in 1803 and attempted a conquest of Canada in 1812. But it is important to realize that this world war was actually a series of wars, most of them quite short, sharp, and distinct. Only Great Britain remained continually at war with France, except for about a year of peace in 1802–1803. Never were the four great powers, Britain, Austria, Russia, and Prussia, simultaneously in the field against France until 1813.

The history of the Napoleonic period would be much simpler if the European governments had fought merely to protect themselves against the aggressive French. Each, however, in its way, was as dynamic and expansive as Napoleon himself. For some generations Great Britain had been building a commercial empire, Russia pushing upon Poland and Turkey, Prussia consolidating its territories and striving for leadership in north Germany. Austria was less aggressive, being somewhat passively preoccupied by the rise of Prussia and Russia, but the Austrians were not without dreams of ascendancy in Germany, the Balkans, and the Adriatic. None of these ambitions ceased during the Napoleonic years. Governments, in pursuit of their own aims, were quite as willing to ally with Napoleon as to fight him. Only gradually, and under repeated provocation, did they conclude that their main interest was to dispose of the French emperor entirely.

47. THE FORMATION OF THE FRENCH IMPERIAL SYSTEM

The Dissolution of the First and Second Coalitions, 1792–1802

The conflicting purposes of the powers had been apparent from the beginning. Leopold of Austria, in issuing the Declaration of Pillnitz in 1791, had believed a general European coalition against France to be impossible. When the First Coalition was formed in 1792, the Austrians and Prussians kept their main forces in eastern Europe, more afraid of each other and of Russia, in the matter of Poland, than of the French revolutionary republic. Indeed, the main accomplishment of the First Coalition was the extermination of the Polish state.[1]

In 1795 the French broke up the coalition. The British withdrew their army from the Continent. The Prussians made a separate peace; the French bought them off by recognizing them as "protectors" of Germany north of the river Main. Spain also made a separate peace in 1795. The world saw the spectacle, outrageous to all ideology or principle, of an alliance between Bourbon Spain and the republic which had guillotined Louis XVI and kept Louis XVIII from his monarchic rights. Spain simply reverted to the eighteenth-century pattern, in allying with France because of hostility to Great Britain, whose possession of Gibraltar, naval influence in the Mediterranean, and attitude toward the Spanish empire were disquieting to the Spanish government. When Austria signed the peace of Campo Formio in 1797 the First Coalition was totally dissipated, only British naval forces remaining engaged with the French.[2]

The Second Coalition of 1799 fared no better. After the British fleet defeated the French at the battle of the Nile, cutting off the French army in Egypt, the Russians saw their ambitions in the Mediterranean blocked mainly by the British,

[1] See pp. 239–240, 372–373.
[2] See p. 382.

and withdrew Suvorov's army from western Europe. The acceptance by Austria of the peace of Lunéville in 1801 dissolved the Second Coalition. In 1802 Great Britain signed the peace of Amiens. For the only time between 1792 and 1814 no European power was at war with another—though the British, to be sure, were at war with some Indian princes, the Russians with some Caucasian tribesmen, and the French with Toussaint l'Ouverture, the black ex-slave who was attempting to found an independent republic in Haiti.

Peace Interim, 1802–1803

Never had a peace been so advantageous to France as the peace of 1802. But Bonaparte gave it no chance. He used peace as he did war to advance his interests. He dispatched a sizable army to Haiti, ostensibly to win back a rebellious French colony, but with the further thought (since Louisiana had been ceded back by Spain to France in 1800) of reviving the French colonial empire in America. He reorganized the Cisalpine Republic into an "Italian" Republic with himself as president. He reorganized the Helvetic Republic, making himself "mediator" of the Confederation of Switzerland. He reorganized Germany; that is to say, he and his agents closely watched the rearrangement of territory which the Germans themselves had been carrying out since 1797.

By the treaty of Campo Formio,[3] it will be recalled, German princes of the Left Bank of the Rhine, expropriated by the annexation of their dominions to the French Republic, were to receive new territories on the Right Bank. The result was a scramble called by patriotic German historians the "shame of the princes." The German rulers, far from opposing Bonaparte or upholding any national interests, competed desperately for the absorption of German territory, each bribing and fawning upon the French (Talleyrand made over 10,000,000 francs in the process) to win French support against other Germans. The Holy Roman Empire was fatally mauled by the Germans themselves. Most of its ecclesiastical principalities and forty-five out of its fifty-one free cities disappeared, annexed by their larger neighbors. The number of states in the Holy Empire was greatly reduced, especially of the Catholic states, so that it could be foreseen that no Catholic Habsburg would again be elected emperor. Prussia, Bavaria, Württemberg, and Baden consolidated and enlarged themselves. These arrangements were ratified in February 1803 by the diet of the Empire. The enlarged German states now depended on Bonaparte for the maintenance of their new position.

Formation of the Third Coalition in 1805

Britain and France went to war again in 1803. Bonaparte, his communications with America menaced by the British navy, and his army in Haiti decimated by disease and by rebellious blacks, suspended his ideas for re-creating an American empire and sold Louisiana to the United States. Great Britain began to seek allies for a Third Coalition. In May 1804 Napoleon pronounced himself Emperor of the French to assure the hereditary permanency of his system, though he had no son. Francis II of Austria, seeing the ruin of the Holy Roman Empire, promulgated the Austrian Empire in August 1804. He thus advanced the long process of inte-

[3] See p. 384.

grating the Danubian monarchy. In 1805 Austria signed an alliance with Great Britain. The Third Coalition was completed by the accession of the Russian Tsar Alexander I, who, after Napoleon himself, was to become the most considerable figure on the European stage.

Alexander was the grandson of Catherine the Great, educated by her to be a kind of enlightened despot on the eighteenth-century model.[4] The Swiss tutor of his boyhood, La Harpe, later turned up as a pro-French revolutionary in the Helvetic Republic of 1798. Alexander became tsar in 1801, at the age of twenty-four, through a palace revolution which implicated him in the murder of his father Paul. He still corresponded with La Harpe, and he surrounded himself with a circle of liberal and zealous young men of various nationalities, of whom the most prominent was a Polish youth, Czartoryski. Alexander regarded the still recent partitions of Poland as a crime.[5] He wished to restore the unity of Poland with himself as its constitutional king. In Germany many who had first warmed to the French Revolution, but had been disillusioned, began to hail the new liberal tsar as the protector of Germany and hope of the future. Alexander conceived of himself as a rival to Napoleon in guiding the destinies of Europe in an age of change. Moralistic and self-righteous, he puzzled and disturbed the statesmen of Europe, who generally saw, behind his humane and republican utterances, either an enthroned leader of all the "Jacobins" of Europe or the familiar specter of Russian aggrandizement.

Yet Alexander, more than his contemporaries, formed a conception of international collective security and the indivisibility of peace. He was shocked when Napoleon in 1804, in order to seize the duke of Enghien, rudely violated the sovereignty of Baden.[6] He declared that the issue in Europe was clearly between law and force—between an international society in which the rights of each member were secured by international agreement and organization, and a society in which all trembled before the rule of cynicism and conquest embodied in the French usurper.

Alexander was therefore ready to enter a Third Coalition with Great Britain. Picturing himself as a future arbiter of central Europe, and with secret designs on the Ottoman Empire and the Mediterranean, he signed a treaty with England in April 1805. The British agreed to pay Russia £1,250,000 for each 100,000 soldiers that the Russians raised.

The Third Coalition, 1805–1807: The Peace of Tilsit

Napoleon meanwhile, since the resumption of hostilities in 1803, had been making preparations to invade England. He concentrated large forces on the Channel coast, together with thousands of boats and barges, in which he gave the troops amphibious training in embarkation and debarkation. He reasoned that if his own fleet could divert or cripple the British fleet for a few days he could place enough soldiers in the defenseless island to force its capitulation. The British, sensing mortal danger, lined their coasts with lookouts and signal beacons and set to drilling a home guard. Their main defense was twofold: the Austro-Russian armies and the British fleet under Lord Nelson. The Russian and Austrian armies moved westward in the summer of 1805. In August Napoleon relieved the pressure upon

---

[4] See p. 330.
[5] See pp. 238–240, 372–373.
[6] See p. 387.

England, shifting seven army corps from the Channel to the upper Danube. On October 15 he surrounded an Austrian force of 50,000 men at Ulm in Bavaria, forcing it to surrender without resistance. On October 21 Lord Nelson, off Cape Trafalgar on the Spanish coast, caught and annihilated the main body of the combined fleets of France and Spain.

The battle of Trafalgar established the supremacy of the British navy for over a century—but only on the proviso that Napoleon be prevented from controlling the bulk of Europe, which would furnish an ample base for eventual construction of a greater navy than the British. And to control Europe was precisely what Napoleon proceeded to do. Moving east from Ulm he came upon the Russian and Austrian armies in Moravia, where on December 2 he won the great victory of Austerlitz. The broken Russian army withdrew into Poland, and Austria made peace. By the treaty of Pressburg Napoleon took Venetia from the Austrians, to whom he had given it in 1797, and annexed it to his kingdom of Italy (the former Cisalpine and Italian Republic), which now included a good deal of Italy north of Rome. Venice and Trieste soon resounded with the hammers of shipwrights rebuilding the Napoleonic fleet. In Germany, early in 1806, the French emperor raised Bavaria and Württemberg to the stature of kingdoms and Baden to a grand duchy. The Holy Roman Empire was finally, formally, and irrevocably dissolved. In its place Napoleon began to gather his German client states into a new kind of Germanic federation, the Confederation of the Rhine, of which he made himself the "protector."

Prussia, at peace with France for ten years, had declined to join the Third Coalition. But as Napoleon's program for controlling Germany became clear after Austerlitz the war party in Prussia became irresistible, and the Prussian government, outwitted and distraught, went to war with the French unaided and alone. The French smashed the famous Prussian army at the battles of Jena and Auerstädt in October 1806. The French cavalry galloped all over north Germany unopposed. The Prussian king and his government took refuge in the east, at Königsberg, where the tsar and the re-forming Russian army might protect them. But the terrible Corsican pursued the Russians also. Marching through western Poland and into East Prussia, he met the Russian army first at the sanguinary but indecisive battle of Eylau and then defeated it on June 14, 1807, at Friedland. Alexander I was unwilling to retreat into Russia. He was unsure of his own resources; if the country were invaded there might be a revolt of the nobles or even of the serfs—for people still remembered Pugachev's rebellion.[7] He feared also merely playing the game of the British. He put aside his war aims of 1804 and signified his willingness to negotiate with Napoleon. The Third Coalition had gone the way of the two before it.

The Emperor of the French and the Autocrat of All the Russias met privately on a raft in the Niemen River, not far from the border between Prussia and Russia, the very easternmost frontier of civilized Europe, as the triumphant Napoleon gleefully imagined it. The hapless Prussian king, Frederick William III, paced nervously on the bank. Bonaparte turned all his charm upon Alexander, denouncing England as the author of all the troubles of Europe and captivating him by flights of Latin imagination, in which he set before Alexander a boundless destiny as Emperor of the East, intimating that his future lay toward Turkey, Persia, Afghanistan, and India. The result of their conversations was the treaty of Tilsit

---

[7] See pp. 325–326.

of July 1807, in many ways the high point of Napoleon's success. The French and Russian empires became allies, mainly against Great Britain. Ostensibly this alliance lasted for five years. Alexander accepted Napoleon as a kind of Emperor of the West. As for Prussia, Napoleon continued to occupy Berlin with his troops, and he took away all Prussian territories west of the Elbe, combining them with others taken from Hanover to make a new kingdom of Westphalia, which became part of his Confederation of the Rhine.

The Continental System and the War in Spain

Hardly had the "peace of the continent" been reestablished, on the foundation of a Franco-Russian alliance, when Napoleon began to have serious trouble. He was bent on subduing the British who, secure in their island, seemed beyond his reach. Since the French naval disaster at Trafalgar, there was no possibility of invading England in the foreseeable future. Napoleon therefore turned to economic warfare. He would fight sea power with land power, using his political control of the Continent to shut out British goods and shipping from all European ports. He would destroy the British trade in exports to Europe, both exports of British products and the profitable British reexport of goods from America and Asia. Thereby, he hoped, he would ruin British commercial firms and cause a violent business depression, marked by overloaded warehouses, unemployment, runs on the banks, a fall of the currency, rising prices, and revolutionary agitation. The British government, which would simultaneously be losing revenues from its customs duties, would thus find itself unable to carry the enormous national debt, or to borrow additional funds from its subjects, or to continue its financial subsidies to the military powers of Europe. At Berlin, in 1806, after the battle of Jena, Napoleon issued the Berlin Decree, forbidding the importation of British goods into any part of Europe allied with or dependent on himself. He thus formally established the Continental System.

To make the Continental System effective Napoleon believed that it must extend to all continental Europe without exception. By the treaty of Tilsit, in 1807, he required both Russia and Prussia to adhere to it. They agreed to exclude all British goods; in fact, in the following months Russia, Prussia, and Austria all declared war on Great Britain. Napoleon then ordered two neutral states, Denmark and Portugal, to adhere. Denmark was an important entrepôt for all central Europe, and the British, fearing Danish compliance, dispatched a fleet to Copenhagen, bombarded the city for four days, and took captive the Danish fleet. The outraged Danes allied with Napoleon and joined the Continental System. Portugal, long a satellite of Britain, refused compliance; Napoleon invaded it. To control the whole European coastline from St. Petersburg around to Trieste he now had only to control the ports of Spain. By a series of deceptions he got both the Bourbon Charles IV and his son Ferdinand to abdicate the Spanish throne. He made his brother Joseph king of Spain in 1808 and reinforced him with a large French army.

He thus involved himself in an entanglement from which he never escaped. The Spanish regarded the Napoleonic soldiers as godless villains who desecrated churches. Fierce guerrillas took the field. Cruelties of one side were answered by atrocities of the other. The British sent an expeditionary force of their small regular army, eventually under the Duke of Wellington, to sustain the Spanish guerrillas; the resulting Peninsular War dragged on for five years. But from the beginning the affair went badly for Napoleon. In July 1808 a French general, for the first time since the Revolution, surrendered an army corps, without fighting, by the capitulation at Baylen. In August another French force surrendered to the British army in Portugal. And these events raised hopes in the rest of Europe. An anti-French movement swept over Germany. It was felt strongly in Austria, where the Habsburg government, undaunted by three defeats, and hoping to lead a general German national resistance, prepared for a fourth time since 1792 to go to war with France.

The Austrian War of Liberation, 1809

Napoleon summoned a general congress which met at Erfurt in Saxony in September 1808. His main purpose was to talk with his ally of a year, Alexander; but he assembled numerous dependent monarchs as well, by whose presence he hoped to overawe the tsar. He even had Talma, the leading actor of the day, play in the theater of Erfurt before "a parterre of kings." Alexander was unimpressed. He was hurt in a sensitive spot because Napoleon, a few months before, had made moves to re-create a Polish state, setting up what was called the Grand Duchy of Warsaw. He had found Napoleon unwilling, despite the grandiose language of Tilsit, really to support his expansion into the Balkans. In addition, Alexander was taken aside by Talleyrand, Napoleon's foreign minister. Talleyrand had concluded that Napoleon was overreaching himself and said so confidentially to the tsar, advising him to wait. Talleyrand thus acted as a traitor, betraying the man whom he ostensibly served, and preparing a safe place for himself in the event of Napoleon's fall; but he acted also as an aristocrat of the prenationalistic Old Regime, seeing his own country as only one part of the whole of Europe, believing a balance among the several parts to be necessary, and holding that peace would be possible only when the exaggerated position of French power should be reduced. For France and Russia, the two strongest states, to combine against all other states was contrary to all principles of the older diplomacy.[8]

Austria proclaimed a war of liberation in April 1809. Napoleon advanced rapidly along the familiar route to Vienna. The German princes, indebted to the French, declined to join in a general German war against him. Alexander stood watchfully on the sidelines. Napoleon won the battle of Wagram in July. In October Austria made peace. The short war of 1809 was over. The Danubian monarchy, by no means as fragile as it seemed, survived a fourth defeat at the hands of the French without internal revolution or disloyalty to the Habsburg house. From it, in punishment, Napoleon took considerable portions of its territory. Part of Austrian Poland was used to enlarge Napoleon's Grand Duchy of Warsaw, and parts of Dalmatia, Slovenia, and Croatia, on the south, were erected into a new creation which Napoleon called the Illyrian Provinces.[9]

Napoleon at His Peak, 1809–1811

The next two years saw the Napoleonic empire at its peak. In Austria after the defeat of 1809 the conduct of foreign affairs fell to a man who was to retain it for forty years. His name was Clemens von Metternich. He was a German from west

---

[8] See pp. 158–159.
[9] See map, p. 401.

of the Rhine, whose ancestral territories had been annexed to the French Republic, but he had entered the Austrian service and even married the granddaughter of Kaunitz,[10] the old model of diplomatic savoir-faire, of which Metternich now became a model himself. Austria had been repeatedly humiliated and even partitioned by Napoleon, most of all in the treaty of 1809. But Metternich was not a man to conduct diplomacy by grudges. Believing that Russia was the really permanent problem for a state situated in the Danube valley, Metternich thought it wise to renew good relations with France. He was quite willing to go along with Napoleon, whom he knew personally, having been Austrian ambassador to Paris before the short war of 1809.

The French emperor, who in 1809 was exactly forty, was increasingly concerned by the fact that he was childless. He had made an empire which he pronounced hereditary. Yet he had no son. Between him and his wife Josephine whom he had married in youth, and who was six years his senior, there had long since ceased to be affection or even fidelity on either side. He divorced her in 1809, though since she had two children by a first husband she naturally protested that Napoleon's childlessness was not her fault. He intended to marry a younger woman who might bear him offspring. He intended also to make a spectacular marriage, to extort for himself, a self-made Corsican army officer, the highest and most exclusive recognition that aristocratic Europe could bestow. He debated between Habsburgs and Romanovs, between an archduchess and a grand duchess. Tactful inquiries at St. Petersburg concerning the availability of Alexander's sister were tactfully rebuffed; the tsar intimated that his mother would never allow it. The Russian alliance again showed its limitations. Napoleon was thrown into the arms of Metternich—and of Marie Louise, the eighteen-year-old daughter of the Austrian emperor and niece of another "Austrian woman," Marie Antoinette. They were married in 1810. In a year she bore him a son, whom he entitled the King of Rome.

Napoleon assumed ever more pompous airs of imperial majesty. He was now, by marriage, the nephew of Louis XVI. He showed more consideration to French noblemen of the Old Regime—only they, he said, knew really how to serve. He surrounded himself with a newly made hereditary Napoleonic nobility, hoping that the new families, as time went on, would bind their own fortunes to the house of Bonaparte. The marshals became dukes and princes, Talleyrand the Prince of Benevento, and the bourgeois Fouché, an Hébertist of '93, and more latterly a police official, was now solemnly addressed as the Duke of Otranto. In foreign affairs also the cycle had been run. With one significant exception all the powers of the successive coalitions were allied with the French, and the Son of the Revolution now gravely referred to the emperor of Austria as "my father."

48. THE GRAND EMPIRE: SPREAD OF THE REVOLUTION

The Organization of the Napoleonic Empire

Territorially Napoleon's influence enjoyed its farthest reach in 1810 and 1811, when it comprehended the entire European mainland except the Balkan peninsula. The Napoleonic domain was in two parts. Its core was the French empire;

---

[10] See pp. 268, 319.

then came thick layers of dependent states, which together with France comprised the Grand Empire. In addition, to the north and east were the "allied states" under their traditional governments—the three great powers, Prussia, Austria, and Russia, and also Denmark and Sweden. The allied states were at war with Great Britain, though not engaged in positive hostilities; their populations were supposed to do without British goods under the Continental System, but otherwise Napoleon had no direct lawful influence upon their internal affairs.

The French empire, as successor to the French Republic, included Belgium and the Left Bank of the Rhine.[11] In addition, by 1810, it had developed two appendages which on a map looked like tentacles outstretched from it. When he proclaimed France an empire, and turned its dependent republics into kingdoms, Napoleon had set up his brother Louis as king of Holland; but Louis had shown such a tendency to ingratiate himself with the Dutch, and such a willingness to let Dutch businessmen trade secretly with the British, that Napoleon dethroned him and incorporated Holland into the French empire. In his endless war upon British goods he found it useful to exert more direct control over the ports of Bremen, Hamburg, Lübeck, Genoa, and Leghorn; he therefore annexed directly to the French empire the German coast as far as the western Baltic, and the Italian coast far enough to include Rome. Rome he desired for its imperial rather than its commercial value. Harking back to traditions as old as Charlemagne, he considered Rome the second city of his empire and entitled his son the "King of Rome"; and when Pope Pius VII protested, Napoleon took him prisoner and interned him in France. The whole French empire, from Lübeck to Rome, was governed directly by departmental prefects who reported to Paris, and the eighty-three departments of France, created by the Constituent Assembly, had risen in 1810 to a hundred and thirty.

The dependent states, forming with France the Grand Empire, were of different kinds. The Swiss federation remained republican in form. The Illyrian Provinces, which included Trieste and the Dalmatian coast, were administered in their brief two years almost like departments of France. In Poland, since the Russians objected to a revived kingdom of Poland, Napoleon called his creation the Grand Duchy of Warsaw. Among the most important of the dependent states in the Grand Empire were the German states organized into the Confederation of the Rhine. Too modestly named, the Confederation included all Germany between what the French annexed on the west and what Prussia and Austria retained on the east. It was a league of all the German princes in this region who were regarded as sovereign, and who now numbered only about twenty, the most important being the four newly made kings—of Saxony, Bavaria, Württemberg, and Westphalia. Westphalia was an entirely new and synthetic state, made up of Hanoverian and Prussian territories and of various atoms of the old Germany. Its king was Napoleon's youngest brother Jerome.

For Napoleon used his family as a means of rule. The Corsican clan became the Bonaparte dynasty. His brother Joseph from 1804 to 1808 functioned as king of Naples and after 1808 as king of Spain. Louis Bonaparte was for six years king of Holland. Jerome was king of Westphalia. Sister Caroline became queen of Naples after brother Joseph's transfer to Spain; for Napoleon, running out of brothers (having quarreled with his remaining brother Lucien), gave the throne of Naples

---

[11] See pp. 380–381, 383–384.

to his brother-in-law, Joachim Murat, a madcap cavalry officer who was Caroline's husband. In the "Kingdom of Italy," which in 1810 included Lombardy, Venetia, and most of the former papal states, Napoleon himself retained the title of king, but set up his stepson, Eugene Beauharnais (Josephine's son) as viceroy. "Uncle Joseph," Napoleon's mother's brother, became Cardinal Fesch. The mother of the Bonapartes, Letitia, who had brought up all these children under very different circumstances in Corsica, was suitably installed at the imperial court as Madame Mère. According to legend she kept repeating to herself, "If only it lasts!"; she outlived Napoleon by fifteen years.

Napoleon and the Spread of the Revolution

In all the states of the Grand Empire the same course of events tended to repeat itself. First came the stage of military conquest and occupation by French troops. Then came the establishment of a native satellite government with the support of local persons who were willing to collaborate with the French and who helped in the drafting of a constitution specifying the powers of the new government and regularizing its relationships with France. In some areas these two stages had been accomplished under the republican governments before Napoleon came to power. In some regions no more than these two stages really occurred, notably in Spain and the Grand Duchy of Warsaw.

The third stage was one of sweeping internal reform and reorganization, modeled on Bonaparte's program for France and hence derivatively on the French Revolution.[12] Belgium and the German territories west of the Rhine underwent this stage most thoroughly, since they were annexed directly to France for twenty years. Italy, and the main bulk of Germany west of Prussia and Austria, also experienced the third stage.

Napoleon considered himself a great reformer and man of the Enlightenment. He called his system "liberal," and though the word to him meant almost the reverse of what it meant later to liberals, he was possibly the first to use it in a political sense. He believed also in "constitutions"; not that he favored representative assemblies or limited government, but he wanted government to be rationally

[12] See pp. 359–364, 388–390.

NAPOLEONIC EUROPE, 1810

Napoleon extended the sphere of French power well beyond the republican expansion of 1798–1799. (See map, p. 383.) By 1810 he dominated the whole continent except Portugal and the Balkan peninsula. Russia, Prussia, and Austria had been forced into alliance with him. He made his brothers kings of Spain, Holland, and Westphalia, his brother-in-law king of Naples, and his stepson viceroy of the kingdom of Italy. He gave the title of king to the German rulers of Bavaria, Württemberg, and Saxony, each of which absorbed smaller German states, while becoming members of Napoleon's Confederation of the Rhine. The old Holy Roman Empire disappeared. In Poland Napoleon, supported by Polish nationalists, undid the partitions of the 1790s by setting up the Grand Duchy of Warsaw.

British troops were fighting in Portugal in 1810, and the British fleet controlled all the islands. To counteract British influence Napoleon extended the borders of the French empire to include the kingdom of Holland and the German cities of Bremen, Hamburg, and Lübeck, and to reach along the Italian coast to a point beyond Rome.

BALTIC SEA

0   100   200 miles

Moscow
Borodino
Riga
COURLAND Vitebsk
Vilna   Smolensk
Tilsit
Königsberg Kovno   Borisov
RUSSIAN EMPIRE
Warsaw   Brest-Litovsk

**Napoleon's Russian Campaign
June to December, 1812**

NORWAY

SWEDEN

FINLAND

St. Petersbu

SCOTLAND

KINGDOM OF DENMARK
AND NORWAY

Edinburgh

ESTONIA

LIVONIA

NORTH SEA

DENMARK •Copenhagen

COURLAND

Memel

IRELAND

GREAT
BRITAIN

HELIGOLAND
(Britain)   Lübeck
Hamburg•
MECKLEN-
BURG

SWEDISH
POMERANIA   Danzig

Königsberg
Tilsit   Niemen
Friedland   •Vilna
Eylau

ENGLAND

KINGDOM OF
HOLLAND   Bremen

Berlin

PRUSSIA

RUSSIA

ATLANTIC OCEAN

London
Dover

Plymouth

Amsterdam•
Antwerp•
Brussels•
K. OF
WESTPHALIA
K. OF
SAXONY

Posen
Oder R.

Warsaw Brest-Litovsk

GRAND DUCHY
OF WARSAW

Vistula R.

ENGLISH CHANNEL Boulogne•
CHANNEL I.   Cherbourg
(Britain)

Amiens•
Cologne•

BERG

Auerstadt
Erfurt Leipzig Dresden
Jena

Breslau

CONFEDERATION
OF THE
RHINE

Cracow GALICIA

Tarna

Nantes•

Seine R.
Paris•
Versailles•
Fontainebleau

Valmy•
Metz•

Mainz•

Prague•

BOHEMIA

Loire R.   Orléans•

Strasbourg•

WÜRTTEM-
BERG
Ulm•
Munich•

Austerlitz•

FRENCH EMPIRE

Rochefort•

Basel•
SWITZERLAND

BADEN

Hohenlinden•
K. OF BAVARIA

Wagram•
Vienna AUSTRIA

CAPE
FINISTERRE

La Coruña•

Bordeaux•

Lyons•

SAVOY

Budapest•

HUNGARY

Rhone R.

PIEDMONT

LOMBARDY
Milan•
VENETIA
Trieste•

Danube R.

AUSTRIA

SLOVENIA

Drave R.

GALICIA

Oporto•
Douro R.

Burgos•

Ebro R.
Toulouse•

Garonne R.

Avignon•

P. OR.
Genoa•

KINGDOM
OF
ITALY

ILLYRIAN
PROVINCES

CROATIA

Save R.

WALLACHI

Belgrade•

Danube

Almeida•
PORTUGAL Ciudad Rodrigo•
Tagus R.

Talavera•   Madrid•

Marseilles•
Nice•
Toulon•

LUCCA
Leghorn• Florence•

DALMATIA

BOSNIA

SERBIA

ADRIATIC SEA

OTTOMAN EMP

MONTENEGRO

Lisbon•
Elvas•

SPAIN •Ocaña
Saragossa•

Barcelona•

CORSICA

ELBA

Rome•

Bari•

ALBANIA

Salonica•

Albuera• Guadiana R.
Baylen•
Seville•
Cadiz•   ANDALUSIA

Valencia•

BALEARIC I.
(Spain)
IVIZA   MAJORCA

MINORCA

KINGDOM OF
SARDINIA

Naples•

KINGDOM
OF NAPLES

Taranto•

CORFU

IONIAN I.
(Britain)

MOREA

TRAFALGAR ×
Tangier• •Gibraltar (Britain)

Cagliari•

Palermo•

STRAIT OF MESSINA

CERIGO

MOROCCO

Algiers•

ALGERIA
(Turkish)

Tunis•

KINGDOM OF
SICILY

MALTA (Britain)

MEDITERRANEAN SEA

TUNISIA
(Turkish)

French Empire

Grand Empire

Allied with Napoleon

0   100   200   300 miles

"constituted," i.e., deliberately mapped out and planned, not merely inherited from the jumble of the past. Man on horseback though he was, he believed firmly in the rule of law. He insisted with the zeal of conviction on transplanting his Civil Code[13] to the dependent states. This code he considered to be based on the very nature of justice and human relationships and to be applicable, therefore, to all countries with no more than minor adaptation. The idea that a country's laws must mirror its peculiar national character and history was foreign to his mind, for he carried over the rationalist and universalist outlook of the Age of Enlightenment. He thought that people everywhere wanted, and deserved, much the same thing. As he wrote to his brother Jerome, on making him king of Westphalia, "the peoples of Germany, as of France, Italy and Spain, want equality and liberal ideas. For some years now I have been managing the affairs of Europe, and I am convinced that the crowing of the privileged classes was everywhere disliked. Be a constitutional king."

The same plan of reform was initiated, with some variation, in all the dependent states from Spain to Poland and from the mouth of the Elbe to the Straits of Messina. The reforms were directed, in a word, against everything feudal. They established the legal equality of individual persons, and gave governments more complete authority over their individual subjects. Legal classes were wiped out, as in France in 1789; the theory of a society made up of "estates of the realm" gave way to the theory of a society made up of legally equal individuals. The nobility lost its privileges in taxation, officeholding, and military command. Careers were "opened to talent."

The manorial system, bulwark of the old aristocracy, was virtually liquidated. Lords lost all legal jurisdiction over their peasants; peasants became subjects of the state, personally free to move, migrate, or marry, and able to bring suit in the courts of law. The manorial fees, along with tithes, were generally abolished, as in France in 1789. But whereas in France the peasants escaped from these burdens without having to pay compensation, because they had themselves risen in rebellion in 1789 and because France passed through a radical popular revolution in 1793, in other parts of the Grand Empire the peasants were committed to payment of indemnities, and the former feudal class continued to receive income from its abolished rights. Only in Belgium and the Rhineland, incorporated into France under the republic, did the manorial regime disappear without compensation as it did in France, leaving a numerous entrenched class of small landowning farmers. East of the Rhine Napoleon had to compromise with the aristocracy which he assailed. In Poland, the only country in the Grand Empire where a thoroughgoing serfdom had prevailed, the peasants received legal freedom during the French occupation; but the Polish landlords remained economically unharmed, since they owned all the land. Napoleon had to conciliate them, for there was no other effective class in Poland to which he could look for support. In general, outside of France, the assault upon feudalism was not socially as revolutionary as it had been in France. The lord was gone, but the landlord remained.

Everywhere in the Grand Empire the church lost its position as a public authority alongside the state. Church courts were abolished or restricted; the Inquisition was outlawed in Spain. Tithes were done away with, church property confiscated, monastic orders dissolved or severely regulated. Toleration became the

[13] See p. 389.

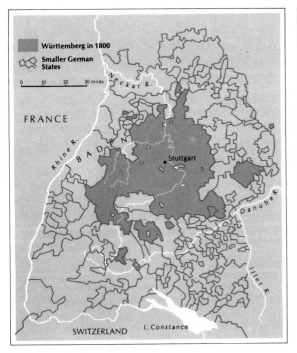
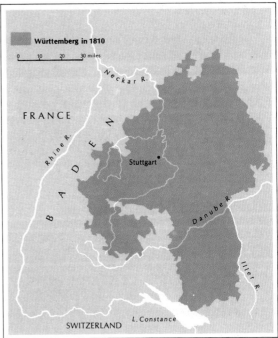

NAPOLEONIC GERMANY

In the panel at the left are shown, by shading, territories of the Duchy of Württemberg in 1800. Note how Württemberg had "islands" of territory unconnected with its main mass, and "holes" or enclaves formed by smaller states enclosed within the mass of Württemberg. Note, too, how Württemberg, itself only fifty miles wide, was surrounded by a mosaic of tiny jurisdictions—free cities, counties, duchies, principalities, abbacies, commanderies, bishoprics, archbishoprics, etc.—all "independent" within the Holy Roman Empire. The right-hand panel shows the Kingdom of Württemberg as consolidated and enlarged in the time of Napoleon. Similar consolidations all over Germany greatly reduced the number of states and added to the efficiency of law and government.

law; Catholics, Protestants, Jews, and unbelievers received the same civil rights. The state was to be based not on the idea of religious community but on the idea of territorial residence. With the nobility, or on economic matters, Napoleon would compromise; but he would not compromise with the Catholic clergy on the principle of a secular state. Even in Spain he insisted on these fundamentals of his system, a sure indication that he was not actuated by expediency only, since it was largely his religious program that provoked the Spanish populace to rebellion.

Guilds were generally abolished or reduced to empty forms, and the individual's right to work was generally proclaimed. Peasants, gaining legal freedom, might learn and enter any trade as they chose. The old town oligarchies and bourgeois patriciates were broken up. Towns and provinces lost their antique liberties and came under general legislation. Internal tariffs were removed, and free trade within state frontiers was encouraged. Some countries shifted to a decimal system of money; and the heterogeneous weights and measures which had originated in the Middle Ages, and of which the Anglo-American bushels, yards, ounces, and pints are living survivals, yielded to the Cartesian regularities of the metric system. Ancient and diverse legal systems gave way to the Napoleonic codes. Law courts were separated from the administration. Hereditary office and the sale of office were done away with. Officials received salaries large enough to shield them from the temptations of corruption. Kings were put on civil lists, with their personal expenses separated from those of the government. Taxes and finances were modernized. The common tax became a land tax, paid by every landowner; and governments knew how much land each owner really possessed, for they developed systematic registration of property and systematic methods of appraisal and assessment. Tax farming was replaced by direct collection. New methods of accounting and of collecting statistics were introduced.

In general, in all countries of the Grand Empire, some of the main principles of the French Revolution were introduced under Napoleon, with the notable exception that there was no self-government through elected legislative bodies. In all countries Napoleon found numerous natives willing to support him, mainly among the commercial and professional men, who were read in the writers of the Enlightenment, often anticlerical, desirous of more equality with the nobility, and eager to break down the old localisms that interfered with trade and with the exchange of ideas. He found supporters also among many progressive nobles and, in the Confederation of the Rhine, among the native rulers. His program appealed to a certain class of people everywhere, and in all parts of the Grand Empire was executed mainly by local persons. Repression went with it, though hardly on a scale to which the twentieth century has become accustomed. There were no vast internment camps, and Fouché's police were engaged more in spying and submitting reports than in the brutalizing of the disaffected. The execution of a single Bavarian bookseller, named Palm, became a famous outrage.

There was, in short, at first, a good deal of pro-Napoleonic feeling in the Grand Empire. The French influence (outside Belgium and the Rhineland) struck deepest in north Italy, where there were no native monarchist traditions, and where the old Italian city-states had produced a strong and often anticlerical burgher class. In south Germany also the French influence was profound. The French system had the least appeal in Spain, where Catholic royalist sentiment produced a kind of counterrevolutionary movement of independence. Nor did it appeal to agrarian eastern Europe, the land of lord and serf. Yet even in Prussia, as will be seen, the state was remodeled along French lines. In Russia, during the Tilsit alliance, Alexander gave his backing to a pro-French reforming minister, Speranski. The Napoleonic influence was pervasive because it carried over the older movement of enlightened despotism and seemed to confer the advantages of the French Revolution without the violence and the disorder. Napoleon, it seemed to Goethe, "was the expression of all that was reasonable, legitimate and European in the revolutionary movement."

But the Napoleonic reforms were also weapons of war. All the dependent states were required by Napoleon to supply him with money and soldiers. Germans, Dutch, Belgians, Italians, Poles, and even Spaniards fought in his armies. In addition, the dependent states defrayed much of the cost of the French army, most of which was stationed outside France. This meant that taxes in France could remain low, to the general satisfaction of the propertied interests that had issued from the Revolution.

49. THE CONTINENTAL SYSTEM: BRITAIN AND EUROPE

Beyond the tributary states of the Grand Empire lay the countries nominally independent, joined under Napoleon in the Continental System. Napoleon thought
of his allies as at best subordinate partners in a common project. The great project was to crush Great Britain, and it was for this purpose that the Continental
System had been established. But the crushing of Britain became in Napoleon's
mind a means to a further end, the unification and mastery of all of Europe. This
in turn, had he achieved it, would doubtless have merely opened the way to further conquests.

At the point where he stood in 1807 or 1810 the unification of continental Europe seemed a not impossible objective. He cast about for an ideology to inspire
both his Grand Empire and his allies. He held out the cosmopolitan doctrines of
the eighteenth century, spoke endlessly of the enlightenment of the age, urged all
peoples to work with him against the medievalism, feudalism, ignorance, and
obscurantism by which they were still surrounded. And while appealing to the
sense of modernity he dwelt also on the grandeur of Roman times. The Roman inspiration reflected itself in the arts of the day. The massive "empire" furniture,
the heroic canvases of David, the church of the Madeleine in Paris, resembling a
classical temple and converted to a Temple of Glory, the Arch of Triumph in the
same city, begun in 1806, all evoked the atmosphere of far-spreading majesty in
which Napoleon would have liked the peoples of Europe to live. In addition, to
arouse an all-European feeling, Napoleon worked upon the latent hostility to
Great Britain. The British, in winning out in the eighteenth-century struggle for
wealth and empire, had made themselves disliked in many quarters. There was
the natural jealousy felt toward the successful and resentment against the high-
handedness by which success had been won and was maintained. Such feelings
were present among almost all Europeans. It was believed that the British were
really using their sea power to win a larger permanent share of the world's seaborne commerce for themselves. Nor, in truth, was this belief mistaken.

British Blockade and Napoleon's Continental System

The British, in the Revolutionary and Napoleonic wars, when they declared
France and its allies in a state of blockade, did not expect either to starve them
or to deprive them of necessary materials of war. Western Europe was still self-
sufficient in food, and armaments were to a large extent produced locally, from
simple materials like iron, copper, and saltpeter. Europe required almost nothing
indispensable from overseas. The chief aim of the British blockade was not, therefore, to keep imports out of enemy countries; it was to keep the trade in such imports out of enemy hands. It was to kill off enemy commerce and shipping, in
order, in the short run, to weaken the war-making powers of the enemy government by undermining its revenues and its navy, and in the long run to weaken the
enemy's position in the markets of the world. Economic warfare was trade warfare. The British were willing enough to have British goods pass through to the
enemy either by smuggling or by the mediation of neutrals.

As early as 1793 the French republicans had denounced England as the "modern Carthage," a ruthless mercantile and profit-seeking power which aspired to

enslave Europe to its financial and commercial system. With the wars, the British in fact obtained a monopoly over the shipment of overseas commodities into Europe. At the same time, being relatively advanced in the Industrial Revolution, they could produce cotton cloth and certain other articles, by power machinery, more cheaply than other peoples of Europe, and so threatened to monopolize the European market for such manufactured goods. There was much feeling in Europe against the modern Carthage, especially among the bourgeois and commercial classes who were in competition with it. The upper classes were perhaps less hostile, not caring where the goods that they consumed had originated, but aristocracies and governments were susceptible to the argument that Britain was a money power, a "nation of shopkeepers" as Napoleon put it, which fought its wars with pounds sterling instead of blood and was always in search of dupes in Europe.

It was on all these feelings that Napoleon played, reiterating time and again that England was the real enemy of all Europe, and that Europe would never be prosperous or independent until relieved of the incubus of British "monopoly." To prevent the flow of goods into Britain was no more the purpose of the Continental System than to prevent the flow of goods into France was the purpose of the British blockade. The purpose of each was to destroy the enemy's commerce, credit, and public revenues by the destruction of his exports—and also to build up markets for oneself.

To destroy British exports Napoleon prohibited, by the Berlin Decree of 1806, the importation of British goods into the continent of Europe. Counted as British, if of British or British colonial origin, were goods brought to Europe in neutral ships as the property of neutrals. The British, in response, ruled by an "order in council" of November 1807 that neutrals might enter Napoleonic ports only if they first stopped in Great Britain, where the regulations were such as to encourage their loading with British goods. The British thus tried to move their exports into enemy territory through neutral channels, which was precisely what Napoleon intended to prevent. He announced, by the Milan Decree of December 1807, that any neutral vessel that had stopped at a British port, or submitted to search by a British warship at sea, would be confiscated upon its appearance in a Continental harbor.

With all Europe at war, virtually the only trading neutral was the United States, which could now trade with neither England nor Europe except by violating the regulations of one belligerent or the other. It would thus become liable to reprisals, and hence to involvement in war. President Jefferson, to avoid war, attempted a self-imposed policy of commercial isolation, which proved so ruinous to American foreign trade that the United States government took steps to renew trade relations with whichever belligerent first removed its controls over neutral commerce. Napoleon offered to do so, on condition that the United States would defend itself against the enforcement of British controls. At the same time an expansionist party among the western Americans, ambitious to annex Canada, considered that with the British army engaged in Spain the time was ripe to complete the War of Independence by driving Britain from the North American mainland. The result was the Anglo-American War of 1812, which had few results, except to demonstrate the distressing inefficiency of military institutions in the new republic.

But the Continental System was more than a device for destroying the export trade of Great Britain. It was also a scheme—today it would be called a "plan"—for developing the economy of continental Europe, around France as its main center. The Continental System, if successful, would replace the national economies with an integrated economy for the Continent as a whole. It would create the framework for a European civilization. And it would ruin the British sea power and commercial monopoly; for a unified Europe, Napoleon thought, would itself soon take to the sea.

The Failure of the Continental System

But the Continental System failed; it was worse than a failure, for it caused widespread antagonism to the Napoleonic regime. The dream of a united Europe, under French rule, was not sufficiently attractive to inspire the necessary sacrifice —even a sacrifice more of comforts than of necessities. As Napoleon impatiently said, one would suppose that the destinies of Europe turned upon a barrel of sugar. It was true, as he and his propagandists insisted, that Britain monopolized the sale of sugar, tobacco, and other overseas goods, but people preferred to deal clandestinely with the British rather than go without them. The charms of America destroyed the Continental System.

British manufactures were somewhat easier than colonial goods to replace. Raw cotton was brought by land from the Levant through the Balkans, and the cotton manufactures of France, Saxony, Switzerland, and north Italy were stimulated by the relief from British competition. There was a great expansion of Danish woolens and German hardware. The cultivation of sugar beets, to replace cane sugar, spread in France, central Europe, Holland, and even Russia. Thus infant industries and investments were built up which, after Napoleon's fall, clamored for tariff protection. In general, the European industrial interests were well disposed toward the Continental System.

Yet they could never adequately replace the British in supplying the market. One obstacle was transportation. Much trading between parts of the Continent had always been done by sea; this coastal traffic was now blocked by the British. Land routes were increasingly used, even in the faraway Balkans and Illyrian Provinces, through which raw cotton was brought; and improved roads were built through the Simplon and Mont Cenis passes in the Alps. No less than 17,000 wheeled vehicles crossed the Mont Cenis pass in 1810. But land transport, at best, was no substitute for the sea. Without railroads, introduced some thirty years later, a purely Continental economy was impossible to maintain.

Another obstacle was tariffs. The idea of a Continental tariff union was put forward by some of his subordinates, but Napoleon never adopted it. The dependent states remained insistent on their ostensible sovereignty. Each had widened its trading area by demolishing former internal tariffs, but each kept a tariff against the others. The kingdoms of Italy and Naples enjoyed no free trade with each other nor did the German states of the Confederation of the Rhine. France remained protectionist; and when Napoleon annexed Holland and parts of Italy to France, he kept them outside the French customs. At the same time Napoleon forbade the satellite states to raise high tariffs against France. France was his base, and he meant to favor French industry, which was much crippled by its loss of its Near Eastern and American markets.

Shippers, shipbuilders, and dealers in overseas goods, a powerful element of the older bourgeoisie, were ruined by the Continental System. The French ports were idle and their populations distressed and disgruntled. The same befell all ports of Europe where the blockade was strictly enforced; at Trieste, total annual tonnage fell from 208,000 in 1807 to 60,000 in 1812. Eastern Europe was especially hard hit. In the West there was the stimulus to new manufactures. The East, long dependent on western Europe for manufactured goods, could no longer obtain them from England legally, nor from France, Germany, or Bohemia because of the difficulties of land transport and the British control of the Baltic. Nor could the landowners of Prussia, Poland, and Russia market their produce. The aristocracy of eastern Europe, which was the principal spending and importing class, had additional reason to dislike the French and to sympathize with the British.

As a war measure against Britain the Continental System also failed. British trade with Europe was significantly reduced. But the loss was made up elsewhere because of British control of the sea. Exports to Latin America rose from £300,000 in 1805 to £6,300,000 in 1809. Here again the existence of the overseas world frustrated the Continental System. Despite the System, export of British cotton goods, rising on a continuous tide of the Industrial Revolution, more than doubled in four years from 1805 to 1809. And while part of the increase was due to mere inflation and rising prices, it is estimated that the annual income of the British people more than doubled in the Revolutionary and Napoleonic wars, leaping from £140,000,000 in 1792 to £335,000,000 in 1814.

50. THE NATIONAL MOVEMENTS: GERMANY

The Resistance to Napoleon: Nationalism

From the beginning, as far back as 1792, the French met with resistance as well as collaboration in the countries they occupied. There was resentment when the invading armies plundered and requisitioned upon the country, when the newly organized states were required to pay tribute of men and money, when their policies were dictated by French residents or ambassadors, and when the Continental System was used for the especial benefit of French manufacturers. Europeans began to feel that Napoleon was employing them merely as tools against England. And in all countries, including France itself, people grew tired of the peace that was no peace, the wars and rumors of war, the conscription and the taxes, the aloof bureaucratic government from on high, the obviously growing and insatiable appetite of Napoleon for power and self-exaltation. Movements of protest and independence showed themselves even within the Napoleonic structure. We have seen how the dependent states protected themselves by tariffs. Even the emperor's proconsuls tried to root themselves in local opinion, as when Louis Bonaparte, king of Holland, tried to defend Dutch interests against Napoleon's demands, or when Murat, king of Naples, appealed to Italian sentiment to secure his own throne.

Nationalism developed as a movement of resistance against the forcible internationalism of the Napoleonic empire. Since the international system was essentially French, the nationalistic movements were anti-French; and since Napoleon was an autocrat, they were antiautocratic. The nationalism of the period was a mixture of the conservative and the liberal. Some nationalists, predominantly conservative, insisted on the value of their own peculiar institutions, customs, folkways, and historical development, which they feared might be obliterated under the French and Napoleonic system. Others, or indeed the same ones, insisted on more self-determination, more participation in government, more representative institutions, more freedom for the individual against the bureaucratic interference of the state. Both conservatism and liberalism rose up against Napoleon, destroyed him, outlasted him, and shaped the history of the following generations.

Nationalism was thus very complex and appeared in different countries in different ways. In England the profound solidarity of the country exhibited itself; all classes rallied and stood shoulder to shoulder against "Boney"; and ideas of reforming Parliament or tampering with historic English liberties were resolutely put aside. It is possible that the Napoleonic wars helped England through a very difficult social crisis, for the Industrial Revolution was causing dislocation, misery, unemployment, and even revolutionary agitation among a small minority, all of which were eclipsed by the patriotic need of resistance to Bonaparte. In Spain, nationalism took the form of implacable resistance to the French armies that desolated the land. Some Spanish nationalists were liberal; a bourgeois group at Cádiz, rebelling against the French regime, proclaimed the Spanish constitution of 1812, modeled on the French constitution of 1791. But Spanish nationalism drew its greatest strength from sentiments that were counterrevolutionary, aiming to restore the clergy and the Bourbons. In Italy the Napoleonic regime was better liked and national feeling was less anti-French than in Spain. Bourgeois of the Italian cities generally prized the efficiency and enlightenment of French methods, and often shared in the anticlericalism of the French Revolution. The French regime, which lasted in Italy from 1796 to 1814, broke the habit of loyalty to the various duchies, oligarchic republics, papal states, and foreign dynasties by which Italy had long been ruled. Napoleon never unified Italy, but he assembled it into only three parts, and the French influence brought the notion of a politically united Italy within the bounds of reasonable aspiration. With the Poles Napoleon positively encouraged national feeling. He repeatedly told them that they might win a restored and united Poland by faithfully fighting in his cause. A few Polish nationalists, like the aging patriot Kosciuzsko, never trusted Napoleon, and some others, like Czartoryski, looked rather to the Russian tsar for a restoration of the Polish kingdom; but in general the Poles, for their own national reasons, were exceptionally devoted to the emperor of the French and lamented his passing.

The Movement of Thought in Napoleonic Germany

By far the most momentous national movement took place in Germany. The Germans rebelled not only against the Napoleonic rule but against the century-old ascendancy of French civilization. They rebelled not only against the French armies but against the philosophy of the Age of Enlightenment. The years of the French Revolution and Napoleon were for Germany the years of its greatest cultural efflorescence, the years of Beethoven, Goethe, and Schiller, of Herder, Kant, Fichte, Hegel, Schleiermacher, and many others. German ideas fell in with all the ferment of fundamental thinking known as "romanticism," which was everywhere challenging the "dry abstractions" of the Age of Reason and about which more will be said in this and the following chapter. Germany became the most "romantic" of all countries, and German influence spread throughout Europe. In the nineteenth century the Germans came to be widely regarded as intellectual leaders, somewhat as the French had been in the century before. And most of the distinctive features of German thought were somehow connected with nationalism in a broad sense.

Formerly, especially in the century following the Peace of Westphalia, the Germans had been the least nationally minded of all the larger European peoples.[14] They prided themselves on their world citizenship or cosmopolitan outlook. Looking out from the tiny states in which they lived, they were conscious of Europe, conscious of other countries, but hardly conscious of Germany. The Holy Roman Empire was a shadow. The German world had no tangible frontiers; the area of German speech simply faded out into Alsace or the Austrian Netherlands, or into Poland, Bohemia, or the upper Balkans. That "Germany" ever did, thought, or hoped anything never crossed the German mind. The upper classes, becoming contemptuous of much that was German, took over French fashions, dress, etiquette, manners, ideas, and language, regarding them as an international norm of civilized living. Frederick the Great hired French tax collectors and wrote his own books in French.

About 1780 signs of a change set in. Even Frederick, in his later years, predicted a golden age of German literature, proudly declaring that Germans could do what other nations had done. In 1784 appeared a book by J. G. Herder, called *Ideas on the Philosophy of the History of Mankind*. Herder was an earnest soul, a Protestant pastor and theologian who thought the French somewhat frivolous. He concluded that imitation of foreign ways made people shallow and artificial. He declared that German ways were indeed different from French but not for that reason the less worthy of respect. All true culture or civilization, he held, must arise from native roots. It must arise also from the life of the common people, the *Volk*, not from the cosmopolitan and denatured life of the upper classes.[15] Each people, he thought, meaning by a people a group sharing the same language, had its own attitudes, spirit, or genius. A sound civilization must express a national character or *Volksgeist*. And the character of each people was special to itself. Herder did not believe the nations to be in conflict; quite the contrary, he simply insisted that they were different. He did not believe German culture to be the best; many other peoples, notably the Slavs, later found his ideas applicable to their own needs. His philosophy of history was very different from Voltaire's. Voltaire and the philosophes had expected all peoples to progress along the same path of reason and enlightenment toward the same civilization. Herder thought that all peoples should develop their own genius in their own way, each slowly unfolding with the inevitability of plant-like growth, avoiding sudden change or distortion by outside influence, and all ultimately reflecting, in their endless diversity, the infinite richness of humanity and of God.

The idea of the *Volksgeist* was reinforced from other and non-German sources and soon passed to other countries in the general movement of romantic thought. Like much else in romanticism, it emphasized genius or intuition rather than

---

[14] See pp. 207–211.
[15] On elite and popular cultures see pp. 242–247.

reason. It stressed the differences rather than the similarity of mankind. It broke down that sense of human similarity which had been characteristic of the Age of Enlightenment,[16] and which revealed itself in French and American doctrines of the rights of man, or again in the law codes of Napoleon. In the past it had been usually thought that what was good was good for all peoples. Good poetry was poetry written according to certain classical principles or "rules" of composition, which were the same for all writers from the Greeks on down. Now, according to Herder and to romantics in all countries, good poetry was poetry that expressed an inner genius, either an individual genius or the genius of a people—there were no more "rules." Good and just laws, according to the older philosophy of natural law, somehow corresponded to a standard of justice that was the same for all men. But now, according to Herder and the romantic school of jurisprudence, good laws were those that reflected local conditions or national idiosyncrasies. Here again there were no "rules," except possibly the rule that each nation should have its own way.

Herder's philosophy set forth a cultural nationalism, without political message. The Germans had long been a nonpolitical people. In the microscopic states of the Holy Roman Empire they had had no significant political questions to think about; in the more sizable ones they had been excluded from public affairs. The French Revolution made the Germans acutely conscious of the state. It showed what a people could do with a state, once they took it over and used it for their own purposes. For one thing, the French had raised themselves to the dignity of citizenship; they had become free men, responsible for themselves, taking part in the affairs of their country. For another, because they had a unified state which included all Frenchmen, and one in which a whole nation surged with a new sense of freedom, they were able to rise above all the other peoples of Europe. Many in Germany were beginning to feel humiliation at the paternalism of their governments. The futilities of the Holy Roman Empire, which had made Germany for centuries the battlefield of Europe, now filled them with shame and indignation. They saw with disgust how their German princes, forever squabbling with each other for control over German subjects, disgraced themselves before the French to promote their own interests. The national awakening in Germany, which set in strongly after 1800, was therefore directed not only against Napoleon and the French, but also against the German rulers and many of the half-Frenchified German upper classes. It was democratic in that it stressed the superior virtue of the common people.

Germans became fascinated by the idea of political unity and national greatness, precisely because they had neither. A great national German state, expressing the deep moral will and distinctive culture of the German people, seemed to them the solution to all their problems. It would give moral dignity to the individual German, solve the vexatious question of the selfish petty princes, protect the deep German *Volksgeist* from violation, and secure the Germans from subjection to outside powers. The nationalist philosophy remained somewhat vague, because in practice there was little that one could do. "Father" Jahn organized a kind of youth movement and became the inventor of what might be termed political gymnastics, having his young men do calisthenics for the Fatherland; he led them on open-air expeditions into the country, where they made fun of aristocrats

[16] See pp. 313–314.

in French costume; and he taught them to be suspicious of foreigners, Jews, and internationalists, and indeed of everything that might corrupt the purity of the German *Volk*. Most Germans thought him too extreme. Others collected wonderful stories of the rich medieval German past. There was an anonymous anti-French work, *Germany in Its Deep Humiliation*, for selling which the publisher Palm was put to death. Others founded the Moral and Scientific Union, generally known as the *Tugendbund* or league of virtue or manliness, whose members, by developing their own moral character, were to contribute to the future of Germany.

The career of J. G. Fichte illustrates the course of German thought in these years. Fichte was a moral and metaphysical philosopher, a professor at the University of Jena. His doctrine, that the inner spirit of the individual creates its own moral universe, was much admired in many countries. In America, for example, it entered into the transcendental philosophy of Ralph Waldo Emerson. Fichte at first was practically without national feeling. He enthusiastically approved of the French Revolution, as did Jahn and Arndt. In 1793, with the Revolution at its height and many foreign observers turning against it, Fichte published a laudatory tract on the French Republic. He saw it as an emancipation of the human spirit, a step upward in the elevation of human dignity and moral stature. He accepted the idea of the Terror, that of "forcing men to be free"; and he shared Rousseau's conception of the state as the embodiment of the sovereign will of a people. He came to see the state as the means of human salvation. In 1800, in his *Closed Commercial State*, he sketched a kind of totalitarian system in which the state planned and operated the whole economy of the country, shutting itself off from the rest of the world in order that, at home, it might freely develop the character of its own citizens. When the French conquered Germany Fichte became intensely and self-consciously German. He took over the idea of the *Volksgeist:* not only did the individual spirit create its own moral universe, but the spirit of a people created a kind of moral universe as well, manifested in its language, arts, folkways, customs, institutions, and ideas.

At Berlin, in 1808, Fichte delivered a series of *Addresses to the German Nation*, declaring that there was an ineradicable German spirit, a primordial and immutable national character, more noble than that of other peoples (thus going beyond Herder), to be kept pure at all costs from all outside influence, either international or French. The German spirit, he held, had always been profoundly different from that of France and western Europe; it had never yet really been heard from but would be some day. The French army commander then occupying the city thought the lectures too academic to be worth suppression. They had, in fact, few hearers; Fichte was considered a firebrand by most Germans; but they later regarded him as a national hero.

Reforms in Prussia

Politically, in the revolt against the French the main transformations came in Prussia. Prussia after the death of Frederick the Great had fallen into a period of satisfied inertia, such as is likely to follow upon rapid growth or spectacular success. Then in 1806, at Jena-Auerstädt, the kingdom collapsed in a single battle. Its western and most of its Polish territories were taken away. It was relegated by Napoleon to its old holdings east of the Elbe. Even here the French remained in occupation, for Napoleon stationed his Ninth Corps in Berlin. But in the eyes of German nationalists Prussia had a moral advantage. Of all the German states it

THE NATIONAL MOVEMENTS: GERMANY 413

was the least compromised by collaboration with the French. Toward Prussia, as toward a haven, German patriots therefore made their way. East-Elbian Prussia, formerly the least German of German lands, became the center of an all-German movement for national freedom. The years after Jena contributed to the "Prussianizing" of Germany; but it is to be observed that neither Fichte nor Hegel, Gneisenau nor Scharnhorst, Stein nor Hardenberg, all rebuilders of Prussia, was a native Prussian.

The main problem for Prussia was military, since Napoleon could be overthrown only by military force. And as always in Prussia, the requirements of the army shaped the form taken by the state.[17] The problem was conceived to be one of morale and personnel. The old Prussia of Frederick, which had fallen ingloriously, had been mechanical, arbitrary, soulless. Its people had lacked the sense of membership in the state, and in the army its soldiers had held no hope of promotion and felt no patriotism or spirit. To produce this spirit was the aim of the army reformers, Scharnhorst and Gneisenau. Gneisenau, a Saxon, had served in one of the British "Hessian" regiments in the War of American Independence, during which he had observed the military value of patriotic feeling in the American soldiers. He was a close observer also of the consequences of the French Revolution, which, he said, had "set in action the national energy of the entire French people, putting the different classes on an equal social and fiscal basis." If Prussia was to strengthen itself against France, or indeed to avoid revolution in the long run in Prussia itself, it must find a means to inspire a similar feeling of equal participation in its own people, and to allow capable individuals to fill important positions in the army and government without regard to their social status.

The reconstruction of the state, prerequisite to the reconstruction of the army, was initiated by Baron Stein and continued by his successor, Hardenberg. Like Metternich, Stein came from western Germany; he had been an imperial knight of the late Holy Roman Empire, who from a bridge near his castle had beheld the domains of no less than eight German princes in one sweep of the eye. Stateless himself, he thought of Germany as a whole; he was long hostile to what he considered the barely civilized Prussia, but finally resorted to it as the hope of the future. Deeply committed to the philosophy of Kant and Fichte, he dwelt on the concepts of duty, service, moral character, and responsibility. He thought that the common people must be awakened to moral life, raised from a brutalized servility to the level of self-determination and membership in the community. This, he believed, required an equality more of duties than of rights.

Under Stein the old caste structure of Prussia became somewhat less rigid. Property became interchangeable between classes; bourgeois were allowed to buy land and serve as officers in the army. The burghers, to develop a sense of citizenship and participation in the state, were given extensive freedom of self-government in the cities; the municipal systems of Prussia, and later of Germany, became a model for much of Europe in the following century. Stein had ideas for parliamentary institutions in Prussia as a whole, thinking they would strengthen the country, but he left office before acting upon them.

His most famous work was the "abolition of serfdom." It was naturally impossible, since the whole reform program was aimed at strengthening Prussia for a war of liberation against the French, to antagonize the Junkers who commanded the army. Stein's ordinance of 1807 abolished serfdom only in that it abolished the

---

[17] See pp. 224–227, 322–323.

"hereditary subjection" of peasants to their manorial lords.[18] It gave peasants the right to move and migrate, marry, and take up trades without the lord's approval. If, however, the peasant remained on the land, he was still subject to all the old services of forced labor in the fields of the lord. Peasants enjoying small tenures of their own continued to be liable for the old dues and fees. By an edict of 1810, a peasant might convert his tenure into private property, getting rid of the manorial obligations, but only on condition that one-third of the land he had held should become the private property of the lord. In the following decades many such conversions took place, of which the result was that the estates of the Junkers grew considerably larger. The reforms in Prussia somewhat reduced the old patriarchal powers of the lords and gave legal status and freedom of movement to the mass of the population, thus laying the foundation for a modern state and modern economy. But the peasants tended to become mere hired agricultural laborers; and the position of the Junkers was heightened, not reduced. Prussia avoided the Revolution. Stein himself, because Napoleon feared him, was obliged to go into exile in 1808, but his reforms endured.

51. THE OVERTHROW OF NAPOLEON: THE CONGRESS OF VIENNA

The situation at the close of 1811 may be summarized as follows. Napoleon had the mainland of Europe in his grip. Russia and Turkey were at war on the Danube, but otherwise there was no war except in Spain, where four years of fighting remained inconclusive. The Continental System was working badly. Britain was hurt by it only negatively, in that, without it, British exports to Europe would have risen rapidly in these years. Well launched in the Industrial Revolution, Great Britain was amassing a vast store of national wealth, accumulating the wherewithal to assist European governments financially against Napoleon. The peoples of Europe were increasingly restless, dreaming increasingly of national freedom. In Germany, especially, many awaited the opportunity to rise in a war of independence. But Napoleon could be overthrown only by the destruction of his army, with which neither British wealth nor British sea power, nor the European patriots and nationalists, nor the Prussian nor the Austrian armed forces were able to cope. All eyes turned to Russia. Alexander I had long been dissatisfied with his French alliance. He had obtained from it nothing but the annexation of Finland in 1809. He received no assistance from France in his war with Turkey; he saw Napoleon marry into the Austrian house; he had to tolerate the existence of a French-oriented Poland at his very door. The articulate classes in Russia, namely, the landowners and serf owners, loudly denounced the French alliance and demanded a resumption of open trade relations with England. An international clientele of émigrés and anti-Bonapartists, including Baron Stein, also gradually congregated at St. Petersburg, where they poured into the tsar's ears the welcome message that Europe looked to him for its salvation.

The Russian Campaign and the War of Liberation

On December 31, 1810, Russia formally withdrew from the Continental System. Anglo-Russian commercial relations were resumed. Napoleon resolved to crush

[18] See p. 123.

the tsar. He concentrated the Grand Army in eastern Germany and Poland, a vast force of 700,000 men, the largest ever assembled up to that time for a single military operation. It was an all-European host. Hardly more than a third was French; another third was German, from German regions annexed to France, from the states of the Confederation of the Rhine, and with token forces from Prussia and Austria; and the remaining third was drawn from all other nationalities of the Grand Empire, including 90,000 Poles. Napoleon at first hoped to meet the Russians in Poland or Prussia. This time, however, they decided to fight on their own ground, and they needed in any case to delay until their forces on the lower Danube could be recalled. In June 1812 Napoleon led the Grand Army into Russia.

He intended a short, sharp war, such as most of his wars had been in the past, and carried with him only three weeks' supplies. But from the beginning everything went wrong. It was Napoleon's principle to force a decisive battle; but the Russian army simply melted away. It was his principle to live on the country, so as to reduce the need for supply trains; but the Russians destroyed as they retreated, and in any case, in Russia, even in the summer, it was hard to find sustenance for so many men and horses. Finally, not far from Moscow, Napoleon was able to join battle with the main Russian force at Borodino. Here again everything miscarried. It was his principle always to outnumber the enemy at the decisive spot; but the Grand Army had left so many detachments along its line of march that at Borodino the Russians outnumbered it. It was Napoleon's principle to concentrate his artillery, but here he scattered it instead, and to throw in his last reserves at the critical moment, but at Borodino, so far from home, he refused the risk of ordering the Old Guard into action. Napoleon won the battle, at a cost of 30,000 men, as against 50,000 lost by the Russians; but the Russian army was able to withdraw in good order.

On September 14, 1812, the French emperor entered Moscow. Almost immediately the city broke into flames. Napoleon found himself camping in a ruin, with troops strewn along a long line all the way back to Poland, and with a hostile army maneuvering near at hand. Baffled, he tried to negotiate with Alexander, who refused all overtures. After five weeks, not knowing what to do, and fearful of remaining isolated in Moscow over the winter, Napoleon ordered a retreat. Prevented by the Russians from taking a more southerly route, the Grand Army retired by the same way it had come. The cold weather set in early and was unusually severe. For a century after 1812 the retreat from Moscow remained the last word in military horror. Men froze and starved, horses slipped and died, vehicles could not be moved, and equipment was abandoned. Discipline broke down toward the end; the army dissolved into a horde of individual fugitives, speaking a babel of languages, harassed by bands of Russian irregulars, picking their way on foot over ice and snow, most of the time in the dark, for the nights are long in these latitudes in December. Of 611,000 who entered Russia 400,000 died of battle casualties, starvation, and exposure, and 100,000 were taken prisoner. The Grand Army no longer existed.

Now at last all the anti-Napoleonic forces rushed together. The Russians pushed westward into central Europe. The Prussian and Austrian governments, which in 1812 had half-heartedly supplied troops for the invasion of Russia, switched over in 1813 and joined the tsar. Throughout Germany the patriots, often half-trained boys, marched off in the War of Liberation, though it was the professional armies of the German states that made the difference. Anti-French riots broke out in Italy.

In Spain Wellington at last pushed rapidly forward; in June 1813 he crossed the Pyrenees into France. The British government, in three years from 1813 to 1815, poured £32,000,000 as subsidies into Europe, more than half of all the funds granted during the twenty-two years of the wars. An incongruous alliance of British capitalism and east-European agrarian feudalism, of the British navy and the Russian army, of Spanish clericalism and German nationalism, of divine-right monarchies and newly aroused democrats and liberals, combined at last to bring the Man of Destiny to the ground.

Napoleon, who had left his army in Russia in December 1812, and rushed across Europe to Paris, by sleigh and coach, in the remarkable time of thirteen days, raised a new army in France in the early months of 1813. But it was untrained and unsteady, and he himself had lost some of his genius for command. His new army was smashed in October at the battle of Leipzig, known to the Germans as the Battle of the Nations, the greatest battle in number of men engaged ever fought until the twentieth century. The allies drove Napoleon back upon France. But the closer they came to defeating him the more they began to fear and distrust each other.

The Restoration of the Bourbons

The coalition already showed signs of splitting. Should the allies, together or singly, negotiate with Napoleon? How strong should the France of the future be? What should be its new frontiers? What form of government should it have? There was no agreement on these questions. Alexander wanted to dethrone Napoleon and dictate peace in Paris, in dramatic retribution for the destruction of Moscow. He had a scheme for giving the French throne to Bernadotte, a former French marshal, now crown prince of Sweden, who as king of France would depend on Russian support. Metternich preferred to keep Napoleon or his son as French emperor, after clearing the French out of central Europe; for a Bonaparte dynasty in a reduced France would be dependent on Austria. The Prussian counsels were divided. The British declared that the French must get out of Belgium, and that Napoleon must go; they held that the French might then choose their own government but believed a restoration of the Bourbons to be the best solution. The three Continental monarchies had no concern for the Bourbons, and both Alexander and Metternich, if they could make France dependent respectively on themselves, were willing to see it remain strong to the extent of including Belgium. In November 1813 Metternich communicated to Napoleon a proposition known as the "Frankfurt proposals," by which Napoleon would remain French emperor, and France would retain its "natural" frontier on the Rhine. There was a chance of peace on this basis, for the allies could not shake off their old fear of Napoleon, the Prussians could be compensated elsewhere, and among the Russians many of the generals and others were impatient to go home. The British, their diplomatic influence reduced by the fact that they had few troops in Europe, faced the appalling prospect that the Continent would again make peace without them—and a peace in which France should again keep Belgium.

The British foreign minister, Viscount Castlereagh, arrived in person on the Continent in January 1814. He held a number of strong cards. For one thing, Napoleon rejected the Frankfurt proposals. He continued to fight, and the allies therefore continued to ask for British financial aid. Castlereagh skillfully used the promise of British subsidies to win acceptance of the British war aims. In addition, he found a common ground for agreement with Metternich, both Britain and Austria fearing the domination of Europe by Russia. Castlereagh's first great problem was to hold the alliance together, for without Continental allies the British could not defeat France. He succeeded, on March 9, 1814, in getting Russia, Prussia, Austria, and Great Britain to sign the treaty of Chaumont. Each power bound itself for twenty years to a Quadruple Alliance against France, and each agreed to provide 150,000 soldiers to enforce such peace terms as might be arrived at. For the first time since 1792 a solid coalition of the four great powers now existed against France. Three weeks later the allies entered Paris, and on April 4 Napoleon abdicated at Fontainebleau.

He was forced to this step by lack of support in France itself. Twenty years before, in 1793 and 1794, France had fought off the combined powers of Europe —minus Russia. It could not and would not do so in 1814. The country cried for peace. Even the imperial marshals advised the emperor's abdication. But what was to follow him? For over twenty-five years the French had had one regime after another. Now there were some who wished a republic, some who wished the empire under Napoleon's infant son, some who wished a constitutional monarchy, and some even who longed for the Old Regime. Talleyrand stepped into the breach. The "legitimate" king, he said, Louis XVIII, was after all the man who would provoke the least factionalism and opposition. The powers, likewise, had by this time concluded in favor of the Bourbons. A Bourbon king would be peaceable, under no impulse to win back the conquests of the republic and empire. He would also, as the native and rightful king of France, need no foreign support to bolster him up, so that the control of France would not arise as an issue to divide the victorious powers.

So the Bourbon dynasty was restored. Louis XVIII, ignored and disregarded for a whole generation, both by most Frenchmen and by the governments of Europe, returned to the throne of his brother and his fathers. He issued a "constitutional charter," partly at the insistence of the liberal tsar, and partly because, having actually learned from his long exile, he sought the support of influential people in France. The charter of 1814 made no concession to the principle of popular or national sovereignty. It was represented as the gracious gift of a theoretically absolute king. But in practice it granted what most Frenchmen wanted. It promised legal equality, eligibility of all to public office without regard to class, and a parliamentary government in two chambers. It recognized the Napoleonic law codes, the Napoleonic settlement with the church, and the redistribution of property effected during the Revolution. It carried over the abolition of feudalism and privilege, manorialism and tithes. It confined the vote, to be sure, to a very few large landowners; but for the time being, except for a few irreconcilables, France settled down to enjoy the blessings of a chastened revolution—and peace.

The Settlement before the Vienna Congress

It was with the government of the restored Bourbons that the powers, on May 30, 1814, signed a treaty. This document, the "first" Treaty of Paris, confined France to its boundaries of 1792, those obtaining before the wars. The allied statesmen disregarded cries for vengeance and punishment, imposed no indemnity or reparations, and even allowed the works of art gathered from Europe during the wars to remain in Paris. It was not the desire of the victors to handicap the new French government on which they placed their hopes. Napoleon meanwhile was exiled to the island of Elba on the Italian coast.

To deal with other questions, the powers had agreed, before signing the Alliance of Chaumont, to hold an international congress at Vienna after defeating Napoleon. The recession of the French flood left the future of much of Europe—Belgium, Holland, Germany, Poland, Italy, Spain—fluid and uncertain. There were many other debatable questions also, including the Russian annexation of Finland and ambitions on the Danube, the disintegration of the Spanish American empire, the British occupation of French, Dutch, and Spanish possessions, and the troublesome issue of the freedom of the seas.

Both Russia and Great Britain, before consenting to a general conference, specified certain matters that they would decide for themselves as not susceptible to international consideration. The Russians refused to discuss Turkey and the Balkans; they retained Bessarabia as the prize of their recent war with the Turks. They also kept Finland, as an autonomous constitutional grand duchy, as well as certain recent conquests in the Caucasus almost unknown to Europe. The British refused any discussion of the freedom of the seas. They also barred all colonial and overseas questions. The revolts in Spanish America were left to run their course. The British government simply announced to Europe which of its colonial and insular conquests it would keep and which it would return.

In Europe, the British remained in possession of Malta, the Ionian Islands, and Heligoland. In America, they kept St. Lucia, Trinidad, and Tobago in the West Indies and reasserted their claims to the Pacific Northwest, or Oregon country, to which claims were also made by Russia, Spain, and the United States. Of former French possessions, the British kept the island of Mauritius in the Indian Ocean. Of former Dutch territories, they kept the Cape of Good Hope and Ceylon, but returned the Netherlands Indies. During the Revolutionary and Napoleonic wars in Europe the British had also made extensive conquests in India, bringing much of the Deccan and the upper Ganges valley under their rule. The British emerged, in 1814, as the controlling power in both India and the Indian Ocean.

Indeed, of all the colonial empires founded by Europeans in the sixteenth and seventeenth centuries, and whose rivalry had been a recurring cause of war in the eighteenth, only the British now remained as a growing and dynamic system. The old French, Spanish, and Portuguese empires were reduced to mere scraps of their former selves; the Dutch still held vast establishments in the East Indies, but all the intermediate positions, the Cape, Ceylon, Mauritius, Singapore, were now British. Nor, in 1814, did any people except the British have a significant navy. With Napoleon and the Continental System defeated, with the Industrial Revolution bringing power machinery to the manufacturers of England, with no rival left in the contest for overseas dominion, and with a virtual monopoly of naval power, whose use they studiously kept free from international regulation, the British embarked on their century of world leadership, which may be said to have lasted from 1814 to 1914.

The Congress of Vienna, 1814–1815

The Congress of Vienna assembled in September 1814. Never had such a brilliant gathering been seen. All the states of Europe sent representatives; and many defunct states, such as the formerly sovereign princes and ecclesiastics of the late Holy Roman Empire, sent lobbyists to urge their restoration. But procedure was so arranged that all important matters were decided by the four triumphant Great Powers. Indeed it was at the Congress of Vienna that the terms great and small powers entered clearly into the diplomatic vocabulary. Europe was at peace, a treaty having been signed with the late enemy; France also was represented at the Congress, by none other than Talleyrand, now minister to Louis XVIII. Castlereagh, Metternich, and Alexander spoke for their respective countries; Prussia was represented by Hardenberg. The Prussians hoped, as always, to enlarge the kingdom of Prussia. Alexander was a question mark: he wanted Poland, he wanted constitutional governments in Europe, he wanted some kind of international system of collective security. Castlereagh and Metternich, with support from Talleyrand, were most especially concerned to produce a balance of power on the Continent. Aristocrats of the Old Regime, they applied eighteenth-century diplomatic principles to the existing problem. They by no means desired to restore the territorial boundaries obtaining before the wars. They did desire, as they put it, to restore the "liberties of Europe," meaning the freedom of European states from domination by a single power.[19] The threat of "universal monarchy," a term which diplomats still sometimes used to signify such a system as Napoleon's, was to be offset by an ingenious calculation of forces, a transfer of territory and "souls" from one government to another, in such a way as to distribute and balance political power among a number of free and sovereign states. It was hoped that a proper balance would also produce a lasting peace.

The chief menace to peace, and most likely claimant for the domination of Europe, naturally seemed to be the late troublemaker, France. The Congress of Vienna, without much disagreement, erected a barrier of strong states along the French eastern frontier. The historic Dutch Republic, extinct since 1795, was revived as the kingdom of the Netherlands, with the house of Orange as a hereditary monarchy; to it was added Belgium, the old Austrian Netherlands with which Austria had long been willing to part. It was hoped that the combined Dutch-Belgian kingdom would be strong enough to discourage the perennial French drive into the Low Countries. On the south, the Italian kingdom of Piedmont was restored and strengthened by the incorporation of the defunct republic of Genoa, extinct since 1797. Behind the Netherlands and Piedmont, and further to discourage a renewal of French pressure upon Germany and Italy, two great powers were installed. Almost all the German Left Bank of the Rhine was ceded to Prussia, which was to be, in Castlereagh's words, a kind of "bridge" spanning central Europe, a bulwark against both France in the West and Russia in the East. In Italy, again as a kind of secondary barrier against France, the Austrians were firmly installed. They not only took back Tuscany and the Milanese, which they had held before 1796, but also annexed the extinct republic of Venice. The Austrian empire now included a Lombardo-Venetian kingdom in north Italy, which lasted for almost half a century. In the rest of Italy the Congress recognized the restoration of the pope in the papal states and of former rulers in the smaller duchies; but it did not insist on a restoration of the Bourbons in the kingdom of Naples. There Napoleon's brother-in-law Murat, with support from Metternich, managed for a time to retain his throne. The Bourbons and Braganzas restored themselves, respectively, in Spain and Portugal and were recognized by the Congress.

As for Germany, the Congress made no attempt to put together again the

[19] See pp. 158–159.

Boundary of the German Confederation

0   100   200 miles

KINGDOM OF NORWAY AND SWEDEN

FINLAND
(Russia, 1808)

Oslo

Stockholm

St. Petersburg

Reval • Novgorod

BALTIC SEA

Riga

Borod

Smolensk

SCOTLAND

Edinburgh

NORTH SEA

UNITED KINGDOM
OF GREAT BRITAIN AND IRELAND

IRELAND • Dublin

ENGLAND

WALES

Copenhagen
DENMARK

SCHLESWIG

HELIGOLAND
(Britain)

HOLSTEIN

Elbe

Hamburg

HANOVER

Niemen R.

EAST
PRUSSIA

• Danzig

LITHUANIA

P R U S S I A

Vistula R.

• Warsaw

London •

KINGDOM OF THE
NETHERLANDS

Berlin

**KINGDOM OF
POLAND**
(1815-1831)

Kiev

ENGLISH CHANNEL

BELGIUM
(Ind. 1831)

Cologne

Rhine

LUX.

HESSE

SAXON
STATES

SAXONY

Breslau

Oder

UKRAINE

GALICIA

Cracow

ATLANTIC OCEAN

Rouen •

Seine R.

Paris R.

Metz

Strasbourg

LORRAINE

ALSACE

BADEN

WÜRT-
TEMBERG

HESSE

BAVARIA

Munich

Prague

AUSTRIA

Vienna

Pressburg

AUSTRIAN EMPIRE

Budapest

HUNGARY

Dniester R.

BESSARABIA
(Russia 1812)

MOLDAVIA
(Autonomous 1829)

Odessa

TRANSYLVANIA

Tours

F R A N C E

Berne

SWITZERLAND

TYROL

Lyons

Bordeaux •

Rhone R.

SAVOY

LOM-
BARDY

Milan

VENETIA

Po R.

PIEDMONT

PARMA

CROATIA

Belgrade

WALLACHIA
(Autonomous 1829)

Danube R.

DOBRUJA

Marseilles

Nice

Genoa

LUCCA

MODENA

SERBIA
*(Autonomous
1829)*

BOSNIA

DALMATIA

Sofia

BULGARIA

Constantinople

Toulon

PYRENEES

Ebro R.

Toulouse •

Barcelona •

KINGDOM OF SARDINIA

ELBA

TUSCANY

PAPAL
STATES

ADRIATIC SEA

MONTENEGRO

O T T O M A N

Salonica •

PORTUGAL

Madrid •

Tagus R.

S P A I N

Valencia

CORSICA
(France)

Rome •

Naples •

BALEARIC I.
(Spain)

SARDINIA

**KINGDOM OF THE
TWO SICILIES**

IONIAN I.
(Britain)

GREECE
(Independent 1829)

AEGEAN SEA

Athens

Smyr

RHODES

Seville

Cadiz

Gibraltar *(Britain)*

Palermo

SICILY

CRETE

Algiers

MOROCCO

ALGERIA *(France, 1830)*

TUNIS
(Turkish)

MALTA
(Britain)

MEDITERRANEAN SEA

bon

Burgos •

TRIPOLI

TRIPOLI

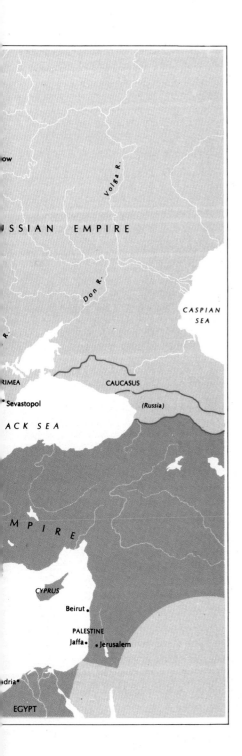

EUROPE, 1815

Boundaries are those set by the Congress of Vienna in 1815. In general, a system of five "great powers" prevailed over the Napoleonic empire. France was reduced to the borders it had had before the Revolutionary-Napoleonic wars. Prussia was firmly installed on both banks of the Rhine, thus obtaining the part of Germany in which industrialization became important fifty years later. South Germany remained as reorganized under Napoleon. Poland was again partitioned. A larger share of Poland than in 1795 now went to Russia, which also acquired Finland and Bessarabia. The Austrians added Venetia to what they had held before 1796.

The union of the Dutch and Belgian Netherlands lasted only until 1831, when the kingdom of Belgium was established. Otherwise, the boundaries of 1815 lasted until the Italian war of 1859 which led to the unification of Italy.

Humpty Dumpty of the Holy Roman Empire. The pleas of the former princelings went unheeded. The French and Napoleonic reorganization of Germany was substantially confirmed. The kings of Bavaria, Württemberg, and Saxony kept the royal crowns that Napoleon had bestowed on them. The king of England, George III, was now recognized as king, not "elector," of Hanover. The German states, thirty-nine in number, including Prussia and Austria, were joined in a loose confederation in which the members remained virtually sovereign. The Congress ignored the yearnings of German nationalists for a great unified Fatherland; Metternich especially feared nationalistic agitation; and in any case the nationalists themselves had no practical answer to concrete questions, such as the institutions of government and the frontiers that a united Germany should have. The Congress did declare, somewhat ineffectually, that in each of the German states there should be a representative legislative body.

The Polish-Saxon Question

The question of Poland, reopened by the fall of Napoleon's Grand Duchy of Warsaw, brought the Congress almost to disaster. Alexander still insisted on undoing the crime of the partitions, which to his mind meant reconstituting the Polish kingdom with himself as constitutional king, in a merely personal union with the Russian empire. A similar arrangement was being initiated in the Grand Duchy of Finland, where Alexander reigned as a constitutional grand duke. To reunite Poland required that Austria and Prussia surrender their respective segments of the old Poland, most of which they had in any case lost to Napoleon. The Prussians were willing, with the proviso, which Alexander supported, that Prussia receive instead the whole of the kingdom of Saxony, which was considered available because the king of Saxony had been the last German ruler to abandon Napoleon. The issue presented itself as the Polish-Saxon question, with Russia and Prussia standing together to demand all Poland for Russia, and all Saxony for Prussia.

Such a prospect horrified Metternich. For Prussia to absorb Saxony would raise Prussia prodigiously in the eyes of all Germans, and it would greatly lengthen the common frontier between Prussia and the Austrian Empire. Furthermore, for Alexander to become king of all Poland, and incidentally the protector of an extended Prussia, would incalculably augment the influence of Russia in the affairs of Europe. Metternich found that Castlereagh shared these views. To Castlereagh it seemed that the main problem at Vienna was to restrain Russia. The British had not fought the French emperor only to have Europe fall to the Russian tsar. For months the Polish-Saxon question was debated, Metternich and Castlereagh exploring every device of argument to dissuade the Russo-Prussian combination from its expansionist designs. Finally they accepted the proffered assistance of Talleyrand, who shrewdly used the rift between the victors to bring France back into the diplomatic circle as a power in its own right. On January 3, 1815, Castlereagh, Metternich, and Talleyrand signed a secret treaty, pledging themselves to go to war if necessary against Russia and Prussia. So, in the very midst of the peace conference, war again reared its head; and, in the very deliberations of the victors, one party among them allied itself with the vanquished.

No sooner had news of the secret treaty leaked out than Alexander offered to compromise. In his mixed nature he was, among other things, a man of peace, and he agreed to content himself with a reduced Polish kingdom. The Congress therefore created a new Poland (called "Congress Poland," which lasted for fifteen years); Alexander became its king, and he gave it a constitution; it comprised much the same area as Napoleon's Grand Duchy, representing in effect a transfer of this region from French to Russian control. It reached 250 miles farther west into Europe than had the Russian segment of the third partition of 1795. Some Poles still remained in Prussia and some in the Austrian Empire; Poland was not reunited. With the tsar thus content, Prussia too had to back down. It received about two-fifths of Saxony, the rest remaining to the Saxon king. The addition of both Saxon and Rhenish territories brought the Prussian monarchy into the most advanced parts of Germany. The net effect of the peace settlement, and of the Napoleonic wars, in this connection, was to shift the center of gravity of both Russia and Prussia farther west, Russia almost to the Oder, Prussia to the borders of France.[20]

With the solution of the Polish-Saxon question the main work of the Congress was completed. Other incidental matters were taken up. The Congress initiated international regulation of certain rivers. It issued a declaration against the Atlantic slave trade, which, however, remained ineffective, since the Continental powers were unwilling to grant the British navy free powers of search at sea, and the British were unwilling to put naval forces at the disposal of an international body. Committees of the Congress set to work to draft the Final Act. And at this point the whole settlement was brought into jeopardy.

The Hundred Days and Their Aftermath

Napoleon escaped from Elba, landed in France on March 1, 1815, and again proclaimed the empire. In the year since the return of the Bourbons discontent had been spreading in France. Louis XVIII proved to be a sensible man, but a swarm of unreasonable and vindictive émigrés had come back with him. Reaction and a "white terror" were raging through the country. Adherents of the Revolution rallied to the emperor on his dramatic reappearance. Napoleon reached Paris, took over the government and army, and headed for Belgium. He would, if he could, disperse the pompous assemblage at Vienna. To the victors of the year before, and to most of Europe, it seemed that the Revolution was again stirring, that the old horror of toppling thrones and recurring warfare might not after all be ended. The opposing forces met in Belgium at Waterloo, where the Duke of Wellington, commanding an allied force, won a great victory. Napoleon again abdicated, and was again exiled, this time to distant St. Helena in the south Atlantic. A new peace treaty was made with France, the "second" Treaty of Paris. It was more severe than the first, since the French seemed to have shown themselves incorrigible and unrepentant. The new treaty imposed minor changes of the frontiers, an indemnity of 700,000,000 francs, and an army of occupation.

The effect of the Hundred Days, as the episode following Napoleon's return from Elba is called, was to renew the dread of revolution, war, and aggression. Britain, Russia, Austria, and Prussia, after being almost at war with each other in January, again joined forces to get rid of the apparition from Elba, and in November 1815 they solemnly reconfirmed the Quadruple Alliance of Chaumont, adding a provision that no Bonaparte should ever govern France. They agreed

[20] See maps on pp. 222–223, 234–235, 328.

also to hold future congresses to review the political situation and enforce the peace. No change was made in the arrangements agreed to at Vienna, except that Murat, who fought for Napoleon during the Hundred Days, was captured and shot, and an extremely unenlightened Bourbon monarchy was restored in Naples. In addition to the Quadruple Alliance of the Great Powers, bound specifically to enforce or amend the terms of the peace treaty by international action, Alexander devised a vaguer scheme which he called the Holy Alliance. Long attracted to the idea of an international order, appalled by the return of Napoleon, and influenced at the moment by the pietistic Baroness von Krüdener, the tsar proposed, for all monarchs to sign, a statement by which they promised to uphold Christian principles of charity and peace. All signed except the pope, the sultan, and the prince regent of Great Britain. The Holy Alliance, probably sincerely meant by Alexander as a condemnation of violence, and at first not taken seriously by the others who signed it, and who thought it absurd to mix Christianity with politics, soon came to signify, in the minds of liberals, a kind of unholy alliance of monarchies against liberty and progress.

The Peace of Vienna, including generally the Treaty of Vienna itself, the treaties of Paris, and the British and colonial settlement, was the most far-reaching diplomatic agreement between the Peace of Westphalia of 1648 and the Peace of Paris which closed the First World War in 1919. It had its strong points and its weak ones. It produced a minimum of resentment in France; the late enemy accepted the new arrangements. It ended almost two centuries of colonial rivalry; for sixty or seventy years no colonial empire seriously challenged the British. Two other causes of friction in the eighteenth century—the control of Poland and the Austro-Prussian dualism in Germany—were smoothed over for fifty years. With past issues the peace of 1815 dealt rather effectively; with future issues, not unnaturally, it was less successful. The Vienna treaty was not illiberal in its day; it was by no means entirely reactionary, for the Congress showed little desire to restore the state of affairs in existence before the wars. The reaction that gathered strength after 1815 was not written into the treaty itself.

But the treaty gave no satisfaction to nationalists and democrats. It was a disappointment even to many liberals, especially in Germany. The transfer of peoples from government to government, without consultation of their wishes, opened the way under nineteenth-century conditions to a good deal of subsequent trouble. The peacemakers were in fact hostile both to nationalism and to democracy, the potent forces of the coming age; they regarded them, with reason, as leading to revolution and war. The problem to which they addressed themselves was to restore the balance of power, the "liberties of Europe," and to make a lasting peace. In this they were successful. They restored the European state system, or system in which a number of sovereign and independent states existed without fear of conquest or domination. And the peace which they made, though some details broke down in 1830, and others in 1848, on the whole subsisted for half a century; and not for a full century, not until 1914, was there a war in Europe that lasted longer than a few months or in which all the great powers were involved. No international disturbance comparable in magnitude to that created by the French Revolution and Napoleonic empire has yet been followed by such a protracted period of peace.

APPENDIXES, BIBLIOGRAPHY, and INDEX

Appendix I:
Chronological Tables

TABLE ONE: TO 1517

EUROPE AS A WHOLE: POLITICAL AND SOCIAL	EUROPE AS A WHOLE: THOUGHT AND LETTERS	BRITISH ISLES
	500–300 B.C. Classical Greek civilization	
146 B.C. Greeks conquered by Rome	427–347 B.C. Plato	
31 B.C. Roman Empire	384–322 B.C. Aristotle	
306–337 Emperor Constantine	106–43 B.C. Cicero	
	2nd century: Ptolemy and Galen	43–410 Roman Empire in Britain
5th century: Germanic migrations	354–430 Saint Augustine	
476 Roman Empire in West ends		
7th century: spread of Islam		596 Conversion of Anglo-Saxons
800 Coronation of Charlemagne		
9th century: Norse and Magyar invasions		871–899 Alfred the Great
1054 Schism of West and East		
	1033–1109 Anselm	
1073–1085 Pope Gregory VII (Hildebrand)		1066 Norman conquest
1095 First Crusade	1079–1142 Abelard	
12th century: rise of towns	12th century: coming of Arabic and Greek science	12th century: development of the monarchy in England
1189 Third Crusade		
1198–1216 Pope Innocent III	12th–13th century: universities, scholasticism	
13th century: rise of parliaments	1215 Fourth Lateran Council	1215 Magna Carta
1294–1303 Pope Boniface VIII	1225–1274 Thomas Aquinas	
		1295 Model Parliament
1348–1349 Black Death		1337–1453 Hundred Years' War
1378–1417 Schism of the West		
	1328–1384 John Wycliffe	
1414–1415 Council of Constance	1415 Death of John Huss	1381 Wat Tyler's rebellion
1453 Roman Empire in East ends	15th century: the Renaissance at its height	1455–1485 Wars of the Roses
	1452–1519 Leonardo da Vinci	
	1454–1455 Printing; Gutenberg Bible	
1492 Discovery of America	1466–1536 Erasmus	*1485–1603 The Tudors*
1498 Portuguese reach India	1469–1527 Machiavelli	1485–1509 Henry VII
1517 Beginnings of Reformation	1517 Luther's 95 Theses	1509–1547 Henry VIII

WESTERN EUROPE	CENTRAL EUROPE	EASTERN EUROPE
		6th–4th century B.C. Greek city-states
		4th–1st century B.C. Hellenistic Age
31 B.C.–476 Roman Empire	31 B.C.–476 Roman Empire in western and southern Germany	31 B.C.–1453 Roman Empire in East
		330 Constantinople founded
496 Conversion of Franks		
	568 Founding of Venice	
711 Muslims in Spain		
732 Muslim defeat at Tours		
768–814 Charlemagne	768–814 Charlemagne	10th century: conversion of Swedes, Poles, Hungarians to Rome; Russians to Constantinople
987–1792 Capetian monarchy in France	*962–1806 Holy Roman Empire*	
		1001–1918 Kingdom of Hungary
	1056–1106 Emperor Henry IV	1054 Schism of East and West
	1075–1122 Investiture struggle	
12th century: development of the monarchy in France		12th century: Teutonic Knights in Prussia
1208 Albigensian Crusade	13th century: failure of the Empire to organize Germany and Italy	13th century: conversion of East Baltic peoples to Rome
1303–1417 Papacy at Avignon		1236 Tartars in Russia
	1356 Golden Bull	1389 Turks in Balkan Peninsula
1337–1453 Hundred Years' War	1420–1431 Hussite Wars	
1412–1431 Joan of Arc	*1438–1918 Habsburg Emperors*	
		1453 Turks take Constantinople; end of Byzantine Empire
1461–1489 Louis XI of France		
1479–1516 Ferdinand and Isabella of Spain		
1494 French invasion of Italy		1480 Ivan the Great ends Tartar control over Russia
1515–1547 Francis I of France	1519–1556 Charles V	

TABLE TWO: 1517–1618

EUROPE AS A WHOLE: POLITICAL AND SOCIAL	EUROPE AS A WHOLE: THOUGHT AND LETTERS	BRITISH ISLES
1517 Beginnings of Reformation	1517 Luther's 95 Theses	1509–1547 Henry VIII
1519–1556 Charles V 1519–1648 Habsburg supremacy 1519–1522 Magellan circumnavigates globe		1521 Henry VIII's *Defense of Seven Sacraments*
1529 Turks besiege Vienna		
	1530 Loyola's *Spiritual Exercises*	
1531 First stock exchange at Antwerp	1534 Luther's German Bible 1536 Calvin's *Institutes of the Christian Religion*	1534 Act of Supremacy 1536–1539 Dissolution of monasteries 1539 Six Articles
1540 Founding of Jesuits 1541–1564 Calvin at Geneva	1543 Copernicus' *Revolutions of Heavenly Orbs* and Vesalius' *Structure of the Human Body*	1547–1553 Edward VI
1545–1563 Council of Trent	1550–1650 Golden age of Spanish literature	1553–1558 Mary I
1555 Peace of Augsburg 1556–1598 Philip II of Spain		1558–1603 Elizabeth I 1559 Knox and the Reformation in Scotland
	1561–1626 Francis Bacon	1563 The 39 Articles
	1564–1642 Galileo 1564–1616 Shakespeare	1569 Norfolk's rebellion
1571 Defeat of Turks at Lepanto	1576 Bodin's *Republic*	1577 Alliance with Netherlands
	1580 Montaigne's *Essays* 1582 Gregorian Calendar	
1588 Spanish Armada	1596–1650 Descartes	1588 Spanish Armada
		1603–1714 The Stuarts 1603–1625 James I
1607 English found Virginia 1608 French found Quebec 1609 Spanish found Santa Fé 1612 Dutch found New York	1611 King James' Bible	

WESTERN EUROPE	CENTRAL EUROPE	EASTERN EUROPE
1515–1547 Francis I of France	1519–1556 Charles V Emperor	
1516 Concordat of Bologna		1520–1566 Suleiman the Magnificent
	1521 Luther banned	
	1526 Charles V at war with Turks	1526 Turks occupy Hungary
	1529 Turks besiege Vienna	
		1533–1584 Ivan the Terrible, first Tsar of Russia
1536 Franco-Turkish alliance against Charles V		1535 First French capitulations in Turkey
1547–1559 Henry II of France	1546–1547 Schmalkaldic War	
		1553 English in White Sea
1556–1598 Philip II of Spain	1555 Peace of Augsburg	
	1556–1564 Ferdinand I	
1559–1589 Weakness of monarchy in France		
1562–1598 Wars of Religion in France		
	1564–1576 Maximilian II	
1566 Netherlands revolt begins		
1572 Massacre of St. Bartholomew		1571 Defeat of Turks at Lepanto
1574–1589 Henry III	1576–1612 Rudolf II	1574 Turks take Tunis
1589–1792 Bourbons in France		
1589–1610 Henry IV		
1598 Edict of Nantes		1604–1613 Time of troubles in Russia
1610–1643 Louis XIII		
	1608 Protestant Union	
	1609 Catholic League	
	1612–1619 Matthias	
	1618 Thirty Years' War	1613–1645 Michael Romanov, Tsar

TABLE THREE: 1618–1714

EUROPE AS A WHOLE: POLITICAL AND SOCIAL	EUROPE AS A WHOLE: THOUGHT AND LETTERS	BRITISH ISLES
	1561–1626 Francis Bacon	*1603–1714 The Stuarts*
	1564–1642 Galileo	1603–1625 James I
	1596–1650 Descartes	
1618–1648 Thirty Years' War		
17th century: English, French, Dutch in America; Dutch in South Africa and Indonesia	1623–1662 Pascal	1625–1649 Charles I
	17th century: flowering of English, French, and Dutch literature	
1619 First African slaves in Virginia	1625 Grotius' *Law of War and Peace*	1637 Ship money case
		1640–1660 Long Parliament
	1642–1727 Isaac Newton	1642–1648 Puritan rebellion and Civil War
1648 Peace of Westphalia		1649 Execution of Charles I
		1649–1658 Rule of Cromwell
1650 World population estimate: 500 million		1649–1653 Commonwealth
		1653–1660 Protectorate
	1660s Beginnings of scientific societies	1660 Restoration
1661–1715 Age of Louis XIV		1660–1685 Charles II
		1670s Rise of Whigs and Tories
		1673 Test Act
1683 Turks threaten Vienna		1685–1688 James II
	1687 Newton's *Principia*	
1689–1697 War of League of Augsburg		1688 "Glorious Revolution"
		1688–1702 William and Mary
	1690 Locke's *Treatises on Government; Human Understanding*	
	1697 Bayle's *Dictionary*	
1701–1714 War of Spanish Succession		1702–1714 Anne
		1707 Union of England and Scotland
1713–1714 Treaties of Utrecht and Rastadt		

WESTERN EUROPE	CENTRAL EUROPE	EASTERN EUROPE
1610–1643 Louis XIII of France	1618–1648 Thirty Years' War 1619 Emperor Ferdinand II 1620 Battle of White Mountain	*1613–1917 Romanovs in Russia* 1613–1645 Tsar Michael Romanov
1624–1642 Richelieu 1629 Peace of Alais 1635 France in Thirty Years' War	1629 Edict of Restitution 1640–1688 Frederick William, Great Elector of Brandenburg	17th century: spread of serfdom in Russia and Eastern Europe
1642–1661 Mazarin 1643–1715 Louis XIV of France 1648 Peace of Westphalia	1648 Peace of Westphalia 17th and 18th centuries: decline in Central Europe	
1652–1674 Three Anglo-Dutch Wars 1659 Peace of Pyrenees		
1665–1700 Charles II of Spain 1667–1668 Louis XIV's War of Devolution 1672–1678 Louis XIV's Dutch war		1667 Russian church reforms: Old Believers 1670 Revolt of Stephen Razin in Russia
1685 Revocation of Edict of Nantes	1683 Turks threaten Vienna	1682–1725 Peter the Great 1683 Turks threaten Vienna 1683–1718 Habsburg victories over Turks
1689–1714 Later wars of Louis XIV		
	1697–1733 Augustus of Saxony King of Poland	1697–1718 Charles XII of Sweden
		1699 Austro-Turkish Peace of Karlowitz
1700–1931 Bourbons in Spain 1700–1746 Philip V of Spain		
	1701–1918 Hohenzollern kings *in Prussia* 1701–1713 Frederick I of Prussia	

TABLE FOUR: 1714–1815

EUROPE AS A WHOLE: POLITICAL AND SOCIAL	EUROPE AS A WHOLE: THOUGHT AND LETTERS	BRITISH ISLES
1713–1714 Treaties of Utrecht and Rastadt	18th century: Age of Enlightenment	*1714–1837 Hanoverians* 1714–1727 George I 1720 South Sea Bubble 1721 Walpole's ministry
1740–1763 British-French colonial wars	1740–1789 Enlightenment at its peak	1727–1760 George II 1739 War of Jenkins' Ear
1740–1748 War of Austrian Succession	1740–1760 Voltaire at his height	
1740–1789 Enlightened despotism in Europe	1748 Montesquieu's *Spirit of Laws*	
		1745 Jacobite Rebellion
1750 World population estimate: 700 million	1751–1768 French *Encyclopedia*	
1754–1763 French and Indian War in America		
1756 Diplomatic Revolution		1760–1820 George III
1756–1763 Seven Years' War	1761 Rousseau's *Social Contract*	
1763 Treaties of Paris and Hubertusburg: British supremacy in Canada and India		1769 Watt's steam engine 1769 Arkwright's waterframe
1776 American Declaration of Independence	1776 Adam Smith's *Wealth of Nations*	1776 American Revolution
1776–1783 War of American Independence		
		1782–1806 Ministries of William Pitt the Younger
1789 French Revolution begins	1784 Herder's *Philosophy of History of Mankind* 1790 Burke's *Reflections on the French Revolution* 1790s Spread of French revolutionary ideas Beginnings of romanticism	
1792–1815 Revolutionary and Napoleonic wars		1793–1814 War with France
1792–1797 War of First Coalition		
1798–1801 War of Second Coalition		1798 Rebellion of Ireland 1801 Union of Great Britain and Ireland 1802–1803 Peace of Amiens
1803–1805 War of Third Coalition		
1804–1814 "Grand Empire"	1804–1811 Napoleonic codes	
1806–1812 Continental System		
		1808–1813 Peninsular War in Spain

WESTERN EUROPE	CENTRAL EUROPE	EASTERN EUROPE
	1711–1740 Charles VI of Austria	1682–1725 Peter the Great
1715–1774 Louis XV of France	1713–1740 Frederick William I	1709 Battle of Poltava
1715–1723 Regency in France	of Prussia	
1720 Mississippi Bubble	1713–1740 Pragmatic Sanction	
		1721 Russo-Swedish Treaty of Nystadt
18th century: culmination of "Old Regime" in France	1740–1786 Frederick II of Prussia	1733–1738 War of Polish Succession
	1740–1780 Maria Theresa of Austria	1739 Austro-Turkish Peace of Belgrade
	1740–1745 Silesian Wars	
	1756 Habsburg-Bourbon Alliance	
	1756–1763 Seven Years' War	
		1762–1796 Catherine II of Russia
		1768–1774 Russo-Turkish War
		1772 First Partition of Poland
1774–1793 Louis XVI of France		1773–1774 Pugachev Rebellion
		1774 Russo-Turkish Treaty of Kuchuk Kainarji
1778 French-American Alliance	1780–1790 Joseph II of Austria	
	1780s Cultural revival of Germany	1787–1792 Russo-Turkish War
1789 French Revolution begins		
1792 First French Republic established		1793 Second Partition of Poland
1793–1794 The Terror	1797 Treaty of Campo Formio	1795 Third Partition of Poland
1795–1799 Directory		1796–1801 Paul I of Russia
1799 Bonaparte's coup	1798–1814 French predominance	
1799–1804 Consulate		
		1801–1825 Alexander I of Russia
1804–1814 Napoleon I: The Empire		
1807 Peace of Tilsit	1806 End of Holy Roman Empire	1806–1812 Russo-Turkish War

EUROPE AS A WHOLE: POLITICAL AND SOCIAL	EUROPE AS A WHOLE: THOUGHT AND LETTERS	BRITISH ISLES
1809–1811 Napoleon at height		
1812 Invasion of Russia, and retreat		
1812 U.S.-British War		
1813 Battle of Leipzig		
1814–1815 Congress of Vienna		1814 Alliance of Chaumont
1815 Waterloo		

WESTERN EUROPE	CENTRAL EUROPE	EASTERN EUROPE
	1806 Confederation of the Rhine	1807 Franco-Russian Alliance
		1812 Napoleon's invasion of Russia
1814 Restoration of Bourbons 1815 Hundred Days; Waterloo	1813–1814 German War of Liberation: Leipzig	

Appendix II:
Rulers and Regimes
In Principal European
Countries since 1500

HOLY ROMAN EMPIRE

Habsburg Line

MAXIMILIAN I	1493–1519
CHARLES V	1519–1556
FERDINAND I	1556–1564
MAXIMILIAN II	1564–1576
RUDOLPH II	1576–1612
MATTHIAS	1612–1619
FERDINAND II	1619–1637
FERDINAND III	1637–1657
LEOPOLD I	1658–1705
JOSEPH I	1705–1711
CHARLES VI	1711–1740

Charles VI was succeeded by a daughter, Maria Theresa, who as a woman could not be elected Holy Roman Emperor. French influence in 1742 secured the election of

Bavarian Line

CHARLES VII	1742–1745

On Charles VII's death the Habsburg control of the Emperorship was resumed.

Lorraine Line

FRANCIS I   1745–1765
(husband of Maria Theresa)

Habsburg-Lorraine Line

JOSEPH II   1765–1790
(son of Francis I and Maria Theresa)
LEOPOLD II   1790–1792
FRANCIS II   1792–1806

The Holy Roman Empire became extinct in 1806.

AUSTRIAN DOMINIONS

The rulers of Austria from 1438 to 1740, and at least titular kings of Hungary from 1526 to 1740, were the same as the Holy Roman Emperors. After 1740:

Habsburg Line (through female heir)

MARIA THERESA	1740–1780
JOSEPH II	1780–1790
LEOPOLD II	1790–1792
FRANCIS II	1792–1835

In 1804 Francis II took the title of Emperor, as Francis I of the Austrian Empire. Austria was declared an "empire" because Napoleon proclaimed France an empire in that year, and because the demise of the Holy Roman Empire could be foreseen.

FERDINAND I	1835–1848
FRANCIS JOSEPH	1848–1916
CHARLES I	1916–1918

The Austrian Empire became extinct in 1918.

BRITISH ISLES

Tudor Line

Kings of England and Ireland
HENRY VII	1485–1509
HENRY VIII	1509–1547
EDWARD VI	1547–1553
MARY I	1553–1558
ELIZABETH I	1558–1603

In 1603 James VI of Scotland, a great-great-grandson of Henry VII, succeeded to the English throne.

Stuart Line

Kings of England and Ireland, and of Scotland

JAMES I	1603–1625
CHARLES I	1625–1649

Republican Interregnum

The Commonwealth	1649–1653
The Protectorate	
OLIVER CROMWELL	1653–1658
Lord Protector	
RICHARD CROMWELL	1658–1660

Restored Stuart Line

CHARLES II	1660–1685
JAMES II	1685–1688

In 1688 James II was forced out of the country, but Parliament kept the crown in a female branch of the Stuart family, calling in Mary, the daughter of James II, and her husband William III of the Netherlands.

WILLIAM III	1689–1702,
AND MARY II	1689–1694
ANNE	1702–1714

In 1707, through the Union of England and Scotland, the royal title became King (or Queen) of Great Britain and Ireland. The Stuart family having no direct Protestant heirs, the throne passed in 1714 to the German George I, Elector of Hanover, a great-grandson of James I.

Hanoverian Line

Kings of Great Britain and Ireland

GEORGE I	1714–1727
GEORGE II	1727–1760
GEORGE III	1760–1820
GEORGE IV	1820–1830
WILLIAM IV	1830–1837

William IV having no heirs, the British throne passed in 1837 to Victoria, a granddaughter of George III. Though the British family has continued in direct descent from George I, it has dropped the Hanoverian designation and is now known as the House of Windsor. From 1877 to 1947 the British rulers bore the additional title of Emperor (or Empress) of India.

VICTORIA	1837–1901
EDWARD VII	1901–1910
GEORGE V	1910–1936
EDWARD VIII	1936
GEORGE VI	1936–1952
ELIZABETH II	1952–

FRANCE

Valois Line

LOUIS XI	1461–1483
CHARLES VIII	1483–1498
LOUIS XII	1498–1515
FRANCIS I	1515–1547
HENRY II	1547–1559
FRANCIS II	1559–1560
CHARLES IX	1560–1574
HENRY III	1574–1589

In 1589 the Valois line became extinct, and the throne passed to Henry of Bourbon, a remote descendant of French kings of the fourteenth century.

Bourbon Line

HENRY IV	1589–1610
LOUIS XIII	1610–1643
LOUIS XIV	1643–1715
LOUIS XV	1715–1774
LOUIS XVI	1774–1792

The Republic

Convention	1792–1795
Directory	1795–1799
Consulate	1799–1804

The Empire

NAPOLEON I	1804–1814
Emperor of the French	
and King of Italy	

Restored Bourbon Line

LOUIS XVIII	1814–1824

(Royalists count a Louis XVII, 1793–1795, and date the reign of Louis XVIII from 1795.)

CHARLES X   1824–1830

The Revolution of 1830 gave the throne to the Duke of Orleans, descendant of Louis XIII.

Orleans Line

LOUIS-PHILIPPE   1830–1848

The Second Republic

1848–1852

The Second Empire

NAPOLEON III   1852–1870
Emperor of the French

The Third Republic

1870–1940

Vichy Regime

1940–1944

Provisional Government

1944–1946

The Fourth Republic

1946–1958

The Fifth Republic

1958–

PRUSSIA (AND GERMANY)

A continuous Hohenzollern line ruled until 1918.

Electors of Brandenburg and Dukes of Prussia

GEORGE WILLIAM   1619–1640
FREDERICK WILLIAM   1640–1688
the "Great Elector"
FREDERICK III   1688–1713

In 1701 Frederick III was permitted by the Holy Roman Emperor to entitle himself King in Prussia, as Frederick I.

Kings of Prussia

FREDERICK I   1701–1713
FREDERICK WILLIAM I   1713–1740
FREDERICK II, the "Great"   1740–1786
FREDERICK WILLIAM II   1786–1797
FREDERICK WILLIAM III   1797–1840
FREDERICK WILLIAM IV   1840–1861
WILLIAM I   1861–1888

In 1871 William I took the title of German Emperor.

German Emperors

WILLIAM I   1871–1888
FREDERICK III   1888
WILLIAM II   1888–1918

The German Empire became extinct in 1918. It was succeeded by the

Weimar Republic

1919–1933

(an unofficial title for what was still called the Deutsches Reich, a phrase not easy to translate accurately)

The Third Reich

1933–1945

(an unofficial title for the Deutsches Reich under Adolf Hitler)
Allied Military Government in 1945 was followed by

German Federal Republic (West Germany)

1949–

German Democratic Republic (East Germany)

1949–

SARDINIA (AND ITALY)

In 1720 Victor Amadeus II, Duke of Savoy, took the title of King of Sardinia, having acquired the island of that name.

Kings of Sardinia

Victor Amadeus II	1720–1730
Charles Emmanuel III	1730–1773
Victor Amadeus III	1773–1796
Charles Emmanuel IV	1796–1802
Victor Emmanuel I	1802–1821
Charles Felix	1821–1831
Charles Albert	1831–1849
Victor Emmanuel II	1849–1878

In 1861 Victor Emmanuel II took the title of King of Italy.

Kings of Italy

Victor Emmanuel II	1861–1878
Humbert I	1878–1900
Victor Emmanuel III	1900–1946
Humbert II	1946

In 1936 Victor Emmanuel III took the title of Emperor of Ethiopia, which became meaningless with British occupation of Ethiopia in 1941. In 1946 the Kingdom of Italy became extinct and was succeeded by the

Italian Republic

1946–

SPAIN

Ferdinand and Isabella   1479–1504/1516

Isabella died in 1504, but Ferdinand lived until 1516, whereupon the Spanish thrones were inherited by their grandson Charles, who became Charles V of the Holy Roman Empire, but was known in Spain as Charles I.

Habsburg Line

Charles I	1516–1556
Philip II	1556–1598
Philip III	1598–1621
Philip IV	1621–1665
Charles II	1665–1700

With Charles II the Spanish Habsburg line became extinct, and the throne passed to the French Bourbon grandson of Louis XIV of France and great-grandson of Philip IV of Spain.

Bourbon Line

Philip V	1700–1746
Ferdinand VI	1746–1759

Charles III	1759–1788
Charles IV	1788–1808

Bonaparte Line

Joseph   1808–1813
(brother of Napoleon)

Restored Bourbon Line

Ferdinand VII	1813–1833
Isabella II	1833–1868

In 1868 Isabella abdicated; after a regency, and a brief reign by Amadeus I (Savoy), 1871–1873, there was a short-lived First Republic, 1873–1874, succeeded by

Alfonso XII	1874–1885
Alfonso XIII	1885–1931

In 1931 a republican revolution unseated Alfonso XIII.

Second Spanish Republic

1931–1936

Spanish Civil War

1936–1939

Regime of General Francisco Franco

1939–1975

Upon the death of Franco the Bourbon family was restored.

Juan Carlos I   1975–

RUSSIA (AND U.S.S.R.)

Grand Dukes of Moscow

Ivan III, the "Great"	1462–1505
Basil III	1505–1533
Ivan IV, the "Terrible"	1533–1584

In 1547 Ivan IV took the title of Tsar of Russia.

Tsars of Russia

Ivan IV, the "Terrible"	1547–1584
Theodore I	1584–1598
Boris Godunov	1598–1605

Time of Troubles

1604–1613

Romanov Line

MICHAEL	1613–1645
ALEXIS	1645–1676
THEODORE II	1676–1682
IVAN V AND PETER I	1682–1689
PETER I, the "Great"	1689–1725
CATHERINE I	1725–1727
PETER II	1727–1730
ANNA	1730–1740
IVAN VI	1740–1741
ELIZABETH	1741–1762
PETER III	1762
CATHERINE II, the "Great"	1762–1796
PAUL	1796–1801
ALEXANDER I	1801–1825

NICHOLAS I	1825–1855
ALEXANDER II	1855–1881
ALEXANDER III	1881–1894
NICHOLAS II	1894–1917

In 1917 the tsardom became extinct.

Provisional Government

1917

Communist Revolution

1917

Union of Soviet Socialist Republics

1922–

Appendix III:
Historical Populations
of Various Countries
and Cities

Figures for dates before the nineteenth century arise from estimates, in some cases subject to a wide margin of error. Those for the nineteenth and twentieth centuries generally reflect census returns, at dates within two or three years before or after the round date indicated. For cities, the figures for 1950 and 1980 refer to "urban agglomerations" as defined in the *United Nations Demographic Yearbook*. Estimates for cities for earlier dates are conveniently assembled in Tertius Chandler and Gerald Fox, *3000 Years of Urban Growth* (New York, 1974).

For countries, the use of the table is mainly for rough comparisons. It shows, for example, that France was about five times as populous as England in the Middle Ages, and was still more populous than all the German states at the time of the French Revolution, or that Spain declined under the Habsburgs in the seventeenth century, and that Ireland lost population after the famine and ensuing emigration. All countries except Ireland grew rapidly in population in the nineteenth century. For Russia, the figures from 1750 to 1950 reflect territorial expansion as well as internal growth. All figures for China are very uncertain, though unquestionably very large.

For 1950 and 1980 the figures for Ireland include both the Republic of Ireland and Northern Ireland, and "Germany" includes both East and West Germany. In 1980 the Irish Republic was about twice as populous as its northern neighbor, and West Germany was over three times as populous as East Germany.

TIES in thousands

	LONDON	MANCHESTER	PARIS	MARSEILLES
4th Century	50	3–	200	
5th Century				
6th Century	100			
7th Century	500	15–	450	50 +
8th Century	750		500	90
1800	959	77	600	111
1850	2681	303	1422	195
1900	6581	544	3670	491
1950	8346	2421	4823	655
1980	6970	2675	8612	1077

	FLORENCE	BERLIN	VIENNA	PRAGUE
4th Century	50 +			
5th Century	60	10–	20	25 +
6th Century	65	12	40 +	40 +
7th Century	75	20	100	40 +
8th Century	75	100	220	75
800	84	172	247	75
50	114	500	444	206
900	206	2712	1675	382
50	374	3337	1766	922
?	464	3044	1590	1191

AMSTERDAM	ANTWERP	LISBON	MADRID	ROME
	5	20 +	5–	30–
20–	35			50–
35	100	100	60	100
100 +	50	73	80	130
150	50	120	120	150
201	62	180	160	153
224	88	240	281	175
511	277	356	540	463
838	584	790	1618	1652
961	1569	1612	3200	2898

WARSAW	BUDAPEST	STOCKHOLM	ST. PETERSBURG LENINGRAD	MOSCOW
70		60	100	
100	54 +	76	220	250
150	178	93	485	365
700	732	301	1150	1000
804	1571	928	3182	4847
1542	2091	1380	4588	8011

OUNTRIES in millions

	ENGLAND AND WALES	SCOTLAND	IRELAND	FRANCE
1300	3.5			15.0
1500	2.8			16.0
1700	5.5	1.2		19.0
1800	8.9	1.6	5.2	27.0
1850	17.9	2.9	6.5	34.2
1900	32.5	4.5	4.5	38.5
1950	43.0	5.0	4.3	41.8
1980	49.2	5.2	4.9	53.7

	SWEDEN	POLAND	RUSSIA U.S.S.R.	CHINA
1300		1.3		
1500		2.0		
1700	1.6		12	200
1800	2.3		30	
1850	3.5		62	400
1900	5.1	28.3	104	
1950	7.0	24.8	180	547
1980	8.3	35.6	265	995

BELGIUM	NETHERLANDS	GERMANY	SPAIN	ITALY
.7	.4	7.0		8.0
		7.0	8.3	6.0
1.6	1.8	15.0	6.0	11.0
3.0	2.0	25.0	10.5	17.2
4.3	3.1	33.8		24.3
6.7	5.1	56.3	19.1	33.6
8.6	10.1	68.3	27.9	46.8
9.9	14.1	78.3	37.4	57.1

JAPAN	EGYPT	MEXICO	BRAZIL	U.S.A.
				.3
	2.5	6.0		5.3
30.0	5.0			23.2
45.0	10.0	13.6	20.0	76.0
83.2	20.0	25.7	52.6	152.0
116.8	42.3	69.3	118.6	228.0

Bibliography

The following reading lists are intended for the convenience of students, teachers, and general readers. Although professional students of history also may find them useful, no attempt has been made to provide comprehensive coverage of any areas or topics. The aim throughout has been to call attention to the most reliable and most recent works, to which the reader may turn for more specialized bibliographies. Classification follows the plan of chapters in the present book. Few titles are intentionally repeated; to find books on some topics, it will sometimes be necessary to look in several places. For reasons of space, works in foreign languages are excluded, as are (with few exceptions) general textbooks, articles in periodicals, and primary source materials.

Many of the titles listed below are now or will be available in paperback; up-to-date lists of such paperbacks may be found in the *Paperback book guide for colleges*, published and distributed by R. R. Bowker Company. An asterisk in the reading lists below indicates availability in a paperback edition.

WORKS OF GENERAL COVERAGE

Bibliographical Guides

There are literally hundreds of thousands of books on historical subjects, and it is difficult to find titles and authors on any particular topic. One useful but now outdated bibliographical tool is the American Historical Association's *Guide to historical literature* (1961). To keep up with the outpouring of historical books in recent years, one must read the book reviews and listings of new books in the *American historical review*, the *Journal of modern history*, and other periodicals; the American Historical Association (AHA) Pamphlets series is often helpful. Some of the most discerning appraisals of new history books are to be found in the (London) *Times literary supplement*.

Brief Reference Works and Atlases

W. L. Langer, *An encyclopedia of world history: ancient, medieval, and modern, chronologically arranged* (rev., 1972), is a vast table of dates and important events. A similar service is performed by S. H. Steinberg, *Historical tables, 58 B.C.-A.D. 1978* (1979), and G. S. P. Freeman-Grenville, *Chronology of world history* (1978). Convenient one-volume reference tools are the *New Columbia encyclopedia* (4th ed., 1975), and the *Random House encyclopedia* (1977).

An excellent atlas that places European history in its world setting is G. Barraclough (ed.), the (London) *Times atlas of world history* (1978). Among many other historical atlases are R. R. Palmer and others, *Atlas of world history* (1957), available also as *Abridged historical atlas** (1958); W. R. Shepherd, *Historical atlas* (rev., 1964); *Muir's Historical atlas—medieval and modern* (rev., 1964); *Chambers historical atlas of the world** (1971); and the *New Oxford atlas* (1975). H. C. Darby and H. Fullard, *Atlas** (1975), is the final volume (vol. 14) of the *New Cambridge modern history*. Geographical information can be readily located through *Webster's geographical dictionary* (rev., 1972), and current developments may be followed in J. P. Cole, *Geography of world affairs* (1979), and M. Kidron and

R. Segal, *The state of the world atlas* (1981). An interesting introduction to cartography is J. N. Wilford, *The mapmakers* (1981).

Geographical influences on history are discussed in D. S. Whittlesey, *Environmental foundations of European history* (1949); C. T. Smith, *An historical geography of Western Europe before 1800* (1967); and E. A. Freeman and J. B. Bury, *The historical geography of Europe* (1974). N. J. G. Pounds, *An historical geography of Europe* (2 vols., 1973–1979), examines economic changes in their geographic setting from 450 B.C. to the mid-nineteenth century. An interesting book stressing unique factors in European development is E. L. Jones, *The European miracle: environments, economies, and geopolitics in the history of Europe and Asia** (1981), while one national setting is examined in E. W. Fox, *History in geographic perspective: the other France* (1971).

Multivolumed Encyclopedias

Among the most useful are the *Encyclopaedia Britannica* [now in its controversial fifteenth edition (1975), of which the nineteen volumes of the *Macropaedia* provide the longer scholarly articles]; the *Encyclopedia Americana, Collier's encyclopedia,* and the *New international encyclopedia.* Each annually publishes a yearbook that covers developments of the previous year. The *Academic American encyclopedia* (1981) is the newest of these multivolumed works of reference. The *International encyclopedia of the social sciences* (17 vols., 1968) may be consulted for many topics. The *Dictionary of the history of ideas* (4 vols., 1973) has substantial articles on important concepts, while the *Encyclopedia of philosophy* (8 vols., 1967) is valuable for philosophical thought. The *Dictionary of scientific biography* (8 vols., 1970–1980) includes scientists from antiquity to the present. The *Dictionary of national biography* (1885–1949) is informative for British figures; a shorter version is the *Concise dictionary of national biography* (2 vols., 1961, 1982).

Multivolumed Collaborative Works and Series on Modern European History

The *Cambridge modern history* (14 vols., 1902–1912) has been superseded by the *New Cambridge modern history** (14 vols., 1957–1979). The volumes, which are described in the appropriate sections below, contain valuable chapters by specialists from all over the world but often fail to provide a synthesis for the period covered; volume 13, a companion volume [Peter Burke (ed.), 1979], is a welcome collection of thematic essays. An *Oxford history of modern Europe,* focusing on individual nations, will also be available soon; seven volumes have been published to date. An important series by American scholars on Europe from 1250 to 1945 is the *Rise of modern Europe* (20 vols. projected, 1936 ff., now all but complete), also known as the "Langer series" for its editor, W. L. Langer; the volumes, each with an extensive bibliography, are discussed in the chapters below. B. C. Shafer is editing *Europe and the world in the age of expansion* (10 vols. projected, 1975 ff.), to cover the thirteenth to twentieth centuries. The multivolumed collaborative *UNESCO history of mankind* (1963 ff.) has suffered from the need to arrive at political consensus on subjects covered. There are a variety of other series.

Interpretive and Large-Scale Histories

Histories recounting and analyzing the human story in order to show that it follows a certain pattern or system, or that it obeys certain laws, are generally regarded with distrust by historians, who are not convinced by the evidence offered. In recent years, the most important grand-scale interpretive account has been A. J. Toynbee's monumental *A study of history** (12 vols., 1934–1961, of which vol. 12 consists of *Reconsiderations*) [abridgment edited by D. C. Somervell, 2 vols., 1947–1957]; Toynbee's *Mankind and mother earth* (1976) was published posthumously. Some objections to Toynbee are discussed in M. F. Ashley-Montagu (ed.), *Toynbee and history: critical essays and reviews* (1956); E. T. Gargan and others, *The intent of Toynbee's history* (1961); and P. Geyl, *Debates with historians* (1956) and *Encounters in history* (1961). The attempt to find patterns or laws in historical evolution is to be distinguished from large-scale efforts to recount the scope of human history. Here two works stand out: H. A. L. Fisher, *A history of Europe* (3 vols., 1935–1936; 2 vols., 1949), an older, notable effort by a single author to tell the whole Western story from the Greeks to the twentieth century, and W. H. McNeill, *The rise of the West: a history of the human community* (1963), a presentation of Western history in its world setting that stresses the interrelationships of human civilization at all stages.

McNeill has also written *The shape of European history* * (1974), a briefer study of Europe from antiquity to the present stressing cultural and technological changes. Ambitious and informative but overly Eurocentric is H. Thomas, *A history of the world* (1979).

General Histories in Special Areas

[Books listed here relate to many or all of the chapters of the present work and provide additional specialized bibliographies as well.] For European economic history, a valuable collaborative work is C. M. Cipolla (ed.), *The Fontana economic history of Europe* * (6 vols., 1972–1976), with chapters contributed by an international roster of experts. A useful, one-volume synthesis is S. B. Clough and R. T. Rapp, *European economic history* (rev., 1975). On economic thought, one may read: E. Roll, *A history of economic thought* (rev., 1946); C. Gide and C. Rist, *A history of economic doctrines* (2nd ed., 1948); R. L. Heilbroner, *The worldly philosophers* * (1953); E. Whittaker, *Schools and streams of economic thought* (1960); E. Heimann, *History of economic doctrines* (1964); H. T. Overton, *Social ideals and economic theories from Quesnay to Keynes* (1962); D. Winch, *Economics and policy: a historical survey* (1972); and H. W. Spiegel, *The growth of economic thought* (rev., 1983).

On rural and agrarian history, the best introduction is D. B. Grigg, *The agricultural systems of the world: an evolutionary approach* * (1974), which may be supplemented by B. H. S. van Bath, *The agrarian history of western Europe, 500–1850* (trans. from Dutch, 1963).

For intellectual and cultural history and the history of ideas one still reads with profit B. Russell, *A history of philosophy* (1945); J. H. Randall, Jr., *Making of the modern mind* (1926, reissued 1976); and the same author's later work, *The career of philosophy* (2 vols., 1962–1965). An impressive comprehensive survey of formal philosophy is F. C. Copleston, *A history of philosophy* (9 vols., 1946–1975). An admirable synthesis for the history of ideas in the modern period is F. L. Baumer, *Modern European thought: continuity and change in ideas, 1600–1950* (1977). C. Brinton's books, *Ideas and men: the story of Western thought* (1950, 1963), published for the modern period as *The shaping of the modern mind* * (1953), and *A history of Western morals* (1959), remain

excellent introductions, as does R. N. Stromberg, *An intellectual history of modern Europe* (rev., 1975). W. W. Wagar, *World views: a study in comparative history* (1977), examines such ideas as rationalism and romanticism in four different cultural settings, while R. Nisbet, *History of the idea of progress* (1980), traces a specific idea from antiquity to the present. Recommended also: J. Bronowski and B. Mazlish, *The Western intellectual tradition: from Leonardo to Hegel* (1960); W. H. Coates, H. V. White, and J. S. Schapiro, *The emergence of liberal humanism* (1966); and the sequel volume by Coates and White, *The ordeal of liberal humanism* (1969).

On political thought, R. Berki, *The history of political thought* * (1977), is an admirable brief introduction, while Q. Skinner, *The foundations of modern political thought* (2 vols., 1978), is a masterful account for the early modern centuries. One still reads with interest G. H. Sabine, *A history of political theory* (1937, reissued 1973). On the need to examine political ideas and political vocabulary in the context of their times, one should read J. G. A. Pocock, *Politics, language, and time: essays on political thought and history* (1971).

Of the many books on the arts, one may turn for syntheses to H. W. and D. J. Janson, *History of art: a survey of the major visual arts from the dawn of history to the present day* (rev., 1977); A. Hauser, *Social history of art* (4 vols., 1963); D. J. Groat, *A history of Western music* (rev., 1973); K. H. Worner, *A history of music* (1973); N. Pevsner, *An outline of European architecture* (rev., 1963); and Pevsner and others, *A dictionary of architecture* (1976).

Books on military history treating war as a social and human phenomenon include the older J. U. Nef, *War and human progress: an essay on the rise of industrial civilization* (1950, 1965); A. Vagts, *A history of militarism: romance and realities of a profession* * (1937); and Q. Wright, *A study of war* (2 vols., 1942; 1 vol. abr., 1965). To these one must add J. Keegan, *The face of battle* (1977); M. Howard, *War in European history* (1976); T. Ropp, *War in the modern world* * (1959, 1962); and R. A. Preston and S. Wise, *Men in arms* * (4th ed., 1979). Other informative books include: A. Corvisier, *Armies and societies in Europe, 1494–1789* (trans. 1979); G. Best, *Humanity in warfare* (1980); B. and F. M. Brodie, *From crossbow to H-bomb* (rev., 1973); W. H. McNeill, *The pursuit of power: technology,* armed force, and society since A.D. 1000 (1982); and S. Mansfield, *The gestalts of war: an inquiry into its origins and meanings as a social institution* (1982).

For strategy and battle history, one may turn to B. H. Liddell Hart, *Strategy: the indirect approach* (1957); J. F. C. Fuller, *A military history of the Western world* (3 vols., 1954–1956); and R. E. and T. N. Dupuy, *Encyclopedia of military history: from 3500 B.C. to the present* (rev., 1977). F. L. Israel has edited *Major peace treaties of modern history, 1648–1967* (4 vols., 1967).

The New Social History

In recent years, stimulated by the *Annales* school of historical writing in France (the name derived from the French periodical *Annales: sociétés, economies, civilisations*) and by newer kinds of working-class history in England, historians have concerned themselves increasingly with aspects of social history distinct from older interests in the history of social classes and of labor and laboring conditions. They have been examining such subjects as the history of the family and of women; the daily lives, diet, and outlook of the urban and rural poor; sexuality and marriage; and popular culture —all viewed as history "from the bottom up." Many of these works are listed below in the appropriate chapters. Three pioneer studies have been P. Ariès, *Centuries of childhood: a social history of family life* (trans. 1962); P. Laslett, *The world we have lost: England before the industrial age* (1965); and E. P. Thompson, *The making of the English working class* (1963).

The family is studied in such recent works as L. Stone, *The family, sex, and marriage in England, 1500–1800* (1977; abr. 1979); R. Trumbach, *The rise of the egalitarian family* (1978); M. Mitterauer and R. Sieder, *The European family: patriarchy to partnership, 1400 to the present* (1982); and E. Shorter, *The making of the modern family* (1975); there are also many collections of essays on the subject, of which a recent one with a useful overview is V. C. Fox and M. H. Quitt (eds.), *Loving, parenting, and dying: the family cycle in England and America, past and present* (1981). A massive bibliographical aid is G. L. Soliday (ed.), *History of family and kinship: a select international bibliography* (1980). Related studies include J. R. Gillis, *Youth and history: tradition and change in European age

relations, 1770 to the present* (rev., 1981); D. Hunt, *Parents and children in history* (1972); and I. Pinchbeck and M. Hewitt, *Children in English society* (2 vols., 1969–1973). A. Esler (ed.), *The youth revolution: the conflict of generations in modern history* (1974), is an interesting anthology.

The best introduction to the history of popular culture is P. Burke, *Popular culture in early modern Europe* (1978), which may be supplemented by J. Beauroy, M. Bertrand, and E. T. Gargan, *The wolf and the lamb: popular culture in France from the Old Regime to the twentieth century* (1977).

General introductions providing samples of the new social history include A. Mitchell and I. Deak (eds.), *Everyman in Europe: essays in social history* (2 vols.; rev., 1981); V. J. Knapp, *Europe in the era of social transformation, 1700 to the present* (1976); R. Z. Bezucha (ed.), *Modern European social history* (1972); and P. Stearns, *European society in upheaval: social history since 1800* (1967).

There has also been a considerable interest, especially by American historians in recent decades, in the history of women. A useful brief introduction to the literature is B. Sicherman, E. W. Monter, J. W. Scott, and K. K. Sklar (eds.), *Recent United States scholarship in the history of women* (1980). Mary Ritter Beard was one of the first to examine the impact of women on history and many of her insights in *Women as a force in history: a study in traditions and realities* (1946) are still provocative. Newer emphases may be sampled in three collaborative collections of essays: R. Bridenthal and C. Koonz (eds.), *Becoming visible: women in European history* (1977), with essays running from ancient times to the twentieth century; M. Hartman and L. W. Banner (eds.), *Clio's consciousness raised: new perspectives on the history of women* (1974); and B. A. Carroll (ed.), *Liberating women's history* (1976), the latter especially valuable. An important monograph is J. W. Scott and L. A. Tilly, *Women, work, and family* (1978), focusing on French and English women in the modern centuries. Two informative collections of essays are P. H. Labalme (ed.), *Beyond their sex: learned women of the European past* (1980), mainly on early modern Europe; and C. R. Berkin and C. M. Lovett (eds.), *Women, war, and revolution* (1980). Two full-length studies are S. G. Bell, *Women: from the Greeks to the French Revolution* (1980), and

P. Stock, *Better than rubies: a history of women's education* (1978), from the Renaissance to the present, incorporating revisions of traditional views of the "progress" made by women in various epochs; recommended also is M. Kinnear, *Daughters of time** (1982). S. Rowbotham, *Women, resistance, and revolution* (1974), is a stimulating series of essays ranging from the English civil wars of the seventeenth century to the twentieth; and J. B. Elstain, *Public man, private woman: women in social and political thought* (1981), is an illuminating survey of political thinkers and their treatment of the subject of women from Aristotle on. Two documentary histories available are E. S. Reimers and J. C. Fout (eds.), *European women: a documentary history, 1789–1945* (1980), and E. O. Hillerstein, L. P. Hume, and K. M. Offen (eds.), *Victorian women: a documentary account of women's lives in England, France, and the United States** (1981), both with interesting selections and extensive bibliographies. An anthology conveying the flavor of an emergent feminism is A. S. Rossi (ed.), *The feminist papers: from [Abigail] Adams to [Simone] de Beauvoir** (1974). Two useful bibliographical studies are J. Kelly, B. A. Engel, and K. Casey, *Bibliography on the history of European women** (1976), and B. Kanner (ed.), *The women of England from Anglo-Saxon times to the present: interpretive bibliographical essays* (1979). [Many other titles are included in the appropriate sections below.]

Other subjects difficult to classify but related to the newer social history are covered in P. Ariès, *Western attitudes toward death: from the Middle Ages to the present* (trans. 1976), a synopsis of his larger work in French completed in 1979 and now being translated; and in three books by M. Foucault: *Madness and civilization* (trans. 1965); *Discipline and punish: the birth of the prison* (trans. 1979); and *A history of sexuality* (trans. 1978), the first volume of a projected larger study. On the latter subject, one may also turn to V. L. Bullough, *Sexual variance in society and history* (1976), and the briefer V. L. and B. Bullough, *Sin, sickness, and sanity: a history of sexual attitudes* (1977).

The Annales School

Although the *Annales* historians have inspired much of the newer social history, they have also been important for their emphasis on long-term factors that slowly and imperceptibly influence the course of historical change, such as geography, environment, resources, climate, population, diet, and disease, which in their view often merit closer attention than "events." Moreover, they have made notable efforts, through the intensive study of limited but valuable sources, to reconstruct the lives and outlook of ordinary men and women. Two outstanding exemplars of the *Annales* school, whose writings are available in English translation, are Fernand Braudel and Emmanuel Le Roy Ladurie.

Braudel's best-known work is *The Mediterranean and the Mediterranean world in the age of Philip II** (2 vols., 1949; rev., 1966; trans. 1972–1974). He has also written *Civilization and capitalism, 15th–18th century* (3 vols., 1977–1979), a revision of an earlier study; the first two volumes are available in English as *The structures of everyday life: the limits of the possible* (trans. 1981), and *The Wheels of Commerce* (trans. 1983). The broad theme of the study as a whole appears in *Afterthoughts on material civilization and capitalism* (trans. 1977).

Two successful books in early modern history by Ladurie skillfully reconstructing ordinary lives are *Montaillou: the promised land of error** (1975, trans. 1978) and *The carnival of Romans, 1579–80** (1979, trans. 1979). He has also written *Times of feast, times of famine: a history of climate since the year 1000* (trans. 1971), and a detailed study, *The peasants of Languedoc** (1974, trans. 1977). His reflections on historical method may be read in *The territory of the historian* (trans. 1979) and *The mind and method of the historian* (trans. 1980). The contributions of the *Annales* historians may be sampled in M. Ferro (ed.), *Social historians in contemporary France: essays from Annales* (1972); P. Burke (ed.), *Economy and society in early modern Europe: essays from Annales* (1972); and in several volumes of selections from *Annales* edited by R. Forster and O. Ranum, among them *Biology of man in history** (1975), *Family and society** (1976), and *Food and drink in history** (1979). An older work in social history that deserves incidental mention is N. Elias, *The civilizing process: the history of manners* (1939; reissued, 2 vols., 1968).

Demography and Related Topics

For demography one may turn to D. V. Glass and D. E. C. Eversley, *Population in history: essays in historical demography* (1965); E. A. Wrigley, *Population and his-*

tory * (1969); C. M. Cipolla, *Economic history of world population* * (1974); and T. McKeown, *The modern rise of population* (1977). A pioneering study, A. M. Carr-Saunders, *World population: past growth and future trends* (1936), is still valuable. To keep up with current trends, one should consult the *United Nations demographic yearbook* and other periodical literature. For the impact of famines, disease, and the movements of peoples, one may read W. H. McNeill, *Plagues and peoples* (1976), the same author's *The human condition: an ecological and historical view* (1981), and the collection of essays, McNeill and R. S. Adams (eds.), *Human migration: patterns and politics* (1978). On famine and food, one may also read E. P. Prentice, *Hunger and history: the influence of hunger on human history* (1939); R. N. Salaman, *The history and social influence of the potato* (1949); E. Forster and R. Forster (eds.), *European diet from preindustrial to modern times* (1975); and R. P. Multhauf, *Neptune's gift: a history of common salt* (1978). T. Chandler and G. Fox provide statistical data and other information on the historical growth of the world's cities in *3000 years of urban growth* (1974), and B. R. Mitchell, *European historical statistics, 1750–1970* * (rev. and abr., 1978), is a valuable compendium of figures on population, trade, and other social and economic topics.

On the subject of literacy, one may read C. M. Cipolla, *Literacy and development in the West* * (1969); and on the origins of higher education from the fourteenth to the twentieth centuries, L. Stone (ed.), *The university in society* (2 vols., 1974).

Historical Manuals and Historiography

Among manuals on methods of research and on the writing of history, a spirited introduction is J. Barzun and H. F. Graff, *The modern researcher* * (rev., 1977); Barzun and G. Dunbar, *Simple and direct: a rhetoric for writers* * (1976), is an excellent guide for all writers. Other introductions include A. Nevins, *The gateway to history* * (rev., 1962); S. Kent, *Writing history* (rev., 1967); and L. Gottschalk, *Understanding history* * (rev., 1969). There is practical information in K. L. Turabian, *A manual for writers of term papers, theses, and dissertations* * (many eds.), an adaptation of a standard guide, the University of Chicago, *A manual of style* (13th ed., 1982); in M. E. Skillin and

others, *Words into type* (3rd ed., 1974); and in M-C. van Leunen, *A handbook for scholars* * (1978).

Examples of books affording insight into the study and writing of history are C. Gustavson, *A preface to history* * (1955), and *The mansion of history* * (1975), the latter on modes of historical thinking; M. Bloch, *The historian's craft* * (1953); A. L. Rowse, *The use of history* * (1946); E. H. Carr, *What is history?* * (1962); G. L. Elton, *The practice of history* (1967); H. S. Hughes, *History as art and science: twin vistas on the past* * (1967); J. H. Hexter, *The history primer* (1971); and A. J. Gilbert (ed.), *In search of a meaningful past* * (1972). For examples of historians confronting evidence, see R. W. Winks (ed.), *The historian as detective: essays on evidence* (1970); L. P. Curtis, Jr. (ed.), *The historian's workshop* * (1971); P. Gay and V. G. Wexler (eds.), *Historians at work* (4 vols., 1972–1975); D. H. Fischer, *Historians' fallacies: toward a logic of historical thought* * (1970); and J. W. Davidson and M. H. Lytle (pseudonyms), *After the fact: the art of historical detection* (1982).

Two informative introductions to the emergence of modern historical writing are H. Butterfield, *The origins of history* (rev., 1981), and D. Hay, *Annalists and historians: Western historiography from the eighth to the eighteenth centuries* (1977). The great historians of the past and the evolution of history are discussed in detail in the encyclopedic M. A. Fitzsimons, A. G. Pundt, and C. E. Nowell (eds.), *The development of historiography* (1954), and in the older J. W. Thompson and B. H. Holm, *A history of historical writing* (2 vols., 1942). A good introductory anthology is F. Stern (ed.), *The varieties of history: from Voltaire to the present* * (1956). Special studies of the historical craft and its practitioners include E. Cochran, *Historians and historiography in the Italian Renaissance* (1981); Donald R. Kelley, *Foundations of modern historical scholarship: language, law, and history in the French Renaissance* (1969); G. P. Gooch, *History and historians in the nineteenth century* (1913); E. E. Neff, *The poetry of history* (1947); B. E. Schmitt (ed.), *Some historians of modern Europe* (1942); and S. W. Halperin (ed.), *Some twentieth-century historians* (1961). For British historians, one may read J. R. Hale (ed.), *The evolution of British historiography: from Bacon to Namier* (1967); and V. Mehta, *The fly and the fly bottle* (1962), an intriguing journalistic account. P. Gay, *Style in history* (1974) and the same author's *Art and act: on causes in history* (1976), are also informative.

The *Annales* writers and others may be examined in T. Stoianovich, *French historical method: the* Annales *paradigm* (1976); W. R. Keylor, *Academy and community: the foundation of the French historical profession* (1975); and in G. G. Iggers, *New directions in European historiography* (1975). J. H. Hexter, *On historians: reappraisals of some of the makers of modern history* (1979), includes a critical appraisal of many writers, including Braudel.

Among other thoughtful reflections by contemporary historians, the following sampling of titles may be suggested: H. S. Commager, *The search for a usable past and other essays in historiography* (1967); P. Smith, *The historian and history** (1964); G. Kitson Clark, *The critical historian* (1967); C. V. Wedgwood, *The sense of the past: thirteen studies in the theory and practice of history* (1960); J. Lukacs, *Historical consciousness: or the remembered past* (1968); J. T. Marcus, *Heaven, hell, and history: a survey of man's faith in history from antiquity to the present* (1967); G. Jackson, *Historian's quest* (1969); M. Duberman, *The uncompleted past* (1970); H. Zinn, *The politics of history** (1970); J. H. Plumb, *The death of the past* (1970); F. E. Manuel, *Freedom from history** (1971); B. Lewis, *History remembered, recovered, invented* (1975); F. Gilbert, *History: choice and commitment* (1977); and L. Stone, *The past and the present* (1981).

Biography may be examined in C. D. Bowen, *Biography: the craft and the calling* (1968), M. Pachter, *Telling lives* (1979), and D. Beales, *History and biography** (1981).

A number of collections of essays provide valuable insights into contemporary trends in historical writing, among them: M. Kammen (ed.), *The past before us: contemporary historical writing in the United States** (1980); C. F. Delzell (ed.), *The future of history* (1977); G. G. Iggers and H. T. Parker (eds.), *International handbook of historical studies: contemporary research and theory* (1979); and T. K. Rabb and R. I. Rothberg (eds.), *The new history: the 1980s and beyond** (1982). Also useful are J. Higham (ed.), *History* (1965); B. C. Shafer (ed.), *Historical study in the West: France, Western Germany, Great Britain, and the United States* (1968); W. Laqueur and G. L. Mosse (eds.), *The new history: trends in historical research and writing since*

*World War II** (1968); and F. Gilbert and S. R. Graubard (eds.), *Historical studies today** (1972).

For relationships to the social sciences, see S. R. Lipset and R. Hofstadter (eds.), *Sociology and history* (1968); D. Landes and C. Tilly (eds.), *History as a social science* (1971); and N. J. Smelser, *Comparative methods in the social sciences* (1976). Contemporary social history owes a good deal to anthropology, where a seminal book with influence on historians has been C. Geertz, *The interpretations of cultures* (1973). One will also read with profit M. Harris, *The rise of anthropological theory* (1968); and two books by R. A. Nisbet, *The sociological tradition* (1967) and *Social change and history: aspects of the Western theory of development* (1969). Examples of quantitative, psychological, and behavioral approaches are to be found in W. O. Aydelotte and others, *The dimensions of quantitative research in history* (1972); V. Lorwin and J. Price (eds.), *Dimensions of the past* (1972); R. Floud, *An introduction to quantitative methods for historians** (rev., 1979); and R. G. Hawks, *Economics for historians** (1980). Psychological dimensions are examined in R. J. Lifton (ed.), *Explorations in psychohistory** (1974); B. Mazlish (ed.), *Psychoanalysis and history* (1963); S. Friedländer, *History and psychoanalysis* (1978); and R. F. Berkhofer, Jr., *A behavioral approach to historical analysis* (1969). A provocative book criticizing the impact of the newer history is J. Barzun, *Clio and the doctors: psycho-history, quanto-history, and history* (1974).

Two books on modern research tools are P. Thompson, *The voice of the past: oral history* (1978), on new ways of tapping neglected sources; and P. Sorlin, *The film in history: restaging the past* (1980).

Philosophy of History

The historical manuals listed above all provide some introduction to the philosophy and theory of history. Two convenient introductions are the anthologies edited by H. Meyerhoff, *The philosophy of history in our time** (1959), and P. Gardiner (ed.), *Theories of history* (1959).

There are many volumes on the philosophy of history written by professional students of philosophy sometimes not directly attuned to the needs and interests of practicing historians. The best scholarly introduction is R. E. Atkinson, *Knowledge and explanation in history: an introduction to the* *philosophy of history**·(1978), which may be compared with two other useful treatments: W. H. Dray, *Philosophy of history** (1964), and W. H. Walsh, *An introduction to the philosophy of history** (1976). Other recommended books are R. Aron, *Introduction to the philosophy of history* (1948, trans. 1961); R. G. Collingwood, *The idea of history** (1946); M. Mandelbaum, *The anatomy of historical knowledge* (1977); A. C. Danto, *Analytical philosophy of history* (1965); R. Martin, *Historical explanation: reenactment and practical inference* (1977); and P. Munz, *The shapes of time: a new look at the philosophy of history* (1977). Two intriguing studies are B. Mazlish, *The riddle of history: the great speculators from Vico to Freud* (1966), and N. O. Brown, *Life against death: the psychoanalytical meaning of history** (1959).

Readings, Source Materials, and Historical Problems

The following titles are intended to give only a sampling of anthologies available for classroom use: Columbia University, *Introduction to contemporary civilization in the West* (2 vols., many revisions), a collection of longer source selections; J. H. Hexter and others, *The traditions of the Western world** (1967); R. P. Stearns, *Pageant of Europe: sources and selections from the Renaissance to the present day** (rev., 1961); F. L. Baumer, *Main currents of Western thought: readings in Western European intellectual history from the Middle Ages to the present** (rev., 1978); E. Weber, *The Western tradition from the ancient world to the atomic age** (1959); L. S. Stavrianos, *The epic of modern man: a collection of readings** (1966), globally oriented; J. K. Sowards, *Makers of the Western tradition: portraits from history* (rev., 1983), focusing on biographical studies; and D. Sherman, *Western civilization: images and interpretations* (2 vols., 1983), with interesting visual sources.

Among the many anthologies that focus on source problems or on conflicting interpretations of historical issues, there are S. B. Clough, P. Gay, C. K. Warner, and J. M. Cammett, *The European past: reappraisals in history** (2 vols.; rev., 1970); B. D. Gooch (ed.), *Interpreting European history** (2 vols., 1967); O. Ranum, *Searching for modern times** (2 vols., 1969); L. W. Spitz and R. W. Lyman (gen. eds.), *Major crises in Western civilization** (2 vols., 1965); and B. Tierney, D. Kagan, and L. P.

Williams (eds.), *Great issues in Western civilization** (2 vols., 1976), available also in separate pamphlets. The Great Lives Observed series* (1968 ff.) consists of sources, contemporary judgments, and latter-day interpretations relating to leading historical personalities.

Two pamphlet series offering divergent interpretations of historical events are the Heath Problems in European Civilization* (1958 ff.) and European Problem Studies* (Holt, Rinehart and Winston, 1963 ff., reprinted by Krieger). By reprinting longer excerpts, the Modern Scholarship on European History series* (New Viewpoints: Franklin Watts, 1971–1978) samples recent scholarship on selected topics.

Anthologies of more specialized coverage include S. Chodorow and P. N. Stearns, *The other side of Western civilization: readings in European civilization* (2 vols., 1979), on social history and popular culture; N. F. Cantor and M. S. Werthman (eds.), *The history of popular culture* (2 vols., 1968); by the same editors, *The English tradition: modern studies in English history* (2 vols., 1967); J. Friugulietti and E. Kennedy, *The shaping of modern France: writings on French history since 1715* (1969); and M. Kranzberg and C. W. Pursell, Jr. (eds.), *Technology in Western civilization* (2 vols., 1967).

There are several series offering brief volumes on selected topics especially suitable for undergraduate reading, among which the Berkshire series has been especially useful; many titles are listed below. Two British series deserve mention: Teach Yourself History, edited by A. L. Rowse, successfully using a biographical approach to lure the reader to historical topics; and the Men in Office series, edited by R. N. Hatton, focusing on key political leaders.

I: THE RISE OF EUROPE

Prehistoric and Ancient Times

[No attempt is made here to suggest more than a few titles.] The reader may wish to consult as useful general introductions: P. Phillips, *The prehistory of Europe* (1980); C. Renfrew, *Before civilization: the radiocarbon revolution and prehistoric Europe* (rev., 1979); J. Hawkes and L. Wooley, *Prehistory and the beginnings of civilization** (rev., 1967), the first volume in the UNESCO History of Mankind series;

J. Hawkes, *The first great civilizations** (1973), on Egypt and the Tigris-Euphrates valley; T. B. Jones, *From the Tigris to the Tiber: an introduction to ancient history** (rev., 1978); and C. G. Starr, *A history of the ancient world* (rev., 1974).

In addition to surveys of classical Greece, such as J. B. Bury and R. Meiggs, *A history of Greece* (rev., 1976), and N. G. Hammond, *A history of Greece to 322 B.C.** (rev., 1967), one may profit from H. D. F. Kitto, *The Greeks** (1951); A. Andrewes, *The Greeks* (1967); and M. I. Finley's books: *The world of Odysseus** (1954), *The ancient Greeks: their life and thought** (1963), *The ancient economy** (1973), and *Ancient slavery and modern ideology* (1980). For Alexander, as an introduction to Hellenistic times, the older standard biography, W. W. Tarn, *Alexander the Great* (1948), may be compared with P. Green, *Alexander of Macedon, 356–323 B.C.** (1973), and with R. L. Fox's admirable account, *Alexander the Great* (1974).

Among many surveys of Rome and Roman civilization, M. Cary and H. H. Scullard, *A history of Rome* (rev., 1976), may be mentioned. A superb volume on the end of the Roman republic is R. Syme, *Roman revolution** (1939), which may be supplemented by A. H. MacDonald, *Republican Rome* (1966), and C. Nicolet, *The world of the citizen in republican Rome* (1976, trans. 1980). Highly recommended are M. Grant's volumes: *The Etruscans* (1981), *History of Rome** (1978), and *The Jews in the Roman world* (1973). Books on later Roman history include M. P. Charlesworth, *The Roman Empire** (1951), and A. H. M. Jones, *The decline of the ancient world** (1966), a condensation of his larger work (3 vols., 1964). On a special subject, one may read S. B. Pomeroy, *Goddesses, whores, wives, and slaves: women in classical antiquity* (1975), a successful effort to reconstruct the lives of women in classical antiquity. For all subjects, the *Oxford classical dictionary* (rev., 1970) is a valuable one-volume collaborative encyclopedia.

On the coming of Christianity, N. H. Baynes, *Constantine the Great and the Christian church* (1931), remains of fundamental importance, but a good, brief account is A. H. M. Jones, *Constantine and the conversion of Europe** (1948), in the Teach Yourself History series. R. A. Markus, *Christianity in the Roman world* (1978), ably traces the growth of Christian self-awareness, while M. Grant reconstructs the historical Jesus in *Jesus: An historian's review of the gospels* (1977). On St. Augustine and his times, there is a sensitive account by P. R. L. Brown, *St. Augustine of Hippo** (1967), and another illuminating study, F. Van der Meer, *Augustine the bishop: church and society at the dawn of the Middle Ages* (1961).

The Middle Ages: The Formation of Europe

Considerable attention has been paid to the emergence of Europe in the early Middle Ages, and a number of illuminating volumes are available. Invaluable as a guide to books written in the last half-century on the Middle Ages is G. C. Boyce (ed.), *Literature of medieval history, 1930–1975* (5 vols., 1981), revising and superseding the older bibliographical guide, long standard, of L. J. Paetow. The first volume of a multivolume *Dictionary of the Middle Ages* has appeared (1982). R. W. Southern, *The making of the Middle Ages** (1953), is fundamental to a reexamination of these years. Among many surveys of the medieval era as a whole, B. Tierney and S. Painter, *Western Europe in the Middle Ages, 300–1475* (rev., 1983), is outstanding; a successful effort emphasizing social history is E. Peters, *Europe: the world of the Middle Ages* (1977), available also in abridged form as *Europe and the Middle Ages** (1983). D. Gerhard, *Old Europe: a study in continuity, 1000–1800* (1981), examines the continuity of medieval institutions in the modern centuries. Illustrative of recent scholarship on the early medieval period are: P. R. L. Brown, *The end of antiquity** (1971); H. R. Trevor-Roper, *The rise of Christian Europe** (1965); D. Hay, *Europe: the emergence of an idea** (rev., 1968); G. Barraclough, *The crucible of Europe: the ninth and tenth centuries in European history** (1976); C. Brooke, *Europe in the Central Middle Ages, 962–1154** (1968); J. M. Wallace-Hadrill, *The barbarian West, 400–1000** (1952); A. R. Lewis, *Emerging medieval Europe, A.D. 400–1000** (1967); G. Duby, *The making of the Christian West, 980–1140* (trans. 1968); and S. R. Packard, *12th century Europe: an interpretive essay* (1973). [Economic histories for the period are listed below.]

C. W. Previté-Orton in the *Shorter Cambridge medieval history* (2 vols., 1952) has condensed for the general reader the eight volumes of the *Cambridge medieval history* (1911–1936). Colorful portraits of medieval life are found in G. G. Coulton's *Medieval panorama* (1938) and his other writings, and in two books by E. E. Power, *Medieval people** (1924, 1935) and *Medieval women** [published posthumously, M. M. Postan (ed.), 1976]; on women in the Middle Ages, one may also read J. Morris, *The lady was a bishop* (1973); S. Wemple, *Women in Frankish society* (1981); and the essays in S. M. Stuard (ed.), *Women in medieval society** (1976).

Intellectual developments are discussed in the volume by R. W. Southern and in many of the books already cited, but are also examined with insight in: D. Knowles, *The evolution of medieval thought** (1962); G. Duby, *The age of the cathedrals: art and society, 980–1420* (trans. 1981); J. LeGoff, *Time, work, and culture in the Middle Ages* (trans. 1981); F. B. Artz, *The mind of the Middle Ages, 200–1500** (3rd ed., 1980); and P. Wolff, *The awakening of Europe** (1968). Other valuable studies include G. Leff, *Medieval thought* (1958), and two works by M. L. Laistner, *Thought and letters in Western Europe, A.D. 500 to 900* (rev., 1957), and *The intellectual heritage of the Early Middle Ages* (1957). On theology, J. Pelikan, *The growth of medieval theology (600–1300)* (1978), volume 2 of his projected five-volume study, *The development of Christian doctrine*, is available. For medieval political philosophy, one still reads with profit C. H. McIlwain, *The growth of political thought in the West: from the Greeks to the end of the Middle Ages* (1932), but also available are J. B. Morrall, *Political thought in medieval times* (1958), a good brief introduction; F. C. Copleston, *Medieval philosophy* (1952); the same author's *Aquinas* (1955); R. S. Hoyt (ed.), *Life and thought in the Early Middle Ages* (1967); and W. Ullmann, *A history of political thought in the Middle Ages** (1965). Useful as a guide to intellectual developments is *The history of ideas: a bibliographical introduction*, vol. 2: *Medieval and early modern Europe* (1977), published under the auspices of the American Bibliographical Center (ABC-Clio).

There are innumerable books dealing with various regions and institutions during the Middle Ages, or covering specific centuries, of which the titles given here are only a sampling. G. Barraclough, *Origins of modern Germany** (1947), is the most valuable introduction to medieval Germany, but F. Heer, *The Holy Roman Empire* (trans. 1968), also merits reading. For the Italian city-states, one may read J. K. Hyde, *Society*

*and politics in medieval Italy . . . 1000–1350** (1973). C. Petit Dutaillis, *The feudal monarchy in France and England, from the tenth to the thirteenth century* (1933, trans. 1936), is a comparative study of the two monarchies, and S. Painter, *Rise of the feudal monarchies** (1951), is an excellent brief introduction.

For English developments, two good introductions are B. Lyon, *A constitutional and legal history of medieval England* (1960), and H. Cam, *England before Elizabeth** (1950). A valuable bibliographical tool is E. B. Graves (ed.), *A bibliography of English history to 1485* (1975). For social developments, one may consult E. Duckett, *Life and death in the tenth century* (1968); D. W. Robertson, Jr., *Chaucer's London** (1968); J. T. Rosenthal, *Angles, angels, and conquerors* (1973), covering the years 400–1154; J. Barnie, *War in medieval English society: social values in the Hundred Years' War, 1337–99* (1974); and M. M. McLaughlin, *Survivors and surrogates: children and parents from the ninth to the thirteenth centuries* (1975). S. L. Thrupp examines the guilds and other subjects in *The merchant class of medieval London, 1300–1500* (1958), and T. H. Lloyd an important economic activity in *The English wool trade in the Middle Ages* (1977). On the Carolingian era and France, see H. Fichtenau, *The Carolingian empire: the age of Charlemagne** (1949, trans. 1957); A. D. Bullough, *The age of Charlemagne* (1965); R. Fawtier, *The Capetian kings of France* (1960); R. Folz, *The coronation of Charlemagne, 25 December 800* (1964, trans. 1975), covering more than the title implies; and P. Riché, *Daily life in the world of Charlemagne** (trans. 1978).

For economic developments, the pioneering books by H. Pirenne on the origins of the cities, revival of trade, and other social and economic developments still merit reading, but they have been superseded by more recent research. Among the most useful of the newer treatments are: R. S. Lopez, *The commercial revolution of the Middle Ages, 950–1350** (rev., 1976); R. Latouche, *The birth of the Western economy** (rev., 1967); and G. Duby, *The growth of the European economy* (1974), all covering social and economic developments. Also useful are N. J. G. Pounds, *An economic history of medieval Europe* (1974), a well-balanced survey; C. M. Cipolla (ed.), *The Middle Ages** (1972, 1977), vol. I of the Fontana Economic History of Europe; the same author's *Before the Industrial Revolution: European society and economy, 1000–1700** (rev., 1980); and M. M. Postan, *Medieval trade and finance* (1973). J. Gimpel, *The medieval machine: the industrial revolution of the Middle Ages* (trans. 1976), is informative but strains to compare the age to contemporary times; it may be compared with L. White, Jr., *Medieval technology and social change** (1962). Important too are the appropriate sections of D. C. North and R. P. Thomas, *Rise of the Western world: a new economic history* (1973), which examines economic growth and other developments from 900 to 1700. The volumes in the collaborative Cambridge Economic History of Europe (1941 ff.) provide authoritative but highly specialized accounts.

The best introduction to the growth of towns is E. Ennen, *The medieval town* (trans. 1979), which incorporates the considerable research completed since Pirenne and is a more complete synthesis than F. Rörig, *The medieval town** (1967). On the complex subjects of feudalism and manorialism, the most informative introduction is F. L. Ganshof, *Feudalism** (rev., 1961). A remarkable effort at comparing ideal models and material realities is G. Duby, *The three orders: feudal society imagined* (trans. 1980); his two other books are also important: *Rural economy and country life in the medieval West* (trans. 1968), and *The early growth of the European economy: warriors and peasants from the seventh to the twelfth century* (trans. 1974). One should also read M. Bloch's important contributions: *Feudal society** (1939–1940, trans. 1961), *French rural history** (trans. 1966), *Land and work in medieval Europe* (trans. 1967), and *Slavery and serfdom in the Middle Ages* (trans. 1975); M. M. Postan, *Essays on medieval agriculture and general problems of the medieval economy* (1973); and J. L. Bolton, *The medieval economy, 1150–1500** (1980). For comparative studies emphasizing the diversity of feudalism in various ages and places, R. Coulborn (ed.), *Feudalism in history* (1956), may be supplemented by J. Critchley, *Feudalism* (1978).

For the Byzantine world, a fundamental work is G. Ostrogorsky, *History of the Byzantine state* (1950), translated in 1956 by J. M. Hussey, who herself has written a good introduction in briefer compass, *The Byzantine world** (1957), and has edited *The Byzantine empire*, vol. IV (rev., 1966–1967), in the Cambridge Medieval History. Among other narrative and topical accounts

are C. Diehl, *Byzantium: greatness and decline** (1919, trans. 1957), an older account; D. Oblensky, *The Byzantine commonwealth: eastern Europe, 500–1453* (1971); P. Lemerle, *A history of Byzantium* (1964); S. Vryonis, Jr., *Byzantium and Europe** (1967); R. Jenkins, *Byzantium: the imperial centuries, A.D. 619–1071* (1966); and D. M. Nicol, *The last centuries of Byzantium, 1261–1453* (1972). An important episode is graphically described in S. Runciman, *The fall of Constantinople, 1453* (1965). A survey stressing socioeconomic trends in the Byzantine and Islamic worlds is E. Ashtor, *A social and economic history of the Near East in the Middle Ages* (1976). Emphasizing cultural interaction is D. J. Geanokoplos, *Medieval Western civilization and the Byzantine and Islamic worlds: interaction of three cultures* (1979). On the theology of eastern Christendom, one may read J. Pelikan, *The spirit of eastern Christendom, 600–1700* (1974), the second volume of his longer study.

Good starting points for the study of Islam include H. A. R. Gibb's succinct *Mohammedanism: an historical survey* (1949); W. M. Watt, *The majesty that was Islam: the Islamic world, 661–1100* (1974); M. G. S. Hodgson, *The venture of Islam: conscience and history in a world civilization** (3 vols., 1974), comprehensive and insightful, from the beginnings to the mid-twentieth century, and free from Eurocentric bias; and B. Lewis, *Islam in history* (1973). Among many accounts of the founder of Islam, three outstanding ones are T. Andrae, *Mohammed: the man and his faith* (trans. 1936, reprinted 1957); W. M. Watt, *Muhammed: prophet and statesman** (1961), a condensation of his detailed two-volume study (1953–1956); and M. Rodenson, *Muhammad** (rev., 1980). Excellent brief surveys of Arab history are B. Lewis, *The Arabs in history** (3rd ed., 1964); B. Lewis (ed.), *Islam and the Arab world* (1978); P. K. Hitti, *The Arabs: a short history* (rev., 1968), the latter a compression of his larger work (rev., 1970); and P. Mansfield, *The Arabs** (1976). S. N. Fisher, *The Middle East: a history* (rev., 1968), covers the region from pre-Islamic times to the twentieth century. G. E. von Grunebaum in his masterful *Medieval Islam: a study in cultural orientation* (1946) compares Islamic with Byzantine and Christian civilizations, while W. C. Smith, *Islam in modern history* (1957), provides indispensable insights on religious themes. N. Daniel, *The Arabs and* *medieval Europe* (rev., 1979), emphasizes the unwillingness and inability of the medieval Latin West to come to terms with Islam. For Islamic philosophy and science and their impact on Europe, there are W. M. Watt's important volumes: *The formative period of Islamic thought* (1973) and *The influence of Islam on medieval Europe* (1972), as well as S. H. Nasr, *Islamic science* (1976). Books focusing on social, economic, and cultural developments include S. D. Gotein, *A Mediterranean society* (3 vols. to date, 1967–   ), informative on the Jewish community in Cairo and the Muslim society surrounding it; I. M. Lapidus, *Muslim cities in the later Middle Ages* (1967); and R. Bulliet, *The camel and the wheel* (1975).

Some biographical accounts for the early Middle Ages are R. Winston, *Charlemagne: from the hammer to the cross** (1954); E. S. Duckett, *Alcuin, friend of Charlemagne* (1951); F. Barlow, *William I and the Norman Conquest* (Teach Yourself History series, 1965); A. R. Kelly, *Eleanor of Aquitaine and the four kings** (1950); E. F. Jacob, *Henry V and the invasion of France** (Teach Yourself History series, 1950); A. S. Ehrenkrentz, *Saladdin* (1978); and J. H. Smith, *Joan of Arc* (1973).

The High Middle Ages

The classic expression of the spiritual unity and harmony of medieval Europe is Henry Adams, *Mont-Saint-Michel and Chartres** (1912, many reprintings). C. Dawson, in *The making of Europe* (1937), *Medieval religion* (1934), and *Medieval essays* (1954), also examines the close communion between medieval European culture and Christianity, as does P. Hughes in the relevant chapters of *A history of the church* (3 vols., 1935–1949). Two recommended books for the advanced reader are D. Matthew, *The medieval European community* (1977), successful in exploring the mentality of the medieval world; and A. Murray, *Reason and society in the Middle Ages* (1978). A valuable introduction to the church as an institution is G. Barraclough, *The medieval papacy** (1968). The appropriate volumes of R. H. Bainton, *The Penguin history of Christianity** (1960 ff.), and H. Chadwick, *The Pelican history of the church** (1967 ff.), both multivolumed works, are recommended. The most comprehensive study of the development of the papacy from the fourth to the twelfth centuries is W. Ullmann, *The growth of papal government in the Middle Ages* (1955,

1962); the same author has also written *A short history of the papacy in the Middle Ages** (1974). An attractive illustrated volume is C. Brooke, *The monastic world, 1000–1300* (1974).

A special subject is treated in A. S. Turberville, *Medieval heresy and the Inquisition* (1920, 1932), and in S. Runciman, *The medieval Manichee* (1961). Both books are more balanced treatments of the Inquisition than H. C. Lea's pioneer work, *History of the Inquisition of the Middle Ages* (3 vols., 1888; abr. ed., 1969*).

Three notable contributions to the study of medieval secular culture are by C. H. Haskins: *Normans in European civilization** (1915), *The Renaissance of the twelfth century* (1927), and *The rise of universities** (1923). The last may be supplemented by H. Rashdall, *Universities of Europe in the Middle Ages* (1895; rev., 1936); and G. Leff, *Paris and Oxford universities in the thirteenth and fourteenth centuries* (1968). Medieval science is examined in A. C. Crombie, *Medieval and early modern science** (2 vols., 1959); D. C. Lindberg (ed.), *Science in the Middle Ages* (1978); and in R. C. Dales, *The scientific achievement of the Middle Ages* (1973). A successful attempt to link medieval society, economic development, and morality is L. K. Little, *Religious poverty and the profit economy in medieval Europe* (1978); and a scholarly exploration of sexual attitudes in the medieval world is J. Boswell, *Christianity, sexual tolerance, and homosexuality: gay people in Western Europe from the beginning of the Christian era to the fourteenth century* (1980).

The Crusades may be approached through the brief Berkshire study, R. A. Newhall, *The Crusades** (1927; rev., 1963), and the detailed, colorful S. Runciman, *A history of the Crusades** (3 vols., 1951–1954). Three volumes of a collaborative, multivolumed *History of the Crusades* (K. M. Setton, gen. ed.) have appeared (1955, 1962, 1975). K. M. Setton's *The papacy and the Levant, 1204–1571* (2 of 3 vols. projected, 1976, 1978) is a monumental account, now complete through the fifteenth century. For all aspects of the expansion of Christianity, the works of K. S. Latourette are indispensable, especially his *History of Christianity* (1953) and his longer *History of the expansion of Christianity* (7 vols., 1937–1945), of which vol. II, *The thousand years of uncertainty, A.D. 500–A.D. 1500*, covers the Middle Ages. S. W. Baron's monumental history, *A social and religious history of the Jews*, covers the years 1200 to 1650 in vols. IX–XVII (rev., 1967–1980); on the same general subject, see also L. Finkelstein (ed.), *The Jews* (2 vols., 1960), and H. H. Ben Sasson (ed.), *A history of the Jewish people* (1976).

Problems and Readings*

Several pamphlets in the various problems series are relevant to this chapter: D. Kagan (ed.), *Decline and fall of the Roman Empire* (1962); A. F. Havighurst (ed.), *The Pirenne thesis* (rev., 1976); J. F. Benton (ed.), *Town origins: the evidence from medieval England* (1968); R. E. Sullivan (ed.), *The coronation of Charlemagne* (1959); R. S. Lopez (ed.), *The tenth century: how dark the Dark Ages?* (1959); C. W. Hollister (ed.), *The twelfth-century Renaissance* (1969); C. R. Young (ed.), *The Renaissance of the twelfth century* (1970); S. Williams (ed.), *The Gregorian epoch* (1966); J. A. Brundage (ed.), *The Crusades* (1964); J. M. Powell (ed.), *Innocent III* (1963); R. E. Herzstein (ed.), *The Holy Roman Empire in the Middle Ages* (1965); and G. P. Bodet (ed.), *Early English parliaments: high courts, royal councils, or representative assemblies?* (1968). M. Chambers, *Ancient Greece* (1973), and E. S. Gruen, *The Roman Republic* (1972), are contributions to the American Historical Association Pamphlets series.

II: THE UPHEAVAL IN CHRISTENDOM, 1300–1560

Important syntheses on the early modern period include M. P. Gilmore, *The world of humanism, 1453–1517** (1952), in the Langer series; W. K. Ferguson, *Europe in transition, 1300–1520** (1963); A. G. Dickens, *The age of humanism and reformation: Europe in the fourteenth to sixteenth centuries** (1972); and S. E. Ozment, *The age of reform, 1250–1550: an intellectual and religious history of late medieval and Reformation Europe* (1980). Other recommended general treatments are D. Hay, *Europe in the fourteenth and fifteenth centuries** (1966); M. Aston, *The fifteenth century: the prospect of Europe** (1968); H. G. Koenigsberger and G. L. Mosse, *Europe in the sixteenth century** (1968); J. R. Hale, *Renaissance Europe: the individual and society, 1480–1520** (1971); M. L. Bush, *Renaissance, Reformation, and the outer world, 1450–1600** (1967); E. P. Rice, Jr., *The foundations of early modern Europe,*

*1460–1559** (1970); L. W. Spitz, *The Renaissance and Reformation movements* (1971); and D. L. Jensen, *Renaissance Europe: age of recovery and reconciliation* (1981). There are informative chapters in G. R. Potter (ed.), *The Renaissance, 1493–1520* (1957), and G. R. Elton (ed.), *The Reformation, 1520–1559* (1958), vols. I and II respectively of the New Cambridge Modern History. The economic basis of the age is examined in H. Miskimin, *The economy of early Renaissance Europe, 1300–1460** (1975), and *The economy of later Renaissance Europe, 1460–1600** (1977), as well as in many of the economic histories listed for the previous chapter. On political thought, there is available a masterful account by Q. Skinner, *The foundations of modern political thought* (2 vols., 1978), the first volume on the Renaissance, the second on the Age of Reformation. C. M. Cipolla explores an interesting subject in *Public health and the medical profession in the Renaissance* (1976), as does G. Mattingly in *Renaissance diplomacy** (1955). E. L. Eisenstein, *The printing press as an agent of change: communications and cultural transformations in early modern Europe* (2 vols., 1979), elaborates the thesis that the truly revolutionary event for the modernization of European culture was the invention of the printing press.

Much of the newer social history has been centered on the early modern centuries. Here P. Burke, *Popular culture in early modern Europe* (1978), cited in the introductory chapter, is fundamental. C. Ginzburg, *The cheese and the worms: the cosmos of a sixteenth-century miller** (trans. from Italian, 1980), is a fascinating effort to reconstruct the mentality and outlook of an obscure Italian miller of the age. Other examples of topics that have been explored include: J. H. Langbein, *Prosecuting crime in the Renaissance: England, Germany, France* (1974); M. Weisser, *Crime and criminality in early modern Europe* (1978); and H. Soly and R. Lis, *Poverty and capitalism in early modern Europe* (1978). R. Kelso, *Doctrine for the lady of the Renaissance* (1956), is an older but still valuable study.

Disasters of the Fourteenth Century

A good brief introduction to the era is R. E. Lerner, *The age of adversity: the fourteenth century** (1968), while a vivid account written for a broad audience and signaling twentieth-century parallels is B. W. Tuchman, *A distant mirror: the calamitous 14th century** (1978). G. Leff, *The dissolution of the medieval outlook: an essay on intellectual change in the fourteenth century* (1976), despite the title, stresses the continuity of medieval thought. The growing restlessness within the church is ably described in P. Hughes, *The revolt against the church: Aquinas to Luther* (1947), an outstanding Catholic account; E. F. Jacob, *Essays on the conciliar epoch* (1943, 1953); and F. Oakley, *The Western church in the later Middle Ages* (1979). National heresies of the fourteenth century may be studied in H. Kaminsky, *A history of the Hussite revolution* (1967); B. Workman, *John Wyclif: a study of the English medieval church* (2 vols., 1926); and the lively K. B. McFarlane, *John Wycliffe and the beginnings of English nonconformity** (Teach Yourself History series, 1952). The fourteenth-century plague that swept Europe and other parts of the globe is examined in W. H. McNeill, *Plagues and peoples* (1976), cited earlier; P. Ziegler, *The black death* (1969); J. Hatcher, *Plague, population, and the English economy, 1348–1530* (1979); and M. W. Dols, *The black death in the Middle East* (1977), where in contrast to Western Europe recovery was considerably slower.

The phenomenon of witchcraft in the early modern centuries has attracted a good deal of scholarly attention. Here K. Thomas, *Religion and the decline of magic** (1971) is of fundamental importance. Other important studies include R. Kieckhefer, *European witch trials: their foundation in popular and learned culture, 1300–1500* (1976); E. W. Monter, *Witchcraft in France and Switzerland: the borderlands during the Reformation* (1976); and J. B. Russell, *A history of witchcraft: sorcerers, heretics, and pagans** (1980). Kieckhefer has also written *Repression of heresy in medieval Germany* (1979), which focuses on the fourteenth century. For the later period one may read H. R. Trevor-Roper, *The European witch craze of the sixteenth and seventeenth centuries** (1969); H. C. E. Midelfort, *Witch hunting in southwestern Germany, 1562–1684* (1972); D. P. Walker, *Unclean spirits: possession and exorcism in France and England in the late sixteenth and early seventeenth centuries* (1981); and C. Larner, *Enemies of God: the witch hunt in Scotland* (1981). Two books that examine the *jacqueries* and other popular revolts are M. Mollat and P. Wolff, *The popular revolutions of the late Middle Ages* (trans. 1972), and G. Fourquin, *The anatomy of popular rebellion in the Middle Ages* (trans. 1978).

The Renaissance in Italy

In addition to the accounts cited at the beginning of this chapter, one may turn to D. Hay, *The Italian Renaissance in its historical background** (rev., 1977); R. S. Lopez, *The three ages of the Italian Renaissance* (1970); J. A. Mazzeo, *Renaissance and revolution: the remaking of European thought* (1969); and B. Pullan, *A history of early Renaissance Italy* (1973). The concept of the "Renaissance" is explored in W. K. Ferguson, *The Renaissance in historical thought: five centuries of interpretation* (1948), in which he examines, among other things, the classical accounts of the Italian Renaissance by J. A. Symonds (7 vols., 1875–1886) and J. Burckhardt (1860; new ed., 1944). An important study stressing continuity rather than rupture with the Middle Ages, and stressing lay culture rather than secularism, is M. Becker, *Medieval Italy: constraints and creativity* (1981).

The fusion of politics and humanism in Renaissance Italy is brilliantly traced in H. Baron, *The crisis of the early Italian Renaissance: civic humanism and republican liberty in an age of classicism and tyranny** (2 vols., 1955; rev. 1 vol. ed., 1966); on this subject, one also may read E. Garin, *Italian humanism: philosophy and civic life in the Renaissance* (1941, trans. 1965). Another successful synthesis stressing the relationships of politics and culture in the age is L. Martines, *Power and imagination: city-states in Renaissance Italy** (1979); here one may also turn to P. Burke, *Culture and society in Renaissance Italy, 1420–1540* (1972). The specialist cannot neglect P. O. Kristeller, *Renaissance thought: the classic, scholastic, and humanist strains* (1961) and *Eight philosophers of the Italian Renaissance* (1964), nor C. Trinkaus, *In our image and likeness: humanity and divinity in Italian humanist thought* (2 vols., 1970). On Machiavelli, there are studies by F. Chabod, *Machiavelli and the Renaissance* (trans. 1958); J. R. Hale, *Machiavelli and Renaissance Italy** (Teach Yourself History series, 1960); and F. Gilbert, *Machiavelli and Guicciardini: politics and history in sixteenth-century Florence* (1965). A profound and provocative study of political thought as it was influenced by the Renaissance from the fifteenth to the eighteenth centuries is J. G. A. Pocock, *The Machiavellian* moment: *Florentine political thought and the Atlantic republican tradition* * (1975). J. R. Hale (ed.), *A concise encyclopedia of the Italian Renaissance* (1981), is a convenient reference tool.

Numerous studies focusing on each of the Italian city-states have helped illuminate the "world of humanism," of which only a few titles can be cited here. Much of the focus has been on Florence, for which three general accounts are available: G. Holmes, *The Florentine enlightenment, 1400–1450* (1969); V. Cronin, *The Florentine Renaissance* (1967); and G. Brucker, *Renaissance Florence* (1969). Among outstanding special studies are G. Brucker, *Florentine politics and society, 1343–1378* (1962), and *The civic world of early Renaissance Florence* (1977), which carries the story to 1430; J. R. Hale, *Florence and the Medici: the pattern of control* (1978), a masterful account; M. Becker, *Florence in transition* (2 vols., 1967–1969); D. Weinstein, *Savanorola and Florence* (1970); C. Fusero, *The Borgias* (trans. 1973); and two books that focus in new ways on relationships between culture and social change: R. C. Trexler, *Public life in Renaissance Florence* (1980), and S. K. Cohen, Jr., *The laboring classes in Renaissance Florence* (1980). R. G. Witt, *Hercules at the crossroads: the life, works, and thought of Coluccio Salutati* (1983), studies an important Florentine humanist. R. A. Goldthwaite, *The building of Renaissance Florence: an economic and social history* (1981), is a thorough account of all aspects of the physical construction of the city, while R. DeRoover explores another specialized subject in *The rise and decline of the Medici bank, 1307–1494* * (1963). E. Cochrane examines the post-Renaissance city in *Florence in the forgotten centuries, 1527–1800* (1973).

Outstanding studies of Venice with varying perspectives include: F. C. Lane, *Venice: a maritime republic* * (1973); W. H. McNeill, *Venice: the hinge of Europe, 1081–1797* (1974); W. Bouwsma, *Venice and the defense of republican liberty: Renaissance values in the age of the Counter Reformation* (1968); B. Pullan, *Rich and poor in Renaissance Venice* (1971); R. Finlay, *Politics in Renaissance Venice* (1980); and J. J. Norwich, *A history of Venice* (1982). On Rome, one may read P. Partner, *The lands of St. Peter: the papal state in the Middle Ages and the early Renaissance* (1972), and *Renaissance Rome, 1500–1559: a portrait of a society* * (1977).

The Renaissance Outside Italy and the New Monarchies

J. Huizinga, *The waning of the Middle Ages . . . life, thought, and art in France and the Netherlands in the fourteenth and fifteenth centuries* * (1924, reissued 1976), and P. S. Allen, *The age of Erasmus* (1914), remain excellent introductions to the northern Renaissance. On Erasmus, there are available the sympathetic P. Smith, *Erasmus* * (1923); J. Huizinga, *Erasmus* * (1924); the brief, spirited M. M. Phillips, *Erasmus and the northern Renaissance* * (Teach Yourself History series, 1950); and R. M. Bainton, *Erasmus of Christendom* (1969). J. D. Tracy, *The politics of Erasmus: a peaceful intellectual and his political milieu* (1978), focuses on his idea of the state. On Christian humanism, one turns to E. H. Harbison, *The Christian scholar in the age of the Reformation* * (1956), and L. Spitz, *The religious renaissance of the German humanists* (1963).

The relations between banking and culture in Germany and elsewhere are examined in R. Ehrenberg, *Capital and finance in the age of the Renaissance: a study of the Fuggers and their connections* (1928), and in J. Strieder, *Jacob Fugger the Rich* (1931). G. M. Trevelyan's *Illustrated English social history* (4 vols., 1949 ff.) and *English social history: a survey of six centuries* * (rev., 1946) discuss the influence of the Continental Renaissance. Two studies by A. B. Ferguson illuminate aspects of the Renaissance in England: *The articulate citizen and the English Renaissance* (1965) and *Clio unbound: perception of the social and cultural past in Renaissance England* (1979). For France, L. Batiffol, *The century of the Renaissance* (trans. 1961), remains useful but see N. Z. Davis, *Society and culture in early modern France: eight essays* (1975), in which the lives and values of ordinary men and women are examined.

Two scholarly biographies of French monarchies are highly recommended: J. M. Tyrrell, *Louis XI* (1980), and R. J. Knecht, *Francis I* (1982), the latter a major work of scholarship. A special subject is explored in M. Wolfe, *The fiscal system of Renaissance France* (1972). The first Tudor monarch is examined in S. B. Chrimes, *Henry VII* (1972), and in M. V. C. Alexander, *The first of the Tudors: a study of Henry VII and his reign* (1980), a lively account. Other books on England, France, and Spain in this period are listed below and in the next chapter.

General Works on the Reformation

Besides the general accounts already listed, syntheses focusing on the Reformation proper include G. R. Elton, *Reformation Europe, 1517–1559** (1963); A. G. Dickens, *Reformation and society in sixteenth century Europe** (1960); O. Chadwick, *The Reformation** (1963); K. Holl, *The cultural significance of the Reformation* (1959); H. J. Grimm, *The Reformation era* (rev., 1965); and H. J. Hillerbrand, *The world of the Reformation* (1973). P. Hughes, *A popular history of the Reformation** (1957), and J. Lortz, *How the Reformation came* (1964), are accounts by eminent Catholic scholars. For the political background, there are H. Holborn, *A history of modern Germany: the Reformation* (1959), the first volume of a three-volume history of Germany; and F. L. Carsten, *Princes and parliaments in Germany* (1959). Two outstanding accounts of the leading ruler of the age are K. Brandi, *The Emperor Charles V** (1939), an older masterly study, and M. Fernandez Alvarez, *Charles V: elected emperor and hereditary ruler* (trans. 1975, in the Men in Office series).

An outstanding biographical account of Luther is E. G. Schwiebert, *Luther and his times* (1950). E. H. Erikson, *Young man Luther: a study in psychoanalysis and history** (1958, 1962), is a pioneering psychoanalytical study. Other lively, scholarly accounts are R. H. Bainton, *Here I stand: a life of Martin Luther* (1950); A. G. Dickens, *Martin Luther and the Reformation** (Teach Yourself History series, 1967); E. G. Rupp, *The progress of Luther to the Diet of Worms, 1521* (1951); R. H. Fife, *The revolt of Martin Luther* (1957); J. Atkinson, *Martin Luther and the birth of Protestantism** (1968); R. Marius, *Luther* (1974); M. U. Edwards, *Luther and the false brethren* (1975); and H. G. Haile, *Luther: an experiment in biography* (1980), which focuses on the reformer in his later years.

P. Blickle, *The revolution of 1525: the German peasants' war from a new perspective* (1977, trans. 1981), studies that event comprehensively but may be supplemented by the essays in B. Scribner and G. Benecke (eds.), *The German peasant war, 1525— new viewpoints* (1979). The appeal of Lutheran ideas to the uneducated classes is skillfully analyzed in R. W. Scribner, *For the sake of simple folk: popular propaganda for the German Reformation* (1981).

Among the best accounts of Calvin and his influence are J. T. McNeill, *The history and character of Calvinism* (1954); F. Wendel, *Calvin: the origins and development of his religious thought* (trans. 1963); and Q. Breen, *John Calvin: a study in French humanism* (1931). There are biographical studies by G. Harkness (1931), R. N. Carew Hunt (1933), and J. MacKinnon (1936). G. R. Potter, *Zwingli* (1977), is an outstanding biography, and W. S. Reid has written *Trumpeter of God: a biography of John Knox* (1974). R. H. Bainton, *Hunted heretic: the life and death of Michael Servetus** (1960), may be compared with J. Friedman, *Michael Servetus: a case study in total heresy* (1978).

The cities in which the major events of the Reformation occurred are examined in G. Strauss, *Nuremberg in the sixteenth century** (1966), and W. Monter, *Calvin's Geneva** (1967); and the urban element in general is analyzed in S. E. Ozment, *The Reformation in the cities: the appeal of Protestantism to sixteenth century Germany and Switzerland** (1975). R. H. Bainton studies the contributions of women to the religious changes of the era in a three-volume study, each covering different parts of Europe, in *Women of the Reformation* (1971–1977), and I. Maclean reviews the images of women in a broad range of early modern thought and writing, including theology, law, and medicine, in *The Renaissance notion of women* (1980).

The Reformation in England and Other Reformation Themes

The course of the Reformation in England may be approached through two outstanding syntheses: A. G. Dickens, *The English Reformation** (1964), and D. H. Pill, *The English Reformation, 1529–58** (1973). Other able accounts are A. G. Dickens, *Thomas Cromwell and the English Reformation* (1959); R. W. Beckingsale, *Thomas Cromwell* (1978); and F. E. Hutchinson, *Cranmer and the English Reformation** (Teach Yourself History series, 1951). Good introductions to England in this age are J. R. Lander, *Government and community: England, 1450–1509* (1980), and G. R. Elton, *Reform and reformation: England, 1509–1558* (1977); both are volumes in the New History of England series. Surveys covering all phases of English religious history are N. Sykes, *The English religious tradition*

(1953), and E. O. James, *A history of Christianity in England* (1949). R. W. Chambers, *Thomas More* (1948), is a sympathetic, moving biography; on More's contribution to his age, one also may read M. Fleisher, *Radical reform and political persuasion in the life and writings of Thomas More* (1973); J. H. Hexter, *The vision of politics on the eve of the Reformation: More, Machiavelli, and Seyssel* (1973); and J. A. Guy, *The public career of Sir Thomas More* (1980). D. Knowles, *Bare ruined choirs: the dissolution of the English monasteries* (1976), a revised version of his earlier work (1959), is informative on an important subject, as are G. W. O. Woodward, *The dissolution of the monasteries* (1967), and J. Youings, *The dissolution of the monasteries* (1971), in which some representative documents are reprinted. A distinguished biography focusing on the king as well as on the events of his reign is J. J. Scarisbrick, *Henry VIII* (1968); one also may read L. B. Smith, *Henry VIII: the mask of royalty* (1971). A detailed account of the famous divorce is provided in G. deC. Parmiter, *The king's great matter: a study of Anglo-papal relations, 1527–1534* (1967), and in H. A. Kelly, *The matrimonial trials of Henry VIII* (1975). On Henry VIII's two immediate successors, one may read W. K. Jordan, *Edward VI* (2 vols., 1968–1970), and D. M. Loades, *The reign of Mary Tudor: politics, government, and religion in England, 1553–1558* (1979). Among books focusing on religion under Elizabeth are P. Collinson, *The Elizabethan Puritan movement* (1967); P. McGrath, *Papists and Puritans under Elizabeth I* (1968); and A. Morey, *The Catholic subjects of Elizabeth I* (1978). The restlessness of the age and of the years that followed is depicted in A. Fletcher, *Tudor rebellions* (1973).

The various forms of Protestantism are placed in historical perspective in E. Troeltsch's masterpiece, *The social teachings of the Christian churches* (2 vols., reissued 1949); J. S. Whale, *The Protestant tradition* (1959); and E. G. Leonard, *A history of Protestantism* (1965). The radical movements of the era may be studied in G. H. Williams, *The radical Reformation* (1962); N. Cohn, *The pursuit of the millennium* (1957; rev., 1964); and M. A. Mulett, *Radical religious movements in early modern Europe* (1980). Another important subject is explored in H. Kamen, *The rise of toleration* (1967).

On the much-debated question concerning the relation between economic change and religious doctrine, see M. Weber, *The Protestant ethic and the spirit of capitalism* * (1904, reissued 1948), which opened the controversy; R. H. Tawney, *Religion and the rise of capitalism* * (1926, 1947), a brilliant work, although somewhat superseded by more recent research; and G. Marshall, *In search of the spirit of capitalism: an essay on Max Weber's Protestant ethic thesis* (1982), a balanced review of the thesis and the debate.

Two provocative books dealing with the social implications of the Reformation for England, among many other subjects, are H. R. Trevor-Roper, *Religion, the Reformation and social change* (1967), and C. Hill, *Reformation to industrial revolution: the making of modern English society* (1967).

Catholicism Reformed and Reorganized

On the Counter Reformation, one may turn to M. R. O'Connell, *The Counter Reformation, 1559–1610* * (1974), in the Langer series; A. G. Dickens, *The Counter Reformation* (1969); H. O. Evennett, *The spirit of the Counter Reformation* (1968); L. Cristiani, *The revolt against the church* (trans. 1962); G. W. Searle, *The Counter Reformation* (1974); P. F. Grendler, *The Roman Inquisition and the Venetian press, 1540–1605* (1977); and P. Hughes, *Rome and the Counter Reformation in England* (1942). H. Jedin, *The Council of Trent* (2 vols., 1957–1961), is an objective treatment, narrating much more than the council itself. An introduction to the large literature on the Society of Jesus is provided in C. Hollis, *The Jesuits* (1968), and one may also read M. Foss, *The founding of the Jesuits, 1540* (1969), and W. V. Bangert, *A history of the Society of Jesus* (1972). There are biographies of Loyola by C. Hollis (1931), P. Dudon (1933), and J. Brodrick (1956).

Problems and Readings*

Among pamphlets in various problems series for subjects covered in this chapter are K. H. Dannenfeldt (ed.), *The Renaissance* (rev., 1975); D. Hay (ed.), *The Renaissance debate* (1963); D. L. Jensen (ed.), *Machiavelli: cynic, patriot, or political scientist?* (1960); L. W. Spitz (ed.), *The Reformation* (rev., 1972); K. C. Sessions (ed.), *Reformation and authority: the meaning of the Peas-*

ants' Revolt (1968); A. J. Slavin (ed.), *The new monarchies* (1964) and *Henry VIII and the English Reformation* (1968); R. W. Green, *Protestantism, capitalism, and social science: the Weber thesis controversy* (rev., 1973); and R. Kingdon, *Calvin and Calvinism: sources of democracy?* (1970). In the Anvil series, there are R. H. Bainton, *The age of the Reformation* (1956), and E. M. Burns, *The Counter Reformation* (1964). Source material and commentary are provided in H. J. Hillerbrand (ed.), *The Protestant Reformation: a narrative history related by contemporary observers and participants* (1964); L. W. Spitz (ed.), *The Protestant Reformation* (1966); and G. R. Elton (ed.), *Renaissance and Reformation, 1300–1648* (1963). S. E. Ozment (ed.), *The Reformation in medieval perspective* (1971), provides examples of recent scholarly writings on the subject. W. J. Bouwsma, *The culture of Renaissance humanism* (1973), and H. J. Grimm, *The Reformation* (1972), are two useful contributions in the American Historical Association Pamphlets series.

III: ECONOMIC RENEWAL AND WARS OF RELIGION, 1560–1648

Of general treatments for these years, covering institutional and international developments, the best guides are J. H. Elliott, *Europe divided, 1559–1598** (1969; rev., 1982); C. Wilson, *The transformation of Europe, 1558–1648* (1976); H. Kamen, *The iron century: social change in Europe, 1550–1660* (1971); R. S. Dunn, *The age of religious wars, 1559–1715** (rev., 1979); and two volumes in the Langer series: M. R. O'Connell, *The Counter Reformation, 1559–1610** (1974), already cited, and C. J. Friedrich, *The age of the baroque, 1610–1660** (1952), which is less useful for political subjects. A richly illustrated collaborative volume with chapters on the non-Western world is H. R. Trevor-Roper (ed.), *The age of expansion: Europe and the world, 1559–1660* (1968). A magisterial work stressing broad geographic, demographic, and economic developments is the study by F. Braudel, *The Mediterranean and the Mediterranean world in the age of Philip II** (2 vols., trans. 1972–1974), cited in the introductory section.

Four analytical treatments focusing on the concept of crisis in the seventeenth century (and useful for this and the following chapter) deserve mention: T. K. Rabb, *The struggle for stability in early modern Europe* (1975); G. Parker and L. M. Smith, *The general crisis of the seventeenth century* (1978); T. Aston (ed.), *Crisis in Europe, 1560–1660** (1966); and R. Forster and J. P. Greene (eds.), *Preconditions of revolution in early modern Europe* (1970). There are informative chapters by specialists in R. B. Wernham (ed.), *The Counter Reformation and price revolution, 1559–1610** (1968), and in J. P. Cooper (ed.), *The decline of Spain and the Thirty Years' War, 1609–1648/59** (1970), vols. III and IV of the New Cambridge Modern History respectively.

The Opening of the Atlantic

The best introductory account is by J. H. Parry, *The age of reconnaissance** (rev., 1981), who also has written *Europe and a wider world, 1415–1715** (1949), and *The discovery of the sea* (1974). Also useful are C. E. Nowell's brief *The great discoveries and the first colonial empires** (1954); G. J. Marcus, *The conquest of the North Atlantic from early times to the late 15th century* (1980); and G. V. Scammell, *The world encompassed: the first European maritime empire, c. 800–1650* (1982). S. E. Morison, *The European discovery of America* (2 vols., 1971, 1974), is indispensable, the first volume on the northern voyages, the second on the southern. Morison also masterfully reconstructed the life and voyages of Columbus in *Admiral of the ocean sea* (1942). C. M. Cipolla stresses the importance of technology for the explorations in *Guns, sails, and empires: 1400–1700** (1965). D. Lach, *Asia in the making of Europe* (2 vols., the second volume in three parts, 1965–1978), is an important work tracing the Asian cultural and intellectual impact on Europe through the sixteenth century.

Portuguese maritime and colonial enterprises are recounted in C. R. Boxer, *Four centuries of Portuguese expansion, 1415–1825** (1961), and *The Portuguese seaborne empire* (1969), on which one may also read B. W. Diffie and G. D. Winius, *Foundations of the Portuguese empire, 1415–1580* (1977), in the series on European expansion edited by B. W. Shafer. On Portugal itself, there are sound histories by H. V. Livermore, *A new history of Portugal** (1977); A. H. De Oliveira Marques, *History of Portugal** (rev., 1976); and on the entire Iberian peninsula, S. G. Payne, *A history of Spain and Portugal* (2 vols., 1973).

Spain in Europe and Overseas

Three books reflecting modern scholarship on Spain for the early modern centuries and superseding older works of which R. B. Merriman's were the best known are J. H. Elliott, *Imperial Spain, 1469–1716** (1964); J. Lynch, *Spain under the Habsburgs 1516–1700* (2 vols., rev., 1981); and I. A. A. Thompson, *War and government in Habsburg Spain, 1560–1620* (1976). Elliott also has written *The revolt of the Catalans: a study in the decline of Spain, 1598–1640* (1963). Recommended also are two books by J. Vicens Vives, *An economic history of Spain from earliest times to the end of the nineteenth century* (1955, trans. 1969), and *Approaches to the history of Spain** (1962, trans. 1967); and a good brief introduction to Spanish economic history is J. Harrison, *An economic history of modern Spain* (1978). R. Herr, *Spain** (1971), thoughtfully views twentieth-century Spain in historical perspective. C. Petrie's *Philip II of Spain* (1963) is an account of Spanish affairs rather than a biography; an impressive scholarly portrait of the king and his times is P. Pierson, *Philip II of Spain* (Men in Office series, 1976). G. Mattingly, *The Armada** (1959), masterfully places the dramatic episode in its European setting.

For the Spanish empire in the new world, excellent accounts are C. Gibson, *Spain in America** (1966); J. H. Parry, *The Spanish seaborne empire* (1966); and J. H. Elliott, *The old world and the new, 1492–1716* (1970). Two vivid accounts are F. A. Kirkpatrick, *The Spanish conquistadores* (1934, 1949), and J. Hemmings, *The conquest of the Incas** (1970).

L. Hanke, *The Spanish struggle for justice in the conquest of America** (1949), questions older views on the Inquisition. Spanish treatment of subject peoples in Latin America also is discussed in L. B. Simpson, *The encomienda in New Spain: forced native labor in the Spanish colonies, 1492–1550* (1929), while a comprehensive study of blacks in Spanish America from 1502 to the present is provided in L. B. Rout, Jr., *The African experience in Spanish America* (1976). F. Tannenbaum, *Slave and citizen: the Negro in the Americas** (1947), argued that in Latin America (unlike North America) there was recognition of the "moral personality" of the slave; see also, on North American attitudes, W. D. Jordan, *White over black: American attitudes toward the Negro, 1550–1812** (1968). Other key studies are D. B. Davis, *The problem of slavery in Western culture* (1966), and its sequel, *The problem of slavery in the age of revolution, 1770–1823* (1975); and E. Williams, *Capitalism and slavery** (1944). The grim story of the slave trade is told in J. Pope-Hennessy, *Sins of the fathers: a study of the Atlantic slave traders, 1441–1807** (1968); D. P. Mannix and M. Cowley, *Black cargoes* (1962); P. D. Curtin, *The Atlantic slave trade** (1969); H. S. Klein, *The middle passage: comparative studies in the Atlantic slave trade** (1978); J. A. Rawley, *The transatlantic slave trade: a history* (1981); H. Gemery and J. Hogendorn (eds.), *The uncommon market: essays in the economic history of the Atlantic slave trade* (1979); and C. A. Palmer, *Human cargoes: the British slave trade to Spanish America, 1700–1739* (1981). A thoughtful analysis is C. D. Rice, *The rise and fall of black slavery* (1975). A pioneer inquiry into the impact of the discovery of silver upon economic changes in Europe is E. J. Hamilton, *American treasure and the price revolution in Spain, 1501–1650* (1934), although some of its conclusions have been modified. The subject also is examined in P. Vilar, *A history of gold and money, 1450–1920* (trans. 1976), and in J. N. Ball, *Merchants and merchandise: the expansion of trade in Europe, 1500–1630* (1977), which explores the upswing in population, trade, and prices in the sixteenth century.

Changing Social Structures, Early Capitalism, Mercantilism

[The general economic histories cited in the introductory section and the general works cited for Chapter II and in the present chapter also should be consulted.] Among the best surveys of preindustrial economic history are R. Davis, *The rise of the Atlantic economies** (1973), covering developments from the mid-fifteenth to the eighteenth centuries; C. M. Cipolla, *Before the industrial revolution: European society and economy, 1000–1700* (1976); and J. DeVries, *The economy of Europe in an age of crisis, 1600–1750** (1976). An important work, influenced by the *Annales* school and especially by F. Braudel, whose works on the emergence of capitalism have been cited in the introductory section, is I. Wallerstein, *The modern world-system:* vol. I, *Capitalist agriculture and the origins of the European world economy in the sixteenth century** (1974), and vol. II, *Mercantilism and the consolidation of the European world econ-*

omy, *1600–1750** (1980); additional volumes are projected. On mercantilism, E. Hecksher, *Mercantilism* (2 vols., 1935), may be supplemented by P. Buck, *The politics of mercantilism* (1942), and C. Wilson, *Profit and power* (1957). Indispensable on social structures is B. Moore, *Origins of democracy and dictatorship: lord and peasant in the making of the modern world** (1966). There are valuable chapters in C. M. Cipolla (ed.), *The Fontana economic history of Europe: the sixteenth and seventeenth centuries** (1974), and in two volumes edited by E. E. Rich and C. H. Wilson: *The economy of expanding Europe in the sixteenth and seventeenth centuries* (1967), and *The economic organization of early modern Europe* (1977), vols. IV and V respectively of the Cambridge Economic History of Europe. For early demography, one may turn to M. W. Flynn, *The European demographic system, 1500–1820* (1981).

J. U. Nef, *Industry and government in France and England, 1540–1640** (1957), argues the case for an early "industrial revolution"; for the English model, it may be compared with L. A. Clarkson, *The pre-industrial economy of England, 1500–1750* (1972); B. A. Holderness, *Pre-industrial England: economy and society, 1500–1750* (1976); and D. C. Coleman, *The economy of England, 1450–1750* (1977). A. O. Hirschman, *The passions and the interests: political arguments for capitalism before its triumph* (1977), explores the changes in intellectual climate that lent respectability to the pursuit of material gain.

Revolt of the Netherlands

G. Parker, *The Dutch revolt* (1977), is an admirable comprehensive study, which may be compared with P. Geyl's masterful longer account: *The revolt of the Netherlands, 1555–1609* (1932, trans. 1958), and *The Netherlands in the seventeenth century, 1609–1715* (2 vols., trans. 1961–1964). C. V. Wedgwood, *William the Silent** (1944), is an excellent, laudatory biography. Other books on the Netherlands appear in the following chapter.

Tudor England

Among many good books, the best recent accounts are G. R. Elton, *Reform and Reformation: England 1509–1558** (1977) cited for Chapter II, sympathetic to the Tudors; J. Hurstfield, *Elizabeth I and the unity of England** (1966), more critical; and P. Williams, *The Tudor regime** (1979), a provocative reassessment. Highly recommended also are two books by W. T. MacCaffrey, *The shaping of the Elizabethan regime** (1968), and *Queen Elizabeth and the making of policy, 1572–1588** (1981); and by J. E. Neale, *The Elizabethan House of Commons* (1949), and *Elizabeth I and her parliaments* (2 vols., 1953–1957). R. B. Wernham, *Before the armada: the emergence of the English nation, 1485–1588** (1972), is important for foreign affairs, as is P. S. Crowson, *Tudor foreign policy* (1973). L. B. Smith, *The Elizabethan world* (1967), is a colorful account. The outstanding biography of Elizabeth remains J. E. Neale's distinguished *Queen Elizabeth I** (1934, 1966), but three other scholarly and readable books deserve mention: E. Jenkins, *Elizabeth the Great** (1959), N. Williams, *Elizabeth the first, queen of England* (1968), and L. B. Smith, *Elizabeth Tudor* (1975). C. Wilson, *Queen Elizabeth and the revolt of the Netherlands* (1970), examines an important episode in her career. A. L. Rowse crowds many subjects into *The Elizabethan age* (2 vols., 1950–1955), and has also written *The Elizabethan Renaissance: the cultural achievement* (1972), as well as a highly controversial *William Shakespeare: a biography** (1963). There is a vivid biography of Mary Tudor by H. F. M. Prescott (rev., 1953) and of Mary Stuart by A. Fraser, *Mary Queen of Scots* (1969).

On the naval and imperial side, one may read J. A. Williamson, *The age of Drake* (1938, 1946), and two books by D. B. Quinn, *Raleigh and the British empire** (Teach Yourself History series, 1947) and *England and the discovery of America, 1481–1620* (1974). The religious connections of English expansionism are pointed out in L. B. Wright, *Religion and empire: the alliance between piety and commerce in English expansion, 1558–1625* (1943). T. K. Rabb, *Enterprise and empire: merchant and gentry investment in the expansion of England, 1575–1630* (1967), is a pioneering effort to apply computer techniques in the study of early modern history. A monograph illuminating more than its topic is C. E. Challis, *The Tudor Coinage* (1978).

Social and economic features of the age are treated in L. Stone, *The crisis of the aristocracy, 1558–1641* (1965; abr. ed., 1967), stressing the decline of the nobility, and a sequel volume, *Family and fortune: studies in aristocratic finance in the sixteenth and* seventeenth centuries (1973). H. R. Trevor-Roper, *The gentry, 1540–1640* (1953), should be read along with J. H. Hexter, *Reappraisals in history: new views on history and society in early modern Europe** (1961), cited in the introductory section. A provocative essay is A. Macfarlane, *The origins of English individualism: the family, property, and social transition** (1978). W. K. Jordan, *Philanthropy in England, 1480–1660* (1959), throws light on the founding of schools and on some of the Oxford and Cambridge colleges; and D. Cressy, *Literacy and the social order: reading and writing in Tudor and Stuart England* (1980), answers other questions about early English education.

New historical research based on the examination of parish records in order to reconstruct the history of the family is brilliantly exemplified in L. Stone, *The family, sex, and marriage in England, 1500–1800** (1977, abr. 1979), cited in the introductory section. Other works focusing on such subjects as trends in illegitimate births since the sixteenth century are P. Laslett, *Family life and illicit love in earlier generations: essays in historical sociology* (1977); and G. R. Quaife, *Wanton wenches and wayward wives: peasants and illicit sex in early seventeenth-century England* (1979). An important demographic study is E. A. Wrigley and R. S. Schofield, *The population history of England, 1541–1871: a reconstruction* (1981).

Disintegration and Reconstruction of France

An informative volume on the religious and dynastic turmoil in sixteenth-century France is J. H. M. Salmon, *Society in crisis: France in the sixteenth century* (rev., 1979); another recommended synthesis is R. Briggs, *Early modern France, 1560–1715** (1977). Two major French works available in abridged translations are R. Mandrou, *Introduction to modern France, 1500–1640: an essay in historical psychology* (trans. 1976), and E. Le Roy Ladurie, *The peasants of Languedoc** (trans. 1974), cited earlier. A survey of French history is provided in G. de Bertier de Sauvigny and D. H. Pinkney, *History of France* (rev., 1983). Other useful books on events, issues, and personalities of the age are: J. E. Neale, *The age of Catherine de Medici and the lost revolution** (1937); N. M. Sutherland, *The massacre of St. Bartholomew and the European conflict,*

1559–1572 (1973); the same author's *The Huguenot struggle for recognition* (1980); R. M. Kingdon, *Geneva and the consolidation of the French Protestant movement, 1564–1572* (1967); D. R. Kelley, *The beginning of ideology: consciousness and society in the French reformation* (1981); and A. N. Galpern, *The religions of the people in sixteenth-century Champagne* (1976), a successful effort to use anthropological techniques. Social history is explored in S. L. Flandrin, *Families in former times: kinship, household, and sexuality in early modern France* (trans. 1979). There are biographies of Henry of Navarre by Q. Hurst (1938) and H. Pearson (1964), and of Henry's mother by N. L. Roelker, *Queen of Navarre: Jeanne d'Albret, 1528–1572* (1968); also available is R. Mousnier, *The assassination of Henry IV* (trans. 1973).

Governmental and constitutional developments are explored in J. R. Major, *Representative government in early modern France* (1980), which stresses the vitality of the early representative bodies; P. Anderson, *Lineages of the absolutist state* (1974); J. M. Haydon, *France and the Estates General of 1614* (1974); and H. H. Rowen, *The king's state: proprietary dynasticism in early modern France* (1980), which argues that the French kings viewed the state as royal property. D. Bitton, *The French nobility in crisis, 1560–1640* (1969), describes arguments for and against nobility two centuries before the French Revolution.

The growth of centralized government is described in D. Buisseret, *Sully and the growth of centralized government in France, 1598–1610* (1968). For Richelieu, one may turn to C. V. Wedgwood's brief and balanced *Richelieu and the French monarchy** (Teach Yourself History series, 1949); G. R. R. Treasure, *Cardinal Richelieu and the development of absolutism* (1972); and W. F. Church, *Richelieu and reason of state* (1972). Other studies include D. Parker, *La Rochelle and the French monarchy: conflict and order in seventeenth-century France* (1980); R. Bonney, *Political change in France under Richelieu and Mazarin, 1624–1661* (1978), especially useful on the role of the *intendants*; and G. Dethan, *The young Mazarin* (1977). Two important specialized studies are O. Ranum, *Richelieu and the councillors of Louis XIII* (1963), and by a Russian scholar, A. D. Lublinskaya, *French absolutism: the crucial phase, 1620–1629* (trans. 1968).

The Thirty Years' War

Vivid and authoritative accounts are C. V. Wedgwood, *The Thirty Years' War** (1938); S. H. Steinberg, *The Thirty Years' War** (1966); and J. V. Polisensky, *The Thirty Years' War* (1971), by a Czech historian, which may be supplemented by his *War and society in Europe, 1618–1648* (1978). Biographical accounts include F. Watson, *Wallenstein: soldier under Saturn* (1938); G. Mann, *Wallenstein: his life narrated* (trans. 1976), a major biographical study; and N. Ahnlund, *Gustav Adolf the Great* (1932, 1940). A detailed treatment of all aspects of Swedish history is to be found in the many books of M. Roberts: *The early Vasas* (1968); *Gustavus Adolphus* (2 vols., 1953–1958); *Essays in Swedish history* (1967); and *The Swedish imperial experience, 1560–1718* (1979). Roberts also has edited *Sweden as a great power: government, society, and foreign policy, 1611–1697* (1968) and *Sweden's age of greatness, 1632–1718* (1973). The story of the conversion to Catholicism of Gustavus Adolphus's daughter and her abdication is told in G. Masson, *Queen Christina* (1968), and in S. Svolpe, *Christina of Sweden*, edited by A. Randall (1966), a condensation of the untranslated larger work by a Swedish historian. A recommended general history of Sweden is F. D. Scott, *Sweden: the nation's history* (1977).

Problems and Readings*

The following will be found useful: D. L. Jensen (ed.), *The expansion of Europe: motives, methods, and meaning* (1967); J. H. Parry (ed.), *The European reconnaissance: selections and documents* (1968); W. E. Minchitan (ed.), *Mercantilism: system or expediency?* (1969); J. M. Levine (ed.), *Elizabeth I* (Great Lives Observed, 1969); R. L. Greaves, *Elizabeth I, Queen of England* (1974); J. C. Rule and J. J. TePaske (eds.), *The character of Philip II: the problem of moral judgments in history* (1963); TePaske (ed.), *Three American empires* (1967); J. F. Bannon (ed.), *Indian labor in the Spanish Indies* (1966); J. H. M. Salmon (ed.), *The French wars of religion* (1967); and T. K. Rabb (ed.), *The Thirty Years' War* (2nd ed., 1981). The Folger Booklets on Tudor and Stuart Civilization, published by the Folger Shakespeare Library, Washington, D.C., treat many historical and literary subjects.

IV: THE ESTABLISHMENT OF WEST-EUROPEAN LEADERSHIP

[Syntheses for these years will often overlap with titles listed at the beginning of Chapter III, which should be consulted.] Informative general works for the seventeenth century include D. Ogg, *Europe in the seventeenth century** (1925, 1961); G. N. Clark, *The seventeenth century** (1929, 1961); M. Beloff, *The age of absolutism, 1660–1815** (1954); R. N. Hatton, *Louis XIV and Europe* (1976); M. Ashley, *The golden century: Europe, 1598–1715* (1969); the same author's *A history of Europe, 1648–1815* (rev., 1973); and W. Doyle, *The old European order, 1660–1800** (1978). Other useful introductions are J. Stoye, *Europe unfolding, 1648–1689** (1969); C. J. Friedrich and C. Blitzer, *The age of power, 1610–1713** (1957); and J. B. Wolf, *Toward a European balance of power, 1620–1715** (1970). Three volumes in the Langer series provide coverage for the seventeenth century: C. J. Friedrich, *The age of the baroque, 1610–1660,** already cited; F. L. Nussbaum, *The triumph of science and reason, 1660–1685** (1953); and J. B. Wolf, *The emergence of the great powers, 1685–1715** (1951).

F. L. Carsten (ed.), *The ascendancy of France, 1648–1688** (1961), and J. S. Bromley (ed.), *The rise of Great Britain and Russia, 1688–1715/25** (1970), vols. V and VI of the New Cambridge Modern History, provide authoritative chapters on many topics. For Europe overseas, one may turn to W. G. Davies, *The North Atlantic world in the seventeenth century* (1974), and for diplomatic practices and institutions of the age, W. J. Roosen, *The age of Louis XIV: the rise of modern diplomacy** (1976).

The Dutch Republic and the Empire

The second part of P. Geyl, *The Netherlands in the seventeenth century, 1609–1715*, already cited, covers the years 1648 to 1715; for seventeenth-century Netherlands' history, there also are available C. Wilson, *The Dutch Republic and the civilization of the seventeenth century** (1968), an attractive, brief introduction; K. H. D. Haley, *The Dutch Republic in the seventeenth century* (1972); and J. L. Price, *Culture and society in the Dutch Republic during the seventeenth century* (1974). Dutch economic influence is explored in the relevant chapters of J. A. van Houtte, *An economic history of* the Low Countries, 800–1800 (1977), and the agrarian economy in J. De Vries, *The Dutch rural economy in the golden age, 1500–1700* (1974). The economic and cultural life of the leading Dutch city is explored in V. Barbour, *Capitalism in Amsterdam in the seventeenth century* (1950); D. Regin, *Traders, artists, burghers: a cultural history of Amsterdam in the 17th century* (1977); and P. Burke, *Venice and Amsterdam* (1974), a comparative study. On William of Orange, the best study is S. B. Baxter, *William III and the defense of European liberty, 1650–1702* (1966). N. A. Robb, *William of Orange: a personal portrait* (2 vols., 1963–1966), is stronger on biographical than on political details, and D. Ogg, *William III* (1956), is a brief sketch. A masterful detailed biography of a leading Dutch statesman is H. H. Rowen, *John de Witt, grand pensionary of Holland, 1625–1672* (1978). On overseas exploration and colonization, an outstanding introduction is C. R. Boxer, *The Dutch seaborne empire, 1600–1800* (1965).

Seventeenth-Century England

[See also the books on England cited in Chapter III.] The best introduction is J. P. Kenyon, *Stuart England* (1978). Other recent histories of high quality are C. Hill, *The century of revolution, 1603–1714* (1962); J. R. Jones, *Country and court: England, 1658–1714* (New History of England series, 1978); B. Coward, *The Stuart age, 1603–1714* (1980); and two books by M. Ashley: *England in the seventeenth century* (rev., 1980), and *The house of Stuart: its rise and fall* (1980). Ashley also has prepared a survey of seventeenth-century social history with many contemporary illustrations in *Life in Stuart England* (1964), and Stuart culture is also well conveyed in G. Parry, *The Golden Age restor'd: the culture of the Stuart court, 1603–1642* (1981). G. M. Straka and L. O. Straka, *A certainty in the succession* (1973), covers the years from 1640 to 1815. For economic developments, one may turn to C. Wilson, *England's apprenticeship, 1603–1763* (1965), and G. N. Clark, *The wealth of England from 1496 to 1760* (1947), while a wider setting is presented in J. R. Jones, *Britain and Europe in the seventeenth century* (1966), and its sequel, *Britain and the world, 1649–1815* (1980). G. E. Aylmer has written two important studies of politics, society, and bureaucracy: *The king's servants: the civil*

service of Charles I, 1625–1642 (1961, 1974), and *The state's servants: the civil service of the English republic, 1649–1660* (1973). Books by L. Stone, H. R. Trevor-Roper, and others on the aristocracy and the gentry have been cited in Chapter III, but one should add G. E. Mingay, *The rise and fall of a ruling class* (1976). The English background to settlement in America is ably sketched in W. Notestein, *The English people on the eve of colonization, 1603–1630* (1954), and in C. W. Bridenbaugh, *Vexed and troubled Englishmen, 1590–1642* (1968). An interesting comparative study in social history is R. Thompson, *Women in Stuart England and America* (1974), and an important addition to the social and economic history of the rural lower classes is A. B. Appleby, *Famine in Tudor and Stuart England* (1978).

On the Great Rebellion and subsequent developments, S. R. Gardiner's older history is justly regarded as a classic, and one still reads it with profit. A commendable, recent effort to recount the dramatic story is A. Fletcher, *The outbreak of the English Civil War* (1981). Other good introductions are L. Stone, *The causes of the English Revolution, 1529–1642* (1972), a brief but informative essay; and P. Zagorin, *The court and the country: the beginning of the English Revolution of the mid-seventeenth century* (1970). Some of the most vivid and perceptive writings on these events have been by C. V. Wedgwood, a strong advocate of the theory that analysis (the "why") ought to flow from detailed, accurate, and lively narrative (the "how"); among her works are a trilogy on the mid-century revolution: *The king's peace, 1637–1641* (1955), *The king's war, 1641–1647* (1959), and *A coffin for King Charles: the trial and execution of Charles I* (1964).

Three recent successful studies of the political and religious conflict are R. Ashton, *The English Civil War: conservatism and revolution, 1603–1649* (1978), which shares historians' conflicting interpretations with the reader; two books by C. Russell, *A crisis of Parliaments* (1971) and *Parliaments and English politics, 1621–1629* (1979); and L. Kaplan, *Politics and religion during the English Revolution: the Scots and the Long Parliament, 1643–1645* (1976).

C. Firth, *Oliver Cromwell and the rule of the Puritans in England* (1900, 1925), is still the best biographical account, but there are other studies by S. R. Gardiner, J. Morley, J. Buchan, M. Ashley, and C. V. Wedgwood. A. Fraser, *Cromwell: the Lord Protector* (1973), is an admirable biography, although less lively than her biography of Mary Stuart; and C. Hill, *God's Englishman** (1972), is a provocative account. C. D. Bowen has sketched a vivid portrait in *The lion and the throne: the life and times of Sir Edward Coke, 1552–1634* (1957). Other important studies are H. R. Trevor-Roper's unsympathetic *Archbishop Laud, 1573–1645* (1940); J. H. Hexter, *The reign of King Pym* (1941); D. Underdown, *Pride's purge* (1971); J. M. MacCormack, *Revolutionary politics in the Long Parliament* (1973); and L. G. Schwoerer, *No standing armies! the anti-army ideology in seventeenth century England* (1974). D. Willson has written a biography of the first Stuart, *King James VI and I** (1956), as has A. Fraser (1975); both may be supplemented by M. Lee, Jr., *Government by pen: Scotland under James VI and I* (1980). E. C. Wingfield-Stratford has written a detailed biography of Charles I (3 vols., 1949–1950), and C. Hibbert a briefer one (1969). B. H. Wormald provides an admirable study in *Clarendon: politics, history, and religion, 1640–1660* (1951), as does B. Worden in *The Rump Parliament, 1648–1653* (1974). The effect of the political turmoil on the English imagination is well conveyed in B. Willey, *The seventeenth century background: studies in the thought of the age in relation to poetry and religion* (1934, 1949); D. M. Wolfe, *Milton in the Puritan revolution* (1941); F. E. Hutchinson, *Milton and the English mind** (Teach Yourself History series, 1946); and C. Hill, *Milton and the English Revolution* (1978), a challenging full-length study.

Much of the interest in Stuart and Commonwealth England is directed to the emergence during that period of some recognizably modern political and social problems. One of the earliest of such efforts was G. P. Gooch, *The history of English democratic ideas in the seventeenth century** (1898; ed. H. J. Laski, 1927). The many provocative books of C. Hill in this connection are especially important; among those not already cited are: *Puritanism and revolution** (1958), *Society and Puritanism in prerevolutionary England** (1964), *Intellectual origins of the English Revolution* (1966), *Anti-Christ in seventeenth-century England* (1971), and *The world turned upside down* (1972). Hill's ideas are ably explored in a series of essays on his writings, D. Pennington and K. Thomas (eds.), *Puritans and revolutionaries: essays in seventeenth-century*

history (1979). B. Manning, *The English people and the English Revolution, 1640–1649* (1976), provides the best evaluation of the Levellers, but see also G. E. Aylmer, *The Levellers in the English Revolution* (1975). Other books include M. Walzer, *The revolution of the saints: a study in the origins of radical politics** (1965); P. G. Rogers, *The Fifth Monarchy men* (1966); J. S. McGee, *The godly man in Stuart England: Anglicans, Puritans, and the two tables, 1620–1670* (1976); W. Schenk, *The concern for social justice in the Puritan revolution* (1948), stressing religious rather than economic compulsions; W. Haller, *The rise of Puritanism** (1938); and M. Ashley, *John Wildman, plotter and postmaster: a study of the English republican movement in the seventeenth century* (1947). An important reassessment of ideology is J. O. Appleby, *Economic thought and ideology in seventeenth century England* (1978), while R. Hamilton, *The liberation of women: a study of patriarchy and capitalism* (1978), explores how preindustrial capitalism redefined the position of women in family and society.

On the Irish question, useful introductions are provided in J. C. Beckett, *The making of modern Ireland* (1966), and L. M. Cullen, *An economic history of Ireland since 1660* (1972); and for the Cromwellian age, there are two important studies: P. B. Ellis, *Ireland, 1652–1660* (1975), and T. C. Barnard, *Cromwellian Ireland: English government and reform in Ireland, 1649–1660* (1975).

Restoration and Revolution of 1688

The background to the Restoration is ably traced in G. Davies, *The restoration of Charles II, 1658–1660* (1955). The best treatment of the Restoration period itself is D. Ogg, *England in the reigns of Charles II, James II, and William III* (3 vols., 1955); a briefer treatment is G. Clark, *The later Stuarts* (rev., 1955). Written from a Tory viewpoint, A. Bryant, *King Charles II* (1932, 1949), makes the best possible case for Charles's relations with Louis XIV. A sympathetic balanced assessment is A. Fraser, *Royal Charles: Charles II and the Restoration** (1979), perhaps the best of her many thoughtful biographies. The nature of monarchy itself is explored in R. Ollard, *The image of the king: Charles I and Charles II* (1980), and a special subject examined in I. M. Green, *The re-establishment of the Church of England, 1660–1663* (1978). F. C. Turner, *James II* (1948), is fair and factual, as is J. Miller, *James II: a study in kingship* (1977), which stresses the monarch's personal integrity but failure as a king.

G. M. Trevelyan, *The English Revolution 1688–1689** (1939, 1946), argues that the revolution strengthened conservatism for the eighteenth century but that the long-run consequences made the revolution a turning point in history; it may be compared with L. Pinkham, *William III and the respectable revolution* (1954); M. Ashley, *The Glorious Revolution of 1688* (1967); J. R. Western, *Monarchy and revolution: the English state in the 1680s* (1972); J. Childs, *The army, James II, and the Glorious Revolution* (1980); S. Prall, *The bloodless revolution: England, 1688* (1972); J. R. Jones, *The Revolution of 1688 in England* (1972); and L. G. Schwoerer, *The Declaration of Rights, 1689* (1981), an admirable study. J. P. Kenyon, *Revolution principles: the politics of party, 1689–1720* (1977), is a subtle study of Lockean and other political theory, and the increased authority of Parliament is discussed in H. Horowitz, *Parliament, policy, and politics in the reign of William III* (1977). Trevelyan's *England under Queen Anne* (3 vols., 1930–1934) vividly portrays the succeeding age, and on the sovereign herself E. Gregg, *Queen Anne* (1980), is excellent. For foreign and military affairs, one may turn to W. S. Churchill, *Marlborough, his life and times* (4 vols., 1933–1938; abr. ed., 1968), and the briefer D. Chandler, *Marlborough as a military commander* (1973). J. H. Clapham, *The Bank of England* (2 vols., 1944), covers the period 1694–1944.

The France of Louis XIV

Many of the general accounts cited at the beginning of this chapter focus on the French predominance in this age. In addition, the following books explore various aspects of Louis XIV and his reign: J. B. Wolf, *Louis XIV** (1968), the most comprehensive biography; D. Ogg, *Louis XIV* (1933), somewhat critical; V. Buranelli, *Louis XIV** (1966), a brief, sympathetic account; M. Ashley, *Louis XIV and the greatness of France** (Teach Yourself History series, 1948); R. M. Hatton, *Louis XIV and absolutism* (1976); and A. Lossky, *Louis XIV and the ascendancy of France* (1977). W. F. Church, *Louis XIV in historical thought: from Voltaire to the* Annales *school* (1976), offers an historiographical assessment. P. Goubert, *Louis XIV and twenty million Frenchmen** (trans. 1972), and his more

detailed *The ancien regime: French society, 1600–1750** (2 vols., 1969–1973; trans. and abr., 1974), are invaluable as studies of French society and the ordinary people of the time by a historian of the *Annales* school; they may be supplemented by R. E. Mousnier, *The institutions of France under the absolute monarchy, 1598–1789: society and state* (trans. 1979), good on institutional development.

Some special studies are A. L. Moote, *The revolt of the judges: the Parlement of Paris and the Fronde, 1643–1652* (1971); E. E. Reynolds, *Bossuet* (1963); E. I. Perry, *From theology to history: French religious controversy and the revocation of the Edict of Nantes* (1973); L. Rothkrug, *Opposition to Louis XIV: the political and social origins of the Enlightenment* (1965); and A. Sedgwick, *Jansenism in seventeenth-century France: voices from the wilderness* (1977). Other interpretive volumes are W. H. Lewis, *The splendid century: life in the France of Louis XIV** (1953); G. R. R. Treasure, *Seventeenth-century France** (1966); V. L. Tapié, *The age of grandeur* (rev., 1966); and O. Ranum, *Paris in the age of absolutism** (1969).

On the French economy and empire, see C. W. Cole, *Colbert and a century of French mercantilism* (2 vols., 1939), his earlier volume, and a sequel that carries the story to 1700; W. Scoville, *The persecution of the Huguenots and French economic development, 1680–1720* (1960); J. Dent, *Crisis in France: crown, financiers, and society in seventeenth-century France* (1973); and R. Bonney, *The king's debts: finance and politics in France, 1589–1661* (1981). On the empire, see H. I. Priestley, *France overseas through the old regime: a study of European expansion* (1939), and W. J. Eccles, *Canada under Louis XIV, 1663–1701* (1964). P. W. Bamford has written two illuminating books, *Forests and French sea power, 1660–1789* (1956) and *Fighting ships and prisons: the Mediterranean galleys of France in the age of Louis XIV* (1973). C. C. Lougee, *Le paradis des femmes: women, salons, and social stratification in seventeenth century France* (1976), examines the relationship of influential women of the age to seventeenth-century society and culture.

On Louis XIV's wars one may read C. Ekberg, *The failure of Louis XIV's Dutch War* (1979), and H. Kamen, *The War of Succession in Spain, 1700–1715* (1969), along with the same author's impressive *Spain in the later seventeenth century, 1665–1700* (1980), in which he sees revival rather than decline on the eve of the French attack. J. Klaits, *Printed propaganda under Louis XIV: absolute monarchy and public opinion* (1977), demonstrates the monarch's efforts to influence public opinion in favor of his wars.

Problems and Readings*

For the debate over events in England, see P. A. M. Taylor (ed.), *The origins of the English Civil War: conspiracy, crusade, or class conflict?* (1960); L. Stone (ed.), *Social change and revolution in England, 1540–1640* (1965); R. E. Boyer (ed.), *Oliver Cromwell and the Puritan revolution: failure of a man or a faith?* (1966); M. Ashley, *Cromwell* (Great Lives Observed series, 1969); G. M. Straka (ed.), *The Revolution of 1688 and the birth of the English political nation* (rev., 1973); and P. Seaver (ed.), *Seventeenth century England: society in an age of revolution** (1976). For France, one may turn to W. F. Church: *The impact of absolutism in France: national experience under Richelieu, Mazarin, and Louis XIV* (1969), and *The greatness of Louis XIV: myth or reality* (rev., 1972); H. G. Judge (ed.), *Louis XIV* (1965); J. C. Rule (ed.), *Louis XIV and the craft of kingship* (1969); and R. F. Kierstead (ed.), *State and society in seventeenth-century France** (1975).

V: THE TRANSFORMATION OF EASTERN EUROPE, 1648–1740

The following are helpful general introductions to the complexities of eastern and east central Europe: F. Dvornik, *The making of central and eastern Europe* (1949) and *Slavs in European history and civilization* (1962); R. Portal, *The Slavs: a cultural and historical survey of the Slavonic people* (1965, trans. 1970); O. Halecki, *Borderlands of Western civilization: a history of east central Europe* (1952); S. H. Cross, *Slavic civilization through the ages* (1948); and W. H. McNeill, *Europe's steppe frontier, 1500–1800* (1964). Two valuable studies are L. S. Stavrianos, *The Balkans since 1453* (1958), and R. Ristelhueber, *A history of the Balkan peoples* (1950; rev. and trans. 1971); they may be supplemented by the background portions of R. L. Wolff, *The Balkans in our time** (rev., 1978); T. Stoianovich, *A study in Balkan civilization** (1967); and D. Djordjevic and S. Fischer-Galati, *The Balkan revolutionary tradition* (1981). J. S. Bromley (ed.), *The rise of Great Britain and Russia, 1688–1725* (1969), vol. VI of the New Cambridge Modern History, mentioned earlier, has informative but highly specialized chapters. A recent effort at a brief synthesis, not completely successful, is L. C. Tihany, *A history of middle Europe: from the earliest times to the age of the world wars* (1976).

The Ottoman Empire

N. Itzkowitz, *Ottoman Empire and Islamic tradition** (1972), is a useful brief introduction for the years 1300 to the late eighteenth century. P. Balfour [Lord Kinross], *The Ottoman centuries: the rise and fall of the Turkish empire* (1977), is a comprehensive narrative, as are S. Shaw, *History of the Ottoman Empire and modern Turkey*, vol. 1: *Empire of the Gazis: the rise and decline of the Ottoman Empire, 1280–1808** (1976), and H. Inalcik, *The Ottoman Empire: the classical age, 1300–1600* (1973). P. F. Sugar, *Southeastern Europe under Ottoman rule, 1354–1804* (1977), is an outstanding study. A careful account of the Turkish role in European affairs is available in D. M. Vaughan, *Europe and the Turk: a pattern of alliances, 1350–1700* (1954), and P. Coles, *The Ottoman impact on Europe, 1350–1699** (1968). Of interest as a special study is R. Schwoebel, *The shadow of the crescent: the Renaissance image of the Turk, 1453–1517* (1967). A popular but sound account of the empire is F. W. Fernau, *Moslems on the march* (trans. 1954). On the sixteenth century, R. O. Merriman, *Suleiman the Magnificent, 1520–1566* (1944) is the best general introduction. B. H. Sumner, *Peter the Great and the Ottoman Empire* (1949), describes early relations between Turkey and Russia, and C. E. Bosworth, *The Islamic dynasties: a chronological and genealogical handbook* (1967), is a useful reference tool.

Austria and the Habsburgs to 1740

Two basic studies are A. Wandruszka, *The house of Habsburg* (1956, trans. 1964), and R. A. Kann, *A history of the Habsburg empire, 1526–1918* (1974). For the early period, one should read H. G. Koenigsberger, *The Habsburgs and Europe, 1516–1660* (1971); R. J. W. Evans, *The making of the Habsburg monarchy, 1550–1700: an interpretation* (1979); and T. W. Barker, *Army, aristocracy, monarchy: essays on war, society, and government in Austria, 1618–1780* (1982). P. Frischauer, *The imperial crown: the rise and fall of the Holy Roman and the*

Austrian empires (1939), is primarily biographical in nature and treats the house of Habsburg to the death of Leopold II in 1792. J. F. Spielman has written *Leopold I of Austria* (1977), a balanced treatment of the seventeenth-century emperor. For Eugene of Savoy, an outstanding biography is D. McKay, *Prince Eugene of Savoy* (Men in Office series, 1977). Two lively studies of the Turkish siege of 1683 are J. Stoye, *The siege of Vienna* (1964), and T. M. Barker, *Double eagle and crescent: Vienna's second Turkish siege and its historical setting* (1967).

Prussia to 1740

Two convenient introductions are F. L. Carsten, *The origins of Prussia* (1954), and S. B. Fay and K. Epstein, *The rise of Brandenburg-Prussia to 1786** (1937; rev., 1964). H. Holborn in his *History of modern Germany, vol. II, 1648–1840* (1964), covers the fluid situation in the Holy Roman Empire after the Thirty Years' War, and E. Sagarra, *A social history of Germany, 1648–1914* (1977), provides fascinating details on the German states. G. Benecke, *Society and politics in Germany, 1500–1750* (1974), presents the case for the empire as a viable constitutional entity, while two important contributions to understanding the formation of the German political tradition are F. L. Carsten, *Princes and parliaments in Germany* (1959), cited earlier, and M. Walker, *German home towns: community, state, and general estate, 1648–1871* (1971).

On the earlier Hohenzollerns, one may read F. Schevill, *The great elector* (1947); R. Ergang, *The Potsdam Führer: Frederick William I, father of Prussian militarism* (1941); and R. A. Derwart, *The administrative reforms of Frederick William I of Prussia* (1953). An invaluable study going well beyond the scope of this chapter is G. A. Craig, *The politics of the Prussian army, 1640–1945** (1956, 1964); it may be compared with K. Demeter, *The German officer corps in society and state, 1650–1945* (1930, 1962; trans. 1965). Important also, especially for the sociological dimension it adds, is H. Rosenberg, *Bureaucracy, aristocracy, and autocracy: the Prussian experience, 1600–1815** (1958), which may be supplemented by J. A. Armstrong, *The European administrative elite** (1973), a comparative study of European bureaucracies during this period.

Russia to 1725

There are many excellent narrative accounts of Russian history, most of which give good coverage of the early years; among those written or revised in recent years are volumes by B. H. Sumner, B. Pares, M. T. Florinsky, J. D. Clarkson, S. Harcave, A. G. Mazour, N. V. Riasanovsky, G. Vernadsky, W. B. Walsh, M. C. Wren, D. Mackenzie and M. W. Curran, and B. Dmytryshyn. A fascinating impressionistic cultural history is J. H. Billington, *The icon and the axe: an interpretive history of Russian culture** (1966). M. T. Florinsky, *Russia: a history and an interpretation* (2 vols., 1953), is perhaps the best general account for the period to 1917; in briefer form, it is available as *Russia: a short history* (1969). G. Vernadsky, *A history of Russia* (5 vols., 1943–1969), covers Russian history in great detail from earliest times to 1682; the final two volumes, *Tsardom of Moscow, 1547–1682* (2 vols., 1969), are relevant here. There are vivid popular narratives by H. Lamb, *The march of Muscovy: Ivan the Terrible and the growth of the Russian empire, 1400–1648* (1948) and *The city and the tsar: Peter the Great and the move to the West, 1648–1762* (1948). On the early rulers, there are available J. Fennell, *Ivan the Great of Moscow* (1961); H. von Eckhardt, *Ivan the Terrible* (1949); I. Grey, *Ivan III and the unification of Russia* (1965); and the same author's *Ivan the Terrible* (1964). A fascinating large-scale study of all the Romanovs, the fifteen men and four women who ruled Russia between 1613 and 1917, is W. B. Lincoln, *Autocrats of all the Russias* (1981).

On Peter and the reforms of his reign, two masterful brief accounts are B. H. Sumner, *Peter the Great and the emergence of Russia** (Teach Yourself History series, 1950), and M. S. Anderson, *Peter the Great* (Men in Office series, 1978). R. K. Massie, *Peter the Great: his life and world* (1980), is a long, vivid, and colorful popular account, criticized by specialists for scholarly inadequacies. Russian expansion is discussed in R. J. Kerner, *The urge to the sea: the course of Russian history* (1942), which emphasizes the significance of trade routes. An important subject is covered in J. Blum, *Lord and peasant in Russia from the ninth to the nineteenth century** (1961), and in R. E. F. Smith, *The origins of farming in Russia* (1960). A remarkable study in comparative cultural history emphasizing Western influences is D. W. Treadgold, *The West in Rus-*

sia and China: religious and secular thought in modern times* (2 vols., 1973), the first volume covering Russia for the years 1472–1917, the second China for the years 1582–1949. Another important comparative study on a very different subject is R. Mousnier, *Peasant uprisings in seventeenth century France, Russia, and China* (trans. 1970).

For Sweden in this age, Voltaire's *History of Charles XII* (1731) still merits reading, but an outstanding modern biography of the Swedish monarch is R. M. Hatton, *Charles XII of Sweden* (1969). A number of important studies by M. Roberts and others have been cited in Chapter III; for these years Roberts, *The Swedish imperial experience, 1560–1718* (1979), deserves mention.

Poland

For Poland in these years, one may turn to the first volume of an important two-volume synthesis, N. Davies, *A history of Poland: God's playground* (2 vols., 1981), vol. I, *The origins to 1795*; and to O. Halecki, *A history of Poland* (rev., 1961). The quarrel over the succession to the Polish throne is told in J. L. Sutton, *The king's honor and the king's Cardinal* [Fleury]: *the War of the Polish Succession* (1980). On the eighteenth-century partitions, one may consult H. H. Kaplan, *The first partition of Poland* (1962), and the older R. H. Lord, *The second partition of Poland* (1915); and for the years that followed, P. Wandycz, *The lands of partitioned Poland, 1795–1918** (1974). S. Konovalov, *Russian-Polish relations: an historical survey* (1945), is a brief, well-organized account, while a special subject is treated in B. D. Weinryb, *The Jews of Poland: a social and economic history of the Jewish community in Poland from 1100 to 1800* (1973).

Problems and Readings*

Various volumes of readings in Russian history and Russian civilization from earliest times to the present are available, among them those edited by W. B. Walsh (3 vols., 4th ed., 1963), T. Riha (3 vols.; rev., 1969), and G. Vernadsky and others (3 vols., 1972). On Peter's innovations, there is M. Raeff, *Peter the Great changes Russia* (rev., 1972). L. J. Oliva has edited *Russia and the West from Peter to Khrushchev* (1965), and W. L. Blackwell, *Russian economic development from Peter the Great to Stalin** (1974). R. V. Burks, *East European history:*

an ethnic approach* (1973), reviews scholarship in this area in the American Historical Association Pamphlets series.

VI: THE STRUGGLE FOR WEALTH AND EMPIRE

For the years covered in this chapter, 1713–1763, the most helpful syntheses are M. S. Anderson, *Europe in the eighteenth century, 1713–1783** (2nd ed., 1977); R. J. Whyte, *Europe in the eighteenth century** (1965); D. Ogg, *Europe of the ancien régime, 1715–1783** (1965); P. Langford, *The eighteenth century, 1688–1815** (1977); and I. Woloch, *Eighteenth century Europe: tradition and progress, 1715–1789** (1982). In the Langer series there are available P. Roberts, *The quest for security, 1715–1740** (1947), and a masterful volume by W. L. Dorn, *Competition for empire, 1740–1763** (1940), particularly good on the relation of the European state system to the overseas expansion and rivalry of the time. J. O. Lindsay (ed.), *The old regime, 1713–1763* (1957), vol. VII in the New Cambridge Modern History, has informative chapters on domestic and international developments.

Popular Culture

It is for the early modern centuries that the differences between elite and popular cultures have been most closely examined, as in P. Burke, *Popular culture in early modern Europe* (1978), and other books cited in the introductory section. Especially useful is F. Braudel, *The structures of everyday life: the limits of the possible* (trans. 1981), the first volume of his three-volume study mentioned earlier. Popular culture is explored also in many of the works on social history, labor history, and women's history cited in the introduction and elsewhere in this bibliography.

The Colonial Empires and Global Economy

Several of the books on European overseas expansion listed for Chapter IV also discuss the eighteenth century. To these must be added H. Furber's superb synthesis, *Rival empires of trade in the Orient, 1600–1800* (1976), a volume in Europe and the World in the Age of Expansion series; J. H. Parry *Trade and dominion: the European oversea empires in the eighteenth century* (1971); G. Williams, *The expansion of Europe in the eighteenth century: overseas rivalry, discovery, and exploitation* (1960); the relevant chapters of D. K. Fieldhouse, *The colonial empires: a comparative survey from the eighteenth century* (1966); the comprehensive C. E. Carrington, *The British overseas: exploits of a nation of shopkeepers* (1950; rev., 1968); and K. M. Pannikar, *Asia and Western dominance: . . . the Vasco da Gama epoch of Asian history, 1498–1945** (rev., 1959), by an Indian scholar. The Dutch role in the global economy is ably portrayed in J. C. Riley, *International government finance and the Amsterdam capital market, 1740–1815* (1980), which supplements C. Wilson, *Anglo-Dutch commerce and finance in the eighteenth century* (1941, 1966).

The eighteenth-century impact of India is explored in H. Furber, *John Company at work: a study of European expansion in India in the late eighteenth century* (1948). In addition, the following works on India may be recommended, although they are not confined to the eighteenth century: S. Wolpert, *A new history of India** (rev., 1982), one of the best introductions; P. Spear, *The Oxford history of modern India, 1740–1975** (2nd ed., 1979); W. N. Brown, *The United States and India, Pakistan, and Bangladesh* (rev., 1972), with perceptive pages on the historical background; P. Woodruff [Mason], *The men who ruled India** (2 vols., 1954–1957); and M. Andrewes, *British India* (1964).

Biographical studies include P. Moon, *Warren Hastings and British India** (Teach Yourself History series, 1947); K. Feiling, *Warren Hastings* (1945); and P. J. Marshall, *The impeachment of Warren Hastings* (1965). An account of these years by Indian scholars is found in R. C. Majumdar (ed.), *The struggle for empire* (1957), the fifth volume in a longer work on Indian history. S. E. Schwartzberg (ed.), *A historical atlas of South Asia* (1978), is a superb collaborative atlas, and J. Nehru, *The discovery of India** (1946), by the Indian statesman, remains an indispensable introduction to Indian history.

The numerous volumes by F. Parkman on the French regime in Canada are classics of nineteenth-century historiography; a standard twentieth-century account is G. M. Wrong, *The rise and fall of New France* (2 vols., 1928), and his various other writings, but the most useful volume is now W. J. Eccles, *France in America* (1972). On the West Indies, there are available two books by N. M. Crouse, *French pioneers in the West Indies, 1624–1664* (1940) and *The French struggle for the West Indies, 1665–1713* (1944); the importance of the West Indies is examined in R. S. Dunn, *Sugar and slaves* (1972).

The British Empire before the American Revolution

J. R. Seeley, *The expansion of England* (1883, 1895), is a classic essay, while W. B. Willcox, *Star of empire: a study of Britain as a world power, 1485–1945* (1950), is rewarding as narrative and analysis. There are numerous older studies of the old colonial system and of mercantilism by G. L. Beer, C. M. Andrews, and H. L. Osgood. For the mid-eighteenth century from 1748 to 1776, there is L. H. Gipson's monumental work in thirteen volumes, *The British Empire before the American Revolution* (1936–1967); vol. XIII contains in part II a summary of the entire work. Another important large-scale treatment is *The Cambridge history of the British Empire* (9 vols., 1929–1959). C. G. Robertson, *Chatham and the British Empire** (1948), and J. A. Williamson, *Cook and the opening of the Pacific** (1948), are two lively studies in the Teach Yourself History series.

British Society and Politics in the Eighteenth Century

Books on eighteenth-century France are listed below in Chapter VIII, but two works should be mentioned here: J. H. Shannon, *Philippe, Duke of Orléans: Regent of France, 1715–1723* (1979), and R. Butler, *Choiseul*, vol. I., *Father and son* (1980), the first volume of a projected three, which vividly portrays the age. Informative recent studies focusing on political parties, political issues, and public opinion in eighteenth-century Britain include W. A. Speck, *Stability and strife: England 1714–1760** (1977), a volume in the New History of England series, which also gives considerable attention to social and economic developments, and the same author's *Tory and Whig: the struggle in the constituencies, 1701–1715* (1968); C. Holmes, *British politics in the age of Anne* (1967); J. H. Plumb, *The origins of political stability: England, 1675–1725* (1967); and B. W. Hall, *The growth of parliamentary parties, 1689–1742* (1976). Recommended books on personalities and events include R. N. Hatton, *George I, Elector and King* (1979); J. H. Plumb, *Sir Robert Walpole* (2 vols., 1956, 1961); the same author's *The first four Georges* * (1956); H. T. Dickinson, *Walpole and the Whig supremacy* (1973); and B. Kemp, *Sir Robert Walpole* (1976). There are three outstanding biographies of the great mid-eighteenth-century statesman: B. Williams, *Life of William Pitt, Earl of Chatham* (2 vols., 1966); S. Ayling, *The elder Pitt, Earl of Chatham* (1976); and P. D. Brown, *William Pitt, Earl of Chatham* (1978). Of special interest is M. Peters, *Pitt and popularity: the patriot minister and London opinion during the Seven Years' War* (1980).

For an institutional approach, one must turn to L. B. Namier's seminal work, *The structure of politics at the accession of George III* (2 vols., 1920; 1 vol., 1957). In progress is a collaborative effort at prosopography, or collective biography, which seeks to reconstruct in minute biographical detail the composition of the modern English parliaments, a project inspired and inaugurated by Namier during his lifetime. An important reassessment of the 1760s is provided in J. Brewer, *Party ideology and popular politics at the accession of George III* (1976).

On social conditions, the following are instructive: L. Kronenberger, *Kings and desperate men: life in eighteenth century England* (1942); G. Rudé, *Hanoverian London, 1714–1808* (1971); B. Malcolmson, *Life and labor in England, 1700–1780* (1981); P. Clark and P. Slack (eds.), *Crisis and order in English towns, 1500–1700* (1972); and D. Marshall's three studies, *The English poor in the eighteenth century* (1926), *Eighteenth-century England* (1962), and *Dr. Johnson's London* * (1967). Several additional books relating to social history in this period are cited in the introductory section of this bibliography, notably works by E. P. Thompson, P. Laslett, L. Stone, R. Trumbach, and others, and additional titles appear in Chapter XI in connection with the Industrial Revolution. On justice in these years, one will find illuminating E. P. Thompson, *Whigs and hunters: the origin of the Black Act* * (1976), and Thompson and others, *Crime and society in eighteenth century England* (1976).

For economic developments, there are important chapters in R. Floud and D. McCloskey (eds.), *The economic history of Britain since 1700* * (2 vols., 1981), of which volume I covers the years 1700 to 1860. On financial subjects a far-reaching book is P. G. M. Dickson, *The financial revolution in England: a study in the development of public credit, 1688–1756* (1967). Two important studies are J. Thirsk, *Economic policy and projects: the development of a consumer society in early modern England* (1978), focusing on schemes to make money from 1540 on, and P. Mathias, *The transformation of England: essays in the economic and social history of England* (1979). The celebrated speculative ventures of the age are graphically described in J. Carswell, *The South Sea bubble* (1960), and in the relevant chapters of C. P. Kindleberger, *Manias, panics, and crashes: a history of financial crises* (1978), which carries the story into the twentieth century. Kindleberger analyzes the formation of financial centers, among other subjects, in *Economic response: comparative studies in trade, finance, and growth* (1978). A very special subject is treated in two books: R. Carr, *English fox-hunting: a history* (1976), and D. C. Itzkowitz, *Peculiar privilege: a social history of English fox-hunting, 1753–1885* (1977). The Jacobite rebellions are ably discussed in B. Lenman, *The Jacobite risings in Britain, 1689–1746* (1980), and F. J. McLynn, *France and the Jacobite rising of 1745* (1981).

Diplomacy and War in Europe, 1740–1763

[Various titles listed at the beginning of this chapter and Chapter V, and in Chapter VIII for enlightened despotism, should also be consulted.] A. Sorel, *Europe under the old regime* * (trans. 1947), the introduction to his study of Europe and the French Revolution (8 vols., 1895 ff.), remains valuable for insights into the European balance of power. C. Petrie, *Diplomatic history, 1713–1933* (1946), provides an overall survey, while C. Duffy, *The army of Maria Theresa: the armed forces of imperial Austria, 1740–1780* (1977), ably explores the nature of the Habsburg army.

On the negotiations ending the Seven Years' War, Z. E. Rashed has written *The Peace of Paris, 1763* (1952). M. Savelle, *The origins of American diplomacy: the international history of Anglo-America, 1492–1763* (1967), covers the diplomacy of these years in a special way.

Problems and Readings*

A sampling of recent scholarship on eighteenth-century English politics and society is provided in D. A. Baugh (ed.), *Aristocratic government and society in eighteenth-century England: the foundations of stability* (1975).

VII: THE SCIENTIFIC VIEW OF THE WORLD

A number of works cited in the introductory section of this bibliography are concerned with various aspects of the history of science, and the reader may wish to consult them. For works in the history of science published in the years 1913–1965, one may consult the *Isis cumulative bibliography* (3 vols., 1971–1976), and for subsequent years the annual bibliographies published in *Isis*.

The Scientific Revolution

The fundamental reorientation of thinking about nature in early modern times has probably had more influence on the later world than any of the specific inventions or technical advances of the period. The best introductions are A. R. Hall, *The scientific revolution, 1500–1800: the formation of the modern scientific attitude** (1954; rev., 1962); H. Butterfield, *The origins of modern science, 1300–1800** (rev., 1965); M. Boas, *The scientific Renaissance, 1450–1630* (1962); W. P. D. Wightman, *Science and the Renaissance* (1963); H. Kearney, *Science and change, 1500–1700** (1971); A. G. R. Smith, *Science and society in the sixteenth and seventeenth centuries* (1972); A. G. Debus, *Man and nature in the Renaissance** (1978); R. S. Westfall, *The construction of modern science** (1978); and R. Mandrou, *From humanism to science, 1480–1700* (1973, trans. 1979). A larger collaborative survey is L. P. Williams and H. J. Steffens (eds.), *The history of science in Western civilization* (3 vols., 1977), from antiquity to the twentieth century. A highly provocative and influential book has been T. S. Kuhn, *The structure of scientific revolutions** (1962), which may be supplemented by the same author's *The essential tension: selected studies in scientific tradition and change* (1977), depicting progress in science as a pull between conservative and innovative forces. Kuhn has also written *The Copernican revolution: planetary astronomy in the development of Western thought* (1956).

E. A. Burtt, *The metaphysical foundations of modern philosophical science** (1925, 1948), is a searching examination of the ideas of scientists from Copernicus to Newton. Other books exploring the theoretical foundations of science include J. B. Conant, *On understanding science: an historical approach* (1947) and *Science and common sense* (1951); S. E. Toulmin, *The philosophy of science* (1953); R. G. Collingwood, *The idea of nature* (1945); A. N. Whitehead, *Science and the modern world* (1925); C. C. Gillispie, *The edge of objectivity: an essay in the history of scientific ideas* (1960); and two books by G. Holton, *Thematic origins of scientific thought: Kepler to Einstein** (1973) and *The scientific imagination: case studies** (1978). I. B. Cohen has written *The Newtonian revolution: with illustrations of the transformation of scientific ideas* (1980), and a more general account, *Album of science: from Leonardo to Lavoisier, 1450–1800* (1980).

Histories of Science

For individual scientists, one will wish to consult the *Dictionary of scientific biography* (8 vols., 1970–1980) cited in the introductory section; R. Taton, *History of science* (4 vols., trans. 1964–1966), or the briefer T. I. Williams, *A biographical dictionary of scientists* (1969). Two excellent introductions are A. R. Hall and M. B. Hall, *Brief history of science* (1961), and S. F. Mason, *A history of the sciences** (1962). Other studies include C. J. Singer, *A short history of scientific ideas to 1900* (rev., 1949); A. C. Crombie, *Medieval and early modern science** (2 vols., 1959), cited in Chapter I; E. Grant, *Physical science in the Middle Ages** (1978); and F. S. Taylor, *A short history of science and scientific thought* (1949). The older pioneering studies of G. Sarton and L. Thorndike remain important for specialists; some of Sarton's general ideas are presented in *The life of science: essays in the history of civilization* (1948) and in *Six wings: men of science in the Renaissance* (1957). A remarkable achievement is the multivolumed study under way by J. Needham, *Science and civilization in China* (5 vols. to date, many in several parts, 1954–   ); some of his important insights are conveyed in *Science in traditional China: a comparative perspective* (1981).

On the history of medicine, one may read H. E. Sigerist, *A history of medicine* (1951); L. S. King, *The growth of medical thought* (1963); and E. H. Ackerknecht, *A short history of medicine* (1955; rev., 1982). A revision of the older F. H. Garrison, *An intro-*

duction to the history of medicine (4th ed., 1929), is in progress.

Scientific Organizations in the Seventeenth Century

On the organization of scientific activity and the spread of new ideas, see M. Ornstein, The role of scientific societies in the seventeenth century (1928); H. Brown, Scientific organizations in seventeenth-century France, 1620–1680 (1934); R. Hahn, The anatomy of a scientific institution: the Paris Academy of Sciences, 1666–1803 (1971); H. Lyons, The Royal Society, 1660–1940 (1944); D. Stimson, Scientists and amateurs: a history of the Royal Society (1948); S. Bethell, The cultural revolution of the seventeenth century (1951); and R. F. Jones, Ancients and moderns: the rise of the scientific movement in seventeenth-century England* (1936, 1961). Of special importance is C. Webster, The great instauration: science, medicine, and reform, 1616–1660 (1976).

Among the books that explore the technological implications of the new science are: A. Wolf, A history of science, technology, and philosophy in the sixteenth and seventeenth centuries (1935) and . . . in the eighteenth century (1939); G. N. Clark, Science and social welfare in the age of Newton (1937); and the stimulating L. Mumford, Technics and civilization (1934).

On technology, one may consult C. Singer and others, A history of technology (5 vols., 1954–1958), from prehistory to about 1900, for which T. I. Williams has edited two additional volumes (1978) for the twentieth century; the briefer T. K. Derry and T. I. Williams, A short history of technology from the earliest times to A.D. 1900 (1961); and W. Beranek, Jr. and G. Ranis, Science, technology, and human development: a historical and comparative study (1978).

Biographical Accounts

The contributions of the pioneer astronomers are described in many of the books cited earlier and in A. Armitage, Copernicus: the founder of modern astronomy (1938) and The world of Copernicus (1947, 1951); J. A. Gade, The life and times of Tycho Brahe (1947); M. Caspar, Kepler (1948, trans. 1959); and the briefer C. Baumgardt, Johannes Kepler: life and letters (1951). F. W. Taylor, Galileo and the freedom of thought (1938), is a dispassionate, carefully documented work, and the

opposition that Galileo aroused is well described in G. de Santillana, The crime of Galileo (1955, 1959). A brief biographical study is L. Fermi and G. Bernardini, Galileo and the scientific revolution* (1961), while a technical study with little attention to the scientist's milieu is S. Drake, Galileo at work: his scientific biography (1978).

Both F. H. Anderson, The philosophy of Francis Bacon (1948), and B. Farrington, Francis Bacon: philosopher of industrial science* (1949), are concerned with Bacon's ideas and impact, while C. D. Bowen has written a sound, vivid biography, Francis Bacon: the temper of the man (1963), which may be supplemented by J. J. Epstein, Francis Bacon: a political biography (1977). E. S. Haldane, Descartes, his life and times (1905), is primarily biographical, and S. H. Mellone, The dawn of modern thought: Descartes, Spinoza, Leibniz (1930), explains the Cartesian system and its influence. For Pascal, see M. Bishop, Pascal: the life of genius (1936); and for Pierre Bayle, see H. Robinson, Bayle the skeptic (1931). F. L. Baumer, Religion and the rise of skepticism (1960), and R. H. Popkin, The history of skepticism from Erasmus to Spinoza* (rev., 1979), both trace the skeptical tradition. Other seventeenth-century scientists are placed in their intellectual setting in L. T. More, The life and works of the Honourable Robert Boyle (1944); M. Boas, Robert Boyle and seventeenth century chemistry (1958); and A. E. Bell, Christian Huygens and the development of science in the seventeenth century (1947). For Newton, a distinguished large-scale biography is R. S. Westfall, Never at rest: a biography of Isaac Newton (1981); there are other biographical accounts by L. T. More (1934), S. Brodetsky (1927), J. Sullivan (1938), E. N. da C. Andrade* (1954), and F. E. Manuel (1968, 1974). The quarrel over the discovery of calculus is portrayed in A. R. Hall, Philosophers at war: the quarrel between Newton and Leibniz (1980).

Two provocative studies focusing on the relationship between seventeenth-century science and its political and social context are J. R. Jacob, Robert Boyle and the English Revolution: a case study in social and intellectual change (1978), and M. C. Jacob, The Newtonians and the English Revolution, 1689–1720 (1978); they may be compared with R. K. Merton, Science, technology, and society in seventeenth century England (1970), which also stresses the close relationship, and with various essays in

C. Webster (ed.), *The intellectual revolution of the seventeenth century* (1974), which do not.

Law, Political Theory, and Natural Law

[The books on political thought cited in the introductory section of the bibliography and in Chapter VIII on the Enlightenment should also be consulted.] The best introductions are the readings in E. A. Burtt (ed.), *The English philosophers from Bacon to Mill* (1939), and E. Barker (ed.), *Social contract: essays by Locke, Hume, and Rousseau* (1947). W. Seagle, *The quest for law* (1941), treats historically the formulation of law and jurisprudence. J. G. A. Pocock, *The Machiavellian moment: Florentine political thought and the Atlantic republican tradition* (1975), cited in Chapter II, is relevant here. On Locke, one may read M. Cranston, *John Locke: a biography* (1957); M. Seliger, *The liberal politics of John Locke* (1969); and J. Dunn, *The political thought of John Locke* (1969). For Hobbes, there is available D. D. Raphael, *Hobbes: morals and politics* (1978). Especially useful for these years is N. O. Keohane, *Philosophy and the state in France: the Renaissance to the Enlightenment* * (1980). W. S. M. Knight has written *The life and works of Hugo Grotius* (1925).

Problems and Readings*

One pamphlet is relevant: G. Basalla, *The rise of modern science: external or internal factors?* (1968). A useful anthology is M. B. Hall (ed.), *Nature and nature's laws: documents of the scientific revolution* (1969), and two interesting older compilations are F. S. Taylor, *The march of mind* (1939), and F. R. Moulton and J. Schifferes (eds.), *The autobiography of science* (1945).

VIII: THE AGE OF ENLIGHTENMENT

For background, the eighteenth-century accounts listed at the beginning of Chapter VI should be consulted, and to them should be added A. Goodwin (ed.), *The American and French revolutions, 1763–1793* * (1965), vol. VIII of the New Cambridge Modern History; L. Gershoy, *From despotism to revolution, 1763–1789* * (1944), in the Langer series, an illuminating account of Europe in the generation before 1789; and the brief L. Krieger, *Kings and philosophers, 1689–1789* * (1970).

Of special interest here is M. S. Anderson, *Historians and eighteenth-century Europe, 1715–1789* (1979), a provocative historiographical study. Additional general accounts are listed in this chapter and the next.

The Thought of the Enlightenment

Although recent research interests have moved away from intellectual history, some of the most interesting historical writing in the past has focused on the ideas of the European Enlightenment. An ambitious effort to interpret the thought of the era on a European-wide scale is P. Gay, *The Enlightenment: an interpretation* (2 vols., 1966–1969), vol. I, *The rise of paganism*, on the use of the classical past to support the struggle for freedom, and vol. II, *The science of freedom*, on the application of science to all areas of human activity, especially the problems of society. Some of his postulates also are explored in his *The party of humanity: essays on the French Enlightenment* (1964). Another large-scale effort, on the French thinkers and thought of the age, is I. O. Wade, *The structure and form of the French Enlightenment* (2 vols., 1977), focusing on the "philosophical spirit" of the age in the first volume and the "revolutionary spirit" in the second.

The older works by the French scholar P. Hazard may still be read with profit: *The European mind: the critical years, 1680–1715* (1935, trans. 1953), and *European thought in the eighteenth century: from Montesquieu to Lessing* (1946, trans. 1954). Historians tend to reject the provocative thesis of C. Becker, in *The heavenly city of the eighteenth-century philosophers* * (1932), that Enlightenment thought, essentially utopian, represented a secularized version of medieval Christian views. Other important interpretations of the Enlightenment are to be found in E. Cassirer, *The philosophy of the Enlightenment* (1932, trans. 1951); A. Cobban, *In search of humanity: the role of the Enlightenment in modern history* (1960); L. G. Crocker, *An age of crisis; man and world in eighteenth century thought* (1959); and N. Hampson, *A cultural history of the Enlightenment* * (1969).

On the Enlightenment theme of progress, three older accounts, J. B. Bury, *The idea of progress: an inquiry into its origin and growth* (1920, reissued 1955); C. Frankel, *The faith of reason: the idea of progress in the French Enlightenment* (1938); and R. V. Sampson, *Progress in the age of reason: the* seventeenth century to the present day (1956), may be compared with R. Nisbet, *History of the idea of progress* (1980), already cited. On economic thought, M. Beer, *An inquiry into physiocracy* (1939), must be supplemented by E. Fox-Genovese, *The origins of physiocracy: economic revolution and social order in eighteenth-century France* (1976). The volume by L. Rothkrug, *Opposition to Louis XIV: the political and social origins of the Enlightenment*, cited in Chapter IV, also examines economic ideas, as does J. Q. C. Macrell, *The attack on feudalism in eighteenth-century France* (1973). H. G. Payne, *The philosophes and the people* (1971), traces the divergent views of the famous writers toward the lower classes, and may be supplemented by H. Chisick, *The limits of reform in the Enlightenment: attitudes toward the education of the lower classes in eighteenth-century France* (1981). On a lesser known *philosophe* sympathetic to the poorer classes, an excellent account is D. G. Levy, *The ideas and careers of Simon-Nicolas-Henri-Linguet* (1980). A forthcoming study is S. Spencer, *French women and the age of Enlightenment*.

On a special subject, A. Hertzberg, *The French Enlightenment and the Jews* (1968), contends that by stressing universal values the *philosophes* contributed to modern anti-Semitism; also critical of the Enlightenment is J. Katz, *Out of the ghetto: the social background of Jewish emancipation, 1770–1870* (1973). R. Mahler, *A history of modern Jewry, 1780–1815* (1971), examines in a different way the impact of the Enlightenment and Revolution on the existing Jewish communities; on European Jewry in this age and since, see H. M. Sachar, *The course of modern Jewish history** (rev., 1977).

The Philosophes

There are numerous good books on each of the leading thinkers of the Enlightenment. On Voltaire: P. Gay, *Voltaire's politics: the poet as realist* (1959), reveals Voltaire's pragmatic, nondoctrinaire reactions to the events of his day. Other recent studies of Voltaire include accounts by I. O. Wade (1970); A. D. Aldridge (1975), a good overview; H. Mason (1981); and a comprehensive biography by T. Bestermann (1969), a leading Swiss authority and editor of Voltaire's correspondence. As a writer of history, Voltaire is ably studied in J. H. Brumfitt, *Voltaire historian* (1958). For Montesquieu there is an outstanding study by R. Shackleton, *Montes-*

quieu: a critical biography (1961). On Diderot, A. M. Wilson's superb biography (2 vols., 1957, 1972) is available, and also L. G. Crocker, *The embattled philosopher: a biography of Denis Diderot* (1954), which may be supplemented by the same author's analytical study, *Diderot's chaotic order: approach to synthesis* (1974). On Rousseau, a good introduction is F. C. Green, *Jean-Jacques Rousseau: a critical study of his life and writings* (1955). In addition to older studies by E. Cassirer (1954) and others, there are available J. Guéhenno, *Jean-Jacques Rousseau* (2 vols., 1948–1962, trans. 1966); W. H. Blanchard, *Rousseau and the spirit of revolt* (1968); R. Grimsley, *Jean-Jacques Rousseau: a study in self-awareness* (1961), and *Rousseau and the religious quest* (1968); J. H. Huizinga, *Rousseau: the self-made man* (1975); and the first volume of M. Cranston's reassessment (1983). On Condorcet, K. M. Baker has written the exhaustive *Condorcet: from natural philosophy to social mathematics* (1975); an older study, J. S. Schapiro, *Condorcet and the rise of liberalism* (1934), is a briefer, general account.

For a sampling of books on other thinkers, see A. L. Lindsay, *Kant* (1934, 1946); D. M. Low, *Edward Gibbon* (1937); N. K. Smith, *The philosophy of David Hume* (1949); and C. Van Doren, *Benjamin Franklin* (1938). On a leading Italian philosopher of the Enlightenment, there are L. Pompa, *Vico: a study of the "new science"* (1975), and G. Tagliocozzo and D. P. Verene (eds.), *Giambattista Vico's science of humanity* (1976). The Enlightenment in general in Italy is studied in F. Venturi, *Italy and the Enlightenment: studies in a cosmopolitan century* (1972).

F. E. Manuel links the eighteenth century to the age that follows in *The prophets of Paris: Turgot, Condorcet, Saint-Simon, Fourier, Comte** (1962), and with F. P. Manuel masterfully traces an important theme in an even wider setting in *Utopian thought in the Western world* (1979). J. Lough, *The contributors to the Encyclopédie* (1973), is a thoughtful brief study. An outstanding effort to explore the most important collaborative work of the French Enlightenment in a new way is R. Darnton, *The business of Enlightenment: a publishing history of the Encyclopédie, 1775–1800* (1979), while the same author's *Mesmerism and the end of the Enlightenment in France* (1968), has stimulated further research into the popular culture of the age. W. Roberts, *Morality and social class in eighteenth-*

century French literature and painting (1974), links the creative arts to political and social life.

G. R. Cragg has written an excellent study of the Enlightenment in its English setting, *Reason and authority in the eighteenth century* (1964), as has J. Redwood, *Reason, radicals, and religion: the age of Enlightenment in England, 1660–1750* (1976), while T. A. Horne, *The social thought of Bernard de Mandeville: virtue and commerce in early eighteenth-century England* (1978), sets one thinker in the framework of English commercial expansion of the era. A valuable introduction to the important Scottish thinkers of the age is A. C. Chitnis, *The Scottish Enlightenment: a social history* (1976), which may be supplemented by K. Haakonssen, *The science of a legislator: the natural jurisprudence of David Hume and Adam Smith* (1981). B. Semmel, *The Methodist Revolution* (1973), argues that Wesleyan theology was the English counterpart to the democratic stirrings in Europe and America. M. C. Jacob, *The radical Enlightenment: pantheists, freemasons, and republicans* (1981), explores radical ideas of English origin that flourished in Dutch literary and publishing circles.

Other books treating the relationship between religion and Enlightenment include G. R. Cragg, *The church and the age of reason* * (1961), a volume in the Pelican History of the Church; J. M. Creed and J. S. Boys Smith, *Religious thought in the eighteenth century* (1934), primarily on English writers; C. E. Elwell, *The influence of the Enlightenment on the Catholic theory of education in France, 1750–1850* (1944); R. R. Palmer, *Catholics and unbelievers in eighteenth century France* * (1939); and S. Todsvig, *Emanuel Swedenborg: scientist and mystic* (1948). F. E. Manuel discusses the attitudes of the age in *The eighteenth century confronts the gods* * (1959), and in *The changing of the gods* (1983); and J. McManners examines a neglected theme in *Death and Enlightenment: changing attitudes to death among Christians and unbelievers in eighteenth century France* (1982). An important episode is studied in D. D. Bien, *The Calas affair: persecution, toleration, and heresy in eighteenth century Toulouse* (1960).

France under the Old Regime (Political and Economic)

C. B. A. Behrens, *The ancien régime* * (1967), and E. N. Williams, *The ancien*

régime in Europe (1970), both study the old regime for its own sake and not merely as a prologue to the revolutionary age. J. Lough, *An introduction to eighteenth-century France* (1960), is useful. The continuing financial crisis is explored in depth in J. F. Bosher, *French finances, 1770–1795: from business to bureacracy* (1970), and on Turgot, one may read D. Dakin, *Turgot and the ancien régime in France* (1965). Several good books on modern France begin with developments in the eighteenth century; among them are A. Cobban, *A history of modern France* * (3 vols., 1957–1965), of which vol. I is *The old regime and revolution 1715–1799* *; G. Wright, *France in modern times: 1760 to the present* * (3rd ed., 1981), with outstanding bibliographical chapters throughout the book; and R. Price, *An economic history of modern France 1730–1914* (1981). For France under the old regime, one still reads with profit Alexis de Tocqueville's study (1856), available as *The old regime and the French Revolution* * (1947), but the best introduction to French demographic, institutional, and social history is P. Goubert, *The ancien régime: French society, 1600–1750* * (trans. and abr., 1974), cited in Chapter IV.

Three impressive special studies published in recent years are J. Kaplow, *The names of kings: Parisian laboring poor in the eighteenth century* (1973); O. Hufton, *The poor of eighteenth-century France, 1750–1789* (1974); and S. L. Kaplan, *Bread, politics and political economy in the reign of Louis XV* (2 vols., 1976). Among many other studies there are: G. T. Matthews, *The royal general farms in eighteenth-century France* (1957); G. P. Gooch, *Louis XV, the monarchy in decline* (1956); and two books on the Parlement of Paris by J. H. Shennan (1968) and B. Stone (1981). Various social classes are examined in F. L. Ford, *Robe and sword: the regrouping of the French aristocracy after Louis XIV* * (1953); E. G. Barber, *The bourgeoisie in eighteenth century France* * (1955); R. Forster, *The nobility of Toulouse in the eighteenth century* (1960); and the same author's two studies of noble families from the time of Louis XIV through the Revolution, *The house of Saulx-Tavanes* (1971), and *Merchants, landlords, magistrates: the Depont family in eighteenth-century France* (1980). Three other books deserve mention: R. Hahn, *The anatomy of a scientific institution: the Paris Academy of Sciences, 1666–1803* (1971), C. C. Gillispie, *Science and polity in France at the end of* the old régime (1981), and T. Gelfand, *Professionalizing modern medicine: Paris surgeons and medical science and institutions in the eighteenth century* (1980). J. F. Traer, *Marriage and the family in eighteenth century France* (1980), focuses mainly on legal questions.

Enlightened Despotism

An informative introductory synthesis is J. G. Gagliardo, *Enlightened despotism** (1967). L. Krieger, *An essay on the theory of enlightenment and despotism* (1975), is a difficult but rewarding analysis. A. Goodwin (ed.), *The European nobility in the eighteenth century* (1953), brings together an important collection of essays. Among many biographies of Frederick the Great, one may turn to G. P. Gooch, *Frederick the Great: the ruler, the writer, the man* (1947); G. Ritter, *Frederick the Great: a historical profile* (1954, trans. 1968), by the German scholar; and D. B. Horn, *Frederick the Great and the rise of Prussia* (1969). His bureaucracy is effectively examined in H. C. Johnson, *Frederick the Great and his officials* (1975), and in W. Hubatsch, *Frederick the Great of Prussia: absolutism and administration* (Men in Office series, trans. 1977). The best general account of German political fragmentation and cultural stirrings is W. G. Bruford, *Germany in the eighteenth century: the social background of the literary revival** (1935); an important study also is F. Hertz, *The development of the German public mind, a social history of German political sentiments, aspirations and ideas: the age of Enlightenment* (1962), part of a larger work. The nature of the Enlightenment and enlightened despotism in the Spanish framework is portrayed in R. Herr, *The eighteenth-century revolution in Spain* (1958), while the broader framework is presented in W. N. Hargreaves-Mawdsley, *Eighteenth-century Spain, 1700–1788: a political, diplomatic, and institutional history* (1979).

The Habsburg rulers between 1740 and 1792 may be approached through: E. Cruikshank, *Maria Theresa* (1969); P. P. Bernard, *Joseph II** (1968), a brief, balanced account; S. K. Padover, *The revolutionary emperor: Joseph the Second, 1741–90* (1934, 1967); and W. C. Langsam, *Francis the Good: the education of an emperor, 1768–1792* (1949). M. Maestro has written a solid biography of the Italian jurist and reformer who served the Austrian state, *Cesare Beccaria and the origins of penal reform* (1973).

Enlightened despotism in Russia is examined in an outstanding, judicious, large-scale study, I. de Madariaga, *Russia in the age of Catherine the Great** (1981), in which she portrays Catherine as giving her subjects reasonable government and greater personal freedom. There are other biographies of Catherine by I. Grey (1962), Z. Oldenbourg (1965), J. Haslip (1977), and V. Cronin (1978). G. S. Thomson, *Catherine the Great and the expansion of Russia* (Teach Yourself History series, 1947), remains a useful introduction. Other valuable studies of eighteenth-century Russia include M. Raeff, *Origins of the Russian intelligentsia: the eighteenth-century nobility** (1966); H. Rogger, *National consciousness in eighteenth-century Russia* (1960); P. Dukes, *Catherine the Great and the Russian nobility* (1966); D. Ransel, *The politics of Catherinean Russia* (1975); and R. Jones, *The emancipation of the Russian nobility, 1762–1785* (1973). Revolts and social stirrings in Russia may be studied in P. Avrich, *Russian rebels, 1600–1800* (1972), and in two books by J. Alexander on the uprising led by Pugachev, *Autocratic politics in a national crisis* (1969) and *Emperor of the Cossacks* (1973). G. L. Freeze, *The Russian Levites: parish clergy in the eighteenth century* (1977), goes well beyond its title in exploring church-state relations and other subjects.

The American Revolution and the Age of the Democratic Revolution

The attempt by R. R. Palmer, J. Godechot, and others to explore the American and French revolutions in a broader eighteenth-century revolutionary setting is described in more detail at the beginning of the next chapter. H. F. May, *The Enlightenment in America* (1976), ably studies the relationship between Enlightenment thought and such elements as Puritanism; of even broader scope is H. S. Commager, *The empire of reason: how Europe imagined and America realized the Enlightenment** (1977). Other efforts to examine North American civilization in the eighteenth century include L. B. Wright, *The Atlantic frontier: colonial American civilization, 1607–1763* (1947); M. Savelle, *Seeds of liberty: the genesis of the American mind* (1948); M. Kraus, *The Atlantic civilization: eighteenth-century origins* (1949); J. Greene, *The ambiguity of the American Revolution* (1968); and two books by B. Bailyn, *The ideological origins of the American Revolution* (1967) and *The origins of American politics* (1968). M. Beloff (ed.), *The debate on the American Revolution 1761–83* (1949), a collection of source materials, discusses the Revolution within the context of the British Empire, while C. L. Becker, *The Declaration of Independence: a study in the history of political ideas* (1922, 1942), is an engaging essay. There are numerous narrative and analytical accounts of the American Revolution; for discussions of current interpretations, see R. B. Morris, *The American Revolution reconsidered** (1967), and I. R. Christie and B. W. Labaree, *Empire or independence, 1760–1776: a British-American dialogue on the coming of the American Revolution* (1976).

Other important books that relate events in America to British internal politics include L. B. Namier, *England in the age of the American Revolution** (1930); G. H. Guttridge, *English Whiggism and the American Revolution* (1942); H. Butterfield, *George III, Lord North, and the people, 1779–80* (1949) and *George III and the historians* (1957); C. R. Ritcheson, *British politics and the American Revolution* (1954); A. B. Donoughue, *British politics and the American Revolution: the path to war, 1773–1775* (1964); J. R. Pole, *Political representation in England and the origins of the American Revolution* (1967); and H. T. Dickinson, *Liberty and property: political ideology in eighteenth-century Britain* (1978). In addition one may read R. Pares, *King George III and the politicians* (1953); J. S. Watson, *The reign of George III, 1760–1815* (1960); R. J. Whyte, *The age of George III* (1968); and J. Brooke, *King George III* (1972). P. D. G. Thomas, *Lord North* (1976), is a brief biography. J. Carswell, *From revolution to revolution: England, 1688–1776* (1973), may be compared with J. G. A. Pocock (ed.), *Three British revolutions, 1641, 1688, 1776** (1979). On parliamentary reform, see also G. Rudé, *Wilkes and political liberty* (1962); I. R. Christie, *Wilkes, Wyvill, and reform* (1963); C. Cone, *The English Jacobins: reformers in late eighteenth century England* (1968); and C. Bonwick, *English radicals and the American Revolution* (1977). A valuable overall account is I. R. Christie, *Wars and revolutions: Britain, 1760–1815* (1982).

On military and naval subjects, one may read J. Dull, *The French navy and American independence: a study of arms and diplomacy* (1975), and L. Kennett, *The*

French forces in America, 1780–1783 (1978). On diplomacy and international affairs, one may consult W. C. Stinchcombe, *The American Revolution and the French alliance* (1969); S. R. Bemis, *The diplomacy of the American Revolution* (1935); I. de Madariaga, *Britain, Russia, and the armed neutrality of 1780* (1962); and on the peace negotiations, R. B. Morris, *The peacemakers: the great powers and American independence* (1965). H. G. Nicholas, *The United States and Britain* (1975), is a perceptive essay on Anglo-American relations since 1776.

An excellent study, the sequel to an earlier volume, both cited earlier, is D. B. Davis, *The problem of slavery in the age of revolution, 1770–1823* (1975), and important on a related subject is R. Anstey, *The Atlantic slave trade and British abolition, 1760–1810* (1975).

Relations between France and America are discussed in L. Gottschalk and D. F. Lach, *Toward the French Revolution: Europe and America in the eighteenth-century world** (1973); A. O. Aldridge, *Franklin and his French contemporaries* (1957); D. Echevarria, *Mirage in the West: a history of the French image of American society to 1815** (1957); C. Lopez, *Mon cher papa: Franklin and the ladies of Paris* (1966); and A. Gerbi, *The dispute of the New World, 1750–1900* (1973), an amusing analysis of European arguments over the significance of the Americas for European life and thought. H. Dippel, *Germany and the American Revolution, 1770–1800: a sociohistorical investigation of late eighteenth century thinking* (1977), explores the impact of the events in America in the German states.

Problems and Readings*

Pamphlets relating to this chapter include R. Wines (ed.), *Enlightened despotism: reform or reaction?* (1967); P. Paret (ed.), *Frederick the Great: a profile* (1972); M. Raeff (ed.), *Catherine the Great: a profile* (1972); E. A. Reitan (ed.), *George III: tyrant or constitutional monarch?* (1964); and W. F. Church (ed.), *The influence of the Enlightenment on the French Revolution: creative, disastrous, or non-existent?* (rev., 1972). In the Anvil series, there are L. L. Snyder, *The age of reason* (1955); P. Gay, *Deism: an anthology* (1968); and M. Kraus, *The North Atlantic civilization* (1957). Two useful anthologies are I. Schneider (ed.), *The Enlightenment* (1965), and P. Gay, *The*

Enlightenment: a comprehensive anthology* (1976).

IX: THE FRENCH REVOLUTION

The French Revolution and the Revolutionary Age

A. Goodwin (ed.), The American and French revolutions, 1763–1793*, vol. VIII of the New Cambridge Modern History, has already been cited; its sequel volume, C. W. Crawley (ed.), War and peace in an age of upheaval, 1793–1830* (1965), also is useful. Some stimulating surveys for the years beginning with the American and French revolutions are G. Rudé, Revolutionary Europe, 1783–1815 (1964); E. J. Hobsbawm, The age of revolution: Europe, 1789–1848* (1962); N. Hampson, The first European revolution, 1776–1850* (1969); and C. Breunig, The age of revolution and reaction, 1789–1850* (rev., 1977).

On the revolutionary developments in France, important general accounts include C. Brinton, A decade of revolution, 1789–1799* (1934; rev., 1962) in the Langer series, critical of the Revolution; C. Lefebvre, The French Revolution* (1951, 2 vols. in trans. 1962–1964), volume I carrying the story to 1793 and volume II to 1799, a balanced account by a distinguished French scholar; L. Gershoy, The French Revolution and Napoleon (1932; rev., 1964); J. M. Thompson, The French Revolution* (1943); N. Hampson, A social history of the French Revolution* (1963), covering more than its title implies; F. Furet and D. Richet, The French Revolution (trans. 1970); and A. Soboul, The French Revolution, 1789–1799: from the storming of the Bastille to Napoleon* (trans. 1975), by a leading French historian of Marxist persuasion. Three excellent brief accounts are M. J. Sydenham, The French Revolution* (1965); A. Goodwin, The French Revolution* (1953); and J. M. Roberts, The French Revolution* (1978). There are numerous older volumes now more important to historiography than to history by such writers of vastly differing viewpoints as J. Michelet, J. Jaurès, H. Taine, L. Madelin, P. Gaxotte, A. Aulard, and A. Mathiez. In that connection, A. Cobban, The myth of the French Revolution (1953) and The social interpretation of the French Revolution* (1964), may be read and compared with F. Furet, Interpreting the French Revolution* (trans. 1981). J. H. Stewart has collected many key documents in

A documentary survey of the French Revolution (1951), while R. Cobb has edited French Revolution documents (1966). A useful collection of essays is D. Johnson, French society and the Revolution (1976), and a unique collection of documents on the role of women in the era is D. G. Levy, H. B. Applewhite, and M. D. Johnson (eds. and translators), Women in revolutionary Paris, 1789–1815* (1981).

Attention has been given in recent years to the Revolution as part of a European and transatlantic movement. The most extensive treatment of the subject is R. R. Palmer, The age of the democratic revolution: a political history of Europe and America, 1760–1800* (2 vols., 1959–1964); the first volume, The challenge, carries the account to 1792, the second, The struggle, to 1800; see also by the same author, The world of the French Revolution* (1970). Some of the conclusions of a French scholar, J. Godechot [La grande nation (2 vols., 1956), and other works], are available in summary form as France and the Atlantic revolution, 1770–1799 (1965).

Developments within France

An excellent introduction to events beginning in 1789 and ably assessing the literature is W. Doyle, Origins of the French Revolution* (1980). On the early events, one may read G. Lefebvre, The coming of the French Revolution* (1939, trans. 1947); the same author's The great fear of 1789: rural panic in revolutionary France* (1932, trans. 1982); and J. Godechot, The taking of the Bastille: July 14, 1789 (trans. 1970). On the efforts to cope with the financial crisis, one should consult J. F. Bosher, French finances, 1770–1793 (1970), cited in the previous chapter, and two books that assess the efforts at reform: R. D. Harris, Necker: reform statesman of the ancien régime (1979), and B. Stone, The Parlement of Paris, 1774–1789 (1981), cited in the last chapter. Two important aspects of the impact of the Revolution are studied in J. McManners, The French Revolution and the church* (1969), and P. Higonnet, Class, ideology, and the rights of nobles during the French Revolution (1981). The counterrevolution may be studied in P. Beik, The French Revolution seen from the right . . . 1789–1799 (1956) and in J. Godechot, The counter-revolution: doctrine and action, 1789–1804* (trans. 1971). A special subject is examined in C. L. Donakowski, A muse for the masses: ritual and music in an age of democratic revolution (1977).

The Lower Classes, the Reign of Terror, and Related Themes

Considerable attention in recent years has been given to the role of the poorer classes in the social history of the times. Here one may read R. C. Cobb, *The police and the people: French popular protest, 1789–1820* (1970); Cobb has also tried to reconstruct the life of the poor by examining four suicides in *Death in Paris* (1978). A. Forrest, *The French Revolution and the poor* (1981), examines the welfare legislation adopted in the revolutionary decade.

The coming of the war and the radicalization of the Revolution may be studied in two books by M. Sydenham: *The Girondins* (1961), and *The first French republic 1792–1804* (1974); A. Patrick, *The men of the first French republic: political alignments in the National Convention of 1792* (1972); and M. L. Kennedy, *The Jacobin clubs in the French Revolution: the first years* (1981). The Terror and related subjects are studied in R. R. Palmer, *Twelve who ruled: the year of the Terror in the French Revolution** (1941, 1958); A. Soboul, *The Parisian sans-culottes and the French Revolution, 1793–1794* (trans. 1964); G. Rudé, *The crowd in the French Revolution** (1959); and R. B. Rose, *The enragés: socialists of the French Revolution?* (1965). More specialized studies include C. Lucas, *The structure of the Terror* (1973); D. M. Greer, *The incidence of the Terror during the French Revolution: a statistical interpretation* (1935), a revealing study of who was actually executed and by what procedures; its sequel, *The incidence of emigration during the French Revolution* (1951); and R. C. Cobb's impressive *Paris and its provinces, 1792–1802* (1975). Two books focusing on popular unrest in both France and England are G. A. Williams, *Artisans and sans-culottes* (1968), and G. Rudé, *The crowd in history: a study of popular disturbances in France and England, 1730–1848* (1964). J. Talmon, *The origins of totalitarian democracy* (1952), sees the roots of later dictatorships in these years, while C. Brinton, *The anatomy of revolution** (1938), is a comparative study of four revolutions: the English, American, French, and Russian. C. Tilly, *The Vendée* (1964), an important sociological analysis of the counterrevolution of 1793, may be supplemented by G. Lewis, *The second Vendée: the continuity of counter-revolution in the department of the Gard, 1789–1815* (1978). The most useful recent study of the Directory is M. Lyons, *France under the Directory* (1975), while the best treatment of the socialist extremist crushed by the Directory is R. B. Rose, *Gracchus Babeuf: the first revolutionary communist* (1978), a balanced and sensitive assessment. I. Woloch, *Jacobin legacy: the democratic movement under the Directory* (1970), analyzes the more numerous constitutional democrats.

Biographies

J. M. Thompson, *Leaders of the French Revolution* (1932), gives sketches of the outstanding personalities, which may be filled out with the following biographical accounts: the somewhat sensational A. Vallentin, *Mirabeau* (1948), which does not entirely supersede L. Barthou, *Mirabeau* (1913); G. C. Van Deusen, *Sieyès: his life and his nationalism* (1932); D. L. Dowd, *Pageant-master of the republic: Jacques-Louis David and the French Revolution* (1948), on art and propaganda during the period; L. Gottschalk, *Jean-Paul Marat: a study in radicalism* (1927, 1966); H. Dupré, *Lazare Carnot, republican patriot* (1940), on the "organizer of victory"; and N. Hampson, *Danton* (1978), which depicts him as a pragmatic and somewhat opportunistic political figure. D. F. Hawke, *Paine* (1974), stressing the revolutionist's career in America, England, and France, may be compared with E. Foner, *Tom Paine and the American Revolution* (1976). Mme. Roland is studied in G. May, *Madame Roland and the age of revolution* (1970). The multivolumed, detailed biography of Lafayette by L. Gottschalk and M. Maddox concludes in its ninth volume (1973) by taking the account to July 1790.

The best-rounded biography of the most prominent figure on the Committee of Public Safety is J. M. Thompson, *Robespierre* (2 vols., 1935), on whom the same author has an excellent brief study in the Teach Yourself History series, *Robespierre and the French Revolution** (1953). One also may read N. Hampson, *The life and opinions of Maximilien Robespierre* (1974), and G. Rudé, *Robespierre: portrait of a revolutionary democrat* (1975). Rudé has also edited *Robespierre** in the Great Lives Observed series (1967). A provocative but not convincing psychoanalytical study is M. Gallo, *Robespierre the incorruptible: a psychobiography* (trans. 1971). On Robespierre's associates, E. N. Curtis has written *Saint-Just: colleague of Robespierre* (1935), and L.

Gershoy, *Bertrand Barère: a reluctant terrorist* (1962).

War and Diplomacy

The war and various diplomatic aspects are discussed in S. T. Ross, *European diplomatic history, 1789–1815: France against Europe* * (1969); the same author's *Quest for victory: French military strategy, 1792–1799* (1973); P. Mackesy, *Statesmen at war: the strategy of overthrow, 1798–1799* (1974), which studies the Second Coalition; H. Mitchell, *The underground war against revolutionary France, 1794–1800* (1965), which traces British diplomacy and espionage; and J. Ehrman, *The British government and commercial negotiations with Europe, 1783–1793* (1962). H. Ragsdale, *Détente in the Napoleonic era: Bonaparte and the Russians* (1980), focuses on the years 1799–1801. Useful for this and the chapter that follows is T. M. Iiams, *Peacemaking from Vergennes to Napoleon: French foreign relations in the revolutionary era, 1774–1814* (1979). On the emergence of Bonaparte, one may turn to G. Ferrero, *The gamble: Bonaparte in Italy, 1796–1797* (1939); P. G. Elgood, *Bonaparte's adventure in Egypt* (1931); and J. C. Herold's vivid *Bonaparte in Egypt* (1962). Additional books on Napoleon are listed in the following chapter.

Effects of the Revolution outside France

The impact of the Revolution and of subsequent events in France is examined in J. M. Diefendorf, *Businessmen and politics in the Rhineland, 1789–1834* (1980); in K. Epstein, *The genesis of German conservatism* (1966), a rewarding study; and in the older book of G. P. Gooch, *Germany and the French Revolution* (1920), and his subsequent work, *Studies in German history* (1948); other books on the German reactions are cited in the following chapter. Events in the Netherlands are examined in S. Schama, *Patriots and liberators: revolution and government in the Netherlands, 1780–1813* (1977), while the Irish rebellion of 1798 is placed in its European setting in M. Elliott, *Partners in revolution: the United Irishmen in France* (1982), and Ireland in this age in general is ably treated in R. B. McDowell, *Ireland in the age of imperialism and revolution, 1760–1801* (1979). For effects in Haiti and the black world, see C. L. R. James, *The black Jacobins: Toussaint l'Ouverture and the San Domingo Revolution* (1938), which must be supplemented by D. P. Geggus, *Slavery, war, and revolution: the British occupation of Saint Domingue, 1793–1798* (1982). An outstanding study of British reaction to the revolutionary events is A. Goodwin, *The friends of liberty: the English democratic movement in the age of the French Revolution* (1979).

Problems and Readings *

Studies in various problems series that relate to this chapter are R. W. Greenlaw (ed.), *The social origins of the French Revolution* (1975); P. Amann (ed.), *The eighteenth century revolution: French or Western?* (1963); R. Bienvenu (ed.), *The ninth of Thermidor: the fall of Robespierre* (1968); and S. Ross (ed.), *The French Revolution: conflict or continuity?* (1971). For a comprehensive survey examining divergent appraisals of all aspects of the Revolution, see F. A. Kafker and M. Laux (eds.), *The French Revolution: conflicting interpretations* (rev., 1983); and for sociologically oriented analyses of various problems, see J. Kaplow (ed.), *New perspectives on the French Revolution: readings in historical sociology* (1965). In the Anvil series, L. Gershoy provides an essay and documents in *The era of the French Revolution, 1789–1799: ten years that shook the world* (1957). A. Cobban has edited *The debate on the French Revolution, 1789–1799* (1949).

X: NAPOLEONIC EUROPE

Three general surveys of Europe in the age of Napoleon are G. Bruun, *Europe and the French imperium, 1799–1814* * (1938; rev., 1957), in the Langer series; J. Godechot, B. Hyslop, and D. Dowd, *The Napoleonic era in Europe* (trans. 1971); and O. Connelly, *The epoch of Napoleon: France and Europe* * (1972); but see also many of the books on the Revolution cited in the previous chapter that continue into the Napoleonic age. P. Geyl, *Napoleon: for and against* * (1949), is a brilliant interpretation by the Dutch historian of what French historians since 1815 have said about Napoleon. *Napoleon self-revealed in 300 selected letters* (1934), edited by J. M. Thompson, gives Bonaparte's own words, as does J. C. Herold (ed.), *The mind of Napoleon* (1955); the same author has written a colorful account of the period in *The age of Napoleon* (1963

Napoleon and Napoleonic France

For Napoleonic France, covering political, economic, and social aspects there is now available L. Bergeron, *France under Napoleon** (1972 trans. 1981), by a French scholar; while I. Collins, *Napoleon and his parliaments, 1800–1815* (1979), examines the survival of political activity in these years.

Of the innumerable biographies and biographically oriented studies of Napoleon, the following are recommended: J. M. Thompson, *Napoleon Bonaparte: his rise and fall* (1952); G. Lefebvre, *Napoleon* (2 vols., 1935; trans. 1969), a major work by a distinguished French historian, the first volume carrying the story to Tilsit, the second to Waterloo; and two books by F. M. Markham, *Napoleon** (1964) and *Napoleon and the awakening of Europe** (Teach Yourself History series, 1954). R. Holtman, *The Napoleonic revolution** (1967), is a brief, judicious assessment. E. V. Tarlé, *Bonaparte* (1937), is a Marxist view of unusual interest, emphasizing economic influences.

Napoleon as a military leader may be studied in G. E. Rothenberg, *The art of warfare in the age of Napoleon* (1978), an excellent overview; D. G. Chandler, *The campaigns of Napoleon* (1966); M. Glover, *The Napoleonic wars: an illustrated history, 1792–1815* (1978); C. Duffy, *Austerlitz, 1805* (1977); H. T. Parker, *Three Napoleonic battles* (rev., 1983); and C. Hibbert, *Waterloo: Napoleon's last campaign* (1967). That Napoleon was defeated by British sea power was the theme of A. T. Mahan's *The influence of sea power on the French Revolution and Empire* (1892, many eds.), a subject treated more recently, and carried down to the contemporary era, in P. M. Kennedy, *The rise and fall of British naval mastery* (1976), and in J. Horsfield, *The art of leadership in war: the Royal Navy from the age of Nelson to the end of World War II* (1980). Related topics are covered in B. Mackesy, *War in the Mediterranean, 1803–1810* (1957), and in R. Glover, *Britain at bay: defence against Bonaparte, 1803–1814* (1973).

Other studies of the Napoleonic age include E. Heckscher, *The continental system* (1922); H. C. Deutsch, *The genesis of Napoleonic imperialism* (1938); and H. H. Walsh, *The Concordat of 1801* (1933). Biographical studies of Talleyrand have been written by A. Duff Cooper* (1932), C. Brinton* (1936), E. Dard (1937), L. Madelin (1948), and J. Orieux (1970, trans. 1974);

and S. Zweig has written *Joseph Fouché: the portrait of a politician* (1930).

On the last phase of Napoleon's career, E. Saunders has written a lively account, *The hundred days* (1964), and A. Brett-James has edited an anthology of eyewitness accounts under the same title (1964). Three biographies of notable women of the era are: E. J. Knapton, *Empress Josephine** (1963); the same author's *The lady of the Holy Alliance; the life of Julie de Krüdener* (1939); and J. C. Herold's *Mistress to an age** (1955), on the influential Mme. de Stael. Napoleon's family is studied in O. Connelly, *The gentle Bonaparte: a biography of Joseph, Napoleon's elder brother* (1968), and in F. Markham, *The Bonapartes* (1975). B. Weider and D. Hopgood, *The murder of Napoleon* (1982), tries to unravel the mystery of how Napoleon died.

Britain in the Time of Napoleon

The patriotic British volumes of A. Bryant, *The years of endurance, 1793–1802* (1942), *The years of victory, 1802–1812* (1944), and *The age of elegance, 1812–1822* (1950), treat the period in detail. The war years receive special attention in J. Ehrman, *William Pitt the Younger* (2 vols. to date, 1969, 1983). The impact of the war and other economic changes of the age are explored in C. Ensley, *British society and the French wars, 1793–1815* (1980), and in A. D. Harvey, *Britain in the early nineteenth century* (1978). C. Oman [Lenanton], *Britain against Napoleon* (1944), is useful; the same author also has written a biography of Nelson (1946), as have C. S. Forester (1929), W. James (1948), R. Grenfell (1949), and others. P. Guedalla (1931) and R. Aldington (1943) have each written good popular biographies of Wellington.

Germany in the Time of Napoleon

Especially useful for Prussian and German nationalism during this era are H. Kohn, *Prelude to nation-states: the French and German experience, 1789–1815* (1967); F. Meinecke, *The age of German liberation, 1795–1815* (trans. 1977); J. G. Gagliardo, *Reich and nation: the Holy Roman Empire as idea and reality, 1763–1806* (1980), on the political writings of the period; H. Brunschwig, *Enlightenment and romanticism in eighteenth-century Prussia* (1974), on politics, thought, and feeling during the revolutionary years; and P. Paret, *Clausewitz and the state* (1976).

For the political, diplomatic, and military developments of the age, one may read G. S. Ford, *Stein and the era of reform in Prussia, 1807–1815* (1922); C. de Grunwald, *Napoleon's nemesis: the life of Baron Stein* (1963); H. A. L. Fisher, *Studies in Napoleonic statesmanship: Germany* (1903); W. O. Shanahan, *Prussian military reforms, 1786–1813* (1945); and the acute assessment of W. M. Simon, *The failure of the Prussian reform movement, 1807–1819* (1955). The able and cynical Gentz has been the subject of biographies by C. S. B. Buckland (1933), P. R. Sweet (1941), and G. Mann (1946).

Other Countries in Napoleonic Times

B. Perkins has written a three-volume study of Anglo-American relations in the three decades from 1795 to 1823: *The first rapprochement* (1955), *Prologue to war* (1961), and *Castlereagh and Adams* (1964). The general diplomatic study of H. C. Allen, *Great Britain and the United States . . . 1783–1952* (1955), is valuable. The American domestic scene is presented in M. Smelser, *The democratic republic, 1801–1815* (1968); and a good account of the U.S.-British military conflict is R. Horsman, *The War of 1812* (1969). Other ramifications in the Western Hemisphere during the revolutionary era are examined in W. S. Robertson, *The life of Miranda* (2 vols., 1929) and *France and Latin American independence* (1939). On Napoleonic influences in other countries, the following also may be mentioned: A. Lobanov-Rostovsky, *Russia and Europe 1789–1825* (1947); E. Tarlé, *Napoleon's invasion of Russia, 1812* (1942), by a leading Soviet historian; G. B. McClellan, *Venice and Bonaparte* (1931); O. Connelly, *Napoleon's satellite kingdoms* (1965); and R. J. Rath, *The fall of the Napoleonic kingdom of Italy* (1941). The best account of Spain in the Napoleonic era is G. H. Lovett, *Napoleon and the birth of modern Spain* (2 vols., 1965). M. Glover, *The Peninsular War, 1807–1814* (1974), is illuminating for

the military events, and J. K. Severn, *A Wellesley affair: Richard Marquess Wellesley and the conduct of Anglo-Spanish diplomacy, 1809–1812* (1981), for the diplomatic background.

Wartime Diplomacy and the Congress of Vienna

Excellent guides on the diplomacy of these years are C. K. Webster, *The foreign policy of Castlereagh, 1812–1815: Britain and the reconstruction of Europe* (1931); C. S. B. Buckland, *Metternich and the British government from 1809 to 1813* (1932), and his shorter parallel study on Gentz (1933); L. I. Strakhovsky, *Alexander I of Russia: the man who defeated Napoleon* (1947); and A. Palmer, *Alexander I: tsar of war and peace* (1975). E. E. Kraehe, *Metternich's German policy*, vol. I, *The contest with Napoleon, 1799–1814* (1963), and vol. II, *The Congress of Vienna, 1814–1815* (1983), is a highly informative and detailed account.

For the Congress of Vienna, one may read C. K. Webster, *The Congress of Vienna, 1814–1815* (1919), a technical study; G. Ferrero, *The reconstruction of Europe: Talleyrand and the Congress of Vienna, 1814–1815* (1914); and on a special subject, H. A. Straus, *The attitude of the Congress of Vienna toward nationalism in Germany, Italy, and Poland* (1949). Important for this and for the chapter that follows on postwar diplomacy are H. Nicolson, *The Congress of Vienna: a study in allied unity, 1812–1822* (1946), and H. Kissinger, *A world restored: Metternich, Castlereagh and the problem of peace, 1812–1822* (1957), by an astute student of contemporary international affairs.

Problems and Readings*

The best problem study here is the volume by P. Geyl, *Napoleon: for and against* (1949), cited earlier. To it should be added D. H. Pinkney (ed.), *Napoleon: historical enigma* (1969). Some of the problem studies mentioned in the previous chapter relate also to Napoleon's impact on Europe.

Illustration
Sources

Index

Dates given after names of rulers and popes are the years of reigns or pontificates; those given for all others are the years of birth and death.

Pronunciation is indicated where it is not obvious. With foreign words the purpose is not to show their exact pronunciation in their own language but to suggest how they may be acceptably pronounced in English. Fully Anglicized pronunciations are indicated by the abbreviation *Angl*. Pronunciation is shown by respelling, not by symbols, except that the following symbols are used for vowel sounds not found in English:

ø   Indicates the sound of ö as in Göttingen. To form this sound, purse the lips as if to say *o*, and then say *ay* as in *ate*.

U   indicates the sound of the French *u*, or of German *ü*. To form this sound, purse the lips as if to say *oo*, and then say *ee* as in *eat*.

aN, oN, uN, iN indicate the sounds of the French nasal vowels. Once learned, these are easily pronounced, roughly as follows: For aN, begin to pronounce the English word *on*, but avoid saying the consonant *n* and "nasalize" the *ah* sound instead. For oN do the same with the English *own*; for uN, with the English prefix *un-*; for iN, with the English word *an*.

The sound of *s* as in the word *treasure* is indicated by *zh*. This sound is common in English, though never found at the beginning or end of a word. *igh* always indicates the so-called long *i* as in *high*. The vowel sound of *hoot* is indicated by *oo*, that of *hood* by *o͝o*.

Compared with English, the European languages are highly regular in their spelling, in that the same letters or combinations of letters are generally pronounced in the same way.

About
the Auth[o]

ROBERT ROSWELL PALMER, Professor Emeritus of History at Yale Univers[ity], born in Chicago in 1909. After graduating from the University of Chicago[, re]ceived his doctorate from Cornell University in 1934. From 1936 to 1[9] taught at Princeton University, and was Dean of the Faculty of Arts and Sc[ience] at Washington University in St. Louis from 1963 to 1966. He was President [of] American Historical Association in 1970. Professor Palmer is the author of *Ca[tho]lics and Unbelievers in Eighteenth Century France* (1939), *Twelve Who Ru[led: The Year of the Terror in the French Revolution* (1941, 1958), and the t[wo-] volume *Age of the Democratic Revolution* (1959 and 1964), both volume[s] which were History Book Club selections and the first of which won the Bancr[oft] Prize in 1960. He has likewise written *The World of the French Revolut[ion]* (1970), which was also published in French in 1968, and *The School of [the] French Revolution* (1975). He edited the *Rand McNally Atlas of World Hist[ory]* (1957) and translated Georges Lefebvre's *Coming of the French Revolut[ion]* (1947) and Louis Bergeron's *France under Napoleon* (1981). He has contribu[ted] to a variety of journals and collaborative volumes in this country and Europ[e].

JOEL COLTON, Professor of History at Duke University, was born in New Y[ork] City. He received his B.A. from the City College of New York and his M.A. a[nd] Ph.D. degrees from Columbia University. In 1947 he joined the Department [of] History at Duke University and chaired the department from 1967 to 1974. Fr[om] 1974 to 1981, he was Director for Humanities at the Rockefeller Foundation. [He] has served on the Board of Editors of the *Journal of Modern History*, the adviso[ry] board of *Historical Abstracts*, several national committees of the American H[is]torical Association, and as a vice-president of the Society for French Histori[cal] Studies and the International Commission on the History of Social Moveme[nts] and Social Structures. He has been awarded Guggenheim, Rockefeller Found[a]tion, and National Endowment for the Humanities fellowships, and is a Fellow [of] the American Academy of Arts and Sciences. He is the author of *Compuls[ory] Labor Arbitration in France, 1936–1939* (1951), *Léon Blum: Humanist in Poli[tics]* (1966, French translation, 1968), for which he received a Mayflower Award, [The] *Twentieth Century* (1968, 1980), in the Time-Life Great Ages of Man series, [and] articles in various journals, encyclopedias, and collaborative volumes. He wa[s ap]pointed to the Phi Beta Kappa Visiting Scholar Program for 1983–1984.

A Note
on the Type

The text of this book is set in CALEDONIA, a Linotype face designed by W. A. Dwiggins, and redesigned for Compugraphic. It belongs to the family of printing types called "modern face" by printers—a term used to mark the change in style of type-letters that occurred about 1800. Caledonia borders on the general design of Scotch Modern, but is more freely drawn than that letter.

This book was composed by Arkotype Inc., New York, N.Y., and printed and bound by Kingsport Press, Kingsport, TN.

The maps were executed by Jean Tremblay.

The text and cover were designed by msl/Levavi & Levavi.

Contemporary Asia

ARCTIC OCEAN

SPITZBERGEN
(Norway)

FRANZ JOSEF
LAND

BARENTS SEA

NOVAYA
ZEMLYA

KARA
SEA

Igar

ATLANTIC
OCEAN

NORWAY

SWEDEN

FINLAND

Archangel

Vorkuta

S. MTS.

E U R O P E

Leningrad

S O V I E T

Toms

Ob R.

Yenisey R.

Moscow

Kiev

Sverdlovsk

Novos

Kuibyshev

Omsk

U R A L

MEDITERRANEAN SEA

BLACK SEA

Istanbul

Ankara

Batum

T U R K E Y

Astrakhan

CASPIAN SEA

Karaganda

L. Balkhash

ARAL
SEA

Urumch

CYPRUS

Baku

Tashkent

SINKIA

LEBANON

SYRIA

Lop

ISRAEL

Cairo
Suez Canal

JORDAN

IRAQ

Teheran

Bukhara

EGYPT

Baghdad

AFGHANISTAN

JAMMU AND
KASHMIR

TIB

SAUDI ARABIA

Basra

KUWAIT

I R A N

Kabul

Lahore

Indus R.

S U D A N

RED SEA

Mecca

BAHRAIN

PERSIAN
GULF

QATAR

Riyadh

UNITED ARAB
EMIRATES

PAKISTAN

NEPAL

New
Delhi

Ganges

Karachi

Muscat

OMAN

I N D I A

Calc

R I C A

YEMEN

SOUTHERN
YEMEN

Bombay

Aden

DJIBOUTI

ARABIAN SEA

Hyderabad

B A
B E N

ETHIOPIA

SOCOTRA
(Britain)

Goa

Madras

SOMALIA

LACCADIVE I.
(India)

Pondicherry

SRI LANKA

KENYA

Colombo

MALDIVE
ISLANDS

TANZANIA

States Recognized as Independent After World War II

0   500   1000 miles

INDIAN OCEAN

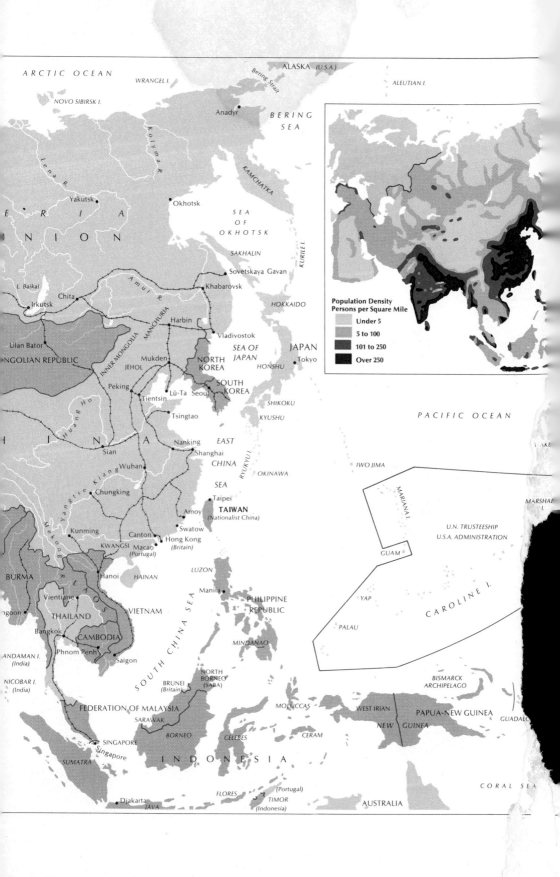

MON I.
(mgn)

ANAL